SHAKESPEARE SURVEY

71

Re-Creating Shakespeare

SHAKESPEARE SURVEY
ADVISORY BOARD

SHAKESPEARE SURVEY

71

Re-Creating Shakespeare

Articles from the World Shakespeare Congress, 2016

EDITED BY

PETER HOLLAND

CAMBRIDGE
UNIVERSITY PRESS

CAMBRIDGE
UNIVERSITY PRESS

University Printing House, Cambridge CB2 8BS, United Kingdom

One Liberty Plaza, 20th Floor, New York, NY 10006, USA

477 Williamstown Road, Port Melbourne, VIC 3207, Australia

314–321, 3rd Floor, Plot 3, Splendor Forum, Jasola District Centre,
New Delhi – 110025, India

79 Anson Road, #06–04/06, Singapore 079906

Cambridge University Press is part of the University of Cambridge.

It furthers the University's mission by disseminating knowledge in the pursuit of
education, learning, and research at the highest international levels of excellence.

www.cambridge.org
Information on this title: www.cambridge.org/9781108470834
DOI: 10.1017/9781108557177

© Cambridge University Press 2018

First published 2018

Printed in the United Kingdom by TJ International Ltd. Padstow Cornwall

A catalogue record for this publication is available from the British Library.

ISBN 978-1-108-47083-4 Hardback
ISSN 0080-9152

EDITOR'S NOTE

This volume of *Shakespeare Survey*, like its predecessor (volume 70), is made up, almost entirely, of articles derived from papers given at the World Shakespeare Congress, held in Stratford-upon-Avon and London in August 2016. Volume 70 focused on 'Creating Shakespeare' and this one focuses on 'Re-Creating Shakespeare', echoing the Congress's title, 'Creating and Re-Creating Shakespeare', though it might be arguable whether some pieces could belong in either volume. I am grateful to Peter Holbrook, then Chair of the International Shakespeare Association, and Nick Walton, its Executive Director, together with all the members of the team, for their tireless labours in organizing the Congress.

Unless otherwise indicated, Shakespeare quotations and references are keyed to *The Complete Works*, ed. Stanley Wells, Gary Taylor, John Jowett and William Montgomery, second edition (Oxford, 2005).

Volume 72 'Shakespeare and War' will be at press by the time this volume appears. The theme of Volume 73 will be 'Shakespeare and the City'. This title covers a wide range of topics including, for example, Shakespeare's representation of cities such as London, Venice, Rome and Athens; the impact on Shakespeare of living and working in London; the history of Shakespeare production in cities world-wide; and many other possibilities. *Shakespeare Survey 74* will be on 'Shakespeare and Education', the topic of the International Shakespeare Conference to be held in 2020. The theme for *Survey 75* will be *'Othello'*.

Submissions should be addressed to the Editor at The Shakespeare Institute, Church Street, Stratford-upon-Avon, Warwickshire CV37 6HP, to arrive at the latest by 1 September 2019 for volume 73, of 2020 for volume 74 and of 2021 for volume 75. Pressures on space are heavy and priority is given to articles related to the theme of a particular volume. Submissions may also be made as e-mail attachments to emma.smith@hertford.ox.ac.uk. All articles submitted are read by the Editor and at least one member of the Advisory Board.

Review copies should be addressed to the Editor as above. In attempting to survey the ever-increasing bulk of Shakespeare publications, our reviewers inevitably have to exercise some selection. We are pleased to receive offprints of articles which help to draw our reviewers' attention to relevant material.

This is my 19th and last volume as Editor for *Shakespeare Survey*, a role I took on with *Shakespeare Survey 53*. I 'inherited' *Survey* from Stanley Wells and hand over now to Emma Smith. The list of people to whom I owe thanks over these years is too long to allow for naming. Let me place them, therefore, into groups. My thanks to all the members of the Advisory Board who have been so unfailingly helpful and supportive; to the many graduate students who have been my outstanding Assistant Editors both at the Shakespeare Institute and at the University of Notre Dame; to all the contributors to these volumes, especially our overburdened reviewers, for their brilliance; and to the extraordinary people at Cambridge University Press who have been involved in the production of these many thousands of pages, especially the eagle-eyed copy-editors.

One person cannot remain unnamed, someone whose name and role do not appear in any of the volumes' prelims, as far as I can see, but whose influence on the success of *Shakespeare Survey* for decades has been greater than anyone else's. Throughout my time as Editor, the person at Cambridge University Press

EDITOR'S NOTE

responsible for *Shakespeare Survey* has been Sarah Stanton and she continues to be so, even though retired from the Press. At a time when the world of publishing seems to mean that people move jobs every few years, her long involvement in the publishing of Shakespeare studies is simply extraordinary. Sarah is, as a result, more learned in the field than 99 per cent of Shakespeare academics and, when it comes to all the myriad details of the processes of assembling and publishing *Shakespeare Survey*, she is, quite simply, the perfect publisher. My deepest thanks to Sarah for ensuring the pleasures of editing *Shakespeare Survey* so far outweighed the pains for, lo, these many years.

PETER HOLLAND

CONTRIBUTORS

POMPA BANERJEE, *University of Colorado Denver*
ASHISH BEESOONDIAL, *Caudan Arts Centre, Mauritius*
IRIS JULIA BÜHRLE, *University of Oxford*
MARK THORNTON BURNETT, *Queen's University Belfast*
JOSEPH CAMPANA, *Rice University*
JONATHAN CREWE, *Dartmouth College*
CARLA DELLA GATTA, *University of Southern California*
KATE DORNEY, *The University of Manchester*
LOUISE GEDDES, *Adelphi University*
ANDREW JAMES HARTLEY, *University of North Carolina Charlotte*
KATHERINE HENNESSEY, *American University of Kuwait*
PETER HOLLAND, *University of Notre Dame*
MARK HUTCHINGS, *University of Reading*
JUDY CELINE ICK, *University of the Philippines Diliman*
RUSSELL JACKSON, *University of Birmingham*
PETER KIRWAN, *University of Nottingham*
AMY LIDSTER, *King's College London*
MARGARET LITVIN, *Boston University*
HAO LIU, *Tsinghua University*
TOM MCALINDON, *University of Hull*
RANDALL MARTIN, *University of New Brunswick*
ALFREDO MICHEL MODENESSI, *Universidad Nacional Autónoma de México*
CYRUS MULREADY, *State University of New York at New Paltz*
STEPHEN PURCELL, *University of Warwick*
CAROL CHILLINGTON RUTTER, *University of Warwick*
KATHERINE WEST SCHEIL, *University of Minnesota*
CHARLOTTE SCOTT, *Goldsmiths College, University of London*
JAMES SHAW, *University of Oxford*
BOIKA SOKOLOVA, *University of Notre Dame*
ROBERT STAGG, *University of Oxford*
KIRILKA STAVREVA, *Cornell College*
MICHIKO SUEMATSU, *Gunma University*
HOLGER SCHOTT SYME, *University of Toronto*
DONNA WOODFORD-GORMLEY, *New Mexico Highlands University*
SANDRA YOUNG, *University of Cape Town*

CONTENTS

ix

CONTENTS

Shakespeare and Other Art Forms

ILLUSTRATIONS

LIST OF ILLUSTRATIONS

SHAKESPEARE'S TRANSCOLONIAL SOLIDARITIES IN THE GLOBAL SOUTH

SANDRA YOUNG

The transformations Shakespearian drama has undergone within the global South allow us to glimpse the rich potential for subversion and renewal within his work. In travelling around the globe, traditional Shakespeare has been dismantled and reimagined, and the result is illuminating for cultural studies attuned to the dynamics at play in an unequal world. However, the temptation to view this capacity for revision as affirming, above all, Shakespeare's exceptionalism has the regrettable effect of obscuring the mutuality of creative innovations that work powerfully to renew Shakespeare and lend his work startling contemporaneity. As theatre-makers across the global South explore affinities between their worlds and Shakespeare's, they allow us to imagine, in sympathy with Shakespeare, the possibility of a transformed critical landscape. It is this capacity for mutual affinity across vast differences in time and space that provides the impetus for my article: the recent renderings of *The Tempest* into the creole forms of Sierre Leone and the Indian Ocean island of Mauritius demonstrate the powerful effect of creolization in this context. These adaptations allow Shakespeare to bear witness to the aftermath of slavery and to play a role in disabling the hateful logic that underpins rigid ethnic classifications.

Contemporary theatre-makers have drawn on Shakespeare in a manner that complicates the dichotomies of earlier cultural histories, that embed Shakespeare within an inimical colonial canon. But scholarship has tended to treat the creative work emerging from non-traditional centres of Shakespeare practice as tangential to mainstream Shakespeare studies, as if it constitutes a welcome and engaging sideshow that affirms, ultimately, Shakespeare's immense appeal and influence. The field of Global Shakespeare has not yet done enough to demonstrate the transformative potential of this creative work and its significance for critical thought and cultural politics.

The conceptual framework of the global South helps to bring into view the connections and affinities between diverse contexts across the world without necessarily reproducing familiar cultural hierarchies. Instead of treating colonialism's abuses and post-colonialism's resistances as the defining moments for vastly different contexts, the framework of the global South opens to view the diverse modes of dominance that obtain across a multiply unequal world. It enables conversations across oceans of difference and points to affinities in terms other than those that were set in place by European colonialism. It invites us to look laterally, across the Indian and Atlantic worlds, for cultural and political resonances, by-passing the endorsement of northern cultural theory.

The global South thus potentially shifts the orientation within which readers might interpret Shakespeare's resonances across the globe. Shakespeare's rich afterlife in non-traditional (and non-English) centres of theatre-making becomes more evident and differently valued within a framework that can more readily acknowledge the texture of innovative cultural work apart from the legitimizing nexus of northern theory. What we understand as 'Shakespeare' is necessarily changed by this shift in perspective, and rendered irreducibly plural. This is not to say that the figure of Shakespeare, as a cultural phenomenon, does not remain one of Britain's most recognizable and marketable icons, represented variously with reference to his imagined person, his characters, his plays and his craft; indeed, it was with Shakespeare's words that well-known British actor Kenneth Branagh (dressed as nineteenth-century British engineer Isambard Kingdom Brunel), invited the world to open themselves to the 'delight' of 'the isle' at the opening ceremony of the London Olympic Games in 2012 and offered the islander's reassurance, 'Be not afeard. The isle is full of noises, / Sounds, and sweet airs, that give delight and hurt not', from *The Tempest*.[1] The quintessentially British Shakespeare, whom viewers around the world encountered in this moment as spokesperson for the British Isles, had been transformed by global anti-colonial politics: the speech with which the Olympic hosts welcomed their audience of 900 million[2] did not belong to the character from *The Tempest* most closely associated in times past with the playwright himself, Prospero, whom Samuel Taylor Coleridge described as 'the very Shakespeare himself'.[3] Instead, it was Caliban's welcome that was extended in 2012 to the imagined visitors to an island world rendered magical and strange through the dreamscape conjured by Prospero's 'Abhorrèd slave' (1.2.354).

The effect of this foregrounding of Caliban is unsettling to the fantasy of world harmony, as Johann Gregory and François-Xavier Gleyzan have argued: 'The sentimental use of Shakespeare in the ceremony, thus, seems to have unconsciously raised the spectre of the colonised Caliban even as it attempted to silence this issue.'[4] In drawing our attention to organizer Danny Boyle's programme notes for the opening ceremony, however, Jem Bloomfield allows us to see how this changing narrative works to transform colonization into something that can be absorbed into a narrative of 'revolution' and global prosperity.[5] According to Boyle, at 'some point in their histories, most nations experience a revolution that changes everything about them. The United Kingdom had a revolution that changed the whole of human existence.' The 'revolution' to which Boyle

refers is a matter of innovation rather than political change but his message appropriates the idealism from the latter sense of 'revolution' to construct an ideal that can be imagined as creating a 'better world' in which all might enjoy 'real freedom and real equality', 'through the prosperity of industry'.[6] Boyle's version of English global influence historically avoids any explicit acknowledgement of its legacy of imperial dominance and the anti-colonial revolutions it faced, but this history haunts the ceremony, not least through Shakespeare's contribution to it.

The fact that Shakespeare gets conscripted to underwrite this myth of global prosperity and well-being is not remarkable. Rather, what is noteworthy is that the world-making taking place on the Olympic stage celebrates, perhaps unwittingly, the power of the dispossessed to create magic and make strange the projection of hegemonic and commodified Englishness. The figure of Caliban-as-Brunel unsettles the attempt to transform a narrative of global domination into a supposedly shared ideal. The kind of unabashed celebration of the English kingdom that was possible in the 1612 Cotswold Olympics, described in Richard Wilson's account of 'Shakespeare's Olympic Game', is revisited in 2012 as a matter of 'pastoral'

---

[1] Quotations from *The Tempest* are taken from William Shakespeare, *The Complete Works*, ed. Stanley Wells, Gary Taylor, John Jowett, and William Montgomery (Oxford, 1986), 3.2.138–9.

[2] Avril Ormsby, 'London 2012 opening ceremony draws 900 million viewers', *Reuters*, 7 August 2012, http://uk.reuters .com/article/uk-oly-ratings-day-idUKBRE8760V820120807.

[3] See Samuel Taylor Coleridge, *Shakespearean Criticism*, vol. 1 (London, 1960), p. 119. The figure of Prospero, played by Sir Ian McKellen, did appear briefly in the opening ceremony for the Paralympics, speaking lines especially scripted for the ceremony.

[4] Johann Gregory and François-Xavier Gleyzan, 'Thinking through Shakespeare: an introduction to Shakespeare and theory', *English Studies* 94.3 (2013), 251–8; p. 253.

[5] Jem Bloomfield, 'Caliban and Brunel: Kenneth Branagh's speech at the Olympics Opening Ceremony', *Words of Power: Reading Shakespeare and the Bible*, 29 July 2012, https://quiteirregular.wordpress.com/2012/07/29/caliban-and-brunel-kenneth -branaghs-speech-at-the-olympics-opening-ceremony.

[6] Danny Boyle, programme notes, quoted in Bloomfield, 'Caliban and Brunel'.

nostalgia rather than fierce competition: as Wilson argues, 'Boyle looked to be idealizing a disarmingly alternative genealogy, and a bucolic rather than heroic sporting culture that had lingered on Dover's Hill', the site of both the 1612 Cotswold Olympics and the 'Olympic Village' in 2012.[7]

This celebration of Englishness places Shakespeare centre-stage, to be sure, but what we encounter in 2012 is an outward-looking and resonant Shakespeare who addresses a global audience through Caliban's words of welcome and Miranda's expression of 'wonder' at this 'brave new world' (as occurred in the opening ceremony of the Paralympic Games).[8] In London's projection of national pride in the summer of 2012 we glimpse something of the haunting presence of the dispossessed within mainstream English culture and the transformation that even canonical Shakespeare has undergone in the face of globalization's cultural disseminations. This transformation is not adequately accounted for through the notion of the post-colony 'speaking back' to the centre, given the varied and uneven histories of cultural and political domination. The study of Shakespeare's changing iterations across the world today requires a more nuanced model of cultural engagement, one that can offer a global mapping of uneven power relations and, at the same time, attend to the texture of local particularities and the surprising affinities and dissonances they yield.

GLOBAL SHAKESPEARE AS SEEN FROM THE SOUTH

There is a case to be made for the global South as a category of analysis for Shakespeare studies, given its presence within cultural studies more broadly. I would like to take a moment here to make some tentative claims about what I consider to be the value, for revisionist scholarship, of the view from the South, not only for those who live and work in the South or who assert an affiliation or a commitment to the politics of the South, but also for critical thought generally. The term 'global South' has developed a certain theoretical purchase in recent years but it has a surprisingly clear

foothold in early modernity as well; early modern geographers wrote explicitly of the people of the 'southern climes' or 'southern nations', or sometimes simply, the 'south', installing as they did so subtle forms of racialization and legitimizing colonial exploitation, as the following two examples attest. Sixteenth-century English compiler Richard Eden writes in a generalized fashion about 'the south partes of the world' when flaunting the extractable wealth and exoticism of regions found 'betwene the two Tropikes under ye Equinoctial or burning lyne'.[9] The seventeenth-century English cartographer Richard Blome sets up a distinction between the 'Southern Nations' of the world and the 'Northern People' in the epistle of his translation of Bernhardus Varenius's *Geographia* in 1682. According to Blome, body and mind are shaped by climate, which explains the unquestionable superiority of the 'Northern People' of the globe, who 'have always been Victorious and predominant over the Meridional or Southern Nations'.[10] I have argued elsewhere at greater length that the distinction between 'South' and 'North' emerged during the early modern expansionist period as a key mechanism for establishing a racial hierarchy on a global scale.[11] The 'south partes' were regions whose natural resources seemed to invite exploitation and whose seemingly primitive peoples warranted the influences of the North.

The term's value for cultural studies today is related to this cultural geography; the global South enables an oblique angle on colonial

---

[7] See Richard Wilson, 'Like an Olympian wrestling: Shakespeare's Olympic Game', *Shakespeare Survey 66* (Cambridge, 2013), pp. 82–95; p. 83.

[8] Actress Nicola Miles-Wildin delivered an excerpt from Miranda's speech from Act 5, scene 1.

[9] Richard Eden, 'Epistle', in *A treatyse of the newe India* (London, 1555), sig. aa.vi.r–v.

[10] Richard Blome, 'Epistle', in Bernhardus Varenius, *Cosmography and geography in two parts*, trans. Richard Blome (London, 1682), sig. A2r.

[11] See Sandra Young, *The Early Modern Global South in Print: Textual Form and the Production of Human Difference as Knowledge* (Farnham, 2015).

modernity or, as Jean Comaroff and John Comaroff have articulated it in their book on *Theory from the South*, an 'ex-centric ... angle of vision'.[12] The global South challenges the normativity of the view from the north, bringing into focus an alternative set of interests and material conditions. Even so, there is a degree of ambivalence surrounding the term, partly as a result of its paternalistic, if somewhat idealistic, early iterations in United Nations 'development' discourse (specifically, a 2003 United Nations Programme, 'Forging a Global South'), even as it sought to encourage 'South–South' connections and self-directed strategies for growth. As Arif Dirlik explains, the 'global South has its roots in earlier third world visions of liberation, and those visions still have an important role to play in restoring human ends to development'.[13] Critics might argue that the term is misleading: the distinction it identifies between a putative 'North' and 'South' cannot in fact be mapped onto a fixed cartographic grid. But the crucial thing about the concept of the global South is that its usefulness lies in the cultural and economic *alignments* it signals, sometimes held in tension within a single nation or region.

The frame provided by the global South is therefore both limited and immensely useful for cultural studies. Arif Dirlik has outlined the 'chaotic' and surprising alignments that frustrate any attempt to map a geographical grid onto the economies of the world.[14] Even so, he finds in the notion of a global South an effective rubric with which to identify the struggles and 'affinities' that potentially challenge the hegemony of a modernity rooted in coloniality: 'There are certain affinities between these societies in terms of mutual recognition of historical experiences with colonialism and neocolonialism.'[15] Most importantly, perhaps, the global South potentially allows for the inclusion, as Dirlik puts it, of 'the voices of the formerly colonized and marginalized in a world that already has been shaped by a colonial modernity to which there is no alternative in sight'.[16] It is this privileging of previously hidden stories that is compelling about the framework provided by the global South, as

well as the space it creates for critical perspectives on race and power. The framework of the global South potentially enables a different perspective on relations of domination and freedom within a world made complex through diasporic mobilities. It focuses on connections and affinities between diverse contexts across the South. It also opens up space for greater nuance as we seek to understand Shakespeare's resonances today.

The emergence of Global Shakespeare has already helped to bring to scholarly attention some of the struggles around race and anti-coloniality across the globe. And yet, while Global Shakespeare thrives as a field of interest, it has not necessarily led to a revision of the critical landscape. While the field has drawn attention to Shakespeare's ongoing presence across the globe, it is not clear to what extent it has transformed the cultural politics of 'Shakespeare'. Certainly, interest in the 'global' has signalled critical openness to non-traditional centres of Shakespeare scholarship and theatre practice. But the value of a recognizably global and plural Shakespeare is not simply its accommodation of a richer variety or its celebration of difference, akin to what Ania Loomba dismissed as the 'simplistic "all is hybrid and multicultural"' approach to cultural studies in her critique of a certain mode of uncritical postcolonial scholarship.[17] Rather, the expanded view and more encompassing methodology have the potential to challenge some assumptions underpinning the field and to liberate scholars, theatre-makers and Shakespeare himself to tell new stories

---

[12] Jean Comaroff and John Comaroff, *Theory from the South: Or, How Euro-America Is Evolving Toward Africa* (Boulder, 2012), p. 2.

[13] Arif Dirlik, *Global Modernity: Modernity in the Age of Global Capitalism* (New York, 2016), p. 150.

[14] Dirlik, *Global Modernity*, p. 138.

[15] Dirlik, *Global Modernity*, p. 139.

[16] Dirlik, *Global Modernity*, p. 147.

[17] Ania Loomba, 'Review of Remapping the Mediterranean World in Early Modern English Writings / Speaking of the Moor: From Alcazar to Othello', *Shakespeare Studies* 38 (2010), 269–70.

entirely, narrated from the 'undersides' of colonial modernity.[18]

SHAKESPEARE AS AN ALLY OF LIBERATION IN AFRICA

What would it mean for us to take seriously the critical frame of the global South and the lateral view it privileges, across the Indian and Atlantic Ocean worlds? Partly in response to that question, this section of my article explores Shakespeare's cultural and political resonances in contemporary Africa and beyond the oceans on either side of its coastlines. It is inspired by the conviction that it is important to resist the impulse to reach for the tired conclusion that Shakespeare's presence across the South affirms, above all, his pre-eminence. While it may be true to say that the creative latitude of contemporary engagements enhances Shakespeare's significance, this is a matter of mutual generation. Shakespeare's evolving presence in Africa speaks to the exciting renewal that is possible when he ceases to be thought of as 'our guru' (as Nobel Laureate Nadine Gordimer once put it) and when he becomes one of many potentially rich experiences of theatre from exciting new writers and theatre-makers.[19]

There is, of course, a long tradition within Africa of invoking Shakespeare as an ally. Despite the resistance to Shakespeare in evidence in post-apartheid and decolonized public culture, and the rise in visibility of new literatures since the Africanist literary movement of the 1970s spearheaded by Ngũgĩ wa Thiong'o and others, Shakespeare has figured as an ally in oppositional politics for a number of African intellectuals during the last century. Shakespeare's language has found its way into the speeches of a number of post-apartheid statesmen, and a narrative has emerged in recent years suggesting that freedom fighters under apartheid felt a keen affinity with Shakespeare. The community of anti-apartheid freedom fighters incarcerated on Robben Island felt drawn to Shakespeare's works and the humanity he seemed to represent; the circulation of *The Alexander Text of the Complete Works of*

Shakespeare, disguised as Hindi scriptures, has recently garnered critical attention, with the publication of monographs by Ashwin Desai and David Schalkwyk.[20] The idea that Shakespeare's value was felt even in the space of the Robben Island prison amongst inmates and liberation heroes, and by Nelson Mandela himself, is compelling: Shakespeare seems to gain a new prescience. But in his moving account of the circulation of the *Complete Works*, Schalkwyk doesn't celebrate Shakespeare's exceptionism in being able to speak into even the dry land of apartheid South Africa. Rather, as Schalkwyk tells it, Shakespeare's words become a device for imagining our way into the lives of the Robben Island prisoners whose signatures next to key passages from Shakespeare's *Completed Works* attest to an imagined solidarity.

There is a long history to this sense of affiliation, for despite Shakespeare's central position within the English colonial canon – and perhaps also because of it – Shakespeare was available as a language for self-expression for an earlier generation of African nationalists, such as Julius Nyerere of Tanzania, and writers, such as Sol Plaatje. But this deployment of Shakespeare as the mechanism of a form of self-assertion in a racist society is an ambivalent matter. It risks reiterating the standing not so much of the translation but of the putative original. Newer generations of African playwrights have tended to produce translations that rewrite, appropriate and transform, working alongside Shakespeare to create a new work. In West Africa, for example, Shakespeare's *Julius Caesar* was reimagined as a powerful figure of Krio democracy in Thomas

---

[18] Comaroff and Comaroff, *Theory from the South*, p. 6.

[19] Nadine Gordimer referred to Shakespeare in this way during a public conversation held at the Centre for the Book in Cape Town in August 2011 in celebration of the publication of her collection of essays, *Telling Times: Writing and Living, 1950–2008* (New York, 2010).

[20] Ashwin Desai, *Reading Revolution: Shakespeare on Robben Island* (Pretoria, 2012); David Schalkwyk, *Hamlet's Dreams: The Robben Island Shakespeare* (London, 2013).

Decker's *Juliohs Siza*.[21] Decker's play unravels the polarity represented by idealization versus resistance. Published just three years after independence in Sierra Leone, it has been praised for its audacity in asserting 'a sort of linguistic authority by means of a Krio appropriation and translation' and an 'African independent theatre'.[22] Now the language of 'everyday life' in Sierra Leone, Krio is a language that has evolved from the multiple influences and traditions at play there. Furthermore, it is neither European nor, strictly speaking, indigenous. The use of Krio thus creates the conditions for a 'linguistic connection' across perceived 'ethnic boundaries'.[23] The possibility for 'linguistic connection' and the crossing of 'boundaries' depends on an engagement with the work that is both lighter and more robust, a veritable creolization of form.

More recently, Mauritian playwright Dev Virahsawmy has entirely refashioned Shakespeare's plays by inserting them into an Indian Ocean world. Virahsawmy's celebration of the language and politics of Mauritian Creole in works such as *Toufann* (an audacious rewriting of *The Tempest*) renders Shakespeare's world irrepressibly polyvocal.[24] This creolization of Shakespeare also has the effect of putting him somehow in relation to slave experience: it insists upon the relation between Shakespeare's world and slavery's traumatic dislocations, marked in the surprising cadences and idioms of Mauritian Creole, in its chaotic temporalities and in the inclusion of contradictory and contesting voices. In the final section of the article, then, I turn briefly to Virahsawmy's reimagining of *The Tempest* in the Indian Ocean world of Mauritius to reflect briefly on the way creole forms bring into view the struggles and the surprising affinities between contexts that differ significantly.

LATERAL AFFINITIES: A CREOLE TEMPEST IN THE INDIAN OCEAN

Working in sympathy with Shakespeare's play, Virahsawmy's *Toufann* explores the anti-colonial and liberatory sentiments within *The Tempest*, while transforming it utterly in 'an irreverent and parodic rewriting', as Roshni Mooneeram puts it.[25]

In Françoise Lionnet's reading, this sympathetic rendering of *The Tempest* is the result of Virahsawmy's sense of affinity, across time and place, between the worlds of post-independence Mauritius and Shakespeare's play. In the new work, the anti-colonial elements of the Shakespearian text are toyed with and reimagined, in an expression of what Lionnet calls 'a "transcolonial" form of solidarity'.[26]

Virahsawmy's activism comes in the wake of the anti-colonial movements of the 1960s and 1970s — in particular, the creolité movement in the Caribbean and its Mauritian counterpart, Khal Torabully's 'coolitude' movement. Coolitude brings into view the more complex stratifications within Indian society and the suffering of the indentured labourers, with their journey across the 'Kala Pani', the black sea of Indian mythology which has frequently been used to refer to the terrifying oceanic crossing, for example in the work of Mauritian writer Ananda Devi.[27] As a cultural and political movement, therefore, coolitude emerges out of the context of the Indian Oceanic world, and the particular history

---

[21] Thomas Decker, *Juliohs Siza* (1964), ed. Neville Shrimpton and Njie Sulayman (Umea, Sweden, 1988).

[22] Tcho Mbaimba Caulker, 'Shakespeare's *Julius Caesar* in Sierra Leone: Thomas Decker's *Juliohs Siza*, Roman politics, and the emergence of a postcolonial African state', *Research in African Literatures* 40.2 (2009), 208–27; p. 213.

[23] Caulker, 'Shakespeare's *Julius Caesar* in Sierra Leone', p. 213.

[24] Dev Virahsawmy, *Toufann: A Mauritian Fantasy*, in *African Theatre: Playwrights and Politics*, ed. Martin Banham, James Gibbs and Femi Osofisan, trans. Nisha Walling and Michael Walling (Oxford, Bloomington, and Johannesburg, 1999), pp. 217–54.

[25] Roshni Mooneeram, 'Literary translations as a tool for critical language planning', *World Englishes* 32.2 (2013), 198–210; p. 203.

[26] Françoise Lionnet, 'Creole vernacular theatre: transcolonial translations', *MLN* 118.4 (2003), 911–32; p. 917.

[27] For a discussion of the history and cultural legacy of Indian indentured labourers and a comparison between the Caribbean and the Indian Ocean island worlds, see Rohini Bannerjee's essay, 'The Kala Pani connection: Francophone migration narratives in the Caribbean writing of Raphaël Confiant and the Mauritian writing of Ananda Devi', *Anthurium: A Caribbean Studies Journal* 7.1 (2010), article 5.

of Mauritius, which occupies a key position along the Indian Ocean spice trade route. It was inhabited by a succession of European traders – the Portuguese, then the Dutch, and finally the French, who created permanent settlements from 1715 and 'a plantation economy reliant on the introduction of slaves mainly from various parts of Africa and Madagascar'.[28] Mauritian Creole is intimately connected to the history and aftermath of slavery in Mauritius. It carries that legacy in its rhythms and richly textured idioms, and in the diverse ethnic identifications of the people, evidence of human mobility over the past four centuries. However, 'coolitude' has been criticized more recently for its celebratory tone and inability to acknowledge the ongoing marginalization of the descendants of African slaves in Mauritius, the group historically associated most closely with creole linguistic and cultural expressions. Virahsawmy's commitment to standardizing Mauritian Creole as a national linguistic identity is not simply a rejoinder to colonial dominance; it also affirms the sense of renewal and inclusivity in the post-independence era, demonstrating the importance of 'notions of inclusion, as opposed to exclusion, of cultural creolisation (métissage), as opposed to (supposed) ethnic purity, of the empowerment of women, as opposed to their oppression', as Shawkat Toorawa has argued.[29]

Shakespeare has become an unlikely accomplice in Virahsawmy's activism on behalf of what is known in Mauritius as Kreol Morisien (or Kreol, as I will refer to it, to distinguish it from other creole forms). Toorawa thinks of Virahsawmy's project as an attempt to 'redeploy' and 'wield Shakespeare in order to elevate Mauritian Creole – the language in which all his plays are written – to the status of a world language'.[30] The elevating effect is mutual, however. In his engagement with The Tempest, Virahsawmy makes Shakespeare an ally in unravelling assumptions about 'ethnicity' and in crafting a new, more inclusive basis for social cohesion in the post-colony.

Shakespeare's play is made to bear witness to the everyday challenges and injustices in Mauritius, in part, through the adoption of Kreol, as I aim to show as I turn to a brief discussion of some aspects

of the play for the remainder of this article. The idiomatic texture of the Kreol makes visible the texture of everyday life on the island in a way that the English translation of this adaptation flattens out somewhat. For example, the boat into which Prospero and his daughter are set loose is a tiny local fisherman's boat called a *lakok pistas*,[31] which in the English translation appears blandly as 'a boat';[32] when the description points to their vulnerability on the water in the face of the cyclone, it registers syntactically as a metaphor: 'in nothing but a nutshell of a boat'.[33] The Kreol, by contrast, recalls the precarity of the life of a fisherman on the waters during an Indian Ocean storm by using the local term for a fisherman's pirogue: 'dan enn siklonn dan enn lakok pistas'.[34] The Kreol idiom used to describe Prospero's prisoners refers to a local shrimp ('sevret') associated with madness or bewilderment, but is rendered as 'fish out of water'[35] in the English translation.[36] Earlier Prospero describes them as 'still infected with evil';[37] in the Kreol version, we are invited to picture their evil still dancing in their head: 'Zot move ankor pe fer bal dan zot latet' (8).[38] In another expression that is not included in the English version, when faced with the impending storm, a sailor warns that 'you pay for your sins on earth' – as the English translation puts it[39] – where the original uses a Kreol idiom ('Pa toulezour fet zako')[40] which warns that 'not every day is a monkey festival'.[41] Even the ubiquitous

[28] 'Mooneeram, 'Literary translations', p. 200.
[29] Shawkat Toorawa, 'Translating *The Tempest*', in *African Theatre: Playwrights and Politics*, ed. Banham, Gibbs and Osofisan, pp. 125–38; p. 128.
[30] Toorawa, 'Translating The Tempest', p. 129.
[31] Dev Virahsawmy, *Toufann: enn Fantezi an 3 Ak* (Rose Hill, 1991), pp. 3, 5, http://boukiebanane.com/toufann.
[32] Virahsawmy, *Toufann*, trans. Walling, p. 220.
[33] Virahsawmy, *Toufann*, trans. Walling, p. 219.
[34] Virahsawmy, *Toufann*, p. 3.
[35] Virahsawmy, *Toufann*, trans. Walling, p. 229.
[36] Virahsawmy, *Toufann*, p. 15.
[37] Virahsawmy, *Toufann*, trans. Walling, p. 224.
[38] Translation by Tasneem Allybokus.
[39] Virahsawmy, *Toufann*, trans. Walling, p. 245.
[40] Virahsawmy, *Toufann*, p. 36.
[41] Translation by Tasneem Allybokus.

exclamation 'Oh my god!' in English[42] carries the trace of a more complex social inheritance in the Kreol 'Baprebab!", a Bhojpuri expression within Kreol, derived from Hindi.

The language of the play – particularly, but not only, in the Kreol version – is scattered with details from everyday life in Mauritius. At the same time, it undermines any sense that contemporary Mauritian existence is located within an unchanging natural world, uncontaminated by global youth culture. To be sure, some images are drawn from an attachment to the natural world and hint at Kreol culture, but this cultural mélange is equally affected by contemporary globalized culture. Dammarro and Kaspalto sing traditional Kreol songs, or sega, by the segatier Alphonse Ravaton, or 'Ti Frère'. The first of these mocks – and celebrates – the impulse to drink banana wine to excess.[43] The next song is also a paean to alcohol and island courtship.[44] The social anthropologist, Caroline Déodat, describes the impact of the sega as a cultural form initially practised by slaves and then post-abolition descendants of slaves; it is a form that evokes the quarrels and struggles of everyday life in Mauritius and subtly controls modes of sociality.[45] Though the sega is traditionally associated with the economically disenfranchised descendants of slaves, analyses of performances of the sega, she argues, present a more complex picture: they 'undermine the essentialist categories inherited from imperialism and colonialism' and 'introduce a relationship with Indianness', disavowing 'a fixed notion of Mauritian creoleness'.[46]

The invocation of the sega in *Toufann* would seem to affirm Déodat's argument, and this is true of both English and Kreol versions of the play, in which both English and Kreol songs remain untranslated. For the English translators, the songs are significant only for the 'folk' elements they bring into view; their literal meanings are not worth clarifying. In a footnote, the translators explain their decision to leave the songs untranslated on the basis of 'their folk quality' and 'the quality of linguistic confusion' that the scene elicits.[47] However, one might equally argue that the 'confusion' is caused not so much by a quality inherent to the traditional genre of the quarrelsome sega, but by the play's refusal to remain within

a coherent cultural field. Immediately after the segas, the characters break into a song associated with a very different popular tradition: the Beatles' 1960s hit 'Lucy in the Sky with Diamonds'. In loud exclamations, the characters celebrate a politics shaped by modern-day drug use: 'Up the Republic of Ecstasy!'[48] – lampooning as they do so the earnest affiliations of contemporary political movements that depend on ethnic or nationalist identifications. This is evident in a comment by King Lir earlier in this scene, when he criticizes the 'politicking' of typical career politicians. In the English version, the critique remains hypothetical, but the Kreol includes an oblique reference to '*proteksion montagn*', echoing a celebrated political speech from 1983 in which, as the translators explain, 'Harish Boodhoo likened the various ethnic groups in Mauritius to monkeys defending their mountains from one another.'[49] In calling for a greater degree of socialist communalism, particularly amongst the marginalized rural communities, during a period of realignment in Mauritian politics, Boodhoo berated Mauritians for privileging ethnicity over class interests, saying it is

---

42 Virahsawmy, *Toufann*, trans. Walling, p. 234.

43 '*Charli O, Charli O. Aret bwar, aret bwar diven banann. Dan diven banan ena bebet sizo*', which would translate as 'Charlie, oh, Charlie, oh. Stop drinking banana wine. In banana wine, you will find scissors bugs': Virahsawmy, *Toufann*, 18. Translated by Tasneem Allybokus.

44 '*Ti mimi lav sa ver la. Lav sa ver la. Met zafer la, koko*', meaning 'Little kitty, wash this cup. Wash this cup. Put the stuff in it, sweetheart' (literally, 'coconut'): Virahsawmy, *Toufann*, p. 18. Translated by Tasneem Allybokus.

45 See Caroline Déodat, 'Troubler le genre du "séga typique": imaginaire et performativité poétique de la créolité mauricienne' ['Disrupting the genre of "typical sega." Imaginary and poetic performativity of Mauritian creoleness'], Centre for South Asian Studies, Paris, June 2016, as described in English in the *Centre for South Asian Studies Newsletter* 14 (Winter 2016/17).

46 Déodat, 'Disrupting the genre of "typical sega"'.

47 Virahsawmy, *Toufann*, trans. Walling, p. 254.

48 Virahsawmy, *Toufann*, trans. Walling, p. 232.

49 They are referring to a speech made by Harish Boodhoo, an outspoken Hindu leader of the Parti Socialiste Mauricien which had merged with a breakaway group from the MMM to form the Mouvement Socialiste Millitant (MSM) when contesting the elections in 1983.

as if 'each monkey has to protect his mountain' (or, '*Sak zako bizin protez so montayn*').[50] In hinting at this critique of mindless ethnic chauvinism, Virahsawmy's creative innovations are thus aligned with the political movement that rejects the structuring logic of ethnicity over a more radical politics that seeks social justice.

A detailed exposition of the play is not possible in this more general discussion of the ways contemporary theatre-makers across the global South invigorate Shakespeare's works by involving them in the project of decolonization. However, I would like to observe that one of Virahsawmy's key strategies for forging a new ethics for the post-colony that is not structured by brutal social hierarchies is in the future he invites us to imagine for Kalibann. Like Shakespeare's Caliban, Kalibann is the figure who most clearly carries the history of slavery in his body and the structural position of servitude he occupies, and yet Virahsawmy's play imagines his speech as reasoned, establishing as it does so his suitability for a life of partnership in love and in political leadership. It is Prospero whose embittered relationship to power appears perverse.

Prospero explains his jaundiced version of their intertwined history to his daughter (who in this play is named Kordelia, invoking the intimacy and independence of Lear's youngest daughter). On this 'small inhabited island, very close to hell', Prospero tells her, '[t]here was a hut, where Bangoya was living with her half-bred batar'[51] or, 'Bangoya ek so batar ti pe viv.'[52] In Kreol, the word *batar* can be used pejoratively to refer to a person born to unmarried parents and 'a "person of mixed race"'; as the English translators note, 'both usages are applied to Kalibann throughout the play'.[53] However, the word *batar* only ever appears during the above exchange, which is the first account of Kalibann's parentage, followed by an explanation that evokes both senses of the word, left untranslated. In effect, this allows both senses to linger simultaneously, literally unhomed in the English version. To suggest this racial complexity, the playwright draws on a wider lexicon: elsewhere Kalibann is referred to as a '*metis*',[54] for example in the stage directions, where it is translated as 'of

mixed race',[55] and in Aryel's account to Poloniouss, where it is translated as 'a mulatto'.[56] The shadow cast by Bangoya's experience of rape, enslavement and abandonment by her pirate owner registers in the vocabulary with which Kalibann himself is presented. Prospero's language is marked by its offensiveness, the worst of which does not bear repeating, except to note his attempt to offer genetics as an explanatory framework for what the audience has already recognized as the power struggle on the island: 'That Kalibann has a very disturbing genetic make-up.'[57]

However, this comment is not left unchallenged. Throughout, the audience is offered alternative perspectives, through Kalibann's own observations and in the responses of other characters. It is Aryel who undoes the spurious association between Kalibann and cannibalism: 'Kalibann is the name of a person', he corrects Poloniouss; 'His father was a white pirate, and his mother a black slave. He's mulatto ... You don't have to feel sorry for him. He knows what he wants.'[58] The play allows us to see Kalibann begin to fulfil that vision. This involves gaining his freedom, but Kalibann requests it rather than claims it: after 'coming out' as lovers, Kalibann and the pregnant Kordelia confront Prospero with an image of his own abuse of power, 'A victim can turn into an aggressor ... You got blinded by your own power, and stopped being able to tell the difference between justice and revenge.'[59] It is then that Kalibann reminds Prospero: 'You promised me my freedom. Since then I've come to understand exactly what that means. Can I ask you to keep your word?', to

---

[50] See Thomas Hylland Eriksen, 'Communicating cultural difference and identity: ethnicity and nationalism in Mauritius', *Oslo Occasional Papers in Social Anthropology* 16.
[51] Virahsawmy, *Toufann*, trans. Walling, p. 221.
[52] Virahsawmy, *Toufann*, p. 5.
[53] Virahsawmy, *Toufann*, trans. Walling, p. 254.
[54] Virahsawmy, *Toufann*, p. 39.
[55] Virahsawmy, *Toufann*, trans. Walling, p. 219.
[56] Virahsawmy, *Toufann*, trans. Walling, p. 248.
[57] Virahsawmy, *Toufann*, trans. Walling, p. 221.
[58] Virahsawmy, *Toufann*, trans. Walling, p. 248.
[59] Virahsawmy, *Toufann*, trans. Walling, p. 251.

which a bewildered Prospero answers, 'Yes, yes'.[60] The elderly patriarch King Lir proposes to Prospero that 'we can make Kalibann King' – for 'this is the way to solve our problem'.[61]

Thus, Kalibann offers not so much an image of a post-revolutionary future as an alternative route to a just future. Prospero emerges as undeniably partisan and manipulative, and racist, at a remove from the cast of younger players who are able to imagine a different kind of future entirely. Virahsawmy's Kalibann presents an alternative, both in his championing of a feminist model of shared leadership with Prospero's daughter, and also in his ability to conceive of transformed social relations without violent revolution. Received ideas of social hierarchy are ridiculed and overturned, and notions of family defined by normative ideas of race, gender and sexuality are rejected outright. This is true not only of Kalibann and Kordelia but also of Ferdjinan and Aryel, for it is their vision that inspires the acknowledgement that dramatic, revolutionary change is within the grasp of those who seek it, regardless of how they have been positioned by the circumstances of their birth. As Ferdjinan exclaims: 'We're free . . . nobody is going to save us'.[62]

However, there is a blind spot in this radical reimagining of a liberated future within the postcolony. Caliban (as Kalibann) can conceivably forge a relationship of mutual love and respect with Miranda (as Kordelia) but the homosexual bond between Aryel and Ferdjinan is doomed to remain without erotic consummation, despite their acknowledgement of desire and despite Ferdjinan's explicit rejection of the heteronormative, reproductive plot laid out for him by the patriarchs, as his retort to his father makes explicit: 'You're so obsessed with getting married and breeding. All this nonsense about inheritance . . . No!'[63]

The play's affirmation, articulated by the ageing King Lir to a contrite Prospero, that 'The young can move life forward in their own way' points to the dawning of a new age, as a result not of adversarial politics, but of the transformative power of a radical and liberated imagination. In fact, the play insists that there are multiple futures and that 'a new ending' could be scripted, with the comic figures Dammarro and Kaspalto as kings, as per the fantasy they had been allowed to indulge in earlier in the play. Aryel promises Dammarro, the comic usurper of King Lir's position, 'I'll get him to write a new story. One where you become king.'[64] Even those marked by the play's comic logic as lowly and absurd are invited to imagine a different future. Their class aspirations are subtly validated and social hierarchy is rendered arbitrary, a matter of scripting rather than birthright, in a moment of irreverence and radical inclusion that extends even to the venerable old patriarchs. Poloniouss urges King Lir to take up his part: 'Majesty – they're writing the script now. Best to play your part in the comedy.'[65] We witness the uncertainties surrounding the scripting of a path for a new post-independence generation.

My impulse to describe the play's ending as 'radical' is misplaced, given its demure treatment of class struggle and sexuality. Still, in inviting us to reflect on its own construction, the play stages (and even celebrates) the plot's unravelling. It recognizes the aspirations of the serving classes and the enslaved from within a set of tensions and possibilities imagined initially in Shakespeare's play, whose plot has been rendered multiple and unbounded.

IN CONCLUSION: RENDERING SHAKESPEARE MULTIPLE

The mode of creolization structuring this work is not one that locates the everyday of Mauritian life in a timeless folk traditionalism. Nor is it structured by defined ethnic or linguistic identifications. Rather, the cultural mélange we witness here acknowledges the global circulation of eclectic forms of contemporary culture and the irreverent mixing of cultural elements, 'folk' and contemporary, local and putatively 'elsewhere'. Shakespeare's work, too, is made subject to the multiple identifications of modern

60 Virahsawmy, *Toufann*, trans. Walling, p. 251.
61 Virahsawmy, *Toufann*, trans. Walling, p. 252.
62 Virahsawmy, *Toufann*, trans. Walling, p. 247.
63 Virahsawmy, *Toufann*, trans. Walling, p. 247.
64 Virahsawmy, *Toufann*, trans. Walling, p. 253.
65 Virahsawmy, *Toufann*, trans. Walling, p. 240.

existence in worlds made more complex by globalization and mixed colonial inheritances.

Such wild reimaginings of Shakespeare do not constitute a disavowal of the Shakespearian text so much as a contribution to its ongoing coming-into-being. This is true even when the intertextual sympathies are only implicit and the new work is far removed from the old, not only in time and space but also in its poetic register, its language and its cultural imagination. The latitude adopted by an adaptation like *Toufann*, with its boldness in transforming the Shakespearian text, is both playful and deadly serious. Shakespearian scholar Christy Desmet challenges us to recognize the seriousness of the culture of 'play' at work in adaptation, even in the stitched-together texts of her analysis and the 'art' of what she calls 'remix': drawing on the terminology of Clifford Geertz, Desmet identifies a kind 'of "deep play" – entrenched in, informed by, and in response to core cultural imperatives'.[66]

Virahsawmy's refashioning of *The Tempest* goes some way towards responding to the cultural imperatives at work in the post-independence Indian Ocean world of Mauritius, its legacy of slavery and settlement legible, nonetheless, in the spaces of its most imaginative reinvention. That Shakespeare's work would provide a fertile place for thinking 'intensely and with freedom', as Stephen Greenblatt put it in relation to 'Shakespeare in Tehran', is of great interest to Shakespeare studies, as it continues to recognize the significance of Shakespeare's resonances within a wider world, and the solidarities that his works have garnered.[67] A creolized Shakespeare is much more than a celebration of multiplicity; to the extent that the aftermath of slavery is legible in creole cultural forms, it is an invitation to bear witness to slavery's brutal legacy of dispossession, dislocation and survival, and to imagine for the post-colony a more just future that resists the ethnocentric logic of colonial modernity.

---

[66] Christy Desmet, 'Appropriation 2.0', in *Shakespeare in Our Time: A Shakespeare Association of America Collection*, ed. Dympna Callaghan and Suzanne Gossett (London, 2016), pp. 236–9; p. 239.

[67] Stephen Greenblatt, 'Afterword: Shakespeare in Tehran', in *Shakespeare in Our Time: A Shakespeare Association of America Collection*, ed. Dympna Callaghan and Suzanne Gossett (London, 2016), pp. 343–52; p. 352.

SHAKESPEARE'S CREOLIZED VOICES

ASHISH BEESOONDIAL

Shakespeare's prominent presence in literary land-scapes of former British colonies in the global South bears testimony to his influence, both during and after the colonial period. Shakespeare currently occupies a ubiquitous status in many literary curricula. Beyond the curricula, however, new Shakespeares, in the form of local literatures, have also been written into existence. The post-independence period in Mauritius, which ushered in a movement of post-colonial writing and identity, has seen the rise of a dual existence for Shakespeare: in the curriculum as well as in the form of local literary productions. There has been a wave of translations and adaptations of Shakespeare there, most notably by local Mauritian playwright, Dev Virahsawmy. A staunch advocate of Kreol Morisien (Mauritian Creole), Virahsawmy has translated a number of texts from the canon into creole in a bid to make these literary works more accessible. His most prominent works, however, feature his adaptations of Shakespeare. This article will examine how Virahsawmy has appropriated and adapted Shakespeare in Kreol Morisien in order to articulate his socio-political vision.

The choice of language is always political. While much literary production in Mauritius has been in English and French, Virahsawmy's purpose in using creole is primarily to valorize the language and to give it the status of a national language, at par with the colonial languages. Inspired by two of his predecessors at the University of Edinburgh, Julius Nyerere of Tanzania and Thomas Decker of Sierra Leone, who translated *Julius Caesar* into Swahili and Kriyo respectively, Virahsawmy first translated *Much Ado About Nothing*. Virahsawmy's mission for

linguistic valorization of Mauritian Creole[1] has to be understood from a historical and cultural context. Successively colonized by the French (1715–1810) and the British (1810–1968), Mauritius, under British rule, allowed the French to remain on the island. Thus, both French and English were to become the main languages there. Slaves were brought to Mauritius mainly under French rule, and out of the communication between slave owners and slaves emerged the creole language – at that time a patois. The abolition of slavery and the beginning of the indentured period saw labourers from different regions of India and China arriving in Mauritius, making it a multi-ethnic, multicultural and multilingual country. While the languages of all these peoples have been given official status and studied in schools, creole was considered to be inadequate for a written language.

The post-independence nationalist spirit and the militant climate that gathered momentum in the 1980s, around a decade after independence, pressed for a Mauritianization of identities, language use and pedagogical curricula. Virahsawmy, who was politically active at that time, sought to prove that his mother tongue, the language that bound all Mauritians, was much more than a patois: it also had the potential to develop as a literary language, one that was capable of articulating philosophical thoughts. His choice of Shakespeare is therefore judicious and bold: while translations meant that Mauritian Creole was a vehicle for the complex

---

[1] See Vicram Ramharai, *La littérature Mauricienne d'expression créole* (Port Louis, 1990).

layers in Shakespeare, his adaptations, however, provided a different perspective. They allowed him, while using creole as a dramatic language, to express his concerns and his vision for his society.

Post-colonial writing often finds expression in an agenda of writing back to the centre. Virahsawmy's writing does not necessarily adhere to this approach. By appropriating Shakespeare, and relocating him in a local, personal and social context, the centre–margin relationship is being redefined. Virahsawmy's adaptations need to be regarded as part of a post-colonial endeavour of deconstructing Shakespeare's monumentalism in order to suit his purpose, which is to express his vision of the local situation. Virahsawmy's adaptations then offer a more reconstructive approach, emanating from a hybridized consciousness,[2] which goes beyond the act of writing back from an anti-colonial perspective. Shakespeare is therefore borrowed, used and relocated to new spaces and, even if Mauritius is not always explicitly mentioned, Virahsawmy brings the Bard closer to home to voice out local concerns and to establish Kreol Morisien as a literary tool. By creolizing Shakespeare, Virahsawmy sought to challenge the bias against a language which needed official recognition.

Extreme liberties are taken with the Bard, as exemplified in the adapted titles of the plays, illustrated below:[3]

Original title	Adapted title	Meaning
Anthony and Cleopatra	*Dernie Vol* (2003)	The Last Flight
Othello	*Prezidan Otelo* (2003)	President Othello
King Lear	*Tabisman Lear* (2003)	Lear's Estate
Hamlet	*Dokter Hamlet* (1996)	Doctor Hamlet
	Hamlet II (1996)	Hamlet II
Romeo and Juliet	*Ramdeo ek so Ziliet* (2012)	Ramdeo and his Juliet
	Ziliet ek so Romeo (2001)	Juliet and her Romeo
The Tempest	*Toufann* (1991)	Cyclone/ Destruction
Macbeth	*Zeneral Makbef* (1980)	General Macbeth
Twelfth Night	*Sir Toby* (1998)	Sir Toby

The meta-narrative of Shakespeare is challenged as the characters are reinvented and placed in different settings across time and space. Ramdeo and Ziliet, for instance, are projected as the Mauritian descendants of Romeo and Juliet, and this play outlines the conflict between the two different communities that Ramdeo and Ziliet belong to – that is, Hindus and Christians, respectively. Zeneral Makbef considers his spiritual gurus to be the three witches of *Macbeth*. In *Toufann*, Virahsawmy transposes the action to a modern, contemporary setting where Prospero's magic books are replaced by his control room and the prison of Prince Ferdinand has surveillance cameras, Aryel is Prospero's invention rather than a spirit. Of greater significance is the representation of Caliban (Kalibann). Far from a demonized 'thing most brutish' (*The Tempest*, 1.2.359), he is here described as intelligent, handsome and a 25-year-old Métis. The valorization of Kalibann is taken to a different level when Prospero gives his consent to the wedding of his daughter to Kalibann who can then become king – in what can be seen as an effort to redress the Manichean dichotomy in Shakespeare's depiction. The other is therefore re-presented as the very symbol of integration and cultural miscegenation.

In transacting with Shakespeare, Virahsawmy also tinkers with the characters, creating new genealogies by borrowing and intermixing them. In *Dokter Hamlet*, Hamlet is the brother of Mrs Ermionn Kapilet (Hermione Capulet) and uncle of Ziliet Kapilet (Juliet). *Toufann* comprises a composite cast of Shakespearian characters: Lir (Lear) replaces Alonso, and Polonius acts as his advisor; Kordelia replaces Miranda; Edmon (Edmund) replaces Sebastian; and, more significantly, Yago (Iago) is used in the place of Antonio. The most notoriously evil of Shakespeare's characters questions his reputation, in what is a direct reproach to his creator: 'Depi ki sa bezsominn Shakespeare finn servi mwa pou li bez Othello ek Desdemona tou

[2] Jane Plastow, *African Theatre: Shakespeare In and Out of Africa* (Woodbridge, 2013), p. x.
[3] See Shawkat Toorawa, *Flame Tree Lane* (London, 2012).

dimoun kwar momem responsab tou problem dan lemon'[4] [Ever since Shakespeare, this son of a bitch, has used me to cause harm to Othello and Desdemona, everyone thinks I am responsible for the troubles in this world]. He goes on to add, 'mo espere ki bann kritik literer konpran ki mo pa move net' (39) [I hope that literary critics understand that I am not all that bad]. These metatextual elements reflect the fact that, in many ways, the characters have been taken from their origins, appropriated and placed in a different context, to suit Virahsawmy's purpose. They develop as personae in their own right within this new context, different from their original portrayal.

Whilst the sense of fun that Virahsawmy has with Shakespeare's characters is palpable, there is a more serious undertone to his adaptations. One of the key themes that stand out in Virahsawmy is power politics. To understand Virahsawmy the playwright, he must first be understood as a politician. He was one of the leaders of a newly formed political party in the post-independence period called the MMM (Mouvement Militant Morisien) – a party with a socialist ideology. He advocated equality of rights and championed the cause of Kreol as a language in a bid to forge a national identity. In 1972, however, Virahsawmy was jailed for nearly a year because of his involvement in nationwide, anti-government strikes. A year later, he resigned from the MMM and, even though he formed his own party, he gradually steered away from party politics, disillusioned by corrupted politics and corrupt politicians. It is from this perspective that Virahsawmy's adaptations have to be read, because Virahsawmy the playwright is shaped by his political beliefs.

Shakespeare's political drama finds echo in Virahsawmy's works: he seeks to interrogate a corrupt body politic by exposing politicians as inept leaders and despots. His approach is a reminder of Wole Soyinka who urges African writers to be more engaged socially and politically in their writing: 'the artist has always functioned in African society as the record of the mores and experiences of his society and as the voice of vision in his own time. It is time for him to respond to this essence himself.'[5]

Zeneral Makbef is a political satire built around Macbeth's 'vaulting ambition' (*Macbeth*, 1.7.27): the rhetoric of humanism and democracy that is sold to the people is paradoxical as Makbef's aim is, in fact, to become emperor. The lust for power knows no limits and the adage of 'power corrupts, absolute power corrupts absolutely' – an important theme in *Toufann* – is typically demonstrated in Virahsawmy's plays. Makbef plans on building a 'Pale-di-Pep' (Palace of the People) and a 'Stad-di-Pep' (Stadium of the People) for ... himself. The irony in the names is obvious. Madam Makbef (Lady Macbeth) is encouraged to enjoy a lavish lifestyle and to roam the cities of London and Paris. And to finance these, money is necessarily taken from the people: farmers and planters are all heavily taxed, the inflation rate shoots up in a classic example of corrupt leadership that numerous post-colonial countries have known. This reference to actual leaders of post-colonial nations is made clearer in Makbef's decision to have his revolutionary reign disseminated in school textbooks.

As is the case in corrupt political establishments that are driven by the desire for personal enrichment rather than a vision for society, infighting for power becomes inevitable. Madam Makbef and Mazor Kaskontour plot to oust Makbef so they can rule jointly. Similar underlying conflicts for political supremacy and personal enrichment are seen in *Tabisman Lir*, where the Rigan–Gomon quartet (made up of Risar, Regann, Goneril, and Edmon – the daughters and sons-in-law of Lear) plot against each other in order to seize power for themselves. In *Sir Toby*, the leadership of Lord Orsino, a visionary, comes under serious threat from despots, and Sir Toby is forced to stay away from politics, which is no doubt an autobiographical reference.

---

[4] Dev Virahsawmy, *Toufann: enn Fantezi an 3 Ak* (Rose Hill, 1991), p. 32. Subsequent page references appear in parentheses in the text.

[5] Wole Soyinka, 'The writer in a modern African state', in *The Writer in Modern Africa*, ed. Per Wästberg (Stockholm, 1968), pp. 14–20.

There is another important facet to the political game that Virahsawmy draws attention to. Political leaders have their way because they are able to manipulate the people, either through rhetoric or by providing enjoyment and entertainment, in order to numb the critical eye and mind. *Sir Toby* opens with 'Zwisans San Fren' – a spirit of limitless enjoyment, with alcohol being provided to the people. Similar endeavours are carried out in *Zeneral Makbef* and *Tabisman Lir* in order to cajole and bribe the people and make them become oblivious to the corruption prevalent in political regimes. Virahsawmy's political plays also demonstrate that evil lies in external forces: he points to global capitalism and uncontrolled globalization as further causes of destruction of society and mankind. The neo-liberalism that his political leaders favour so that they can get more money is but a form of neo-colonization, which has negative repercussions on local markets.

It is Virahsawmy's treatment of these forces that makes his stance interesting: after taking over Lear's estate, the Rigan–Gomon quartet becomes the biggest multinational on the planet, holding the majority of shares in the media, thus enabling them to manipulate public opinion. In *Prezidan Otelo*, Yago (Iago), who holds the post of Prime Minister, is bent on striking a deal with the Gridi Empire – a twist of the word 'greedy' – so that the latter can invade the local market with its products. The representatives of the Gridi Empire are depicted as mafia agents, dressed as Al Capone, and the dominant ideology is that all countries will be governed by one supreme leader. The idea of global supremacy also surfaces in *Sir Toby*, where rival political leaders need to work with the Paren-en-Sef (Supreme Mind) or the Godfather of the Mafia, and in *Ziliet ek so Romeo*, where a much-changed and modern Romeo, benefitting from the support of the mafia, wants to take over Ziliet's business and strike a deal with them to open a chain of restaurants and hotels. Virahsawmy is clearly highlighting the dangers of globalization. By associating evil characters with the supreme powers of the global world, he is targeting not only local politicians but also countries that have established themselves as super-powers, whose foreign policies promote their own interests at the cost of others'.

Much like Soyinka, he uses satire as his weapon to castigate the power seekers. Makbef's contradictory leitmotif of self-professed love and sacrifice for the country is rendered meaningless and ridiculous through frequent repetitions. Makbef and his followers are exposed as inefficient and corrupt through their empty, paradoxical discourse. He describes his political regimes as built upon the principles of freedom and democracy, using a socialist-humanist approach and speaking of 'revolutionary re-education' of the people, when he actually wants this to be a way to brainwash them and assert his authority in order to make them accept all his decisions unilaterally. Virahsawmy also uses a number of farcical situations to mock the political leaders. In *Toufann*, both Lir and Edmon go berserk on hearing voices – which could be Prospero's voice or their own conscience – and Lir's resulting confession can be read as an important statement by the playwright: 'Mo abdike. Power corrupts, absolute power corrupts absolutely. Donn pouvwar lepep. Organiz eleksion' (22) [I give up. Power corrupts, absolute power corrupts absolutely. Give power to the people. Organize elections]. His naming technique is equally effective in caricaturizing the leaders: Makbef is a combination of two words in creole, *Mak* and *Bef*, which refer to 'stooge' and 'ox', respectively. And this name is derived from the commonly used Mauritian maxim, 'donn dizef, pran bef' or 'give an egg, take the ox in return' – a maxim that aptly catches Makbef's leadership. Other names, such as Lakord Pandi (hangman's noose), Kaskontour (U-Turn), and Marto (hammer), are all derived from popular parlance and would easily invite laughter from a local audience. Virahsawmy's sarcasm is exacerbated in his portrayal of such characters as sexual deviants: there is a sentimental erotic melody that accompanies Zeneral Marto, while other protagonists are often likened to paedophiles. Song and dance are also used to ridicule the characters as they give foolish renderings, such as Kleomatari's erotic military dance in *Sir Toby*.

In his depiction of political leaders, Virahsawmy uses hyperbole to good effect. In *Sir Toby*, the despots decide to spread the HIV virus in order to fight off any opposition to their aspirations for power. Yago in *Prezidan Otelo*, for instance, is seen to be waking up from a coffin, vampire-like. In many respects, Virahsawmy's exaggeration should not be read from a realistic perspective. He uses hyperbole to reinforce his idea of nepotism and, by reducing characters to types, he invites mockery of them. His approach here is radically different to Shakespeare's. There is no psychological depth and inner conflict in Virahsawmy's characters – they are character types, because they need to represent different elements that the playwright wants to bring out in his socio-political vision.

This vision from a reconstructive perspective is that of a just and egalitarian society, and so feminism and human rights are of particular concern for Virahsawmy. He points to a male-dominated society imbued with a patriarchal mind-set as Beatrice–Shakti gives up on her belief that she can usher in a new era and philosophy in society, because people are not ready to accept a female Prime Minister in the country. *Ziliet ek so Romeo*, which is a rewriting of the myth of the Garden of Eden, situating the characters in Balfour Garden in Mauritius, is a play with strong feminist undertones, written in response to the view that Eve caused the downfall of Man. The play instead depicts Romeo as the one who, selfishly drawn to a superficial life of glamour, loses his way. Similarly, Otelo as President adopts a more holistic view of society, fighting against all kinds of discrimination, including that against gay marriage, in order to promote free love.

Virahsawmy also uses Shakespeare's characters to deal with issues that have been considered taboo in Mauritius. Otelo himself is gay, which Yago considers to be a form of sexual perversion. Kleopatra in *Dernie Vol* has AIDS because she has been a sex worker, and Kordelia in *Tabisman Lir* is HIV-positive, yet she is accepted by her partner and trade unionist Jaysee, and leads a normal, happy life. By associating his protagonists with the so-called 'taboo issues', he is giving the marginalized a voice: no matter what the prejudice, even they can be leaders and play prominent roles in society.

Addressing social issues and confronting prejudice comes across clearly in both Hamlet plays. Doctor Hamlet is Virahsawmy's symbol for open-mindedness. He wants to live an open relationship with his mistress, Orfelia (Ophelia), who herself is free-thinking and expecting Hamlet's child. Hamlet also takes the bold decision to euthanize his terminally ill mother, albeit not without emotional struggle. In another scene, he is discussing the issue of abortion with his niece Ziliet Kapilet. Through Doctor Hamlet and his other protagonists, Virahsawmy is holding up a mirror to his society, and by addressing the taboo topics in his plays, he is making his readers/audience confront the same issues.

Hamlet, however, is hounded as a result of political manipulation, because his open-mindedness is a threat to the political establishment. He reappears briefly in *Hamlet II* as a fugitive – but his role and influence are telling. *Hamlet II* uses the metaphor of crossroads to show the social prejudices and narrow-mindedness that people are caught up in. The fact that he is the only one able to convince Gounna to detach herself from her surroundings and to move out of her house located at the crossroads projects him as a liberator from mental enslavement and prejudice. In his quest to expose social prejudice, Virahsawmy's statement is clear-cut: individuals have the ability to go beyond narrow-mindedness and to effect change, on their own, at a societal level. The role of Sooklall in *Zeneral Makbef*, therefore, is of great significance. He becomes Virahsawmy's mouthpiece and, in a Brechtian-style address to the readers, he exhorts them not to be passive spectators, but to show leadership on their own and chart their own future. Virahsawmy knows that the challenge of creating leaders is not an easy one. Varrouna in *Romeo ek so Ziliet* and Shakti Devi are both killed by the ruling power because of the threat they pose and because of what they represent: freedom and power to the people.

The sensitive social fabric of Mauritius also occupies a central role in *Ramdeo ek so Ziliet*. Communal differences between Hindus and Christians are the root cause of social division in the play, but the solution is provided by Sheikh Soufi (Virahsawmy's adaptation of Friar Lawrence), who belongs to the Muslim-Sufi religion. By making the lovers disappear for a year, he makes their respective families regret their actions. The child of Ziliet and Ramdeo bears the name of both families: Saroj Zorzet Kapilet-Moutalou. While this may seem to be an easy solution to the conflict, the message of Virahsawmy is fundamental to communal harmony: the future lies in both biological and cultural inter-mixing, rather than in ethnic essentialism.

Adapting Shakespeare in creole has allowed Virahsawmy to give the language an added value: that of a medium of literary and dramatic expression. Virahsawmy's contribution to the formalization and standardization of the creole language as a written form in recent years has been well documented. His use of creole as a literary language, however, has brought a degree of vibrancy to the language and to the stage. His creative use of 'Sirandann', or riddles, and local idioms and expressions have been considered refreshing, aptly capturing and conveying a Mauritian spirit in literature. He has also included a variety of expressions from Bhojpuri (another dialect in Mauritius, used by Indian immigrants and their descendants) in his use of creole, thus broadening the scope of the mother tongue. His use of songs (the local sega, for instance) has given his plays a degree of syncretism that typifies performances in countries of the global South. Virahsawmy's belief about using Shakespeare is appropriately conveyed in his own words: 'I have often leant on Shakespeare to build a dramatic literature as part of the national culture of New Mauritius. Language planning, nation building and the teaching of basic values are done through tears, laughter, songs and dances.'[6]

---

[6] Plastow, *African Theatre*, p. 88.

'ACCENTS YET UNKNOWN': *HAIDER* AND *HAMLET* IN KASHMIR

POMPA BANERJEE

Recent adaptations of *Hamlet*, in 'accents yet unknown'[1] in early modern England, draw attention to the way global reworkings of the play realign the cultural authority of Shakespeare and, in doing so, revise the role of the English language in a newly reconfigured world. Vishal Bhardwaj's film, *Haider*, a 2014 adaptation of *Hamlet* co-written with Basharat Peer, is a case in point. The film is set in Kashmir in the 1990s, at the contested border between India and Pakistan. *Haider* yokes *Hamlet* to the concerns of the militarized zone of conflict and violence in Kashmir. In this way, the film renegotiates Shakespeare's cultural authority in the global marketplace. Shakespeare's play about a melancholy Danish prince, left restless by the meddlesome ghost of his father, becomes one among many 'foreign' bodies that complicate seemingly local concerns in Kashmir. While *Hamlet* is made to engage in a conflict that many still consider to be a regional skirmish between India and Pakistan, the play's iconic status and Shakespeare's cultural capital among global audiences ensure that Kashmir's tense war-zone, agitated by decades of hostilities between two states armed with nuclear weapons, is projected as an international, not a regional, concern.

Haider's insertion of Shakespeare into Kashmir repositions the English language as well. Displaced in a diverse linguistic community of multiple languages (Kashmiri, Urdu, Arabic, and Hindi, among others), English is detached from the civilizing mission that brought *Hamlet* and English studies to colonial India. Nineteenth-century colonial intervention in Indian education, such as Macaulay's 'Minute on Indian Education' (1835),

advanced Shakespeare's plays and the English language to reinforce cultural and racial hierarchies.[2] *Haider*, however, destabilizes the role of English in modern, multilingual India by reminding audiences that, far from being the master language, English is only one language among many. But, if English cannot adequately express the fractured reality of Kashmir, neither, the film suggests, can other languages bear the burden of expression. Consequently, language itself is put under scrutiny.

These realignments of cultural authority and language produce a rich afterlife for *Hamlet*, one achieved through a process of 'transformation and renewal'.[3] As Derrida's note on Benjamin's translator suggests, such an adaptation 'modifies the original even as it also modifies the translating language'.[4] By offering up Shakespeare's play in new languages and new geopolitical realities,

---

[1] *Julius Caesar*, 3.1.114. All quotations from Shakespeare's plays are from *William Shakespeare: The Complete Works*, ed. Stanley Wells, Gary Taylor, John Jowett, and William Montgomery (Oxford, 1986).

[2] Gauri Viswanathan, *Masks of Conquest: Literary Study and British Rule in India* (New York, 1989), pp. 57–80; Jyotsna Singh, *Colonial Narratives, Cultural Dialogues: 'Discoveries' of India in the Language of Colonialism* (London, 1996), p. 121; Michael Neill, 'Post-colonial Shakespeare? Writing away from the centre', in *Post-colonial Shakespeares*, ed. Ania Loomba and Martin Orkin (London, 1998), pp. 168, 180; and Ania Loomba, *Gender, Race, and Colonialism* (Oxford, 2002), p. 22.

[3] Walter Benjamin, *Illuminations* (New York, 1968), p. 73.

[4] Jacques Derrida, *The Ear of the Other: Otobiography, Transference, Translation: Texts and Discussions with Jacques Derrida*, ed. Christie McDonald (Lincoln, NE, 1988), p. 122.

Haider creates disruption; it shifts 'the foundation so that new angles, vantages, and perspectives are created',[5] and Shakespeare in revised form reaches unanticipated audiences across linguistic and cultural borders through the global reach of Bollywood.

WORDING KASHMIR

Shakespeare's play shifts to a new terrain in *Haider*. Adopting Craig Latrell's commentary on Indonesian theatre, one might say that, to tell the story of Kashmir, Shakespeare's play has been 'studied, borrowed, reworked, reinterpreted, and combined with pre-existing local styles to produce something which is novel yet recognizable to local audiences'.[6] Shakespeare is enmeshed in indigenous concerns where '[L]ocal particularities' – in this case, the chronicles of blood and loss in Kashmir – 'become transplanted to new ground, and something new and hybrid results'.[7] This new ground, *Haider*'s Kashmir, is riven by decades of conflict. A harsh military outfit disciplines this claustrophobic, heavily armed zone through an emergency decree, AFSPA, the Armed Forces Special Powers Act. AFSPA suspends civil liberties in the Indian-controlled part of Kashmir under a special emergency anti-terrorism measure. The army routinely performs body searches and compulsory roll-calls of residents to ferret out terrorists, insurgents and sympathizers with suspected agitators seeking freedom from Indian control. People are 'disappeared' or go missing without official explanation. Haider/Hamlet has been at university, far from his home in Indian-controlled Kashmir. When his father, Dr Meer, disappears after performing surgery on a suspected insurgent, Haider returns to Kashmir to look for his missing parent.

Haider's search for his father in the brutal geopolitical reality of Kashmir is parallelled by a steady destabilization of language. The film words Kashmir by pressing language into new forms. Shakespeare's English is unable to express the scope of violence and loss in Kashmir; other languages falter as well. *Haider* employs linguistic dislocations, word replacements, signs, neologisms and foreign words to create a language of disruption that calls attention to its own inadequacies. Words become indeterminate; their import does not always attach to concrete objects or places. In some instances, words do not always indicate the same meaning to every speaker (or listener). The most effective example of the film's destabilization of both language and space appears in Haider/Hamlet's response to the security force's question at the roadblock outside his hometown in Kashmir: 'Which town do you belong to?' When Haider responds that he is from Islamabad, the soldiers detain him. An explanation arrives with his fiancée Arshee: Islamabad does not refer to the capital city of Pakistan, but to a place in Indian-controlled Kashmir known to the locals as both Anantnag and Islamabad. Some Hindus call the town Anantnag, and some Muslims call it Islamabad. Words, in this instance, telescope the unstable history of space and time. In a place where people frequently disappear, words do not necessarily designate a precise geographical marker of space. By redirecting our focus to the land, 'This other Eden, demi-paradise' of Shakespeare's history plays (*Richard II*, 2.1.42), *Haider* also indicates that, while the disputed land of the film, this other Paradise of Kashmir, can be fenced off, bordered variously, fought over, blood-sodden and called by different names, it endures beyond language.

Paranoia accompanies a further destabilization of language as Haider continues to search for his father in burial grounds where words are often replaced by something else. Signs and placards flag the missing body of Dr Meer. In Illustration 1, at top right, nailed to a tree, the anonymous gravesites are overseen by a green sign. In Urdu, the words spell out an address: Shahid Chowk, Regee Pura. While the space of the bleak cemetery

---

[5] Ayanna Thompson, *Passing Strange: Shakespeare, Race and Contemporary America* (Oxford, 2011), pp. 17–18.

[6] Craig Latrell, 'After appropriation', *The Drama Review* 44.4 (Winter 2000), 52.

[7] Linda Hutcheon, *A Theory of Adaptation*, 2nd edn with Siobhan O'Flynn (London, 2013), p. 150.

1. Haider finds an address for mourning. Screen capture from *Haider*, directed by Vishal Bhardwaj (2014).

2. Haider kneels before Grave 318. Screen capture from *Haider*, directed by Vishal Bhardwaj (2014).

is marked and named, the corpses in the graves remain unclaimed and unmemorialized.

In Illustration 2, numbers appear as placeholders for words: one sees the faint appearance of the number 318 instead of a headstone with words, which are delayed.

Eventually, Dr Meer's remains shift from the anonymity of a 'disappeared' corpse assigned a numbered grave to a burial place marked with a headstone inscribed in multiple languages.

In Illustration 3, a new tombstone replaces the number 318. Several languages collectively offer context and identity for the body under the slab. On the top of this image, the first underlined text engraves the number 786, the numerical representation of the Arabic 'Bismillah' (in the name of Allah/God). The text below the number declares in Arabic, 'Ho'val–Baaqi', or 'He [Allah] is that who remains' or 'only He is the immortal one'. Below the Arabic inscription, the body under the

3. From number to word. Screen capture from *Haider*, directed by Vishal Bhardwaj (2014).

headstone is finally identified. The name Hilaal Meer appears, first in English, accompanied by 'Dr.', the abbreviated sign of his profession, and then in Urdu. The ensuing text in Urdu notes the *vafaat*, the date of death, as 15 December 1995. A small sign after the date indicates the initial letter for 'Eesavi' (of Christ) distinguishing the Christian calendar from the Islamic or Hijri calendar. Below the date, the inscription 'Allah aap ko jannat naseeb kare' [May Allah grant you peace and paradise] bestows a benediction on the spectator viewing the tombstone, and the film.[8] The viewer must piece together the narrative of Haider's missing father in Urdu, Arabic and English. In this multi-lingual graveyard, English depends on Urdu and Arabic to draw out the context surrounding Dr Meer's death.

The film employs other ways of placing language under scrutiny. It reminds viewers that *Haider* and Kashmir are not 'passive receivers of Western ideas and images but active manipulators of such influences, that intercultural borrowing is not simply a one-way process, but something far more interestingly dialogic'.[9] This dialogue does not necessarily lead to an exchange or negotiation. Instead, at particular moments, the film pointedly refuses to enter an exchange. In the scene leading up to Dr Meer performing surgery on the insurgent

pursued by the army, the tension of the moment is transferred to a telephone call that is not answered, at least not then. The wanted militant needs emergency surgery. The hospital is not an option. Haider's father, Dr Meer, brings him to his home for surgery. His wife Ghazala/Gertrude is terrified. The patient's companion silently places a container with bloody napkins on the bed by her. She vomits. The phone rings. She descends the stairs and looks at the telephone that continues to ring in the silence. The lack of communication between Ghazala and the unseen caller at the other end of the telephone line points to her unspoken fears about the hunted militant her husband insists on healing and the official retribution that must surely follow.

The inevitable reprisal recasts the dialogic relationship between Shakespeare's play and the reality of Kashmir. A wordless exchange passes for a 'conversation' that resists language by substituting words with sounds that telegraph meaning. A non-vocalized or mechanical sound replaces language – in this case, a car horn. The army rounds up the

---

[8] I am grateful to Sheeraz Mohammed, Rahul Bjorn Parson, and Rob Adler Peckerar for their kind assistance with translations.

[9] Latrell, 'After appropriation', p. 46.

4. A lesson in power: Wajura Primary School. Screen capture from *Haider*, directed by Vishal Bhardwaj (2014).

citizens in search of the militants known to be in the village. The viewer is aware that Dr Meer has refused to turn away a wanted man because he was in need of surgery. As Dr Meer joins the stream of men holding up their identity cards for roll-call, each man is forced to pause in front of a parked vehicle. A silent, masked figure sits inside the jeep and watches the men pass in single file. If he shakes his head to indicate 'no', then the car horn stays silent, and the man before him is allowed to pass. If, on the other hand, the masked man nods his head to confirm the man's guilt, then the car horn blares this verdict, and the soldiers seize upon him and drag him to a room to administer punishment.

Words are redundant in this impromptu military trial, which does away with language as a direct means of communication. Words do not articulate or affirm guilt, pronounce judgement, or invite retribution. No dialogues punctuate the action with words justifying the violence. No verbal testimony is offered, and the accused do not speak. When words appear, they flash on signboards, asking viewers to draw their own conclusions.

In Illustration 4, the signboard in the background locates the summary trial and punishment in Wajura Primary School, reinforcing the educational value, the lesson, of this exercise in power. The car horn speaks for the masked figure. He is the sole judge of the proceedings, and he has absolute power over the man called before him. The only prominent background sound is the vicious beating of the nameless person in line before Dr Meer, a person identified as a problem by the car horn. The few words heard in response to the beating of the nameless man are 'I don't know.' Words are uttered only to deny knowledge and deflect communication, which bypasses language and is decided by the arbitrary horn controlled by the masked figure inside the jeep.

Haider/Hamlet's search for his father, the missing Dr Meer, also tracks the shifting role of the English language in Kashmir. On road signs, billboards, and shop fronts, English words are usually accompanied by translations in Urdu and other languages. On the rare occasions when English appears without the support of other languages, the intended viewers of those signs reside outside of Kashmir.

In Illustration 5 the crowd outside the gates of the United Nations compound in Kashmir holds up English-only signs. The mostly handwritten notices, posters, and placards chronicle the plight of the disappeared people and their families: 'My father, where is he?'; 'Where are our loved ones?'; 'Stop crime against humanity'; 'What am I posthumous or orphan?' The absence of the other languages that fill billboards everywhere else in the film suggests that the crowd employs English to mediate the transfer

5. Where did they go? Screen captures from *Haider*, directed by Vishal Bhardwaj (2014).

of their seemingly local concerns to a global body of viewers. Through these scenes, *Haider* takes a 'broad ownership of Shakespeare', making *Hamlet* 'productively intertextual', and allowing Shakespeare 'to function as a collocation of meanings that resonate with the world'.[10] Addressed to an international audience, the United Nations, as well as the worldwide consumers of televised wars and disasters, the English words register their authors' loss on the consciousness of the world.

Away from the UN gates, however, no single language, such as English, can bear witness to events.

In Kashmir, English is inadequate, behind the times, because '[S]tandard English is simply not capable of giving adequate expression to the fractured narrative of our times.'[11] Words bend to the needs of the moment. New words are coined and thrown into the circulation: 'half-widows', for instance – the wives of disappeared men – or 'suffocracy', a suffocating democracy. No language offers words to describe the perplexing symptoms of a 'new disease' that compels men to stand by their door, unable to cross the threshold into their own home. In Illustration 6, victims of the yet-unnamed 'new disease' are able to enter their homes only after they have been patted down, searched and declared 'safe'.

Perhaps the film's most significant dislocation of both Shakespeare and English occurs in its radical implantation of a foreign word, *chutzpah*, in Haider/Hamlet's supposedly deranged rant in the town square. Speaking before an appreciative audience, Haider uses the word *chutzpah* to draw attention to the violence and the contempt of civil law permitted under AFSPA. Mispronouncing the word as *CHutzpah*, Haider explains the meaning of the foreign word with examples – for instance, the *chutzpah* of the bank robber who steals cash from one bank counter, then saunters to the next counter to open an account with the stolen money.

Pronounced as *CHutzpah* in the film, the word may sound like a local swearword, but there is also another form of disruption that is worth examining. *Chutzpah* as brazen insolence is relatively recently recorded – in 1892 – in the *Oxford English Dictionary*. As insolence, *chutzpah* appears after 'mouth', as in 'mouthing off', in 1891, and before 'crust', also as in insolence, in 1900.[12] In the Kashmir of the 1990s, this deliberate (and awkward) implantation of the word as *CHutzpah* alerts the viewer that English may be irrelevant in this

---

[10] Mark Thornton Burnett, *Shakespeare and World Cinema* (Cambridge, 2013), pp. 1, 55.

[11] Jatinder Verma, 'Classical Binglish in the twenty-first century', in *Shakespeare, Race, and Performance: The Diverse Bard*, ed. Delia Jarret-Macauley (New York, 2016), p. 40.

[12] chutzpah, *n.*, *OED Online*, September 2016.

6. Permission to enter my home. Screen capture from *Haider*, directed by Vishal Bhardwaj (2014).

situation, because it is unable to mediate between cultures and languages. There is no English phonetic equivalent to the Hebrew CH/KH sound. However, the KH sound does exist in Urdu, for example, as in 'Khuda Hafiz' ('May God be your guardian', and/or 'good bye').[13] In that sense, *CHutzpah/chutzpah* bypasses English altogether. In the Kashmiri marketplace, Hebrew – through Yiddish – speaks to Urdu. The foreign word *chutzpah* is transported in contested Kashmir to transfer the concerns of one embattled diaspora to another. It illustrates the way words and ideas migrate in different forms to mediate between local and global. Moreover, Shakespeare is estranged. Both *chutzpah* and Shakespeare are foreign entities in the Kashmiri market square. Shakespeare is made unfamiliar but becomes uncannily familiar and recognizable in an altered and renegotiated afterlife in Kashmir.

Haider's realignment of Shakespeare's cultural authority and the English language helps us understand that Shakespearian adaptations are not one-way transmissions from West to East but collaborations across time, culture and language.[14] Through these 'collaborations', the film creates a space to refashion the dynamic community of early modern theatre that produced texts voiced severally by the multiple authors, actors, censors, editors, publishers,

translators and audiences. In such performances, 'Local and foreign sources of authority coexist in performance, with neither authority subsuming, or erasing the other.'[15] This sort of hybridity, Linda Hutcheon suggests, produces a dialogue between the adapted text (*Hamlet*) and adaptation (*Haider*), as well as the cultures that produced them. Together both text and adaptation negotiate a new kind of language, and 'both are in dialogue with the words themselves'.[16]

Haider complicates the idea of English as the master language of the colonist, and allows us to think about cross-cultural transfers. The film does not silence or erase the language of Shakespeare but adds to it in significant ways; it is 'not a Shakespeare emptied of words', but one 'with added languages and additional resonances, both linguistic and performative'.[17] The film makes a case for

---

[13] I am grateful to Rob Adler Peckerar for his lively commentary on chutzpah.

[14] Julie Sanders, *Adaptation and Appropriation* (New York, 2006), p. 47.

[15] James R. Brandon, 'Other Shakespeares in Asia: an overview,' in *Re-Playing Shakespeare in Asia*, ed. Poonam Trivedi and Minami Ryuta (New York, 2010), p. 31.

[16] Hutcheon, *Theory of Adaptation*, pp. 149–50.

[17] Trivedi and Ryuta, eds., *Replaying Shakespeare in Asia*, p. 15.

a renewed Shakespeare. Adaptations are, after all, 'about seeing things come back to us in as many forms as possible'.[18] The film also renegotiates Shakespeare's place in the global market. On the one hand, Shakespearian texts are catalysts, 'foreign' bodies that animate specifically indigenous concerns. On the other hand, through 'the act of siting', the foreign becomes local.[19] If *Hamlet* was once a British import instrumental in expressing the colonizer's values, then *Haider* transforms the once-familiar text into a specifically Indian cultural export. Shakespeare is stretched, challenged, and made 'the sum of the critical and creative responses elicited by his work'.[20] In 1817, Hazlitt asserted, 'It is *we* who are Hamlet',[21] but *Haider* rewrites the 'we' of Hazlitt's confident assertion. Shakespeare's play is made new and meaningful, and assured a 'continued life'[22] among multilingual and diasporic audiences numbering hundreds of millions, many of whom are under the age of 35, and for whom English is only one language among many. Transculturated and indigenized, *Hamlet*, in turn, reenergizes both cultures. *Haider* then evokes a web of influences and offers the capacity to foster a genuine conversation, in multiple languages, in which *Hamlet* informs Kashmir, and Kashmir inflects *Hamlet*, even as the film expands the interpretation of Shakespeare's play.

---

[18] Sanders, *Adaptation and Appropriation*, p. 160.

[19] Sonia Massai, 'Defining local Shakespeares', in *World-wide Shakespeares: Local Appropriations in Film and Performance*, ed. Sonia Massai (London, 2005), p. 3.

[20] Massai, 'Defining local Shakespeares', p. 6.

[21] William Hazlitt, *The Round Table: Characters of Shakespeare* (London, 1969), p. 232.

[22] Benjamin, *Illuminations*, p. 71.

THE FORESTS OF SILENCE: GLOBAL SHAKESPEARE IN THE PHILIPPINES, THE PHILIPPINES IN GLOBAL SHAKESPEARE

JUDY CELINE ICK [1]

I consider myself an outsider to Global Shakespeare, although, in some ways, I could easily pass for its poster child. I have a German last name – thanks to a German-Filipino father who married my Spanish-American-Filipino mother. I live and work in Asia, albeit that part of Asia that often feels like Latin America on the wrong side of the Pacific, teaching Shakespeare to Filipino students in English. This rather diverse biological and cultural *mestiza* background certainly justifies my claim to the label 'global'. Also, I have been teaching Shakespeare at my university for the better part of three decades. And yet, when I teach Shakespeare, I simply teach 'Shakespeare', not 'Global Shakespeare'. When I work on productions – whether as an actor or as a dramaturg – my colleagues and I see ourselves as doing a Shakespeare play, not a Global Shakespeare play. Although I work on Shakespeare from a particular place on the globe, that doesn't seem to be enough to merit the adjective 'global' for, indeed, any Shakespeare produced from the planet Earth would qualify for what would ultimately be a meaningless label. I do wonder then: when does Shakespeare cease to be just 'Shakespeare', and when does it become 'Global Shakespeare'?

One might argue, of course, that Shakespeare was global from the get-go – his plays often set in worlds other than his native England, the expanse of the universe embedded in the architecture of his very own Globe. One might further point out, as Graham Holderness and Brian Loughrey do, that even his early audiences included travellers from outside England, who have left the most significant

records of the theatre of Shakespeare's time.[2] More strictly speaking, however, one might situate Global Shakespeare as the critical approach or theoretical movement that evolved from the limits of the inter-cultural or post-colonial approaches to Shakespeare studies that preceded it. David Schalkwyk, who heads the Global Shakespeare Program at the University of Warwick, goes as far as to posit Global Shakespeare as the potential heir to new historicism as the dominant force in Shakespeare studies.[3]

Even among its leading practitioners and theorists, however, there seems to be no consensus about exactly what Global Shakespeare is. In her ground-breaking anthology, *World-wide Shakespeares*, Sonia

---

[1] A shorter version of this article was delivered as part of the panel, "'I'll put a girdle round about the earth": interrogating Global Shakespeare' at the 2016 World Shakespeare Congress in London. I would like to acknowledge the Office of the Vice-President for Academic Affairs of the University of the Philippines (Emerging Interdisciplinary Research Grant) and the International Shakespeare Association for the grants that facilitated research for this article and my attendance at the conference.

[2] Graham Holderness and Brian Loughrey, 'Arabesque: Shakespeare and globalisation', *MIT Global Shakespeares*, http://globalShakespeares.mit.edu/blog/2013/07/25/arabesque. Originally published in *Globalization and its Discontents: Writing the Global Culture, Essays and Studies*, ed. S. Smith (Cambridge, 2006), pp. 24–46.

[3] David Schalkwyk, 'Reconstructed closing remarks: "Shakespeare as global cultural heritage"', New York University, Abu Dhabi, April 2015, p. 3, www2.warwick.ac.uk/fac/cross_fac/iatl/activities/projects/globalShakespeare/news/reconstructed_closing_remarks.pdf.

26

Massai claims that the growing attention focused on Shakespearian productions from beyond the Anglophone world suggests that 'Shakespeare has effectively become a successful logo or brand name', operating in contrast to the locally produced as universal brands do in a globalized world.[4] The rise of Shakespeare as a global icon and the consequent development of Global Shakespeare as some sort of academic brand highlights how 'the field of Shakespeare Studies has been radically transformed by the emergence of significant world-wide localities, within which Shakespeare is made to signify anew'.[5] Although she does not use the label 'Global Shakespeare', Massai nonetheless provides a useful theoretical lens (via Bourdieu) of a symbiotic, if volatile, relationship between the local and the global in the cultural production of the field of Shakespeare studies. Shakespeare, according to Massai, has inevitably become 'a global cultural field'.[6] Alexa Huang [Joubin], co-curator – along with Peter Donaldson – of the influential *Global Shakespeares* digital archive, on the other hand, emphasizes the pluralities enabled by a global appreciation of Shakespeare, and describes 'Global Shakespeares' as 'a body of travelling cultural texts and a liminal space where migrating people and ideas meet', which holds great promise as a methodology continuously 'energized by the sheer multiplicity of genres, cultures, representations of diverse time periods, and artistic and academic investments in performances as multilingual affairs'.[7] Writing on Shakespeare and globalization, Graham Holderness and Brian Loughery trace a history of sorts of Global Shakespeare and demonstrate how, by the early twenty-first century, Shakespeare becomes 'the substance of a global conversation'.[8]

Regardless of its point of origin or whether it is properly defined as a cultural field, a methodology or a conversation, what is clear about Global Shakespeare is the fact of its ubiquity. *Hic et ubique* – it is here and everywhere. Global Shakespeare exists as graduate degrees in leading educational institutions, as courses or subjects in universities across the globe, as a popular topic of professional conference panels, with its core set of books and

anthologies, journals and journal special issues. It thrives in virtual space as well as in databases, popular blogs, and even as a travel portal for Expedia. My own vantage point into Global Shakespeare is one of a voyeur who exists outside its more institutional manifestations, and yet its very ubiquity allows me to form general impressions by reading books and journals, surfing through websites, and poring over course syllabi available online that all lay claim in some way or other to the label Global Shakespeare.

Apparently, using the term 'global' alongside 'Shakespeare' is just too delicious a temptation for most academics and artists to pass up. The conjuring of the Shakespearian ground zero, of its point of artistic origin, and the simultaneous invocation of its contemporary world-wide influence makes the phrase 'Global Shakespeare' almost too good to be true. As wide open and inclusive as the label seems to be, however, certain dominant characteristics have emerged that serve to define and limit the field. In terms of its privileged productions, an informal canon of works that are readily associated with Global Shakespeare – a canon that includes names such as Kurosawa, Kozintsev, Ninagawa, Msomi, Ong, Suzuki, Al-Bassam, Bhardwaj, etc. – seems to be a predominantly foreign or non-Anglophone Shakespeare, usually in a language other than English. This 'loss' of language, furthermore, relegates the communication of meanings to the realm of the visual, or a reliance on a heavily visual theatricality. Hence, exemplary productions of Global Shakespeare tend to offer either spectacle – song and dance, lavish costumes, ancient theatrical traditions – or varying degrees of shock, such as we find in avant-garde, Brechtian, or postmodernist productions. The rationale behind productions admitted into the Global Shakespeare canons

---

[4] *World-wide Shakespeares: Local Appropriations in Film and Performance*, ed. Sonia Massai (London, 2005), p. 4.

[5] Massai, ed., *World-wide Shakespeares*, p. 8.

[6] Massai, ed., *World-wide Shakespeares*, p. 6.

[7] Alexa Huang [Joubin], 'Global Shakespeares as methodology', *Shakespeare* 9.3 (2013), 273–90; pp. 286–7.

[8] Holderness and Loughrey, 'Arabesque'.

seems to be presenting not so much 'a Shakespeare we've never heard before' as much as 'a Shakespeare we've never *seen* before'. The more unfamiliar, the more global?

Looking through its catalogues and canons, one wonders whether Global Shakespeare is not merely non-English or non-Anglophone Shakespeare given a celebratory label to occlude the guilt of the post-colonial or, worse, in an attempt to return to the naiveté of the universal. After all, the focus on spectacle allows Shakespeare to be universal, speaking in the language of images rather than tongues, even as it maintains the language of origin as the exclusive domain of the English. Holderness and Loughrey raise several important questions: Is global Shakespeare then still imperial Shakespeare? Has the Shakespeare myth simply extended itself into what Bourdieu called '"the justificatory myth" of globalization'?[9] It would seem that, on some levels, the invocation of 'global' alongside Shakespeare is also fraught with controversy, carrying with it the baggage of globalization's dark side – its perceived presentist bias, its inherent threat of homogeneity, its thinly veiled Eurocentrism, and the economic inequalities it either fails to account for or even creates. While less than 'celebratory', these questions haunt the critical debates that surround the productions of Global Shakespeare, and that questioning is not necessarily a bad thing.

Aside from a predilection for the elements of spectacle or shock, censorship also seems to be a recurring trait in some productions identified with Global Shakespeare. A production endangered in its local circumstance often finds asylum in Global Shakespeare. Productions or films that are banned in their home countries, usually for speaking out against repressive regimes, are championed. Perhaps it is because we want to imagine our guy William as a freedom fighter or a mouthpiece for liberal democracies everywhere. Again, this perspective allies Global Shakespeare with a more celebratory sense of globalization and its effects.

In any case, given these characteristics that outline, however vaguely, the contours of Global Shakespeare, I wonder why Philippine productions remain on the outside. Let me name a few examples from fairly recent history that could have laid claim to the label – beginning with a 1984 *Macbeth* by one of the country's leading theatre companies, the Philippine Educational Theater Association (PETA), in collaboration with the East German director Fritz Bennewitz, who was then the director of the Weimar National Theatre. Staged in the waning years of the Marcos dictatorship, the production was highly political, as it was very easy to make the connections between the Scottish butcher and his fiend-like queen and the then-current dictatorship. Given Bennewitz's artistic inclinations, the production used a Marxist/Brechtian approach that proved to be highly influential in the company's later productions. Some of its leading artists credit this collaboration with Bennewitz as formative in their own careers. Brenda Fajardo, one of the company's most important designers, for example, talks about how, together with Bennewitz, she was able to develop the company's trademark design principle, which she labels as an 'aesthetics of poverty'.[10] Rody Vera, who translated *Macbeth* for this production and went on to become one of the country's leading playwrights and translators, names Bennewitz as a pivotal mentor.[11] This landmark production would certainly fulfil the requirements of Global Shakespeare – being a tantalizingly political Brechtian production in a language other than English – except that in 1984, when this production was mounted, no one knew that Global Shakespeare would emerge. At best, this would

[9] Holderness and Loughrey, 'Arabesque'.

[10] Brenda Fajardo, 'The aesthetics of poverty: a rationale in designing for Philippine People's Theater 1973–1986', *Kritika Kultura* 15 (2010), 179–94; http://journals.ateneo.edu/ojs/index.php/kk/article/view/1452.

[11] 'Fritz became my mentor in translating and adapting Shakespeare as well. And under him I had undergone a full course on play analysis and dramaturgy, which for me, became the most significant lesson in my career as a playwright', Rodolfo Vera, 'Playwriting in the time of exigency', *Kritika Kultura* 14 (2010), 103–10; p. 107; http://journals.ateneo.edu/ojs/index.php/kk/article/view/1466/1491.

have been labelled cross-cultural, or maybe inter-cultural, theatre.

Looking further down the line, another version of *Macbeth*, Josefina Estrella's *Makbet* (Dulaang Unibersidad ng Pilipinas, 1994) – which set the Scottish play in the Philippine highlands, recasting the play's power struggles among warring indigenous tribes – makes a strong case for inclusion among the cultural texts that comprise Global Shakespeare. It was a spectacular production, featuring authentic costumes of intricately woven fabrics, lavish headdresses, elaborate spears and shields, that incorporated indigenous rituals, music, chanting and dance. It certainly capitalized upon the visual splendour of the exotic, as the local culture on display was far removed from its more westernized Manila audiences. An excellent example of Shakespeare relocated and made strange, it might have merited the label 'Global Shakespeare' had it been performed elsewhere. Staged exclusively in Manila, however, this production might be more correctly classified as an example of intra-cultural theatre, following Rustom Bharucha's conception of a theatrical practice between and among diverse ethnicities or cultures within a nation-state.[12]

Ricardo Abad's bilingual production of *Taming of the Shrew* in 2002 (*Ang Pagpapaamo sa Maldita*, Tanghalang Ateneo) used Shakespeare's play as an allegory of American colonialism in the Philippines. Petruchio was played as the conquering American soldier, and Katarina as the feisty local girl who stood for the Motherland, following the conventions of the early twentieth-century seditious plays in the Philippines. This is another possible claimant to the Global Shakespeare label – except that, given its explicit juxtaposition of Shakespeare's power struggles within the marital bond and the American colonial occupation of the Philippines, this production might have been more correctly labelled 'post-colonial'. Indeed, Abad himself unequivocally makes that claim.

What I wanted to do with Shakespeare's *Taming of the Shrew* was to stage the play in the eyes of Philippine history. How the production eventually became a postcolonial discourse of Philippine–American

relations at the turn of the 20th century was a fortuitous convergence of several events and ideas . . . In this reading, the taming of the shrew is seen as a metaphor for the attempted taming of the Filipino by the American colonial power in the Philippines during the first decade and a half of the last century. It is a reading that represents the business of reinterpreting Shakespeare, and this business, to paraphrase Loomba and Orkin (1998:3), is part of the business of reinterpreting and changing our Filipino social world.[13]

Of course, save for a few academics and reviewers – all based in the Philippines – the play did not receive any such attention outside the country. Like the Philippines itself in the theoretical landscapes of post-colonialism that very often focused on the aftermath of the British (but not the American) empire, Abad's *Taming* remained unnoticed, nowhere near the radar of post-colonial Shakespearian theorists. While he references Ania Loomba and Martin Orkin and their landmark work on post-colonial Shakespeare, Loomba and Orkin have in all likelihood never referenced Abad, because, sadly, this excellent piece of post-colonial Shakespeare stayed home.[14]

And that's part of the problem – none of these productions travelled, either literally or virtually. While these Philippine productions and others like them might have contributed richly to debates and theorizations of intercultural, intracultural or post-colonial Shakespeare, they didn't. They remained outside the consciousness of those involved in those theoretical conversations. Moreover, this seems to be happening again in the developing field of Global Shakespeare. Why is there precious

---

[12] Rustom Bharucha, *Theatre and the World: Performance and the Politics of Culture* (London and New York, 1993).

[13] Ricardo Abad, 'A postcolonial view of Shakespeare's Shrew', *The Loyola Schools Review* 2 (2002), 1–12; p. 1.

[14] For a fuller discussion of this and other Abad productions and their relationship to post-colonial theory, see Judy Celine Ick, 'And never the twain shall meet? Shakespeare and Philippine performance traditions', in *Re-Playing Shakespeare: Performance in Asian Theatre Forms*, ed. Poonam Trivedi and Minami Riyuta (New York, 2010), pp. 181–99.

little about the Philippines in discussions of Global Shakespeare? And how can that absence help us further understand this emergent field?

One easy answer to my first question, of course, is economics. More than adhering to a specific aesthetics or politics, Global Shakespeare is powerfully driven by an economics. Global Shakespeare is, after all, a function of place – or, more precisely, a function of places, of moving from place to place. Global Shakespeare entails migration and travel – whether actual or virtual, real or digital. This, in turn, requires privilege. Freedom of movement is most often an economically driven privilege. One needs money to travel to conferences, for instance, in order to converse with other academics and practitioners, to join in their relevant conversations. One needs money to tour productions and ensure their visibility to a wider audience. Even barring physical travel, one needs money adequately to record and display performances on appropriate digital platforms. And, similarly, one needs money to access them. Hence, we must not be too quick to celebrate the digital as the champion of Global Shakespeare when access to these technologies remains unequal throughout the globe. To use the example of Asian Shakespeare, for instance, is it any accident that the countries in Asia with some of the lowest rates of Internet penetration – Laos, Cambodia, and Myanmar – are those we don't see on the maps of Global Shakespeare?[15] As Geoffrey Way argues in 'Peeking behind the digital curtains':

We cannot focus solely on the amount of Shakespearean content available for online audiences at the expense of understanding and theorizing how that content is accessed by audiences. For example, we may have more filmed versions of Shakespearean stage performances available now than we have had access to at any time in the past. However, if those performances are accessible only through technologies that mimic traditional notions of access (e.g., expensive paywalls or programs and websites with specific technological requirements), then no significant shift in access has occurred.[16]

But while a simple economics of access or absence of resources explains much, it also fails to account for the more complex role the global

and attendant idea of globalization plays in the field of Global Shakespeare. It would be simplistic to conclude that rich nations have Global Shakespeare while poor nations have to settle for Local Shakespeare. After all, wherever one stands in the global wealth spectrum, globalization ensnares all in an all-encompassing world market.

And it is perhaps through the lens of the market that a more nuanced understanding of Global Shakespeare can come about. Very often, too much attention is paid to its producers (those who create the productions of Global Shakespeare) and less attention is paid to its consumers. Who is Global Shakespeare produced for? Who are its audiences and how do productions vary with reference to these audiences rather than to its creative artists? Another way of approaching the question of Global Shakespeare would be to look at it as a function of audience. Considering who these plays are produced for and who its target consumers are reveals much more complex ways in which the global figures into Shakespeare and vice versa. Two recent productions from the Philippines begin to illustrate this point.

Ricardo Abad's *Sintang Dalisay* (Tanghalang Ateneo, 2011) is a verse and dance version of *Romeo and Juliet* using the *igal*, an indigenous dance form of the Sama-Bajau people of the Southern Philippines and other parts of maritime Southeast Asia, to re-tell the story of Shakespeare's star-crossed lovers. Now recast as Rashiddin and

---

[15] According to the latest available reports (June 2017) on Internet World Stats, the Internet penetration rates of the general population in Laos (21.9%), Myanmar (25.9%), and Cambodia (25.6%) fall far behind Asian leaders like South Korea (92.7%), Japan (94%), Taiwan (88%), and Singapore (81.2%). These leading countries are also the leading representatives of Asia in the field of Global Shakespeare. The Philippines also lags behind at 55.5%: www .internetworldstats.com/stats3.htm#asia.

[16] Geoffrey Way, 'Peeking behind the digital curtains: Shakespearean performance institutions, social media, and access', *Borrowers and Lenders: The Journal of Shakespeare and Appropriation* 10.1 (2016), www.borrowers.uga.edu/1756/ show.

Jamila of the Mustaffa and Kalimuddin families, Abad relocates Shakespeare's tragedy in a fictional Muslim community called Semporna. Purposefully intercultural, the narrative hews closely to Shakespeare's play even as elements of the performance deliberately conform to indigenous cultural conventions. The Friar Lawrence figure is now an Imam who also serves as apothecary, chorus, and storyteller. True to its theatrical roots in Southeast Asia where purity of genre is an alien concept, tragedy is thwarted by an epilogue that serves as the play's end. True to the conventions of the *igal* and its uses in community celebrations, the production includes an epilogue featuring the resurrection and reunion of Rashiddin and Jamila in the spirit world, who are then joined by members of the cast and audience in a final celebratory dance amidst butterflies. Dance, music and spectacle – rather than Shakespearian text – take centre stage in this production. An indigenous orchestra of gongs and drums is present onstage to accompany the chanting and dancing and, occasionally, to punctuate dialogue. Despite a minimal set, the production is nonetheless visually stunning owing to the lavish costumes – bright, shimmery silks, elaborate jewellery, intricately woven fabrics – designed by the Filipino National Artist for Theater Design, Salvador Bernal.

Sintang Dalisay readily fits the bill of Global Shakespeare not only in terms of the production's inherent characteristics, but also because it holds the distinction of being the Philippine production most performed outside the country. It did so on a grand total of four occasions. It was originally conceived as a 30-minute, three-actor piece for the UNESCO-ITI Theater Expo at the Shanghai Theater Academy in 2009. A slightly expanded version received a 2nd-place award at the 9th Teatralny Koufar International Student Theater Festival at the IXth World Congress of the International University Theater Association (IUTA) in Belarus in 2012. In 2014, a full-length version was staged at the Asian Shakespeare Association inaugural conference in Taiwan. And in 2016, it found its way to Vietnam as part of the 3rd International Experimental Theater Festival in

Hanoi. Deliberately conceived for an international audience, and in keeping with these performance contexts, the production looks very much like the showcase productions expected of these types of events and festivals – a spectacular rearticulation of Shakespearian texts in indigenous performance grammars, much like the use of forms such as Noh, Kabuki and Beijing Opera by more established Global Shakespeare productions. Abad himself, it must be said, was very cautious about employing the *igal*, a dance form of a minority group exotic even to the Manila audiences the play was initially intended for. He has sometimes expressed a mixture of discomfort at self-consciously showcasing a local culture for the consumption of world audiences, displaying an ambivalence between self-orientalizing guilt and nationalist pride.[17]

While receiving some exposure on the global stage and a measure of success at home with over 60 performances to date (where typical theatrical runs average around 15–20 performances), *Sintang Dalisay*'s performance record pales beside the over-200 and still-going performance run of a Filipino rap musical called *William*. *William*, an original play written by Ronan Capinding for PETA in 2011, essays the travails of five typical High School Juniors – an honour student, a jock, a spoiled rich girl, a student leader, and a painfully shy underachiever – as they strive to fulfil an English class assignment on Shakespeare. The formulaic stories of adolescents coming to self-awareness unfold with the aid of rap music and dance, making the production reminiscent of current pop culture staples like *Glee* or *High School Musical* rather than any particular local performance tradition. None of the

---

[17] A full account of Abad's deliberate process of working with indigenous culture and his analysis of the play's reception can be found in Ricardo Abad and MCM Santamaria, 'Reconfiguring folk performance for the contemporary stage: *Sintang Dalisay* and the *igal* of the Sama-Bajau in Southern Philippines', paper prepared for the SAC International Conference on the theme 'Folk performing arts in ASEAN', Sirindhorn Anthropology Center, Bangkok, Thailand, September 2016.

political, linguistic or historical issues concerning the teaching of Shakespeare to 21st-century Filipino students is probed with great depth; instead, the play features an almost fairy-tale-like series of magical transformations of these students from Shakespeare loathers to hard-core Bard believers. These transformations take place through performance. Most of the performances take the form of the recital of set pieces in the typical classroom oratorical exercise and are staged with appropriate reverential awe – replete with the isolated lighting and resultant hush in a heretofore almost rowdy audience. They serve, as well, as plot turning points: the student leader who is outed by another classmate finds expression and acceptance for his sexuality via Shylock's 'Hath not a Jew eyes' oration from *Merchant of Venice*, the honour student finds forgiveness for a mother who abandons her for a new family in London (a situation partially alluding to the Filipino diaspora) via Portia's 'quality of mercy' piece, and the social-climbing beauty queen rejects superficiality via Juliet's 'What's in a name?' speech. A happy ending is ensured for all, as enacted in the final scene – the junior prom with a Renaissance Ball theme, reminiscent of the celebratory endings of Shakespearian comedies themselves. As the production is targeted at youth audiences and marketed to schools as an aid to pedagogy, any specific cultural/local traces are less important than the elements and tropes from global culture that are far more palatable to young people.

Both of these productions exhibit varying relations to the idea of a Shakespearian market, of trading in Shakespeare. On the one hand, *Sintang Dalisay* was expressly created for an international market, a Philippine Shakespeare for export as it were. *William*, on the other hand, was commissioned and staged by PETA at the beginning of what it described as its Shakespeare season, which later featured productions of *King Lear* and *Twelfth Night*. Its mission – to popularize, and generate enthusiasm for, Shakespeare among its predominantly young audiences – was succinctly captured in the production's subtitle: 'from Shakes-fear to Shakes-peer'. It was, in some sense, a marketing tool that allows PETA entrance into the global

commerce in Shakespeare – albeit, to date, exclusively in local markets – where Shakespeare, alongside hip hop and rap, is transposed into a Filipino milieu, like imported goods adjusted to local tastes. Selling Shakespeare, of course, means not problematizing it, eliding prolonged critical engagement with the hard questions, evading probing questions of politics and language, and, as this production did, selling copies of *No Fear Shakespeare* in the theatre lobby.

Looking through the lenses of its target audiences or consumers, *Sintang Dalisay* and *William* represent two modes of Global Shakespeare. *Sintang Dalisay* is its more familiar and recognizable face. Staged for global, but highly specific, audiences, these productions emphatically illustrate Shakespeare's spread across the globe by fusing Shakespearian narratives with local theatrical forms. *William*, on the other hand, espouses the globalized aesthetics of hip hop and teen dramas for larger local audiences and is, therefore, less recognized as Global Shakespeare. More often than not, the label "global" is appended to Shakespeare for, at or with reference to its site of consumption. Too often, productions that travel out into the world are instantly recognizable and quickly admitted into Global Shakespeare canons; productions where the globe travels in – in forms including, but not limited to, Shakespeare – are not, as, for instance, in a play like *William*, or even in nontheatrical productions like manga or anime where Shakespearian characters and plots coexist with zombies and vampire-slayers. Since, in these types of productions, Shakespeare's role is less than privileged, such productions exist largely beneath the Global Shakespeare radar. Put another way: Shakespeare as export trumps Shakespeare as import.

One reason that the reverse traffic in Shakespeare may have been obscured from view is that, of late, the binary of local/global has given way to the more inclusive paradigms of networks, or, to use Douglas Lanier's highly useful concept, a rhizomatics of Shakespeare, based on Deleuze and Guattari's botanically inspired 'image of thought' that resists the hierarchical organization of binary and instead uses the rhizome – a network of random roots and their offshoots – as a model for how knowledge grows and develops. 'The Shakespearean rhizome', Lanier explains,

is never a stable object but an aggregated field in a perpetual state of becoming, ever being reconfigured as new adaptations intersect with and grow from it. Articulating the Shakespearean rhizome's changing lines of energy and difference, the myriad interactions, affiliations, contestations, collusions, ruptures, and, yes, appropriations among adaptations without privileging Shakespeare's 'original' text as a determining or final adjudicatory force, serves as the *raison d'être* for Shakespearean rhizomatics as a field.[18]

This is, of course, a welcome shift. Moving beyond a simplistic binary of centres and peripheries is indeed helpful, and the metaphor of networks certainly captures the complexity of global cultural exchanges more precisely. In addition, the distinctions between local and global are increasingly difficult to pin down, as this binary always leaves the question: 'local for whom?' A far greater number of contemporary Filipinos, for instance, would be more at home with rap and hip hop than they would be with the *igal*. The homogeneity of global popular cultures absorbed into different cultures throughout the world, an undeniable effect of globalization, complicates notions of the local a great deal.

But there remains some danger, as well, in using the concepts of networks or rhizomatics to theorize about Global Shakespeare. First, a rhizomatics, relying as it does on a constant state of becoming, carries with it the danger of concentrating on the present, to the always becoming *now*. While the paradigm does not preclude history – indeed, Lanier himself is explicit about how relations within a Shakespearian rhizomatics 'are certainly fraught with forms of cultural power' – it does little to bring temporality to the fore, being a predominantly spatial paradigm.[19] If one does not exercise due diligence in introducing the dimension of time, the concept of networks threatens to obscure or elide histories and their embedded power relations. In 'Shakespeare without borders', Sandra Young cautions that 'the turn to the "global" is, however, equally vulnerable to the

reductiveness that has at times robbed postcolonialism of its critical acuity'.[20] 'If it is to be meaningful as a critical paradigm', she adds,

'global Shakespeare' has to go further than adding superficial race-based interest' to the early modern period. Its real value ... is to be found in its invitation to recognize with greater perspicacity the ideological dimensions of cultural and critical life and the fundamental asymmetries of power relations at work ... Critical sensitivity to the impact of the 'global' calls for *more* careful historicism, not less. Without an attentiveness to the myriad of 'locals' within the global, it may have the effect of universalising what is culturally dominant.[21]

The call for a stronger sense of historicism in Global Shakespeare cannot be overemphasized. As a rhizomatics of Shakespeare seeks to make connections between related nodes of cultural production and exemplify the breadth and entanglements of the network, it must also consider the historical depth of each of these nodes and uncover relations between them that are embedded in their pasts.

Second, the creation and growth, or propagation, of a field of study such as Global Shakespeare is still primarily a human activity, and, as such, is given to the 'thousand natural shocks that flesh is heir to' (*Hamlet*, 3.1.64–5) – limitations of vision and judgements, inherent inequalities, varying degrees of influence and ignorance, etc. Let's face it: while no single entity is responsible for the development of the field of Global Shakespeare, some nodes in its rhizomatics are more influential than others. While the paradigm of networks seems to guarantee a reassuring multi-centredness, the embeddedness of institutions of academic and

---

[18] Douglas Lanier, 'Shakespearean rhizomatics: adaptation, ethics, value', in *Shakespeare and the Ethics of Appropriation*, ed. Alexa Huang [Joubin] and Elizabeth Rivlin (New York, 2014), 21–40; p. 30.

[19] Lanier, 'Shakespearean rhizomatics', p. 36.

[20] Sandra Young, 'Shakespeare without borders', in *South African Essays on 'Universal' Shakespeare*, ed. Chris Thurman (Farnham, 2014), 39–52; p. 46.

[21] Young, 'Shakespeare without borders', p. 47.

cultural production of Shakespeare within the realities of uneven, if globalized, economies still means that some centres are simply more central. There are places in these complex networks that act as 'filtering agents', that have a greater power of bestowing labels and legitimacy to certain productions while ignoring others. Bruno Latour's explanation of the network metaphor may serve to clarify this point:

What I have always found great in the metaphor of the net is that it is then easy to insist on its fragility, the empty spot it leaves around (a net is made first of all of empty space), . . . but above all, what it does with universality: the area 'covered' by any network is 'universal' but just as long and just where there are enough antennas, relays, repeaters, and so on, to sustain the activation of any work.[22]

In a sense, the institutions of Global Shakespeare act like Latour's antennas, relays and repeaters: propping up an encompassing sense of the universal or global onto Shakespeare even as they are surrounded by vast empty spaces.

In the end, Shakespeare undeniably can and does travel the globe, but unless these Shakespearian productions travel through the institutions that grant them greater visibility among stakeholders in the field, they remain outliers. The Philippines provides a case in point. Despite a long, rich history of Shakespearian productions, it remains almost invisible in the Global Shakespeare field. Admittedly, my appearance as part of the World Shakespeare Congress represents a significant signal boost, a manner of breaking the silence. Yet I wonder how many more are out there, how many mute onlookers there might be eavesdropping on the global conversation and who remain nonparticipants in the networks of roots and more like full-grown trees falling in the forest of Global Shakespeare's archival silences.

---

[22] Bruno Latour, 'Networks, societies, spheres: reflections of an actor-network theorist', keynote speech for the 'International Seminar on Network Theory: Network Multidimensionality in the Digital Age', Annenberg School for Communication and Journalism, Los Angeles, 19 February 2010, www.bruno-latour.fr/sites/default/files/121-CASTELLS-GB.pdf.

ARAB SHAKESPEARES AT THE WORLD SHAKESPEARE CONGRESS

KATHERINE HENNESSEY AND MARGARET LITVIN

[A]ny resemblance or allegory to a particular ex-president is unintentional. It is merely a coincidence.[1]
 (actor Yaḥyā al-Fakharānī, on playing Lear in Egypt)

Why and how do contemporary theatre practitioners from across 'the Arab world' – a misleadingly simple shorthand for a vast, diverse and rapidly changing region of the globe – adapt and perform Shakespeare? On Friday 5 August in the Great Hall of King's College London, the 2016 World Shakespeare Congress (WSC) 'Arab Shakespeares' panel convened to analyse the significance, the challenges and the creative innovations of translations, appropriations and productions of Shakespeare's works in the Middle East, North Africa, and the Arabian Peninsula. The panel provided a lively set of perspectives on the myriad ways in which Shakespeare is currently being re-cast, re-set and re-created in the Arab world.

What follows is a brief summary of the panel's content. Presentations were quite short – each speaker was given approximately 12 minutes – but full-length versions of all of the participants' papers have since been published in a special 'Arab Shakespeares' issue of *Critical Survey* (28.3, December 2016), co-edited by panel organizer and chair Katherine Hennessey and discussant Margaret Litvin.

After Hennessey welcomed the audience to the Great Hall, David C. Moberly of the University of Minnesota stepped to the podium to deliver a lecture entitled 'The taming of the tigress: Faṭima Rushdī and the first performance of *Shrew* in Arabic', which opened with the fascinating story of a young girl born into a struggling family in

Alexandria, who rose to become one of Egypt's most celebrated actresses.[2] By the age of 22, as Moberly notes, Faṭima Rushdī had been nick-named 'the Sarah Bernhardt of the East', and was co-owner and manager of a large and acclaimed theatre troupe that bore her name. In 1929, she recited the role of Mark Antony in her company's high-profile production of *Julius Caesar*, and the title role in *Hamlet*. The following year, she played Katharine in an Egyptian translation of *The Taming of the Shrew*, pointedly re-titled *The Giantess*.

Moberly's detailed research on contemporary reviews of this production demonstrates both that it met with widespread praise for Rushdī's performance and that it sparked a fierce linguistic controversy, provoked by translator Bishara Wakim's effectively unprecedented decision to render Shakespeare's lines in *'ammiyya* (Egyptian dialect) rather than *fuṣḥa* (formal literary Arabic). Critical responses to Wakim's use of the colloquial ranged from 'Shame on [him]!' for debasing Shakespeare's eloquence to the language of the Egyptian street, to defence of the choice based on the grounds that this play was a comedy, not a weighty tragedy, and that its lightness was better communicated by rough-

---

[1] Yaḥyā al-Fakharānī, interview by 'Amr Ṣaḥṣāḥ, 'My character in Dahsha is by coincidence allegorical to Arab rulers', *Youm7.com*, 8 August 2014; translated and cited by Noha Mohamad Mohamad Ibraheem in "Abd al-Raḥīm Kamāl's *Dahsha*: an Upper Egyptian *Lear*, *Critical Survey* 28.3 (2016), 67–85; p. 77.

[2] David C. Moberly, 'The taming of the tigress: Faṭima Rushdī and the first performance of *Shrew* in Arabic', *Critical Survey* 28.3 (December 2016), 8–26.

and-tumble *'ammiyya*. Moberly highlights the gendered undertones of this debate, in which comedy and dialect were perceived primarily as appertaining to feminine or domestic spheres, and therefore lacking the gravity and socio-political significance of both tragedy and *fusha*. The 'taming' of Katharine in Shakespeare's play thus parallels both an undercurrent of critical condescension towards Rushdī's own accomplishments as a groundbreaking figure in Egyptian theatre, and the rather pompous bias towards tragedy that continues to characterize both Arab engagement with Shakespeare, and critical evaluations of that engagement by Arab and Western scholars.

Noha Mohamad Mohamad Ibraheem of Cairo University spoke next, on "Abd al-Raḥīm Kamāl's *Dahsha*: an Upper Egyptian *Lear*'.[3] Ibraheem's presentation began with a video clip of a scene from *Dahsha*, a 2014 television series that sets Shakespeare's play in Upper Egypt in the early twentieth century, while presenting social and political issues pertinent to the twenty-first. In the video clip, Yaḥyā al-Fakharānī, who plays Basil (Lear), laments the cruelty of his two daughters, who have driven him out of their homes, forcing him to cross a stretch of scorching sand in his bare feet. Like Moberly, Ibraheem meticulously analyses an extensive cache of critical reviews, and she finds that the television series has provoked a similar debate – a recurrent one in Egyptian criticism, it seems – about the validity of adapting Shakespeare into colloquial and peripheral frames and forms. Some critics praised director 'Abd al-Ra-ḥīm Kamāl for his complex and thoughtful reproduction of *Lear*'s plots and subplots within its new setting, while others complained that he had rendered Shakespeare's play as mere gloomy melodrama rather than towering tragedy.

Ibraheem elected in her remarks at the WSC to push her analysis of one particular plot element further than she does in her *Critical Survey* article. She notes, intriguingly, that Basil equates his patriarchal authority with divine order – in the video clip that Ibraheem showed, the lamenting Basil claims that 'a father is a god' – and that he alludes to Qur'anic verses urging respect and obedience to

one's parents to buttress his complaints against his undutiful daughters. One wonders how the average Egyptian viewer might have interpreted such a recourse to religious precepts, given the series's repeated depictions of Basil as hot-tempered, vengeful, and willing to defy both man-made and divine law. Certainly, it is a moment that could provoke debate about a highly sensitive subject, i.e. the propensity of certain groups and individuals to invoke Islamic Holy Writ only insofar as it furthers their own ends. As Ibraheem points out, though Kamāl is not a political propagandist, and though al-Fakharānī went to some length in an interview to deny that the story contained any contemporary political allegory, the series seems, gingerly, to hold certain tantalizing propositions like this one up for debate. Ibraheem also perceives in *Dahsha* additional issues of relevance to contemporary Egypt, including gender inequality, rural poverty, and the stigma that is attached, to this day, to children born out of wedlock.

The presentation by Katherine Hennessey of Global Shakespeare (University of Warwick / Queen Mary University of London) shifted the panel's geographical terrain from Egypt to the Arabian Peninsula – to Oman, a country which has received little attention to date within studies of Arab Shakespeare. Her paper, '*Othello* in Oman: Ahmad al-Izki's fusion of Shakespeare and classical Arab epic',[4] examined a recent literary mash-up entitled *Al-Layla al-Halika* by Omani playwright Ahmad al-Izki, in which Othello meets his counterpart from pre-Islamic Arabian literature, the poet and warrior-hero 'Antara Ibn Shaddad. Though passionately in love with the beautiful 'Abla, 'Antara is considered unworthy of her because of his part-African heritage, which causes his 'purebred' Arab fellow tribesmen to treat him with contempt.

Hennessey argues that, by juxtaposing 'Antara with Othello, al-Izki's play reminds audiences on

---

[3] Ibraheem, "Abd al-Rahim Kamal's *Dahsha*'.

[4] Katherine Hennessey, '*Othello* in Oman: Ahmad al-Izki's fusion of Shakespeare and Classical Arab Epic'. *Critical Survey* 28.3 (December 2016), 47–66.

the Arabian Peninsula that they need to address the racial discrimination that continues to exist in their societies against African migrants, and against residents whose appearance implies African rather than 'pure Arab' ancestry. Moreover, she connects the issue of racism to entrenched systems of division across the Gulf, from the imposition of gender segregation to zoning and districting practices that separate citizens from foreigners, Sunni from Shi'a, the rich from the poor. According to Hennessey, this play's heroes demonstrate their virtue and their intelligence by transcending such barriers and by treating each other with trust and respect, despite the villainous Iago's attempts to sow discord and suspicion between them. They likewise prove themselves worthy of roles as leaders and protectors of their community – a cipher for the greater political participation sought by some residents of Oman and the wider Arab Gulf during and since the so-called 'Arab Spring' of 2011.

Distinguished scholar Graham Holderness of the University of Hertfordshire delivered the panel's final presentation, 'Sulayman Al-Bassam and questions of Shakespearean adaptation'. In his remarks, Holderness wished Arab Shakespeare a happy birthday, noting that it had been a full decade since the first-ever WSC panel on Arab Shakespeares (Brisbane, 2006) 'began to shape a new field of inquiry'.[5] Holderness's own interest in the topic was piqued by a performance of Al-Bassam's *The Al-Hamlet Summit* in Hammersmith in 2004, prompting him to contact the author, with whom he has since collaborated extensively. Reflecting on his communication with Al-Bassam as the latter was composing *Richard III: An Arab Tragedy* and *The Speaker's Progress* (an adaptation of *Twelfth Night* that turned Malvolio into an Islamist on a cue from a Holderness article on 'Shakespeare and Terrorism'[6]), Holderness recalled 'talking to the writer as he was in the process of creating the work, receiving successive drafts and commenting on them, feeding critical ideas into the creative process'.[7] Holderness suggested that his and Al-Bassam's experience models a process whereby 'artists can become more critical, and critics more creative'.[8]

Margaret Litvin of Boston University, who had convened the original 2006 Arab Shakespeares WSC panel ten years earlier and translated Jawad al-Assadi's *Forget Hamlet* for performance there,[9] opened her remarks as discussant by noting that this year's WSC had scheduled a trio of its 'global' panels for the same day and timeslot, 'as though scholars working on Arab, Latin American, and Indian Shakespeares had nothing to learn from each other'! She summarized how Shakespeare adaptation has provided a slippery but convenient 'playable surface' for Arab artists during an extremely challenging decade (including the Arab uprisings and their aftermath) and continues to offer Western scholars and audiences a way to understand Arab artists' work as well as their lives.[10] Hailing the diversity and quality of emerging scholars, and the broader interest in Arab Shakespeares from mainstream theatre companies and centres of scholarly authority such as journals and conferences, she expressed her hope that this maturing field would continue to grow sharper, more historically sophisticated and more comparative with other regions.

Litvin's remarks led into a lively discussion session. Ibraheem fielded inquiries about how obvious and how recognizable the *Lear* subtext of *Dahsha* would have been to an Egyptian audience (quite so for many viewers, given Yaḥyā al-Fakharānī's long-running performance in the title role of *King Lear* in Arabic translation at the National Theatre in Cairo). Hennessey was asked to

---

5 Graham Holderness, 'Afterword', *Critical Survey* 28.3 (2016), 209–12; p. 209.
6 Graham Holderness and Bryan Loughrey, 'Rudely interrupted: Shakespeare and terrorism', *Critical Survey* 19.3 (2007), 107–23.
7 Holderness, 'Afterword', p. 210.
8 Holderness, 'Afterword', p. 211.
9 See *Four Arab Hamlet Plays*, eds. Marvin Carlson and Margaret Litvin (with Joy Arab), New York: Martin E. Segal Center, 2016.
10 On 'playable surfaces', see Margaret Litvin, 'For the record: interview with Sulayman Al-Bassam', in *Shakespeare and the Ethics of Appropriation*, ed. Alexa Huang [Joubin] and Elizabeth Rivlin (New York, 2014), pp. 221–40.

elaborate upon the effect that al-Izki's integration of elements of *Othello* into a play that ends happily would have had upon local audiences (startling and thought-provoking, but not perhaps to the same degree as al-Izki's unorthodox portrayal of 'Antara, a great romantic hero whom most Gulf Arabs would consider a part of their own literary heritage, and whom al-Izki depicts as momentarily attracted to Desdemona). And audience member Christian Smith commented that this panel was one of the most important ones he had attended at the 2016 Congress, since it addressed urgent issues of diversity and inequality in Shakespeare-inspired representation and performance.

While the representation of women and people of colour within the upper echelons of the WSC, and of Shakespeare studies in general, was the subject of some debate at this year's Congress,[11] this panel had three female contributors (including in the key roles of chair/organizer and discussant) and two male; its participants were British, American and Egyptian, and its presenters ranged from very early career to well-established. Moreover, the presentations, on the whole, strove to recuperate or shed light on figures (such as actress Rushdī, screenwriter Kamāl, and playwright al-Izki), genres (comedy and television), and geographies (Oman, Upper Egypt) that have until now remained on the periphery of Arab Shakespeare studies.

Elsewhere in the Congress – in seminars and workshops on Shakespeare in cinema, for example, or in non-Anglo-Saxon cultures – scholarship on Arab Shakespeares seemed under-represented. One exception was graduate student Madiha Hannachi's contribution to the seminar on 'Reading Shakespeare adaptations historically', led by Deborah Cartmell (De Montfort University) and Maurizio Calbi (University of Salerno). Hannachi, of the University of Montreal, circulated to the seminar a paper entitled 'Reversal of the early modern pattern of representation in contemporary Arab adaptations of Shakespeare', which posits that, since the 1990s, Arab writers have been 'embracing Shakespeare to resolve contemporary local struggles', a thesis through which she interprets the presentation of Arab characters in Al-Bassam's *Al-Hamlet Summit* and *Richard III*.

As noted, each of the Arab Shakespeares panel's four presentations has now been published in *Critical Survey* 28.3. The special issue also includes features on Shakespeare in Palestinian, Moroccan and Swedish-Arab theatre, in Egyptian film and in Lebanese Anglophone novels, and contributions from two esteemed translators of Shakespeare's complete sonnets into Arabic. It is an extensive publication – the online version runs to 212 pages, and includes eight articles, an interview, two short essays, and four reviews – and its contributions reflect the remarkable geographic, linguistic and generic diversity of studies of 'Arab Shakespeares' in 2016 to a degree that a four-presentation panel could not.

Yet the limitations of time and number that governed the composition of the WSC panel worked, in certain ways, to its advantage. For instance, the tighter focus illuminated the thematic similarities between Moberly's and Ibraheem's examinations of Egyptian adaptations of Shakespeare in different media (stage vs small screen) and at vastly different historical moments (1930 vs 2014), allowing audience members at least a glimpse of the performative and critical trajectories that link them. Moberly's nuancing of Egyptian Shakespeare adaptations by genre and linguistic register encouraged audience members to consider the significance of *Lear* rewritten as serialized television melodrama, or of an Othello and a Desdemona who can escape the tragic ending of Shakespeare's play when wrenched out of their own narrative and dropped into a Bedouin warrior's epic romance. And Holderness's remarks reminded all of us of the remarkable opportunity that the study of Arab Shakespeares offers – the opportunity to shape, intervene in, and contribute expertise to a swiftly expanding field.

---

[11] See, for example, Nora Williams's *NotInOurStars* blog post 'The *Taming of the Shrew*, *Cymbeline*, and the World Shakespeare Congress'.

THE DUAL TRADITION OF BARDOLATRY IN CHINA

HAO LIU

In *The Revenge of Prince Zi Dan*,[1] the Peking opera adaptation of *Hamlet* applauded by audiences from thirteen countries in the last ten years, the God of Justice, a new character in this adaptation, tells the story of regicide in the opening scene. The moral exposition by the new character does not duplicate the essence of Shakespeare that 'frustrates and fulfills expectations simultaneously'.[2] The narrative explicitness and the sharp contrast between good and evil is a far cry from the moral ambiguity in Shakespeare, but *The Revenge* epitomizes the century-long tradition of adapting Shakespeare to Chinese sensibilities.

The reception of Shakespeare is pertinent to the discussion of the renaissance of Chinese culture ever since the late Qing dynasty. Introduced to China in a time of cultural progress and transition, Shakespeare could never circumvent the confrontation between the 'old' and the 'new' cultures in the making of a modern nation. The reception of Shakespeare in China follows a binary course which reflects the intellectual preoccupation of the last century with the 'new' and the 'old' trends in culture. Instead of assimilating exclusively into either side of the opposite cultural groups, Shakespeare has been a convenient symbol for the 'new' ideas, and at the same time a reminder of the 'old' values.

This article begins by discussing the reception of Shakespeare in China in the first half of the twentieth century, and then it fast-forwards to the revival of enthusiasm in Shakespeare since the late 1970s. A variety of commentary and stage productions in the last century testifies to a dual tradition in the early reception of Shakespeare. Shakespeare symbolizes paradoxically both the 'new' and the 'old' in Chinese culture. This dual meaning is rooted in the divided and shifting attitudes of Chinese intellectuals during different historical periods towards traditional and anti-traditional elements. After the Cultural Revolution, and since the late 1970s, Shakespeare becomes laden with the dual meaning in the Chinese discourse of globalization and cultural exchange again, though the implications of the 'old' and the 'new' are now different and at times amalgamated.

To know the reason why Shakespeare has seemed both 'old' and 'new' in China, we need to know the Chinese intellectual currents in the early twentieth century, namely the 'new' and the 'old' trends. As the Qing dynasty was weakened by the Opium Wars in the mid nineteenth century, the Chinese elite began to see the advantages of Western civilization. A group of intellectuals turned to Western culture, hoping to remedy social ills with imported ideas. Change became the leitmotif in the early twentieth-century culture. The early reception of Shakespeare was preceded by the dawn of economic

This research is supported by the Youth Foundation of the Ministry of Education of China for Humanities and Social Sciences (16YJC752013). My thanks to King-Kok Cheung for much advice on the revision of the article.

1 *The Revenge of Prince Zi Dan*, performed by Shanghai Peking Opera Theatre (2005; Shanghai, Guangzhou: Beauty Culture Communication Co. Ltd, 2008), DVD.

2 Stephen Booth, 'On the value of Hamlet', in *Shakespeare: An Anthology of Criticism and Theory 1945–2000*, ed. Russ McDonald (Malden, MA, 2004), p. 26.

and cultural prosperity in Europe. The idea of the Renaissance introduced by Christian missionaries as early as the late sixteenth century[3] inspired the reformation of Chinese culture. European history was promoted by leading scholars as paradigms to expound their own views on how to rejuvenate their culture.[4]

Therefore, in the early reception of Shakespeare, the 'new' trend was usually not only anti-traditional but also tied to Western cultural paradigms. On the other hand, the conservative intellectuals continued to champion traditional Chinese values. They were not totally opposed to imported ideas but they believed change should be made by modifying, not by displacing, the national tradition. These intellectuals for the 'old' not only advocated traditional Chinese values but also held that imported ideas should be assimilated into the system of traditional values. In both the 'new' and the 'old' narratives, as the next section demonstrates, there are constant allusions to Shakespeare, and manifestations of bardolatry.

SHAKESPEARE AS A MODEL
OF THE 'NEW' CULTURE

In the early reception of Shakespeare in China, the reformists and radical intellectuals, though not always commenting on the specific merits of his works, kept chanting his name. As the modernization of China was a major intellectual concern, Shakespeare was turned into 'utopian visions of universal figures of modernity'.[5] Shakespeare was lauded for his literary achievements in publications that introduced the Western countries and their cultures in the mid and late nineteenth century and was gradually adopted as a model of Western values at the turn of the century. Li Hongzhang, a politician and diplomat of the Qing dynasty who was considered a pioneer in the industrial modernization of China, in a speech in 1896, venerated Shakespeare as one of those who could make the nation powerful and the people wealthy.[6] Lu Xun, a leading figure of modern literature, related Shakespeare to the new civilization, saying that people needed Shakespeare to 'preserve humanity

and balance it, which led to today's civilization'.[7] Among the leading scholars who thought highly of Shakespeare and commented on him in their public writings were Yan Fu, the translator who was famous for introducing Western ideas (especially the Darwinian theory), and Liang Qichao, the leading reformist whose writing inspired a generation of Chinese scholars.[8] It is telling that, in 1922, *Hamlet* was the first faithful translation of a Shakespeare play, published in the magazine *The Young China*, indicating on which side Shakespeare was positioned in the confrontation between the old and the new cultures.

The furtherance of the bardolatry in China had much to do with the controversies over reforming Chinese drama, and Shakespeare was adopted as a model of a better type of drama that was to take the place of traditional Chinese dramatic conventions, imparting new ideas to the masses. At the turn of the twentieth century, being aware of the power of literature, some intellectual reformers held drama to be a good means to educate the common people.[9] Chen Duxiu, a revolutionary intellectual and later dean of Humanities at Peking University and co-founder of the Chinese Communist Party, and Liu Yazi, a renowned poet, wrote articles for the popular journals *Twentieth-Century Stage* and *The New Fiction* in 1904 to put forward their

---

[3] Nicolas Standaert, 'The transmission of Renaissance culture in seventeenth-century China', in *Asian Travel in the Renaissance*, ed. Daniel Carey (Oxford, 2004), pp. 42–66.

[4] Luo Zhitian, *Tradition in Fission: Chinese Culture and Scholarship in the Early Twentieth Century* (Beijing, 2003), pp. 51–8.

[5] Alexa Huang [Joubin], *Chinese Shakespeares: Two Centuries of Cultural Exchange* (New York, 2009), p. 18.

[6] Cai Erkang, *Tours of Li Hongzhang in Europe and America* (Changsha, 1986), p. 138.

[7] Lu Xun, 'On the History of Science', in *The Complete Works of Lu Xun*, vol. 1 (Beijing, 1981), p. 17.

[8] T. H. Huxley, *Evolution and Ethics*, trans. Yan Fu (Beijing, 1971), p. 57; Liang Qichao, *Uncollected Essays*, vol. 1: *The Collected Works of Yinbingshi*, ed. Xia Xiaohong (Beijing, 2005), p. 126.

[9] Wang Jimin, *The Scientific Trend of Thought and Scientific Criticism of Literature in the Late Qing Dynasty and the Early Period in the Republic of China* (Beijing, 2004), pp. 80–1.

objections to traditional Chinese drama.[10] Such famous actors and Peking opera singers as Wang Xiaonong, Tan Xinpei and Mei Lanfang starred in Chinese operas of modern costume, which were all the rage. Liang Qichao and Liu Yazi tried their hands at writing new plays too. In the late 1910s and 1920s, some Chinese intellectuals argued fiercely over upholding or abolishing traditional Chinese drama. Hu Shih, Qian Xuantong, Liu Bannong, Chen Duxiu, Fu Sinian and Ouyang Yuqian launched harsh criticism against the themes and aesthetics of traditional drama in *The New Youth*, some even saying that Chinese drama contained 'no aesthetic value at all' and should be abolished.[11]

In this context, Shakespeare, Henrik Ibsen and Bernard Shaw became paragons for Chinese dramatists to use as weapons against tradition. According to the reformers, the remedies for the withering of Chinese drama were the scripts and theories of Western drama.[12] The pioneers of Chinese modern theatre (the early form of which – 1907–18 – is known as *wenming xi* or 'the civilized drama') started to perform Shakespeare's plays before any faithful and complete translation was published. Shakespeare's plays were used as examples for the Chinese playwrights to follow.[13] The playwright and drama theorist Yu Shangyuan considered the translation of Shakespeare to be 'the starting point' of new drama in China.[14] In Liang Qichao's play, *New Rome*, Shakespeare even appears as a divine character who rides on a cloud.

Applauded by intellectuals and dramatists who spared no effort in promoting imported ideas, Shakespeare was successfully moulded into an image of the 'new', and radical intellectuals wanted to hold up the image so their compatriots could see by contrast what changes were needed in Chinese culture.

SHAKESPEARE AS LADEN WITH THE 'OLD' CULTURE

Alongside the recognition of the foreignness of Shakespeare was the indigenization of the Bard throughout the history of the reception of Shakespeare. The affiliation of Shakespeare with traditional Chinese writers can be traced back a century and a half. Since then, writers and scholars have been trying to assimilate his works into the Chinese tradition.

From the early twentieth century, directors have attempted to blend Shakespeare and Chinese traditional opera, using Chinese opera to familiarize Shakespeare or weaving Shakespeare into the dramatic tradition of China. Shakespeare's plays have been adapted to Kun opera, Peking opera, Yue opera, Huangmei opera, Guangdong Yue opera, Tanci, and other varieties of Chinese operas. Traditional Chinese flavour was even seen in the *wenming xi* (civilized drama) and *huaju* (spoken drama) adaptations. For example, *The Traitor of the State* (an adaptation based on *Hamlet*) was advertised through the press with typical Chinese expressions and moral concerns – 'He betrays his king and his country; he steals his brother's wife and his crown.'[15] The advertisement for an adaptation of *The Merchant of Venice* in the 1930s was a verse of four lines in stylized Chinese,[16] immediately reminiscent of the style of poems as a convention to start or end a chapter in traditional Chinese drama. It seemed that a play geared towards a traditional Chinese mind-set might appeal more readily to the common people.

While Shakespeare's plays were recast into traditional Chinese plays, titles had been bestowed on

---

[10] Chen Duxiu (San Ai), 'On Chinese opera', *Anhui Vernacular Journal* 11 (1904), 1–6; Ya Lu (Liu Yazi), 'Forward', *Twentieth-Century Stage* 1 (1904), 1–5.

[11] Fu Sinian, 'My views on the reformation of drama', *The New Youth* 5.4 (1918), 349–60.

[12] Ouyang Yuqian, 'My views on the reformation of drama', *The New Youth* 5.4 (1918), 341–3; Chen (San Ai), 'On Chinese opera'.

[13] Yuan Sheng (Huang Yuansheng), ed. and trans., 'On new drama', *Monthly Journal of Fictions* 5.1 (1914), 1–2; and 2 (1914), 3–6.

[14] Yu Shangyuan, 'On translating Shakespeare', *Crescent* 3.5 and 6 (10 April 1931), 11–12.

[15] *News Daily of the Republic of China* (11 March 1916).

[16] *A Special Issue to Introduce Shakespeare*, published by the National Drama School (1937), inside the front cover.

the playwright by intellectuals of either the new or the conservative schools, and some of the early commentaries connected the Bard with Chinese poets and scholars. Some early critics approached Shakespearian works in the same way they appreciated traditional Chinese literary works. Lin Shu and Su Manshu both compared Shakespeare with Du Fu, the poet-sage of China in the Tang dynasty.[17] In a poem about London theatre, Kang Youwei, a prominent scholar and political thinker, compared the Bard to Qu Yuan, the patriotic Chinese poet who lived 2,000 years ago.[18] Zhao Jingshen started the tradition of comparative study of the Chinese playwright Tang Xianzu and Shakespeare in 1946.[19] When Shakespeare became better read and studied in China, aspects of Shakespearian drama started to be examined in comparison with Chinese dramatic conventions. Unlike the comparison between Tang Xianzu, the playwright, and Shakespeare, his contemporary, the parallels drawn by Kang Youwei, Lin Shu and Su Manshu between Shakespeare and Du Fu, the poet-sage, or Qu Yuan, the forefather of Chinese poets, elevated Shakespeare to an even higher literary rank.

Several early translations or adaptations of Shakespeare tended to indigenize his works with a classical style of language, conventions of Chinese fictions or translator's notes. In *Xie Wai Qi Tan* [Strange Overseas Tales], Shakespeare's plots were rendered into stereotypical Chinese tales in classical Chinese by an anonymous translator in 1903. *Yin Bian Yan Yu* [Tales from Shakespeare] was one of the most famous and influential translations of Shakespeare in China. Published in 1904, it boasted the elegance of the classical style of the renowned traditionalist scholar, Lin Shu. In *Tian Chou Ji* [Heavenly Revenge], a classical-Chinese translation of *Hamlet* published in 1924, the translator Shao Ting never hesitated to comment on the moral vision or break the dramatic suspense in his translator's notes.

It is especially interesting that Lin Shu, known as the 'king of translators', strove to draw readers back to the beauty of classical Chinese. Holding that Shakespeare was representative of the 'old' cultural tradition of the West, and that the Shakespearian style was as archaic as a historical relic, Lin Shu tried to justify the position of traditional Chinese culture in a modern age by alluding to Shakespeare's time-honoured position in the West.[20] Lin made several interesting changes to Shakespeare's stories to accommodate the taste of Chinese readers. His translation was so popular that it became the basis for many performances of *wenming xi*.

It seems that Shakespeare was readily accepted as a quasi-Chinese playwright and consumed by the common audience and readers. However, in the early phases of introduction and adaptation, both the cultural conservatives and cultural radicals took Shakespeare as a springboard for their beliefs and ideological claims. Shakespeare began to merge into modern Chinese culture in the dual tradition of being received as a model of the new culture and as a trophy of the old heritage.

HAMLET AS A SYMBOL OF DILEMMA

As Shakespeare continued to be used as a bifurcated cultural symbol, *Hamlet*, in particular, epitomized the dilemma of Chinese intellectuals in the 1930s and the 1940s.

Chinese intellectuals who were distressed by the cultural uncertainty of the time identified with Hamlet and turned him into a token of the struggle between the old and the new, echoed in the conflict between contemplation and action. In a short story by Ba Jin, Hamlet was construed as the archetype of young intellectuals who yearned for the courage to act and advance but ended up in

---

[17] Lin Shu, preface to Charles Lamb and Mary Lamb, *Yin Bian Yan Yu* [Tales from Shakespeare], trans. Lin Shu and Wei Yi (Beijing, 1981) (first published 1904), p. 1; Su Manshu, *Duan Hong Ling Yan Ji* [Stray Swan Geese], first published in 1912, Kindle edition (Hangzhou, 2013), p. 171.

[18] Kang Youwei, *The Complete Words of Kang Youwei*, vol. 12 (Beijing, 2007), p. 306.

[19] Zhao Jingshen, 'Tang Xianzu and Shakespeare', *Literature and Art Review* 2.2 (1946), 5–9.

[20] Lin Shu, preface to Lamb and Lamb, *Yin Bian Yan Yu*, p. 1.

contemplation and retreat.[21] Lao She's short story, 'New Hamlet', was possibly the earliest parody of *Hamlet* in China,[22] and in Lao She's plan for his play *Gui Qu Lai Xi* [Returning], which would have been named 'New Hamlet', he had designed a plot about a 'wise, contemplative, sceptical, pessimistic man who cannot take action'.[23] Jiao Juyin, a prominent director and theatre theorist, and Liao Mosha, a famous essayist, related *Hamlet* more explicitly to the character of Chinese people, saying that the Chinese were 'often too prudent to do anything demanding courage',[24] and that a 'Hamletian' tragedy would be full of Chinese intellectuals.[25] There were more literary works in the 1930s and 1940s that alluded to Hamlet, who 'had been an indispensable reference for the Chinese writers when they pondered over the fate of Chinese intellectuals'.[26]

Inability to act had caused melancholy in Chinese intellectuals who grew up to face a time of cultural transition, and their loss of power was a result of both ideological confusions and the nullification of the imperial examination system, which previous generations of orthodox intellectuals had engaged in for over 1,000 years. The fact that Hamlet was used as a symbol for the mental pains and uncertainty of that period testifies not only to the popularity of the Bard among Chinese intellectuals but also to the ambiguity of bardolatry in China.

DUAL VISION IN A NEW AGE

The competition between the new and the old trends had long been an intellectual preoccupation in China's transformation towards modernity, and Shakespeare was adopted by both sides as a symbol of heterogeneous or homogeneous values vis-à-vis China. Although there was an interruption in Shakespeare studies in the 1960s and 1970s due to the Cultural Revolution, the enthusiasm for Shakespeare in mainland China revived soon after 1976. Since the late 1970s and the 1980s, the reception of Shakespeare in mainland China has entered a new phase. Shakespeare is still a bridge between the old and the new,

though the meanings of 'old' and 'new' have been transformed.

After the late 1970s, Shakespeare was embraced again as a sign of the 'new'. However, this did not so much signify the importation of ideas (although this enthusiasm was a kind of recognition of the values of Western literature) as celebrate the revival of a broad worldview and love for literature that had been officially restricted and censored. In 1979, the Shanghai Youth Theatre launched a production of *Much Ado About Nothing*, which marked the flourishing new age of Shakespeare on Chinese stage.[27] Shakespeare was the first foreign writer to have his complete works published in mainland China after the Cultural Revolution. The 1986 Shakespeare Festival in China was the most influential Shakespeare event in that decade, with twenty-eight productions of Shakespeare plays.[28] Eight years after the 1986 Festival, an International Shakespeare Festival was held in Shanghai. With lectures, seminars, publications and stage presentations, the Chinese people's passion for Shakespeare and Western literatures was officially rekindled.

---

[21] Ba Jin, 'Spring rain', in *The Complete Works of Ba Jin*, vol. 10 (Beijing, 1989), 246–7; first published in *Mercury* 1.1 (10 October 1934). Qian Liqun points out the connection between this story and Hamlet in his book *The Rich Pains: The Eastward Moves of Don Quixote and Shakespeare* (Beijing, 2007), 247.

[22] Huang, *Chinese Shakespeares*, p. 87.

[23] Lao She, 'On my seven plays', in *The Collected Plays of Lao She*, vol. 1 (Beijing, 1982), 556–7.

[24] Jiao Juyin, 'Shakespeare and Hamlet', in *The Collected Works of Jiao Juyin*, vol. 2 (Beijing, 1998), 172.

[25] Huai Xiang (Liao Mosha), 'The Hamletian tragedy', in *The Collected Works of Liao Mosha*, vol. 1 (Beijing, 1986), 256; first published in *Xinhua Supplement of Xinhua Daily* (7 October 1943).

[26] Qian Liqun, *The Rich Pains*, pp. 247, 249.

[27] J. Norman Wilkinson, 'Shakespeare in China', *New England Theatre Journal* 2.1 (1991), 39–58.

[28] Ruru Li, 'The Bard in the Middle Kingdom', *Asian Theatre Journal* 12.1 (Spring 1995), 50–84; Zhang Xiaoyang, *Shakespeare in China: A Comparative Study of Two Traditions and Cultures* (Newark and London, 1996), p. 115.

As mainland China was eager to rebuild the link with world culture after the Cultural Revolution, Shakespeare's plays betokened the Chinese people's zeal for communicating with what was then 'new' to them after the interruption – the fruits of other cultures and the cultural prosperity of a globalized age. An essay published in *Shakespeare Quarterly* in 1988 was entitled 'Shakespeare renaissance in China', and it relates that in 1976 'queues formed in the streets for copies of Shakespeare's most popular play in China, *The Pound of Flesh* [*The Merchant of Venice*]'.[29]

On the other hand, Shakespeare again signified the recognition of the aesthetic tradition in Chinese drama. At the 1994 Shakespeare festival, a variety of Chinese productions of Shakespeare transmitted a new message when they were presented to a world audience. Different from the Chinese-opera adaptations in the early half of the twentieth century, the new-age productions were designed both to revive Shakespeare and to highlight the unique Chinese theatrical heritage, so as to announce the fruitful return of mainland China to world culture. Shakespeare's plays continued to be treated as a counterpart of Chinese dramatic traditions and were infused with Chinese aesthetics and morals. Though Marxist approaches had been the main trend since the 1950s, alternate perspectives emerged in that new age, and the unique views of Chinese scholars were especially encouraged. Cao Yu, the first president of the Shakespeare Association of China, proposed in his 'Inaugural observations' for *Shakespeare Studies* that 'we are reading the world giant Shakespeare from the point of view of a modern China involved in its own recent history'.[30]

In the new age after the late 1970s, the Janus-faced symbol of Shakespeare has a lot to do with China's global outlook, in addition to the opposition between the traditional and anti-traditional schools in the early twentieth century. The mainstream intellectuals of mainland China eagerly imbibed Western values, while at the same time they cherished the idea of China's cultural renaissance, which is based on the re-discovery of traditional values.

CONCLUSION: SHAKESPEARE BIFURCATED AND RE-CREATED

The image of Shakespeare in China reflects the rivalry of the anti-traditional culture and the conservative culture. Both sides applauded Shakespeare and used him as a convenient resource to prove their own worth. Besides the richness of Shakespeare's works, the following factors may have accounted for the binary course of bardolatry in China.

First, the 'old' and 'new' camps of the early twentieth century overlapped with each other in academic background and aesthetic taste. And the impact of Western cultural trends, especially of Shakespeare, was so profound that both the radicals and the conservatives had been under the influence of Western culture and could not dismiss Shakespeare as irrelevant. Some of the leading scholars of the conservative camp, such as Wu Mi, even considered themselves inheritors of Western cultural tradition.[31]

Second, before 1921, there was no complete and serious Chinese translation of any Shakespeare play. In the 1930s, the translation of the complete works of Shakespeare was just starting in China. Except for some scholars who read the original English version, people referred to Shakespeare without knowing specific lines from his plays. On the other hand, European aesthetics by the eighteenth century had turned away from the art object towards the artist as an independent figure, and 'one of the first signs of western literary influence in China' was the 'new respectability of the writer'.[32] Therefore, in the first few dozen years of Shakespeare's introduction into China, he was romanticized and turned into a convenient and flexible symbol for the opposing sides of the ideological warfare.

---

29 J. Philip Brockbank, 'Shakespeare renaissance in China', *Shakespeare Quarterly* 39.2 (summer 1988), 197.
30 Murray J. Levith, *Shakespeare in China* (London and New York, 2004), p. 60.
31 Wu Mi, *Poems and Notes on Poetry* (Xi'an, 1992), pp. 250–1.
32 Bonnie S. McDougall, 'The impact of Western literary trends', in *Modern Chinese Literature in the May Fourth Era*, ed. Merle Goldman (Cambridge, 1977), p. 38.

Third, and most important, the dual meaning in the Chinese bardolatry is rooted in the Chinese idea of the mutuality of the old and the new in traditional philosophy. The intellectuals of the last century favoured the idea of the Renaissance, in which they saw the new growing out of the old.[33] The traditional Chinese notion that the new grows organically from the old was reiterated by the leading scholars of that century. According to Liang Qichao, a culture develops by inheriting and sublimating its tradition and by adopting from other cultures what it lacks.[34] Hu Shih claimed that the new is not made by abandoning the old, but that a new culture in China should be built by the balance of the new and the old, and the mix of Chinese and Western thoughts.[35]

The dual meaning of the 'new' and the 'old' invested in Shakespeare has evolved over the last century into the dual vision of both reaching out to the world and recognizing the domestic tradition. When Chinese operas were popular 100 years ago, Shakespeare was at once enshrined as the 'other' and domesticated to be consumed. Now, with more and more young people estranged from traditional Chinese operas but well-read in Shakespearian masterpieces, the meanings of the 'old' and the 'new' are different. In *The Revenge of Prince Zi Dan*, for example, the Hamletian procrastination runs afoul of the Chinese morals represented by the God of Justice; in a Peking opera adaptation of *King Lear*,[36] the youngest princess speaks eloquently against the division of the country. In the new interpretations of Shakespeare, the co-existence of global values and domestic values is no longer a dilemma, but promises multi-faceted re-creations of Shakespeare in a polyglot world.

---

[33] Luo Zhitian, *Tradition in Fission*, pp. 73–4.

[34] Liang Qichao, 'The new people', in *Political Essays in the Ten Years Before Xinhai Revolution*, vol. 1:1, ed. Zhang Nan and Wang Renzhi (Beijing, 1960), p. 122.

[35] Hu Shih, 'An argument against studying abroad', in *The Collected Academic Essays*, ed. Jiang Yihua (Beijing, 1998), p. 14.

[36] *King Qi's Dream*, performed by Shanghai Peking Opera Theatre (1995; Guangzhou: Beauty Culture Communication Co. Ltd, 2006), DVD.

A CATALYST FOR THEATRICAL REINVENTION: CONTEMPORARY TRAVELLING COMPANIES AT THE TOKYO GLOBE THEATRE

MICHIKO SUEMATSU

Travelling companies are culturally out-of-place. In the theatre, the actors who travel and the audiences who take in the theatre companies' performances both have out-of-place cultural experiences. The actors bring and stage a production from home in an alien space, tearing it away from its original cultural *mise-en-scène*; simultaneously, the audience's theatre-going habits in their familiar theatre are disrupted by encountering unfamiliar, and sometimes unconventional, performances from overseas. This is entirely different from a theatre-going experience in which one travels overseas and goes to see a performance among the local audiences. The sense of cultural displacement created by travelling companies is mutual and more dynamic. Theatre history has shown that, from time to time, this cultural displacement has worked as a powerful catalyst for reinvention of Shakespeare.

In the Japanese history of Shakespeare production, for instance, travelling companies from overseas twice effected their decisive influence and reinvented Shakespeare: first, in the late nineteenth century when Japan opened its ports to Western powers after its 200-year-long *sakoku*, or national isolation policy; and second, about 100 years later in the 1980s, when an influx of touring productions began at the Tokyo Globe Theatre. The chief aim of this article is to assess the second instance of travelling companies' impact on today's Japanese Shakespeare performance, examining how it differs from that of a century earlier. A comparison with the first instance of travelling companies in Japan, which Kaori Kobayashi has detailed in her paper '"The Actors Are Come Hither": Shakespeare productions by travelling companies in Asia', can provide significant insight into the implications of travelling companies in shifting historical and cultural contexts.[1] Kobayashi's paper focuses on two travelling companies formed by two British actors, George Crichton Miln and Allan Wilkie. Both the Miln Company and the Allan Wilkie Company toured widely in and beyond the British Empire at the turn of the twentieth century. By examining the first-hand records of these companies, as well as the notes left by some audience members, Kobayashi gave an account of the companies' Shakespeare performances and explored how they influenced the development of Shakespearian performance in Asia, particularly in Japan and India.

In the case of Japan, because the travelling companies' shows were staged primarily within the foreign settlements, such as Yokohama and Kobe, audiences

[1] As a leader of the panel '"The Actors Are Come Hither": Shakespearean productions by travelling companies in the British Empire and Asia' at the World Shakespeare Congress 2016, Kaori Kobayashi, who passed away in September 2015, intended to report the results of her research on British companies' early twentieth-century theatrical expeditions in Japan and India. See Kaori Kobayashi, '"The Actors Are Come Hither": Shakespeare productions by travelling companies in Asia', *New Theatre Quarterly* 32.1 (2016), 49–60.

were extremely limited. Luckily, however, among them were a small number of the Japanese cultural elite, including Shoyo Tsubouchi, one of the pioneers of modern Japanese theatre, who first translated the entire Shakespeare canon into Japanese. Tsubouchi saw some of the Miln Company productions in 1891 and the Alan Wilkie productions in 1912. Considering that these travelling productions prompted Tsubouchi to forsake his earlier attempts to Westernize Kabuki with Shakespearian plots – an effort he began at the urging of the Meiji government's Westernization policy – these shows, which intended to re-create 'the culture of the motherland for the British, or English-speaking people in the settlements', helped to lay the foundations for modern Japanese Shakespeare, or *Shingeki* Shakespeare.[2] Tsubouchi proceeded to stage full productions of Shakespeare using his own translations, the first of which was the 1911 production of *Hamlet*. Kobayashi notes that, for Tsubouchi, the experience of directly seeing touring productions by Miln and Wilkie was an 'awe-inspiring experience almost like travelling abroad', and that with this in-the-flesh experience came the revelation of the decisive difference between the dramaturgy of Kabuki and Shakespeare.[3] Tsuboushi wanted to stage unique Japanese Shakespeare, but it became clear that Shakespeare had to be staged using completely new theatrical idioms and vocabulary: not in the old Kabuki style, but in *Shingeki* style, literally a 'new theatre' style that conforms to Western dramaturgy. The 'practical ways of directing Western drama', and 'performance techniques such as dialogue, expression, elocutions' in staging Shakespeare that Tsubouchi learned from the travelling companies helped him immensely in directing the 1911 *Hamlet*.[4]

Thus, the initial encounter with British travelling companies at the dawn of modern Japan gave the 'substance' to Shakespeare's language on the printed page, allowing a successful shift from pre-modern to modern performance practice. However, in spite of Tsubouchi's intention to stage new, characteristically Japanese, Shakespeare productions, the first encounter ironically marked the beginning of the subsequent Japanese Shakespeare performance history, which was devoted to re-creation of Western models, with the enduring admiration for and adherence to the 'original'.

About half a century later, after the interruption of World War II, travelling companies from overseas resumed their touring to Japan. Aside from occasional visits by educational companies such as the London Shakespeare Group, which have performed regularly at schools since the 1960s, prior to the 1980s seeing performances by overseas companies was still a rare opportunity for Japanese audiences. Then, the opening of the Tokyo Globe Theatre in 1988 triggered an avalanche of visits from travelling companies from across the globe. The present Tokyo Globe Theatre was re-launched in 2004 with a new, more commercialized concept to stage musicals and straight plays featuring young pop idols; the original Tokyo Globe Theatre discussed in this article operated from 1988 to 2002, exclusively staging Shakespeare and adaptations of Shakespeare. Seeing live stage performances by overseas travelling companies remained a rare experience in Japan; however, by the 1980s, a century-long history of cultural negotiation had considerably altered Shakespeare's position in Japanese culture. For one thing, *Shingeki*, an institution dedicated to Western realism that came to constitute the backbone of Japanese Shakespeare performance, was becoming marginalized and outdated by the radical underground theatre movement of the 1960s, making room for unconventional, alternative Shakespeare; for another, the highbrow, canonical status of Shakespeare himself was increasingly threatened by rapid popularization and commercialization of Japanese theatre in the 1970s. The Tokyo Globe Theatre opened against the backdrop of this changing cultural and economic climate.

If asked which contemporary international touring production prompted a new reinvention of Shakespeare, most Japanese would immediately cite Peter Brook's legendary *A Midsummer Night's Dream* in 1973 as the touring Shakespeare

---

[2] Kobayashi, 'The Actors Are Come Hither', p. 50.
[3] Kobayashi, 'The Actors Are Come Hither', p. 59.
[4] Kobayashi, 'The Actors Are Come Hither', p. 59.

production that changed Japanese Shakespeare forever. Certainly, *Brook's Dream*, a stunning embodiment of Jan Kott's argument, illuminated Japanese audiences by demonstrating Shakespeare's viability as a vehicle for engagement with the present. Directors such as Yukio Ninagawa and Hideki Noda openly admitted that the production utterly renewed their ideas of Shakespeare performance. However, in the cultural context of Shakespeare's localization in Japan, the continuous existence of travelling companies at the Tokyo Globe over that decade has had a greater and more profound impact. This is because the long-term, extensive exposure to travelling companies' productions, or sustained cultural displacement, resulted in a paradigm shift in the negotiation for cultural authority between Shakespeare and Japanese culture.

Suddenly, a cultural enclave appeared in central Tokyo in the form of the Tokyo Globe Theatre, where anyone could regularly watch Shakespeare performances staged by illustrious visiting foreign companies at reasonable prices. In its fourteen-year history, the Tokyo Globe's most phenomenal season remained the opening one in 1988. In that year alone, the Tokyo Globe staged seventeen productions, fourteen of which were touring productions from overseas. They included the English Shakespeare Company's *The Wars of the Roses*, the Royal Shakespeare Company's *Unnatural and Unkind*, the National Theatre's *Cymbeline, The Winter's Tale* and *The Tempest* directed by Peter Hall, and The Royal Dramatic Theatre Company of Sweden's *Hamlet*.

The opening productions, the English Shakespeare Company's *The Wars of the Roses*, which consisted of seven history plays, were by themselves a theatrical feat.[5] When staged in sequence over a weekend, the performances lasted for nearly 30 hours. This was the first production ever to stage the history cycle consecutively in Japan, let alone in English. The epic scale, the sheer modernity of staging and sets, and the dynamic ensemble acting that characterized the performances were all beyond audiences' expectations. Toshiro Murakami, a leading Shakespeare

scholar, remarked at the time that he had never imagined that the days would come when he could see such Shakespeare productions in Japan, and this sentiment was shared by most audience members.[6]

Among about 200 Shakespeare productions that were staged at the Tokyo Globe Theatre over fourteen years, nearly one-third of them were performances by travelling companies from abroad.[7] Although the number of foreign travelling-company productions dwindled towards the theatre's closure, in the first decade they were staged on average every other month or more frequently – enough to make them a regular part of the Tokyo theatre scene. British theatre companies that repeatedly visited the Tokyo Globe include the Royal Shakespeare Company (1988, 1991, 1993, 1994, 1995, 1998, 2000, 2001 and 2002), the National Theatre (1988, 1989, 1990 and 1991), the Renaissance Theatre Company (1990), the Compass Theatre Company (1990, 1991, 1992, 1993 and 1995), Cheek By Jowl (1992 and 1994), the Watermill Theatre Company (1992 and 1995), Nottingham Playhouse (1995) and Shared Experience (1996). Visiting companies from countries other than Britain also staged Shakespeare productions that created a huge impact on the audience. Directors such as Ingmar Bergman (Sweden, 1988), Andrej Wajda (Poland, 1990), Silviu Purcărete (Romania, 1992), Robert Lepage (Canada, 1993) and Lin Zhaohua (China, 1995) brought their companies to the Tokyo Globe. As Table 1, below, shows, the overall production number at the venue reached its peak in 1993, and then it gradually decreased until the venue closed

---

[5] The English Shakespeare Company, led by Michael Bogdanov, toured extensively with this production in the UK, Europe, the USA, Australia and Asia throughout 1987 and 1988.

[6] Toshiro Murakami, 'Stream of the "history", stream of the "play": watching *The Wars of the Roses*', *Shingeki* 35.7 (1988), 100.

[7] For the details of productions staged at the Tokyo Globe Theatre, see Michiko Suematsu, 'The Tokyo Globe years: 1988–2002', in *Shakespeare in Hollywood, Asia, and Cyberspace*, ed. Alexa C. Y. Huang [Joubin] and Charles S. Ross (Indiana, 2009), pp. 121–8.

Table 1 The Number of Productions at the Tokyo Globe Theatre: 1988–2002[8]

	Total	1988	1989	1990	1991	1992	1993	1994	1995	1996	1997	1998	1999	2000	2001	2002
Total	192	17	12	14	22	17	24	21	18	12	10	6	7	4	5	3
Travelling companies	69	14	1	7	5	7	9	7	6	2	2	3	1	2	2	1
Japanese productions	101	3	10	6	15	7	10	10	10	9	6	3	5	2	3	2
Others	22	0	1	1	2	3	5	4	2	1	2	0	1	0	0	0

in 2002. Having received no subsidy from the government, the theatre was left with no other choice than to close down when it failed to resolve financial issues after its major sponsor, Panasonic, pulled out in Japan's economic stagnation in the late 1990s.

All in all, the Tokyo Globe experience strengthened the sense of Japanese ownership of Shakespeare in two ways. First, the regular stagings by British theatre companies with a wide stylistic range – from Cheek by Jowl's all-male *As You Like It* (1992) to Shared Experience's *The Tempest*, rich in fantastic visual imagery (1996) – challenged the notion and authority of the quintessentially 'British Shakespeare'. British Shakespeare, just like Japanese Shakespeare or Korean Shakespeare, is no more than a sum of one culture's efforts in the name of Shakespeare, each performance trying to represent the contemporary and specific through Shakespeare. First-hand encounters with these Shakespeare productions by overseas travelling companies at the Tokyo Globe – not exclusive to cultural elites but open to the general public – liberated the Japanese from the century-long servitude to the authority and authenticity of the West, and this assured them of their right to stage their own Shakespeare.[9] Second, the process of building the Tokyo Globe Theatre itself challenged cultural assumptions regarding the West's ownership of Shakespeare. During the Japanese economic boom in the 1980s, superfluous market capital flowed into the theatre industry, enabling the building of a number of new theatres in the Tokyo area. One land development corporation, Toyama Kaihatsu, chose to build a new Globe Theatre in Tokyo to make it another Shakespearian mecca by

staging Shakespeare productions throughout the year and inviting a large number of world-renowned theatre companies. The Tokyo Globe was a showcase of Shakespeare, the most marketable cultural commodity. Like many other examples of Japanese cultural ransacking during the period of the 'Bubble Economy', the Tokyo Globe Theatre comprised, in part, a marketing scheme to show Tokyo as a global economic and cultural capital.

The Tokyo Globe Theatre thus represented the economic and cultural confidence of Japan at the time. Moreover, the venue incorporated Japanese audiences into the global theatre circuit, giving them a sense of immediacy and contemporaneity with the world that they had never experienced before. For instance, in the 1970s, they had to wait three years to see Brook's *A Midsummer Night's Dream* after its premiere in the UK, while, after the Tokyo Globe's opening, the touring companies began to bring shows straight from home. Though they still geographically remained in the Far East, they were no longer behind.

As noted earlier, an initial encounter with travelling companies at the turn of the twentieth century inspired headlong Japanese commitment to duplicating 'authentic' British Shakespeare productions in the *Shingeki* style. Even half a century later, in the 1950s, attempts to recreate onstage Western models faithfully by performing with red wigs and padded noses, or replicating overseas directors' concept and style of productions,

---

8 Suematsu, 'The Tokyo Globe years', p. 124.
9 Suematsu, 'The Tokyo Globe years', p. 122.

continued.[10] The 'Japaneseness' in these performance would remain as inconspicuous as possible, because only by 'borrowing' Western cultural authority could *Shingeki* theatre companies, the agent of Western cultural hegemony, stage 'authentic' Shakespeare. Against this cultural imperialism of *Shingeki*, the underground theatre movement in the 1960s reacted and staged radically localized and historicized performances of Western plays, which culminated with *Ninagawa Macbeth* (1980) and Tadashi Suzuki's *The Tale of Lear* (1984). However, although compelling enough to convince audiences of the legitimacy of a localized approach to Shakespeare, these productions were generally regarded as the unique individual achievements of highly talented directors. *Shingeki* and what it stands for still prevailed until Japanese Shakespeare was exposed to continuous cultural transactions facilitated by diverse travelling companies. The second encounter with travelling companies at the Tokyo Globe Theatre collectively allowed Japanese Shakespeare finally to break away from its servitude to the authority of Western models and the illusion of homogeneous British Shakespeare or any one culture's Shakespeare. This revelation led to a 'plurality' of self-conscious localization of Shakespeare in Japan.[11] The ensuing reinvention of Shakespeare took the form of numerous appropriations and adaptations in both traditional and non-traditional performance modes, staged at and beyond the Tokyo Globe Theatre. *Hamuretto Yamato Nishikie*, or *Kabuki Hamlet* (1991), and *Hora-Samurai*, or the Kyogen version of *The Merry Wives of Windsor* (1994), which premiered at the Tokyo Globe, were the earliest examples of productions reasserting through Shakespeare the value of indigenous theatre traditions. Young directors such as Takeshi Kawamura and Hideki Noda opted for radical, modern adaptations retaining only a hint of the original plots, such as *A Man Named Macbeth* (1990), and *Sandaime Richard* – or *Richard III* –

(1990), which were Shakespeare reinvented in the wildest sense. Moreover, the legitimacy of staging Shakespeare as a straight play also came to be challenged by the performance of Shakespeare in a variety of genres including opera, musical, dance, ballet, puppet show and *Rakugo*, or traditional Japanese comic storytelling by a lone storyteller.

The closing of the Tokyo Globe Theatre in 2002 heralded the end of the golden age of touring Shakespeare productions in Japan. The number of professional visiting companies from overseas has dropped dramatically since then, with one production per year on average. For instance, the last visit by the Royal Shakespeare Company, one of the most frequent visitors to the Tokyo Globe, was in 2004, more than a decade ago. However, the post-Globe years have seen an increase in a new type of 'intercultural' Shakespeare productions, neither entirely foreign nor entirely Japanese. The mode of intercultural collaboration is again heterogeneous or 'plural': a Columbian director with a mixed Swiss and Japanese cast, or a Japanese director with a mixed Korean, Chinese and Japanese cast, and so on.[12] What they invariably reflect is the landscape of Japanese cultural transactions today, which calls into question the validity of simple binary oppositions between East and West.

---

[10] The most famous example is the 1955/6 production of *Hamlet* by Bungakuza, one of the leading *Shingeki* theatre companies, which was an almost exact copy of the Old Vic production (1953/4) with Richard Burton.

[11] For 'pluralism' of localization in Shakespeare performance, see John Gillies, 'Afterward: Shakespeare removed: some reflections on the localization of Shakespeare in Japan', in *Performing Shakespeare in Japan*, ed. Ryuta Minami, Ian Carruthers, and John Gillies (Cambridge, 2001), pp. 236–48.

[12] Omar Porras, a Columbian director, directed *Romeo and Juliet* in 2013 and 2016, while Junnosuke Tada, a Japanese director, directed *Taifu Kitan*, or *The Tempest*, in 2015.

'BOTH ALIKE IN DIGNITY': HAVANA AND MEXICO CITY PLAY *ROMEO AND JULIET*

ALFREDO MICHEL MODENESSI

On 25 November 2016, Fidel Castro died. What an opportune irony: almost sixty years after his victory, the head of the Cuban Revolution – deemed a hero as much as a dictator – passed on roughly two weeks after a TV excuse for a despot was elected to rule the USA, a country built on the pledge of never yielding to a despot. To boot, the USA was at a crucial stage in re-establishing relations with Cuba, the nearest thorn in their side – other than the pain down their southern end called Mexico, my homeland, so vilified by the aforementioned reality-TV host. The timing of Fidel's demise may be justifiably brought to attention herein because I mean to explore two films based on *Romeo and Juliet* made in those troubled Latin American countries: *Shakespeare in Avana: Altri Romeo, Altre Guiliette* [Shakespeare in Havana: Other Romeos, Other Juliets] (2011)[1] and *Besos de azúcar* [Sugar Kisses] (2013). But I have personal reasons, too: Fidel died in Havana shortly after my father did so in Mexico City. I hope this tale of two [un]fair Veronas that I love will be substantial, albeit brief.

When I was a child, my dad told me that Havana and Mexico City were loving partners. But in the 1950s – he added – sinister people forced them asunder. During the first half of the twentieth century, artists from Cuba and Mexico often worked together, contributing to an amazing era of Latin American music. Between 1950 and 1985, my father was the lead singer in a popular Mexican trio. Thus, in the 1960s, as Cuba grew isolated and my father's tours ceased, what I heard from him was that *we* would progress inside the 'free world', while *they*, our brethren still, would drown in a red wave of communist slavery. But I grew up, and since the Cuban Revolution started on a 26 July, and I was born on a 27 July, as a youngster I saw myself as the child of 'a new day' in Latin America. Later, after confronting some harsh realities of the Cuban Revolution, my enthusiasm waned. It cannot be denied that alien barriers and local hurdles (Fidel included) have kept from Cuba the peace needed to build a just society. But the same applies to all of Latin America. Our region is an 'unfinished project, hybrid, transculturated, marginalized, and positioned as dependent within the asymmetrical structures of globalization'.[2] Ironically, now that I am fatherless in fact, and also an orphan of a dream of passion, Cuba, wearied, deprived and *dazed*, is looking to go 'global'. Yet, given the violence, corruption and lawlessness that affect Mexico – far longer mired in the same 'global' delusion – it is easy to see which of these two 'households' is worse off.[3] True, despite evident merits in health, education

---

[1] For a detailed discussion of this film, see my '"Victim of improvisation" in Latin America: Shakespeare out-sourced and in-taken', in *The Oxford Companion to Shakespeare in Performance*, ed. James C. Bulman (Oxford, 2017), pp. 549–67.

[2] Joanna Page, *Crisis and Capitalism in Contemporary Argentine Cinema* (Durham, 2009), p. 16.

[3] Contrary to fallacious but highly successful white-supremacist propaganda in the USA, not all Mexicans are rapists and drug dealers. Moreover, many 'aliens' who cross the border with criminal intentions do so with the complicity of many Americans who share their interests – the simple fact being that the only nationality of capital is capital itself, whether its business is 'legitimate' or criminal.

and self-esteem, Cuba endures many forms of injustice. Nevertheless, Mexico is visibly as bad and, on top, despite harbouring world-class-obscene fortunes, remains unable to provide for millions at home, and for the thousands who look for options north of our border and half-find them – at enormous risk, and because their labour comes much cheaper to American companies.

Many inside and outside Havana and Mexico City worry over the future of our young, who exist at 'the border where the colonial difference emerges, making visible the variety of local histories that Western thought, from the right and the left, hid and suppressed'.[4] The makers of the films I will explore address this concern through Shakespeare's tragedy of young life but, as Latin Americans often do, transcreating[5] the native, European and African arts that cannot be called ours and yet are the roots of the only arts we can call our own: 'in-between'[6] creative practices where *anthropophagy* plays a major role. As cultural concept, anthropophagy emerged in Brazil, where indigenous peoples 'used anthropophagic practices as gestural metaphors for negotiating group boundaries, while artistic vanguards used the anthropophagic metaphor to appropriate and invert relations to European culture'.[7] The metaphor then extended to theoretical and artistic practices beyond Brazil. A fundamental question underlies them all: 'Can originality be grasped if it is considered exclusively in terms of the artist's indebtedness to a model imported from the metropolis?'[8]

Anthropophagic endeavours do not conceal their appropriation of the foreign. Rather, by embracing 'its transformative potential as an agent of cultural hybridization, anthropophagy can engage in cultural appropriation without taking on a subaltern position ... The self-conscious nature of anthropophagy ... distinguish[es] it from an unconscious mimicry of the colonizer'.[9] Since the mid twentieth century, the best Latin American Shakespeares have been staged with a freshness entailing that, in our region, 'the concepts of *unity* and *purity* lose the precise contours of their meaning, lose their crushing weight, their sign of

cultural superiority'.[10] Our history is a process of endless 're-originalization'[11] in endless sync with one of repression. Hence, Latin America 'establishes its place on the map of Western civilization by actively and destructively diverting the European norm and resignifying pre-established and immutable elements that were exported to the New World by the Europeans'.[12] Our films bear witness to this.

David Riondino, the film-maker of *Shakespeare in Avana*, is an Italian playwright, actor, director, composer and *improvvisatore*. But the visible force in the film is the Cuban poet Alexis Díaz-Pimienta, the leading performer, theorist and teacher of a tradition of extempore poetry in Cuba called *repentismo* (sudden-ism). Impromptu poetry in Spanish originated in medieval Spain from contact with Arab forms, spread to the Canary Islands and the colonial Atlantic, and remains widely practised. *Repentismo* is frequently prompted cold by a premise or line, and often sung, with or without music. It demands improvising stanzas of ten octosyllables with a symmetrical scheme of perfect rhymes (*abbaaccddc*) called *décimas* (ten-liners), which abound in the history of poetry and popular culture in Spanish. Early in the film, the final *décima* of Díaz-Pimienta's extempore introduction to this 'update of *Romeo and Juliet* through performance', announces:

---

[4] Walter Mignolo, 'The geopolitics of knowledge and the colonial difference', *The South Atlantic Quarterly* 101.1 (Winter 2002), 66.

[5] See Haroldo de Campos, 'Da tradução como criação e como crítica', in *Metalinguagem: Ensaios de teoria e crítica literaria* (Petrópolis, 1967), pp. 21–38.

[6] See Silviano Santiago, *The Space In-Between: Essays on Latin American Culture*, ed. Ana Lúcia Gazzola (Durham, 2001).

[7] Gazi Islam, 'Can the subaltern eat? Anthropophagic culture as a Brazilian lens on post colonial theory', *Organization* 19.2 (2011), 4.

[8] Santiago, *The Space In-Between*, p. 31.

[9] Islam, 'Can the subaltern eat?' p. 11.

[10] Santiago, *The Space In-Between*, p. 30.

[11] See Aníbal Quijano, 'Colonialidad del poder, cultura y conocimiento en América Latina', *Anuario Mariateguiano* 9 (1997), 113–22.

[12] Santiago, *The Space In-Between*, p. 30.

... una pasión, una muerte,
Eros y Tánatos juntos,
apasionados difuntos:
tragedia que se convierte
en una lírica suerte
de bien que termina mal.
En este poema oral
van a ver, en El Vedado,
a Shakespeare cubanizado,
con su drama universal.

[... passion and death,
Eros and Thanatos together,
the passionate deceased:
a tragedy that becomes
a sort of lyrical fate,
of right ending up wrong.
In this oral poem
you will see, in El Vedado [a famous Havana
    neighbourhood],
how Shakespeare is 'Cubanized',
with his universal drama.][13]

The film, then, mainly documents an 'oral rewrite' of the play by means of acts of *repentismo*, called *repentinas*, prompted *in situ* by select 'scenes' from *Romeo and Juliet*, interspersed with other performances by outstanding practitioners (*repentistas*). For the rest of the article, I will stress only two aspects that the films significantly share: the way both re-direct the ending of Shakespeare's plot, and how their settings bear on the modified narratives.

The 'Cuban rewrite' of *Romeo and Juliet* follows Shakespeare's plot loosely. Díaz-Pimienta improvises a prologue, and then acts as mediator for 'scenes' by others which are either broadly recognizable (e.g. the duel of Tybalt and Mercutio) or made-up (conversations among 'friends' of Romeo or Juliet). This is consistent with the fact that, nowadays, 'versions' of *Romeo and Juliet* may stem from just a summary or a widespread perception of the play, i.e. from 'echoes of an *agent* of Shakespeare's cultural authority long embedded and fiercely dominant in its own hypotext'.[14] The improvisational nature of this rewrite also precludes illusionistic settings; moreover, the performers do not act, dress or characterize their parts, but simply improvise in their present voices and

wardrobe. The scenes are wholly made of live words actively reaching our senses in meta-medial fashion: we are able to witness a series of strictly localized poetic experiences that would otherwise vanish as they are enjoyed only because an outsider/insider chose to inscribe them in a documentary.

Through this mediatization, Riondino advances a narrative of his own: a tribute to Havana and its culture as mobile, non-theatrical stages, apt for 'investigating the spatial dimension of contemporary identities'.[15] Shunning facile 'pro-revolutionary' propaganda, between scenes Riondino films ruined façades, worn-out corners, and unassuming inhabitants of a city where time stopped and the resources to 're-start' it are wanting – they will come, but at great costs, material and spiritual. Riondino does not sweeten the squalor of Cuban society. Instead, his film suggests that the weight and continuity of a hybrid tradition like *repentismo* allows that society to rejoice in pleasures immune to external aggression and internal collapse – better yet, with an 'alien' like Shakespeare as input and provocation: in Latin America, 'national and foreign, original and imitative ... are unreal oppositions which do not allow us to see the share of the foreign in the nationally specific, of the imitative in the original, and of the original in the imitative'.[16]

Díaz-Pimienta's 'prologue', for example, may be construed as a surrogate for the opening sonnet, but it also bespeaks anthropophagic transcreation. Díaz-Pimienta does not affirm that Shakespeare will be 'played' as much as that he 'will speak

---

[13] All literal transcriptions from Spanish are mine.
[14] Alfredo Michel Modenessi, 'Cliché "by any other name": *Romeo and Juliet, the Telenovela*', in *Shakespearean Echoes*, ed. Adam Hansen and Kevin Wetmore Jr. (New York, 2015), p. 80.
[15] Fiona Wilkie, 'The production of "site": site-specific theatre', in *A Concise Companion to Contemporary British and Irish Drama*, ed. Nadine Holdsworth and Mary Luckhurst (Malden, 2008), p. 89.
[16] Roberto Schwarz, 'Brazilian culture: nationalism by elimination', *New Left Review* 167 (January–February 1988), 90.

again', that Romeo and Juliet 'come back'. The oral performance re-invigorates and discards its source at one and the same time; it follows *Romeo and Juliet* as much as it interacts and intersects with what it is made of. To wit, a staple of Shakespeare's treatment of the hypotext's fundamentals – his frequent use of verbal sparring – not only provides a fitting correlative for *repentismo*, which thrives on formally challenging repartee, but actually shares roots with it. *Repentismo* allows competing parties to cut into each other's *décimas*, creating witty oppositional dialogues called *controversias*. Parts of this 'oral rewrite' of *Romeo and Juliet* take the form of *controversias*, foregrounding resources common to both source and derivative while focusing on their own methods. The death of Mercutio illustrates this: what in Shakespeare proceeds from quick verbal sparring to tragic action, in *Shakespeare in Avana* becomes an elaborate exchange of *décimas*, with an aggressive Tybalt gradually dominating a strangely peace-seeking Mercutio. The scene ends with a gestural 'stab' and an *indicial* 'death', as befits the medium: improvised verse, not poetic drama.

But the main detour from Shakespeare's 'original' involves the ending. As Riondino films a love song to this besieged and oppressed, but ever fair, Verona, his ending looks up to the skies, not down to 'Capel's monument'. The rewrite includes a brilliantly simple 'death scene', where the lovers just hold hands and shut their eyes to signify death after their closing *décimas*. But, later, Díaz-Pimienta's epilogue suggests that the 'original' ending may not be 'it':

> En todos estos asuntos
> en una isla del caribe,
> aunque Shakespeare ya no escribe,
> sólo algo voy a decir:
> el cuerpo puede morir,
> pero el amor sobrevive.
>
> [Regarding these affairs
> on a Caribbean island,
> though Shakespeare no longer writes,
> this is all I'd like to say:
> the body may pass away,
> but love stays alive.]

Accordingly, the film closes with two venerable *repentistas* on a roof-top, improvising joyful rhymes about their readiness to die *of* and *for* love, and about love everlasting beyond time and grave. Thus, contrasting with the improvisation corresponding to Shakespeare's finale by a young couple – who still prove that this tradition is alive and thriving – we hear, instead, the experienced voices of an elderly couple who are not split by death, and who were there before Cuba's times of change, expressing a joyful and fierce will to carry on regardless of present or oncoming penuries. Fittingly, their celebration is followed by several final shots of Havana, lovingly 'in-taken' by Riondino's modest lens.

This was meaningful enough in 2011, but it may be even more so in the aftermath of Fidel's death and whatever may occur in a mock-totalitarian USA. In this 'Cuban rewrite', a design from *outside* meets anthropophagic resistance because Latin American formations are 'inevitably "out of the frame", if the frame is to be given by the self-idealizations of advanced Europe'.[17] The illusion of 'doing Shakespeare right' has gradually vanished from the Latin American stages and screens after projects with Western models sank under military and neocolonialist rapaciousness in the mid twentieth century. Now the task is to find what in Shakespeare matters to the social, political and cultural diversity of the world that transcreates him. *Shakespeare in Avana* tries. *Besos de azúcar* tries as well.

Unlike the Cuban/Italian celebration, *Besos de azúcar*, directed by the Mexican Carlos Cuarón, seems bereft of hope. In the end, its pubescent protagonists duly jump hand-in-hand off the top of a building in Mexico City's downtown neighbourhood of Tepito, where the streets are an endless informal market trading in everything from exotic lingerie, sex toys and pirated DVDs to pot-smoking paraphernalia, hard drugs and whatever follows. A crucial screenwriting detail must be

---

[17] Roberto Schwarz, 'Competing readings in world literature', *New Left Review* 48 (November–December 2007), 105.

borne in mind, however: like the old Cuban *repentistas*, the Mexican teens are on a roof and ultimately act *together*.

Carlos Cuarón's virtues as a screenwriter stand out in films by his brother Alfonso, especially *Y tu mamá también* (2001). He has also directed a handful of movies, albeit substantially rougher than his sibling's.[18] *Besos de azúcar* is uneven – at times, awkward. Still, Cuarón and co-writer Luis Usabiaga's knack for creating appealing characters in odd situations appears everywhere. The odd situations start with a close shot of a filthy mattress on an all-dirt football pitch, strangely surrounded by clear skies and quiet streets. Although opening credits run against lively marketplace noise, all we hear now is a Beethoven piano composition, one of several constituting the only background music of the film. A young boy rises from under the mattress and carries it on his shoulders. *Besos de azúcar* is chiefly told from the angle of 'Nacho' (short for Ignacio), our Romeo, 13 years old. He belongs to a typically big family – with his mother, step-brother and step-sister, step-father, and the latter's mom – huddling up in a two-bedroom flat in a *vecindad*: a decayed building – occasionally a run-down colonial mansion – adapted to hold as many people as possible, regardless of comfort or hygiene. As Nacho makes his way home, the neighbourhood becomes its boisterous, real, self. 'Cacayo', his Mercutio (only known by nickname), helps him carry the filthy object through the streets, all the way up to the flat. But Nacho's dreams of no longer sharing a bed with four people are crushed by his mom, who forces him to take 'that piece of shit' out of her house by knocking some sense into his head – her and her husband's favourite educational method.

So Nacho takes his treasure to the roof of an empty building, seeking to turn the ruins into his refuge. Eventually, the cherished object is twice desecrated by bullies from Nacho's school, who always call him homophobic names and occasionally beat him: one time, they set it on fire; another, they pee on it, and on Nacho, as he sleeps off a heartache. By his family's standards, Nacho is oddly sensitive: a boy looking for a peaceful spot away from step-folks who mock his otherness with intrusive crassness, and from his crooked transit-cop mom, who ranks Nacho well below her new husband – Joao, a trader in 'originally pirated DVDs' – and calls Nacho's dad an 'asshole that couldn't even make it across the border [with the USA]'. No one knows what became of him, but Nacho fantasizes about joining him some day.

Mayra, our Juliet, is a girl who, for the standards of the neighbourhood, 'has it all', except room to be herself, as her family keeps a close grip on her – to say the least for now. She is the daughter of Doña Leticia, aka 'La Diabla' (the She-Devil), one of the 'social leaders' feuding for control of the bootlegging rings. La Diabla 'owns' Joao and many others who are pathetically subservient when she comes to collect her rent. She is rich, and deeply feared: rumour has it that she killed her husband, who, in her words, was 'just as soft' as his daughter Mayra. When Mayra dyes a tuft of her hair pink, La Diabla forces her to change it, reminding her that she sends her to a private school to learn 'how to be a princess, not a fucking whore, you shit-head slut' – or something with that affectionate feel. Everyone speaks like this with, to or around the teens. In her mother's large house, Mayra has a room to herself, but not a place of her own. As may be surmised from Shakespeare's plotline, Mayra and Nacho eventually share an instant of freedom on the mattress, atop the empty building, which makes the opening sequence more pointed. But in this film, not everything is what it seems.

In keeping with its Tepito setting, *Besos de azúcar* could be described as a 're-boot-leg' of *Romeo and Juliet*. For instance, a still mirroring the iconic image of the lovers touching palm to palm was used for promotion, but the image is not in the actual release; rather, when Nacho finally approaches Mayra, he offers his hand, but she rejects it – in good fun; she is, throughout, firmly in control. There is no ball but a dancing match at an arcade: a dare initiated by Nacho but, again,

---

[18] See www.imdb.com/name/nm0190860/?ref_=nv_sr_1#director.

finally managed by Mayra. In one 'balcony scene', conventional expectations are blown up and away, as we shall see. The film features a now-familiar top shot of the kids lying side by side and face to face, similar to the 'chamber scenes' in the films of Zeffirelli and Luhrmann, and even in an earlier Mexican version called *Amar te duele* [Loving Hurts You],[19] but Mayra and Nacho never have sex. These and other 'high points' in the plotline of *Romeo and Juliet* are rebooted with a refreshingly anthropophagic treatment. But space only allows my discussing how *Besos de azúcar* may not be, after all, devoid of hope.

Cuarón and Usabiaga's refashioning of the main parts is generally remarkable. Tybalt becomes 'Brayan' (*Brah-jan*, a disyllabic, Mexican 'Brian'): the apple of La Diabla's murderous eye – her driver, bodyguard and enforcer. His looks are a detailed replica of a Tepito gangbanger. The streets of Tepito, lined with tarpaulin-canopied stands where, as mentioned, anything can be bought or sold, are home to all degrees of crime and criminals. Tepito is likewise famous for the cult of 'La Santa Muerte',[20] patroness of all things demonized in conventional society. But Tepito is also the proud home of major artistic groups and enterprises of popular arts and crafts, as well as the birthplace of many world boxing champions. It also borders on the *barrio* where I grew up, the 'Colonia Guerrero', which boasts equally violent and dangerous, but also positive, credentials, although less famously. I can bear direct witness, then, to an alarmingly major way my country has changed in the past half-century.

Back then, criminality was of the kind expected in any big city: callous and cruel. But it was not as frighteningly pervasive – and, worse, as deceptively rewarding – among the deprived youth in large and small Mexican towns alike. Hence, it was not as widespread or widely spreading. Nowadays, staples of social and cultural identity are being replaced by violent forms of immediate and inane 'recompense' among the young. Missing out on solid education and perspectives, many Mexican youngsters are lured into not caring about the lives of others – or even their own – by what crime can *ipso*

facto provide; the most power-hungry will not hesitate to destroy even their own blood in horrifying ways, to obtain 'all they need': gadgets, clothes, drugs, cars, worldwide or simply web-based celebrity and, on top, a 'licence to kill' far more remorselessly and savagely than ever – things obsessively advertised and coveted in 'global' consumer culture, where the paradigms of prestige are 'free and beautiful people', hardly ever native-looking. In this framework, Cuarón and Usabiaga endow Brayan with the fake swagger and true cowardice that simultaneously characterize his type, and take his spiritual depletion to the limit: he tries to rape his own sister – our Juliet, Mayra – twice.

The protagonists of *Besos de azúcar* are not simple-mindedly portrayed as immaculate souls, but they are, indeed, as pure as pure can be in their complex reality: not infallible but deserving of respect and support for and of their flaws. Bullied at school and home, Nacho acts his fantasy-loaded age, uses the innocuously filthy language of most teens, and is as well informed regarding sex as may be expected of one whose sole advisor is Cacayo, a technician in a porn-pirating den who is at least a decade older but collects photos of nude women so he can draw bras on them. The purity of Nacho's soul is not a matter of behaviour, then, but of demonstrable integrity in the midst of the minor and major, material and spiritual, corruption that engulfs him: his mother's, his step-father's, his half-siblings', his schoolmates', La Diabla's, and the local cops'. He is just as pristinely constant in his sudden love for 'a true queen'. Nacho tries to eroticize his practically non-existent relationship with Mayra only as a matter of course. He knows no better, nor could have: his advisor is unaware that sex involves more than grabbing body parts. But Cacayo is no Mercutio when it comes to

---

[19] See my 'Looking for Mr GoodWill in "Rancho Grande" and beyond', *Revista Alicantina de Estudios Ingleses* 25 (2012), 97–112.

[20] For an introduction in English, see R. Andrew Chesnut, *Devoted to Death: Santa Muerte, the Skeleton Saint* (Oxford, 2012).

helping his friend out: he offers his room (at his mother's) in case the lovers ever need privacy.

Up to this point, Mayra has been a riddle. Soon she shows, however, that she is strong and will be who she wants, not what her mother tells her to be. On a clandestine first visit to her balcony, Nacho witnesses the risks she runs even inside her room. Brayan tries to rape her but is frustrated by the fortuitous first combined action of Nacho and Mayra: he throws a stone at her window, and she locks her brother out of the house after he chases Nacho away. But when Nacho is padlocked in his house for displeasing Joao, Mayra comes to *his* window, in a reversed 'balcony scene'. *She* frees *him* from his home prison, and they go to Cacayo's place. In what may be construed as a bold rewrite of the sonnet scene, Nacho's awkward sexual advances are promptly checked and corrected by Mayra. Then he, like Romeo, honestly prays for a second chance. The day takes them to the roof, a lovely first kiss, a long talk side by side on the mattress, and sleep – which leads to worry and hurry, because La Diabla is waiting for Mayra at home. La Diabla duly sends Mayra inside, and Nacho to hell. A third balcony scene then marks the turning point, after Nacho is now locked *out* of his no-home for his escape. Signs of a beating show on Mayra's face when Nacho appears outside her window again. She sends him packing with language that clearly belongs in her mother's mouth but comes out of hers. Upon his baffled insistence, she fakes a call to her would-be rapist. Her evident efforts to protect him are confirmed by her deep sadness as he leaves in fear. Nacho curls up to weep in his refuge. The shot recalls one of Romeo framed by the cinema ruins early in Luhrmann's film. But Nacho is no Di Caprio's moody-poet heartthrob, just a heartbroken kid.

These details show the extent of Cuarón's acquaintance with the play and its versions, and the firm care with which he made transcreative decisions. The teens act together. Mayra shows far more agency than Juliet. She suffers physical violence, however. That leads to her brutally obscene dismissal of Nacho at the balcony – all of which, in turn, is a complete reversal and, at the same time, a literalization of the potential in Shakespeare's 'own' scenes. Even the allusion to Luhrmann's film is a sharp 'rewrite', insofar as it de-glamorizes Nacho's fantasies of being a Romeo to a Juliet: he is unfit for a Hollywood ending, as one of Mayra's schoolmates and himself at some point objectively acknowledge. The kids in *Besos de azúcar* are made of strong stuff, though. Impurely pure of heart and soul – especially after he showers off the bullies' urine – Nacho packs his bags, ready to elope with Mayra. This time she lets him in, and he notices her bruised lip and eye before hiding under her bed. Mayra denounces Brayan's assault to her mother, but all she merits is a new slap and curse, now for telling 'a fucking lie' and 'surely being a teasing whore'. La Diabla storms out, and soon Brayan attacks again. After fighting him off, Nacho and Mayra begin their getaway helped by the providential fall of a statue of La Santa Muerte that La Diabla keeps in her foyer. A major, self-evident, point is made: Nacho proposes going *north* in search of his long-gone father, but Mayra prevails over his fantasy – it will be best to join her beloved paternal grandmother in the *south* of the country. The final sequence ensues.

Brayan's attempts at rape – more repulsive for being indifferently carefree, on top of beastly – embody the evil threatening the impure purity of Nacho and Mayra: they are besieged by the indiscriminate depravity that haunts Mexico, and by everything that colludes with it. But the best work of Carlos Cuarón relies on his caustic and often puzzling sense of humour. His take on these miseries is neither pathetic nor parodic. He aims at a narrow bandwidth of irony between playfulness and shock that turns the film into a keen exercise in allegory. The final sequence is one degree from cartoonish, featuring a long chase through streets and oddly communicating buildings all the way to Nacho's never-sacred sanctuary, punctuated by the *presto agitato* of Beethoven's Piano Sonata 14, often used in similar cases. Cuarón's humour is not misplaced or light-hearted but enlightening; it fosters meaningful extrapolation from situations that could be deplored for their seeming lack of truthfulness but that actually prompt the realization of how much worse they are in reality. Cuarón does not conceal that his movie delivers by artificial courier. He goes for self-conscious comedy, not so much bittersweet as revealingly dark; he looks back at Truffaut's *400 Blows*, but through a garish plastic curtain, disturbingly funny.

The ending invites a strong, if mixed, reaction to a veritable life-threatening situation, even in the tail-end of a ludicrous pursuit. Earlier in the film, Mayra and Nacho looked down from the roof and wondered whether the tarpaulin over a stand, and the underwear sold therein, could cushion and save them if they fell. In the end, the rooftop cannot shelter them anymore, because La Diabla and her revered Brayan also get there, and point their guns at them. They cannot fire at Nacho, as Mayra is too close and will not budge. So Mayra and Nacho decide to take a 'leap of faith'[21] together. They hold hands and smile as they fall, in slow motion, fading out in mid-air to the closing notes of the *arietta* from Beethoven's Sonata 32. However, the film will never reveal what happens; after a blackout come the end-credits. Maybe Cuarón recalled that Juliet's balcony is a perfect metaphor of her condition: a spot with a view to all she might be or desire that, nonetheless, keeps her apart from all she can be or desire, 'saintly' in wait of 'worship'? And maybe, therefore, in anthropophagic fashion, he also chose to give Mayra, and *her* Romeo, the privilege of a plunge, feet first?

Perhaps he means that the kids' impure purity of imagination – similar to what gives Mexico City its devil-may-care beauty – somehow helped them survive beyond the hellish circle of disregard for life where they were trapped? Either way, there will be no answer. The young vanish from view, let us think, for the best. One can sustain that hope in this land.

The 'oral rewrite' of *Shakespeare in Avana* pays playful and thoughtful mind to the rich contribution of Shakespeare, eschewing tiresome demands for canonized 'authenticity', and pointing to joyful renewal. *Besos de azúcar*, a Romeo-and-Juliet fable in a wilderness of she-devils and spoiled miscreants, pays at once self-deprecating and self-affirming tribute, too; and with similar thoughtfulness, if in more ambiguous terms, it also looks to the young for hope. Together, these films remind us that, in Latin America, 'copying is not a false problem, so long as we treat it pragmatically, from an aesthetic and political point of view freed from the mythical requirement of creation *ex nihilo*'.[22] In the end, both succeed in not going 'by the book', but voraciously reinventing Shakespeare as a truly significant other.

---

[21] This phrase plays a major role in the title song; the slogan of the film uses the phrase 'Love is a leap into the void.'

[22] Schwarz, 'Brazilian culture', p. 90.

CUBAN IMPROVISATIONS: REVERSE COLONIZATION VIA SHAKESPEARE

DONNA WOODFORD-GORMLEY

Cuban adaptations of Shakespeare have ranged from very traditional performances to versions that use loose associations to Shakespeare plays to explore concerns in contemporary Cuban life. There have been dance interpretations of Shakespeare choreographed and performed by the Ballet Nacional de Cuba; plays which, while translated into Spanish, were otherwise fairly faithful to Shakespeare's texts; and other plays which borrow characters and ideas but radically change Shakespeare's plots, portraying Othello, Iago, and Desdemona in a love triangle set in post-revolutionary Cuba[1] or having Prospero and his shipmates encounter Cuban Orishas, or deities, who are the daughters of Sycorax and the sisters of Caliban.[2] There has even famously been an essay which both criticized the dependence of Latin American writers on European authors, and used a Shakespearian character as the symbol of Latin America.[3] In all of these approaches, however, Cubanized or Classic, Shakespeare remains a foreign import and not a native Cuban art form.

This situation is less vexed than it might be in other post-colonial nations, such as India or the former British colonies in the Caribbean, where Shakespeare was used as a tool of colonization, a way of teaching British superiority. The British did control Havana for 11 months between 1762 and 1763, but it has been the long Spanish colonial control and the later threat of US influence that have left a much greater mark on Cuban history. However, while Shakespeare was never a tool of colonization in Cuba as he was in British colonies,

and while he is not a cultural relic of either Spain or the US, he is European and could be seen as a symbol of that from which Cubans have struggled to liberate themselves. Rine Leal, the noted Cuban scholar of theatre history, observed that in the late 1960s and 1970s there was an effort in the newly independent Cuba to focus 'el esfuerzo creador en nuestras propias formas y valores culturales revolucionarios, en el conocimiento de los valores artísticas de los pueblos latinoamericanos, en la asimilación de lo mejor de la cultura universal, sin que nos lo impongan desde afuera' [the creative force on our own forms and revolutionary cultural values, on the knowledge of the artistic values of the Latin American peoples, on the assimilation of the best of universal culture, without it being

---

[1] Tomás González, *El bello arte de ser y otras obras* (Havana, 2005), 137–92.

[2] Raquel Carrió and Flora Lauten, *Otra tempestad* (Havana, 2000).

[3] Roberto Fernandez Retamar, 'Caliban: notes towards a discussion of culture in our America', *Massachusetts Review: A Quarterly of Literature, The Arts and Public Affairs* 15.1–2 (1974), 7–72. For a discussion of these works and other Cuban adaptations of Shakespeare, see Donna Woodford-Gormley, 'CUBA', in *The Stanford Global Shakespeare Encyclopedia*, online, forthcoming; Donna Woodford-Gormley, 'Devouring Shakespeare: Cuba, cannibalism, and Caliban', *Critical and Cultural Transformations: Shakespeare's The Tempest – 1611 to the Present. REAL: Yearbook of Research in English and American Literature* 29 (2013), 131–48. Woodford-Gormley, '"In fair Havana, where we lay our scene": *Romeo and Juliet* in Cuba', in *Native Shakespeares*, ed. Craig Dionne and Parmita Kapadia (London, 2008), pp. 201–11.

imposed on us from outside].[4] So, while Cuba does not have a lengthy history of British imperialism to overcome, it does have a proud tradition of preserving and promoting its own artistic forms and of bringing in outside forms only when it can do so on its own terms. The films explored here, *Shakespeare in Avana: Altri Romeo, altre Giuliette* [Shakespeare in Havana: Other Romeos, Other Juliets] and *Otello all'improvviso*, do just that – they marry an outside form, Shakespeare, with a Cuban artistic form, *Repentismo*, or improvisational poetry.[5]

Otello all'improvviso and *Shakespeare in Havana*, collaborations between Italian film director David Riondino and Cuban poet Alexis Díaz-Pimienta, explore Cuban *repentismo* by giving prompts drawn from Shakespeare plays and then asking poets to improvise the response of Romeo, Othello, Juliet, or another Shakespearian character. A poet, for example, might take a shot of rum and then improvise a *décima* in which he offers Romeo relationship advice. Instead of merely importing Shakespeare to Cuba, these films, and the European tour that followed, allow Cuba to export to Europe an art form that has developed and been nurtured in the global South. These films represent a reverse colonization, taking a stanza that was originally Spanish and a poet who was English, combining them with a thriving Cuban art form, and using these films and a tour to spread the word about this art form back to Europe.

Repentismo, the improvisation of a poetic stanza known as the *décima*, is an important part of Cuban culture, but that is not to suggest that either the improvisation or the stanza are unique to or native to Cuba. The *décima* is a stanza of poetry containing ten octosyllabic lines with a rhyme scheme of abbaaccddc. The *décima* has its roots in Andalusian literature, and it is a stanza now used commonly throughout the Spanish-speaking world. In Cuba, it is the 'national Cuban stanza', and it is the stanza used in *Repentismo*, or improvisational poetry.[6]

Improvisational poetry is also not unique to Cuba. In fact, Pimienta asserts that improvisational poetry is a universal art form, which all languages have some form of. It is, however, an art form that

is deeply engrained in Cuban culture and an art form that has flourished and developed in Cuba. Improvisational verse, says Pimienta, commonly has its roots in the *campesinos*, or farmers, who may have no formal education but who gather to improvise poetry. In Cuba, these poetic gatherings, or *peñas*, also began with the *campesinos*, and there continue to be *peñas* of *campesinos*, though currently there are also many flourishing urban *peñas*.[7] In *Otello all'improvviso*, Pimienta comments that, when he was a child, there wasn't a day of the week when there wasn't at least one *peña*, and sometimes there were two in a day. Currently, he says there are at least five *peñas* each weekend in Havana, two more in Matanzas, and at least three more in the provinces. With twenty to thirty poets at each *peña*, this means that there are hundreds of poets improvising each week in Cuba; there are even schools dedicated to improvisational poetry. Cuban *repentismo* is also often broadcast on radio and television, and since the revolution there have been poets who have received a monthly salary and a retirement pension, becoming 'obreros del verso' or workers of verse.[8] Thus, while the *décima* and the tradition of improvisational poetry are not uniquely Cuban, they are an important part of Cuban culture, and Cuba has certainly aided in their continued development.

Shakespeare in Havana and *Otello all'improvviso* are part of a larger, longer collaboration between Pimienta and Riondino. For years, they have been collaborating on projects that fuse film, theatre and *Repentismo*. They have produced several documentary films about Cuban *Repentismo*, and in 2009 they created the first of these to involve

4 Rine Leal, *Breve historia del teatro cubano* (Havana, Cuba, 1980), p. 152.
5 *Otello all'improvviso*, directed by David Riondino in collaboration with Alexis Díaz-Pimienta (Giano Produzioni, 2008), DVD; *Shakespeare in Avana: Altri Romeo, altre Giuliette*, directed by David Riondino in collaboration with Alexis Díaz-Pimienta (Giano Produzioni, 2011), DVD.
6 *Otello all'improvviso*, 2008.
7 Alexis Díaz-Pimienta, *Teoría de la improvisación poética* (Almería, Spain, 2014), pp. 140–2; *Otello all'improvviso*, 2008.
8 *Otello all'improvviso*, 2008.

Shakespeare: *Otello all'improvviso*. *Shakespeare in Havana* followed in 2010, and in 2013 they formed an experimental theatre company of *repentistas* called AEDOS, or 'Bards'. This group toured Italy and Spain in 2015, performing improvised scenes from *Romeo and Juliet* in seven cities in Italy and one in Spain, and a film chronicling this tour is currently in production.[9] The goal of this group of bards has been to form an international theatrical company of *repentistas*, experimenting with the fusion of theatre and improvised poetry, and to leave documentary evidence of their improvised versions of great, 'universal' works of theatre.[10]

The collaborations by Riondino and Pimienta have not been limited to Shakespeare. As Pimienta notes in *Shakespeare in Havana*, 'cualquier dramaturgo está en peligro en este momento. Cualquier dramaturgo puede ser victima de nuestra *repentismo*' [any playwright is in danger at this moment. Any playwright could be victim of our improvisation].[11] However, he acknowledges, 'comenzamos por Shakespeare dada su importancia y universalidad' [we started with Shakespeare given his importance and universality].[12]

The term 'universal' may seem troubling, reminiscent as it is of the justifications frequently used for the imposition of Shakespeare on British colonies. However, during a series of lectures and classroom visits at New Mexico Highlands University in November of 2014,[13] Pimienta regularly made it clear that, when he talked about choosing Shakespeare for his universality, he was not suggesting that Shakespeare should be taught and performed in Cuba to impose an idea of English or foreign superiority, as it was in colonial India or in the British Caribbean. Rather, he and Riondino chose Shakespeare as the starting point of their improvisational collaborations because they knew that Shakespeare was universally known in the rest of the world, and they therefore knew that they would gain a wider audience for their documentary about Cuban improvisational poetry by linking it to Shakespeare. This is less a matter of imposing Shakespeare on Cuba than a case of using Shakespeare to bring Cuban art to the rest of the world.

Indeed, the first film in which Pimienta and Riondino incorporated Shakespeare, *Otello all'improvviso*, was far from relying on a universal Cuban knowledge of Shakespeare. Rather, Pimienta had to play a sort of trick on his Cuban friends. He invited a group of poets and musicians to his house, told them he had some friends visiting from Italy, and said that they would all drink together and improvise a bit. He didn't mention anything about Shakespeare or *Othello* because he didn't want to scare them off. Most of these poets had never read *Othello*, or had read it years ago. Perhaps they had seen a film of it, but none of them was a professional actor or Shakespeare scholar, and none had extensive knowledge of the play. However, one of the beauties of Cuban *Repentismo* is that *campesinos* who have never seen a play performed in a theatre have probably witnessed and participated in local performances of *Repentismo*. While they might have resisted the idea of performing a Shakespeare play, they were happy to come to improvise. They showed up, ready for a night of poetry and festivity, and by the time Pimienta explained that they would be improvising *décimas* based on a Shakespeare play, they were generally willing to participate.

This film is the first step in this process of reverse colonization, and although Shakespeare's *Othello* is the subject of the improvisations, at times the poetry and the film drift away from the play, focusing more on introducing a non-Cuban audience to the *décima* and to *Repentismo*. We often hear lengthy discussions of *Repentismo*, the sources of

---

[9] *Aedos – el mundo en versos. Romeo y Julieta en décimas*, directed by David Riondino with Alexis Díaz-Pimienta (Giano Produzioni, forthcoming).

[10] Alexis Díaz-Pimienta, emailed letter to Donna Woodford-Gormley, 'Desde La Habana', 2013.

[11] *Shakespeare in Havana*, 2011.

[12] Díaz-Pimienta, email, 2013.

[13] From 1 to 14 November 2014, Alexis Díaz-Pimienta was the Ballen Visiting Scholar at New Mexico Highlands University. During his visit, he screened films and held question-and-answer sessions about them, gave lectures about improvisational poetry in Cuba, led workshops on improvisation, gave readings of his poetry, fiction, and children's literature, and visited classes.

inspiration, and the process of improvising, which, while fascinating, have nothing to do with Shakespeare or Othello. However, in the film and in the booklet containing the *décimas* improvised in the film, there are also *décimas* that reinvent, and Cubanize, *Othello*.

There is, for instance, this improvised version of a monologue by Othello, in which the Malecón, the iconic seawall of Havana, becomes a character in the play, the only one who, with his unquiet waters, can understand the suffering in the veins and heart of Othello:

> Solamente el Malecón
> con aguas poco serenas
> sabe como están mis venas
> y como mi corazón.
>
> [Only the Malecón
> With its unquiet waters
> knows how I feel in my veins
> and in my heart.][14]

Cuba itself becomes a character in this Cubanization of a Shakespeare play, listening to and empathizing with the tragic hero.

If *Otello all'improvviso* is the first step in bringing the Shakespearian *décima* back to Europe, that journey of reverse colonization continues in Riondino and Pimienta's next collaboration, *Shakespeare in Havana: Other Romeos, Other Juliets*.

Shakespeare in Havana shows various *repentistas*, or improvisational poets, in the act of spontaneously translating Shakespeare. Some of these poets are given group identities such as Romeo's friends, Juliet's friends, the Montagues or the Capulets. Others are given specific roles such as Juliet, Romeo, Mercutio or Tybalt. Some of the groups, such as that representing the friends of Juliet, work together, with each poet creating a line or two until the *décima* is complete. In other cases, one poet improvises while the others in the group respond. In the case of an argument between the Montagues and Capulets, for example, the groups were told that the only thing they all agreed on was that the couple could not marry. One poet would improvise some *décimas*, and the other family members would respond with either cheers or jeers.

Frequently the tradition of *Repentismo* as a verbal duel between two poets is incorporated, which seems particularly appropriate when the poets are improvising the words of characters who actually would be in a duel, as in the case of Tybalt and Mercutio. The use of this tradition of the verbal duel also offers an interesting twist on the repartee between Juliet and Romeo. Instead of just romance, there is a bit of a competitive edge to the balcony scene between this Cuban Juliet and her Romeo, as she both repulses his flirtatious banter and outdoes him in their poetic repartee.

And the tradition of duelling poets is not the only Cubanization of the balcony scene, which is performed on a roof-top in Havana. Before the improvisation begins, Riondino and Pimienta point out some of the 'beautiful' and 'dramatic' images and metaphors used in the Shakespeare play, but they also assure the poets that they have 'absolute liberty' to either use these images or to 'modernize' and 'Cubanize' them.[15]

Also interspersed throughout these scenes of improvised Shakespeare are scenes of Pimienta, sometimes talking with Riondino and sometimes improvising *décimas* that give an overview of the project and tie the separate scenes together. While Pimienta praises Shakespeare's universality, he also makes it very clear that the film is set in Cuba. In his opening *décimas*, for example, he continually shifts between invoking the spirit of Shakespeare and reminding his audience that he is in Cuba:

> Nos Hallamos en la Havana
> Tierra de una luz secreta
> Vuelvan Romeo y Julieta
> En una versión Cubana
> La décima nos hermana
> Shakespeare regrese al Caribe
> Y esta historia inmensa vive
> En nuestra improvisación
> Con el olor del Malecón
> Con algo que no me inhibe

---

[14] David Riondino and Alexis Díaz-Pimienta, *Otello all'improvviso: viaggio tra i poeti improvvisatori di Cuba* (Florence, 2007), p. 40; *Otello all'improvviso*, 2008.

[15] *Shakespeare in Havana*, 2011.

Aunque esté in este lugar
Que algo tiene en esta historia.
Shakespeare recobra la memoria
Oyendome improvisar.
Veremos amar, pelear,
Morir, discutir, sufrir
Shakespeare volverá a decir
Pero en décima guajira
Lo que siente y lo que admira
El pecho al verse latir

Una pasión, una muerte
Eros y Tánatos juntos
Apasionados difuntos
Tragedia que se convierte
en una lírica suerte
El bien que termina mal
En este poema oral
Van a ver en el Vedado
A Shakespeare Cubanizado
Con su drama universal.

[We are in Havana
Land of a secret light
Romeo and Juliet return
In a Cuban version
The *décima* makes us brothers
Shakespeare returns to the Caribbean
This great story lives
In our improvisation
With the scent of the Malecón
With something that doesn't inhibit me

Although I'm in this place
Which has something to do with this story
Shakespeare recovers the memory
Hearing me improvise
We will see loving, fighting,
Dying, arguing, suffering.
Shakespeare speaks again,
But in *décima guajira*
What is felt and admired
By the beating heart

A passion, a death
Eros and Thanatos together
The passionate deceased
Tragedy that turns to
A lyrical destiny
The good that ends bad
In this oral poem
We are going to see in Vedado

Shakespeare Cubanized
With his universal drama.][16]

As Pimienta speaks these lines, he walks through the Cemetario de Colon, a large cemetery full of beautiful monuments. It is a landmark of Havana, and memorable to anyone who has seen it. With this location as his backdrop, he is undeniably in Cuba and, to eliminate any doubt, he calls attention to his location. He refers to how he is not inhibited, although he is in 'este lugar' (this place). But then he also asserts that this place is relevant to the story. The Cemetario is not only a background that evokes Havana; it is also a fitting scene for a tragedy that will end in a tomb and the erecting of monuments. The Cemetario thus serves two functions, simultaneously signalling that the film is set in Havana and reminding viewers of the link to Shakespeare.

Many of Pimienta's improvised verses perform similar functions, pointing at once to Shakespeare and to Cuba. He begins by asserting that we are in Havana, but two lines later he informs us that that Romeo and Juliet are returning. They are returning, however, in a Cuban version, and this great story is now infused with the scent of Havana's Malecón, or sea wall. Pimienta furthermore places himself, the Cuban poet, in a position of authority and control when he notes that Shakespeare comes back to life or, literally, 'recovers memory' upon hearing Pimienta improvise, and Shakespeare will speak once more, but in a 'guajira' or Cuban *décima*. Throughout these stanzas, Pimienta reminds us that what we are seeing and hearing is both Shakespeare and Cuban, or 'Shakespeare Cubanizado'.

If this project of reverse colonization began with a film that was more focused on Cuban *repentismo* than on Shakespeare, and continued with a documentary that repeatedly emphasized the Cubanization of Shakespeare, it has continued with Riondino and Pimienta's most recent Shakespearian endeavour, a European tour by Cuban *repentistas* improvising scenes from

---

[16] *Shakespeare in Havana*, 2011.

Romeo and Juliet, and another film documenting this tour. The original idea for this tour was, again, not limited to Shakespeare. The plan was to take a group of Cuban *repentistas* on a European tour, and, each night, let the audience choose whether they would improvise Shakespeare, Boccacio, Ibsen, Calderon de la Barca or other playwrights. However, they decided this might prove too complicated for a first tour, and they chose Shakespeare again for his universality. Thus, they decided to improvise scenes from Romeo and Juliet, and each night the audience was able to choose who would be Romeo, who Mercutio, and so on. Pimienta served as a narrator, but at times he would be chosen to be Romeo, and then he would play both parts at once. Although it was always *Romeo and Juliet* that they were performing, each performance was unique because it was improvised in the moment.[17] The tour, they assert, in a Facebook post about the event in Barcelona, was 'una manera de revivir y difundir en todo el mundo el antiguo arte Cubano de la improvisación en verso ... y así crear un puente cultural hacia esta hermosa isla en un momento histórico de grandes cambios y apertura del país' [a way of reviving and spreading throughout the world the ancient Cuban art of poetic improvisation ... and so creating a cultural bridge to this beautiful island at a historic moment of great changes and opening up of the country]. The tour, the post claims, 'quiere contribuir a la difusión de esta forma de arte que se originó en España y quiere ser un vínculo entre una Cuba finalmente abierta al mundo y una Europa que

redescubre sus artes nativos ya casi olvidados' [wants to contribute to the diffusion of this art form that originated in Spain and to be a link between a Cuba that is finally open to the world and a Europe that is rediscovering its now almost forgotten native arts].[18] The tour completes the project of reverse colonization, allowing Cuban poets to share their own work even as they reinvigorate and adapt European art forms.

While some versions of Shakespeare in the global South may still carry the colonial legacy, and while many adaptations of the bard may be anticolonial, these documentaries and the tour that has sprung from them are actually a colonization of Shakespeare by Cuban *repentistas* for the purpose of spreading knowledge of Cuban *repentismo* to Europe. The tour brings the project of reverse colonization full circle: a group of Cuban *repentistas* uses a stanza that originated in Spain and a play written by an English playwright and set in Italy. They tour Europe, bringing their own, Cubanized version of Shakespeare from the global South, back to Italy and Spain, in the hopes of creating a cultural bridge. If the English Bard has travelled the world as his works were performed, read, adapted and translated, these Cuban bards follow in his footsteps, using Shakespeare Cubanizado to bring their own art form to the rest of the world.

---

[17] Alexis Díaz-Pimienta, emailed letter to Donna Woodford-Gormley, 'Chamaquiili en el Oeste'.
[18] Alexis Díaz-Pimienta and David Riondino, 'Shakespeare In Havana', Facebook.com, 29 Nov. 2016, https://www.facebook.com/events/789953784404626.

MIXING MEMORY WITH DESIRE: STAGING
HAMLET Q1

ANDREW JAMES HARTLEY

Paul Menzer has remarked that the success of the first or 'bad' quarto of *Hamlet* on stage is one of Shakespeare's most predictable surprises.[1] No matter how many times it is staged and how many times directors, actors, critics and reviewers remark on the surprise of its success, that success continues – apparently – to surprise. I'm not interested in arguing about the quarto's 'good' or 'bad' status, or about championing the text as especially performable (even, surprisingly so); rather, I'm intrigued by the text's unique position in the theatrical landscape as one which engages with memory (personal and cultural) and with forgetting – some of it necessary – in ways that conspire to engineer that sense of surprise. In the process, I want to explore not just what audiences think they know about *Hamlet* coming in to the theatre, but what they want from it, which leads me to the (perhaps unsurprising) discovery that the very things that make a script work as a piece of theatre might be seen to be its failings as a piece of 'Shakespeare'.

This particular graveyard meditation emerges from a particular death: the end of our fall 2015 production of the play, directed on the University of North Carolina–Charlotte campus by James Vesce with an all-student cast, a production for which I served as live-in dramaturg. I want to use a consideration of our staging as a way of looking at how the status of a 'bad quarto' shifts when the presence of Shakespeare in the larger culture changes, notably as that culture forgets the high art of its past and renegotiates its sense of what we value in that which remains.

I would like to start with two contradictory observations. The first comes from the local paper's publicity piece penned in advance of the event (the writer, Lawrence Toppman, who is the *Charlotte Observer*'s primary theatre reviewer, did not see the production in any form and so this piece is the only official record of the show in any print newspaper other than the campus one).

For readers familiar with the common version of the masterpiece, the Q1 text may seem plain. Compare the speeches of King Claudius at prayer, mulling over his sin of fratricide:

Q1: 'O, these are sins that are unpardonable. Why, say thy sins were blacker than is jet, Yet may contrition make them as white as snow. Ay, but still to persevere in a sin, It is an act 'gainst the universal power. Most wretched man, stoop, bend thee to thy prayer. Ask grace of heaven to keep thee from despair.'

Version we know: 'Try what repentance can. What can it not? Yet what can it, when one can not repent? O wretched state! O bosom black as death! O limèd soul that, struggling to be free, art more engaged! Help, angels. Make assay. Bow, stubborn knees, and heart with strings of steel, be soft as sinews of the newborn babe.'

Now, that second guy is really sweating his fate.

Still, people who love Shakespeare enjoy knowing his first thoughts (if they are, indeed, HIS first thoughts). So the UNCC show, which runs through Nov. 15 at the Lab Theater in Robinson Hall, will be an intriguing

---

[1] The phrase came from his preshow talk during the run of our production, 'Every bad quarto deserves a good theory', and will appear in his forthcoming book *Shakespeare's Uglies: A History of Taste*.

curiosity – even if famous speeches show up in unexpected places and in forms that don't sound 'right' to us.[2]

This is the iteration of the piece as it was edited after I communicated with the writer in an attempt to complicate and mitigate some of his assumptions (based largely on old-fashioned scholarship about bad quartos). The original article was even more damning of the text than this revised excerpt makes it. My concern at the time was at least partly about marketing, since the article seemed to raise (somewhat derisively) a real question as to why anyone would bother staging a work which was so clearly shoddy. The sample above shows that much of that sentiment survived the subsequent revision, preserving as it does the problematic assumption that Q1 represents an early draft of the play while the Folio represents the finished version (there's no mention of Q2, and no sense that in key respects Q1 is actually closer to F than is Q2), and hinting that Q1 might not be authorial in the way the later text/texts is/are ('if they are, indeed, HIS first thoughts').

The article's comparison of (to my mind, oddly selected) lines from the King's repentance speech also raises questions, since they are presented as self-evidently assessable in terms of quality. Q1 is 'plain' while the 'version we know' (more Q2 than F) represents a man 'really sweating his fate'. But does it? Yes, in some ways the verse is richer, but is it better being fuller, more poetic, or does it seem more abstract, more aestheticized, more philosophical, and therefore, perhaps, the opposite of one 'sweating his fate'? Is anyone this eloquent in despair and mental torment, or is the terse version manifested in Q1 more theatrically plausible? I say *theatrically* on purpose and not simply as a way of gaining status for a text that cannot compare to the poetic richness of the texts published after it. The textual comparison Toppman offers is, after all, in specific response to a theatrical event, and his casual evocation of 'this guy' 'really sweating' imagines the King not as an abstraction but as a real person, and in contemporary terms, so that he sounds more like a mobster than a king.

The paradox as I see it is that, when it comes to *Hamlet*, what is familiar (the 'version we know') is assumed to trump all comers in literary, poetic and theatrical terms, whether or not it actually does. Indeed, the example above is not so much an investigation designed to reach a conclusion as evidence of an assumption on which the comparison is predicated, as Toppman demonstrates:

An admirer once insisted to Ben Jonson that Shakespeare never blotted a line in writing his masterworks. 'Would that he had blotted a thousand!' came the reply. The existence of these quartos, however exact they may or may not be, suggests that 'Hamlet' and 'Lear' did not pop out of his brain fully formed, and that rewriting may have made him the greatest writer in the English language.

The argument ignores all recent scholarship on the relationship between the different textual variants in order to enact a teleology of quality in which *printed* earlier means 'first draft' and later means 'polished for publication'. Shakespeare the man evolves into Shakespeare the myth with a little common-sensical flourish, and the only reason to look at the Q1 *Hamlet* script at all is as a kind of biographical curiosity, because it shows how far Shakespeare still had to go.

I want to balance this self-performed 'learned' approach to the textual issue with that of my students as a way of further complicating the 'version we know'. I taught a class using all three major *Hamlet* texts concurrently with the rehearsal period, and most of the principal actors took the course as a form of parallel dramaturgy. Because of the class schedule, and because I didn't want to confuse the performers with multiple versions of the text until the show was up and running, beyond some general discussion of the major variances and the history of the texts themselves, we confined ourselves to Q1 in the first part of the semester, only approaching Q2 and F in the final third.[3]

---

[2] www.charlotteobserver.com/entertainment/ent-columns-blogs/state-of-the-art/article42999738.html.

[3] It wasn't a good structural model. The show closed with over a month still to go in the class, by which time everyone was thoroughly burned out on the play and resistant to looking at it in ways that weren't clearly complimentary of the choices we had just made. Next time I run such a class, I'll do it in the semester prior to the one in which the show is mounted.

What was then clear was that the actors had bonded with their lines as actors tend to, and saw the later texts as baroque, digressive and interpolative to the point of violating the 'original' (which is to say Q1, i.e. theirs). I do not offer this as any kind of proof of anything except to poke at the house of cards which is the 'version we know'. These were undergraduate theatre students. They clearly had no real knowledge of *any Hamlet* text before entering the class or rehearsal. They knew odd lines or fragments of lines, but staging Q1 did not require the unlearning of Q2/F, which I had expected, because they had never learned it (including those who had 'read' the play in high school[4]). The version they knew was the one we staged, and others seemed to them unnecessarily difficult, convoluted and lacking in urgency.

The production's audience showed no signs of being better informed. Though we explained the textual choice and its nature in programme notes, preshow lectures and post-show discussions, I didn't hear a single valid cavil about the nature of the script's digression from the 'version we know' from any general audience member. I should say that the majority of our audiences are students and the family members of those involved in the show, plus a scattering of faculty and a smaller scattering of people from 'the community' – which is to say, the Charlotte metro area. The faculty (mostly) knew better than to complain about the script, but my instinct was that few of the rest of the audience really noticed any difference at all beyond 'To be, or not to be – ay, there's the point' (7.115).[5] Indeed, when we got questions from the audience in post-show discussions, they seemed to have quite misunderstood the textual variant debate even more profoundly than Toppman in the *Observer*. Several seemed to think we had modernized the text extensively, confusing the largely contemporary setting of the production (and its diverse racial casting) with some more radically adaptive editorial strategy regarding the script. They then professed themselves amazed that they 'got' the story 'in the original'. Again, my point is

not to claim an inherent playability about Q1, and even less to make any argument about transcending history or culture or what have you (such arguments are, I think, nearly always spurious, Bardolatrous and self-serving), but to problematize the notion of the 'version we know'. So far as I could tell, practically no one who saw the show knew anything substantial about *Hamlet*, and they knew even less about the text, even when they worried about or mocked the notion of staging Q1. And let's be clear: Charlotte may not be London or New York, but it's no Podunk backwater either; it's a substantial city (pop. 2.4 million, the largest city in the state, and the third-fastest-growing city in the United States), a transportation hub, a financial centre and a beacon of the New South.

This might, I suppose, be a prelude for some Bloomian (Harold, not Leopold) rant about the state of culture and education but I prefer to see the upside in this (surprising?) ignorance about the world's most famous play. For a theatre person, after all, it is all quite liberating, and the idea of *Hamlet* being not the graveyard pored over (or pawed over?) by academics till every mote of dust, every fragment of bone has been thoroughly deconstructed, but an undiscovered country, is exciting. Our audiences (and our actors) came to see 'Hamlet', which is a kind of charcoal grey cultural smear of half-remembered quotations, a skull, a drowned girlfriend, a dead father, and a suicidal revenger who talks a lot about death. Maybe. Some of my students seemed to know

---

[4] A process that is equal parts film clips (often from the same film) and *No Fear Shakespeare* (or equivalent), which means minimal grappling with the actual words of any early text. While this may well not be representative of most high school teaching of Shakespeare, it is – at least in my experience – a persistent feature. The percentage of theatre students coming into my classes who have real and detailed knowledge of any Shakespeare is in the single digits and, while the numbers are higher for my English majors, the notion that any significant number carry with them the kind of Shakespeare data from which they can quote, for instance, is nonsense.

[5] Citations and line numbers from Q1 are taken from *Hamlet: The Texts of 1603 and 1623*, ed. Ann Thompson and Neil Taylor (London, 2006).

even less than that. What I think they all knew was that 'Hamlet' was Famous, Tedious and Depressing, and that, I would argue, is really the 'version we know', and Toppman's use of 'we' is actually a kind of false modesty, a polite extension of the mantle of cultural superiority to an unknowing populace who thus feel slightly stupider and slightly more impressed by the knowledge of the critic, as they then appropriate his informed sneer.

That rhetorical sleight of hand seems to haunt a lot of the discussion about bad quartos in the non-academic sphere, of course, because it serves the master narrative of Shakespeare's inalienable genius, the differences between the good and the bad wheeled out as self-evident (as Toppman's example shows). The result is a bit like the story of the Emperor's New Clothes, where disputing the genius of the one risks revealing a paucity of judgment in the doubtful observer. Again, I'm not saying that

such qualitative differences cannot be laid out in accord with clear criteria – rather, that the impulse to find such marks of superiority and inferiority is often part of a larger agenda tied to the cultural status of the judge, not the utility or power of the art object in question.

Let me return to the specifics of our show to reinforce the idea of the material conditions that surround the staging of the playtext before returning to a consideration of how we used that playtext. Paula Garofalo's costume designs – contemporary, eclectic and slightly larger than life (Rosencraft and Guilderstone, for instance, were preppie Eurotrash in pastels, hats and sockless Docksiders) – established the play's world as one contrasting a slightly stuffy court with a younger, hipper crowd who resembled the students in the audience. The set, designed by Gordon W. Olson (who also did the lights), resembled something between an abandoned

7. Hamlet (Noah Tepper) sees the ghost. Photograph by Gordon W. Olson.

8. The king (Tony Heard, centre) and court watch the play-within-the-play. With (from left to right) Chester Wolfaardt (Corambis), Jessica Boyles (Ofelia), Jennifer Huddleston (Gertred), and Noah Tepper (Hamlet). Photograph by Gordon W. Olson.

temple and a derelict car park, its concrete pillars fractured to reveal the rebar beneath and to avoid blocking sightlines in the show's arena configuration. The result was that the lab theatre felt almost like a found space, and the world of the play felt both stark and transitional, a remnant of former grandeur long run to seed. Sound, by Alex Gilland and James Vesce, emphasized atmospherics – wind and ambient noises that were less natural – and music which was contemporary and obscure, so as not to trigger audience association. Fog was used extensively and the whole had an eerie, claustrophobic quality (the theatre as configured held fewer than a hundred), which lent itself to some startling moments, as when the ghost of Old Hamlet appeared (in full military dress uniform) sitting in the house, though the compactness of the space limited some physical action, as in the final Hamlet/Leartes duel, which had to be tightly constrained for safety reasons.

The production involved video sequences designed and shot by Jay Morong in consultation with the director, James Vesce, and projected on several surfaces around the house so that they felt immersive. Sometimes they showed simple background atmospherics, but during Ofelia's mad scenes they conflated both what she had been doing (running through the woods, picking flowers, etc.) with what was in her head – trippy, kaleidoscopic images through which Ofelia fell. The projection surfaces also served for bulletins such as the King's first announcement of his marriage (taken from Q2), the first Fortenbrasse scene and the play within the play, but also provided live streaming from security cameras dotted around the building. These were running when the audience first entered the space, so that they could see themselves on the screens in ways emphasizing, paradoxically, the liveness and meta-theatricality of the

9. The closet scene with Noah Tepper and Jennifer Huddleston. The images on the screen behind them are live pictures of the hall where Corambis was just killed. Photograph by Gordon W. Olson.

digital image. One of these later showed Hamlet's brutal beating of the eavesdropping Corambis in the hallway outside the theatre, but their general mode was to show patrolling sentries and hence to reinforce the sense of a state under constant self-policing surveillance.

The production was planned from the outset as one that would speak to our campus conditions, and it was cast accordingly. Almost half of the actors (six of fourteen) were people of colour, though last-minute casting changes made it impossible to honour family units in racial terms, and the production was effectively colour-blind. Voltemar and Horatio were played by women (as women), and our sexually ambiguous Hamlet might have been as romantically interested in Leartes as he was in Ofelia (pronounced oh-*Fail*-ya), who played on her phone and texted when she got distracted. Every conscious choice the cast and design team made aimed to feel as close as was possible to a telling of the story which our students might have generated out of their own experience, and it consciously resisted choices that felt overly familiar. We were trying to make the play feel new, and that meant no tired Oedipal dynamics or somnambulant soliloquizing. We also wanted to foreground the production as a particular iteration within a long and changing tradition, so the show was framed as a narrative event; an interpolated prologue by Horatio anticipated the play's final moments as she promised to tell Hamlet's story, then left the script (the Arden 3 Q1/F edition) on stage to be used as a prop thereafter, as the show proper began.

The choice of that performance script was made in the hope that it too would help us to sidestep the ponderous weight of the more familiar and quotable texts, giving us something that would complement the show's other design and casting choices, something that felt contemporary, tense and immediate. Along with such conceptual justification, however, we chose Q1 because we thought it would be easier for undergraduate actors, less cluttered, less obscure in its references, and less weighed down by intimidating cultural baggage.

We were wrong in every respect.

The Q1 text is not easier. It is more direct and less mellifluous, but its prosy quality is as much the result of broken or erratic verse as it is actual prose. Those actors who had done some Shakespeare before struggled to make their work on scansion helpful and got bogged down trying to hold on to rhythms that confused not just the meter of the line but its sense as well. Those less attuned to meter would either end-stop their lines or read to punctuation points just as they would with Q2/F, so the 'looser' verse of Q1 made no significant difference. And, yes, the Q1 script is less cluttered and digressive, requiring fewer trips in the dramaturgical ambulance, but it isn't necessarily clearer, and there are moments which go beyond baffling syntax when actual plot seems confounded (such as the crucial scene in which Horatio relays Hamlet's return from England to the Queen [Gertred], which, in omitting Q2's convenient pirates, makes the tale of what actually happened to Hamlet and how he got back to Denmark bewildering). As to that cultural baggage we thought we were sidestepping, that came with the title alone, none of the cast knowing much of anything about the play that inhered solely in Q2 or F. My class made much of the way Gertred declared her ignorance of her husband's murder in ways Gertrude never actually does, and the way Gertred promises to assist Hamlet's vengeful intents, but such things only stand out by comparison, neither moment actually altering the plot of the story. Indeed, the actress playing Gertred struggled to make sense of her character's apparent inaction in the final scene, having pledged active assistance only a few scenes earlier. Those crucial lines of support Gertred gives to Horatio, which seemed, before rehearsals, to make Gertred clearer and more active as an agent than Gertrude,

wound up making her more opaque when she doesn't clearly deliver on her promise. We considered various kinds of business during the duel to allow her to make good on her earlier words, but it always felt like an overreach, probably because the director and I couldn't shake assumptions about the story that grew out of the other texts.

That said, Q1 is simpler and shorter. Ours was a fairly tech-heavy show, which included the aforementioned video sequences but still came in at under 2 hours (with a ten-minute intermission), with no substantive cutting. Whether or not the actors felt the absence of Q2/F's aesthetic and philosophical digression, the show had pace, driven by its core plot to brisk conclusion, and one of the show's achievements, I thought, was that the majority of the text sounded clear and comprehensible in the mouths of our fairly inexperienced cast. As everyone always says about the Q1 text, it moves on stage, feels focused, (ironically) decisive and material in ways its more famous textual versions do not. It works as story even if it stumbles as poetry or philosophy.

And there's the rub. Because its successes and failures are symbiotically related, to be or not to be really is the question – or the point – because to truly *be* on stage requires a liveness, an energetic presence, and sense of purpose that I think we found in Q1, not in spite of, but because of, the play's failings as poetry and philosophy. Our actors were young people (it was an entirely undergraduate cast) in a tale of passion and action, and they inhabited their roles with the ease of those who understood the urgency of the emotions in the play. One of the reasons we had opted to use the Q1 text is that it never clarifies Hamlet's age as Q2 does, revealing in the graveyard that he is in fact 30.[6] Part of Q1's appeal was that it allowed us to

---

[6] Or at least he is so at this point in the story. While the actual timeline of the play appears to take days or weeks at most, this is one of those very Shakespearian moments when time seems subject to character and plot. Hamlet feels younger earlier in the play when his actual age is left unpointed for the nonce, suddenly 'becoming' 30 just as the play takes a turn for the more experienced, contemplative and resigned to mortality.

10. Hamlet (Noah Tepper) offers his hand to Leartes (Shawn Jones) prior to the duel in the final scene. Photograph by Gordon W. Olson.

play the title character as an 18- or 19-year-old, the play becoming a kind of *Young Adult Hamlet*, and like all good YA art, its feelings are raw, its sense of outrage is heightened, and the personal seems to confirm the universal. Its simplicity comes in part from its refusal constantly to second-guess itself as the soliloquies of Q2 and F tend to (especially the 'rogue and peasant slave' and 'How all occasions do inform against me' speeches). The text of Q1, like its protagonist and our adolescent actors, is confused, impetuous, passionate and absolute. Everything is black or white, greyness itself a kind of moral failing, even when the character and text are themselves bewildered into straying between points. It does not intrinsically value reflection, contemplation or the indecision so central to much of the play's cultural baggage, and is thus – and this is the heart of what makes Q1 surprising, I suspect – not very *Hamlet*-like. So, what makes it

work as theatre might be seen to make it less as art object, as rumination, even as *Shakespeare*, since those qualities are tied to the cultural memory, or assumption, of what *Hamlet* is.

For *Hamlet* to be un-*Hamlet*-like creates a kind of cultural vertigo, a dizzying anxiety about what one is experiencing, one Toppman's confused but passionate dismissal of the Q1 text also embodies. We know, or think we know, what *Hamlet* is, so when we are presented with a *Hamlet* that is not those things, we suffer a species of epistemological crisis akin to that of the play's hero. We know not seems. We are forced to interrogate every utterance, every action, for signs of its meaning, and – in the intensely

---

The fact of his age hasn't simply been reserved to this point. The truth of the theatrical moment has altered it, even if the play never actually said he was younger.

moralistic world of both *Hamlet* and culture criticism – demand to know its worth. If the play we are watching isn't what we expected, were our expectations at fault? Have we invested time and energy in something bereft of the Bardic imprimatur which is the ultimate source of its value as cultural experience? If all our assumptions about *Hamlet* are suddenly shown to be problematic, what does that do to Shakespeare's cultural standing? Or our own?

In other words, the staging of the Q1 text takes Shakespeare's standing, his genius, and troubles it in the most immediate and visceral way, unravelling much of the narrative tapestry of artistic greatness and the ambient glow in which some of the cultural elite are pleased to bask. This unsettling of texts, of Shakespeares, of notions of cultural production and of artistic merit, triggers a kind of rearguard action. The staging of 'bad' quartos is a political act, like the telling of stories from outside the canon or productions that challenge that canon from the perspectives of those marginalized by it (think of *The Wind Done Gone* or even *Wicked*), not solely because they champion the marginalized, but because they tease at the notions of fixity, familiarity and authority. They worry at our assumptions and the values which undergird them, exposing the 'version we know' as a fiction tied to cultural status, to power, and the anxiety that both are fading as the world changes. My students did not know *Hamlet*. Now they do. But

their *Hamlet* is not the one most people think – in a fuzzy, unspecific way – that they know, and some people find that worrying.

Staging *Hamlet* Q1 mixes, in Eliot's phrase, memory and desire, because insofar as we know the play, or think we know the play, we cannot unremember the 'version we know'. Q1 is always, for better and worse, deprived of ontological status and can only be known by comparison. After the fact, I kicked myself for not allowing Gertred some wordless act that would have shown how she tried to aid her son's revenge as she had said she would, but at the time I just couldn't shake Q2/F's more passive queen. She, like the rest of the play, had wormed her way into my head (poison in jest, the leprous distillment taken through the portals of my ears), and I couldn't unlearn her. Q1 is not the *Ur-Hamlet* but the *UnHamlet*, and as such it fulfils some desires (such as one for more drive and focus in the plot on stage) while confounding others – desire which would not exist without a 'prior' text already in mind, however imprecisely. The only audience members who can experience the Q1 text as a play in its own right are those who know next to nothing about 'Hamlet', though such people are, perhaps, rather more common than we might like to believe. In spite of the extensive rhetoric to the contrary, and at least in terms of an audience discovering the play in performance for the first time, that may not be a bad thing.

SHAKESPEARE, RACE AND 'OTHER' ENGLISHES: THE Q BROTHERS' *OTHELLO: THE REMIX*

CARLA DELLA GATTA

The 2015 announcement of the Oregon Shakespeare Festival (OSF) *Play On!* project, which said that Shakespeare's plays would be translated into contemporary English by thirty-six American playwrights assisted by dramaturgs, was met with both curiosity and disdain, with some scholars taking to public forums to express their outrage. There was worry that these new translations would be prioritized for the stage over the originals, concern that theatres should help actors to continue to master technique rather than employ writers to translate the scripts into an 'easier' language, and, in many cases, dismay at the suggestion that Shakespeare's language requires translation. In his essay on the history of adapting Shakespeare's dialogue, Daniel Pollack-Pelzner concludes that 'in its combination of updating and deference, O.S.F.'s commission looks like an eighteenth-century project couched in nineteenth-century terms', a reference to changing the language without the intention of altering the play.[1] Although there is a theatrical legacy for altering Shakespeare's language, in the last century the conception that Shakespeare's language is definitive of his drama has been an earmark of his plays, leading James Shapiro to state: 'The only thing Shakespearean about his plays *is* the language.'[2]

Later in 2015, the language debate expanded to the United Kingdom. Julian Fellowes, whose 2013 film adaptation of *Romeo and Juliet* flopped in large part due to its modernized English, backtracked on his previous claim that only a university education could provide access to comprehending Shakespeare. When defending the textual changes to his film, he had stated that he could understand Shakespeare '"because I had a very expensive education. I went to Cambridge; not everyone did."'[3] Antony Sher took issue with Fellowes's comment, and Fellowes backed down, only for Ian McKellen to pronounce that Shakespeare should be seen in the theatre and not read, and Anthony Hopkins then contrarily to urge people to read the plays.[4]

The *Play On!* announcement coincided with the launch of the Hogarth Shakespeare series, a new line of book adaptations of Shakespeare's plays. The project was described in similar terms: the plays would be 'reimagined by some of today's bestselling and most celebrated writers. The books will be true to the spirit of the original plays, while giving authors an exciting opportunity to do something new.'[5] In April 2016, Arden released *On Shakespeare's Sonnets: A Poets' Celebration*, with renditions and responses to the sonnets by thirty contemporary English, Scottish and Irish poets. In both cases, the Hogarth and Arden projects received none of the vitriol heaved at OSF's project.

---

[1] Daniel Pollack-Pelzner, 'Why we (mostly) stopped messing with Shakespeare's language', *The New Yorker*, 6 October 2015.

[2] James Shapiro, 'Shakespeare in modern English?' *New York Times*, 7 October 2015.

[3] Quoted in Chris Hastings, 'No Julian, you DON'T need a degree to enjoy Shakespeare, says furious Antony Sher', *Daily Mail*, 31 October 2015.

[4] Hastings, 'No Julian'.

[5] 'The Hogarth Shakespeare', *Vintage Books*.

One of the primary reasons that Hogarth and Arden did not suffer from retaliation was that they commissioned translations into non-theatrical genres, and novels and poems cannot replace Shakespeare's scripts for performance. But another factor cannot be ignored. OSF touted that its playwrights for the project were 'more than 50 percent female and more than 50 percent writers of color, [who] will bring a range of diverse voices and perspectives to the works of Shakespeare'.[6] This is in sharp contrast to Hogarth's range of writers. Of the eight authors whose works had been announced to be published through 2021 at the time of this article's writing (June 2018), over 62 per cent are women and 0 per cent are people of colour. Of the thirty artists included in the Arden collection, 33 per cent are women and 10 per cent are people of colour.

All of these English-to-English translation projects challenged dominant structures to recognize translation of Shakespeare into English, and people of colour as qualified translators. Shakespeare studies has largely embraced the global – with Global Shakespeares investigating Shakespeare in non-English-speaking countries – but it retains a distance from the diversified local. Pollack-Pelzner writes, 'What is genuinely radical in [OSF's] commission is not the process but the people involved',[7] referencing the diversity of the playwrights. From Stephen Greenblatt, who reminisced that he fell in love with Shakespeare 'not through the charm of performance but through the hallucinatory power of his language',[8] to Ralph Alan Cohen, who voiced concern that 'the OSF project takes actors and directors off the hook'[9] by modernizing the language, scholars designated poetic language as the primary value and artistry of Shakespeare.[10]

But what eluded the public debate was a candid discussion about the relationship of race to ideological precepts about language. James Shapiro closes his critique of the OSF project by lamenting that 'when you attend a Shakespeare production these days, you find listed in the program a fight director, a dramaturg, a choreographer and lighting, set and scenery designers – but rarely an expert steeped in

Shakespeare's language and culture'. For Shapiro, the foundation funding the project would better 'spend its money hiring such experts and enabling those 36 promising American playwrights to devote themselves to writing the next Broadway hit like "Hamilton", rather than waste their time stripping away what's Shakespearian about "King Lear" or "Hamlet"'.[11] The five key value judgements associated with the project, or, more largely, with the role of language and theatre in a dominant valuation of Shakespeare, are embedded in Shapiro's closing statement. The role of the dramaturg varies by theatre, production and individual, but a dramaturg is undoubtedly one who should be 'steeped in Shakespeare's language and culture'. In the case of the OSF project, the dramaturgs include Ph.D.s, playwrights, directors, translators, literary managers, artistic directors, MFAs, producers and more, whose diverse backgrounds and experiences offer a breadth of access points to Shakespeare's language and culture. Also, OSF is spending the money of a wealthy entrepreneur who has the power to commission the United States' largest repertory theatre to employ more than seventy people, create a canon of modern work and influence theatre across the country (if not later the world), as several theatres have already committed to producing some of the translations. Although wealthy patrons have sponsored the arts from the Greeks through Shakespeare to now, the

---

6 Bill Rauch, 'Why we're translating Shakespeare', *American Theatre*, 14 October 2015.

7 Pollack-Pelzner, 'Why we (mostly) stopped messing with Shakespeare's language'.

8 Stephen Greenblatt, 'Teaching a different Shakespeare from the one I love', *New York Times*, 11 September 2015.

9 Ralph Alan Cohen, 'American Shakespeare Center Director of Mission's response to the Shakespeare translation project', American Shakespeare Center, asc-blogs, 9 October 2015.

10 Cohen is co-founder of the American Shakespeare Center (ASC). In April 2017, the ASC announced their 'Shakespeare's New Contemporaries' contest, commissioning thirty-eight fan-fiction plays and awarding $25,000 and a staging for each winner. Shapiro proclaimed his support for this rival initiative in various public announcements.

11 Shapiro, 'Shakespeare in modern English?'

ethical question and capitalist paradigm of accepting not just funding, but the idea and direction for a project itself, from someone, based merely on their ability to pay for it, has warranted little discussion in comparison to the desire to protect Shakespeare's plays from translation.

Shapiro characterizes the translators as 'promising', as many in fact are up-and-coming playwrights. But it remains a curious term for the thirty-eight writers who together have received over eighty playwriting awards, plus a myriad of others for directing, translating, producing and beyond, and it illustrates how contemporary American playwrights are valued when compared to standard-bearers such as Shakespeare. Further, his suggestion that they write 'the next Broadway hit like "Hamilton"' refers to a show that has achieved greater theatrical and financial success than any single Shakespeare production, recently winning eleven Tony awards and the Pulitzer Prize. It is a tale of one of the Founding Fathers, penned by a Latino, and performed by the most diverse cast on Broadway through a mixture of musical genres that include rap, soul, and R&B. But what is commercially advertised, popular, on Broadway, and, most critically, inclusive, diverse, and 'ethnic', seems at odds with Shapiro's esteem of Shakespeare's language and the historical legacy of white-dominated American Shakespearian performance, and Shapiro's phrasing relegates it to a lower level of importance. Finally, Shapiro devalues the rigor and creativity involved in translation, arguing that the playwrights will waste 'their time stripping away' Shakespeare's language, rather than achieve their task of creating an original aesthetic for the dialogue. His statement follows Stanley Wells's implication that translation involves simplification – that 'to dilute some of Shakespeare's complexities would be like simplifying Bach's counterpoint'.[12]

One place where these issues have been unfolding for the past few decades is in the genre of hip hop Shakespeares. Hip hop is more than a musical style used to adapt Shakespeare, it is also a visual and phenomenological experience, resulting in an innovative way of encountering the text. A close look at the most successful hip hop Shakespearian production illuminates a cultural moment in which aurality confuses the traditional definitions and recognition of the Other. The Q Brothers' *Othello: The Remix* is a hip hop version of Shakespeare's *Othello* that premiered in 2012 and introduced the genre of hip hop Shakespeares to the world stage. The Q Brothers, named for Gregory and Jeffrey Qayium (GQ and JQ), began adapting Shakespeare's plays into full-length musicals nearly twenty years ago. It is through the employment of hip hop as both performance genre and subject matter that *Othello: The Remix* utilizes a Shakespearian story to loosen the perceived equation of hip hop and black culture. The Q Brothers' *Othello: The Remix* illuminates Shakespeare as a viable conduit for breaking down stereotypes of hip hop, and hip hop storytelling as a device to complicate ideas about Shakespeare and race.

***

Othello: The Remix was the American contribution to the 2012 Globe to Globe Festival, a theatre festival that brought together thirty-eight theatre companies from around the world to perform all of Shakespeare's plays. Similar to OSF's *Play On!*, the Globe to Globe Festival established a set of rules for the participants, with language restrictions integral to the design of the festival. Only the Globe players were given the freedom to claim the stage by employing the use of spoken English, as the festival mandated that all other theatre companies translate Shakespeare's plays, thereby removing the element that critics of *Play On!* claimed was the very essence of Shakespeare. *Henry V* by the Globe actors was the only play in spoken English heard on the Globe stage during the festival, re-normalizing British Shakespearian performance through its proprietary claim on the English language. The United Kingdom's other production, *Love's Labour's Lost*, was performed in British Sign Language, while the production of *Troilus and Cressida* from English-dominant New Zealand was performed in the

---

[12] Stanley Wells, Twitter, 15 September 2016.

indigenous language of Maori. The Globe to Globe mandated that each company use a language other than English, thus in order to invite an American troupe, hip hop was deemed a 'language', although it was the only language in the festival that is not recognized by linguists as such.

But hip hop is more than a language; it is also a contested discursive strategy that carries the legacies of African folk storytelling, New York DJs and graffiti artists of Latinx and Latin descent,[13] urban vernacular and, most recently, global corporate culture. Thematically, hip hop often includes critiques of stereotypes of absent fathers and junkie mothers, gangs, and references to 'ghetto life'. Hip hop is also a performance style, one that references a visual component that cannot be made distinct from its language and sound. In his study of hip hop performativity, Christopher Holmes Smith argues that hip hop aurality has an 'inherently visual capacity'.[14] To view hip hop as merely a language is to posit that the Q Brothers' work is solely a linguistic translation, while not acknowledging the performance style, which can have repercussions for the affective response to hip hop. Scholar Marcus Tan writes, 'In other words, considering sound/music as language, while useful, inhibits one's ability to evaluate sound/music as a phenomenological experience.'[15] The rhythm, shared lines and beat boxing that contributed to the aural soundscape of *Othello: The Remix* were interwoven with the graffiti walls, costuming and choreography that made this production hip hop both aurally and visually.[16] Hip hop is aural and visual, and it is racially charged. So, what then is hip hop Shakespeare?

The genealogy of hip hop Shakespeares is composed of five intersecting threads. The first descends from within the academy, largely instigated by white, male scholars attempting to use hip hop as a point of accessibility for teaching Shakespeare. Examples of pedagogical tools include Sitomer and Cirelli's 2004 book *Hip Hop Poetry and the Classics*, and Flocabulary's 2007 compact disc endorsed by Stephen Greenblatt, *Shakespeare is Hip-Hop*.[17] More recently, entrepreneurs have picked up where the scholars left off. Jacob Salamon and Jared Bauer formed the company Wisecrack in

2012 and created *Thug Notes*, a series of YouTube videos that showcase African American comedian Greg Edwards as 'Sparky Sweets, PhD', who raps summaries of literature from Dr Seuss to Jane Austen, as well as a number of Shakespeare plays.

The second is from black artists who rap Shakespeare to demonstrate both mastery and appropriation of *the* white status symbol in an effort to empower black youths. This type of advocacy work is referred to as 'Hood Work', and 'involves educational and prosocial messaging for youths that are enacted within and through hip-hop'.[18] Black artists who use Shakespeare in this manner include British rapper Akala, who founded The Hip-hop Shakespeare Company (THSC) in 2008, and New York's The Sonnet Man (Devon Glover).

The third takes the form of theatre outreach programmes and workshops, as well as summer camps run by practitioners to engage teenagers. Outreach programmes include Hartford's Breakdancing Shakespeare, started in 2006, which offers an annual funded six-week intensive summer course. These

---

[13] Although hip hop is strongly associated with black culture, Latinxs were prominent rappers and DJs in the early stages of hip hop. See Juan Flores, 'Puerto rocks: rap, roots, and amnesia', in *That's the Joint! The Hip-Hop Studies Reader*, ed. Murray Forman and Mark Anthony Neal (New York, 2012), pp. 74–91. D. G. Kelley also notes that the first prominent hip hop graffiti artist was of Greek descent, in D. G. Kelley, 'Foreword', in *The Vinyl Ain't Final: Hip Hop and the Globalization of Black Popular Culture*, ed. Dipannita Basu and Sidney J. Lemelle (London, 2006), pp. xi–xvii.

[14] Christopher Holmes Smith, 'Method in the madness: exploring the boundaries of identity in hip hop performativity', *Social Identities: Journal for the Study of Race, Nation and Culture* 3 (October 1997), 345–74; p. 345.

[15] Marcus Tan, *Acoustic Interculturalism* (New York, 2012), p. 36.

[16] The 'four elements' of hip hop include DJing, MCing, graffiti and breaking, as defined by Tricia Rose in her seminal work on rap. See Tricia Rose, *Black Noise: Rap Music and Black Culture in Contemporary America* (Middletown, 1994), p. 34.

[17] See also Michael King's 2008 documentary, *Rapping with Shakespeare*, regarding this type of pedagogy.

[18] Murray Forman, 'Hood work: hip-hop, youth advocacy, and model citizenry', *Communication, Culture & Critique* 6 (2013), 244–57; p. 245.

three strands of engagement converge in the desire for a cutting-edge pedagogy that is predicated, to some extent, on the idea that Shakespearian language requires a 21st-century musical conduit to be understood by young people.

The fourth is from black theatres or repertories that pen a cultural adaptation of a Shakespearian play that includes hip hop, such as *Revenge of a King* (*Hamlet*) in Phoenix in 2009 and *Macbreezy* (*Macbeth*) in Los Angeles in 2010. Finally, the fifth, more recent, is from practitioners who employ the musical genre for adaptation. Theatrical hip hop musicals include *Clay* (2008) and *Venice* (1999), hip hop adaptations of *Henry IV* and *Othello*, respectively, both of which were produced by Matt Sax and Eric Rosen.[19]

Standing adjacent to these threads is the Q Brothers' canon of work, which began in an academic setting through artistic development, not pedagogy. The Q Brothers had their first hit with *The Bomb-itty of Errors* (1999), borne out of GQ's senior thesis at NYU's Tisch Experimental Theatre Wing. At Tisch, GQ needed more than his own original work for his senior project, so he went 'to the master adapter, Shakespeare'.[20] *Bomb-itty* went on to become a successful off-Broadway show, and was followed by *Funk It Up About Nothin'*, which debuted at Edinburgh Fringe in 2008. Post *Othello*, the Q Brothers created their *The Two Gentlemen of Verona* adaptation, *Q Gents*,[21] and stepped outside of Shakespeare for their first time with their adaptation of Dickens's *A Christmas Carol*, which had its official premiere in 2014. Since then, the Q Brothers' success as professional and collaborative theatre-makers has led to the production of *I♡Juliet* at Illinois Shakespeare, *Rome Sweet Rome* (*Julius Caesar*) developed with students at University of Iowa, *Long Way Home* (Homer's *Odyssey*) with the Chicago Children's Choir, a workshop production at the Getty Villa of *The Madness of Love Mixtape* (Plato's *The Phaedrus*) and *Ms. Estrada* (Aristophanes' *Lysistrata*) that premiered in New York in 2018 with a large co-ed cast that included none of the members of the Q Brothers collective.

***

Othello: The Remix stood outside the norms of the Globe to Globe not simply as a metaphorical gesture to differentiate the American production from the British, but also in that it was the only musical in the festival and the only self-proclaimed adaptation.[22] But the experience of the American *Othello* was more analogous to early modern Globe playgoing than any other production in the festival, with its use of a stylized, fast-paced, contemporary English, dozens of current cultural references, a re-making of an older tale, actors in multiple roles, men (though not boys) playing women, audience address, pre-show musical entertainment, a short rehearsal time, a collaborative playwriting style, and more than enough bawdiness to keep the groundlings entertained for the less-than-2 hours they were there. Though the United Kingdom staged *Henry V* in Renaissance costuming and used the original dialogue, the Q Brothers in many ways provided a more precise simulacrum of the early modern theatre-going experience for audience members.

To adapt Shakespeare into a hip hop musical, the Q Brothers employed a process that retained the pace and order of Shakespeare's tragedy. They

19 For reviews and analysis of hip hop Shakespearian productions, see Todd Landon Barnes, 'Hip hop Macbeths, "Digitized Blackness", and the Millennial Minstrel: illegal culture sharing in the virtual classroom', in *Weyward Macbeth: Intersections of Race and Performance*, ed. Scott L. Newstok and Ayanna Thompson (New York, 2010), pp. 161–72; Landon Barnes, 'MacB: the Macbeth Project (review)', *Shakespeare Bulletin* 27.3 (Fall 2009), 462–8; Peter Meineck, 'Live from New York: hip hop Aeschylus and operatic Aristophanes', *Arion* 14.1 (Spring/ Summer 2006), 145–67; Bradley D. Ryner, 'Revenge of a King (review)', *Shakespeare Bulletin* 27.3 (Fall 2009), 457–62; and Kevin J. Wetmore Jr, '"Big Willie Style" staging hip hop Shakespeare and being down with the Bard', in *Shakespeare and Youth Culture*, ed. Jennifer Hulbert, Kevin J. Wetmore Jr, and Robert L. York (New York, 2006), pp. 147–70.

20 Gregory Qaiyum, personal interview, Chicago, 3 April 2013.

21 The Q Brothers' *Q Gents* has now been added to the OSF *Play On!* project.

22 The production involved a lot of firsts for the Globe. It was the first hip hop musical on the stage, the first use of speakers at the Globe, the first production with amplified sound, and the first time they had a DJ.

started by constructing a direct line-for-line remake in rhyme, using the *OED* and different copies of the play. The first draft retained about 80 per cent of Shakespeare's language. They then translated the rhyme into hip hop, adapting the narrative at this stage of the process. Shakespeare's verse makes only one appearance in the Q Brothers' script. Iago's sexualized phrase about Othello, which he speaks to Brabantio, 'I am one, sir, that comes to tell you your daughter and the Moor are now making the beast with two backs',[23] was echoed in 'You and I know it for a fact / You and her will make the beast with two backs.'[24] But the line was transposed to Iago's motivating speech to Roderigo as a hopeful image of Roderigo and Desdemona in bed. The Q Brothers shifted this imagined visual of a biracial pairing to a uniracial, white one, and, in this rewriting, repurposed it to complicate the association of that line with miscegenation.

The Q Brothers said, 'after going through over thirty drafts, we fight until we are all happy. Absolute collaboration.'[25] Specifics of characterization and the adapted storyline resulted from their process of translating the dialogue from Shakespeare, through the *OED*, and then into hip hop. There were no major cuts or alterations to the plot of *Othello*, but the action was placed in a modern consumerist culture of hip hop performers and moguls.[26] The Q Brothers employed the genre of hip hop hermetically to set the action within a hip hop crew; hip hop culture was both the medium for conveying the story and the story itself. The Q Brothers depicted MC Othello as a black man who had lived a stereotypically 'inner city' childhood, but they did not make this element of Othello's blackness a performed part of the show. Themes and cultural references associated with hip hop were all an (offstage) part of Othello's tale of his past at the outset of the production. Othello successfully transposed his story of overcoming displacement into his financially lucrative mainstream music, in much the same way that the Q Brothers called upon a tradition of undervalued hip hop Shakespeares when they created their financially lucrative show about a hip hop Othello.

Othello was the mainstream rapper, Iago an old-school hip hop artist and the best lyricist, while Cassio was a green boy-band type who prioritized his dancing and entertainment over a sophisticated hip hop sound. Roderigo was characterized as a gamer nerd, obsessed with science fiction almost more than he was with Desdemona, and Loco Vito was portrayed as a shady hip hop CEO from Los Angeles who consistently analogized events to professional tennis from the 1980s and 1990s, and who later had to leave the country for 'undisclosed reasons'.[27] The setting was modernized and tertiary characters were rewritten as comic character roles, and, without any significant cuts to the plot, the production ran a fast-paced 90 minutes.

The Q Brothers created a narrative frame that allowed them to shift between their roles as rappers and characters. The actors entered the stage as performance artists, then shifted to hip hop concert performers, energizing the crowd with 'Throw your hands up'[28] eight times before transitioning to actors who depict a story. The audience participated in the experience as theatre patrons, concertgoers, and sometimes co-creators of the beat, with the performers consistently changing their relationship with the audience and with each other (as multiple

---

[23] "The Tragedy of Othello the Moor of Venice', by William Shakespeare in *William Shakespeare: The Complete Works*, ed. Stanley Wells, Gary Taylor, John Jowett, and William Montgomery (Oxford, 1986), 1.1.117–18.

[24] Q Brothers, *Othello: The Remix*, unpublished script (2012), p. 26.

[25] Shakespeare's Globe, 'Unpublished interview with the Q Brothers', Archive at Shakespeare's Globe, 5 May 2012.

[26] All references to the production and script are from the Globe to Globe Festival in 2012 and may differ slightly from the published script (forthcoming). Changes were made following the run at the Globe but they did not significantly alter the dialogue, music, or choreography. The performers were GQ, JQ, Postell Pringle, Jackson Doran, and the DJ Clayton Stamper who mixed the music offstage. When the actors perform as narrators, they will be represented as GQ, JQ, POS, and JAX, respectively. Otherwise, the dialogue will be credited to the character.

[27] Q Brothers, *Othello*, p. 56. [28] Q Brothers, *Othello*, p. 4.

characters and also narrators) throughout. When the plot advanced quickly, the narrators moved time backward saying,

ALL: Rewind!
JQ: Let's do that over slower cuz I think they fell
ALL: behind[29]

The constant fluctuation between mimesis and diegesis invited comedic commentary, and some critics felt that the Q Brothers had not effectuated tragic elements sufficiently.[30] But, more importantly, this adaptation made explicit that the characters themselves are performers. In Ayanna Thompson's new introduction to the Arden *Othello*, she illustrates how Othello and Iago are both successful storytellers, concluding that 'the play teaches us to be sceptical of adhering to one frame, or one story'.[31] Having multiple narrators and narrative voices interspliced with the action, the audience was forced to confront the racialized bodies of the actors as both storytellers and characters.

The most surprising change for most audience members and reviewers was that, following in the tradition of *Othello* adaptations that omit major characters, Desdemona was not a physical character on stage. Djanet Sears's *Harlem Duet* (1997) includes male and female characters yet only a glimpse of [Desde]Mona's elbow and her voice only heard from offstage; Paula Vogel's *Desdemona, a Play about a Handkerchief* (1994) consists only of three actresses who portray the three female characters; and Toni Morrison's *Desdemona* (2012) involves only female actors and musicians, who also voice some of the male characters. Although the 1962 film adaptation *All Night Long* (dir. Basil Dearden), includes all of the major characters, Delia (Desdemona) does not 'take the stage' like all of the other musicians in the jazz club and instead performs her song offstage. Thompson argues that *Othello* 'is a play that invites revision',[32] and the omission of characters is a key component of the theatrical legacy of its adaptations.

While each actor took on multiple roles, and both Bianca and Emilia appeared in the show, Desdemona was represented only through the sound of her singing voice. Her backstory was filled in, yet she remained a negative space in performance. The DJ played her singing voice offstage from a pre-recorded track. She sang background for Othello, so when her voice was first heard, it was as an echo of his. As the action progressed, Desdemona no longer articulated words, only sounds. During the final bedroom scene when Othello strangled Desdemona, he said,

OTHELLO: I know you're awake
DESDEMONA: ⸺
OTHELLO: Don't even try me.[33]

Othello finished the shared lines in lieu of a dialogue between the two characters. The narrators eerily sang the song's chorus in low tones, repeating 'You made your bed', a refrain that Othello would sometimes complete with 'now sleep in it'.[34] This refrain shifted Desdemona's failed defence into the mouths of the male performers. Othello then mounted the sole piece of furniture on the stage, a graffiti-covered musicians' trunk, which transformed into a bed in the imaginations of both actors and audience. Placing a pillow over the invisible Desdemona's head, he smothered her. This moment raised the question of the importance of having Desdemona present at all, especially for her own death. It may seem obvious to lament the visual absence of a climactic scene, but audiences responded with gasps and horror at the pantomimed violence. Death by smothering gained even more traction when it was also the silencing of a character who had a voice and no body.

---

[29] Q Brothers, *Othello*, p. 44.
[30] See reviews by Reiss, Skantze, and Yates on the 'less tragic' aspect of the show: Edward Reiss, 'Globe to Globe: 37 plays, 37 languages', *Shakespeare Quarterly* 64.2 (Summer 2013), 200–32; P. A. Skantze, 'O-thell-O: styling syllables, donning wigs, late capitalist, national "scariotypes"', in *Shakespeare Beyond English: A Global Experiment*, ed. Susan Bennett and Christie Carson (Cambridge, 2013), pp. 129–38; and Kieran Yates, 'Othello – review', *Guardian*, 7 May 2012.
[31] Ayanna Thompson, 'Introduction', in *Othello: Revised Edition*, ed. E. A. J. Honigman (London, 2016), pp. 1–116; p. 3.
[32] Thompson, 'Introduction', p. 5.
[33] Q Brothers, *Othello*, p. 73. [34] Q Brothers, *Othello*, p. 73.

The absent Desdemona and the 'sassy' Latina Bianca proved problematic for some viewers due to the fraternal aspect of the Q Brothers' performance and hip hop's history as a male-dominated genre. Some of that critique also had to do with identification; the innocent white victim was nowhere to be seen. Thompson argues that Shakespeare's *Othello* stimulates a desire for agency on the audience's part: 'a desire to protect Desdemona from an unjust death'.[35] In the case of *Othello: The Remix*, although the audience's gasps responded to the brutality of Desdemona's murder, she was not visually present. Compounding her absence was Iago's increased stage time and the fact that the greatest use of direct address was given to Iago and to the actor GQ as a narrator, making the audience all the more complicit in the violence towards the other characters.

Countering Wells's claim that Shakespearian translation involves simplification, which he expressed though musical analogy, the use of music in *Othello: The Remix* accented the linguistic delivery of the dialogue. JQ describes the complexity of having a live DJ to manipulate the two-bar and four-bar musical loops, which requires that the performer land a punch line on the front half of the beat. He goes on to state that the beats are kept as a frame to allow the actor to lead over the music.[36] This type of musical intricacy is part of hip hop, and when transposed to the theatrical performance of a Shakespeare translation, it accentuates the timing for line delivery. Within this hip hop soundscape, musical differentiation was key to characterization: the old-school rap of Iago, the boy-group pop of Cassio and the mainstream rap of Othello. As a language, hip hop is diverse; Marina Terkourafi writes, 'polyphony and fragmentation can be found at its very core'.[37] The Q Brothers' hip hop adaptation included a range of rap styles and some non-hip hop music as well. Emilia's speech about marital relationships was transposed to a post-Motown R&B number, a riff on James Brown's 'It's a Man's Man's Man's World', in which she took centre stage. Here, instead of the higher-pitched voice that actor Jackson Doran used for Emilia's spoken dialogue, he sang in his masculine voice, conveying that Emilia feels 'like an analog girl in a world that's / Digital'.[38] The other non-hip hop number occurred at the end of the show, with Othello leading an a cappella song (that the remaining actors joined him in), entitled 'Love Will Set You Free', about the 'cold, dark, unforgiving system' and his destiny in a tough world.[39] Both of these non-hip hop musical numbers, outside the primary musical genre of the show, solidified Emilia's and Othello's feelings of loneliness and isolation in that world.

Music was key to characterization, but aural differentiation was central to performances of race and ethnicity. For example, Bianca was portrayed as Latina through a Spanish-inflected English rather than a musical style or costume. In addition, the Q Brothers expanded their intricate aural strategy beyond music and accent to language, complicating ideas about race and ethnicity. Othello was made linguistically distinct from the other characters, signifying his racial difference. Through a sophisticated differentiation of hip hop and African American Vernacular English (AAVE), the Q Brothers disassociated both AAVE and hip hop from blackness, while simultaneously making Othello a linguistic Other. AAVE is also referred to as African American English (AAE), Black Vernacular English (BVE), and Ebonics, the last of which is a particularly polarizing term. The 1996 Oakland Ebonics controversy centred on a secondary school board in California that passed legislation recognizing that Ebonics needed to be preserved and taught. Opponents suggested that this move was motivated by a desire to attain funding for bilingual education and that Ebonics was a style of slang. Proponents argued that Ebonics was a dialect, and Ebonics was even

---

35 Thompson, 'Introduction', pp. 42–3.
36 GQ and JQ, 'Something then in rhyme', *Shakespeare Unlimited Podcast*, Folger Shakespeare Library, 10 January 2017.
37 Marina Terkourafi, 'Introduction' in *Languages of Global Hip Hop*, ed. Marina Terkourafi (New York, 2010), pp. 1–18; p. 3.
38 Q Brothers, *Othello*, p. 61. 39 Q Brothers, *Othello*, p. 85.

recognized by the Linguistic Society of America, which noted the regularity of the linguistic system and the 'grammar and pronunciation patterns' over 'the past thirty years'.[40] As with the Globe to Globe's decision to name hip hop a language to invite an American troupe while keeping with the rules of the festival, language determinations are highly political, and, for that reason, language itself, whether it is hip hop, AAVE, or the contemporary English of the OSF playwrights, is semiotic and must be read accordingly.

Though hip hop owes much of its origins to 1970s African American youth culture in the Bronx, it does not linguistically define itself by the rules of AAVE. One characteristic of AAVE is that it drops the preterite ending from verbs[41] and uses verb tenses, especially 'to be', differently from Standard American English. In *Othello: The Remix*, the whole hip hop crew spoke AAVE, evidenced in phrases such as Iago's 'We don't know if she's guilty till we see what she do',[42] Roderigo's 'You been stringin me along',[43] Bianca's 'You gonna get famous',[44] Loco Vito's 'All I got is sherry',[45] and Cassio's 'Don't be mad at how I be!'[46] These characters, who were not from the same black urban background as Othello, adopted this linguistic pattern that Othello also employs when he says, 'I got some good news',[47] illustrating AAVE's widespread influence on the vernacular.

The Q Brothers flipped the presumed association of AAVE and black culture, challenging audience expectations and illustrating the mainstreaming of AAVE. Although the other characters employed speech patterns associated with AAVE, the Q Brothers used Othello to foreground its variations, as it was Othello who was made linguistically distinct. The only time a character was confused by verbal utterances in the production was when Iago suggested that Othello should fire Cassio:

IAGO: You just gotta axe him
OTHELLO: Axe him what?
IAGO: No, axed from the line-up, like he needs to get cut, you know, fired?
OTHELLO: Oh that kinda axin.[48]

This linguistic confusion in which Othello hears 'axe' as 'ask' rather than as 'cut' clearly demonstrates that, despite Othello's mainstream success, his vocal patterns are still contrastive from others in his crew. Although the entire production was in hip hop and non-black characters employed AAVE – as both hip hop and AAVE have been appropriated by mainstream culture – it was only Othello, the black man, who needed to be given verbal clarification. The Q Brothers' sophisticated translation transposed the moment of Othello's epileptic breakdown in Shakespeare's script, which offers a visual of a commanding military officer losing physical and verbal control, into a linguistic breakdown for a master hip hop lyricist. The Q Brothers depicted Othello as not only visually confused, mistaking the reason that his gold chain is in Cassio's possession, but also linguistically confused, needing aural clarification within the hip hop culture he dominates.

Characters were differentiated musically and aurally but popular culture brought them all together. Aside from Bianca's reference to 'Coronas on the beach'[49] that adhered to a stereotype of Latinxs, cultural references did not communicate ethnicity or race; rather, a bevy of references repositioned this hip hop narrative as part of a wider mainstream commodification culture. There were allusions to the Beastie Boys, the 1987 film *Can't Buy Me Love*, the late 1970s television show *Mork and Mindy*, a host of tennis players from the 1970s through the 1990s, the 1992 film *A Few Good Men*, He-Man, *The Princess Bride*, *Crocodile Dundee*, various soap operas, *Harry Potter*, *Star Trek*, video games, the fall of the Berlin

---

[40] 'Resolution on the Oakland "Ebonics" issue unanimously adopted at the Annual Meeting of the Linguistic Society of America', Linguistic Society of America, 3 Jan. 1997.
[41] John R. Rickford, 'Geographical diversity, residential segregation, and the vitality of African American Vernacular English and its speakers', *Transforming Anthropology* 18.1 (2010), 28–34; pp. 29–30.
[42] Q Brothers, *Othello*, p. 42. [43] Q Brothers, *Othello*, p. 63.
[44] Q Brothers, *Othello*, p. 21. [45] Q Brothers, *Othello*, p. 23.
[46] Q Brothers, *Othello*, p. 29. [47] Q Brothers, *Othello*, p. 23.
[48] Q Brothers, *Othello*, p. 43. [49] Q Brothers, *Othello*, p. 45.

Wall, Madonna, and *Resident Evil*, to name a few. Although some black celebrities were mentioned, they were those whose influence reached broadly in mainstream culture, including Michael Jackson, Eddie Murphy, and the NFL wide receiver Devin Hester. Most of these references would be familiar to English-speaking audiences in their 30s or 40s of any race.

Like the cultural references, one of the few material props to appear onstage connoted the centrality of Othello's materialism. Othello's handkerchief that provides the 'ocular proof'[50] was transformed into an embellished gold chain, itself a monetarily valuable object. As Thompson explains, in Shakespeare's script, 'The handkerchief knits together Othello and Desdemona with his African past and her European present; it weaves their love together... and it unravels their lives'.[51] The gold chain in *Othello: The Remix*, by contrast, is a symbol of Othello's recent fame and wealth. He has no physical memento of his disadvantaged (read: black) past. The gold chain is, rather, a memento of Othello's ten platinum records – 'ten times plat'[52] – which he earned for hip hop songs that repackaged the early struggles of his life. Founding his success story on his own displacement, Othello commodifies the stereotyped black life so well that he is later named CEO and promoted out of his career as an artist. In writing about Shakespeare's play, Ian Smith argues against the long-standing belief that the handkerchief is white and tied closely to Desdemona (and her stained wedding sheets), suggesting instead that the handkerchief 'dyed in mummy' is in fact black – 'a substitute self for Othello'.[53] The gold chain in *Othello: The Remix* leaves open the question of this debate. As MC Othello's object adorning his body, a gold status symbol of his journey, it never becomes visually associated with the absent Desdemona as the handkerchief is in Shakespeare's play.[54]

Othello: The Remix tells the story of how race relations undergird the successful commercialization and rebranding of an artistic genre. In Iago's song, 'Why I Hate the Moor', the chorus repeats,

> Othello's rich but he keeps me poor
> And now it's time to settle the score
> He never lets me get my foot in the door
> and
>> ALL this is why I hate the Moor.[55]

Iago does not identify his racial bias as motivation for his disdain for Othello, emphasizing work politics instead. Iago drew a stylistic difference between Cassio, who 'makes music for little teenage white chicks', and himself, who is 'half-man half-Beastie Boy'[56] and thereby musically superior. It was not merely disdain for Cassio's style, but also for the fact that Iago was considered to be lesser, 'Opening for the opener ... this is just pathetic'.[57] Iago took all of his anger out on Othello, even though he acknowledged that systemic problems within the hip hop industry caused much of his resentment. After seeing the money that Cassio's album earned, he exclaimed,

IAGO: What is this? Damn!
        A rapper should be a rapper, not a business man.[58]

Iago blamed Othello rather than conceding that the line-up merely reflected that sales of Cassio's music exceeded his own. But implicit in Iago's dissatisfaction was the determination by the CEO (Loco Vito) that Iago's way of rapping was now only popular with 'the underground fans, you know the hard-core'.[59] The story mirrored that of late 1990s hip hop, a time when it had achieved widespread popularity but was subject to a growing

---

[50] Shakespeare, *Othello*, 3.3.365.
[51] Thompson, 'Introduction', p. 50.
[52] Q Brothers, *Othello*, p. 4.
[53] Ian Smith, 'Othello's black handkerchief', *Shakespeare Quarterly* 64.1 (2013), 1–25; p. 20.
[54] The gold chain in *Othello: The Remix* has the same function as the handkerchief in Shakespeare's *Othello*; it is the 'ocular proof' that Cassio has a personal item that Othello gave to Desdemona.
[55] Q Brothers, *Othello*, pp. 13–14.
[56] Q Brothers, *Othello*, p. 13. [57] Q Brothers, *Othello*, p. 14.
[58] Q Brothers, *Othello*, p. 14. [59] Q Brothers, *Othello*, p. 23.

divide between those interested in financial success and those interested in artistic acclaim.[60] The Q Brothers used Shakespeare to tell the history of hip hop, setting *Othello: The Remix* in the era after Notorious B.I.G. and Tupac Shakur had died, and Puff Daddy (Sean Combs) had transitioned to promoting 'more fabricated and poppy' rappers.[61] For that reason, most of the beats were reminiscent of the late 1990s, but they sometimes echoed 'gangsta rap' sounds when Iago spoke.

Othello: The Remix was an internationally commissioned production that told a Shakespearian story through hip hop in order to perform the history of the commodification of hip hop. But it is also *Othello*, and this re-contextualization goes well beyond a mere resetting of the play, to force a powerful dialogue between Shakespearian drama and hip hop. The subtext was that putting a hip hop Shakespearian production on the Globe stage signalled the mainstream commodification of not hip hop, but Shakespeare. The Q Brothers' Iago served as the harbinger of fidelity criticism, lamenting the new popular version of his art. Comparable to the critics of *Play On!* and *Othello: The Remix*, Iago spoke out against the current aesthetic, concluding that what is now popular to a wide group does not retain the complexity of the earlier language and form. This strategy downplayed Iago's racism towards Othello and foregrounded his aesthetic and linguistic concerns. Authenticity and the theme of 'keepin it real'[62] are standard themes in hip hop. Perhaps they are in Shakespeare as well, as he continues to appeal to, and to be adapted and performed by, a wider, more diverse population.

Despite the definitive statement in the Q Brothers' script that Iago was unhappy with Othello because of career suppression, in performance Othello was portrayed by the one African American actor in the cast. This casting caused a racially motivated antagonism to persist. GQ said, 'There is still an unspoken racial element in there. Iago thinks he is a better rapper but he's white.'[63] Although real-life brothers JQ and GQ are half Indian and half German, they and the blond Jackson Doran playing Cassio appeared in visual opposition to Postell Pringle's Othello. When asked about the casting choices, the Q Brothers stated that originally JQ was Othello, 'but then it looked as if [we] were making a statement. We fell into roles, and played to [our] strengths.'[64] Bound by visual conventions of performing race, the Q Brothers made casting choices that propelled the complex racial histories they were enacting onstage.

Racial hatred remained present but ancillary in the character of Brabantio,[65] who was 'set in the ways of a different generation'.[66] Brabantio had the fewest lines and only appeared for one speech, but he expressed explicit racial hatred, harping on the disparity between his daughter and Othello: 'But bunnies don't befriend big bears, it's just wrong.'[67] Following a line that ended with the word 'bigger', Brabantio left out the last word of the next line. After a pause, he said, 'I was gonna say rapper.'[68] Brabantio did not articulate the racial epithet, but both the audience and the characters onstage could fill in the blank.

As racism was not made a dominant motivation for propelling the action, reading race became more complicated. Within a hip hop storyline and genre, the strategy of aural differentiation used to convey Bianca as Latina and Othello as a linguistic Other also led to a question of race for Desdemona. The dependence on sound to convey Desdemona's persona raised the question of her visual appearance, and, unique to hip hop adaptation, the question of her race, though her father and husband referenced it. Brabantio described her

[60] Gregory Qaiyum, personal interview.
[61] Q Brothers, 'Post-show talkback', Chicago Shakespeare Theater, 10 April 2013.
[62] Terkourafi, 'Introduction', p. 5.
[63] Gregory Qaiyum, personal interview.
[64] Gregory and Jeffrey Qaiyum, personal interview, Chicago, 3 April 2013.
[65] GQ portrayed both Brabantio and Iago. This doubling placed the explicit racial hatred of Brabantio and implicit hatred of Iago into the body of one actor.
[66] Q Brothers, *Othello*, p. 11. [67] Q Brothers, *Othello*, p. 11.
[68] Q Brothers, *Othello*, p. 11.

as 'lily-white'[69] and Othello alluded to their differ-ence by what they could produce together, rap-ping, 'When she singin I'm picturin offspring with skin of cinnamon.'[70] Despite this pronouncement of her whiteness in the Q Brothers' production, the textual certainty of it in Shakespeare's script, and the legacy of performance of Desdemona as a white woman, some critics and viewers questioned Desdemona's whiteness because of the soulful quality of her voice and the very association of hip hop with black culture. P. A. Skantze describes Desdemona as one who '"sounds" black, though in the commercial music moment in which we are living this could be a girl trained to sing black at a young age'.[71] Kieran Yates did not mention Desdemona at all in her review for the *Guardian*, but a commenter imagined her as black – or as not black enough – writing: 'I think the production would have benefited with a Desdemona that combined the sass and attitude of, say, Beyonce, Nikki Minaj, and Rihanna.'[72] These comments reflect how Desdemona's invisibility was offensive from a certain perspective; the whiteness of Desdemona is as important as the blackness of Othello in contemporary performance.[73] In actuality, a white woman, Sophie Grimm, recorded Desdemona's tracks,[74] and the Q Brothers used a white man, then Globe artistic director Dominic Dromgoole, as the visual focal point for the actors to engage when picturing Desdemona. What the Q Brothers' production illuminated was that, in the absence of a white body onstage, the ongoing association of black culture, soulfulness, and hip hop could cause even Desdemona's race to be questioned.

But the Q Brothers challenged this stronghold through their own biracialism, even if it was not legible to the audience. Their presence onstage upheld a sense of elite academic authority (their work began during GQ's study at NYU) while firmly upsetting it (GQ and JQ are first-generation – the group was racially and ethnically diverse, and they didn't attempt to cater to a particular group as pedagogy or entertainment). Terkourafi writes, 'This dual role of *expert/outsider* is often assumed by immigrants and/or bilinguals,

who naturally find themselves at the juncture between different communities and cultures, enabling them to function as conduits for the transmission of the genre.'[75] This description applies not only to the Q Brothers' ensemble, but to the character of Othello in Shakespeare's script. Othello is both converted Christian and Moor, lauded warrior and outcast, murderer and victim. Notably, when Brabantio and his men go to arrest Othello, it is Othello who is the Jesus figure, the representative Christian, and Iago his Judas.[76] Shakespeare pushed on notions of typol-ogy, making Othello both the standard white and black characters, confusing expectations of race through his story, structure and dialogue. The Q Brothers' adaptation followed suit.

The Globe had reserved *Othello* for the Americans, and there was an implication that American race issues would best be addressed through this Shakespearian play.[77] The Globe designated the language of hip hop for *Othello* due to hip hop's association with black culture, which Othello is tied to in contemporary stagings. But the Q Brothers overturned the norms of racial performance and the expectation of the visual of an American performance of miscegenation. Rather than staging racial tension through the bodies of the two actors playing Othello and Desdemona, the Q Brothers created it musically and aurally, insin-uating that Shakespeare has extended beyond

---

[69] Q Brothers, *Othello*, p. 11. [70] Q Brothers, *Othello*, p. 34.
[71] Skantze, 'O-thell-O', p. 130. [72] Yates, '*Othello*'.
[73] This also reflects a risk-averse attitude amongst primarily white scholars and critics to engage in a frank discussion on the performance of race. Skantze describes actor Postell Pringle as 'Othello-ey looking' and GQ and JG as 'two with less easy to define physical and racial characteristics' ('O-thell-O', p. 130).
[74] Grimm's vocals were used for the Globe to Globe Festival through all of the subsequent runs until the show moved to off-Broadway at the close of 2015, when they were replaced by vocals by Typhanie Monique, who is also white.
[75] Terkourafi, 'Introduction', p. 5.
[76] See Thompson for how Shakespeare subverts aspects of the morality play ('Introduction', p. 10).
[77] Gregory Qaiyum, personal interview.

11. Back from left to right: Jackson Doran (Cassio), GQ (Iago) and JQ (Loco Vito) listen to Postell Pringle (Othello) debut a new track featuring Desdemona in Chicago Shakespeare Theater's production of *Othello: The Remix*, written, directed and composed by the Q Brothers. Photograph by Michael Brosilow.

whiteness and his style of English, as hip hop has extended past racial lines. The spoken word and a mix of ethnoracial bodies onstage made liminal the reading of identity, and thwarted the desire by some for clearly demarcated racial boundaries.

The black body of Othello appeared onstage, but all others around him became difficult for some scholars and critics to read, nodding to a sense of superiority that redirects through infantilizing language and how the complexity of musicality can override sight as a marker. As the Q Brothers' Iago refers to Cassio as a 'kid [who] is just an actor' and that 'he belong in a boy band',[78] P. A. Skantze refers to the actors in the Q Brothers ensemble as 'guys' and 'boys' repeatedly, echoing Shapiro's pejorative use of the word 'promising' to describe the group of OSF playwrights who are largely middle-aged, with some in their 60s, 70s and 80s. This language says, in a sense, that contemporary modes of production are implicitly measured as childish and adolescent, in contrast to Shakespeare's imagined maturity.

Playing to sold-out Globe audiences, *Othello: The Remix* then proceeded to an international tour that the creators of any Shakespearian – or for that matter, theatrical – production would envy. After the premiere at the Globe to Globe, it had a short run in Germany, and it then spent a month at the Edinburgh Fringe, where the actors

---

[78] Q Brothers, *Othello*, p. 13.

refined the show. It moved to Chicago Shakespeare Theater (CST) in March 2013, where it later won Jeff Awards for Best Ensemble and Large Theater Sound Design. The run was extended through August 2013, and it was also performed for inmates at the Cook County Jail in Chicago, before travelling to South Korea, London and Sydney. In 2014, *Othello: The Remix* was performed at the Gdańsk Shakespeare Festival for the opening of their Gdańsk Shakespeare Theatre. The show travelled to Melbourne, the United Arab Emirates and New Zealand in 2015. In 2016, it returned for a run at CST for the 400th anniversary celebration and, later that same year, actor and producer John Leguizamo took the show to Off-Broadway. The Off-Broadway run resulted in GQ and JQ receiving a Drama Desk Award nomination for Outstanding Lyrics.

Othello: The Remix worked throughout to break down theatrical boundaries in hip hop Shakespeares, causing the audience to rely more on a nuanced listening over a mimetic visual characterization. The interracial origins of hip hop, its global appeal and the perception of hip hop Shakespeares, all point to a bigger issue of how we conceptualize racial division in the world. If hip hop has previously served as a pedagogical tool for young people to understand Shakespeare, this production suggested that Shakespeare could be the necessary entrance point for white culture to learn about the history of hip hop and its mode of storytelling. Describing both *Othello: The Remix* and *Play On!* as translation projects downplays how linguistic translation cannot be separated from a discussion of culture. What both projects point to is the need to embrace the collapsing of suspect assumptions about translation and adaptation, canonical and non-canonical forms, and who gets to adapt whom. Everyone wants to own hip hop, but nobody does. The same goes for Shakespeare.

'MINGLED YARN': *THE MERCHANT OF VENICE* EAST OF BERLIN AND THE LEGACY OF 'EASTERN EUROPE'

BOIKA SOKOLOVA

A 'STRANGE EVENTFUL HISTORY', OR WHAT HAPPENED TO 'THE MERCHANT OF VENICE' UNDER COMMUNISM

Late in 2015, a BBC documentary entitled *Shylock's Ghost* asserted that *The Merchant of Venice* was 'Shakespeare's most performed play'.[1] At that point I was looking into post-communist productions, which involved taking a longer view of the situation before 1989, and the statement made in the documentary ran counter to the situation in a large part of Europe. My reading soon confirmed what had been only a hunch, that the history of the reception of the play is rather complicated and needs further investigation.

Though my focus is on post-communism, the first part of this article briefly surveys the situation before 1989, the cut-off line for the socio-political transition in a region involving almost half of the countries on the European continent. Needless to say, my data is not complete, nor does it cover all former communist countries, though tendencies seem to emerge. In the second part, I consider several post-communist productions which, to my mind, capture the intense pressures of the moment of their creation. In the case of countries like Hungary and Poland, where the play has had a dynamic stage life after 1989, choosing a single example has been difficult, and the choice is, perhaps, one-sided, but I have tried to identify productions that have taken the play, locally or internationally, in new directions. In a project like this, a major difficulty is posed by the multilingual nature of the scholarship involved, and I am

deeply grateful for the generous help of colleagues from the European Shakespeare Research Association. Without their expertise and intellectual generosity, even this preliminary study would not have materialized. And this overview *is* preliminary, although it hopes to inspire more transnational work on the subject of the stage life of *Merchant* – a profoundly European play about anti-Semitism, racism, xenophobia, and the way societies use mechanisms of Othering.

Even the most cursory look at the spread of the play before World War II on the stages east of Berlin shows that it had a rather rich life, though it was hardly 'the most performed' play. Moving geographically from west to east, the curve of its popularity moves from high (Hungary, Czechoslovakia), to moderate (Poland) to low-ish (Balkans, Russia), a situation that changed dramatically with the arrival of the new social order, which interrupted its performance history.[2] Different as they are in their inherited cultural

---

[1] Shylock's Ghost, dir. Alan Yentob (BBC 4, 2015), www.bbc.co.uk/programmes/b06myq5v.

[2] Even in Hungary, a country with a high incidence of Shakespeare productions, the count on the centenary of the National Theatre of Budapest in 1937 does not list *Merchant* among the top six (where the counting stops). See Anthony Németh, 'The cult of the Shakespearean drama in Hungary', *Danubian Review* 5.4 (1937), 29–33. There was one more production before World War II: Zoltán Márkus, 'Der Merchant von Velence: The Merchant in London, Berlin, and Budapest during World War II', in *Shakespeare and European Politics*, ed. Dirk Delabastita, Jozef De Vos, and Paul Franssen (Newark, 2008), pp. 143–57.

traditions, most countries that became 'Eastern Europe' after 1945 stayed, for decades, practically *Merchant*-free. This situation is in strong contrast to, say, that in post-war West Germany where, in time, the socio-political debate about war guilt actively involved *The Merchant of Venice*, so much so that it became a 'litmus test' for the relationship between Germany and its Jews. The ensuing intense debate claimed it diversely, as 'a text damaged by history, as a vehicle of confronting history and as a means of bypassing history'.[3] At the same time, in Eastern Europe, it was a text banished from history. Elinor Shaffer defines such 'editing out' of a particular work as antagonistic reception, which is usually maintained through the levers of censorship and can result in long-term distortions and delays.[4]

Indeed, the ground started to shift soon after the 1917 revolution in Russia. After nearly sixty years of stage life in the pre-revolutionary Russia,[5] in the period between 1920 and 1991, when the Soviet Union ceased to exist, there were no *Merchant*s on the Russian stage.[6] Aleksey Bartoshevich explains that, though there was no official ban, any 'attempt to touch on the historical fortunes of the Jews was met with suspicion and nipped in the bud'.[7] He attributes this to the capacity of the text 'to awaken dangerous associations' in the minds of audiences living 'in a country of pogroms, where everything related to the Jewish theme required particular delicacy'.[8] Mark Sokolyansky has drawn attention to another element of the antagonistic reception reflected in the tenuousness of critical attention, and even the removal of *The Merchant of Venice* from lists of Shakespeare's plays. He further proposes that the frequent textual occurrence of words like 'Jew' and 'Hebrew', which are not always used with a negative connotation, would have worried ideologists who feared that stage interpretations could offer 'a *sui generis* apology of ethical Jews'.[9]

Thus, Alexandre Benois's 1920 production at the newly established Bolshoi Dramaticheskii Teatr in Petrograd (St Petersburg) was destined to draw the curtain over the play for nearly eighty years. In the midst of a civil war, political overhaul,

and the concomitant politicized struggles over artistic styles, Benois's deliquescent, sunny Venice, where 'poetry triumphed over the darkness of life' was at odds with both the revolutionary romanticism of the theatre's artistic platform and the reality of the hungry city outside.[10] Nor could its rarefied beauty evade awakening 'dangerous associations' (however unintended). A contemporary review describes Shylock as a 'dark cloud' fleetingly passing over the majestic landscape, 'not as a conscience, but as a dream of perverted humanity'.[11] In the years to come, Stalinist terror, along with the lightly veiled anti-Semitism of the regime, made the play toxic, and theatres avoided it

---

3 Zeno Ackermann, 'At the threshold – remembrance and topicality in recent productions of *The Merchant of Venice* in Germany', in *Reinventing the Renaissance: Shakespeare and his Contemporaries in Adaptation and Performance*, ed. Sarah Brown, Robert Lublin, and Lynsey McCulloch (New York, 2013), pp. 143–61.

4 Elinor Shaffer, 'Affinities and antagonisms: the processes of reception', in *Confrontations and Interactions: Essays on Cultural Memory*, ed. Bálint Gárdos, Ágnes Péter, Natália Pikli, and Maté Vince (Budapest, 2011), pp. 71–86; p. 79.

5 I've counted eleven different productions in the fifty-seven years before 1917: https://ru.wikipedia.org/wiki Венецианский купец.

6 In 1926 and 1940, the play was put on in Yerevan, the capital of Armenia, a country which has a time-honoured tradition of performing *Merchant* with a compassionate Shylock. A third production was in Perm, to which I've only found cursory references.

7 Aleksey Bartoshevich, 'A Venetian Jew on the Russian stage', *Toronto Slavic Quarterly* 4 (2003), http://sites.utoronto.ca/tsq/04/index04.shtml.

8 Aleksey Bartoshevich (2001), 'Венецианский еврей на русской сцене' [A Venetian Jew on the Russian stage] http://mxatschool.theatre.ru/press/articles/archive/747. Though Bartoshevich makes this comment in relation to a 1916 production, the anti-Semitism latent in Russian society, to which he refers, would hardly have evaporated in the four years to Benois's staging in 1920.

9 Mark Sokolyansky, 'The half-forbidden play in Soviet Shakespeare criticism, 1920–1950', *Multicultural Shakespeare: Translation, Appropriation and Performance* 6.7 (2010), 71–9.

10 Nadezhda Hmeleva, '*Mir iskusstva* artists at the Bolshoi Dramatic Theatre', *Nashe Nasledie* 73 (2005), www.nasledie-rus.ru/podshivka/7316.php.

11 Hmeleva quotes M. Kuzmin, '*The Merchant of Venice* at the Bolshoi Dramaticheskii Teatr', *Zhizn iskusstva* (1920), 1.

long after Stalin's death. As late as the 1990s, a Moscow director would decline to put it on.[12] Distortion and delay thus kept their stranglehold on it for the better part of a century.

When the political construct of 'Eastern Europe' was forged out of the victory deal of the Allies in 1945, and the Soviet space was extended, performances plummeted across the board. Of course, in the wake of the Holocaust, *The Merchant of Venice* was a painfully problematic text. However, a comparison across East European countries suggests that the reasons are only partly to do with post-war sensitivities and that the totalitarian control over societal discourse affected its fortunes.

Numerical comparisons for the period from 1945 to the collapse of the communist system in 1989 clearly bear this out. Bulgaria and Romania, where the reception was low to medium, both had only one production, away from the capital. Poland had two. In Hungary, where the pre-war reception was high, no fewer than three attempts to put on the play during the 1970s were foiled by the authorities, while the three that actually happened are all close to 1989, when the system was beginning to weaken.[13] In Yugoslavia, similar processes were under way. After a flurry of five post-war productions on the stage of the Belgrade National Theatre between 1945 and 1964, a hiatus of forty years between 1964 and 2004 ensued. On the Croatian stages, too, the play sustained a performance gap of several decades.[14]

Data collected by the team led by Sabine Schülting at the Freie Universität, Berlin, reveals a conspicuous numerical difference between the two German states. In contrast to the over 100 productions in West Germany, those in the German Democratic Republic (between 1949 and 1990, when it ceased to exist) are consistent in their paucity with other communist countries. After a resounding silence between 1945 and 1976, the play cautiously returned to the stages in the 1980s.[15]

Czechoslovakia seems to be the exception that proves the rule. High as the reception was there between 1918 and 1945, it doubled after that date, a fact that needs further scholarly attention. Another interesting fluctuation is that all

productions, bar one, were in Czech and outside the capital Prague. The only Prague production came in 1954, during the tense years after Rudolf Slánský's show-trial, which, as Ivona Mišterová has shown, coloured the critical perception of Shylock as a villain requiring punishment.[16] At the same time, in both pre- and post-war Slovakia, the stage life of the *Merchant* was scarce.[17]

With the collapse of communism, in 1989, *The Merchant of Venice* returned to the east European stages in a world of radical change.

THE RETURN OF THE REPRESSED:
POST-1989 HISTORIES

At the end of the 1980s, *The Merchant of Venice* emerged on post-communist stages from a time

---

[12] According to Elena Yampolskaya, Kozakov's idea of bringing *Merchant* to Russia was originally declined. See 'Mikhail Kozakov's Jewish question', *Novie izvestia*, 12 July 1999, www.mossoveta.ru/truppa/actors/goloborodko/1943.

[13] I am indebted for this information to Dr Julia Paraisz.

[14] Alen Biskupović, 'Coping with the greatest for over 100 Years', *European Stages* 7.1 (2016), http://europeanstages .org/2016/10/19/coping-with-the-greatest-for-over-100- years.

[15] 'Shylock in Germany: The Reception of Shakespeare's *The Merchant of Venice* after 1945', a project led by Sabine Schülting, has produced an exemplary database and other publications. See www.geisteswissenschaften.fu-berlin.de /en/v/shylock.

[16] On the connection between this production and then-current politics, see Ivona Mišterová, *Angloamerické drama na plzeňských scénách* [Anglo-American Theatre Performances on the Pilsen Stages] (Pilsen, 2013), pp. 103–4. Rudolf Slánský and his supporters – most of whom, including Slánský himself, were Jewish – were tried and executed for anti-state conspiracy. This trial was the Czech version of the string of show trials of the 1940s and 1950s which brought Stalinism to all countries handed over to the Soviets. Their aim was to instate people loyal to Moscow in the national communist parties and oust local communist leaders who refused to follow blindly the Moscow line. Throughout Eastern Europe, this was a period of terror when thousands of people were sent to labour camps, while the higher-profile leaders were sentenced to death on trumped-up charges.

[17] Jana Wild has drawn my attention to this disparity. Private communication.

warp of semi-enforced obscurity into a changed socio-political landscape. In the aftermath of the Holocaust, its performance tradition, as developed in particular in West Germany, had changed, especially in the representation of Shylock and in the perception of the play's genre as comedy.[18]

Of course, the former East European countries had war histories and guilts different from Germany's, but in practically all of them there had been crimes against Jews during the war period. However, since the play returned to the stages relatively late, and the world it encountered was in a new political convulsion, it addressed current concerns. Historian of the Balkans Maria Todorova defines the aftermath of the political changes initiated in 1989 as a process during which East Europeans were confronted with 'Eastern Europe as legacy', common to all of them in spite of other historical differences, or geographical position.[19] Among the elements of this common legacy were the drastic economic reconfiguration of society, leading to loss of status for vast swathes of the population (which became a fertile ground for conspiracy theories and any conceivable form of divisive Othering), destabilized institutional structures, and the emergence of new media.[20] Territorial divisions created uncertainties about identity which stoked up populist ideologies; ethnic tensions spawned 'aliens' on a daily basis; media frenzy fogged meaningful discourse. Stable political entities, like the Soviet Union, Czechoslovakia, and Yugoslavia, disappeared from the map, with often cataclysmic effects for their populations. For the first time since World War II, war showed its ugly face in Europe, and is still brewing on its edges.

Positive counter-processes were also at work. Many post-communist countries joined the EU and re-geared their legislative systems in accordance with its rules, which involve the implementation of laws against ethnic, racial and gender discrimination within a democratic framework. During the last decade, however, a backlash of conservative and nationalistic ideologies has brought to power parties that try to row back on democratic principles. Dealing with the 'East European' legacy has led to a rather mixed bag of co-existing contradictory, even toxic, attitudes.

When it reappeared, *The Merchant of Venice* took root in a reality of unbridled greed, instability and moral collapse. Later on, it confronted the resurrection of dormant patriarchal ideologies and xenophobia of many stripes, those time-honoured alternatives for 'resuscitating' society to 'stability and health' through the controls of fear. The post-Holocaust re-shaping of *Merchant* became the received model to which new theatrical styles brought disquieting abrasiveness. Homophobia, xenophobia and gender issues came to the fore, along with a renewed focus on anti-Semitism, while the memory of the Holocaust that had 'damaged' the comedy remained as a subtext. East European *Merchant*s project intolerant, violent, loveless, modern worlds where Shylocks mostly do not survive and where no one is a sympathetic character. It is a play about rupture, trauma, even hopelessness, articulating the 'form and pressure' (*Hamlet*, 3.2.24) of a social transition.

During the last twenty-five years, the play has experienced something of a performance renaissance: Hungary has had sixteen productions, Poland fourteen, and the numbers are changing as I write. Bulgaria, Romania, Serbia and Russia have had fewer, but they have defined important moments in their transitions. In the following pages, I look at productions from different countries in relation to their particular contexts. The arrangement is chronological, a chronology that to some extent traces the fluctuation of processes across this period.

Directed in 1992 by Zdravko Mitkov at the Ivan Vazov National Theatre in Sofia, *The Merchant of Venice* was a play about the here and now of the

---

[18] Manfred Pfister, 'The Merchant of Venice', in *Shakespeare Handbuch*, ed. Ina Schabert (Stuttgart, 2000), pp. 411–17.

[19] Maria Todorova, 'Re-imagining the Balkans', in *Welcome to the Desert of Post-Socialism: Radical Politics after Yugoslavia*, ed. Srećko Horvat and Igor Štiks (London, 2015), pp. 85–102; p. 94.

[20] Marcus Stan, 'Postcommunism and its rocky road to transition: the case of Romania', in *An Atomizing Theatre*, ed. Jerzy Limon and Agnieszka Żukowska (Gdansk, 2014), p. 133.

giddy early years of post-communism. Seeing the present through the lens of a rarely performed Shakespeare play about greed and wealth re-distribution, after a 54-year absence from the stage, was refreshing and well timed.[21] In an inter-view, the director shared that anti-Semitism had not been on his mind, since he did not think the subject was relevant in the Bulgarian context.[22] Instead, he saw other, contemporary, implications. According to Evgenia Pancheva, this production captured a moment characterized by 'a paranoid fear of manipulation', 'conflicting legislative ideol-ogies', and 'debate[s] on property and the morality of confiscation and restitution'. In the flux of the early 1990s, it allowed for the re-enactment of 'the triumph of law and the collapse of justice'.[23]

At that time, Bulgarians knew that, though the country had been a German ally during World War II, the planned deportation of 48,000 Bulgarian Jews in 1943 had been prevented.[24] Helping Jewish com-patriots was part of the lived experience of many people in the older generation and was well publicized.[25] So, when Stefan Danailov's handsome Shylock walked the boards as an Orthodox Jew, he presented a sign that did not jog historic memories – reviews tend to read the production outside the context of anti-Semitism, local or otherwise, while all note its contemporary social pathos. Mitkov's Venice was a modern city dominated by a Coca-Cola sign perched on the glass façade of a high-rise that dwarfed the portico of Shylock's home. The city buzzed with sharp-suited young fortune-seekers, ruthless *arrivistes* with whom the old-fashioned money-lender dealt with a queasy super-iority. Religion gave Shylock backbone and moral anchor, all qualities that the young men lacked, and compensated for with a general boorishness. For his part, Shylock was not intimidated by this new lot and was trying to do business as usual. Furthermore, textual cuts toned down the religious subtext and Shylock's own hatred. His soliloquy in 1.3, the Duke's disparaging remarks at the beginning of 4.1, Jessica's desire to 'Become a Christian' (2.3.21), as well as her worries about salvation in 3.5, were cut, and she was not referred to as an 'infidel' in Belmont (3.2.216).[26]

Instead, the play's focus was on the greed and manipulation permeating the structures of friend-ship, family, legislature, and the state. The casket mystery was cracked by a serial con in which Lancelot impersonated Morocco, and Gratiano impersonated Aragon, to whom Bassanio had whispered: 'The golden casket has already been tried.'[27] The trial scene was an apotheosis of the tragedy of an individual caught in the clutches of a system capable of devising tailor-made legislation in favour of a powerful clique. Shylock was a man hopelessly trying to challenge its implacable arro-gance with a pathetic pen-knife. Conversion was a demeaning insult from Antonio, who could not have cared less about religion, but who saw an opportunity to humiliate his enemy. At the end, Shylock looked like a man who had had a heart-attack. Critics noted the strong audience identifi-cation with him, as the only character of integrity, defeated by underhand twisting of the law. Shylock

21 The last pre-war performance was in 1938, in a Reinhardt-influenced adaptation, whose thrust was to debunk the idea of the venality of the Jew. See Alexander Shurbanov and Boika Sokolova, *Painting Shakespeare Red: An East-European Appropriation* (Newark, 2001), pp. 76–82.

22 Boika Sokolova, personal interview with Zdravko Mitkov, December 2015.

23 Evgenia Pancheva, 'Nothings, Merchants, Tempests: trimming Shakespeare for the 1992 Bulgarian stage', in *Shakespeare in the New Europe*, ed. Michael Hattaway, Boika Sokolova, and Derek Roper (Sheffield, 1994), pp. 247–60.

24 The literature on the subject is considerable. See Esther Benbassa and Aron Rodrigue, *The Jews of the Balkans: The Judeo-Spanish Community, 15th–20th Centuries* (Oxford, 1995), pp. 173–9; Tzvetan Todorov, *The Fragility of Goodness: Why Bulgarian Jews Survived the Holocaust* (London, 2001).

25 Apart from publicizing the help of individual citizens, in the post-World War II period the Communist Party claimed it alone played a role in saving the Jews. In fact, the decisive role belonged to committed local councillors, to several parliamentarians, and personally to Mr Alexander Peshev, MP. Leaders of the Bulgarian Orthodox Church also played a crucial part in stopping the trains. See documents in Todorov, *The Fragility of Goodness*.

26 Quotations from *Merchant* refer to *William Shakespeare: The Complete Works*, ed. Stanley Wells *et al.*, 2nd edn (Oxford, 2005).

27 Pancheva, 'Nothings, Merchants, Tempests', p. 252.

was us, the audience, who were struggling to survive the whirlwinds of wild capitalism, lashing with impunity through their lives.

Belmont in Act 5 was a cold white space, suffused in Chekhovian gloom, where a heavily pregnant Jessica bickered with a disgruntled Lorenzo. In a finely understated manner, Mitkov hinted at another perfidy underlying the future of the new families. Portia and Nerissa, who used to share a bath, were involved with each other and engineered the saving of their unromantic marriages as a compromise necessary to sustain a public face. Interestingly, this was not picked up in the reviews – apart from the presence of the bath – which is typical of the relative blindness to such issues at the time, and of the dominant preoccupation with greed, legal corruption, and manipulation.

There have been no Bulgarian *Merchant*s since. However, in 2013, a huge hole opened up in the comforting story of the fate of Bulgarian Jews when two scholars published documents related to deportations from the territories where Bulgaria was an occupying force during World War II, the lists of property taken away from those who were not deported, and that property's re-distribution.[28] An obfuscated past came to light in the year of the seventieth anniversary of the Holocaust. The political response to the revelations, however, was rather muted. Not only did the government shy away from lending support to the publication, but the declaration that passed through parliament on the occasion of the anniversary tip-toed around the complicity of the pre-war administration.[29] In perfectly good faith, the 1992 production and its reviewers had seen the play through a different, contemporary lens. Perhaps some further *Merchant* will reach into this as-yet-unvisited, painful area or grapple with the plight of the refugees currently crossing into the country, or with the disturbing rise of nauseating xenophobia. It will be an indication of the painfully slow evolution of a functioning civic society.

In the late 1990s, when domestic politics across eastern Europe swung to the right, productions started to engage with the resurgence of anti-Semitism and conservative attitudes towards gender and race. Robert Alföldi's 1998 Budapest

production provides a good example. A programme note describes the context in which it appeared as a time when 'all the hatred and opposition that had been suppressed for forty years was brought to the surface, and minorities, such as Jews and homosexuals, became the target of . . . the hatred that [had] accumulated'.[30] Alföldi did not seek to recall Hungary's past, marked by the deportation and death of hundreds of thousands of its Jewish citizens, but to engage the audience with its here and now.[31] His ground-breaking *Merchant* at the Tivoli Theatre homed in on the depravities unleashed by the transition. Like Mitkov, he was concerned with the way greed dehumanizes society, but he also forged a connection between violence, anti-Semitism and homophobia, and the role of the media in whipping up hatred.[32] Alföldi

---

[28] *The Deportation of the Jews from Western Thrace, Vardar Macedonia and Pirot*, ed. Nadya Danova and Roumen Avramov (Sofia, 2013); Roumen Avramov, 'Salvation' and Fall (Sofia, 2012). On the ambiguities in the politics of the current Bulgarian government, see Roumen Avramov, interview by Hristo Butsev, *Liberalen pregled*, 25 August 2013, www.librev.com/index.php/discussion-bulgaria-publisher/2153–2013-08-25-13–02-10.

[29] Here is the problematic statement: 'We denounce this criminal act, undertaken by Hitler's command and express our regrets for the fact that *the local Bulgarian administration had not been in a position to stop this act.*' See 'Declaration', 8 March 2013, http://shalompr.org/parlamentt-prie-edinodushno-deklaraciya-po-povod-70-godishninata-ot-spasyavaneto-na-blgarskite-evrei-i-pochitane-na-pametta-na-zhertvite-na-holokosta.

[30] Programme note for the production at the Newmark Theatre, Portland Centre Stage, Oregon, 10–29 February 2004, quoted in Michael W. Shurgot, review of The Merchant of Venice, *Shakespeare Bulletin* 22.2 (2004), 98.

[31] On the fate of Hungarian Jews, see Randolph L. Braham, *The Politics of Genocide: The Holocaust in Hungary* (Detroit, 2000). It has interesting chapters on the reactions in several European countries to the events unfolding in 1944.

[32] In my reconstruction of the production, I have used several sources: Aniko Szucs, 'The relativization of victim and perpetrator in the Hungarian productions of *The Merchant of Venice* and *Mein Kampf*', in *Jews and Theater in an Intercultural Context*, ed. Edna Nahshon (Leiden, 2012), pp. 297–318; Karin Magaldi, review of The Merchant of Venice, *Theatre Journal* 56 (2004), 496–8; Shurgot, review of *The Merchant of Venice*.

also embraced the abrasive theatricality typical of the 1990s. Aggressive and discomforting on many levels, his production provocatively drew the audience into moments of complicity with the onstage acts of anti-Semitism.[33]

Aniko Szucs aptly sums up Alföldi's approach as revealing the *process* that transforms a group of modern young people into thugs. He showed how aggression, humiliation and hatred create the Other, who, 'although in this case ... a Jew, as has been the case many times in Hungarian history, ... could just as well have been a Gypsy, black, or a foreigner'.[34] The performance also suggested that the dehumanizing of society worked both ways, by 'relativizing' the positions of victim and perpetrator, though the cumulative effect of the indignities suffered by Shylock justified his cruelty. Not only that: his lynching and death at the end inevitably brought to mind the Holocaust.[35]

Alföldi's rocking, 'yuppie', Venice was fast, furious, homophobic and bigoted. Shylock and Antonio were two successful young businessmen with no reason to be enemies other than the anti-Semitic hang-ups of the city milieu and its venality. Slighting and humiliating the Jewish merchant was an act of brainless ostracism, which, stage by stage, changed him into a heartless and willing murderer. By 4.1, Shylock and Antonio were mirror images of each other: both stripped to the waist for the cutting of flesh, their common humanity in full view. Yet, they were emblematically marked as mutually irreconcilable – a chasm signalled by Antonio's tattoo and Shylock's thuggishly shaven head under his yarmulke. Though the production followed the text, it did not avoid death. Shylock was brutally attacked and beaten to death in the courtroom, with the events transmitted on TV.

Nor did the rapacious world of the modern-day city allow room for conventional romance. As in the Bulgarian production, the contest was a con. Bassanio got the right casket by changing disguises, which allowed him to perform ugly stereotypes of Otherness. He, of course, knew nothing about value, apart from monetary value. In a final display of aggressive cupidity, the fear that the lost rings might jeopardize their hard-won 'golden fleece' drove the

two husbands to rough up their wives before a horrified Portia could produce the explanatory letters. Earlier, Lorenzo had raped Jessica. Shylock's dead body remained on the stage throughout 5.1.

A barrage of in-your-face images of violence, male nudity, sexual intercourse, along with warped and amplified versions of on-stage events, dwarfed moments of direct expression of emotion and empathy. Shylock's pained speech in 3.1 was paralleled by distorted anti-Semitic images of his face on the screens, provoking disturbing audience laughter at the display of racism.[36]

When his success elevated him to the directorship of the National Theatre in Budapest, Alföldi brought to the table an agenda of contemporary urgency, which characterized his 1998 *Merchant*: 'to hold up a mirror, to make us see ourselves ... to make us WANT to see what is ... here, now'.[37] In spite of his enormous success during his term, he became a target for the far right and was bombarded with homophobic and anti-Semitic slurs. In what has been described as ensuing culture wars, the government tried to define an ideological and aesthetic framework within which national cultural institutions, including the National Theatre, should function.[38] As part of a robust public response, the Hungarian Theatre Critics'

---

[33] Szucs, 'The relativization of victim and perpetrator'; Magaldi, review of *The Merchant of Venice*.

[34] Szucs, 'The relativization of victim and perpetrator', p. 308.

[35] Szucs, 'The relativization of victim and perpetrator', pp. 306–8.

[36] Magaldi (review of *The Merchant of Venice*), Shurgot (review of *The Merchant of Venice*), and Szucs, 'The relativization of victim and perpetrator', all pay attention to this moment.

[37] Quoted after Natália Pikli, 'Politics, prejudice and text in recent theatrical productions of *The Merchant of Venice* in Hungary', a paper presented at the ESRA Congress, Gdansk, 27–31 July 2017. I wish to thank the author for allowing me to use her work in manuscript.

[38] The situation is strangely reminiscent of similar attempts through the nineteenth century to police the play, discussed in Katalin Agnes Bartha, '*The Merchant of Venice* in Pest and Cluj (Kolozsvár) during the Habsburg neo-absolutism', in *Shakespeare and Tyranny: Regimes of Reading in Europe and Beyond*, ed. Keith Gregor (Cambridge, 2014), pp. 77–104.

Association came out in Alföldi's defence, against the accusations of deviancy and treason, and the smearing of his work as 'obscene, pornographic, anti-national, and anti-Hungarian'.[39] Many marched in support, but his contract was not renewed.[40]

In the meantime, Hungarian productions of *The Merchant of Venice* have proliferated, and many of them sustain the alarming now-ness of Alföldi's approach. By returning again and again to Shakespeare's 'offensive' play, even by 'offending' with it, the theatre continues to challenge the dangerous divisive phobias which have raised their heads in politics and society.[41]

Almost a decade after the collapse of the Soviet Union, two productions appeared back-to-back on the Moscow stage in 1999–2000.[42] At the end of a decade marked by the rise of oligarchs, the return of *Merchant* coincided with yet another transformation: Russia's turning again into a more introverted society. In the few months separating the plays, Vladimir Putin quietly stepped into the shoes of President Boris Yeltsin, the Second Chechen War was in full force, the NATO bombings of Yugoslavia fostered Russian isolationism, and the fight for control over the media intensified.[43]

In both cases, the impulse for mounting the play came from people who had experienced displacement. The suggestion for the production, directed by Andrey Zhitinkin on the Mossovet stage, came from Mikhail Kozakov, a prominent actor whose Shylock announced his return to Russia after a sojourn in Israel.[44] The other production was created by Robert Sturua, the most important Soviet director working in the post-Soviet period, who, as a Georgian in Moscow, was a foreigner in what used to be his country. He brought to the Et-Cetera theatre a cut and re-assembled version of the play entitled *Shylock*, billing it as an exploration of 'the irrational impulse of xenophobia'.[45]

The critical discourse triggered by the first production inevitably addressed the reasons for the long absence of the play. Explanations varied. Some suggested that it was due to the frequent use of the word *zhid*, a derogatory Russian usage

---

39 See 'Letter from the Hungarian Theatre Critics' Association', *Hungarian Watch* 30 (November 2010), https://hungarian watch.wordpress.com/voices-from-hungary/letter-from-the -hungarian-theatre-critics-association.

40 One of many illuminating articles about government and other pressures on the Hungarian press and theatres, and about Holocaust denial at the time referred to above, is Philipp Oehmke, 'Hungary's right-wing war on culture', *Spiegel Online*, 16 December 2011, www.spiegel.de/interna tional/europe/revanchism-in-budapest-hungary-s-right-wing -war-on-culture-a-803865.html. See also Walter Mayr, 'The Goulash archipelago: EU remains silent as Hungary veers off course', *Spiegel Online*, 19 August 2011, www .spiegel.de/international/europe/the-goulash-archipelago-eu- remains-silent-as-hungary-veers-off-course-a-780794.html.

41 While it is a member of the EU and is working towards the restoration of Jewish communities, Hungary is also experi- encing the rise of fascist ideologies. Jobbik, an ultra- nationalist party aligning itself with the pre-war fascists, has gained a number of parliamentary seats. To the question, put to one of its leaders, of whether Hungary should apologise for its role in the Holocaust, Marton Gyongyosi, a spokesperson for Jobbik, responded: 'Me, should I say sorry for this, when 70 years later I am still reminded ... every hour about it? Let's get over it, for Christ's sake. I find this question outrageous.' See Orlando Radice, 'Hungary's far-right: Jews not welcome here', *The Jewish Chronicle*, 2 February 2012, www.thejc.com/news/world-news /62968/hungarys-far-right-jews-not-welcome-here.

42 The first post-Soviet production was directed by Abu Hassan in Kazan, the capital of the Tartar region, in 1993. Entitled *Shylock*, it featured a Mafioso-like modern Venice and, by including local Tartar actors, focused on xenophobia. On this, see Vera Shamina, 'Shakespeare's play The Merchant of Venice on the international and home stage', *Bridge: Language and Culture* 225 (2010), 1–13, http://repository.kpfu .ru/?p_id=23824. I have also come across a record of a 1993 film, *Shylock*, directed by Boris Blank, but I have not been able to obtain any information about it beyond a single Wikipedia reference. In the history of Russian reception, starting with Stanislavski, the play is often given the name of its Jewish character.

43 Arakady Ostrovsky, *The Invention of Russia: The Journey from Gorbachov's Freedom to Putin's War* (London, 2015).

44 Zhitinkin's world was one of oligarchs, of whom Shylock was one, which partly explains the forcefulness of his court appearance. Zhitinkin is the first director I am aware of to have turned the choice of caskets into a reality TV show.

45 Oleg Zintsov, 'An interpretation of dreams', *Vedomosti*, 25 April 2000, quotes Sturua: https://et-cetera.ru/press/ review/tolkovanie-snovideniy.

for 'Jew'.[46] Others expressed an unease prompted by fears of religious extremists – a particular group had just been banned – and reported a swastika smeared on the theatre poster along with catcalls during the first performance, which upset Kozakov.[47] Yet, for many, the excitement was symptomatic of another problem: the malaise of ingrained Russian xenophobia vis-à-vis the current ethnic conflicts in Russia.[48] Even those who criticized Zhitinkin's production found in it contemporary resonances going beyond the relationship between Christians and Jews. The implacable khaki-uniformed Shylock of its end was likened to 'a terrorist from the Caucasus, taking a justified cruel revenge';[49] one critic referred to him as Shamil (a typical Chechen name).[50] Some openly questioned the claims of tactfulness as an explanation for the long absence of *The Merchant of Venice* and hailed its appearance as a sign of growing civic maturity and as a channel for a public discourse about Russia's past and present. A critic stated that the events on the stage enjoined the audience to think about the rewards 'we reap by searching for . . . [Others] in the crowd and by trying to conceal, yet again, prosaic ends with lofty religious arguments and state interests'.[51] The idea that open debate is the antidote to poisonous nationalisms is voiced by others, too.[52] Similarly, Sturua's *Shylock* was applauded as an act of courage, enabling the theatre to speak about the irrationality of hatred fuelled by the parcelling of the country.[53]

Sturua's trademark metaphoric theatricality, his love for outlandish devices and the absurd, the unstable, dream-like worlds he creates add up to a well-honed instrument for probing the irrational. As is his wont, he bent the text to his needs through deep cuts and re-arrangements, which turned the play into an eternally repetitive black comedy. Through juxtapositions of word and image, musical cues, rhythmical movement, signature gestures, emblematic properties, comic gags, and a fantasy-space made of familiar objects, he created a surrealist version of Shakespeare's play. Trees blossomed over computer screens; inside and outside were reversible; characters materialized from unexpected corners; iconic images out of René

Magritte's paintings – bowler hat, apple, cloud – were used as stylistic cues. Characters were puppet-like. As in a *noir* mystery, a Borsalino-wearing Mafioso – an elusive, menacing manipulator – hovered in the background and controlled properties and TV screens. Costuming was modern, but Shylock and the anonymous manipulator were dressed in a 1930s style. Another absurdist touch was the presence of an internal audience of ever more visible full-sized animal dummies – cow, pig, and goat – seemingly frozen in wonder at the sapience of humans.

Alexandr Kalyagin's Chaplinesque, bowler-hatted Shylock negotiated the various obstacles of space and plot with the rotund charm of a roly-poly toy, bouncing back after every hit. And hit he was, and often. Though he was a well-heeled gentleman who fitted in, the darkly comic logic of the production made him into a perpetual scapegoat, mocked and beaten after Jessica's elopement, then beaten again after the trial and mounted backwards on a cow in a Georgian ritual of shaming.[54]

Theatricality was the key offered to the audience from the very start when a silent, sceptical clown

[46] Yampolskaya, 'Mikhail Kozakov's Jewish question'. Published on http://mossoveta.ru/truppa/actors/ilyin/ 1943, p. 1. Both productions used T. L Shchepkina-Kuprenik's translation, made in 1937 and reworked in the 1950s.

[47] Yampolskaya, 'Mikhail Kozakov's Jewish question'.

[48] Dina Kinarskaya, 'Shylock transformed', *Moskovskie novosti*, December 1999, 21–7; Roman Dolzhanskii, 'A play about un-returned credit', *Kommersant*, 25 April 2000, www.smotr .ru/1999/1999_etc_shey.htm.

[49] Pavel Rudnev, 'Shylock against the Carnival', *Nezavisimaya gazeta*, 10 December 1999, www.smotr.ru/pressa/rec/mos sovet_vc.htm#ng.

[50] Natalia Kaminskaya, 'A Shylock whose name could be Shamil', *Kultura* (December 1999), 9–15.

[51] Kaminskaya, 'A Shylock whose name could be Shamil'.

[52] Dina Kinarskaya, 'When there's a problem, just don't mention it: Robert Sturua's Shylock', *Vremya MN*, 26 April 2000, https://www.et-cetera.ru/press/review/u-kogo-chego-bolit-tot-o-tom-ne-govorit.

[53] Zintsov, 'An interpretation of dreams'.

[54] Natalia Kaminskaya, 'There's no justice here on earth. Nor up above, either', *Kultura*, 27 April 2000, www.et-cetera.ru /press/review/net-pravdy-na-zemle-no-pravdy-net-i-vyshe

lifted up the curtain to the strange reality where Antonio sat on a low platform in the middle of a stock market office, daydreaming about Bassanio. Little by little, through the agency of the manipulator, the daydream acquired a reality. From a trap door, he handed out objects that triggered actions: a magic wand to conjure up Portia and Shylock; a quill for signing the bond; long-forgotten religious attire. As the wand changed hands, power relations shifted. At the end, Portia wielded it with relish before a soporific representative of the law, but lost control and the courtroom erupted in violence.

Sturua's production homed in on the ways religion can be manipulated for retaliation. Jewishness, as a visible difference, was 'thrust upon' Shylock. After Jessica's flight, a moth-eaten tallith was delivered through the trapdoor, and the manipulator handed Shylock a menorah, thus linking revenge and religion. Nor was Antonio a Christian engaged in a rusty ancient grudge. He sought solace in Oriental meditation, which diffused the opposition Christian/Jew. The single line given to Antonio, 'Let him presently become a Christian' (a version of 4.1.384), was drowned in the mayhem of the courtroom. The men who beat the Jew were the young 'Christians' of Bassanio's gaggle of friends, sporting guns, crosses, and designer clothes. Disguised as bank robbers for Jessica's elopement, they hastened to hang a cross around her neck, much to Lorenzo's distress.

Kalyagin's masterfully balanced acting oscillated between man and clown, creating an emotionally malleable character across a spectrum of states ranging from comic absurdity to heart-rending pathos.

Instead of Act 5, a *da capo* ending brought Antonio and Shylock back to the stage. Wrapped in his Oriental coat, Antonio settled down to daydream about Bassanio. Smart in his three-piece suit, Shylock slowly appeared through a brightly lit back door, like a cloud from a Magritte painting.[55] The two men looked at each other as if wondering whether they were in or out of their roles, whether the play had really ended, or whether they had to perform it once again. Sturua's finale underscored the absurdly repetitive nature of the antagonism.

A collage of lines from 5.1 gave Antonio and Shylock closing statements, which meant the same, but sounded as a disagreement: 'What a night!', exclaimed Shylock. 'This night, methinks, is but the daylight sick', responded Antonio (5.1.124). 'No', objected Shylock, ''Tis a day / Such as the day is when the sun is hid' (5.1.125–6). The manipulator lit up the TV screens with an image of the single candle burning on Shylock's balcony while the menorah lay on the floor; a chorus intoned, 'Oh Heavenly Salvation'. As at the end of a Beckett play, unanswered – perhaps unanswerable – questions stood before the bewildered characters and spectators. Is a resolution ever possible? Who is in control of our lives? Who are the 'dark forces' of division? *Quo vadis*, Russia?

Reflecting on the play fifteen years after these productions, Aleksey Bartoshevich noted its new disappearance from the Russian stage and concluded that this was symptomatic of the acuteness of national problems.[56] In the meantime, *Shylock* has received numerous accolades at festivals and continues to live in a free-access HD recording on the theatre site. As Robert Sturua noted, 'to be able to talk about evil is to fight evil'.[57] His theatre does just that.[58]

Just like Sturua's production, Egon Savin's 2004 *Merchant of Venice* closed a long, forty-year gap on the stage of Yugoslav Dramatic Theatre and, just like the Russian production, it appeared in the aftermath of ethnic wars.[59] According to political scientist Jovan Byford, the early 2000s in

---

55 It reminded the author of Magritte's 1939 *Victory*.
56 Aleksey Bartoshevich, 'Judeophobes consider the play philo-Semitic, Judeophiles – anti-Semitic. Four centuries of Shylock's wanderings in the streets', *Kommersant.ru*, 17 April 2015.
57 Kinarskaya, 'When there's a problem, just don't mention it: Robert Sturua's *Shylock*'.
58 I have since located one further production in Russia. In 2011, the play was directed by Roman Samgin in Perm. It played to moderate reviews, suggesting an eclectic approach. I owe a special debt of gratitude to Professor Galina Rebel from the State Pedagogical University in Perm for her generous answers to my questions.
59 The production was still playing in 2017, thirteen years later.

Serbia were characterized by an unexpected rise in anti-Semitic hate crime, rather unusual in a country with low levels of anti-Semitism, despite the variety of ideologies of hate directed against other groups. Byford attributes this sea change to a combination of factors, including the rise of anti-Semitism in the West and the rise of local inward-looking political conservatism and clerical nationalism. The latter, among other things, is aggressively homophobic. After the collapse of Yugoslavia and the ousting of Slobodan Milošević, conspiracy theories that earlier served to explain the NATO bombings as an Anglo-American-Jewish plot, became obsessed with the enemy within.[60] Unlike the productions discussed so far, this one was not set in a contemporary city, but in a self-indulgent 1930s Venice on the brink of fascism, thus enabling a link between past and present. Predrag Ejdus's Shylock was a humiliated and exasperated man, trying to restore his self-respect and dignity, something that the turn of events in Venice would not allow to anyone who was different. In Savin's version, ethnic, sexual and gender difference abounded – along with a gay Antonio and bisexual Bassanio, Solanio and Salarino were a gay couple, enjoying their lifestyle. The casting of a male actor, Dragan Mićanović, who masterfully performed Portia as a woman, underscored the made-up nature of difference. Though Mićanović's character sustained a sense of the comic and romantic, the end of the play made it clear that the xenophobic and homophobic rot had turned dangerously political, and comedy could not triumph. A directorial intervention revealed disturbing developments on the edges of the golden world. Dressed in the uniform of an Italian fascist, the servant Lancelot, the man from the depths of Venetian society, emerged as a force to be reckoned with. He molested Jessica and threw gay Antonio out of the villa. Even Portia was powerless to protect him; the future under the likes of this new man of power boded ill for all.[61] The real enemy within was not the stranger, but one of Venice's own. Zorica Bećanović-

Nikolić sums up the production as revealing how, 'in a religiously, racially and nationally unified community with a clearly dominant national, or religious denomination', anyone belonging to a minority has a problem.[62] Savin's production was acclaimed as a reminder of the past and a warning for the future.[63] Like many of his East European colleagues, he believes that '[t]he role of theatre is to destroy prejudice' – though, as he admits, 'by its very nature, it cannot change the world'.[64] He is right on both counts.

In post-1989 Poland, *The Merchant of Venice* is an often-performed play, which makes choosing a single example difficult. However, Krzysztof Warlikowski's work is hard to bypass, not only because his theatre has achieved international fame but, more importantly, because it is indicative of the road travelled by his audience in engaging in new ideas.[65] According to Grzegorz Niziołek, Warlikowski's theatre 'exposes what is perceived as different, other and even hostile in Polish culture', and its impact goes beyond the discussion of aesthetic issues.[66]

No less significantly, his approach to *The Merchant of Venice* in *African Tales from Shakespeare* (2011) is radically transformative. Like Sturua's *Shylock*, *African Tales* stresses the absurd,

[60] Jovan Byford, 'Anti-Semitism and the Christian Right in post-Milošević Yugoslavia: from conspiracy theory to hate crime', *Internet Journal of Criminology* (2003), 1–27.

[61] Ivan Medenica, 'Portia, a master class in acting', *Vreme*, 12 February 2004, www.vreme.com/cms/view.php?id=367866.

[62] Zorica Bećanović-Nikolić, 'Interpretation as existential choice in *The Merchant of Venice* and as aesthetic and ethical statement in theatre productions', paper presented at the ESRA Congress, Gdansk, 29 July – 3 August 2017. With thanks to the author for allowing me to quote from her manuscript.

[63] Vladimir Stamenković, 'A radical modernization', *Theatre*, 12 February 2004, n.p.

[64] Egon Savin, interview by Aida Tipura, 'Theatre destroys prejudice', *Nezavisnenovine*, 8 June 2009, www.nezavisne.com/magazin/jet-set/Egon-Savin.

[65] Grzegorz Niziołek, *Warlikowski: Extra Ecclesiam*, trans. Soren Gauger (Frankfurt, 2015), p. 10.

[66] Niziołek, *Warlikowski*, p. 9.

uses a rewritten text, and has had considerable international exposure, having been commissioned for a series of cultural events promoting a European culture beyond national borders.[67] In this post-dramatic reworking, *The Merchant of Venice* is re-scripted by Piotr Gruszczyński and collated with other Shakespeare plots and non-Shakespeare texts.[68] For Warlikowski, Shakespeare is someone who 'refus[es] to compromise' and who tries to 'describe the entire world, rather than a mere fragment of reality'.[69] In *African Tales*, Shakespeare is 'material', a source of stories embedded in European consciousness; it is also a 'piece of coal', in Peter Brook's sense – a fuel for uncompromising theatrical craftsmanship.[70] The result is a multi-layered, complex, controversial and intellectually intense five-hour rollercoaster. Throughout his career, Warlikowski has sought to engage with homophobia, Jewishness and the endemic conservatism surrounding gender.[71] This particular production also entered another debate: the national soul-searching related to Poland's relationship with its Jews during the Holocaust, a debate fuelled by a 2001 book, entitled *Neighbours*. It brought to light the suppressed history of a 1941 murder of Jews in the small Polish town of Jedwabne, which was perpetrated by local men,[72] and helped to unlock memories of similar incidents, during and after the war, which were buried in the national consciousness.[73] The traumatic legacy of World War II, particularly devastating in this country, has made the subject of Polish guilt difficult to discuss.[74] Still, though slowly, successive governments have addressed it. On the sixtieth anniversary of the Jedwabne tragedy, President Aleksander Kwaśniewski spoke about responsibility, reconciliation and forgiveness.[75] *African Tales*, which coincided with the seventieth anniversary, artistically grapples with the Polish Holocaust legacy, contemporary anti-Semitism and gender problems.[76]

Aleksandra Sakowska has written brilliantly about the 'liquidity' of Warlikowksi's theatre, of the richly suggestive, theoretically complex web of ideas behind his work, and of the receptiveness of Polish audiences to it.[77] I shall discuss only three moments of the section that is based on *The Merchant of Venice*:

Shylock's decision to demand the payment of the bond, Antonio's speech in court, and the resolution of the Portia plot.

For the moment of Shylock's decision, Warlikowski created a web of images from popular culture, which transcend the narrowly national. He achieved this by a visual gesture to Art

---

[67] The project includes theatres from Luxembourg, France, Belgium, Germany, Italy, Portugal, and Finland.

[68] *African Tales from Shakespeare* includes *Othello*, *The Merchant of Venice*, *King Lear*, an adaptation of J. M. Coetzee's *Summertime*, and video materials. Early in his career, in 1994, Warlikowski directed the play in Toruń with a focus on the tragic solitude of Jew and homosexual, both 'legal but unaccepted' Others in a bigoted modern society, as defined by Krystyna Duniec in 'Sposoby na Shylocka' [Ways to do Shylock], *Dialog* (September 2008), 38–52; p. 47.

[69] *Theatre Notebook*, 2003, quoted in Monika Mokrzycka-Pokora, 'Krzysztof Warlikowski', *Culture* (February 2004), http://culture.pl/en/artist/krzysztof-warlikowski.

[70] I am referring here to Peter Brook, *The Empty Space* (London, 1968).

[71] The 'black protests' against the anti-abortion law are only the currently visible tip of a rather large iceberg. See Christina Davies, 'Women to go on strike in Poland in protest at planned abortion law', *Guardian*, 3 October 2016, https://www.theguardian.com/world/2016/oct/02/women-to-go-on-strike-in-poland-abortion-law. On the history of anti-feminist developments in Poland, see Katheryn Detwiler and Ann Snitow, 'Gender trouble in Poland', *Dissent* (Fall 2016), https://www.dissentmagazine.org/article/gender-trouble-poland-pis-abortion-ban.

[72] Jan T. Gross, *Neighbours: The Destruction of the Jewish Community in Jedwabne, Poland* (Sejny, 2000).

[73] Antony Marcel, 'Jedwabne and reviled victims', *TLS*, Letters to the Editor, 10 June 2016, p. 6.

[74] See Piotr Gontarczyk, 'Jan Tomasz Gross "is no historian"', Radio Poland, 10 July 2016, www.thenews.pl/1/9/Artykul/260790.

[75] President Aleksander Kwaśniewski's speech is widely available. In spite of the unevenness of the processes, concerted efforts have been made to restore Jewish communities and place the discourse about the past in the framework of education.

[76] The Polish Parliament has passed a law that imposes a prison sentence for ascribing Holocaust atrocities to the Polish nation or state.

[77] Aleksandra Sakowska, '"Liquid Shakespeare": adapting Shakespeare's works in twenty-first-century Poland' (Ph.D. thesis, King's College London, 2014). I would also wish to thank Aleksandra for the DVD of the production at Nowy Teatr in Warsaw.

Spiegelman's comic book *Maus*, which relates Spiegelman's Polish father's experiences in a concentration camp. Its – now iconic – animal images portray the Germans as pigs and the Jews as mice. In addition to this memorial imagery, Warlikowski's stage layout enabled him to handle simultaneously different temporalities, a feature typical of the cartoon strip. For Spiegelman, the strip is a spatially organized time sequence, where each box presents a different moment, allowing for different temporalities to be observed simultaneously.[78] In the production, characters step from one scene, or story, into another, within a horizontally arranged space, divided into sections – not unlike frames – which allow access to simultaneously existing realities. On the occasion in question, Shylock, a butcher by profession, is confronted by two half-naked men wearing pigs' heads, who enter a 'frame' he shares with a *Maus*-headed Tubal. Unceremoniously, the pigs declare that they are 'neighbours' who have arrived to celebrate Jessica's elopement. On the table – a property central to Warlikowski – where in an earlier scene Shylock plied his trade and the bond was agreed, the pigs engage in a lewd enactment of Jessica's imagined sexual experiences. In a separate frame, set downstage by the audience, Antonio delivers a rabid anti-Semitic diatribe. Simultaneously, a line of *Maus* characters is projected onto the back wall. The audience is hit by a triple set of images showcasing the unspeakable vulgarity of the pigs, Antonio's close-range anti-Semitic rant, and a string of memorial Holocaust images, with Shylock inside the hallucinatory blend. Co-existent events/times produce an intensely disturbing time-warp fully expressive of the artistic conception behind the set as 'head space'.[79] Indeed, the later court scene directly engages with the irrational nature of anti-Semitism. There, Antonio is allowed to prove that his irrational hatred for Jews is, in fact, totally rational. A piece of inspired writing captures the essence of anti-Semitism and xenophobia as a displacement of other existential fears. From the fear of change to that of old age, from the realization of one's own insignificance to the dread of rejection, fear finds a distorted rationale in hatred for the Jew. 'And', as Antonio concludes, 'this fear is totally rational'.[80]

Masterfully and provocatively layered history also lurks under the seemingly playful surface of the production poster, which caused moral outrage in some circles when it appeared on the streets of Warsaw.[81] It features two naked white men covered in 'African' body paint; in front of them, an Asian-looking tourist is being photographed. Buried underneath the apparent silliness lies another memory. From under the composition – created by conceptual artist Zbigniew Libera (author of a provocative Lego concentration camp installation) – peeps the bone structure of one of Leni Riefenstahl's images from her Nuba series. Shot twenty years after World War II, during which she used prisoners for her films, her stunning African photographs exquisitely overlay her unseemly past as Hitler's favourite cinematographer.[82] If this is anything to go by, *African Tales* offers an endless series of masks which it revels in tearing off, reversing and flaunting.

In the final movement of the *Merchant* section of *African Tales*, Warlikowski throws at the audience the play's most contested image: the pound of flesh. Freed from her legal disguise, Portia slowly ingests a pound of flesh-like substance at the very spot where, earlier, Antonio performed his rant. The process is painful to watch as the audience can see the actual physical effort required from the actress to ingest the substance. Having thus literally 'eaten' the discourse associated with it, she delivers a non-guilty verdict for Shylock's homoerotic desire for his enemy's flesh.

---

[78] Spiegelman is quoted in Hillary Chute, 'The shadow of a past time: history and graphic representation in Maus', *Twentieth Century Literature* 52 (2006), 199–230; p. 201.

[79] Grzegorz Niziołek, *Warlikowski*, p. 153, where he quotes the set designer Małgorzata Szczęśniak.

[80] Quoted from the subtitles of the DVD of the production.

[81] Sakowska, '"Liquid Shakespeare"', p. 266.

[82] Stephen C. Feinstein, 'Zbigniew Libera's Lego concentration camp: iconoclasm in conceptual art about the Shoah', *Other Voices* 2 (2000), www.othervoices.org/2.1/feinstein/auschwitz.php.

Warlikowski then engages with one of the few remaining idealisms of the play's ending: instead of marrying Bassanio, Portia commits herself to God. Her own Otherness in the play's male world thus underscored, she is entrusted to another system of patriarchal subjugation. The loop remains closed, something which critics have found problematic.[83] Perhaps the refusal to give an illusion of atonement suggests that characters cannot achieve it, or that, in the terms of their worlds, it is unattainable. Such a conclusion might be depressing, but no more so than the world where women's rights are traded for political gain, a world not that far from the threshold of Warlikowski's theatre.

CODA: THE LEGACY OF A SKULL

In December 2008, British media broadcast the news that the then-ongoing production of Shakespeare's *Hamlet* was using a real skull as a prop in the Gravedigger scene.[84] As it turned out, it was part of the remains of the Polish-born pianist André Tchaikowsky, who had died in Britain in 1982, bequeathing it to the RSC for their *Hamlet* performances. Twenty-five years after his death, the skull was duly delivered to the company, which, in fulfilment of his wish, used it in the performance. Though sometimes self-righteously moralistic, the journalistic hullaballoo helped to revive Tchaikowsky's memory as a composer and also his only opera, *The Merchant of Venice*, finished in 1982. In 2013, it was finally co-produced by the Bregenz Festival in Austria and the Polish National Opera in Warsaw. In 2014, recast, it opened in Warsaw, and thus, in the strange ways of history, the composer's skull enabled his posthumous return to the stage, and to Poland, in a grand manner.

Tchaikowsky's personal life is itself a testament to the atrocity of last century's anti-Semitism and racism. Born in Poland in 1935, he was smuggled out of the Warsaw Ghetto, survived, studied music in Lodz and Paris, and ended up in Britain as a virtuoso pianist. A brilliant, gay, depressive man, his *Merchant of Venice* rings with the disjunctive

atonality of twentieth-century music. Antonio's countertenor piercingly conveys his vulnerability and neurotic instability, which are counterpointed by Shylock's baritone. The choric scenes speak of a society permeated by anti-Semitism and xenophobia: choruses mock Portia's failed lovers, as well as Shylock after Jessica's elopement. In the end, however – and unlike most recent productions – the opera allows lovers to overcome the hurdles of Act 5 through a musical invocation of a romantic world.

Keith Warner's elegant production placed events at the turn of the twentieth century and, through a legible succession of images, metaphorically connected it with the disasters of the 1930s that followed the excesses of the era. An imposing movable wall of numbered boxes – resembling bank safes, prisoners' or medical files – represented the compartmentalized business world of Venice. In front of it, clerks conducted business. Behind it, Shylock and Jessica inhabited a caged space. Shylock's humiliation was effectively staged by a posse of women and children wearing masks with cartoon noses, imputing a stereotyped Jewishness at a grotesque remove from the face of Shylock. The same properties were effective in the Warsaw version where Shylock's part was sung by the African-American baritone Lester Lynch, and underscored the similarity between anti-Semitism and racism. Though visited by Shylock's ghost, Act 5 ended in hard-earned harmony with all couples going to bed, leaving Antonio outside.

The production, however, delicately complicated the tone by the use of silent framing, which linked the romantic, pecuniary, and memorial strands by way of three human-sized caskets. In the opening scene, Antonio appeared to be undergoing therapy with a Freud-like figure, while the caskets floated around like painful obsessions. Bassanio emerged out of one, only to be

---

[83] Aleksandra Sakowska, "'Liquid Shakespeare'", p. 266.

[84] The production was directed by Gregory Doran with David Tennant as Hamlet. For materials about Tchaikowsky, see the ever-expanding and very informative http://andretchaikowsky.com website.

pushed back by Portia, who slammed the door shut. Another contained Shylock, his gaze fixed on Antonio through the open door. During the final scene of a similar psychotherapy session, only Shylock's casket is on stage, open and empty.[85] With a start, Antonio remembers something, searches his wallet, and throws a ring into the casket. Is that the one he had bought from Solanio, who had boasted he got it in Genoa for a monkey? Under the beams of the enormous romantic moon, Shylock's casket remains silent.

This international production of Tchaikowsky's opera was justly described as 'a restitution to remember'.[86] His opera, like its post-communist East European theatrical counterparts, has overcome a long silence and started its travels on the world stages. That a man like Tchaikowsky, whose life was blighted by one of the great horrors of the twentieth century, could write a hopeful future for the lovers of Venice and Belmont, is an important and potent legacy.[87]

As this brief survey suggests, post-1989 East European performances of *The Merchant of Venice* indicate that the play will be troublesome for some time to come. As its memorial function is now entwined with a relentless contemporariness, it confronts new forms of intolerance and cruelty. Too many figures in the European carpet look like skulls, too much history pushes under the masks of our civilization, and productions reverberate with these tensions. In the hands of a new generation of directors committed to the problems of their world, they serve as a constant reminder of what we, normal human beings, are capable of, and the furiousness which the East European legacy has injected into the old play continues to challenge complacency.

---

[85] The production showed Shylock symbolically dying in the trial scene, disappearing under a sheet on the stage floor. He re-emerged as a ghost that did not want to poison his daughter's happiness, but disappeared into one of the caskets, which in the production was marked as a site of memory and female emancipation – both Portia and Nerissa threw their wedding rings into it in a gesture of autonomy from their husbands.

[86] John Allison, review of *Die Zauberflöte / The Merchant of Venice*, *Telegraph*, 28 July 2013, www.telegraph.co.uk/cul ture/music/classicalmusic/10205054/Die-ZauberflöteThe-Merchant-of-Venice-review.html.

[87] The opera was rejected by the English National Opera in Tchaikowsky's lifetime. After Bregenz and Warsaw, it has been to Cardiff and Covent Garden in 2017.

ARIEL'S GROANS, OR, PERFORMING PROTEAN GENDER ON THE BULGARIAN POST-COMMUNIST STAGE

KIRILKA STAVREVA

Any serious reflection on how Shakespeare enters our lives is bound to consider performance, 'whether on film, stage, or classroom', contends Sarah Werner in an inspiring study of the colliding and overlapping theatre practices that shape how we relate to Shakespeare's plays.[1] As for changing lives, since Bertolt Brecht at least, we have looked to formally experimental performances as particularly well suited for impressing upon audiences the possibility that social hierarchies and relationships – including gender and sexual hierarchies – can shift. With the life-changing capacity of the theatre in mind, I discuss the evolving portrayal of Ariel's gender in recent Bulgarian productions of Shakespeare's *The Tempest*: from the representation of the spirit, early in the post-communist transition, as an overly feminized character of repressed emotions and a feeble claim to identity, to an Ariel (and Ariels) of protean and exuberant performativity in more recent years.

Since the 1990s, *The Tempest*, along with *Hamlet*, has held an important place in Bulgarian theatre. Such sustained interest in the play by post-communist Bulgarian theatre-makers is unusual given the fact that it had been staged just twice during the communist era: a mainstage production in the 1950s and a puppet production in 1987.[2] Partially, the surge of interest is a matter of individual artistic choice. The first director to stage the play shortly after the fall of the Berlin Wall was the widely popular Alexander Morfov, who created a radically fragmented and collaged production for La Strada Theatre in 1992. Four years later, Morfov mounted a new version for the Ivan Vazov National Theatre,

whose artistic director he had become. It enjoyed over 150 performances. (*The Tempest* appears to have a permanent hold upon Morfov's imagination, as he went on to stage it again in 1998 for the Komissarchevskaya Theatre in Saint Petersburg, Russia, and yet again in 2014 for the National Theatre in Bucharest, Romania.) Likewise, individual fascination with the play may have been the impetus for the 2004 Varna Puppetry Theatre production directed by Petar Pashov, one of two directors to have staged the play in the communist era.

With the proliferation of *Tempest* productions in the post-communist era and the play's growing popularity among diverse and expanding audiences, professional recognition did not lag far behind. Pashov's second *Tempest*, whose precarious beauty and poignant social and popular allusions engaged a mixed audience of young and old spectators, was selected in 2005 for the Varna Summer International Theatre Festival. That year, the Festival featured another *Tempest*: a terror-ridden experimental production by the Turkish Adana Theatre, directed by Javor Gardev, one of the most prolific and admired Bulgarian directors, and with a Bulgarian composer

---

[1] Sarah Werner, *Shakespeare and Feminist Performance: Ideology on Stage* (London, 2001), p. 3.

[2] Boika Sokolova, 'Relocating and dislocating Shakespeare in Robert Sturua's *Twelfth Night* and Alexander Morfov's *The Tempest*', in *World-Wide Shakespeares: Local Appropriations in Film and Performance*, ed. Sonia Massai (London, 2005), pp. 57–64; Teodora Simova, 'Shakespeare and puppet theater in Bulgaria', slide presentation, 5 May 2014, https://prezi.com/i4katsu4c8te/presentation.

and set designer. Although the brief festival run that the production had in Bulgaria and the multinational character of its creative team place it beyond the scope of this study, it is worth noting that Gardev's *Tempest* drew not only the usual theatre sophisticates and cultural tourists but also a largely working-class audience of Turkish Bulgarians. In 2013, Katya Petrova's production of *The Tempest*, with puppet and scene design by Rin Yamamura, a Japanese artist residing in Bulgaria, opened at the State Puppet Theatre in Sofia. It garnered the national Ikar Prize for best puppet show of the year. In 2014, Stoyan Radev directed the play for the amateur Studio Teatar in Varna; the production was featured on the main stage of the city's Stoyan Bachvarov Theatre on that year's European Night of the Theatre. Petrova's and Radev's productions engaged (but were not restricted to) young audiences on the local level, in the theatres and training studios in which spectators and aspiring actors grow up. For a small country where Shakespeare is neither a national poet nor a sure draw for theatre-goers, such wide-ranging and enduring attention to a previously ignored play is worth exploring.

The Tempest and its characters, I would suggest, have entered the Bulgarian artistic vocabulary of cultural change. And while *The Tempest*s of the late 1990s and early 2000s foreground a local, unheroic Prospero who remains on the island upon realizing that Milan is either unattainable or undesirable, the two latest productions shift their focus to Ariel.[3] Notably, the surge in creative attention to Ariel's character came at a time when young people and a good part of Bulgaria's creative intelligentsia took to the streets with public calls for ethical responsibility in politics – a moral revolution that was part of an unfolding global phenomenon that calls for a large-scale political analysis. The massive street protests in Bulgaria's capital and some of the major cities, although overshadowed in world news by the violence-ridden 2013 protests in Brazil, Egypt, and Turkey, were a remarkable event. They started on 14 June 2013 and continued, peacefully, for some 400 days. In the case of the new Ariels, theatre and civic unrest took parallel paths.

Central to Ariel's character is, of course, its elusive gender – and, arguably, it is the elusiveness of a central identity marker that presents an irresistible challenge to theatre artists working in conditions of unsettling and unpredictable cultural change. Yet, in production, a gender of some sort must be assigned to Ariel. This decision, for a character that has come to signify the freedom of the imagination, has posed productive challenges to actors and directors. If, as Juliet Dusinberre argues regarding *Antony and Cleopatra*, Shakespeare's highlighting of the boy's part and 'the oscillating construction of the masculine and the feminine ... pushed the boy actor to his limits, and possibly beyond them', the challenge to the boy actor playing Ariel has been no less formidable – and exhilarating.[4] In addition to taking on the second longest part in *The Tempest*, and either overlooking or driving the action in every scene, the *character* Ariel performs in three plays within the play – as sea nymph, harpy and Ceres.[5] In at least two of these, the boy actor would have taken on parts traditionally played by girls and women in the court masques of the era. In other words, he would have had to oscillate between playing a genderless spirit and performing as a girl playing a female part in a Jacobean masque – certainly an overdetermined part in terms of gender.[6]

---

[3] On the range of anti-nostalgic revisions of Prospero on the Bulgarian stage at the turn of the twenty-first century, from a little man in need of making peace with his past, to a neurotic with severed ties to reality, to a Balkan colonizer/colonized haunted by historical narratives of annihilation, see Kirilka Stavreva, 'Dream loops and short-circuited nightmares: post-Brechtian Tempests in post-communist Bulgaria', *Borrowers and Lenders: The Journal of Shakespeare and Appropriation* 3.2 (2008).

[4] Juliet Dusinberre, 'Squeaking Cleopatras: gender and performance in *Antony and Cleopatra*', in *Shakespeare, Theory, and Performance*, ed. James C. Bulman (London, 1996), pp. 46–7.

[5] Virginia Mason Vaughan, in *The Tempest: Shakespeare in Performance* (Manchester, 2011), p. 8, remarks on Ariel's omnipresence in each of the play's scenes and labels him 'the second most important character in the play with 210 lines (more if s/he personates Ceres in the masque in 4.1)'.

[6] Deanne Williams, 'Prospero's girls', *Borrowers and Lenders: The Journal of Shakespeare and Appropriation* 9.1 (2014), p. 12, explains that 'Ariel's disguise as a sea-nymph may allude to the

To the director, the part of 'Ariel and all his quality' (1.2.194) presents a similarly exhilarating challenge. The character list refers to Ariel as 'an airy spirit of the island, servant to Prospero': neither a dead human (ghost), nor an anthropomorphic creature from a popular belief system (witch, fairy); a character from a different realm, yet one with a measure of humanity. Since the early modern era, '*his* quality' has been portrayed as female, male, and sexually ambiguous, as singular and multiple, young and old, invisible, delicate, athletic, saccharine, portly, hyper-masculine, femininely seductive, androgynously provocative, vocally enchanting or discomforting, submissive, stoic, dedicated, resentful and more. Because of Ariel's close relationship with Prospero, gendering the part has been instrumental in articulating *and* subverting Prospero's political and patriarchal power, as Christine Dymkowski claims.[7] In the case of the Bulgarian renditions of Ariel analysed below, however, gendering Ariel is not a vehicle for upholding Prospero's power, nor for formulating an ideological opposition to it. Rather, in the earlier set of post-communist productions, Ariel's melancholic femininity becomes emblematic of the Duke's own entrapment and inability to break loose from inherited identity narratives. In the two most recent productions, however, both Ariel's gender and the master–servant relationship are imaginatively reconceived as Prospero's character gets subsumed by an Ariel (and Ariels) of protean gender performativity. At stake in all of these productions is the future not of Milan, nor of its Duke, but of the island. And while none of the Bulgarian Ariels offer solutions to the island's problems, some dream of ways of achieving them.

ARIEL AS A SAD GIRL

In Morfov's production of *The Tempest* for the National Theatre, Ariel is unmistakably female. Performed by Reni Vrangova, who also plays Miranda, this Ariel comes across as a dejected survivor. In this, she resembles not only Prospero but almost all of those stranded on the island. What these characters yearn for is someone to lend

a sympathetic ear to their life story – and they fail to find such a listener. Thus, Miranda may be a captive audience for Prospero's tale of betrayal and survival, with which the play opens and ends, but she would much rather be listening to the imaginary voices in the sea conches she presses against her ear. Nor does Prospero pay any attention to his daughter's wistful rehearsal of an imaginary falling-in-love – her lines from her first encounter with Ferdinand in Shakespeare's playtext. These lines are uttered here at the opening of the play but not when Ferdinand finally appears, as both get deprived of voice and voluntary movement by the spirits manipulating them in this scene.

There is little power that Vrangova's Ariel holds. Her harpy's crescendo in the enchanted banquet scene is reduced to farcical havoc after a bout of communal smoking by the Neapolitans and the spirits, who appear in straw skirts and native headdress. The masque of the three goddesses, the supreme theatrical accomplishment of Shakespeare's Ariel, is cut in Morfov's production. (So is Miranda's game of chess, the one overt assertion of the female political and sexual power of Ariel's double.) Ariel has even been denied the fascination of the audience, largely due to Vrangova's doubling as Miranda, which undermines both characters' cohesiveness and frustrates emotional identification with them.[8]

Ironically, the one shred of power left to the *spirit* Ariel is her resistance to becoming what philosopher Branka Arsić describes as a spectralized subject. A spectralized subject denies to the Other a part of its already-constituted world; this subject constitutes its subjectivity not as interpellated by

performance of Prince Henry's teenaged sister, Elizabeth, as a sea nymph in Samuel Daniel's *Tethys' Festival*, performed for her brother's investiture in 1610'. She also suggests that it is plausible to read the lyrics of 'Come Unto these Yellow Sands' as 'a thumbnail sketch of girls' performances as dancers in the Jacobean court masque'.

7 William Shakespeare, *The Tempest*, ed. Christine Dymkowski, Shakespeare in Production series (Cambridge, 2000), p. 48.

8 Stavreva, 'Dream loops', p. 14.

the Other, but instead in response to 'a little other (produced by the subject itself)' – in other words, in response to figments of a solipsistic imagination experienced as exterior reality.[9] Spectralization, endemic in Morfov's rendition of *The Tempest*, is manifested most poignantly when the bookish Prospero, himself a prisoner of the island, chains a bookish Caliban like a dangerous beast into a confining cage and hoists him up, fully aware of Caliban's terror of heights. Ariel herself has been subjected to the abuse of a spectralized Prospero, when he tightens her long silk scarf around her head, even as he threatens: 'If thou murmur'st, I will rend an oak, / And peg thee in his knotty entrails till / Thou hast howled away twelve winters' (1.2.295–7). Yet, impervious to Prospero's sexual or filial attraction as this Ariel may be, she is the only character attentive to his emotional crisis, unfolding even as his project 'gather[s] to a head' (5.1.1), and offers him a lifeline: 'The rarer action is / In virtue than in vengeance' (5.1.27–8). At this point in the play, Ariel is the one character in this *Tempest* who constitutes her subjectivity through emotional identification with *and* reasoned differentiation from her Other, Prospero, for her emotional statement about the rare value of virtue and the denial of vengeance, I posit, connects the core of her identity to that of her oppressive Other.

Does it matter that the only non-spectralized subject in Morfov's production of *The Tempest* is gendered feminine? Perhaps, but then only to the extent that it underscores the futile entrapment of the male Prospero, and the rest of the old and new islanders, into old identity narratives. Regrettably, there is no Miranda in the grand finale of the play even to hint at gender optimism regarding the 'brave new world' to come (5.1.186). Nor does Prospero take up Ariel's invitation to 'the rarer action'. The production eschews the catharsis of forgiveness and, instead of the promise of fair winds and truths told, it circles back to the beginning of the play as the revolving stage shows the Neapolitans descending on the island from the back of Prospero's ship.

ARIEL'S FEMININITY, REVEALED

If, in Morfov's *Tempest*, Ariel's identity was blurred with Miranda's, in Petar Pashov's 2004 puppet production, it is further submerged by making Ariel, literally, part of the set. For almost the entire play, the spirit remains beneath the blue parachute silk covering the island, its movement shaping the magical topography. Other characters in Pashov's *Tempest* are also associated with the set and props. The dramatic action is triggered when Prospero drops his book of magic on the ground. Its scattered pages eventually metamorphose into archetypal aspects of the characters: thus, Alonso's chess-piece crown, Ferdinand's knightly mantle and empty codpiece, Miranda's wild, stubborn hair are all made out of paper. Yet, paper-clad as these characters may be, their identity is never in question. Not so in the case of Ariel, whose humanity and gender, hidden beneath the parachute silk, remain, for almost the entire play, allegorized qualities of the island.

The balance of power on this magical island is precarious. On the one hand, Ariel is trapped under its surface, futilely pushing against it. Even as a harpy, the terror Ariel instils in the Neapolitans is matched by the palpable terror of her constraint, antithetical to the nature of a free spirit (Illustration 12). At the same time, the very shape of the island is determined by Ariel's 'quality', or movement. The Duke's footing on this morphing surface is doubly insecure, as part of the action unfolds on a precariously balanced platform. Momentary peace, when achieved, is the doing of Ariel. It is the under-cover spirit, for instance, who quenches Miranda's adolescent rebellion, embracing her and rocking her to sleep, to Prospero's visible relief.

As I have argued elsewhere, Prospero's precarious control of the island and his daughter satirize the Western myth of the multi-talented Renaissance Man supposed to have a firm grip of

---

[9] Branka Arsić, 'Queer Serbs', in *Balkan as Metaphor: Between Globalization and Fragmentation*, ed. Dušan I. Bjelić and Obrad Savić (London, 2002), p. 258.

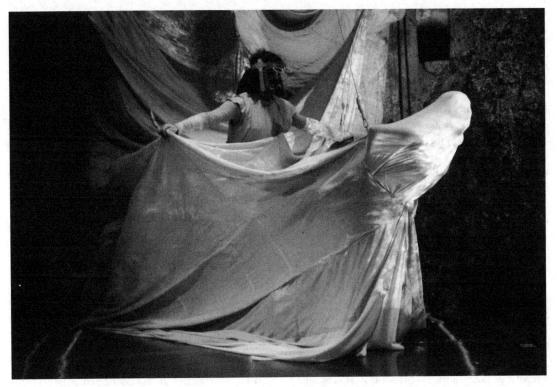

12. Ariel's harpy. *The Tempest*, directed by Petar Pashov, Varna Puppetry Theatre, 2004.

his world and life-story.[10] At the end of the play, this Duke (like the one in Morfov's production) remains on the island, and his reconciliation to this beautiful and volatile, small world is dramatized when Ariel breaks through the membrane of blue silk to embrace him. The production culminates with a tableau of forgiveness, but this is Ariel's, not Prospero's, forgiveness.

As Ariel's humanity is revealed, so is her femininity – a choice similar to Julie Taymor's in her 1986 production for New York's Theater for a New Audience, when Louise Smith, the puppeteer operating Ariel's bunraku puppet, took off the black covering of her face that had rendered her invisible as the creator of magic.[11] Yet, unlike Smith's Ariel, the one performed by Emilia Petkova does not take flight through the audience; she remains on stage, holding Prospero from behind as he utters his Epilogue. In a production in which Ariel's female humanity was not only

constrained but rendered invisible – a social construct too familiar in a society battered by acute economic depravity, entrenched patriarchal mentality, and lip service to gender equality – claiming the moral high ground from Prospero is valiant indeed. This Ariel does not find her voice, and her gender performance is marked by long-suffering gentleness. Yet before we write off the final tableau as rehashing the terms of the old heterosexual romance featuring a long-suffering and forgiving woman, we should note two of its formal aspects. First, for all its tenderness, the ending gives Ariel the higher ethical ground; more

[10] Stavreva, 'Dream loops', p. 12.

[11] On Taymor's production, see D. J. R. Bruckner, 'Stage: *The Tempest* at New Audience', *New York Times*, 27 March 1986, and Vaughan, *The Tempest: Shakespeare in Performance*, p. 184.

importantly, it places the *release* for which Prospero asks not only in the hands of the audience, but, literally, in Ariel's hands.

TRIUMPHANT ARIELS

Unlike the downplaying or concealment of gender in the Bulgarian *Tempest*s from the turn of the century, when Stoyan Radev staged the play in the fall of 2014, he placed gender at the centre of the articulation and contestation of power. Moreover, the gendering of the Prospero–Ariel conflict driving this production is neither conventional nor rigid. The director and his youthful cast, I argue, play joyful havoc with gender norms.

As 'the representation of freedom and its curtailment', in Radev's words, Ariel is in a tense and dynamic relationship with the island's ruler, the Duchess Prospera.[12] Four years after Helen Mirren brought Prospera to cinema screens the world over, re-gendering the Duke of Milan no longer surprises. Yet Radev's casting sends an even clearer message than Taymor's about gender stereotypes and power. Not only is absolute power on the island – including sexual domineering over Caliban – gendered female, but the coup in Milan is the work of Prospera's sister, Antonia, another woman adept at wielding sexual and political power. Among Prospera, Antonia, and the feisty Miranda, this is a world where women have little patience for prescriptive gender narratives.

Ariel is here both one and many. The character is performed by seven male and sixteen female actors, one of whom is visibly pregnant. The Bulgarian dialogue translates 'his quality' as 'his aria of spirits, nymphs, elves and little fairies'. And while the chorus often speaks as one, there are exceptions, which render Ariel a character of complex, unreconciled motivations (Illustration 13). Constantly on stage, Ariel functions as a chorus modelling the audience's response to the action, and as an evolving character intermittently intertwined with Prospera's.

The multiplicity (or, perhaps, multipotentiality) of Ariel's gender is underplayed in the opening, when the spirit chorus performs in synch with Prospera's witch-like revelling in her destructive power. Except for accentuating movement through stomping and clapping, this is a silent Ariel, with no audible gender signifiers. Overwritten by a performance script authored by Prospera, the Ariels illustrate the Duchess's absolute power, though they are alienated from it. At the same time, the gender of the Duchess is played as something out of an old-time fairy tale about voracious femininity.

Such voracious femininity gets a stereotypical aural expression during the pursuit of 'Caliban and his confederates' (4.1.140). The hound-chasing scene in Radev's *Tempest*, purely comical, opens up with Ariel's and Prospera's taunts, overlaid by their laughter. It culminates with what the ancient Greeks called *ololyga* as Prospera leads the Neapolitan party on stage to declare, 'At this hour / Lies at my mercy all mine enemies' (4.1.260–1). *Ololyga* is a singularly feminine ritual cry marking the high points in rituals (e.g. sacrifice) or in real life (e.g. childbirth or loss). It has no representational content, but rather expresses pure pleasure and/or pain.[13] Prospera's aural incontinence is certainly gender-stereotypical, especially since it is followed by a frantic verbal outburst in which she takes over Ariel's response to her own question about the time. 'How's the day? / On the sixth hour', she answers in the same breath (5.1.3–4).

In spite of the Ariels' penchant for the kind of noise-making associated with the animal world and the lower-body strata (cries and fake farts), the chorus lets Prospera's harpy-like shriek ring out on its own. Contrasted to the Duchess's gender-stereotypical lack of measure in voice and movement is the quiet, attentive stillness of the Ariel chorus flanking her, as well as that of Miranda, who remains immersed in her game of chess downstage throughout the chase scene. Yet neither Ariel nor Miranda in this youthful production are

---

[12] Stoyan Radev, personal interview, Varna, Bulgaria, 27 August 2015.

[13] See Anne Carson's chapter, 'The gender of sound', in *Glass, Irony and God* (New York, 1995), esp. pp. 124–6.

13. The Ariels. *The Tempest*, directed by Stoyan Radev, Studio Teatar, Varna, 2014. Photograph by Toni Perec.

paragons of submissiveness. Moreover, their contesta-tion of Prospera's power is clearly gendered. For instance, Ariel's challenge to Prospera's extortion of more 'toil' (1.2.243) is voiced by two women, who step out of the cowering chorus to demand liberty in no meek terms. This is despite the physical pain which Prospera inflicts on the spirit, communicated through the silent contortions of a male Ariel beneath her left (sinister) hand. The Bulgarian word for 'spirit' is gendered masculine, and the rebellious female Ariels stick to this gender designation when arguing 'his' faithful service, but Prospera genders Ariel's ungratefulness feminine, countering with a line that would translate as 'You gal, dost thou forget / From what a torment I did free thee?' (1.2.251–2).

In the end, Prospera never gets to release Ariel. Rather, the Ariel chorus takes charge of orchestrat-ing the resolution of the romance and their own freedom, as Prospera, somewhat inexplicably,

abandons her revenge plans and, along with them, the script of witchy femininity. First, the Ariel chorus, this time completely unprompted, switches into the prophetic performance mode of a harpy to affirm the authenticity of Prospera's self-narrative (modifying the Shakespearian playtext to fit the revised gender of the characters):

> But howsoe'er you have
> Been jostled from your senses, know for certain
> That this is Prospera that very Duchess
> Which was thrust forth of Milan by her sister
>   Antonia . . .
> Welcome to her island.

Next, in the revelation scene, the Ariels explode the convention of narrative theatre that has dominated the production so far, as they dive right into Ferdinand's courtship dance to the tune of the Queen song 'Mustafa Ibrahim'. Eventually, they take the action into the audience (and, rather to Miranda's consternation, they take Ferdinand along as well). The dance is, of course, no less of a performance than the tableaux of power previously staged by Prospera. Certainly, it is a far cry from Robert Johnson's seventeenth-century composition 'Where the bee sucks'. Yet, like Freddie Mercury's provocative mixture, in the song, of a Muslim call to prayer with rock rhythms, of Arabic, English and nonsense phrases, Ariel's dance is likewise marked by gender fluidity, stylistic hybridity and improvisation. The play ends with a variation of Prospero's Epilogue, laced with local references to the area's golden sands and quiet sea coast, and delivered by the entire cast. Visually, the ensemble is crowned by a female Ariel. As for the Duchess, she is positioned, slightly isolated, in the inconspicuous second row. Written with the bodies of the young actors is a playful and dynamic concept of age, gender and power – a rare gift to an audience starved for new cultural and political narratives.

ARIEL PLAYS ON

Further collapsing the power differential between master and servant, in Katya Petrova's puppet *Tempest*, a female-gendered Ariel acts more like Prospero's partner and, eventually, his alter ego. Like Radev's vision, here, too, Ariel is an instrument and impetus of change; she teaches Prospero and the audience the courage to own up to one's actions. Director Petrova writes for the production's programme: 'When we were little, we played with masks. Later, when we grew up, each of us put on a mask, which transformed and deformed us so that we no longer resemble ... who we are, what we are'. Her production features an Ariel capable of questioning and resisting power hierarchies and pressures. A sharp observer of the deeds of the island's power players, she not only sees through the social masks they have donned, but manages to imbue Prospero with her signature playful and irreverent attitude to language and habits of mind.

Maya Bezhanska's Ariel, child-like as she may appear with her diminutive stature, quick movements, high-pitched voice and paper wings, is a far cry from the traditional 'breeches' part of Prospero's 'modest and seductive side-kick'.[14] Hers is a wise child, confident in magic-making and jazz-like improvisations upon Shakespeare's language, which she transforms into 'something rich and strange' (1.2.404). Somewhat reminiscent in her gliding movements of Giulia Lazzerini's petite gamine Ariel in Giorgio Strehler's historic 1978 *Tempesta*, Bezhanska's Ariel offers little in the way of conscientious servitude. The morbid sensuality of Ariel's love–hate relationship with Prospero in the Italian production is here replaced by tricksy competitiveness and Ariel's incessant, humorous testing of Prospero's power.

Like the rest of the characters in Petrova's production, Ariel is first introduced through her mask – a stylized, ungendered child's drawing, the face with which she is known to the world. Unlike the rest of the characters, however, she rarely hides behind the mask. On the few occasions this happens, she dons it with meta-theatrical aplomb, gesturing pointedly at Prospero's overblown assertions of power over his 'industrious servant' (4.1.33). Thus, when summoned to produce the masque entertainment for Miranda and Ferdinand, she tosses the mask into Prospero's hands and leans back behind it in a parodic imitation of complete surrender to the master's wishes. Scoffing about the amount of labour the masque production calls for, Ariel proceeds to underscore with comic earnestness Prospero's mixed-up pronunciation of 'the vanity of mine art' (4.1.41). 'What have you decided?' she improvises, 'I do not understand it', before prompting him to join her in a silly display of spirit-conjuring for the benefit of Ferdinand and Miranda. Masks are good to play with, though not for long, suggests Ariel's performance.

Instead of a mask, Ariel favours her pop glasses, which feature the same stylized child's drawing of

---

[14] Dymkowski, ed., *The Tempest*, p. 37.

14. The jazz duo of Ariel (Maya Bejanska) and Prospero (Georgi Stoyanov) in *The Tempest*, directed by Katya Petrova, State Puppet Theatre, Sofia, 2013. Photograph by Ivan Grigorov.

a face. She uses her glasses as part statement about her quasi-human nature, part vehicle for candid investigation of those incapable of breaking out of their social scripts and defences. Her fascination with the Italian characters is often tempered when she strikes a pose of comic incredulity at their actions.

In Petrova's staging of *The Tempest*, it is hard to determine whether Ariel is Prospero's side-kick or the other way around. When first called, Ariel puts Prospero through a comic chase, something the two have clearly done before. They have developed not only a physical routine but also a common language repertoire, riffing off each other in jazzy nonsensical phrases. The culmination of the jazz performance of this duo comes when Prospero renounces his 'rough magic' (5.1.50). In Petrova's *Tempest*, this is not the

grand declaration of the magus's resumé, but, rather, a performance of the Ariel–Prospero duo, telling about, enacting and sounding magic that is shared, exulted in and reviled (Illustration 14). The scene is remarkable not only for its performance value but also because it restores a female voice to a speech in which, as feminist scholars have pointed out, Shakespeare's Prospero ventriloquizes the magical vaunting of Ovid's Medea.[15]

---

[15] Mary Ellen Lamb, 'Engendering the narrative act: old wives' tales in *The Winter's Tale*, *Macbeth*, and *The Tempest*', *Criticism* 40 (1998), pp. 546–7; Kirilka Stavreva, *Words Like Daggers: Violent Female Speech in Early Modern England* (Lincoln, 2015), pp. 124–6; Judith Buchanan, 'Not Sycorax', in *Women Making Shakespeare: Text, Reception and Performance* (London, 2014), p. 340.

Eventually, jazzy trickster Ariel changes Prospero – so much so that the Duke connives with Miranda, swaps masks with her, and then hops into Ferdinand's arms just before blessing (provisionally) the marriage. But Ariel is also aware of the need to get the audience to look through old masks and tired scripts and to start poking fun at them. So, she takes her place in the auditorium during Ferdinand's trial, commenting and interfering with the stage action, and calling on Prospero to make sure that he counts her among the humans that Miranda had seen before Ferdinand.

As is typically the case with post-communist Shakespeare productions, in the shows I have discussed, the playtext is not only cut and re-arranged but at times liberally rewritten. They belong to a tradition that evokes Shakespeare as a cultural authority in order to underwrite (the directors') creativity and commentary on social and cultural phenomena. Unlike in British, US and post-colonial traditions, Caliban gets short shrift in these productions. Notable, too, is the eventual waning of interest in Prospero. Confronted by the ongoing crisis of the never-ending post-communist transition and the surging challenges to American and European moral identity and political unity, Bulgarian directors have started to place their hopes for the future of the magical island in feisty Mirandas and youthful Ariels capable of joyful gender transformations.

DRESSING THE HISTORY 'BOYS': HARRY'S MASKS, FALSTAFF'S UNDERPANTS

CAROL CHILLINGTON RUTTER

By mid-2016, the UK Shakespeare community had experienced, one after the other, a spate of anniversaries and national celebrations that put Shakespeare, iconically, at their centre: the 450th anniversary of his birth in 2014; the 400th anniversary of his death in 2016; the opening ceremony of the 2012 London Olympics; the 2012 Cultural Olympiad; the 2014–16 Globe to Globe *Hamlet* tour. This activity, much of it conscripting Shakespeare to 'do' political work in the national self-interest, has prompted me to think about how the UK uses Shakespeare to frame its national self-image and to publish that image to the world. More specifically, I have been interested to observe how the Shakespeare theatre industry in England has aligned itself with this national cultural project by putting on view a particular view of 'England' in recent productions of Shakespeare's *Henry IV* plays. This, in turn, sent me to revisit the site of original work done by Barbara Hodgdon in the Royal Shakespeare Company Costume Collection, to return to questions she posed in her seminal essay 'Shopping in the archives'.[1] I was in search of an iconic costume and led there by other, more recent costumes that I'd seen in performances over the past few years, costumes that required me to ask questions about how current productions of Shakespeare's history plays were remembering history. If costumes are the stuff of production memory and preserve the material remains of stories told, what, I wondered, was the archive telling us about the England that has been on view to England (and the world) of late, particularly in those two plays that Shakespeare used so ambiguously to put England on view to *his* audiences, the two parts of *Henry IV*?

The results of a UK referendum in July 2016 to leave the European Union invested my research with a new political urgency. How, I asked myself, have recent theatrical fashionings of medieval English history anticipated, even contributed or held up a mirror to, the frame of mind that led Britons to support Brexit? In asking how England uses Shakespeare to view England, and what England our major Shakespeare producing house, the RSC, is not just putting on view locally to audiences in the theatre in Stratford-upon-Avon but beaming to global audiences in real-time video links 'Live from Stratford', I was conscious that all European eyes were now fixed – in astonishment, in horror, with baleful bemusement – on a Britain that looked determined to renounce 'Great'-ness for borders (and sovereignty) that would restore 'little England' by pulling her back inside the outlines of a map drawn to John of Gaunt's measure: a map that figures in the *Henry IV* plays. How theatre might be implicated in the making and the exporting of national self-fashioning, imagining and fantasizing was suddenly a very live political issue.

I've spent most of my working life with Shakespeare, writing about performance. I regularly come out of the theatre with a burr

---

[1] In Peter Holland, ed., *Shakespeare, Memory and Performance* (Cambridge, 2006), pp. 135–67. Hodgdon's seminal work has reached its culmination in a monograph, *Shakespeare, Performance and the Archive* (London, 2016). This article is dedicated to the memory of a magnificent scholar and dear friend who in a lifetime's work set the agenda for Shakespeare performance studies.

under my saddle and a bee in my bonnet. That's how I left Gregory Doran's 2014 productions of the *Henry IV*s, with Jasper Britton as the King, Alex Hassell as Prince Hal, Antony Sher as Falstaff, and with Oliver Ford Davies and Jim Hooper giving show-stopping performances as that geriatric double act, those 'rural fellows' from Gloucestershire, memory-maundering Justice Shallow and his aphasic cousin, Slender. Doran's *Henry*s were beautifully set in something like period costume (the designer: Stephen Brimson Lewis), where 'period' was faux late-Elizabethan. The low-lifers in the Boar's Head, like the place itself, were rendered in specific detail (down to the turkey carpet on the table and the napkin at serving man Francis's neck). Hassell's Hal wore leather; Falstaff, a filthy dowlas shirt, sagging boots, and a greasy surcoat over breeches held up by a belt that showed the strain of competing with the paunch. He entered the play from under a tangle of sheets in a bed already occupied by the prince and a pair of doxies who were vigorously servicing him. Reviewing them, I described Doran's *Henry*s as 'richly upholstered costume dramas'.[2] I was registering my admiration for the skill of the designer and of the costume cutters, dyers, seamstresses and wardrobe mistresses who were playing a simulation game, realizing on stage a visual world Shakespeare creates in words, giving us access to the historical time of the narrative and tuning our ears by focusing our eyes. But I was also registering resistance, using 'costume drama' as a term of critique whereby 'design concept' functions as an act of complacency, safely locating history as 'Ago' in an England preserved by the heritage industry, an England that votes Tory – if not UKIP (that is, the ultra-right-wing United Kingdom Independence Party that campaigned loudly on the 'Leave' side of the referendum).

But I've always understood the *Henry IV* plays to be historically bi-focal, creating for costume consistency as big a headache for the designer as *King Lear* does, that play juggling scenes set in prehistoric and post-Renaissance Britain. *Henry IV* intercuts 1399 with 1599.[3] The King's play dramatizes history out of Holinshed. But in Hal's play, the play set in

Eastcheap, Shakespeare writes about *today*, an Eastcheap of his own time, ostlers grooming horses, poulterers sending turkeys to market, travellers complaining of fleabites, pots being filled, slates being scored. The plays unroll a map that 'we' recognize – the City, Westminster, Coventry, Sutton Coldfield, the Severn, the Trent, Shrewsbury, the Inns of Court, the lanes behind them where the 'bona robas' hang out. The politics discussed are a politics of the moment (which 'we' recognize as a politics of our own moment, these plays dwelling in a perpetual time present): rebellion at home, threat of invasion from abroad, taxation, legitimate government, the draft – topics (under different names) no doubt current in 1399 but discussed in the *Henry IV* plays in ways specific to 1599, most tellingly in that impromptu that refashions interrogation as play, 'Do thou stand for my father' (*1 Henry IV*, 2.4.366) (Illustration 15).

Shakespeare's *Henry*s, then, do not consign history to the past. History is *also* about now. The few records of costumes we have surviving from the period – Peacham's drawing of *Titus Andronicus*[4] – or implied as stage directions – Cleopatra's command 'Cut my lace, Charmian'[5] – suggest to us the

---

[2] Carol Chillington Rutter, 'Shakespeare performances in England 2014', *Shakespeare Survey 68* (Cambridge, 2015), pp. 368–407; p. 376.

[3] See James C. Bulman's 'Introduction' to the Arden Third Series *King Henry IV Part 2* (London, 2016). Bulman writes of 'events dramatized in the political plot' sitting side by side 'anachronistically' with a view of 'English society in the 1590s'. 'Drawing on oral traditions and popular nostalgia as a counterweight to the authority of chronicle narratives', *Part 2* 'creates a world rich in the quotidian life of Elizabethan subcultures and populated by characters more authentically realized than many of those drawn from chronicles ... who collectively paint a picture of contemporary English society more inclusive than one finds in any other Shakespeare history play' (p. 3). My quotations of the two plays come from this and from *King Henry IV Part 1*, ed. David Scott Kastan (London, 2002).

[4] Manuscript held in the library of the Marquess of Bath at Longleat; image reproduced in R. A. Foakes, *Illustrations of the English Stage 1580–1642* (Stanford, 1985).

[5] *Antony and Cleopatra*, 1.3.71. Quotations from plays other than *Henry IV* are from *William Shakespeare: The Complete Works*, ed. Stanley Wells et al. (Oxford, 1986).

15. *Henry IV Part 1*. Hal (Alex Hassell) and Falstaff (Antony Sher) hold court in Eastcheap. RSC (2014), directed by Gregory Doran. Photograph by Kwame Lestrade. ©RSC Images.

visual 'now-ness' of early modern performance, productions staged in some version of modern dress, or as mash-ups, Roman sash over Elizabethan armour. Of course, if history is about *now* (as well as *then*), it is about live issues. That means it's dangerous. And that's my gripe with 'costume drama' Shakespeare. Whether it aims to or not, it instantiates nostalgia. It traps Shakespeare in a single time zone – *then*. It pictorializes history and pictures history as finished. 'Costume drama' Shakespeare gives as conversations long over and done what the plays stage as urgent topical debates.

Reflecting on Doran, and rifling through the back-catalogue of images stored in my personal memory bank, some collected in the theatre, some accessed in the RSC's performance archive held in Stratford in the Shakespeare Birthplace Trust, I had to ask, 'Has it always been thus with the *Henry IV*s?' There have been seven productions of the two parts of *Henry IV* in Stratford in the past forty-eight years, all of them in 'period' dress. Illustration 16 shows the Boar's Head gang in Terry Hands's five-star production of 1975 where Alan Howard's Hal is, like Alex Hassell's in 2014, a youth in faux early modern boots and leather, and where Brewster Mason's 'sanguine coward', 'bed-presser', 'horse-back-breaker' Falstaff sartorially begets Antony Sher's 'trunk of humours', 'huge bombard of sack', 'grey Iniquity', 'father Ruffian' and 'Vanity in years' (*1 Henry IV*, 2.4.235–6, 437–42). To extend the

16. *Henry IV Part 1*. Hal (Alan Howard) and Falstaff (Brewster Mason) hold court in Eastcheap. RSC (1975), directed by Terry Hands. Photograph by Tom Holte. © Shakespeare Birthplace Trust.

'period' comparisons we see in these images, we can go beyond the RSC to the Peter Hall Company (2011) with Desmond Barrit as Falstaff (Illustration 17) and the Globe (2010) with Roger Allam (Illustration 18).

Of course, I knew the answer to my question, 'Has it always been thus?' No. Over the same weeks in 2014 that Doran's *Henry*s were on stage at the Royal Shakespeare Theatre (RST), Harriet Walter was playing the King, directed by Phyllida Lloyd, at the Donmar Warehouse in London. The conceit of Lloyd's all-female, bang-up-to-date production was that we were observing inmates in a women's prison rehearse Shakespeare's play under the watchful gaze of Her Majesty's enforcers. This was make-shift theatre as rehabilitation, simulating in-yer-face confrontation, staging fake violence as an alternative to actual

grievous bodily harm. All the lags had parts. And when they started speaking, their voices made us hear the prison as a microcosm of the nation (what Shakespeare does in *Henry V* when he brings on the four captains, Fluellen, Macmorris, Jamie, and Gower). Hal (Clare Dunne) had an Irish accent. Hotspur and Poins (Jade Anouka, Cynthia Erivo) were a pair of bad-ass 'saaf Lundun' girls who flaunted their black 'gangsta' credentials; Kate Percy (Sharon Rooney) came from one of Glasgow's slums, probably the Gorbals; Falstaff (Ashley McGuire) was a distant East End relative of the Krays, a kind of androgynous bloat of breast sagged into belly, a face hardened by fags, booze, and punch-ups on Bethnal Green. Harriet Walter's 'posh' voice – she'd clearly been sent down for some kind of white-collar offence like credit card fraud – reminded us that 'nobs', too, commit

17. *Henry IV Part 1*. Falstaff (Desmond Barrit) plays the king to Hal (Tom Mison). Peter Hall Company (2011), directed by Peter Hall. Photograph by Geraint Lewis.

crimes: bankers, TV entertainers, members of Parliament.[6]

Putting Shakespeare's words into this setting made these plays about us, about the current state of the nation, and this reanimated the urgency of the head-to-head confrontations they stage. This setting knew all about the rivalries that seethe in the *Henry IV*s (where they explode in civil war, as in contemporary England, with rioting on the streets of London in 2011): it knew about territoriality, tribalism, gang warfare, loyalty, promise-breaking, betrayal, the instant combustion of insult and aggro, and it played them to the personal high stakes they demand in Shakespeare's writing. In Doran, Antony Sher's bulked-up Falstaff in his fat suit was a lovable rogue – Hassell's Hal clearly adored him. But that string of epithets (most dangerously, 'misleader of youth' (*1 Henry IV*, 2.4.450)) was, in his case, a comic flourish. The larks he got up to with Hal (like that initial

'dirty' turn in the sheets) were boys' own japes. Delinquency couldn't stick to Hassell's teflon-coated Hal. (He kept his early modern boxer shorts on in bed.) The Father of Lies' lies were laughed off as entertainment. In Lloyd, McGuire's Falstaff was also a buffoon – wanting to play Peter Pan as Indian Chief in feathered headdress to a crew of doting boys, except that, here, doting was actually addiction. The production's first scenic cut to Falstaff ('Now, Hal, what time of day is it, lad?' (*1 Henry IV*, 1.2.1)) showed McGuire's Falstaff snorting a line of coke – and pushing charlie onto the un-

---

[6] See Bulman's *King Henry IV Part 2* for more on this production in which the King and the Prince were 'played by white actors' while 'the rebels' were 'black' or 'Asian': 'Rebellion thus wears a dark face', and, just as 'The prisoners and the actors who play them ... represent the different races, ethnic histories and types of poverty and oppression to be found in the UK today', so (Bulman quotes the *Observer* reviewer, Susannah Clapp) 'the state is embodied on stage' (p. 503).

18. *Henry IV Part 1.* Falstaff (Roger Allam) prepares for the battle of Shrewsbury. Shakespeare's Globe (2010), directed by Dominic Dromgoole. Photograph by John Haynes.

resisting Prince. Delinquency, riot, stain, waste: these weren't just metaphors; they were descriptors of bodies in jeopardy. The claim Hassell's Hal made so confidently, 'I know you all, and will awhile uphold / The unyoked humour of your idleness' (*1 Henry IV*, 1.2.185–6), trapped Dunne's Hal in a much more dangerous territory. For Dunne's Hal, delinquency was a drug. Would he kick the

habit? *Could* he kick the habit? Falstaff's extended howl on 'I know thee not, old man' (*2 Henry IV*, 5.5.46) in this production, as he was dragged off, was the incredulous rage of the pusher who never expected to get the elbow.

Most impressively, Phyllida Lloyd's production, making this a play that makes a play that makes a play, multiplying the original meta-

19. *Henry IV*. Harriet Walter plays the king. Donmar Warehouse (2014), directed by Phyllida Lloyd. Photograph by Helen Maybanks.

theatricality Shakespeare stages in the *Henry IV*s, defamiliarized meta-theatricality. Taking the *Henry IV*s out of period costume, showing us all the materials of performance to be fakes and stand-ins (like the crown that can be seen sitting on the chair next to Walter's King Henry in Illustration 19, looking like it's made out of scrounged cornflakes packages with aluminium milk bottle tops stuck on for jewels), Lloyd's production gave us access to one of Shakespeare's big ideas in *Henry IV*, an idea that's absolutely about our own present: that is, the constructedness of authority, the staginess of its symbols of power, the way the person disappears behind layers and layers of manipulated personae. Power always wears a mask – as we saw in Lloyd's production at the battle of Shrewsbury (Illustration 20).[7]

Which England, then, is put on view in *Henry IV*? Doran gave us comfortable types, huggable buffoons. (We've learned to look at buffoonery in high places differently in the intervening years, not least in England and the USA in the 2016 Brexit

and presidential election campaigns.) Doran's England was the 'little England' that is rendered iconically in John of Gaunt's dying breath, the 'sceptered isle', the 'happy breed of men' living in a 'little world' or 'fortress' protected from 'infection' from 'less happier lands' by the English Channel, which serves it as a 'wall' or 'moat' to keep out Johnny foreigner (*Richard II*, 2.1.40–9). By contrast, Lloyd's inmate actors (only slightly disguised with the trappings of 'then') performed scenarios of political disaffection 'now', using Shakespeare's words to give voice to the politically ignored, the excluded, the disenfranchised. They were trash Britain biting back, sticking two fingers up to the self-absorbed political class who populate the Westminster 'bubble'. From different angles, both of these productions predicted Brexit.

---

[7] For anyone in the audience who knew *1 Henry IV* and could summon to mind text that Lloyd cut, these masks neatly troped the king's battlefield tactic to confuse the enemy by 'Semblably furnish[ing]' many 'like … himself', so that 'many' are seen 'marching in his coats' (5.3.21, 25).

20. *Henry IV*. The battle of Shrewsbury. Donmar Warehouse (2014), directed by Phyllida Lloyd. Photograph by Helen Maybanks.

Seeing King Henry's masks in Lloyd's production, I experienced a rush of *déjà vu*. They triggered a memory. And that's where this article turns (finally) to the costume archive. I've been talking as though productions of the *Henry IVs* staged in period dress give an untroubled view of the past, insulating us from the ways these plays contest contemporary politics and so stripping from them the power to promote our own contestatory politics. That may be true – and, if it is true, we'd most likely see such complacency registered at the moment in Shakespeare's play of regime change, when Harry's person, translated into the personage of the king, loses self-hood, loses personal history as he's subsumed into the history of England – when, dressed in the coronation robes that make Harry, after his father, 'Henry', he takes on Justice as his new surrogate father, discarding Riot and Vanity:

'I know thee not, old man.' In Doran's production, this moment was uncontroversial. Harry-becoming-Henry changed leather breeches for gorgeously woven robes, a tousled mop for hair bound in by a plain gold coronet. The rejection of Falstaff was a personal decision, made face to face. It was consistent with what had gone before; it preserved design continuity, provoked no trouble for interpretation. That same moment in period-dress *Henry IV*, Terry Hands's in 1975, staged the rejection to make it mean very differently, a staging that radically disturbed the visual surface of the production. As the king's brothers knelt (stage right) and Falstaff and his cronies huddled expectantly (stage left), the newly crowned king entered down stage. He was a Thing of Gold. The stage – solid black for the preceding ten acts of the two parts – had been transformed, shrouded in an eye-

21. *Henry IV Part 2*. Hal (Alan Howard) enters crowned as King Henry in golden armour. RSC (1975), directed by Terry Hands.
Photograph by Joe Cocks. © Shakespeare Birthplace Trust.

blinding white cloth. A few rushes strewn down stage and the naked twisted branches of a tree (behind) reminded us of a natural world, but only fleetingly. Harry was gone. Masked behind gold that replaced his visage, he no longer faced Falstaff as a person (Illustration 21).[8]

In 1975, this costume (designed by Terry Hands's closest design collaborator, Farrah) ruptured design continuity by breathtakingly introducing into the 'period' production radical inconsistency, stylistic incongruity, an image that forced interrogation. Never on stage for longer than three minutes, this costume was an assault on the spectatory retina that left viewers both dazzled and battered. It didn't just say something about power in the play. It suddenly fast-forwarded its way of thinking into the present, to project an image of the facelessness, the remoteness, the machine-like inhumanness of power as the audience experienced it in *their* time. In the final

minutes of 6 hours of playing time, the golden costume made Hands's *Henry*s about the production's audience. In that year, a Labour-led government gave the nation a vote in a referendum asking whether the UK should remain in the European Economic Community. Opposed by the Labour Party itself 2 to 1, and by extreme right-wingers who marched through north London protesting against integration with Europe and complaining of job losses to economic migrants, the referendum was won by the 'remain' campaign with 67 per cent of the vote. In that year, Maggie Thatcher became leader of the Tory Party; the British economy went into double-dip recession; the Vietnam war ended – ending, too, eight years of anti-government protests and radical insurrection in the USA, particularly on university campuses

---

[8] I am grateful to Terry Hands for talking me through the final scene of this production (May 2016).

where students had had enough of the 'old men' they saw as appalling 'misleader[s] of youth', 'grey iniquit[ies]'.

Now preserved in the RSC's Costume Collection, the gold costume is kept in several archive boxes that perforce dismember the gorgeous ceremonial body politic, boots in one box, helmet in another, mask, gloves, cloak in others. Displayed on a tailor's dummy or examined up close in the store, the costume shows itself an extraordinary work of art, hand-crafted from cloth-of-sequins, each tiny metal disc (of hundreds of thousands) a surface reflecting light in a dazzle of gold (Illustration 22). It materializes costliness. 'Sequin' is itself derived from 'chequin', as early modern English travellers to Venice had corrupted the local currency, the 'ducato di zecca' or 'zecchino'. A costume of 'sequins' is one made literally of money. And it materializes power not just in performance (working the transformation of Harry) but in production. It demonstrates the power of the director. Only someone as self-assured as Terry Hands, already aiming at the RSC's top job (which he'd secure three years later, partly on the triumph of his *Henry IV*s), would stake so much expense on so fleeting an encounter between spectacle and spectator.

It is perhaps because Alan Howard wore this costume for less than three minutes per performance – he appeared for the curtain call in something like a bathrobe – that it contains (to my eyes and nose) none of the actorly residue Barbara Hodgdon longs to encounter in the RSC's costume archive, where she writes of 'the thrill of touching a costume's fabric, feeling its weight and drape in one's hand': 'some of these clothes whisper, some sing or shout'; 'seeing them is like talking softly with someone'.[9] My encounter with the golden costume was of a completely different order. In the archive, it feels as remote as the act of alienation it performed on stage. There's no wear in the gloves, no sweat on the mask, no pressure marks of feet being shoved into boots during a quick change. No sign of Big Al's presence. No conversation, even whispered.

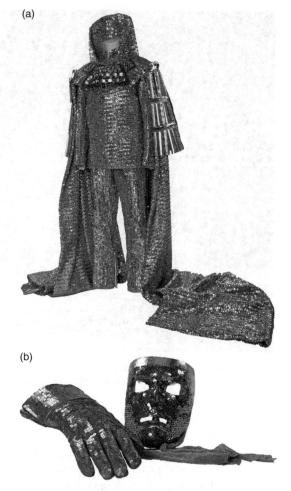

(a)

(b)

22. Harry's golden armour, RSC Costume Collection. Photograph by RSC. © RSC Images.

Question: what, then, does the costume archive remember? It doesn't remember. But it anchors the memories we bring to it. (The young curator opened archive boxes for me, unwrapped tissue. I lifted out gloves, the face mask; I talked about Alan Howard, remembering that magnificent actor of Shakespeare's English kings from Henry VI to Richard III, who'd died only a few months earlier. 'I had no idea', she said. Can objects, can texts, talk if we don't do the talking?)

---

[9] Hodgdon, 'Shopping in the archives', p. 140.

Still, if Harry's mask didn't speak to me, the work it performed upon spectators in 1975 got me thinking about the 'original' work for which Shakespeare required 'stuff' to perform upon *his* spectators of the *Henry IV* plays – objects, properties, costumes, the materials of performance that, for instance, were inventoried in lists (creating something like an early modern production archive) by Philip Henslowe for the Admiral's Men in 1599.[10] How might those English spectators have looked at an England Shakespeare staged as one mapped by rebels, a map put in view not just carved up and turned to new sovereignty, but squabbled over, its very rivers 'turned' (*1 Henry IV*, 3.1.132)? What might they have made of an England troped in a crown that we see figured in a shabby cushion worn threadbare by the weight of many men's buttocks (*1 Henry IV*, 2.4.369) and, later, in a golden manifestation, a 'polished perturbation', made of torturing metal that 'scald'st' the brows it encircles like 'armour worn in heat of day', a sort of elemental corrosive, not 'Preserving life in med'cine potable' but a chemical cannibal that 'Hath eat' the 'bearer up' (*2 Henry IV*, 4.3.154, 161–2, 292, 294)? Was the England he was gesturing at with these 'properties' the England of 1399 – or 1599?

I've claimed that Shakespeare wrote his *own* – his own time, people, London – into the *Henry IV*s, that he encouraged spectators to see themselves in the plays. But what if, like modern audiences watching 'heritage' Shakespeare today and failing to connect, Shakespeare's own audiences missed that recognition? Is it fanciful to suggest that he might have hit upon Falstaff, that spectacular embodiment or reification of so much conflicted history in these plays, to feature in a subsequent performance that would serve as the troublesome mechanism to align history 'ago' with 'now' and make Elizabethans see themselves? Shakespeare invents an afterlife for Falstaff. Post-rejection, Falstaff is sent, we remember, into banishment, owing poor Justice Shallow £1,000, though it is anyone's guess how Falstaff managed to shed £1,000 between Gloucestershire and Westminster, when they didn't even pause to change horses or shirts. By the time we see Falstaff

again, he's escaped from a boyhood serving John of Gaunt (d. 1399) as a page and from rogue service as an adult at Shrewsbury (fought in 1403), and he's miraculously emerged into a chancer's 'third age'. He's on the loose and on the make in Elizabethan Windsor, aiming to settle old debts in new times. In his disgracefully laddish feudal past, he ambushed the medieval king's exchequer and fabricated fabulous stories of derring-do and martial combat. In his Elizabethan present, he turns his attention to women, to fabulous flatteries, and to *marital* combat, aiming to prise open the groaning coffers of the well-heeled Windsor gentry by seducing their wives. Collapsing history into his capacious body, Falstaff makes *The Merry Wives of Windsor* all about 'us'. Could any Elizabethan mis-recognize 'us'?

In Desmond Barrit's performance at the RSC in 2014 – Barrit having played Falstaff in Peter Hall's *Henry IV*s in 2011 and in Michael Attenborough's at the RSC in 2000 – Falstaff in *Merry Wives* showed us the new face of power. The politics were local. The economy was domestic. The rhetoric was persuasive, and the costume was a kind of mask (like Harry's golden one) that revealed even as it concealed. We saw the contemplative predator, cranking up the charm for one more sting, sitting on the edge of his iron-frame bed in the charmless garret he rented at the Garter, holding up to his girth what he'd dug out of his suitcase. Falstaff considered his underpants – a pair of seducer-ware boxer shorts that he clearly hadn't worn since the days when he was an 'eagle's talon in the waist' (*1 Henry IV*, 2.4.321). Here he needed a mirror to see over his mountainous corpulence to check the fit (Illustration 23). How macro the belly; how micro the 'yard'. Yet how dangerous the intent. This personal costume archive disturbed Falstaff's image of who he was – observed by a theatre full of spectators.

---

[10] These inventories, now lost, are printed as Appendix 2 in R. A. Foakes and R. T. Rickert, *Henslowe's Diary* (Cambridge, 1968), pp. 316–25.

23. *The Merry Wives of Windsor*. Falstaff (Desmond Barrit) sizes up his underpants. RSC (2012), directed by Phillip Breen. Photograph by Pete Le May. © RSC Images.

Dressing the history 'boys', Phillip Breen, the director of *The Merry Wives of Windsor*, with Max Jones (his designer), like Phyllida Lloyd of the *Henry IV*s and her designer Deborah Andrews, used costume as Hands and Farrah did, precisely to that end: to disturb England's image of itself. It would be gratifying to report that the RSC's Costume Collection recognizes the equivalent political work the dressing did in these productions. It doesn't. The golden costume is archived. Harry's mask is carefully preserved. But Falstaff's underpants? They aren't there. More troublingly for my purposes in this article, the collection preserves row upon row of 'heritage history' costumes, costumes that say that England is about her gorgeous, vanished past; that her history is about well-padded, elaborately decorated Westminster elites. Gazing on all those remains of the history 'boys' across the years spilling out at me from untied muslin costume bags (like the guts of so many English subjects, hanged and drawn on traitors' scaffolds), I mused upon the kind of betrayal we perform upon these plays – and upon England – by settling for nostalgia, for looking backward. Post-Brexit, England has entered a period of profound – and profoundly conflicted – self-scrutiny that has to look forward. If they're produced as plays about the present as much as about the past, about Eastcheap as much as Westminster, about Gloucestershire, Wales and Northumberland as much as London, Shakespeare's *Henry IV*s can offer a powerful lens for conducting that scrutiny. Figured in Harry's masks and Falstaff's underpants, they give us England the golden – and the grubby.

SHOPPING FOR THE ARCHIVES: FASHIONING A COSTUME COLLECTION

KATE DORNEY

My title comes from Barbara Hodgdon's 'Shopping in the archives', which begins with an anecdote in which she is looking at two Sargent paintings in the Boston Museum of Fine Arts. One is *The Daughters of Edward Darley Boit*, and the other is an unnamed and now unidentifiable portrait of a young girl in a pink dress 'which clouds around her, radiating like an open peony blossom'.[1] A curator overhears her discussing the dress and tells her that, after he gave a gallery talk about the painting, a mysterious box arrived for him containing the peony dress along with a note from Sargent's model who had heard the talk.[2] I had a similar experience during my decade working as a curator at the Victoria & Albert Museum (V&A). At the end of a study day I'd arranged to celebrate the acquisition of Peter Brook's archive, I was seeing the Brooks into a taxi when Mary Rutherford, who played Hermia in the 1970 *A Midsummer Night's Dream*, thrust an orange Sainsbury's carrier bag into my hand explaining it was her costume. Then she disappeared before I could get her to complete any of the paperwork. I was left not with a peony dress, but with a white, woollen, A-line, ankle-length kaftan decorated with splashes of green. The shape of the costume and the quality of the fabric brought to mind the rack of Elders' costumes from the Ballets Russes *Rite of Spring* that hang in the V&A stores: surprisingly thick and blanket-like for roles that demand physical exertion. Rutherford's costume reflects the (then) contemporary fashion for kaftans, reminding me also of the extraordinary afterlife of some of Ballets Russes's costumes: modelled as hippie gear in

The Sunday Times to publicize the now-legendary Sotheby's sales of the 1960s and 1970s, and bought by the denizens of swinging London to wear at parties.[3]

The tales of the peony dress and the Rutherford kaftan reflect the serendipitous and unofficial nature of some museum acquisitions. One item or collection acts as a talisman that attracts (and sometimes repels) others. I assume Rutherford donated the costume because the V&A had a body of material relating to Brook and the production, and it seemed like a fitting home. As well as the recently acquired archive, the museum already counted several other costumes and a variety of props from the production, as well as costume designs and a set model remade by designer Sally Jacobs specifically for display, among its collection. When I made the acquisition file for the new costume, I justified its accession by explaining the significance of the production, how it complemented the museum's existing holdings of Brook's papers, Jacob's designs, props and other costumes. The peony dress and the kaftan also raise questions of

[1] Barbara Hodgdon, 'Shopping in the archives: material memories', in *Shakespeare, Memory, Performance*, ed. Peter Holland (Cambridge, 2006), pp. 135–66; p. 135.

[2] Hodgdon notes, 'curiously enough neither I nor the present MFA curator can identify, from exhibit catalogues or listings, what I once saw about which I once had listened to another's story of a memorable encounter' (p. 136).

[3] Jane Pritchard, 'Diaghilev under the hammer', in *Diaghilev and the Golden Age of the Ballets Russes*, ed. J. Pritchard (London, 2010), pp. 166–7.

attribution, of provenance. Unlike a conventional work of art or unique object, the provenance of items like these can be hard to establish and is often largely dependent on testimony. In the case of Hermia's costume, Rutherford told me she wore it in the production, it had a wardrobe label that said the same thing, it was showing wear consonant with life in a physically demanding production, so I deemed it an authentic item. But, as this article will discuss, the problem with performance remains like props and costume is that they're slippery – not always what they seem, even when they come from well-known, well-documented productions. Without secondary evidence or the resources and time of a science conservation laboratory, it can be hard to distinguish the costume from the first production from the costume for the tour or the understudy. They do not come with a signature like a design does, or a date like a book, or an impress like a print, and their wearability means they can, and do, walk away from the wardrobe department. Unlike Rutherford's simple kaftan, a single costume may have many parts to it as well as accessories, and, after a show ends, the separate costume parts may be stored separately, ready to be reused. Early in my curatorial career, I went to a Royal Shakespeare Company wardrobe sale and quickly realized that they were aimed not at browsing curators but at opera and theatre companies. The costumes are separated into their component parts or assigned a grouping based on role requirements – it is not the kind of sale at which one can reassemble a costume from a particular production but one at which you could clothe a production. This very recyclability makes shopping for the archive tricky, so curators tend to do their costume shopping in auction houses, actors' homes (and sometimes their sheds) and, occasionally, direct from a theatre or production company or a third party associated with the performer.[4]

Performers are good at preserving material because they like to have mementos from shows and they also like the idea of passing on, or receiving, talismanic objects. Hodgdon demonstrates this through her discussion of 'The Peggy', a long brown cardigan worn by Peggy Ashcroft in *All's Well That Ends Well*, then

by Estelle Kohler in *A Winter's Tale*, and Alexandra Gilbreath in *The Taming of the Shrew*.[5] A more spectacular example in the V&A is the Chinese Conjuror costume from *Parade*, made between 1917 and 1920 for either Léonide Massine or Léon Woizikovsky – the fact that we cannot be sure testifies again to the tricky nature of costume – which survived World War II buried in a garden in Poland (given that the house burned down, the survival is even more miraculous). Serge Lifar then bought the costume from Woizikovsky and the V&A bought it, silk shattered, knees ripped, from Sotheby's.[6] Although we cannot be completely sure whether the costume was made for Massine or Woizikovsky, we know what the costume is for because it is an iconic Ballets Russes production, much photographed and talked about. Just like Brook's *Dream*.

Rutherford's Hermia costume is not the only performer's gift from the show. Patricia Doyle, who understudied Sara Kestelman's Titania and played one of the Fairies on the 1972 tour, also donated costumes to the museum. A note on the acquisitions file records that she told the acquiring curator that 'most costumes were burned at the end of the world tour as Brook felt the production had come to the end of its natural life'.[7] Brook may have felt, or wished, that the production was at the end of its natural life, but memories and appetite for it have lived on and its remnants are constantly in demand to stand in for, commemorate and reactivate the show. At the time of writing, Doyle's Titania costume, a green synthetic silk kaftan, is on display in the museum's permanent theatre gallery, while Kestelman's had a recent tour of duty in the British Library's *Shakespeare in Ten Acts* exhibition, in which the production loomed

[4] Hodgdon begins her most recent work, *Shakespeare, Performance and the Archive* (London, 2016), with an account of the rehearsal of the Nine Worthies scene in John Borton's 1972 production of *Love's Labour's Lost* that draws on numerous other past productions for props and costumes.

[5] Hodgdon, 'Shopping in the archives', pp. 160–1.

[6] For more on the costume, see 'Need to know', *Selvedge* 37 (2010), 6.

[7] V&A Registered File.

large. Even more recently, a rehearsal shot by Laurence Burns provides the cover of Barbara Hodgdon's *Shakespeare, Performance and the Archive* while, inside, his shots enable her to recreate and re-interrogate the performance. Some productions are sticky, lodged in the collective memory and sometimes so familiar that they seem preserved in amber, so that the fine grains and textures are no longer distinguishable. Hodgdon skilfully reanimates Brook's *Dream* using Burns's photographs and her own memories of the show. Here I want to try to re-texturize and contextualize Harley Granville Barker's *Twelfth Night* (1912) and, to a lesser extent, *A Midsummer Night's Dream* (1914) through a close reading of costumes, photographs and archival material from those productions and the textures of those productions – more precisely, the textures of the textile and paint that created the visual effects of the performance revealed by the collections of the V&A.

The V&A had officially collected theatre material since 1924, when it accepted Gabrielle Enthoven's collection of playbills, prints and engravings into the Department of Engravings, Illustrations and Designs. Along with the collection, it took their collector and her money, but it limited acquisitions to two-dimensional material, which may explain why a portion of Henry Irving's stage wardrobe ended up at the Museum of London (MoL) in 1938 instead of at the V&A, and why some costumes from *Twelfth Night* are also there. Enthoven died in 1950 and, soon after, two pressure groups began acquiring a wider range of material, including props and costumes, as part of a strategic plan to force the government into creating a separate museum of performance. The British Theatre Museum Association gathered, among others, Lillah McCarthy's archive and costumes from *Androcles and the Lion*, *The Witch*, *Twelfth Night*, and *A Midsummer Night's Dream*, as well an evening gown worn by Elenora Duse and some Ballets Russes costumes. The Friends of the National Museum for Performing Arts bought Ballets Russes costumes and cloths from a succession of Sotheby's auctions between 1967 and 1968.[8]

The convergence of McCarthy's costumes and those of the Ballets Russes at the point of acquisition is pleasingly serendipitous given the contiguity of the productions and the noted influence of Ballets Russes designers Alexandre Benois and Leon Bakst on Norman Wilkinson of Four Oaks, who designed the set and costumes for Harley Granville Barker's *Twelfth Night* and *A Midsummer Night's Dream*. Both sets of costumes also went on display within ten years of each other: Richard Buckle created his first exhibition of displayed Ballets Russes material in the 1950s, and McCarthy's costumes went on display at the British Theatre Museum in Leighton House in the mid-1960s. A generation too young to have seen the shows now had the opportunity to see the costumes and realize their composition for the first time.

Russell Jackson is one of many scholars who has noted how *Twelfth Night* combined

authenticity in the use of an apron stage and stylized settings with an adoption of Elizabethan costume that was qualified by a degree of exoticism: his Viola is in doublet and knee breeches, as are Malvolio, Sebastian, Sir Toby and Sir Andrew, but Orsino's court is that of a (vaguely) Eastern potentate. The 'authentic' costumes are themselves stylized, redolent of the work of designers for Diaghilev's *Ballets Russes* – such as Leon Bakst and Alexander Benois – the colours and patterns of fabrics are distinctively of the new movements in the visual arts.[9]

I would add to Jackson's observation that the *Twelfth Night* costumes also reveal the symbiotic nature of the relations between stage costume and fashionable dress in the same way that Jacob's costumes for *A Midsummer Night's Dream* do, but

---

[8] Among the acquisitions were Vladimirov's costume from *The Sleeping Princess*, the Buffoon and his Wife from *Chout*, Max Frohman's costume for a lover in *Le Dieu bleu*, and the blue, white, and brick costume for a guest in *Le Bal* (Jane Pritchard, www.vam.ac.uk/blog/diaghilev-and-ballets-russes/adventures-costumes).

[9] Russell Jackson, 'Brief overview: a stage history of Shakespeare and costume', in *Shakespeare and Costume*, ed. Patricia Lennox and Bella Mirabella (London, 2015), pp. 9–20; p. 16.

more of that later. What the V&A holdings on the Savoy Shakespeares and Ballets Russes reveal is the utility of collecting costumes and other three-dimensional materials alongside the more familiar performance remains of reviews, photographs and archival material. Among the McCarthy material at the V&A is an account book detailing all the money spent on the Savoy Season, which, when read alongside the remaining costumes and the numerous photographs that featured in the illustrated journals *Play Pictorial* and the *Sketch*, provides a tactile dimension to the reimagining of the production, as well as a re-colouring of it. Dennis Kennedy has vividly described the clash of colours and Wilkinson's mix of East and West in the appearance and decoration of Olivia's house and garden and Orsino's court:

Wilkinson used a colour scheme to contrast the mourning of Olivia's house, principally in black, to the mooning passion of the Duke's court, principally in carmine ... Wilkinson said he sought after 'romance and smartness' in the costumes (*Evening News* 12 Nov. 1912, p. 7) by combining a basic Elizabethan style with the exoticism of a Persian seraglio, apparent in Orsino's cape and turban ... For the final scene a pair of golden gates was inserted at mid stage level, the box trees and baldecchino having been struck; the gates and walls had an East–West hybrid look that matched that of the clothes. The Duke's soldiers were like Swiss Guards, with high Spanish helmets and shiny breastplates.[10]

Susan Carlson has further suggested that the cerise and green colour scheme is a sign of Granville Barker and McCarthy's sympathy with the suffrage cause – cerise and green being the colours of the Actresses' Franchise League (AFL).[11] I like this idea very much, but it seems strange that an outspoken suffragist like McCarthy would not mention it anywhere, even in her memoirs.

Given *Twelfth Night's* 'obsessive discourse of materials and material goods',[12] it is not surprising that the Savoy production should offer so much scope for the analysis of costume and textures. Building on Kennedy and Jackson, I suggest that Orsino's Orientalized court retinue has much in common with Bakst's *Schéhérazade* (1910) – harem

pants, turbans, billowing tunics, all trimmed with pearls (Illustrations 24 and 25: souvenir figures from *Schéhérazade*, Victoria & Albert Museum, London) – but, through him, with fashion. In the 1910s, Bakst was well on his way to becoming a 'legislator of fashion', while Parisian designer Paul Poiret had been popularizing 'tassels and bold Ottoman embroidery, Indian-inspired turbans and oversized "Chinese" opera cloaks in sumptuous fabrics, in an eclectic melange of influences'.[13] In an interview in the *Evening News*, Wilkinson declared: 'a feature of the costumes will be the number and variety of cloaks' (*Evening News*, 12 Nov. 1912, p. 7), and in 'Modes of Mayfair' in the *Play Pictorial* special edition on *Twelfth Night*, Rita Detmold reminds readers that: 'At the moment, the Russian and Eastern influences are still paramount ... Both in the beautiful and elaborate fabrics and the quaint touches of gorgeous bits of colour are these effects conceived.'[14]

Bearing all this in mind, we might then view Orsino's court not as that of an 'Eastern potentate' but as an enthusiastic (perhaps over-enthusiastic) follower of fashion. Orsino's costume is described in the account book as a cerise velvet tunic and knickers trimmed with pearls and silver braid, and a cerise corded silk coat stencilled in gold. The production photographs suggest that the softness of the velvet is mitigated by the stiffness of the paint, pearl, and braid so that he presents a hard surface in comparison to Cesario's silken doublet and breeches (of which more later). The facings of

---

[10] Dennis Kennedy, *Harley Granville Barker and the Dream of Theatre* (Cambridge, 1985), p. 146.

[11] Susan Carlson, 'Politicizing Harley Granville Barker: suffragists and Shakespeare', *New Theatre Quarterly* 22.2 (2006), 122–40; p. 134.

[12] Keir Elam, 'Introduction', in Arden Shakespeare's *Twelfth Night*, 3rd edn (London, 2008), unpaginated (accessed via Dramaonline).

[13] John E. Bowlt, 'Leon Bakst, Natalia Goncharova and Pablo Picasso', in Pritchard, ed., *Diaghilev*, pp. 103–15, p. 104; Claire Wilcox, 'Paul Poiret and the Ballets Russes', in Pritchard, ed., *Diaghilev*, pp. 64–5, p. 64.

[14] Rita Detmold, 'Modes of Mayfair', *Play Pictorial* 21.26 (1912), iv.

24. Wooden souvenir figure of The Grand Eunuch in *Schéhérazade*, designed by Vera Willoughby (also Petrovna). Victoria & Albert Museum, London.

gown with a brocade overcoat, a plaid gauze turban and red morocco shoes, and the production suggests that Viola did her shopping in Paris or Mayfair. The costume bears a marked resemblance to Poiret's 'Lavallière' evening dress, and McCarthy could have strolled off the stage and down the street in this like a fashionable woman about town.[15]

All the extant costumes emphasize the fact that, from the play's opening to its end, Viola is all smooth silk to Orsino's pearls and painted velvet. There is some debate over McCarthy's opening costume. I take it to be the fashionable green Chinese silk gown and turban described in the account book as the 'first dress'. Wilkinson states that 'Viola, played by Miss Lillah McCarthy, makes her appearance in a Persian dress, wearing a burnous [a loose Arabian cloak] in which green, white and gold will be noted, and on her head a turban' (Wilkinson, *Evening News*, 12 Nov. 1912, p. 7). The *Play Pictorial* picture of McCarthy in this costume however, is captioned 'Let me see thee in thy woman's weeds' (*Play Pictorial*, 126, 68), and appears at the end of the feature, implying she wears it, or reassumes it, in Act 5. Working from *Play Pictorial*, Christine Dymkowski describes 'a Viola who finally appears in woman's weeds of vampy caftan, blousy long robe of patterned silk, and turban'.[16] In her edition of *Twelfth Night*, Schafer suggests this is the case – 'Occasionally Viola reappears in a dress e.g. in Craig (1907) (*Boston Transcript* 5 Jan 1907); Lillah McCarthy in Barker (1912)'[17] – but there is no mention of the exit and reappearance of Viola in Kelly's account of the prompt books.[18] In his 1968

[15] The 'Lavallière' is illustrated in Wilcox, 'Paul Poiret', p. 65.

[16] Christine Dymkowski, *Harley Granville Barker: A Preface to Modern Shakespeare* (London, 1986), p. 48.

[17] *Twelfth Night*, ed. Elizabeth Schafer, Shakespeare in Production (Cambridge, 2009), p. 224.

[18] Without access to a copy of the prompt, housed at University of Michigan, I have relied on Kelly's thesis (Helen M. Kelly, 'The Granville-Barker productions: a study based on the promptbooks' (unpublished Ph.D. thesis, University of Michigan, 1965)), Schafer's edition of the play, and the latter's kind responses to my enquiries.

one of McCarthy's extant costumes suggests that 'cerise' is close to Schiaparelli's shocking pink – another reminder of the ever close association, and sometimes overlapping, of fashion and costume design. Viola's costume reinforces this. The account book describes a green Chinese silk

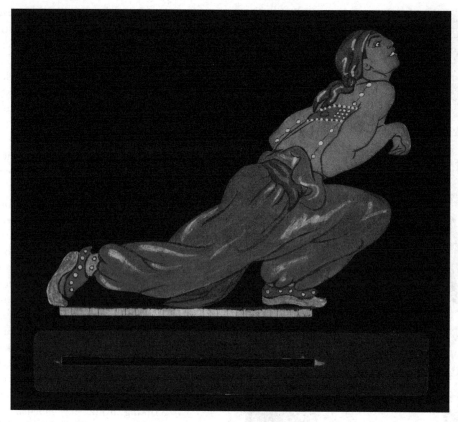

25. Wooden souvenir figure of Massine as the Favourite Slave in *Schéhérazade*, designed by Vera Willoughby (also Petrovna). Victoria & Albert Museum, London.

catalogue of MoL stage costumes, M. R. Holmes suggests the 'Large cloak with armholes, cream brocade trimmed with green silk and silver lace, and lined with black poplin' was probably for her first appearance when shipwrecked.[19] But close reading of the production photographs, photographs from MoL, and the account book suggests this cloak is actually part of the 'third dress' described as 'white brocade cloak trimmed with green braid and silver braid, lined black silk', which McCarthy is pictured wearing in 5.1 alongside her identically dressed brother.

Like Sebastian and Viola, the *Twelfth Night* costumes were separated, but, unlike the twins, are unlikely to be reunited and, appropriately, the confusion intensifies when it comes to breeches/trunks. In his preface to the 1912 acting edition of

Twelfth Night, one senses Barker's disapproval of actresses who 'seize every chance of reminding the audience that they are girls dressed up, to impress on one moreover, by childish by-play as to legs and petticoats or the absence of them'.[20] McCarthy records how, on Barker's instructions, she suppressed 'her urge to let Viola betray the woman in her'.[21] This might explain why Viola and Sebastian wear boots with their breeches while every other man but Toby wears stockings and shoes. If the

[19] M. R. Holmes, *London Museum Stage Costume and Accessories* (London, 1968), p. 63.
[20] *Twelfth Night*, ed. Harley Granville Barker (London, 1912), p. vii.
[21] Lillah McCarthy, *Myself and My Friends* (London, 1933), p. 161.

production photographs are any kind of record, it seems unlikely that McCarthy's legs were ever visible as her knee-high brown boots were met by her knee-length black and green slashed silk breeches and matching doublet. The account book records two sets of 'trunks' and two matching doublets for Viola, along with 'One silver brocade coat. Five black velvet hats, trimmed pearls. Six pairs of white kid gloves trimmed cerise and silver. Two pairs black silk stockings. One cerise plush brocade cloak lined with gold tinsel. Sword and belt. Two pairs black silk opera hose' (Savoy Theatre Account Book, V&A). But what exists is a crudely sewn together doublet and trunks in the V&A (along with a matching outfit for her brother), while MoL has a pair of trunks joined to a white chemise and a separate doublet, along with a 'Knee-length cassock of silver-grey brocade trimmed with magenta. Short bell sleeves with close black and green sleeves inset, simulating the sleeves of the preceding doublet.'[22] The inset sleeves turn the cassock into an intriguing hybrid that is designed to be worn instead of a doublet rather than over it. It isn't clear when McCarthy first appears in the cassock – the photographs in *Play Pictorial* and the *Sketch* suggest that she wears only doublet and breeches at Orsino's court, and the cassock with breeches underneath in the scenes with Olivia. So, between 1.4 and 1.5, she has to discard the tunic for the cassock, which we might read in several ways at the same time: as an 'outdoor' garment; as livery, symbolizing that she is part of Orsino's retinue; but also as a feminine garment. Unlike the loose flowing cloaks worn by the rest of Orsino's court, the cassock buttons up to the chin, is nipped in at the waist by a belt and flares out below the waist. I assume that she puts on the separate doublet to match the breeches for 2.4 with Orsino, swaps doublet for cassock at 3.1 through to 3.4, and then puts the doublet *and* cassock back on after exiting at 266,[23] before returning to the stage for the duel, for which 'she removed her coat and placed it on the right proscenium seat'.[24] In photographs of 5.1, she is still in tunic and breeches with the addition of the cream brocade cloak of the third costume. I thought that

the V&A conjoined doublet and hose was a quick-change garment, but it actually requires more fastening than the separate items, so it is hard to work out its role. The stitching at the waistband is crude and irregular, so it is possible that the alteration came later in its life – its inscrutability is a prime example of the slipperiness of costume.

A more glaring spare, the 'Antonio', if you will, is a beautiful silver brocade tunic with cerise facings donated to the V&A along with the other McCarthy costumes. The account book describes a 'cerise plush brocade cloak lined with gold tinsel' and specifies that it should be made from '6 ¾ yds cerise and gold velvet tissue' (Savoy Account Book). But what exists is a silver brocade coat with cerise silk facings (Illustration 26) clearly showing considerable signs of wear – it surely had a role in the performance, but there is nothing in the prompt, production photographs or press accounts to suggest what it might have been. I have yet to find a picture of McCarthy wearing it; previous curators have always assumed she wore it over the doublet and breeches, but I cannot find any evidence to support this. If she did change back into her 'woman's weeds' for the end of the play, it is possible she wore the coat over the dress, cementing the union between her and Orsino. Or that she wore the 'cerise plush cloak' described in the account book, which would match his own cerise and gold costume. It is also possible that the V&A coat was made for the Savoy company's 'Twelfth Night' ball, or the Three Arts Club ball where she appeared in her Cesario costume, or for the performance of *Twelfth Night* at Middle Temple put on in 1914 in aid of the Red Cross, but I have yet to find any accounts of this with images.

The gold-hued *A Midsummer Night's Dream* of 1914 is a more straightforward affair, perhaps

---

[22] Holmes, *London Museum Stage Costume*, p. 63.

[23] Schafer notes that the promptbook records Viola's exit but does not mention that removing her cassock is part of the 'Bus[iness] of preparing them for the duel' – that is, saluting, measuring ground, etc. (Schafer, ed., *Twelfth Night*, pp. 187 and 251).

[24] Kelly, 'The Granville-Barker productions', p. 214.

26. Costume worn by Lillah McCarthy as Viola in *Twelfth Night*, designed by Norman Wilkinson of Four Oaks. Victoria & Albert Museum, London.

because only one costume is extant. McCarthy recalls her pale gold hair 'fresh from Clarkson [the theatrical wig makers], in a cardboard box, delivered daily. One such golden thread was all that Ariadne had. I had a wig full.'[25] She delighted in her long golden hair, but the gold theme was not uniformly delightful. Titania and Oberon's attendants were all dressed in bronze and gold with golden hair and faces. A terrific photo album given by Beryl Hoare, one of the attendants, contains a short account of the gilding process, which cost a shilling per fairy per performance:

Our gold leaf make up came in books of 12 small sheets. We 4 could use 6 a performance so were allowed out between the matinee and evening performance. The adult principals were not so lucky as they used more sheets than we did. We started the show by using a gold dust which we put on our faces with hare's foot. But, and I think it was through Christine Silver that we gave it up, as it affected her complexion badly. I was only 11 years old so wouldn't like to be too sure about anything. My only thought was: –
   Whose turn is it to tie up Dennis Neilson-Terry's gold gaiters as we took it in turns. He was so sweet to the four of us.[26]

The fairy haze of gold is revealed to have prosaic implications: the gold dust causes break-outs, or worse, in Titania's skin, despite being applied with the soft hare's foot – a staple of actors' make-up boxes. Neilson Terry's gaiters look scratchy and uncomfortable and liable to constantly fall down. At least the fairies had a soft velvet mound to sit on, but everything else about them was stiff and otherworldly. Their golden corkscrew curls were made of curled and painted buckram – a fabric more usually employed to stiffen books or other fabrics. The effect of the gold paint and the stiff fabric had critics describing them as brass or ormolou figures, or, as *The Times* noted,

Is it Titania's 'Indian Boy' that has given Mr Wilkinson his notion of Orientalising Shakespeare's fairies? Or is Bakst? Anyhow, they look like Cambodian idols and posture like Njinsky in *Le Dieu Bleu* ... they are all gold ... One with a scimitar stalks like the black marionette, with *his*

[25] McCarthy, *Myself and My Friends*, p. 174.
[26] Beryl Hoare Collection, THM/386, V&A.

27. Costume for a Little God in *Le Dieu Bleu*, designed by Leon Bakst. Victoria & Albert Museum, London.

scimitar in *Petrouchka* [*sic*]. Evidently the Russian ballet, which has transformed so much in London, has transmogrified Shakespeare.[27]

There are certainly similarities between individual figures in Titania's and Oberon's retinues. The white and gold costume for a Little God from *Le Dieu bleu* is festooned with swags and coils (Illustration 27) as are some of the *A Midsummer Night's Dream* attendants. The scimitar-wielding fairy is not only reminiscent of the marionette in

Petrushka, his costume also prompts memories of *Schéhérazade* and, indeed, *Twelfth Night*. They are not, I would say, posturing in a particularly Njinsky-like way in the extant photographs. One doesn't nowadays think of Njinsky posturing, but his careful, precise movements and the *placement* represented in photographs and souvenirs might well account for the

[27] *The Times*, 7 February 1914, p. 8.

133

word choice. The Ballets Russes influence can also be seen in Helena's Act 5 crêpe de chine silk dress designed by Wilkinson, which is strikingly similar to Bakst's design for Likenion in *Daphnis and Chloe*.[28] Greek costume, it seems, looks the same whether you were born in Grodno or Birmingham. Helena's two silk dresses, incidentally, were far more expensive than the gold accessories and paint, costing £23 6s 9½d – more than £2,000 at today's prices. Only one of the dresses made it to the V&A, and it's likely that this one survived because McCarthy spent most of her time in it reclining on a couch during Act 5. A former colleague gave an account of the Theatre and Performance department's origins memorably titled 'Accidents of survival', and this is certainly true of performance costume – survival is a mixture of luck and foresight.[29] Woizikovsky had the foresight to bury his *Parade* costume and, through luck, it survived the attention of rodents and insects while buried in a Polish garden – not to mention the fire that engulfed the house. Someone, perhaps McCarthy, made the decision to keep the costumes from the Savoy Shakespeares, whether for pragmatic reasons or sentimental ones, or both, and then to pass them

on, just as Rutherford, Doyle and Kestelman did with their Brook *Dream* costumes decades later. Their foresight and generosity allow us to re-read those performances, to puzzle over the processes that created them, and to remind ourselves that, through material culture, fantasy can always be traced back to reality.[30]

[28] And also in the illustration for Detmold's 'Modes of Mayfair' in *Play Pictorial*, mentioned above.

[29] Catherine Haill, 'Accidents of survival: finding a place in the V&A's theatre and performance archives', in *Scrapbooks, Snapshots and Memorabilia: Hidden Archives of Performance*, ed. Glen McGillivray (Bern, 2011), pp. 105–28.

[30] I dedicate this article to Barbara Hodgdon, an inspiration and fellow quester in the archives. Without the generosity of my former colleagues, particularly Janet Birkett, Veronica Castro, and Beverley Hart at the V&A, and Beatrice Behlen at MoL, who hauled out costumes, photographed them, and speculated with me, it would have been impossible to produce this account. Thanks also to Veronica Isaac and Lou Taylor, without whom I would know very little about dress history and textiles, and to Christine Dymkowski and Elizabeth Schafer for sharing their own archives and memories with me regarding their excavations in Barker's *Twelfth Night*.

PASTICHE OR ARCHETYPE? THE SAM WANAMAKER PLAYHOUSE AND THE PROJECT OF THEATRICAL RECONSTRUCTION

HOLGER SCHOTT SYME

An actor speaks a speech written 400 years ago, using her 21st-century voice and body, surrounded by a few hundred similarly modern bodies and their minds. She might do this from a stage stretching out deep behind her and the proscenium arch framing her. She might do it from a platform surrounded on all sides by spectators. Perhaps she is lit by a sharply focused spot. Perhaps she is speaking with the aid of a microphone, her voice coming at the audience's ears separated from the body that their eyes observe. But no matter how it is framed, produced, contextualized or interpreted, the moment always involves a clash of cultures: the words are manifestly neither the actor's nor the audience's; they sound nothing like the words these bodies would use in their everyday lives. They do, in an obvious if rarely acknowledged sense, not belong. From a scholarly perspective, it is apparent enough how studying such modern theatrical transactions would yield insights about contemporary performance cultures; it may be less obvious how they could offer up new perspectives on the dramatic works themselves, given that the particular clash they necessarily produce and have to negotiate is an effect of historical distance, not of a deeper immersion in or closer proximity to the text being staged. What, however, if a performance could reduce that distance, at least in certain respects? What if we could recreate the spaces for which those 400-year-old plays were written, reproduce the visual and aural conditions of their original performances, give actors opportunities to leave as much as possible of their 21st-century selves behind and address their (irreducibly modern) audiences from a perspective that limits

the sense that a historical gap separates text and performer?

That dream lies behind most efforts at theatrical reconstruction, no matter whether they adopt a rigorous 'original practices' approach, stretching to the replication of accents and early modern all-male casting practices, or whether they merely seek to recreate some of the physical conditions of staging early modern plays. Put Shakespeare's plays on an outdoor thrust stage, the thinking goes, in a theatre that tries to resemble the original Globe – stage them in an indoor space approximating the performance environment of a seventeenth-century hall, using only simulated daylight and candles – and something will reveal itself about the plays; something about their theatre-historical moment of origin that eludes other scholarly or theatrical approaches will become tangible.[1]

In this article, I am primarily concerned with what we might be able to discover about early modern indoor performance from contemporary theatrical engagements. Broadly, I will ask whether we can in fact learn anything about playacting 400 years ago by playacting now; more specifically,

---

[1] Essays that engage critically with this idea include Jeremy Lopez, 'A partial theory of original practice', *Shakespeare Survey 61* (Cambridge, 2008), pp. 302–17; Abigail Rokinson, 'Authenticity in the twenty-first century: Propeller and Shakespeare's Globe', in *Shakespeare in Stages: New Theatre Histories*, ed. Christine Dymkowski and Christie Carson (Cambridge, 2010), pp. 71–90; and my 'Where is the theatre in original practice?' Dispositio.net, 25 July 2014, www.dispositio.net/archives/1942.

whether we can learn anything about Jacobean indoor playing from the Sam Wanamaker Playhouse (SWP), the indoor space at Shakespeare's Globe in London that opened in 2014.

The SWP is obviously a gorgeous theatre. The paper on which this article is based was delivered from the Wanamaker's stage and could let the space speak for itself; readers unfamiliar with the venue will have to take my word for it. It is a beautiful venue for performance, despite the discomforts of some of its seats (because of the curved benches in the semi-circular pit, spectators seated there have to twist their bodies and crane their necks to manage a straight view of the stage).[2] The sensual experience this theatre offers is quite extraordinary. Its smells, of wood and beeswax candles (more intense four years ago than now, since the building has aged a little); the texture of the candlelight; the physical proximity of the actors: all of this amounts to an atmosphere and a mode of theatre that is not readily available elsewhere.[3] The other major attempt at reconstructing an early modern hall playhouse, the Blackfriars replica in Staunton, VA, has a very different effect – partly because it is larger, partly because it uses electrical lighting.[4] By most accounts, actors love the SWP, too: every single one interviewed for the Globe's 'Adopt an Actor' podcast series praises the intimacy of the theatre, the connection they can establish with the audience, and the vocal flexibility it allows.[5] However, as interesting a venue as the SWP may be, it is not at all clear that it is a replica of a 'Jacobean playhouse' in any meaningful sense.

'REIMAGINING' A JACOBEAN THEATRE

When the bricks-and-mortar shell surrounding the theatre was built as part of the Globe reconstruction in the mid 1990s, its footprint and external features were based on a set of drawings from Worcester College – drawings that at the time had been dated to around 1616 and were believed to be by Inigo Jones. To realize how important those plans were to the initial conception of the

Globe's indoor theatre, one only needs to consult John Orrell's chapter on 'The Inigo Jones designs'

---

[2] Many early reviews of the space commented on the uncomfortable seating arrangements; one critic noted that 'a good half to two thirds of the seats are facing the centre of the auditorium. This means that in order to see the stage you have to turn in your seat to watch what is going on' (Rev Stan, 'The Sam Wanamaker Playhouse experience (or why?)', *Rev Stan's Theatre Blog*, 8 March 2014, http://theatre.revstan.com/2014/03/the-sam-wanamaker-playhouse-experience-or-why.html. Andrew Gurr has argued, in conversation with Martin White, that the SWP's layout speaks to a 'three-dimensional' understanding of theatre, 'in which the centre of the theatre is where you group everybody around and that curvature of the seating in the pit reflected precisely that' – as if all the seats were oriented towards an actor speaking from the centre of the stage's fore-edge ('Interpreting the evidence: Prof. Andrew Gurr', *Chamber of Demonstrations* (Bristol, 2009), DVD, 7:25-8:00). This might be a reasonable description of the relationship between the orchestra and the seating area in an ancient Greek theatre, but it is manifestly not how the SWP is set up. Instead, the seats in the pit, precisely *because* of the curved benches, point *away* from the stage (as do the galleries on the side of the pit), making it necessary for spectators to twist their necks and bodies to see the action. Arranging the pit benches parallel to the stage edge would achieve the effect Gurr describes far more effectively than a semi-circular auditorium in which the majority of seats do not point towards the stage (as is the case in the SWP).

[3] For photos of the interior, see www.shakespearesglobe.com/support-us/sam-wanamaker-playhouse, as well as production photos of past shows, at www.shakespearesglobe.com/discovery-space/previous-productions. The opening show, *The Duchess of Malfi*, is available on video at https://globeplayer.tv/videos/the-duchess-of-malfi.

[4] For a Google Streetview walk-through of the Blackfriars Playhouse, see https://goo.gl/maps/gDudSbojBsAZ.

[5] See www.Shakespearesglobe.com/discovery-space/adopt-an-actor/archive. As Will Tosh, postdoctoral research fellow at Shakespeare's Globe, noted in a paper delivered as part of the 'Settling In: Reflecting on the Move Indoors' panel at the World Shakespeare Congress 2016 in London, these publicly available interviews tend to be somewhat more positive in tone than the extensive interviews with cast members conducted by the Globe's 'Indoor Performance Practice Project'. In the latter conversations, actors have reflected more critically on the challenges of the space, in particular the difficulty of vocally reaching the upper galleries when the proximity of the pit and the lower galleries invites a more reduced style of acting.

in *Rebuilding Shakespeare's Globe*, the programmatic volume he co-authored with Andrew Gurr.[6] In fact, it was thanks to their existence that reconstructing the indoor space appeared a less fraught undertaking than the 'rebuilding' of 'Shakespeare's' Globe itself.[7] The Worcester College drawings 'show something remarkably like the Blackfriars', Orrell wrote (p. 130); 'Jones's drawings provide us with the kind of concrete certainty that all Elizabethan theatre studies unfortunately lack ... Here for once the English theatre historian can leave his guesswork and address two sheets of paper generously spilling over with unimpeachable facts' (p. 132). The confidence that the drawings showed a theatre 'almost exactly like the Blackfriars' (p. 129) was probably misplaced even in 1989: Orrell knew, after all, that the theatre they depicted measured 40 by 55 feet from outer wall to outer wall (excluding the stair turrets), whereas the Blackfriars was 46 feet wide and at least 66 feet long *internally* – unquestionably a much bigger space. But the purported similarity between the drawings and the King's Men's own indoor venue was clearly a key aspect of the allure of those plans, and part of the justification for including a reconstruction of a hall playhouse based on them in the Shakespeare's Globe complex. For Orrell, who argued that the drawings represent Christopher Beeston's Cockpit (which opened in 1617), it was significant that the Cockpit 'began life as a regular private house of the *Blackfriars type*' (p. 139, my italics). Reconstructing the theatre depicted in the drawings, therefore, would not simply mean rebuilding the Cockpit but 'the equivalent of the Blackfriars': 'if we build the Jones Cockpit playhouse to these precise and original designs we shall possess a structure which comes as close as we dare hope to the staging conditions established at the Blackfriars by James Burbage in 1596 and inherited by Shakespeare in 1609' (p. 148).[8] Andrew Gurr is using similar language when he describes the planned 'Inigo Jones playhouse' in glowing terms as 'an absolutely authentic original design, a close neighbour and rival to the Blackfriars, an indoor playhouse, a bridge between Shakespeare and

modern theatre designs'.[9] And, more recently, Martin White has suggested that the drawings, no matter when they were made, represent 'a playhouse that looks exactly like a playhouse you would design in 1616'.[10]

There is what should be an obvious problem with those arguments: as Orrell himself notes, a reconstruction of the Blackfriars itself would be highly 'speculative', since 'almost every part of the structure would be based on analogical rather than direct evidence' (p. 129). However, once one admits that nobody really knows what the Blackfriars looked like, the claim that the Worcester College designs *resemble* the Blackfriars becomes necessarily meaningless: how, after all, can we know that something resembles something else if only one of the two somethings is known? White's assertion that the Worcester College images look 'exactly' like a 1616 theatre is similarly baffling, simply because no-one can say what such a theatre would have looked like. And the broader allegation that there was such a thing as a 'Blackfriars type' is possibly even more problematic: if we only have one actual exemplar of an indoor theatre (taking the Worcester images as that

---

6 Andrew Gurr, with John Orrell, *Rebuilding Shakespeare's Globe* (London, 1989), pp. 125–48.

7 Identifying both theatres as 'Shakespeare's' was justified by Orrell's extraordinary claim that 'it is certain that [the Globe and the Blackfriars] were both developed with the presentation of [Shakespeare's] plays in mind' (Gurr and Orrell, *Rebuilding*, p. 125) – a statement that presupposes an utter centrality of Shakespeare's drama to the Chamberlain's and King's Men's repertory, for which we have no real evidence.

8 Given that the actual dimensions of the Blackfriars are known, and, as I discuss below, differ markedly from those of the building in the Worcester College designs, as well as from those that have been proposed for Beeston's playhouse, the leap from reconstructing the Cockpit to building something approximating the Blackfriars is a precarious manoeuvre even before considering other problems with the drawings.

9 Gurr, 'The Inigo Jones Playhouse', in Gurr and Orrell, *Rebuilding*, pp. 167–71; esp. p. 171.

10 'Interpreting the evidence: Dr Gordon Higgott – the Worcester College drawings', Chamber of Demonstrations, 8:55.

for now), how can we derive from that a 'type'? And why would such a 'type' be named *not* after the depicted theatre, but after one with which it purportedly shares many features, even though far too little is known about that other playhouse to assess what its essential features were and whether or not they were 'typical'? I will return to the problem of typicality below; for now, though, I want to note that the very notion that the Worcester plans capture not just a particular playhouse, but an entire *category* of playhouse, was a crucial aspect of their appeal to the reconstructionists. It made rebuilding something *like* the Blackfriars, the Globe's natural indoor sibling, a tangible possibility.

Unfortunately, in the intervening years, the very 'concrete certainty' of the Worcester College document that Orrell welcomed so enthusiastically has also faded away, along with the longed-for 'unimpeachable facts'. The notion that the drawings represent the Cockpit was already difficult to maintain in 1989, in the face of an essay published the previous year in which Graham Barlow showed conclusively that the plot on which that theatre was constructed was too small to accommodate the building outlined in the plans.[11] For that reason alone, Glynne Wickham's belief that the drawings in fact depicted the Salisbury Court playhouse of 1629 was certainly a far safer bet than Orrell's identification of the building as a Jacobean theatre.[12]

By now, however, even the identification of the building in the designs as an actual Caroline theatre has become virtually untenable. Gordon Higgott has shown beyond reasonable doubt that the Worcester College drawings are not by Inigo Jones but by his assistant John Webb. Jones never employed the specific techniques on display in the drawings, and he certainly had not mastered the skill with which they were made in the 1610s. Webb, on the other hand, only entered Jones's service after he finished his schooling in 1628; he, too, did not develop the techniques used to produce the Worcester College images until later. It is therefore a near-certainty that they do not depict the 1629

Salisbury Court. Stylistically, the drawings correspond most closely to Webb's work after the late 1640s. Higgott argues that they in fact date from around 1660 and do not represent a theatre that was ever built; in a 2005 paper, he tentatively suggested that they were prepared for Sir William Davenant's mission in the spring of 1660 to gain permission for the construction of a new theatre and the establishment of a new company.[13] However, based on both internal and external evidence, he concluded that they were more akin to a vision statement than to actual plans: 'the cleanliness of the drawings and the inconsistencies in the treatment of levels and door openings in the plan and sections, point to

---

[11] Graham Barlow, 'Wenceslas Hollar and Christopher Beeston's Phoenix Theatre in Drury Lane', *Theatre Research International* 13 (1988), 30–44. Orrell dismissed Barlow's arguments as 'far from definite', but without fully arguing that assertion. In fact, although the evidence Barlow musters allows for a number of different interpretations, his extremely detailed and exhaustive analysis of the legal documents concerning the Cockpit location leaves little doubt that the plot could not have been larger than 60 by 65 feet. On that site were located not only the playhouse, but also a smaller adjacent house, a lane, and a small orchard. Given that the Worcester drawings show a building that measures 40 by 72 feet (including the stair turrets), it is difficult to see how it could possibly have been designed for the Cockpit site.

[12] See Glynne Wickham, *Early English Stages, 1300–1660*, vol. 2: *1576 to 1660, Part II* (London and New York, 1972), pp. 144–7. The Salisbury Court plot, which measured 42 by 140 feet, could easily have accommodated the playhouse in the designs. The room for a dancing school built in 1660 as an additional storey measured 40 feet square – dimensions that would fit quite neatly over the rectangular section of the plan before the rounded apse (p. 147).

[13] Higgott's research, which significantly expands and revises arguments he first put forth in his unpublished 1988 Ph.D. thesis, remains accessible only in the form of conference papers and an interview on the *Chamber of Demonstrations* DVD edited by Martin White ('Interpreting the evidence: Dr Gordon Higgott'). The fullest account can be found in Higgott, 'Reassessing the drawings for the Inigo Jones theatre: a restoration project by John Webb?' (paper presented at Shakespeare's Globe, 13 February 2005, www.bris .ac.uk/drama/jacobean/Reassessing_the_Worcester_College_ Drawings.pdf).

their being an initial project design that was never worked up for construction'.[14]

Once the design of the SWP began in earnest in 2012, it became clear that Higgott's assessment was right: the drawings did not depict a structure that *could* have been built as drawn. As Jon Greenfield and Peter McCurdy, the architect and timber framing specialist who worked on both the Globe and the SWP, have shown, Webb's designs seem unconcerned with 'solving the construction geometry' of the building he imagines;[15] his drawings cannot in fact serve as a 'blueprint' for a real edifice. Instead, they should be treated as a 'useful guide' in 'reimagining' a Jacobean indoor playhouse (p. 37). The space within which that reimagining would take place, however, was fixed: when the Shakespeare's Globe complex was constructed in 1995, the outer shell of the SWP was quite literally set in stone, based on the Worcester College plans, but enlarged to accommodate fire exit routes. Constructed as it was in Portland stone and brick, it proved too solid and permanent to alter after the fact. Putting a positive spin on things, Greenfield and McCurdy argue that this challenge in fact had

the *unanticipated advantage* [my italics] of making this project much more like the project undertaken by James Burbage when he was faced with converting the Blackfriars monastic hall into a commercial indoor theatre in 1596 ... [T]here are strong parallels with the Blackfriars project undertaken four hundred years ago: a late Elizabethan/early Jacobean set-up of galleries, *frons scenae* and stage in a pre-existing mediaeval interior; a neo-Jacobean set-up of galleries, *frons scenae* and stage in a pre-existing masonry interior.   (p. 38)

Turning a manifest liability – the necessary use of a space without real theatre-historical warrant – into a positive advantage earns high marks for PR acrobatics. As an argument, though, the idea that *any* project that involves building something inside a pre-existing shell has 'strong parallels' to the construction of the Blackfriars Playhouse is as flimsy as the notion that the existence of a roof over the auditorium creates a 'type' of indoor theatre. In reality, the construction of the SWP required an exercise in counterfactual history-

making: what might someone interested in constructing a theatre in 1610 or thereabouts, inside a shell based on a 1660 drawing and with the guidance of interior designs made that same year, have ended up building? Nothing about that situation resembles that of James Burbage in 1596, the group associated with the Whitefriars Playhouse in 1606–7, the Blackfriars consortium in 1609, Christopher Beeston in 1616, or Richard Gunnell and William Blagrave at the Salisbury Court in 1629.

To be fair, the Globe includes an account of the SWP's difficult history in all programmes for shows in the space.[16] (Although the same programmes also contain an essay about the Blackfriars Theatre, which might mislead an inattentive reader into thinking that there is some connection between that playhouse and the replica.[17]) The notion that the replica's construction closely mirrors that of the Blackfriars is not foregrounded in the Globe's own publicity materials. Instead, what takes centre stage is the assertion that the SWP is 'an archetypal indoor theatre of the period'.[18] Similar formulations abound in the collection of essays published to coincide with the opening of the new venue, *Moving Shakespeare Indoors*. Greenfield and McCurdy, for instance, describe their 'new design brief' as the creation of

---

[14] Higgott, 'Reassessing', p. 8.

[15] Jon Greenfield and Peter McCurdy, 'Practical evidence for a reimagined indoor Jacobean theatre', in *Moving Shakespeare Indoors: Performance and Repertoire in the Jacobean Playhouse*, ed. Andrew Gurr and Farah Karim-Cooper (Cambridge, 2014), pp. 32–64; p. 44.

[16] Heather Neill, 'Building the Sam Wanamaker Playhouse', in *The Duchess of Malfi Programme* (London, 2014), pp. 4–10, and, with a slightly modified text, in subsequent programmes.

[17] Sarah Dustagheer, 'The Blackfriars Playhouse: Shakespeare's indoor theatre', in *The Duchess of Malfi Programme* (London, 2014), pp. 2–3, and subsequent programmes.

[18] Farah Karim-Cooper and Will Tosh, 'The Indoor Performance Practice Project', *The Changeling Programme* (London, 2015), pp. 10–11; p. 10. For similar formulations, see also Sarah Dustagheer, 'Anticipating the Sam Wanamaker Playhouse', *Cahiers Élisabéthains* 88 (2015), 139–53; p. 140.

'a *simulacrum*, an *archetype* of an indoor Jacobean playhouse' – a building in which 'the look and feel of the space' are to be guided by 'accounts of the Blackfriars', even as the 'arrangement of space is given by the Worcester College drawings' (p. 37). The goal, thus, was not the rebuilding of 'one particular indoor Jacobean theatre' but 'an analogue of one' (pp. 63–4). In their introduction to the volume, Farah Karim-Cooper and Andrew Gurr argue that 'the new playhouse ... will invoke a version of the indoor playhouse Shakespeare's company occupied from 1609 to 1642' – more broadly, it will tackle the 'task of building ... a "Jacobean ideal"'.[19]

The language of the archetype or the ideal in these essays takes the place of the discourse of typicality in the earlier publications I discussed above; it inherits the problems of that discourse and adds a few new ones. What, after all, does it mean to call a reconstruction an archetype? How can something that is made to resemble a lost original built hundreds of years ago be presented as 'the original pattern or model from which copies are made'?[20] If anything, the claim that the SWP should be regarded as an archetype seems to respond to the loss of the certainty previously associated with the Worcester College drawings by upping the ante: the 'reimagined' theatre is not merely a reconstruction of the Cockpit but actually something more valuable and more profound: a copy of the quintessence of *all* indoor playhouses. The trouble with such a claim, beyond the logical incoherence of identifying a copy as an archetype, is that there is no way of ascertaining its credibility: since we know virtually no details about any of the indoor playhouses and their interior designs, we cannot possibly determine what may or may not have been a 'typical' feature, let alone an archetypal one.

COMPARING INDOOR THEATRES

There is one exception to this lack of factual information: we do have a reasonably clear sense of how large most of the indoor theatres were. By that standard, however, the SWP falls far short

of being 'typical'. As it stands, the new playhouse measures about 40 by 55 feet, including the tiring house. From the *frons scenae* to the inner back wall of the galleries, the inside measures roughly 40 by 38 feet. This is a much smaller space than the King's Men's Blackfriars. While little is known with any certainty, the external dimensions of the hall purchased by James Burbage are well established: it was 107 feet long and 52 feet wide. An early Jacobean assessment gives the theatre's *interior* dimensions as 66 by 46 feet – the latter figure revealing the thickness of the walls.[21] Scholars have generally supposed that the *frons* was 66 feet from the back wall of the galleries; Irwin Smith's influential reconstruction of the space makes that assumption, proposing a stage depth of 22 feet, and an auditorium 44 feet deep.[22] (The SWP's auditorium is a mere 25 feet deep.) By area, ignoring the (conjectured) size of the stage, the Blackfriars provided 3,036 square feet; the SWP has around 1,520. In other words, the reimagined playhouse is at best half the size of the Blackfriars, even without taking into account the possibility that the latter had three galleries, as opposed to the SWP's two.[23]

Like all aspects of theatre history not directly linked to Shakespeare, the other Jacobean indoor theatres have received somewhat more limited scholarly attention. Here is what we know, more or less.

---

[19] Gurr and Karim-Cooper, 'Introduction', in Gurr and Karim-Cooper, eds., *Moving Shakespeare Indoors*, pp. 1–12; p. 1. I have discussed the highly tendentious narrative of the Blackfriars history and the 'move indoors' offered by Gurr in this introduction elsewhere; see 'Fact and factitiousness: theatre history and irresponsible scholarship', *Dispositio*, 9 November 2014, www.dispositio.net/archives/2012.

[20] 'archetype, n.' *OED Online*, December 2016, www.oed .com.myaccess.library.utoronto.ca/view/Entry/10344? redirectedFrom=archetype.

[21] See Oliver Jones, 'Documentary evidence for an indoor Jacobean theatre', in Gurr and Karim-Cooper, eds., *Moving Shakespeare Indoors*, pp. 65–78; esp. p. 67.

[22] Irwin Smith, *Shakespeare's Blackfriars Playhouse: Its History and Its Design* (New York, 1964), p. 309.

[23] See Jones, 'Evidence', pp. 68–9.

The Whitefriars, the first 'new' indoor space to open during James I's reign, was constructed inside a medieval hall that once housed the library of a Carmelite monastery near Fleet Street. It was a very narrow but rather long space measuring about 17 by 90 feet; Julian Bowsher has hypothesized (on very slim archaeological basis) that it might have had a stage of around 17 by 15 feet, with an auditorium 56 feet deep. The overall *frons* to back wall depth of the room thus might have been 71 feet, for an area of roughly 1,200 square feet. The SWP is *larger* than that, but in the arrangement of its space, it is a very different venue: it is not even clear whether the Whitefriars had galleries, and it certainly was a long and narrow room, very likely set up with the entire audience facing the stage.[24]

The Cockpit, which opened in 1617 just off Drury Lane, was almost immediately destroyed by rioting apprentices, and re-opened as the Phoenix in 1618. It was built at least in part on the foundations of – or as an extension to – an existing cock-fighting arena. As noted above and assuming Graham Barlow's analysis of the legal documents is correct, the Phoenix measured at most 40 by 58 feet on the outside. If Barlow's confidence in Wenceslas Hollar's *View of West London* is justified, the Phoenix was a square, two-storeyed building of 40 by 40 feet.[25] Nothing is known about the interior of the building; if Hollar's engraving can be trusted, it probably had only two levels of galleries. Without internal measurements, and without even tentative ideas about the size of the tiring house, it is difficult to compare the Cockpit/Phoenix to the SWP.[26] But, given that the reimagined playhouse was based on a drawing that was long held to represent the Phoenix, it is perhaps not surprising that the measurement of the new theatre come closest to those of the playhouse in Drury Lane. Most likely, the SWP is somewhat larger and less square than the Phoenix was.

Finally, the Salisbury Court, the only Caroline playhouse, was constructed between 1629 and 1630 on a plot 42 feet wide and 140 feet long.

To build it, William Blagrave and Richard Gunnell converted an existing barn on the site, but little is known of the size or design of their playhouse. At a minimum, it measured 40 by 40 feet, since in 1660 two carpenters were contracted to 'build and erect on the said theatre or stage a large Roome or Chamber for a danceing school of forty foote square'.[27] Curiously, even though it seems to have been at least as large as the Phoenix, the Salisbury Court appears to have had

---

[24] See Bowsher, *Shakespeare's London Theatreland: Archaeology, History, and Drama* (London, 2012), p. 124; Glynne Wickham, Herbert Berry, and William Ingram, eds., *English Professional Theatre, 1530–1660* (Cambridge, 2000), pp. 547–50.

[25] See also Wickham *et al.*, eds., *English Professional Theatre*, pp. 623–6. Bowsher argues that the original Cockpit was likely a wooden structure, and that the new theatre, which had a brick exterior, was a wholesale replacement (*Theatreland*, p. 129).

[26] As the recently discovered remains of the Curtain in Shoreditch suggest, we may have to rethink how the backstage areas of early modern playhouses were organized. The Curtain appears to have had only a shallow passage behind the *frons scenae*, no deeper than 5 feet; however, there were larger rooms on either side of the stage that probably served as tiring houses (Heather Knight (Senior Archaeologist, Museum of London Archeology), personal communication, 23 November 2016). It is certainly possible that a relatively wide but not especially deep space such as the Cockpit adopted a similar set-up to minimize the stage's thrust and to avoid wasting precious room for audience members seated facing the stage. In general, the Curtain dig should make theatre historians reconsider whether a more 'frontal' performance style may have been common in rectangular playhouses – and whether those theatres, both indoors and outdoors, had more in common with each other than has generally been assumed. It is certainly instructive that the Queen's Servants frequently moved between three venues – the Curtain, the Red Bull, and the Cockpit/ Phoenix – that have traditionally been seen as unlike one another (because one was indoors, the others open to the elements), but that may now be reconsidered as spaces similar in their rectangularity. Finally, it is worth noting that the Staunton Blackfriars, with a stage 22 feet deep and 29 feet wide, has a tiring house that is less than 14 feet deep – as compared to the SWP's, which is deeper than the stage itself (at roughly 17 feet, as opposed to the 15 feet of the stage).

[27] Gerald Eades Bentley, *The Jacobean and Caroline Stage*, vol. 6 (Oxford, 1968), p. 92.

a reputation as a 'little House' – G. E. Bentley offers a range of evidence for its 'inferior size'.[28] Whether this reflects the actual physical size of the theatre, or the seating arrangements inside it (and whether a 'little House' might have been one that used its space inefficiently, cramming fewer spectators in than could be accommodated) is unclear; the most one can say is that the SWP is as wide as the Salisbury Court probably was.

Beyond these very limited facts, nothing can be established with any certainty: how many galleries these indoor theatres had or what size their stages were is as unknown as the shape or the height of their ceilings – pretty much the only thing we can be sure of is that they *had* ceilings. And then there are the things we will never know, but about which one can reasonably speculate on the basis of architectural analogues, such as questions about decoration and materials.[29]

It is unclear to me what an archetypal original underlying all four of these playhouses might have looked like. Since at least two of them, but possibly all four, used elements of pre-existing structures or were set up inside another building, their specific features were presumably dictated at least in part by the physical conditions set by those earlier structures. But even ignoring that factor, it is evident that the Blackfriars was not a 'type' but quite unlike the other three indoor playhouses; that the Whitefriars shape was nothing like the other three; and that the Phoenix and Salisbury Court *may* have been somewhat similar to each other, even though one was perceived as small while the other was not. Diversity rather than typicality seems to be what characterized the early modern indoor playhouse. Admittedly, the SWP, in its quest to copy an imaginary archetype, seems to have succeeded in resembling two of four indoor theatres more closely than the other two – but that is a fairly odd definition of typicality. It is also worth noting that the new theatre certainly fails to achieve the modified goal of building a theatre 'Shakespeare may have recognized'.[30] After all, the only indoor playhouses it might

resemble were both built after Shakespeare's death, in 1617 and 1629/30.

WHAT CAN A SPACE TEACH A SCHOLAR?

I take it the notional justification for constructing an 'archetypal' space for historically informed performance is that it allows one to test out theories without insisting that the conditions of the experiment replicate those in any one specific space. But if it seems that those conditions either do not replicate *any* early modern playing space, or in fact resemble only those in one or two *specific* early modern playhouses, does that rationale not lose most of its appeal? We may learn something about the effects of candle light in the SWP, for instance – but how can we transfer that new knowledge to our broader discussions about early modern playhouses with any confidence, given that in a space nearly twice the size of the Wanamaker lights would surely have quite different effects, in part because distances from the stage would necessarily increase? How about a venue such as the Whitefriars, where the depth of the hall would have created lighting conditions rather unlike those in the SWP? Isn't the same true of acoustics, of the use of music, of the number of actors the stage will comfortably hold, and so on? In other words, even if we do in fact learn something about the theatrical impact more-or-less early modern visual and aural effects have *in the Sam Wanamaker Playhouse*, do we really gain more than an insight into the workings of a specific *modern* space – or, fingers crossed, a specific early modern venue?

If, however, the best hope for the SWP is that it might reveal something about how its closest historical analogue, the Phoenix, may have been used, the programming of the first three seasons has been

---

[28] Bentley, *The Jacobean and Caroline Stage*, p. 93 (quoting Thomas Nabbes's 1633 *Tottenham Court*).

[29] For informed speculation on those counts, see Greenfield and McCurdy, 'Practical evidence', pp. 55–62; and Jones, 'Evidence', pp. 72–8.

[30] Neill, 'Building', p. 4.

distinctly odd. Only two Phoenix plays have in fact been staged there so far: *The Changeling* and *'Tis Pity She's a Whore*. Most of the Wanamaker shows have been Blackfriars plays – plays, that is, from the theatre that makes for the *poorest* comparison with the SWP.[31] Admittedly, not all that many Phoenix plays survive, let alone Jacobean Phoenix plays. But, in putting those plays on that stage, one might at least make a reasonable claim for reconstructing the spatial conditions under which they were first performed. There is little reason to believe, on the other hand, that *The Duchess of Malfi* in the SWP, effective as the production may have been, bore much of a resemblance to what Webster's play would have looked, sounded and felt like in the Blackfriars.

That said, I also cannot really claim that I found *The Changeling* in 2015 a more revelatory show than *The Duchess of Malfi* in 2014: both were interesting in their own ways, but neither struck me as more successful at mimicking an early modern performance than the other. Did *The Changeling* obviously belong in the slightly claustrophobic space of the SWP in a way that *Duchess* obviously did not? Not to my eyes and ears.[32] Does that make *The Changeling* more of a 'Phoenix play' than Webster's tragedy is a 'Blackfriars play'? Or does it simply mean that both *productions* used the theatre they were working with to the best of their abilities, as most modern performances would?

I have seen four productions in the Wanamaker: *The Duchess*, *The Changeling*, *The Knight of the Burning Pestle* and *Othello*. None of them seemed particularly concerned with exploring how a space such as the SWP would have been used in Jacobean London – let alone with probing whether these particular plays were written 'for' a space particularly like the SWP. Rather, all four shows made use of the entire building, sometimes including the space left by the modern fire exit routes. All four featured exits and entrances through the auditorium. At least one had actors climbing on the gallery bannisters. In other words, all four used the Wanamaker *as* the Wanamaker (not as an archetype of a 400-year-old mode of indoor theatre), approaching the venue from the perspective of

contemporary performers rather than that of participants in an experiment in reconstruction. And as a matter of staging a show in the twenty-first century, none of these decisions is in the least bit problematic. As a matter of quasi-historical inquiry, though, they are disabling: turning features that we know only exist in the modern replica into integral elements of the staging means that the space the production can access differs categorically from one an early modern company might have had at its disposal; having actors make use of that space in a way for which we have no historical warrant similarly distorts how that space may have read and functioned for Jacobean performers and audiences. In effect, the modern actors' and directors' instincts to make the most of the venue either jettisons the historical inquiry altogether or assumes that theatremakers 400 years ago would similarly have taken all performative opportunities afforded by a specific playhouse, even if we have no documentary evidence to support such an assumption. What this approach forestalls is a confrontation with the particular features of the SWP as productive limitations – not limitations that must be overcome, but that need to be respected if any 'learning' is to take place (and the 'learning' might just be that – at least from our

---

31 To date, the following plays have been staged in fully mounted productions in the SWP: *The Duchess of Malfi* (Blackfriars/Globe), 2014; *The Knight of the Burning Pestle* (Blackfriars), 2014; *The Malcontent* (Blackfriars/Globe), 2014; *'Tis Pity She's a Whore* (Phoenix; Caroline), 2015; *The Changeling* (Phoenix), 2015; *The Broken Heart* (Blackfriars), 2015; *Dido, Queen of Carthage* (Court[?]; Elizabethan), 2015; *Cymbeline* (Blackfriars/Globe), 2015; *Pericles* (Blackfriars/Globe), 2016; *The Winter's Tale* (Blackfriars/Globe), 2016; *The Tempest* (Blackfriars/Globe), 2016; *Comus* (Ludlow Castle; Caroline), 2016; *The White Devil* (Curtain or Red Bull), 2017; *Othello* (Blackfriars/Globe), 2017. Over a third of the fourteen plays staged so far at the SWP were almost certainly not written for an indoor venue at all, although they were probably eventually performed in one; a further two were not written for performance in a commercial theatre.

32 An impossibly subjective response, no doubt, but how could such an assessment ever be anything but subjective?

modern perspective – the limitations are simply too severe to allow a show to go on).

I have now shaded into my second, larger question, of course: whether we can learn anything about early modern theatre at all from modern performances – performances we ineluctably make with modern bodies and watch with modern eyes. And that modernity may be more pronounced in the SWP than on the Globe stage. Take the two Jacobean tragedies I have mentioned. Both featured a cast, and especially female leads, with rich experience in theatre, TV and film: Beatrice-Joanna in *The Changeling*, for instance, was played by Hattie Morahan, an actor who has had some of her greatest successes in collaborating with the director Katie Mitchell, who works in a thoroughly contemporary aesthetic informed by both psychological realism and avant-garde sensibilities. The Wanamaker, despite its visuals, seems to provide a fruitful environment for performers operating in such a modern artistic idiom. Listening to the many, fascinating interviews with actors on the Globe website, it is evident that the current discourse of 'storytelling', 'relatability', identification with a character's emotional states and backstory, and so on, deeply informs their work. Performing in the Wanamaker seems to allow for the nuance and reduced theatricality of expression that makes a greater degree of realism possible.

I do not mean to suggest that all actors in all SWP productions follow this approach; on the contrary, one of my quibbles with *Duchess* was the sheer diversity of acting styles.[33] But it is surely the case that most performers approach their work as modern actors, trained in a specific set of skills and within a specific ideology of what makes for 'good acting'. How those actors move, speak and think necessarily has little to do with how their ancestors moved, spoke and thought in spaces perhaps not completely unlike the Wanamaker 400 years ago. But if that is the case, how can we learn something about those actors of the past from actors of the present? Can we learn much about wainwrights from studying car mechanics? Or about early

modern cobblers from watching modern artisans making shoes in Northampton?

By the same token, the mechanics of the SWP and their aesthetic effects can feel revelatory, even startling. But would they have the same impact if we all still lived by candlelight? Would discovering that a surprisingly small number of candles can light a stage actually be a discovery at all – or would it pass unnoticed, because we would all know how candlelight works from daily experience? In other words, can we distance ourselves from our modern responses to what we are witnessing in this theatre sufficiently to gain a sense of how those same effects might have affected an early modern audience?[34] And if it is *distance* rather than experience that will allow us to develop that sense, what then is the added value of having the experience in the first place? What exactly are we 'discovering', and about whom?

My point is not to dismiss the enterprise of staging plays in the SWP. I meant what I wrote above: it is a beautiful theatre and a space in which rich theatrical experiences can be had. The darkness in the dead-hand-scene in *Duchess* was unlike most darknesses I had previously sat through in a theatre, and it did change how I was affected by that scene. But I do not know if my experience bears much of a resemblance to that an audience member in 1613 would have had. The rich variety of candlelight effects absolutely has been a revelation. Personally, I did not anticipate that hand-held candelabra could be used to light faces in an early modern version of a follow-spot. That is something I learned in the Wanamaker, though I could also have learned it elsewhere, since it merely confirmed arguments other theatre historians had already made. And I still do not know whether such effects would have worked similarly well in differently

---

[33] I have written about that production at great length on *Dispositio*, 15 February 2014, www.dispositio.net/archives/1854.

[34] Dustagheer considers some of these concerns in 'Anticipating the Sam Wanamaker Playhouse', esp. pp. 143 and 147–8.

configured spaces, particularly the Blackfriars or Whitefriars. I was impressed with how little of a problem the mock-battle scenes in *Knight of the Burning Pestle* were on the SWP's small and shallow stage – though I do not think that should have surprised me. We do know, after all, that being able to adapt to often radically different spaces was a key skill for early modern actors well into the seventeenth century. That the plays they performed did not utterly depend on Globe-sized stages should not really be remarkable.[35] Similarly, it can hardly be surprising that the SWP has proved to be 'hospitable to a wide variety of genres and forms', as Farah Karim-Cooper and Will Tosh write in a programme note.[36] The opposite would have been much more shocking and would have been so badly at odds with everything we believe about the early modern repertory that it probably would have confirmed the anachronism of either the venue or the 'discovery'.

On the other hand, that music can be placed more precisely in space in the SWP than in the Globe and that loud instruments can in fact be used, as that same programme note points out, are noteworthy insights, as they run counter to what scholars previously held: they seem to 'pu[t] paid to the assumption that "drum and trumpet" musical styles were impossible in indoor theatres' (p. 11). Interestingly, it is the very limitations of the SWP that makes this a persuasive observation: if even as small a theatre as this can employ noisy music without overwhelming an audience, surely a space twice its size, such as the Blackfriars, could have done the same. Assuming, that is, that early modern ears responded to noise similarly to our own.

But, for the most part, the central problem I have identified above remains: in observing performances at the Wanamaker, how can we know that something we find remarkable is not *just* a feature of the Wanamaker? How can we know that it is an 'archetypal' effect rather than one specific to this particular space? How can we say that the powerful, remarkable theatrical experiences and insights we can have and gain in this playhouse are more than experiences and

insights related to seeing a 21st-century performance in a 21st-century building? More problematically still, once we have learned that loud music can be played in small spaces, is there a justification for repeating the same experiment over and over again? How can the results of such an experiment possibly be falsified or verified? And how can such 'discoveries' justify the existence of an entire permanent building – let alone one as fraught with conceptual problems as the SWP?

The Sam Wanamaker Playhouse is a space in which powerful theatrical events can take place, no matter what its flaws might be as a tool for theatre-historical inquiry. Perhaps it is those experiences that should be the grounds on which to justify its existence: even if the building can reveal little about early modern indoor playing, and although it would be a serious fallacy to treat 'discoveries' made there as newly unearthed facts about Jacobean staging practices, it is still a venue that can bring old plays to new life. If the make-believe that those revivification acts have something to do with a special connection to the past established by a modern reimagining of a building that never existed helps modern audiences, there is presumably no harm in maintaining that illusion: make-believe is, after all, one of the reasons theatre exists. But, given the space's capacity for generating powerful experiences, it would seem perverse to try to distance ourselves from those experiences in order to distill from them credible

---

35 If anything, the SWP may serve as a helpful reminder that the surviving information about stage sizes also suggests variety rather than typicality as the norm – the Rose (less than 50 square metres, and only a little larger than that after the 1592 remodelling) and the Curtain (*c.* 70 square metres) had much smaller stages than the Fortune (110 square metres), with the Boar's Head occupying a middle ground (*c.* 92 square metres). Nothing is known about the size of the stage at the Theatre, the Swan, the Globe, the Red Bull, the Hope or any of the indoor theatres, although various more or less creditable hypotheses have been proposed (some of which I have cited above).

36 Karim-Cooper and Tosh, 'Performance Practice Project', p. 10.

scholarly insights that rarely, if ever, actually *require* spectatorial witnessing – even if our modern experiences in the Wanamaker are necessarily the single most inauthentic and anachronistic aspect of the entire enterprise. As a scholarly undertaking, the SWP is fraught with problems; but, as a playhouse, it is thriving. Why not then use the place in a way that plays to its strengths: as a living laboratory for modern performance; an intimate venue for exploring the continued, continually changing lives of old plays in the modern world; and a theatre that daily demonstrates that a return to the historical origins towards which its very physical fabric gestures is made impossible by the realities of its existence as a modern performance space?

EVOLUTIONARY NATURALISM AND EMBODIED ECOLOGY IN SHAKESPEARIAN PERFORMANCE (WITH A SCENE FROM *KING JOHN*)

RANDALL MARTIN

They seemed almost, with staring on one another, to tear the cases of their eyes; there was speech in their dumbness, language in their very gesture …

(*The Winter's Tale*, 5.2.11–14)[1]

Anybody looking up Darwin and Shakespeare quickly discovers that their relationship has been defined by two contrasting comments made by the former in an addendum to his *Autobiography*, a year before his death. Discussing his literary reading, Darwin first says:

Up to the age of thirty, or beyond it, poetry of many kinds, such as the works of Milton, Gray, Byron, Wordsworth, Coleridge, & Shelley, gave me great pleasure, & even as a schoolboy I took intense delight in Shakespeare, especially in the historical plays.[2]

He adds that 'pictures [also] gave me considerable, & music very great delight'. But now in his 70s, Darwin regrets the 'curious & lamentable loss of the higher aesthetic tastes': 'for many years I cannot endure to read a line of poetry: I have tried lately to read Shakespeare, & found it so intolerably dull that it nauseated me. I have also almost lost any taste for pictures or music.' Most commentators have concluded that Darwin's interests in literature fell off rapidly in middle age. Gillian Beer has challenged this assumption, however, by showing from Darwin's Notebooks in the 1830s to 1850s that his literary reading remained diverse and substantial, and included plays across the Shakespeare canon. While Beer argues that such works stimulated the abstract development of Darwin's scientific ideas,[3] *On the Origin of Species* (1859) did not actually mention or

allude to Shakespeare; so, reading back from Darwin's second remark in his *Autobiography*, commentators might well have assumed that any direct intellectual relationship with the playwright had ended.[4] But in *The Descent of Man* (1871), Darwin cites Shakespeare and Newton together as exemplars of evolved human capacity for conceptual thought.[5]

---

[1] Quoted by Charles Darwin, *The Expression of the Emotions in Man and Animals* (1872), ed. Joe Cain and Sharon Messenger (London, 2009), p. 258. All quotations from *Expression* are taken from this edition. While quotations of Shakespeare from *Expression* are verbatim, line numbers (which Darwin did not include with act and scene references) are taken from *The Complete Works*, ed. Stanley Wells, Gary Taylor, John Jowett, and William Montgomery, 2nd edn (Oxford, 2005). Shakespeare quotations other than from Darwin's work are also taken from this edition.

[2] 'Recollections of the development of my mind & character', as Darwin titled his *Autobiography: Darwin Online*, http://darwin-online.org.uk/content/frameset?pageseq=1&itemID=CUL-DAR26.1–121&viewtype=text, Addendum 114–116.

[3] *Darwin's Plots: Evolutionary Narrative in Darwin, George Eliot and Nineteenth-Century Fiction* (Cambridge, 2000), pp. 26–8.

[4] Darwin did not list Shakespeare in the original indices of any of his major works, and modern editions follow suit, although Paul Ekman's edition of *The Expression of the Emotions* (see below, n. 11) is an exception.

[5] *The Descent of Man*, ed. James Moore and Adrian Desmond (London, 2004), p. 86. Thomas Woolner's sculpture of Puck from *A Midsummer Night's Dream* (1845–7) represented the variably inherited point or thickening in the inner edge of the upper ear which some humans share homologously with the pointy ears of primates (*Descent*, p. 32). Darwin named this vestigial feature the 'Woolnerian Tip' (now also known as Darwin's tubercle). Image: www.victorianweb.org/sculpture/woolner/puck.html.

And in *The Expression of the Emotions in Man and Animals* – the focus of this article – Darwin quotes from Shakespeare's plays fifteen times to illustrate and imaginatively extend his analysis of human facial and bodily gestures related to a 'community of certain expressions' inherited by 'descent from a common progenitor' (*Expression*, p. 23). Evidently, Darwin continued to read and think about Shakespeare at least into his 60s. He seems to have recognized that the playwright's work could serve as a wide-ranging source for the physical language of emotion, just as contemporaries subsequently saw *Expression* as a potential manual for artists.[6] (I do not have room here to discuss all of Darwin's quotations, nor all of Darwin's instances of non-verbal expression that might be illustrated by Shakespeare, and will therefore be selective.) Early in Chapter 1, for example, Darwin cites Norfolk's report of Cardinal Wolsey's turmoiled reactions to Henry VIII's demand to see his financial accounts. Darwin describes Wolsey's gestures as signs of an 'involuntary over-flow of nerve-force':

> Some strange commotion
> Is in his brain: he bites his lip and starts;
> Stops on a sudden, looks upon the ground,
> Then, lays his finger on his temple; straight,
> Springs out into fast gait; then, stops again,
> Strikes his breast hard; and anon, he casts
> His eye against the moon: in most strange postures
> We have seen him set himself.
> (*Expression*, p. 41; *Henry VIII*, 3.2.113–20)

While this passage served partly to outline the character-performance of Wolsey's bodily distress, it also introduced several of Darwin's later arguments that specific gestures – biting the lip to keep it from trembling in fear, instinctive movements away from danger, striking the chest to keep a terrified heart from beating violently, and eyes rolling in an ecstasy of fear verging on madness – are inherited and involuntary physical responses to environmental stimuli. At the other end of *Expression*, Darwin's final page quotes Hamlet's passionate amazement at the First Player's performance of Hecuba's grief to sum up another key point – that simulated emotions communicated through facial and bodily gestures can create mental

and physical affects in spectators as real and moving as naturally produced ones:[7]

> Is it not monstrous that this player here,
> But in a fiction, in a dream of passion,
> Could force his soul to his own conceit,
> That, from her working, all his visage wann'd;
> Tears in his eyes, distraction in 's aspect,
> A broken voice, and his whole function suiting
> With forms to his conceit? And all for nothing!
> (*Expression*, p. 334; *Hamlet*, 2.2.553–9)

Hamlet confirms Darwin's arguments (like those of early moderns before him) that imagined emotions may work on the heart and nervous system to generate a life-like expression, which can be intensified by the free physical movement 'of [its] outward signs', as the First Player's affectively embodied performance demonstrates (*Expression*, p. 333).[8] At the same time, Darwin suggests, inherited involuntary expressions and gestures that are generated in the course of bodily interaction with other players or spectators in live performance stimulate 'natural', improvised and virtuoso artistry in the individual 'personing' of character.

I'd like to continue exploring Darwin's uses of Shakespeare in *Expression*, the last and arguably most original of his major works on human and non-human evolution. I'll begin historically by showing how Darwin's use of Shakespeare implicitly

---

[6] Review of *The Expression*, *Journal of the Anthropological Institute of Great Britain and Ireland* 2 (1873), 444–6.

[7] In his discussion of early modern theories of passionate rhetoric and acting, Joseph R. Roach, *The Player's Passion: Studies in the Science of Acting* (Newark, 1985), p. 45, pairs Hamlet's speech with Thomas Wright's anticipation of Darwin's physiological insights: 'Thus we moove, because by passion thus wee are moved, and as [passion] hath wrought in us so it ought to worke in you' (*The Passions of the Mind in General* [1604], p. 176). Darwin also cites 'a family famous for having produced an extraordinary number of great actors and actresses' (i.e. the Kembles), who are able to control facial muscles and mimic natural expressions to convey emotion organically (*Expression*, p. 170; Roach, *Player's Passion*, p. 177).

[8] See Evelyn Tribble's discussion of this speech in terms of the First Player's creative expression of embodied memory-images: *Cognition in the Globe: Attention and Memory in Shakespeare's Theatre* (New York, 2011), pp. 90–4.

revealed the co-evolved origins of performance communication, and how Shakespeare helped Darwin to convey his ideas persuasively to contemporary readers. My article will then consider how *Expression*'s use of both naturalizing and metatheatrical photographs parallels the ecological phenomenology of Shakespearian theatrical relations. Out of these discussions, I'll make two arguments: that perceiving either the harmony or discrepancies between instinctive and learned gestures constitutes a critical perspective for judging the performance of

character as 'natural'; that an ethologically conscious Shakespeare has the potential to open contemporary audiences' imaginations to ecological values and environmentalist choices. I'll attempt to illustrate these arguments by examining *King John*, 4.1.

THE ETHOLOGY OF PERFORMANCE

The Expression of the Emotions in Man and Animals analyses the manifold continuities between humans and animals in their physical signalling of emotions.

Fig. 15. Cat terrified at a dog. From life, by Mr. Wood.

28. Charles Darwin, *The Expression of the Emotions in Man and Animals* (1872), Figure 15. Terrified cat with fur standing on end.

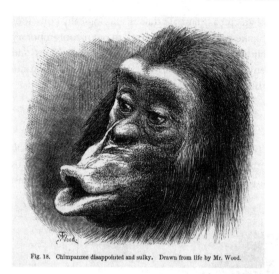

Fig. 18. Chimpanzee disappointed and sulky. Drawn from life by Mr. Wood.

29. Charles Darwin, *The Expression of the Emotions in Man and Animals* (1872), Figure 18. Sulky chimpanzee expressing disappointment.

Darwin's interspecies study inaugurates the modern science of ethology, the comparative investigation of evolved animal and human behaviour.[9] It thereby contributed to his career-long project of demonstrating that humans have evolved structurally with animals on every level. Innate human facial and body movements are extensions of those found in animals, while animal expressions of emotion have many human-like qualities (Illustrations 28 and 29).[10] Darwin's other overarching goal was to show that the chief human emotions and expressions – sadness and grief, joy and tenderness, sulkiness and frowning, anger and hatred, disgust and contempt, fear and terror – are shared by humans universally and not differentiated according to alleged racial subspecies.[11] In other words, *Expression* concentrates on primary similarities across human cultures and generations, secondary characteristics among ethnic groups arising from sexual selection having been covered in *The Descent of Man*.

Darwin's semiotics of physical affect consists of comparing the muscular mechanics of facial expressions (foreheads wrinkling; eyes opening and closing; eyebrows shifting; nostrils, lips and mouths moving; teeth being exposed), and related body reflexes in people and non-human animals.

Working in his usual methodical and cautious way – he is the original 'slow' scholar – Darwin built up evidence from decades of personal observation as well as a vast research network of friends, colleagues, and global correspondents, who supplied evidence using a questionnaire Darwin designed for his purposes (*Expression*, pp. 339–40). His Shakespeare citations add the expressions of the playwright's characters to this record of empirical observation. When describing fear and terror and one of its outward signs, 'The erection of the hair', for instance, Darwin refers to Brutus's reaction to the appearance of Caesar's ghost: 'Art thou some god, some angel, or some devil, / That mak'st my blood cold, and my hair to stare' (*Expression*, p. 273; *Julius Caesar*, 4.2.330–1). He also cites Cardinal Winchester's death-bed ravings about the Duke of Gloucester's murder: 'Comb down his hair – look, look, it stands upright' (*Expression*, p. 273; *Henry VI Part Two*, 3.3.15).[12] These passages lead Darwin to consider whether bristling hair is not just a poetic commonplace but an involuntary physical reflex. For Shakespeare's detailed descriptions of physical expression suggested to Darwin that the playwright had observed this reaction occurring naturally in animals and people as well as in stage actors performing fear. Combining ideas gathered from his earlier analysis of dogs and cats raising their hackles with reports sent to him about the behaviour of asylum inmates (i.e. human subjects acting in supposedly more socially unguarded and less self-conscious ways), Darwin concludes that Shakespeare recognized that hair standing on end is not just a hoary cliché but a true and imitable response (i.e., perceptions or the memory of danger acting on the nerves to cause the involuntary contraction of

---

9 This is not the discredited early twentieth-century ethology of Western-defined universalism and racial hierarchies, but the modern global study of genetic and physiological affinities.

10 Joe Cain, Introduction to Cain and Messenger, eds., *The Expression*, p. xix.

11 Paul Ekman, Introduction to *The Expression of the Emotions in Man and Animals*, ed. P. Ekman (London, 1998), p. xxxiv.

12 Darwin, *Expression*, p. 273. Also pp. 95–9.

minute muscles underlying hair follicles (*Expression*, p. 273)). During a person's lifetime, involuntary expressions are adapted or suppressed, often unconsciously, under the influence of parental upbringing, social customs and cultural attitudes (*Expression*, p. 323). But an actor's dedicated representation of her character's emotional expression draws on and re-creates the double life of embodied affect. This happens because, although the main human emotions and their expressions are inherited and involuntary, 'once acquired, such movements may be voluntarily and consciously employed as a means of communication' (*Expression*, p. 325). Darwin illustrates these innate and imaginary capacities by citing Henry V's advice to his soldiers at Harfleur, with his quotation again serving to confirm Shakespeare's precise knowledge of the nervous and muscular signalling of 'extreme rage' that Darwin has been describing in his text:

> In peace there's nothing so becomes a man
> As modest stillness and humility;
> But when the blast of war blows in our ears,
> Then imitate the action of the tiger:
> Stiffen the sinews, summon up the blood,
> Then lend the eye a terrible aspect;
> Now set the teeth, and stretch the nostril wide,
> Hold hard the breath, and bend up every spirit
> To his full height! On, on, you noblest English.
> (*Expression*, pp. 219–20; *Henry V*, 3.1.3–7, 9, 15–17)

Simulated facial and bodily affects are transferable to spectators and may be reciprocated by them just as readily as natural involuntary expressions, as Hamlet shows by responding frenetically to the First Player's performance of grief over Hecuba, culminating in 'O vengeance!' (*Hamlet*, 2.2.584). Moreover, whether naturally produced or simulated, observers in conducive circumstances can react to affective gestures as true signs of emotion. As Darwin observed, 'Sympathy with the distresses of others, even with the imaginary distresses of a heroine in a pathetic story, for whom we feel no affection, readily excites tears' (*Expression*, p. 199; also pp. 23, 328, 333). Such insights recall early modern theorists of the passions: interlocutors and spectators are not passive recipients of emotion, but

perceive, absorb and re-express its physio-cognitively generated state (as Shakespeare's Bottom recognizes: 'the audience [will have to] look to their eyes', he vows, when he summons up tears in the 'true performing' of Pyramus (*A Midsummer Night's Dream*, 1.2.21–2)). The embodied knowledge of such exchanges allows observers to judge emotional expressions experientially – often at micro levels or unconsciously – as true or false. On this last point, Darwin's conclusions recall those of Thomas Heywood in his *Apology for Actors* (1612) when he affirms spectators' imaginative capacities for evaluating the stage performance of a 'person personated' as either life-like or something less than fully true or natural.[13] Darwin's use of Shakespearian evidence thus presents a meditation on the ethological origins of theatrical representation by implying that human physical and emotional co-evolution with animals makes the affective performances of characters such as Wolsey or Brutus both universally recognizable and innately compelling.

Alan Read calls this pre- or non-verbal level of communication 'the unaddressed'. Like Darwin before him, he identifies it in child- and animal-like playfulness and shared human–animal impulses to display and perform. In the theatre, these behaviours manifest as spontaneous, involuntary and unscripted expressions and gestures, in contrast to what Read calls 'the addressed, the licensed, the staged, the celebrated'. It is the human actor's heritage of an affective kinship with non-human animals that makes live stage performance uniquely in the moment, and unpredictably generative compared to technologically mediated and/or artfully shaped forms of performance.[14] *Expression* underpins Read's study by documenting the ethological and physiological roots of natural performance. Darwin related this potential for life-like mimesis to the dramatic naturalism of nineteenth-century actors, while Shakespeare's audiences admired it in the

---

[13] *An Apology for Actors* (1612), B3v–B4r.
[14] *Theatre, Intimacy & Engagement: The Last Human Venue* (London, 2008), pp. 102–19, citation 104. Also pp. 15–78.

embodied pathos of Richard Burbage, who probably performed Brutus and Wolsey.[15] Darwinian ethology thus offers an epistemological platform for recovering the phenomenology of embodied expression in Shakespearian performance, then and now.[16]

DARWIN'S UNNATURALLY NATURAL PERFORMANCES

Instinctive facial and gestural affect establishes an expressive threshold that may serve either to naturalize or to contradict the willed intentions of theatrical representation by both actors and scriptwriters. Darwin became highly aware of this ambidextrous capacity when he pondered how to present his arguments in ways that would win over sceptical readers. *On the Origins of Species* and *The Descent of Man* had attracted fierce public resistance; but, unlike his 'bull–dog' defender of evolution, T. H. Huxley, Darwin was not a combative man. *Expression* was also competing with anatomist and natural theologian Sir Charles Bell's widely admired book *Essays on the Anatomy and Philosophy of Expression* (1824), which was abundantly illustrated with drawings, one of which Darwin reproduced in *Expression* (p. 33, Figure 1). To support his scientific descriptions of evolved continuities between animal and human expressions of emotion, Darwin enlisted Shakespeare's Romantic reputation as a close observer of nature. Victorian readers' familiarity with the playwright's characters also helped to illustrate Darwin's case studies of facial and body anatomy with easily recognizable comparisons. Shakespeare's function in *Expression* was therefore rhetorical as well as evidential, comparable to the drawings of animals that populated the book's first five chapters on 'General Principles of Expression'. His presence may have contributed to *Expression*'s publishing success: 9,000 copies were sold in the first four months.[17]

On the Origins of Species famously contained only one image: the fan-like 'tree' (or, as Darwin also called it, 'coral') of life, illustrating evolutionary and extinctive developments. *The Descent of Man* presented many drawings of fish, birds and animals, but only a single human image: 'Woolner's ear'. The intensive focus on facial movements in *Expression* presented technical challenges that required a new mode of communication. Human expressions were difficult to capture and hard to study, 'owing to the movements being often extremely slight, and of a fleeting nature' (*Expression*, p. 23). But Darwin also recognized that most facial signs can be imitated to the point of being accepted by observers as authentically life-like. Here, his knowledge of Shakespeare and contemporary acquaintance with Victorian actors may have suggested theatrical mimicry as a means of isolating facial reflexes, in combination with the emergent technology of photography. It was able to capture fleeting human expression with an apparent neutrality that the hundreds of pictures from Western art and scores of commercial photographs Darwin initially sorted through for his project could not do satisfactorily.[18] Their pictorial contexts either interfered with detached scrutiny, or would lead observers to prejudge and/or sympathize with the emotions they perceived.[19] Unfortunately, photography in the 1860s and 1870s required long exposure times of up to two minutes. This obliged natural human expressions to be artificially held and/or manipulated. As Philip Prodger's pioneering research on Darwin and visual culture has shown, very few of the thirty photographic images in *Expression* were strictly 'natural' or unaltered. Many were commissioned to illustrate specific expressions performed by the fashionable artistic photographer Oscar Rejlander or other actors.

---

[15] Stanley Wells, *Great Shakespeare Actors: From Burbage to Branagh* (Oxford, 2015), pp. 18–19.

[16] Bruce R. Smith, *Phenomenal Shakespeare* (Oxford, 2010), p. xvi.

[17] Ekman, ed., *Expression*, p. xxix. A review in *The Athenaeum*, Saturday 9 November 1872, p. 591, was cautiously supportive of Darwin's use of shared animal and human expression as positive evidence for evolution.

[18] Phillip Prodger, *Darwin's Camera: Art and Photography in the Theory of Evolution* (Oxford, 2009), pp. 8–9.

[19] Phillip Prodger, 'Photography and The Expression', in Ekman, ed., *Expression*, Appendix 3, pp. 399–415, citation 403.

From today's perspective, this situation raises questions about both the accuracy of Darwin's images and whether they constitute legitimate scientific evidence. Prodger argues that Darwin's photographs must be judged according to the technical capabilities and scientific standards of the day, before shorter exposure times and stricter protocols of objectivity were developed (and leaving aside the theoretical scruple that all photography mediates its object). *Expression* not only was one of the first books to introduce photographs for scientific purposes, but also began to shape the methodology of using photos as empirical evidence. This came about because Darwin drew explicit attention to the constructedness and artificiality of his evidence. His candour established methodological self-scrutiny as a critical strength (or re-established it, since these principles recall Francis Bacon's attention to the inductive situatedness of the observer[20]). Because Darwin highlighted some images as photographic performances, he also pointed to metatheatrical estrangement as a shared Shakespearian effect. This aspect of his commentary made the reader aware of the epistemological and temporal differences between an originary moment, its present perception and its interpretive future(s), thereby revealing its ecological relations.[21]

At the beginning of the book, a note at the bottom of the List of Illustrations (added as a handwritten insertion to Darwin's corrected proofs[22]) stated that 'Several of the figures in these seven Heliotype Plates' were reproduced from photographs rather than 'the original negatives'; consequently, they are 'somewhat indistinct', albeit Darwin assured readers they were 'faithful copies' and 'much superior to any drawing' (*Expression*, p. 10). Later, he revealed that certain images had been performed by Rejlander and/or other actors for the express purpose of illustrating the facial muscles and bodily gestures he was describing. Although Darwin asked for signs of electric instruments to be removed in certain images, in some either they were retained or the histrionic quality and

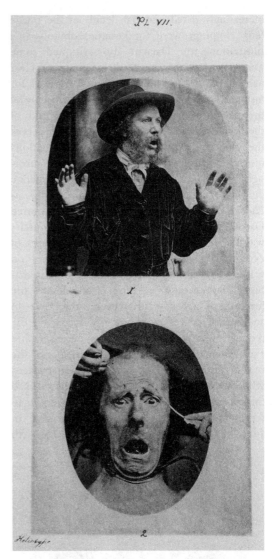

30. Charles Darwin, *The Expression of the Emotions in Man and Animals* (1872), Plate 7, Figures 1 & 2. (Top) Photographer Oscar Rejlander performing astonishment. (Bottom) An unnamed old man being stimulated with electrical instruments to express fear. Photograph sent to Darwin by French neurologist Guillaume-Benjamin-Armand Duchenne de Boulogne.

[20] Smith, *Phenomenal Shakespeare*, pp. 16, 185–6.
[21] Richard Hornby, *Drama, Metadrama, Perception* (Lewisburg, PA, 1986), pp. 99–100, 113–45.
[22] Fisher Library, University of Toronto, shelfmark Dar.D36 E86 1872, original proof sheets of *Expression*.

increasingly dated material details of the image (e.g. clothing) were (or became) obvious (see Illustration 30). Darwin also critiqued some images as less than perfectly accurate or clear presentations.[23] When discussing grief, for instance, and its chief facial signs – furrowing of the central forehead, raising of the inner ends of the eyebrows and drawing down of the corners of the mouth – Darwin revealed the production-history of a photograph he received from neurologist Guillaume-Benjamin-Armand Duchenne de Boulogne, whose treatise *The Mechanism of Human Facial Expression* (1862) supported Darwin's ideas that the operation of facial muscles was the result of a long-accumulated series of evolutionary changes, and that facial expression was a universal non-verbal language inherited at birth (Illustration 31).[24] This photo depicts the forehead of 'a young lady who has the power in an unusual degree of voluntarily acting on the requisite [grief-]muscles'. But because 'her expression was not at all one of grief' (i.e. the rest of her face did not appear grief-stricken) while she was being photographed, Darwin had the image cropped from the eyebrows down to represent 'the forehead alone' (*Expression*, p. 167).[25] Darwin then compares this image with

two other photographs reproduced 'on a reduced scale' from Duchenne's *Mechanism* (Illustration 32). They are of 'a young man who was a good actor', first with his face in a relaxed state, and then simulating grief. Darwin judges the latter expression not to be completely natural because the actor 'was not able to act equally on both his eyebrows' – that is, he raised them asymmetrically.[26] In her control of certain facial muscles, Darwin observes that the young lady is in some respects a better performer, even though she is not a professional actor. Yet, remarkably, when Darwin showed the photos of the young man to fifteen people and asked them to identify the emotion being expressed, fourteen of them answered 'despairing sorrow', 'suffering endurance', 'melancholy and so forth' (*Expression*, p. 169). While recognizing the semiotic instability of his photographic evidence, Darwin concludes from these responses that the 'expression is true', even though he has just pointed out to the reader that it is somewhat false. And that is the epistemological paradox of Darwin's theatricalized presentations: that human emotional expressions are universally inherited, and their skilful and

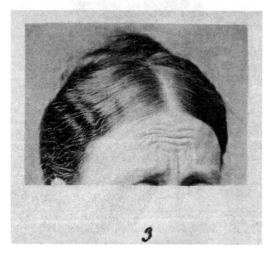

31. Charles Darwin, *The Expression of the Emotions in Man and Animals* (1872), Plate 2, Figure 3. Forehead muscles contracted when expressing grief.

[23] Prodger, 'Photography and *The Expression*', p. 409.
[24] Cain and Messenger, eds., *Expression*, p. xxviii.
[25] Prodger, *Darwin's Camera*, p. 232, reproduces the entire photograph from Duchenne, in which the woman appears to be concentrating but looks rather impassive. For simulation of natural expression according to an imagined fictional scenario, see Plate 5, Figure 1. Darwin remarks: '[The photograph] represents a young lady, who is supposed to be tearing up the photograph of a despised lover' (*Expression*, p. 232). The image shows only her disdainful face, whose accuracy of expression Darwin approves. Darwin also mentions that Plate 6, Figures 3 and 4, in which the photographer Oscar Rejlander illustrates shrugging of the shoulders, is 'successfully acted' (*Expression*, p. 245).
[26] Paul Ekman's scientific research has confirmed Darwin's observations. See Ekman's notes to Plate 7, Figure 2, and Plate 3, Figures 5 and 6 (Ekman, ed., *Expression*, pp. 182, 202, corresponding to images in Cain and Messenger's edn, pp. 186–8). Also Joseph C. Hager and Paul Ekman, 'The asymmetry of facial actions is inconsistent with models of hemispheric specialization', *Psychophysiology* 22.3 (1985), 307–18.

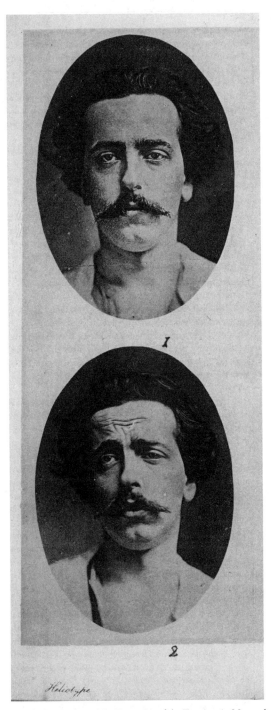

affective personation creates life-like signs in contexts conducive to them being judged natural; but the meaning of facial signals always remains semiotically indeterminate until observers either validate them as life-like or deprecate them as artificial or not fully adequate. *Expression* demonstrates that representational fidelity in the service of scientific objectivity involves contingent negotiations of values and perceptions, as Darwin judges the photos for their naturalistic performance rather than their visual truthfulness. Darwin's implied phenomenology of the perceiver as 'co-investigator' privileges artificially over naturally produced life-likeness if it serves the rhetorical goals of communicating his ideas to readers convincingly.[27] Meanwhile, bringing objectivity and fidelity into stricter scientific alignment had to wait for technical progress in photography later in the century. Fidelity and mimesis depend in *Expression* on dialogue with readers as collaborative scientific evaluators, just as, in live stage performance, effect and meaning rely on the co-operative perception and responses of spectators to 'hold … the mirror up to nature' (*Hamlet*, 3.2.22). Darwin productively blurs the lines between 'true' origins, artificial means and 'faithful' ends.

ETHOLOGY AND NATURALISM IN SHAKESPEARIAN PERFORMANCE

Darwin's self-critical re-creation of expressions of emotion suggests a conceptual framework for evaluating natural performance in live stagings of Shakespeare. In both contexts, naturalism is related to, but not identical with, stage traditions of nineteenth-century naturalism. For the remainder of this article, I shall use the term to refer to instinctively or unconsciously embodied gestures of feeling and emotion. Their co-evolutionary heritage mingles with the intentional or epiphenomenal

32. Charles Darwin, *The Expression of the Emotions in Man and Animals* (1872), Plate 2, Figures 1 & 2. (Top) Unnamed actor with face relaxed. (Bottom) Actor simulating grief.

[27] Prodger, *Darwin's Camera*, pp. 30–3, 155, 202, 218–21.

agencies of the individual performer, social and dramatic embodiment through training and rehearsal, and spectator interaction, to create an extensively layered and dynamic ontology of character.[28] On stage, it is analysable as what Farah Karim-Cooper calls a 'polysemous system' in her illuminating study of hand gestures on the early modern stage.[29] My first proposition from Darwin is that perceiving either the congruence or disjunction between instinctive and acquired gestures constitutes a critical viewpoint for judging the life-likeness of character performance – that is, whether the mirror is being held up 'truly' to nature.[30] Such a distinction seems possible because simulated expressions are physiologically not exactly identical to involuntary ones. Deliberately performing a muscle movement in the face, for example, normally produces lateral asymmetries, often slight but detectable. The differences between spontaneous and simulated micro-expressions may become more perceptible when an actor tries deliberately to control the discrepancies or 'leakage' between natural and intentional gestures (Malvolio's exaggerated smiling in *Twelfth Night* exploits this gap comically).[31] Spectators' critical perceptions may also be sharpened by metadramatic attention to the distinction between an actor's personal body and his or her dramatic character, such as when King Edward in *Henry VI Part Three* threatens to grab Warwick's head by his 'coal-black hair' before cutting it off (5.1.54–5).[32] My reading of instinctive expressions of emotion (or passion as early moderns called it) in *King John* also builds on Stacey Alaimo's insight that posthumanist studies of the interconnectedness of beings and things, which try to reconceptualize organic and non-organic relations ecologically, can be deepened historically and ontologically by recalling Darwinian ethology.[33]

My second reason for identifying a Shakespearian ethology of natural performance is to address a current gap between environmental awareness and performance. During this anniversary year,

[28] My definition extends Andrew James Hartley's suggestive idea of a performance habitus, which he defines as a Bourdieuesque interplay of individually chosen and socially inculcated behaviour, to a third, ecologically vital, ontology of stage action and perception: human kinship with non-human origins: ' Character, agency and the familiar actor', in *Shakespeare and Character: Theory, History, Performance and Theatrical Persons*, ed. Paul Yachnin and Jessica Slights (London, 2009), pp. 158–76.

[29] Farah Karim-Cooper, *The Hand on the Shakespearean Stage* (London, 2016), pp. 114–15. Like Karim-Cooper, Darwin drew on studies of physical expression by John Bulwer, such as *Chirologia* and *Pathomyotomia* (e.g., cited on the opening page of *Expression*, p. 13).

[30] *Hamlet*, 3.2.15–33; Darwin, *Expression*, pp. 191, 257, 265; Heywood, *Apology for Actors*, B4r, C4r; Leonore Leiblein, 'Embodied intersubjectivity and the creation of early modern character', in Yachnin and Slights, eds., *Shakespeare and Character*, pp. 117–35, citation pp. 124–5.

[31] Ekman, Introduction to *Expression*, pp. 172–202.

[32] The same detail occurs in the earlier version of the play, *The True Tragedy of Richard Duke of York* (1594) (Oxford, 1985), line 2022. Another instance occurs when spectators watching *As You Like It* may notice that Celia is *not* noticeably shorter than Rosalind, who describes herself as 'more than common tall' (1.3.114). See also John H. Astington, 'Actors and the body: meta-theatrical rhetoric in Shakespeare', *Gesture* 6.2 (2006), 241–59.

[33] Stacey Alaimo, *Bodily Natures: Science, Environmentalism, and the Material Self* (Bloomington, 2010), pp. 147–58. For early modern humoral physiology, phenomenology, and affective and cognitive relationships in theatre, see, e.g., Gail Kern Paster, *Humoring the Body: Emotions and the Shakespearean Stage* (Chicago, 2004); Gail Kern Paster, Katherine Rowe, and Mary Floyd-Wilson, eds., *Reading the Early Modern Passions: Essays in the Cultural History of Emotions* (Philadelphia, 2004); Mary Floyd-Wilson and Garrett A. Sullivan Jr, eds., *Environment and Embodiment in Early Modern England* (Basingstoke, 2007); Laurie Johnson, John Sutton, and Evelyn Tribble, eds., *Embodied Cognition and Shakespeare's Theatre: The Early Modern Body–Mind* (London, 2014); Allison Hobgood, *Passionate Playgoing in Early Modern England* (Cambridge, 2014); Charis Charalampous, *Rethinking the Mind–Body Relationship in Early Modern Literature, Philosophy and Medicine* (London, 2016). For animal–human relations in Shakespeare, see the pioneering research of my fellow panelists Andreas Höfele, *Stage, Stake, & Scaffold: Humans & Animals in Shakespeare's Theatre* (Oxford, 2011); Scott Maisano, 'Rise of the poet of the apes', *Shakespeare Studies* 41 (2013), 64–76; Laurie Shannon, *The Accommodated Animal: Cosmopolity in Shakespearean Locales* (Chicago, 2013). Also Erica Fudge, *Brutal Reasoning: Animals, Rationality, and Humanity in Early*

commentators from Philomena Cunk to Stephen Greenblatt have riffed on the theme of Shakespeare's ever-refashionable modernity. But where is Shakespeare our *eco*-contemporary? While there have been several notable eco-themed productions, such as Rupert Goold's 'arctic desert' *Tempest* for the RSC in 2006, on the whole directors have been – in the words of modern-drama scholar Steve Bottoms – 'slow to pick up the ecological baton'.[34] Since Bottoms made this observation in 2010, contemporary playwrights and companies have upped their engagement with environmental issues.[35] But eco-Shakespeare is not generally part of what Gregory Doran called the imperative 'now' of contemporary productions in his 2016 World Shakespeare Congress plenary talk. Among the reasons for this reluctance seem to be the persistence of Shakespeare's reputation as an icon of traditional Western humanism and social relations (i.e. anthropocentrism); distaste for green agitprop, whose catastrophic ethos tends to produce feelings of indifference or resentment among today's theatre companies, audiences and critics; and the simple fact that Shakespeare (unlike Ibsen, for example, in *An Enemy of the People*) did not write environmentalist narratives, even though his work displays extensive awareness of emerging ecological modernity.[36] Even outdoor immersive productions of Shakespeare, often regarded as conducive to environmental consciousness, do not inevitably foster ecocritical thinking in audiences or performers, although they can tell us significant things about embodied expression and receptive affects, as the groundbreaking research of Evelyn O'Malley has shown.[37]

We can also relate this situation to Jacques Rancière's call for an 'emancipatory' theatre that reconfigures the traditional epistemology of informed playwright and performer, and pre-critical spectator, and more specifically to his provocation that there is 'no direct road from intellectual awareness to political action' in the modern theatre.[38] Baz Kershaw and Alan Read have explored Rancière's arguments in case studies

Modern England (Ithaca, 2006); Todd Andrew Borlik, '"The Chameleon's Dish": Shakespeare and the omnivore's dilemma', *Early English Studies* 2 (2009), 1–25; Bruce Thomas Boehrer, *Animal Characters: Nonhuman Beings in Early Modern Literature* (Philadelphia, 2010); Sharon O'Dair, '"To fright the animals and to kill them up": Shakespeare and ecology', *Shakespeare Studies* 39 (2011), 74–83; Karen Raber, *Animal Bodies, Renaissance Culture* (Philadelphia, 2013). All these scholars have shown how Shakespeare narrows or dissolves the distance between human and non-human ontologies in ways that anticipate post-Cartesian and Darwinian anti-exceptionalism.

34 Stephen Bottoms, review of Baz Kershaw, 'Theatre Ecology: Environments and Performance Events', *Research in Drama Education: The Journal of Applied Theatre and Performance* 15.1 (2010), 121–6; citation p. 121. Bottoms's comments echo those of Erika Munk, Una Chaudhuri, and Theresa J. May on 'playwrights' silence on the environment as a political issue'. See Munk, 'A beginning and end', *Theater* 25.1 (1994), 5–6, cited by May, 'Beyond Bambi: toward a dangerous ecocriticism in Theatre Studies', *Theatre Topics* 17.2 (September 2007), 95–110, citation p. 95; May, 'Greening the theater: taking ecocriticism from page to stage', *Interdisciplinary Literary Studies* 7.1 (Fall 2005), 84–103; Chaudhuri, '"There must be a lot of fish in that lake": toward an ecological theater', *Theater* 25.1 (1994), 25–31. Also Stephen Bottoms, Aaron Franks, and Paula Kramer, 'On ecology', *Performance Research* 17.4 (2012), 1–4; Downing Cless, *Ecology and Environment in European Drama* (London, 2010); 'Ecodirecting canonical plays', in *Readings in Performance and Ecology*, ed. Wendy Aarons and Theresa J. May (New York, 2012), pp. 159–68; Deirdre Heddon and Sally Kelly, 'Environmentalism, performance and applications: uncertainties and emancipations', *Research in Drama Education: The Journal of Applied Theatre and Performance* 17.2 (2012), 163–92.

35 Ray Schultz and Jess Larson, 'Staging sustainable Shakespeare: "Greening the Bard" while advancing institutional mission', in *Performance on Behalf of the Environment*, ed. Richard D. Besel and Jnan A. Blau (Lanham, MD, 2014), pp. 211–33.

36 Monographs include: Gabriel Egan, *Green Shakespeare: From Ecopolitics to Ecocriticism* (London, 2006); Simon Estok, *Ecocriticism and Ecophobia* (Basingstoke, 2011); Todd Andrew Borlik, *Ecocriticism and Early Modern English Literature* (London, 2011); Randall Martin, *Shakespeare and Ecology* (Oxford, 2015).

37 'Weathering Shakespeare: outdoor Shakespeares, audiences, and ecocriticism', paper presented at the meeting of the Shakespeare Association of America, New Orleans, March 2016.

38 Jacques Rancière, *The Emancipated Spectator*, trans. Gregory Elliot (London, 2009), p. 75 and *passim*. Kendra Fraconi has similarly argued that 'Thematic resonance is not enough' to make theatre ecologically effectual: 'Place remembers', *Canadian Theatre Review* 145 (2011), 97–9.

showing that resistance to environmentalist theatre is related to that of instrumentalist drama more broadly.[39] Didactic approaches suffer from a tendency to impose premature closure on complex problems that require flexible and consilient understanding of human and non-human stakeholders, cross-disciplinary knowledge, and local site-specific conditions.[40] As Read observes, 'theatre cannot do politics but does do the social ... because it is excellent at tracing the connections between controversies while wholly unable to settle controversies'.[41] Top-down promotion of environmental awareness, as Bruno Latour, Val Plumwood and Greg Garrard likewise argue, tends to perpetuate, rather than undo, the epistemological dualisms that have excluded non-human life from ethical consideration, and treated the physical world as inert and exploitable.[42] In this respect, eco-allegories may resemble the crude biological determinism that social Darwinists used to construct politically regressive world-views. This environmentally damaging ideology continues today in the predator-and-survivor ethos of business and management theories (not to mention of certain politicians).

An alternative approach is to seek ecological insights from human–non-human relations in performance that expose the universal kinship of ethologically related behaviour and perception.[43] In this article, I suggest this kind of pre-propositional environmentalism can be generated by encouraging actors and spectators to double-back ethologically and environmentally to re-discover their co-evolutionary heritage of affective and material relations, with a view to translating their perceptions into progressive attitudes and future action. In these regards, Shakespeare's plays possess a dual capacity for recursive and forward-thinking power. They pay detailed attention to physically communicated emotion in collaboration with physiologically reciprocating spectators, a characteristic Darwin noticed partly because Shakespeare sometimes associates such signalling with animal metaphors and/or human–animal expression, such as when Henry V refers to his tensed-up soldiers standing 'like greyhounds in the slips' (*Expression*, p. 220; *Henry V*, 3.1.31; see above,

p. 151). Shakespeare's plays also suggest ecological presence and futurity because of their meta-theatricality, in which actors' performing bodies and contemporary stage environments are often juxtaposed with a play's dramatic fictions, as when Romeo observes 'Famine', 'Need and oppression' in the Apothecary's eyes and cheeks (*Romeo and Juliet*, 5.1.69–70), or the mechanicals in *A Midsummer Night's Dream* imaginatively re-green the bare stage boards, thereby performing a symbolic act of reforestation during a period of climate change and accelerating woodland depletion (3.1.2–5). Darwin himself recognized that the ethological study of emotional expression had present-day implications. *Expression*'s final paragraph declared that 'the language of emotions ... is certainly of importance for the welfare of mankind', including the 'specific and sub-specific unity of the several races' (p. 334).[44] In inherited affinities and contrasts with non-human animals, we can discover an ethological epistemology that foregrounds our primary physiological relationships with non-human nature; that engages today's politically aware but ecologically contemplative Shakespearian performers and audiences; and that opens universally evolved affects to audiences' perceptions of new subjective commitments to

---

[39] Baz Kershaw, *Theatre Ecology: Environments and Performance Events* (Cambridge, 2009); Read, *Theatre, Intimacy & Engagement*.

[40] Edward O. Wilson, *Consilience: The Unity of Knowledge* (New York, 1999), p. 7 and *passim*.

[41] Read, *Theatre, Intimacy & Engagement*, p. 44.

[42] Bruno Latour, *We Have Never Been Modern* (Cambridge, MA, 1993); Val Plumwood, *Environmental Culture: The Ecological Crisis of Reason* (London, 2002); Greg Garrard, 'Ecocriticism and education for sustainability', *Pedagogy: Critical Approaches to Teaching Literature, Language, Composition, and Culture* 7.3 (2007), 359–83.

[43] The environmental uncertainty and risk that characterize the anthropocene are critical and artistic resources for actors and audiences (Heddon and Kelly, 'Environmentalism, performance and applications', pp. 170–5); in Shakespeare, they are troped by storms and unseasonable weather.

[44] 'and sub-specific' (i.e. traits underlying secondary characteristics) added by Darwin in original proof corrections. See n. 22 above.

biocentric values and choices. To illustrate the kind of ethologically focused performance that might expose such affective ecological relations, I'll conclude with a brief discussion of a scene of physically enhanced expression in *King John* – Hubert's attempt to carry out King John's orders to put out Prince Arthur's eyes with hot irons (4.1): 'All things that you should use to do me wrong / Deny their office' (*King John*, 4.1.117–18). Arthur's confrontation with Hubert looks forward to the animalized dynamics of Gloucester's blinding in *King Lear*,[45] beginning with King John's bestialization of Arthur as a 'serpent' (3.3.61). But in *King John* the outcome is different, because Arthur successfully divides Hubert's sympathetic passions from his murderous intent by reading his unintended facial and bodily gestures as signs of a somatically disruptive subjectivity. After they exchange curt 'good morrows', Arthur immediately observes Hubert's 'sad' and 'pale' looks. Although Hubert tries to suppress these signs by resolving to shut out Arthur's 'innocent prate' (4.1.9–11, 25, 28–9), the actor's body language betrays the character's verbalized will. For when Hubert silently passes John's warrant to Arthur to avoid naming the violence he must inflict, he simultaneously pushes away a dreadful object and possibly shrinks back physically. These are life-like signs, as Darwin showed, of fear and terror (*Expression*, p. 283). Hubert likewise weeps in mental distress and sympathy at the thought of Arthur's suffering ('How now: foolish rheum, / Turning dispiteous torture out of door?' (4.1.33–4)). The actor simulating Hubert's weeping passions could appear naturalistic by deepening the furrow which runs from the wings of the nostrils to the corners of the mouth and tensing up the vertical lines between the eyebrows (*Expression*, pp. 139–40).

Shakespeare's representation of Hubert's body independently opposing his will is characteristic of the pre-Cartesian bi-subjectivity that Charis Charalampous has shown was common to Galenic physiology and early modern theories about the autokinetic and cognitive body.[46] Arthur re-presents Hubert's instinctive empathy,

making him an observer of his own body's sentient reason to overthrow the dehumanizing script of John's bloody commission. As Charalampous explains, it is the early modern (and Darwinian) body's capacities for pre-linguistic memory and inter-species communication that enable transcorporeal communication between an actor's non-verbal performances and spectators' somatic memories.[47] This common physical identification allows the group to feel for and approve Hubert's instinctively rebellious body, as well as Arthur's endangered one.[48]

Arthur's decoding of Hubert's inner feelings suggests an ethological as well as idealized childhood power of intuition. One way in which this kind of naturalistic viewpoint became accessible to early modern spectators was through memories of the dramatic template for Shakespeare's scene: the medieval play of Abraham and Isaac, in which Abraham's faith is tested by God's command to sacrifice his son, before an angel intervenes at the last moment to save the boy and substitute a young ram. The cross-over scenario with *King John* is of an innocent child threatened by a father-figure torn between obedience to a higher authority and humane compassion. Among the many intertextual signs of the mystery play in *King John* are Isaac's and Arthur's reading of Abraham's and Hubert's faces for instinctive passions that contradict their willed intentions, as well as Isaac's and Arthur's animal consciousness in their self-identification

---

[45] See Andreas Höfele's analysis in *Stage, Stake, & Scaffold*, pp. 188–209.

[46] *Rethinking the Mind–Body Relationship*, p. 29. Charalampous's pre-history of the thinking body advances recent scholarship about early modern physiology and cognition (see n. 33 above), while showing its many anticipations of Darwinian research into shared animal and human emotional gestures and still-evolving scientific and posthuman scholarship.

[47] *Expression*, pp. 62–8, 86–8, 114–15, 326–7. For transactional affects in the theatre, see Garrett A. Sullivan Jr, 'Subjectivity – the mind–body: extending the self on the Renaissance stage', in Johnson *et al.*, eds., *Embodied Cognition and Shakespeare's Theatre*, pp. 67–70.

[48] Hobgood, *Passionate Playgoing*, pp. 1–5, 25–32, 43–57; Leiblein, 'Embodied intersubjectivity', pp. 119–24.

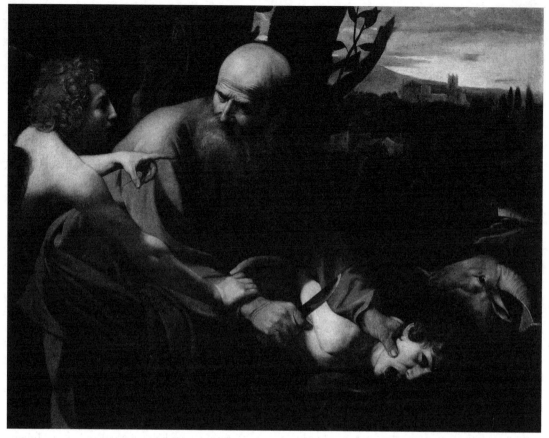

33. Caravaggio, *Sacrifice of Isaac* (*c.* 1602), Uffizi Gallery, Florence, Italy, https://en.wikipedia.org/wiki/Sacrifice_of_Isaac_(Caravaggio) #/media/File:Sacrifice_of_Isaac-Caravaggio_(Uffizi).jpg.

with sheep as symbols of sacrifice (Arthur: 'I will sit as quiet as a lamb' (*King John*, 4.1.79)).[49]

In both Genesis 22 and the medieval play, the ram and Isaac are physically interchangeable. But the anonymous dramatist of the Brome version of *Abraham and Isaac* uses Isaac's animal shadow to heighten the naturalistic tension between the boy's instinctive fears and the typological framework that erases any real threat to him, ostensibly obviating audience sympathy for his anticipated killing. (We know these naturalistic tendencies undermined the play's theological symbolism in performance because the Doctor in the Brome version admonishes parents not to grieve for the premature deaths of their children which they mournfully relived in the near-death experience of Isaac and Abraham's agonies.)[50]

[49] Other intertextual connections: Abraham's and Hubert's psychologically revealing asides and uncontrollable weeping for the death they foresee; Isaac's Marian image of his grieving mother and Arthur's maternal concern for Hubert; Isaac's and Arthur's Christ-like vow to forgive their killers ('I'll forgive you, / Whatever torment you do put me to' (*King John*, 4.1.82–3)); the juxtaposition of Hubert's murderous intent against his physical and reflexively feminized body ('I strike my foot / Upon the bosom of this ground' (4.1.2–3); also 4.2.255–6); the merciful angel that stops Abraham's blow and the notional cruel angel which Arthur disavows (4.1.68); the blindfold which Abraham applies to Isaac in the play and the 'pair of eyes' which Arthur persuades Hubert to spare (4.1.90–8).

[50] https://www.wwnorton.com/college/english/nael/noa/pdf/13BromePlay_1_12.pdf.

Isaac's ovine surrogate is also an awkward witness to the fact that, while the earth's animals fell with Adam and Eve, they will be left out of the *commedia* of human redemption that Abraham's faith and Isaac's willing sacrifice anticipate. Instead, animals will become hostages to the Western subjection of the earth's creatures and environments. An audience's ethological recognition of Isaac's and Arthur's animal otherness thus generates a latent counter-history of environmental justice. This emancipating potential within the story's affective conflicts – a potential independently realized by parental spectators against the Doctor's interpretive bullying – is illuminated by Renaissance images such as Caravaggio's *The Sacrifice of Isaac* (c. 1602; Illustration 33) and, in turn, clarifies the ethological similarities and differences between the medieval play and *King John*.

Caravaggio visually contrasts Isaac's terror and the ram's serenity to mingle affective compassion for the animal-human subject doubly threatened by the patriarch's knife. What I find particularly interesting about this depiction is the silent dialogue between angel and ram. The ram is neither backdrop nor an unfortunate bystander as he is in Genesis (where his circumstance of being 'caught in a thicket' diverts responsibility for his death to a supposedly accidental order of nature). The angel obliviously marks the ram's destiny as the unredeemable Other of human violence. The ram rebuffs the angel's pointed finger with impassive and guiltless defiance. Caught within their mute ontological dialogue, Isaac becomes proleptically ram-like in his non-verbal but powerfully articulate open-mouthed cries of terror. Spectators respond to this juxtaposition with their own animal-memory feelings of life-and-death threats. In *King John*, we hear such vocal modes when Arthur 'passions' in intelligibly sentient sounds that are shared with animals, and which both precede and exceed human language.[51] These are the meta-verbal 'Ohs', 'Ahs', and 'Los' that respond to Hubert's threatening iron, and subsequent relief after he turns

kind.[52] Shakespeare makes the life and death of Isaac's ram somatically immanent and ethologically retraceable in Arthur's animal-human expressions.

Arthur further unsettles Hubert's intention to burn out his eyes with synaesthetic dialogue about what they touch and feel, as well as what they see:

ARTHUR Is there no remedy?

HUBERT None but to lose your eyes.

ARTHUR O God, that there were but a mote in yours,
    A grain, a dust, a gnat, a wandering hair,
    Any annoyance in that precious sense,
    Then, feeling what small things are boisterous there,
    Your vile intent must needs seem horrible.

HUBERT Is this your promise? Go to, hold your tongue!

ARTHUR Hubert, the utterance of a brace of tongues
    Must needs want pleading for a pair of eyes.
                    (4.1.90–8)

This exchange suggests that verbal language – for early moderns, the supreme sign of human rationality – cannot find a fully embodied discourse for eyes because the latter act independently as body-subjects. In these moments, the actors playing Arthur and Hubert stage a pre-discursive dialogue between 'stern looks' and 'gentle heart' that the Executioners will re-present in half-spoken words and silent gestures (4.1.6, 74, 84–5: 'I am best pleased to be from such a deed' (85)). Shakespeare then underlines the scenes' environmental relationality by connecting the subjective independence of human eyes as thinking objects

---

[51] David Abrams, *The Spell of the Sensuous: Perception and Language in a More-than-Human World* (New York, 1997).

[52] *King John*, 4.1.60, 72, 101, 103, 125. Richard Schechner, 'Ethology and theater: animal–human performance continuities', in *Performance Theory*, rev. edn (New York, 1988), pp. 199–242; p. 212. Schechner concludes that animal–human performances form 'a single bio-aesthetic web' (p. 239). Arthur's sounds anticipate the 'Ohs' of quarto *King Lear*, 5.3.303, to cite just one other well-known instance.

and feeling subjects to the red-hot iron which Hubert takes from one of the Executioners out of the brazier-fire (which the Folio text implies stood behind a stage arras and was revealed at 4.1.71). Through personification, Arthur converts the iron from a fearsome weapon into a compassionate friend by noting its change in colour as it cools ('the fire is dead with grief, / Being create for comfort … There is no malice in this burning coal' (4.1.105–6, 108)). The iron becomes part of the scene's materially distributed system of cognition as well as a non-human participant in the theatrical training of the adolescent male actor.[53] Spectators may also notice the stage prop seeming to act physically before Arthur's personification: by 'remembering' its former experiences of being heated for cruel deeds, the iron's cooling shift disables its own harm in a show of compassion for its fire-threatened victim. Sympathy, like horror, as Darwin notes and early modern physiologists before him affirmed, is a naturally transforming emotion: 'our sufferings are thus mitigated … and mutual good feeling is thus strengthened' (*Expression*, p. 333). The iron too thus appears to have a 'stern look' when heated by human agents, but shows a 'gentle heart' when materially left to its natural state. Moreover, Shakespeare again possibly recalls the material–allegorical duality of *Abraham and Isaac* when Arthur draws Hubert's attention to the fire's agency: 'The breath of heaven hath blown his spirit out, / And strewn repentant ashes on its head' (109–10). The passage recalls the paradoxical ontology of Richard II's

> senseless brands [that] will sympathize
> The heavy accent of thy moving tongue,
> And in compassion weep the fire out;
> And some will mourn in ashes, some coal black.
> (*Richard II*, 5.1.46–9)

Finally, Arthur captures the non-human sentience of iron and fire by comparing Hubert and 'his' iron to a dog forced by its master to fight: the dog 'Snatch[es] at [him] that doth tarre him on' (4.1.116). Prioritizing its sympathetic instincts and defying its belligerent owner, Arthur's dog-iron behaves more humanely than Hubert in distinguishing rationally between cruelty and kindness (a moment that anticipates the 'dog'-like Servant who comes to Gloucester's defence in *King Lear* 3.7.70–7). And this transmaterial sensibility is again contagious: the iron and fire's 'compassion' eventually 'gives life' to Hubert's. Whereas he apparently looked 'rude exteriorly', like a 'fellow by the hand of nature marked' 'to do a deed of shame', according to King John (4.2.258, 222–3), Arthur reinterprets his accumulating signs of instinctive compassion as co-evolved expressions of animal and physical subjectivity: 'O, now you look like Hubert. All this while / You were disguisèd' (4.1.125–6). In persuading Hubert to abandon his cruelty, Arthur shows Hubert's instinctive body becoming humanized through animally embodied self-awareness and cross-species and transmaterial reciprocity.

Watching the affective shifts and ethical transformations develop in Arthur and Hubert's ethologically framed encounter reveals what Darwin called a 'community of descent' acting interdependently in response to environmental factors, and works to confound the essentialist divide between people and other animals. In these and other physiologically heightened moments of human–animal affect, Shakespeare seems to anticipate the research of Darwinian ethology, while *The Expression of the Emotions in Man and Animals* confirms the playwright's pre-scientific insights that human and non-human animals respond to external conditions and perceptions with kindred bodies and minds. This shared corporeal habitus is the foundation of natural performance in the theatre, and indeed the physiological origin of theatrical impersonation itself. Shakespeare's attention to these ecologies of co-extensive emotion and belonging reorients audiences away from the false notion that humans respond to environmental conditions in

---

[53] Tribble, *Cognition in the Globe*, pp. 136–42.

exceptional ways that justify their exclusive domination of the planet. And Shakespeare's affective networking of actor, spectator, and theatre relations creates opportunities for stage practitioners to discover the ecological propositions which contemporary spectators might imaginatively reciprocate in locally adapted and environmentally oriented productions.[54]

[54] I am grateful to Madeline Bassnett, Jane Freeman, Stephen Heard, Margaret Jane Kidnie, Evelyn O'Malley, Gretchen Minton, and Deanne Williams for commenting on earlier versions of this article, first presented at the 2016 World Shakespeare Congress in Stratford-upon-Avon, and for making improving suggestions. I should also like to thank The Fisher Library of the University of Toronto for permission to reproduce original images from Darwin's *Expression* and his proof corrections of the book.

OF DANCE AND DISARTICULATION: JULIET DEAD AND ALIVE

JOSEPH CAMPANA

'Star-crossed' is what lovers are in *Romeo and Juliet*, just as 'death-marked' is what love is between the issue of the 'fatal loins' of the Capulets and the Montagues (Prologue 5–9). As tragic lovers *par excellence*, matched in renown perhaps only by the likes of Tristan and Isolde or Antony and Cleopatra, Romeo and Juliet are not only at cross purposes but doomed from the start. Although it was Tristan and Isolde who provided the paradigm for what Denis de Rougemont describes as a fatal love, he might well have been discussing *Romeo and Juliet*. 'Happy love', he argues,

has no history. Romance only comes into existence where love is fatal, frowned upon and doomed by life itself. What stirs lyrical poets to their finest flights is neither the delight of the senses nor the fruitful contentment of the settled couple; not the satisfactions of love, but its *passion*. And passion means suffering. There we have the fundamental fact.[1]

Just as suffering casts a shadow over love, so too tragedy casts a fatal shadow over all the players on its stages. Some will escape, but none will be untouched by death, the great disarticulator about which tragedy has been, historically, so articulate. Even corpses manage remarkable volubility in this empire of silence and cessation.[2]

The houses of Capulet and Montague may be 'alike in dignity', but their scions seem to sustain remarkably different relationships to the idea of death. For Romeo, death is little more than the logical extension of love. He assumes, quite conventionally, that he will die for love, since that is what love is for. His response to the opening brawl turns quickly away from what Julia Kristeva, in response to de Rougemont, describes in her analysis of *Romeo and Juliet* as 'the intrinsic presence of hatred in amatory feeling'.[3]

> Here's much to do with hate, but more with love.
> Why then, O brawling love, O loving hate,
> O anything of nothing first create;
> O heavy lightness, serious vanity,
> Misshapen chaos of well-seeming forms,
> Feather of lead, bright smoke, cold fire, sick health,
> Still-waking sleep, that is not what it is!
> This love feel I, that feel no love in this.
>
> (*Romeo* 1.1.172–9)

The conventional oxymorons of Petrarchan love ('Feather of lead, bright smoke, cold fire, sick health') evoke not merely contradictory feelings but a penchant for negation. Each experience 'is not what it is', just as Romeo feels love as 'no love'. And on the other side of these 'well-seeming forms', or literary conventions, lies 'Misshapen chaos'. Romeo's understanding of *eros* is fully saturated with visions of *thanatos*, which seems to be the condition of love as in the eerie chorus that opens two acts and witnesses in the wake of his arbitrary forswearing of Rosaline:

---

[1] Denis de Rougemont, *Love in the Western World* (New York, 1974), p. 15.

[2] For an account of dead flesh on the Renaissance stage, see Susan Zimmerman, *The Early Modern Corpse and Shakespeare's Theatre* (Edinburgh, 2005). For a recent account of the cultural utility of corpses, see Margaret Schwartz, *Dead Matter: The Meaning of Iconic Corpses* (Minneapolis, 2015).

[3] Julia Kristeva, *Tales of Love* (New York, 1987), p. 222.

Now old desire doth in his death-bed lie,
And young affection gapes to be his heir.
That fair for which love groaned for and would die,
With tender Juliet matched, is now not fair.

(*Romeo* 2.0.1–4)

In the wake of Tybalt's demise, Capulet's delay of the wooing Paris provokes the sententious certainty of the sentiment, 'Well, we were born to die' (3.4.4). William Carroll argues in an essay especially attuned to this line that '*Romeo and Juliet* goes to great lengths to stress the inevitability of Capulet's vision.'[4] The play is death-soaked from its beginning – the proximity between love, sex and death so intense as to annihilate thought. But death is not just the drama of self-extinguishing love or a particularly masculine melancholy of mortality. It is possessed of a certain heft easily obscured by the sentiments surrounding it.

Eventually Romeo does die, not from the easy world-negating melodrama of his own affections, or from a kind of cultural resignation to mortality, but in despair in a tomb at the end of the play from the administration of the apothecary's quick drugs. Juliet, however, seems simultaneously more in tune with death and more capable of thinking with its wordless weight. What to make of the spectacle and sensibility associated with her death? Elisabeth Bronfen considers 'the western culture dream of beautiful dead women' and a persistent 'interrelation between femininity and death', which serves to 'repress its knowledge of death', and which marks the female body as the site of utter alterity.[5] However, she makes reference to neither Shakespeare nor Juliet, neither opera nor ballet. Although she too makes no reference to Juliet, Catherine Clément diagnoses the root aesthetic pleasure of opera as the death or undoing of women: 'Opera concerns women. No, there is no feminist version; no there is no liberation. Quite the contrary: they suffer, they cry, they die.'[6] Kristeva, on the other hand, suggests there is something Lady Macbeth-like about the young Juliet. 'Because it is Juliet who reveals that infernal quickening leading to the night of death, a quickening peculiar to amorous feeling', she argues, 'this does not only signify that

a woman is, as they say, in direct contact with rhythm. More imaginatively, feminine desire is perhaps more closely umbilicated with death; it may be that the matrical source of life knows how much it is within her power to destroy life.'[7] Although it is hard to imagine Juliet smashing the brains of her own child against a wall, rhythm suggests that death spurs movement, corporeal activity, and Juliet does seem to be in touch also with the peculiar way that, in tragedy, death is not the end of a trajectory but an incitement to recurrence. Death is the switch by which reiteration begins.

How many times, after all, does Juliet die? Once, twice, thrice?

Once: Juliet takes her life after waking alone in a cold and gruesome tomb where she discovers Romeo not ready to whisk her away into romantic exile but self-slain. 'O happy dagger!' she cries. 'This is thy sheath! There rust, and let me die' (5.3. 168–9).

Twice: earlier, Juliet 'dies' at her own hands, thanks not to the quick drugs of an apothecary but to the only seemingly mortal draught of the botanically inclined friar. 'A sleeping potion', he later informs the prince and the lovers' parents, 'which so took effect / As I intended, for it wrought on her / The form of death' (5.3.243–5). In this easily overlooked moment, the Friar unleashes a chilling interplay between various meanings of 'form'. He might be referring to the shape of death, the mere appearance or likeness of death, or, in a now-obsolete usage operative in Shakespeare's era, the beauty or comeliness of death. Is the form of death a shaping reality, mere appearance, or the aesthetically appealing end of tragedy?

---

4 William Carroll, '"We were born to die": Romeo and Juliet', *Comparative Literature* 15.1 (1981), 54–71; p. 55.
5 Elisabeth Bronfen, *Over Her Dead Body: Death, Femininity, and the Aesthetic* (Manchester, 1992), p. xi.
6 Catherine Clément, *Opera: The Undoing of Women*, trans. Betsy Wing (Minneapolis, 1988), p. 11.
7 Kristeva, *Tales*, p. 214.

Thrice: earlier still, Juliet anticipates disaster in the tomb. The friar might poison her. She might 'wake before the time' and 'be stifled in the vault, / To whose foul mouth no healthsome air breathes in, / And there die strangled ere my Romeo comes' (4.3.30, 32–4). She might be driven mad by stench and corpses and gloom and 'with some great kinsman's bone / As with a club dash out my desp'rate brains' (4.3.52–3). In her mind, she has already died.

How many times *does* Juliet die? Final answer: Juliet is always dying, as is Romeo, although Juliet seems to do so with greater frequency and self-awareness. These lovers, like the protagonists of any work capable of reiteration, exist in a loop of recurrence, dying daily and nightly across a dizzying array of media every time the fatal engine of the story *Romeo and Juliet* starts up, every time and on whatever platform – be it on a page, on a stage, on a screen, in a feed, or, in fact, anytime a body executes that series of algorithms and consequences that is *Romeo and Juliet*. John Neumeier's balletic *Romeo and Juliet* (1974) emphasizes this quality of queasy repetition. In a public street scene, Juliet encounters a travelling troupe who delight Verona with dumb-show-like puppet re-enactments of great stories. While Ludovico Ariosto's romance, *Orlando Furioso*, to this day still provides the archive of stories for travelling puppet theatres in Sicily, the tale Juliet spectates is her own: the tragedy of *Romeo and Juliet*. Such a metatheatrical moment offers audiences the pleasure of a poignant moment redolent with foreboding, but Neumeier's choice also highlights the revelatory nature of death, which occurs as a tragic loop in which the lovers, knowingly or unknowingly, are caught. Juliet comes closest to an awareness of this cycle of recurrence just as, I argue here, choreographic treatments of Juliet's death, especially balletic ones, accomplish a special kind of thinking about death and recurrence, on the one hand, and the tension between the monumentalization of tragic protagonists and the corpses concealed by monuments, on the other.

Long before Romeo's death, Juliet, as Cleopatra will for Antony, imagines, in anticipation of a time when Romeo has shuffled off his mortal coil, her lover monumentalized:

> Give me my Romeo, and when I shall die,
> Take him and cut him out in little stars,
> And he will make the face of heaven so fine
> That all the world will be in love with night
> And pay no worship to the garish sun.
>
> (*Romeo*, 3.2.21–5)

In her stirring and iconic soliloquy, Juliet renders Romeo a starry monument. While the likes of Walter Benjamin and Theodor Adorno found in 'constellation' a way of describing conceptual articulation and linking, it is a process that accomplishes through violence a series of operations: extraction, fixation, abstraction and reification. The beauty of stellification relies on force and implies the elimination of movement and change. Stellification obfuscates – one might say beautifies – the consequences and remainders of death, especially those that figure prominently in *Romeo and Juliet*'s tomb scenes. Beneath fire and music, flame and star dust, corpses lie. Moreover, when Juliet vows she will cut Romeo out in little stars, she aspires to memorialize him *before* his death. In a perhaps uncharacteristic gesture of good taste, Cleopatra at least waits until after Antony's demise before imagining his apotheosis: 'His face was as the heav'ns, and therein stuck / A sun and moon, which kept their course and lighted / The little O o'th' earth' (*Antony* 5.2.78–80).

For Robert N. Watson, the contemplation of death in early modern England sparked a particular crisis, as 'the fear of death as annihilation' threatened 'traditional promises of immortality'.[8] Tragedy, according to Michael Neill's powerful account, not only was about 'the discovery of death and the mapping of its meanings' but constituted 'a crucial part of' a 'secularizing process' of death in the era and thus became 'among the principal instruments by which the culture of early

---

[8] Robert N. Watson, *The Rest is Silence: Death as Annihilation in the English Renaissance* (Berkeley, 1994), p. 1.

modern England reinvented death'.[9] In so doing, Neill argues, tragedy combatted several overwhelming facets of the experience of mortality, including the shame of being stripped naked to one's base body, the violation of that body after death, and the indifference of death, which constitutes 'a condition of dreadful *disfigurement*' that strips away status and identity to leave behind little more than carrion.[10] The often-ennobling nature of tragic action could make, as Cleopatra put it, 'death proud to take us' (4.16.90). And it is in this vein that Juliet's strategy of stellification operates. She and Romeo are no longer children crushed by their parents (or circumstances) but become starry edifices to be named and recollected and admired. What Jonathan Dollimore argues of Juliet's apparently dead body might also apply to the stellified Romeo. 'This spectacle of death', he suggests, 'is unbearable yet not undesired, because here death arrests beauty; transience, decay, decline, failure (including parental impotence) are pre-empted in and through "untimely" death.'[11]

The morbidity of Juliet's anticipation of Romeo's posthumous life is striking. After all, constellation requires his death. But Juliet's body – anticipating its death, then apparently dead, and then actually dead – has proved even more striking, especially to choreographers. Juliet certainly joins figures from the late plays – Innogen (disguised as Fidele), Hermione and Thaisa – arrested in death-like states. The repertoire of story ballets also includes tantalizing proximate, but not quite analogous, figures. *Sleeping Beauty*'s Aurora dances into slumber after pricking herself on the spinning wheel and later wakes from that death-like sleep after the prince's kiss. Ghosts dance about, like the vengeful spirits of wronged women in *Giselle* or the exquisite dream-like vision of temple dancers, the iconic Kingdom of the Shades scene in *Bayadère*, which also features dead lovers reunited as spirits at the end. The frequent translation of *Romeo and Juliet* into choreography highlights Juliet's (apparently) dead flesh as a problem and a challenge. More than merely morbid, *Romeo and Juliet* and its legacy in dance directs our attention to the violence of disarticulation endemic to myth-

making and to the recalcitrant corporeality of death, which versions of this most popular of Shakespeare's plays in the world of dance emphasize. As choreographers grapple with Juliet's body, they display the utility of notions of disarticulation and reanimation for understanding of the afterlives of Shakespeare.

Why these terms? Disarticulation is clearly a function of tragedy, the dissecting of the social body that purportedly may lead to the revelation and extirpation of diseased segments. And in addition to the impressive body counts of so many tragedies, many also focus on the literal disassembly of bodies (as, famously, in *Titus Andronicus*).[12] More recently, Bruce Smith's *Shakespeare / Cut* marshals 'cut' and 'cutwork' to refer to a range of significant excisions and media crossings.[13] Here I want to use 'disarticulation' to refer more broadly to the physicality of live or once-live performing bodies. First, ballet radically *dis-articulates* Shakespeare by rendering him wordless, a fact so obvious its significance can be elusive. The wordlessness of a choreographic Shakespeare may encourage a certain fantasy of communicability; this is a work whose universality and timelessness conveys feelings and truths so powerful they may be conveyed in the absence of language. But wordlessness witnesses an intensification of that sense of corporeality shared with – but not identical to – other, especially theatrical, iterations of *Romeo and Juliet*. The more that balletic versions of *Romeo and Juliet* pay attention to Juliet's body, the more they suggest the importance of an urgent corporeality irreducible to familiar narrative, characterological and emotive frameworks of meaning, which,

---

[9] Michael Neill, *Issues of Death: Mortality and Identity in English Renaissance Tragedy* (Oxford, 1997), pp. 1, 3.

[10] Neill, *Issues*, p. 9.

[11] Jonathan Dollimore, *Death, Desire, and Loss in Western Culture* (London, 1994), p. 112.

[12] For the critical preoccupation with disarticulated bodies, see *The Body in Parts: Fantasies of Corporeality in Early Modern Europe*, ed. David Hillman and Carla Mazzio (London, 1998).

[13] Bruce Smith, *Shakespeare / Cut: Rethinking Cutwork in an Age of Distraction* (Oxford, 2016).

however potent or enjoyable, conceal a problematic body in the process of death and reanimation. Second, while many of the choreographic versions of *Romeo and Juliet* work firmly in the narrative tradition of the story ballet, some versions disarticulate Juliet by cutting her off from and pulling her out of the familiar plot and setting, forcing us to ask ourselves what Juliet is without Romeo and, in a sense, without tragedy. In the era of the empire of adaptation – a term that, however useful, too easily strips away media specificity and arts technique to locate all significance in an essential narrative kernel[14] – disarticulation draws attention to aspects of a mythic structure not reducible to elements of narrative and which become subject to dis- and re-assembly, while reanimation signals the recalcitrant corporeality without which the afterlives of a work of art cannot be understood. Indeed, in the hyper-mediated world we live in, remembering the physicality of performance, its former liveness, is critical.[15] In what follows, I consider how choreographers treat the anticipation of Juliet's death, the liminal moment in the tomb when Juliet appears to be dead, Romeo's interaction with her in this apparent death, and then her actual death. In these moments, Juliet's body poses a challenge and an opportunity worth thinking through not just narratively but choreographically.

Of the many decisions, large and small, required to stage the final tomb scene, one rushes to the fore: what, if anything, is to be done with Juliet's body? While 'nothing' might be the answer – many productions are content to leave her on a slab until her awakening – this question primarily has arisen as one of narrative. Does Juliet wake after Romeo dies, as indicated by the text, or does she rise before Romeo dies? It may be the case, as Ramie Targoff argues, that this textual gesture indicates 'Shakespeare's refusal to give the lovers the kind of posthumous intimacy that early modern couples so often desired for their bodies, he in effect doubles the force of the tragedy'.[16] But in the case of other stagings, narrative alteration impacts plot sequence, timing, and the resulting emotional impact, all of which

may even more enhance our sense of this work as a tragedy of miscommunication and missed connections. Even Baz Luhrmann's cinematic *Romeo + Juliet* notably stages just such an overlap of awareness. Rather than Juliet waking after Romeo's death, she wakes suddenly, not soon enough to prevent his death but, rather, just in time for the instant to see him take the poison and painfully watch him die. But in addition to a narrative question, there is, here, what I will call a choreographic question, one that arises in any configuration of bodies, but most intensely when body conveys significance in the absence of language. Does Juliet merely lie inert as Romeo enters, mourns, encounters and fights Paris, mourns some more, and then takes his life? If not, how and where is she moved, in what manner, and by what agency? Does Juliet seem corpse-like or merely sleeping? Whether she moves, is moved or not, prior to awakening, is the physicality of resuscitation emphasized? What can be said of the weight, gait, manipulation and movement of the body is absolutely a theatrical question, but it is one taken up with heightened intensity in a balletic tradition on a wordless stage on which corporeal events, as much as character performance, create meaning. How easy it is to forget that most captivating of features of most performance, the body, which seems so solid and yet remains a fleeting trace. As Peggy Phelan argues, 'Historical bodies and bodies moving on the stage fascinate us because they fade.'[17] Susan

---

[14] For an overview of tendencies in the choreographic staging of *Romeo and Juliet*, and for my discussion of the overly narrative emphasis of adaptation studies, see Joseph Campana, 'Dancing Will: the case of Romeo and Juliet', in *Romeo and Juliet: A Critical Reader*, ed. Julia Lupton (London, 2016), pp. 153–76.

[15] See Philip Auslander, *Liveness: Performance in a Mediatized Culture* (London, 2008).

[16] Ramie Targoff, *Posthumous Love* (Chicago, 2014), p. 5.

[17] Peggy Phelan, 'Thirteen ways of looking at choreographing writing', in *Choreographing History*, ed. Susan Leigh Foster (Indianapolis, 1995), p. 200.

Leigh Foster has written extensively of the 'articulate physicality'[18] of the dancing body and suggests attention to that body, 'its habits and stances, gestures and demonstrations, every action of its various regions, areas and parts – all these emerge out of cultural practices, verbal or not, that construct corporeal meanings'.[19]

However ephemeral, however textual, and even however seemingly immaterial, corporeality doesn't so much endure as it recurs, nightly resurrected even, itself a medium of significance and specificity, whenever a performance begins. What, then, is it to be a body on a choreographic stage? When and to what end does choreographic language break down? When, how and to what effect do lapses of articulation of the choreographed body occur, whose deployment of the architecture of an idiosyncratic movement idiom (the postures and positions of its system) differentiates it from other forms of theatrical or everyday motion? Despite the dominance of narrative represented by the inheritance of the story ballet, ballet offers more than just another vehicle for story, character and emotional expression. It offers resources for understanding the attunement of body, which includes distinct movement vocabularies (out of whose grammar significance might be created) and an intense concentration on the wordless weight of the body. The staging of Juliet's body in the tomb occurs not only relative to reiterations of *Romeo and Juliet* in worlds most familiar to Shakespearians (like theatre and film) but also in conversation with balletic tradition, which has accumulated its own share of lovers, dead and alive, although analogous moments remain fleeting.[20] Death is staged all the time in ballet, but when does death disarticulate the balletic body, whose ideal figure – in spite of decades of choreography that works counter to this ideality – prides itself on artful, exquisite athleticism that disavows a grosser sense of corporeality even in the midst of extreme exertion? Lifts are effortless, landings silent, and death gorgeously sculpted.

In making a claim for the specificity of choreographic language with respect to iterations of *Romeo and Juliet*, this article both builds on and works in tension with tendencies I can only here mention briefly. First, the thrust of adaptation studies enshrines narrative transformation, transmission, and practises a strategic indifference to medium specificity.[21] At the same time, the rise of a wonderfully varied and sophisticated body of work in media studies – about a shocking array of media, new and old – coincides with a swerve away from formerly known artistic specificities. In other words, the arts may be the casualties of an age of media. Second, the practice and theory of choreography have worked towards an ever-greater expansiveness of that term. Choreography is more than a century beyond the strictures of ballet. Choreographers build movement vocabularies from a stunning array of movements, from extravagant to ordinary. And 'the choreographic' tends to be used capaciously to refer far beyond what happens on a choreographic stage, including a politically self-consciousness awareness of corporeality and public space.[22] Here I use it to refer literally to choreography in dance and to a broader sense of significance attached to bodies, still or in motion, for which movement is part of a concerted pattern of strategies and idioms, whether as codified in the traditional positions of ballet or in the idiosyncratic vocabularies developed by those who inherit and diverge from classical technique.

---

18 Susan Leigh Foster, *Choreography and Narrative* (Indianapolis, 1996), p. xvi.

19 Susan Leigh Foster, 'Manifesto for bodies living and dead', in *Choreographing History*, ed. Susan Leigh Foster (Indianapolis, 1995), p. 3.

20 Many ballets stage a relationship between love and death. Some end with a *liebestod* gesture: the lovers may be united only in and through death, as in some versions of the end of *Swan Lake*. In others, a dead lover becomes a ghost or shade, as in *Giselle*, where the title character turns into a Willi, or vengeful female spirit, yet spares her former lover.

21 Campana, 'Dancing Will', pp. 158–9.

22 Recently, Jenn Joy argues that 'choreography invites a rethinking of orientation in relationship to space, to language, to composition, to articulation, and to ethics': *The Choreographic* (Cambridge, MA, 2014), p. 1.

It is hard to overestimate the centrality of *Romeo and Juliet* in the world of dance. As Roslyn Sulcas argues:

'Romeo and Juliet' is near ubiquitous in the ballet repertory. Although the best-known versions are by John Cranko and Kenneth MacMillan, virtually every self-respecting artistic director is aching to present an individual take on the story. There are productions with multiple Romeos and Juliets (Angelin Preljocaj's); with Friar Lawrence as the central figure (Jean-Christophe Maillot's); that eschew Renaissance settings (Peter Martins's). Matthew Bourne is working on a gay version. But it's likely that even a Romeo and Julian will fulfill the one requirement that seems inviolate, whatever the production: the tragic, cathartic end, with its terrible sense of waste and loss.[23]

Elsewhere, I have examined the evolution of the choreographic *Romeo and Juliet* from the narrative strictures of the original collaboration between choreographer Leonid Lavrosky, composer Sergei Prokofiev, dramaturg Adrian Piotrovsky, and director Sergey Radlov towards innovative non-narrative iterations that do not necessarily sustain the 'inviolate' principle Sulcas names 'the tragic, cathartic end, with its terrible sense of waste and loss'.[24] From the dozen or so choreographic iterations of *Romeo and Juliet* I considered for this article, several distinct treatments of the dead Juliet emerge: the sleepwalker, the corpse, the revenant, and the survivor.

The sleepwalker witnesses a Juliet who, although not awakened by a kiss as in the *Sleeping Beauty* fantasy, seems to retain control over her body and the capacity to move within the strictures of ballet while she is, at least in Romeo's mind, dead. She has none of the automatism of, say, George Balanchine's *La Sonnambula*, which features the odd female sleepwalker, whose movement for most of that ballet resembles that of a wind-up machine occasionally colliding, but not interacting, with the world around her until she draws the slain protagonist into her ghostly world at the end. In many versions, although in differing degrees, Romeo lifts Juliet into what appears to be a postmortem pas de deux. Take, for instance, Kenneth MacMillan's version, which

is perhaps the most frequently performed balletic *Romeo and Juliet*. Many productions have moderate to elaborate sets, including, in the iconic 1966 film starring Rudolf Nureyev and Margot Fonteyn, a tomb replete with grisly monuments to which a long line of mourners process with Juliet's body. Entering the dark tomb, Romeo discovers his love. Romeo hauls her up and carries her with one arm. Although she is 'dead', her body is partly taut – her legs straight, her feet pointed. All the bend is at the waist as her upper body remains slack. With the apparent corpse of Juliet, Romeo reprises gestures from the balcony pas de deux that seals their love, lifting her up as she arches her back over his head before reversing into the same fish dive as before. Romeo keeps trying to catapult her into motion until finally he gives up, drags her body across the floor by her arm and hauls her back onto her funeral bier. He poisons himself and collapses on the ground just below her prone body. Juliet wakes to discover a different gory spectacle from the one that the textual Juliet imagined: not the bones of Tybalt but the corpse of her beloved Romeo. Grief-stricken, and with no poison left, she stabs herself, crawls back on the funeral bier and arduously reaches down to haul Romeo's body up just enough to plant a kiss on his lips before collapsing into death. Juliet may evince more control and coordination once she wakes, but even death does not inhibit the elegant articulation of the balletic body.

MacMillan's predecessor Frederick Ashton features a similarly sleep-walking Juliet, elegantly limp, as do reconstructions of Leonid Lavrosky's original choreography.

The sleepwalker suggests the triumph of stellification, the elegance of art that not only survives but thrives in the face of death. The corpse, on the contrary, insists upon the loss of bodily articulation in the face of death. In what feels a violation of the corporeal architecture of ballet, the body is merely

---

23 Roslyn Sulcas, 'O Romeo, Romeo, wilst thou smile at this finale?' *New York Times*, 29 June 2008.
24 Campana, 'Dancing Will', pp. 168–79.

meat, and an attempt at quasi-naturalistic movement replaces choreography. Instead of pointe work or partnering, Juliet (and sometimes also Romeo) presents awkward and heavy flesh to be manipulated. John Cranko's noted, if now less frequently performed, production not only concentrates on the dead weight of Juliet but also seems to anticipate an inert Juliet in the tomb. At the Capulet ball, Mercutio and Benvolio lure the guests away to enable a private moment between the would-be lovers. Those couples partner one another far upstage beyond some arches and gates in what suggests a ritualized social dance fit for a party. The main stage clears, leaving Romeo and Juliet alone for their first pas de deux, one eventually interrupted by Tybalt. At one point, Romeo lifts Juliet over his head. She flattens out, her back nearly horizontal, her legs dangling, as if she were dead weight. This seems distinct from more common lifts in which the ballerina either sustains a formal position or arches her back yet seems to sink into the ecstasy of partnering. Those moments can seem looser or more relaxed but still require a fair amount of articulation and body control. Moments later, having been held awkwardly above as if she were a corpse on a funeral bier, she shifts her legs and arms, which are now held in more articulate positions as would be the case for a more conventional lift. Later, in the tomb, both lovers collapse under the weight of impending death. Romeo lifts Juliet off the slab. He wants to carry her somewhere, away from death, perhaps, but there is nowhere to go. He drops her on the floor awkwardly, picks her up again and places her back on the funeral dais. Romeo kisses Juliet, but Sleeping Beauty does not wake. He stabs himself and collapses on the dais but around her body. Moments later, Juliet wakes, seeming ecstatic to be alive and perhaps expecting to find Romeo and the Friar. She senses the weight of Romeo's flesh and tries to wrap his arms around her, as if the two were merely taking a nap together. When she realizes he is dead, she shakes the dead weight of his corpse. She is, at first, inconsolable and gesticulates wildly. She composes herself enough to locate a knife a few feet away and

stabs herself with it. She climbs up on the slab, and tries to haul Romeo's body up. Juliet leans Romeo against her body and collapses into death, her body making a heap with his.

Rudi Van Dantzig (1967) similarly emphasizes Juliet's corpse when Romeo enters the tomb to find her body is covered by white fabric. He lifts her and carries her away from the slab. She is dead weight in his arms, her own arms dangling down lifelessly. He sets her back on the dais. He stabs himself and collapses some distance from Juliet's body. Moments later, she wakes, looks in horror around her at the interior of the tomb. Finally, she casts her eyes upon Romeo's body and responds with shock. She runs to him and tries to haul his heavy body up. Clearly, he is dead. She stabs herself and collapses, grabbing his arms to force a final embrace. After the death, two black-cloaked figures appear – the ghosts of Tybalt and Mercutio – to attend the lovers' passing. With a sweep of cloaks, they cover the bodies, hiding them as the curtain closes.

More recent choreographies build significantly from the dead weight of the body noted and gestured towards in choreographies by Cranko and Van Dantzig. Angelin Preljocaj (1992) creates an intentionally awkward corpse choreography from Juliet's apparent death. She lies on a square slab in a red dress, her legs straight and her arms flung out to her sides. She is attended by two young women who sit in chairs downstage from the body. Romeo walks in, passing the attendants who do not seem to notice him at first. When they take note, they stand up and walk upstage to exit. Romeo kneels by the body, crawls up to her to take her hand. With his mouth, he moves her arms to cross them over her chest. He grabs her body and clutches it to his chest. He moves her to a chair and then leans heavily against her seemingly dead body. He throws her arms over him as in an embrace. He sits in the chair across from her as she is laid out – still seemingly dead – in the chair. He does a series of more complicated gestures with what is, to him, Juliet's corpse. He rolls across the floor with her. Lying flat on his back with her on top of him, Romeo lifts Juliet up in the air with his arms and one leg. He rolls her off him, wrestles her back onto the slab, and strips off her red coat. He leans on and over her as he drives a knife into himself, leaving his dead body to collapse on hers. Moments later, she slowly wakes with Romeo's dead weight pressing down on her. She reaches out to caress him but realizes something isn't right. She tries to haul him up to kiss him and checks to see if he's alive, after which she flops his body awkwardly on the floor and wrestles him over to one of the chairs. She sits on his lap and embraces his dead body. Juliet takes his hand as she backs away from him. She begins to run away from the chair and then back to leap against his body on the chair. She sits on his lap again, grabs his hand and forces it to caress her body, and then leans into his embrace and places his arms around her. Eventually she walks over, not to a sword or knife, but to a razor blade and slices her wrist after the music has stopped. The razor drops loudly on the floor. She embraces him one last time and dies. Their end is gruesome, intentionally awkward, and they are insistently dead with little glimmer of stellification in sight.

Sasha Waltz (2007) and Mats Ek (2013) convey the weight of the dead body by burying and implanting Juliet's body. Waltz's ballet sets the operatic *Romeo and Juliet* of Hector Berlioz. Her production is by no means wordless, but the scenes of Romeo's discovery of Juliet's body are. Gestures of burial, including funerary stones deployed in the scene, convey the weight of the corpse left by erotic disaster. Juliet's body is lifted by two men and then placed in a pit, lit from below, in the centre of the stage. She is surrounded by a huge crowd, some of whom are the singers who will separate themselves by voice from the dancers. The mourners pour stones over her – just as some mourners now still cast flowers or earth upon a coffin. At times, the primary sound is neither singing nor the movement of feet, but the lithic retorts of these burial gestures. Three men in black carry in black bags full of stones and pour them over her. Romeo whirls on stage dramatically in a coat with a long trailing tail, making wildly grief-stricken gestures. He collapses on the edge of the

stage, crawls towards her grave, then crawls away in horror. He stares at the body, crawls back to it and lays his head on the stones that cover her; all the while, the stones continue to vocalize. He seems to lean over and kiss her, lifts his arms to caress his face with her hand, and then takes the poison, which does not kill him instantly. As he collapses over her, she reaches up her hand to caress him. He rises, pulls her out of the grave, seizes and twirls her about, lifting her into the air. She still seems half-dead in the air but manages to run and leap with him. He lifts her a few more times, always from behind so that in the air she seems paralyzed or like captured prey. Romeo finally collapses in the grave on the stones. Juliet, in disbelief, hauls his torso up to her, drops heavily upon him before kissing him. She seems to stab herself then collapses on his body as a huge cast of singers and dancers emerges to mourn.

In Ek's version, Romeo and Juliet relate to one another over a sort of discovery space, a square concavity into which Juliet partly sinks. At a certain point, they reprise a gesture repeated throughout the work as she and Romeo both put their feet up in the air as if to surrender and to die and to be planted in the ground all at once. In the case of Waltz and Ek, Romeo and Juliet enact a corpse dance that emphasizes the implantation and entombment of their bodies. Memorialization occurs, but stones, not stars, dominate.

Waltz's choice to allow Romeo and Juliet some moments together as she revives and he dies signals another strategy of imagining the lovers neither dead nor alive entirely but caught in some odd twilight in the tomb. In this case, the lover is a revenant, and other choreographers emphasize not the zombie-like in-between-ness but rather the reanimation of the dead. For Jean-Christophe Maillot (1996), resuscitation occurs briefly and incompletely. Romeo, kneeling on the angled plinth on which Juliet's body rests, kisses his prone and, in his mind, dead beloved. As he does, he gradually raises his torso away from her. Her body follows. She arches her back, meets the kiss, and when the kiss ends she collapses back onto the plinth as Romeo staggers to the side. For Mauro

Bigonzetti (2006), the reanimation of the body is not merely a momentary tug at the heartstrings or a canny reprise of *Sleeping Beauty*. Although he also uses Prokofiev's iconic score, he distances himself from the story itself, as did Maillot, whose website describes that 'based on the assumption that everyone is familiar with *Romeo and Juliet*, Jean-Christophe Maillot took a choreographic approach that avoids paraphrasing Shakespeare's literary masterpiece'.[25] Bigonzetti even more powerfully disarticulates the narrative, his entire focus on velocity and violence. Bigonzetti insists, 'We didn't want to tell the Romeo and Juliet story.'[26] Instead, this choreography conveys the peril of city life, which mars and kills youthful flesh. Anyone might be Romeo or Juliet. No firm distinctions are drawn between the various couples on the stage, and the iconic status of singular lovers comes to be outscaled by the surroundings. One particularly notable pas de deux takes place in and around a massive industrial fan. Bigonzetti turns *Romeo and Juliet* into a story of death and resurrection. In Bigonzetti's realization, a figure in black – a death figure – dances alone at the beginning. A series of slabs with dead or sleeping bodies appear in eerie red light. The figures writhe, reach out to one another, which is perhaps one sign that the tragedy is about to begin again. Bigonzetti flags the process by which life floods back into dead bodies and thus gestures to corporeal reanimation as the best analogy for the process by which any iconic work of art comes to be reperformed. Lovers die over and over so they may be resurrected for viewers. Bigonzetti choreographs it as an endless loop of violent exertion, expiration and resuscitation.

Juliet is a sleepwalker, a corpse, a revenant, and at times she is also a survivor. Indeed, it was not merely the post-Restoration stage that recrafted Shakespeare's tragedies, replacing disasters with survival. Mark Morris (2008) restored the original score and happy ending from the 1940 première of Prokofiev's *Romeo and Juliet*.[27] Morris's full-length R&J is in the choreographer's own movement idiom, not ballet. Dancers are not en pointe. The centre of gravity is noticeably lower, and the upper body is less active and erect in jumps, spins and turns. Unlike the world of classical ballet, Morris distinguishes genders much less strictly. For example, Juliet and Romeo lift each other in their first pas de deux. For viewers, across media, weaned on the tragic end, the most remarkable transformation occurs with respect to the narrative, which avoids the tomb altogether. After Juliet takes the Friar's potion, she collapses on her bed. She is found by the nurse the next morning, as is the case in most productions. When the nurse rushes out in grief to report on Juliet's death, Romeo suddenly appears in the bedroom and finds the dead Juliet. He comes back earlier than in other versions, but he has not received the Friar's message. Romeo lifts Juliet's arm, holds her hand, but there is no sign of life. He dances a slightly overwrought solo but, just before he stabs himself, the Friar bursts in, grabs the knife, and wrests it from him. After breathing a sigh of relief, the Friar pantomimes the plan. Romeo waits nervously. Gradually, Juliet wakes as if from an ordinary slumber. The Friar rings a bell stage left, repeatedly, to summon the household. The lovers dance, and then leave stage right through what looks like a window. The household arrives – but the body is gone. The entire community eventually assembles: Montague, Capulet, prince. The Friar communicates the tale (pantomime of birds flying away), and suddenly everyone is reconciled, with embraces and kisses all round.

---

[25] www.balletsdemontecarlo.com/en/romeo-and-juliet.

[26] Romeo and Juliet, choreographed by Mauro Bigonzetti (2006; Halle: Arthaus, 2010), DVD.

[27] As Sulcas reports, 'The "new" score was turned up by Simon Morrison, a music historian at Princeton ... he had made a fascinating discovery while working at the Russian State Archive of Literature and Art in Moscow: a "Romeo and Juliet" score from 1935 that predated the familiar version. Not only did this original score, notated for orchestration, have different passages (and that different ending), it was accompanied by a detailed libretto by Prokofiev and the dramatist Sergei Radlov that diverged in important ways from Shakespeare's play. But the Soviet cultural authorities were horrified when Prokofiev presented his score, and he was forced to rewrite the ending, insert new solos in the ball and balcony scenes and thicken the orchestration before the ballet was finally given its Russian premiere at the Kirov Ballet in Leningrad in 1940' ('O Romeo, Romeo').

The curtain falls. Rises again on a spare space – all blue panels with stars – which sets the scene for a final pas de deux. This final ending replaces tragedy with a fortunate escape. There is no need to worry about poison or corpses or corpse brides. The scent of roses replaces the stench of death emanating from the tomb. We never even enter the tomb, so there is no need to figure out how to exit from it. The final pas de deux reprises music from the balcony scene. At the very end, the lovers spin and turn palm to palm in a circle as the curtain closes. Juliet never stops dancing, nor does Romeo. The body is stilled by neither death nor time nor the end of music. The two spin on and on and on, an instance of never-dying love that replaces the story of tragic ends.

Unlike Morris, the innovative Edward Clug (2005) images Juliet living on, but she does so alone, after the tragedy. The Romanian-born artistic director of the Slovenian company Ballet Maribor, created *Radio and Juliet*, set to the music of Radiohead. Clug's *Radio and Juliet* also radically disarticulates the narrative. Clug insists, 'Everyone knows the story so well. I found no reason to tell it again.'[28] Not only does he set aside the Prokofiev score and its powerful narrative structure, but he also insists upon interchangeability. Six Romeos partner one Juliet. Iconic scenes appear – a party, the wedding – but storytelling is not a priority. Two film sequences introduce new material and reiterate live movement. *Radio and Juliet* opens with a film clip

that Clug edited himself in collaboration with a film-maker. Juliet inhabits a bare apartment. We find her lying on a stripped bed on the floor. The camera pans over Juliet's body before flashing forward to action yet to be seen. Clug describes this as a Juliet after the disaster. How she feels, we cannot say, but Romeo is absent. Juliet is the constant in Clug's choreography, the stable focus of the film sequences, and the only survivor. Juliet seems always to be the centre of gravity in choreographic productions of *Romeo and Juliet*, and in this Clug's distinctive vision swears fealty to Juliet's ascendancy and centuries of ballerina-centred dance.

Shakespearians are no strangers to the fantasy that eternity might be found in love and in art, as well as in heaven. Here on earth, the fact that death is only the beginning for *Romeo and Juliet* seems ever more obvious, as that work, even more so than its lovers, has emerged as perhaps the brightest Shakespearian constellation. The sleepwalker, the corpse, the revenant and the survivor remind us that behind the starry and increasingly virtual edifices of *Romeo and Juliet* lie stubborn corporealities, echoes of violence and shades of life and death without which what we call Shakespeare could not be recreated and re-embodied – in pages, on stages, across screens and in feeds – daily and nightly, over and over again.

---

[28] Edward Clug, interview by Maura Keefe, Jacob's Pillow Dance Festival, Beckett, Massachusetts, 4 July 2009.

TITANIA'S DREAM: THREE CHOREOGRAPHIC *MIDSUMMER NIGHT'S DREAMS* OF THE TWENTIETH CENTURY

IRIS JULIA BÜHRLE

A Midsummer Night's Dream is by far William Shakespeare's most frequently adapted comedy on ballet stages worldwide. Several of its themes and situations are particularly well suited for a choreographic transposition, such as the wide range of depicted emotions and the triple wedding at the end. In fact, the play includes more dancing than any other work by Shakespeare,[1] and Peter Holland even compares its entire action to a dance.[2]

This article analyses three significant ballet adaptations of *A Midsummer Night's Dream*, by George Balanchine (New York City Ballet, 1962), Frederick Ashton (Royal Ballet, 1965), and John Neumeier (Hamburg Ballet, 1977).[3] It argues that the first two works are deeply rooted in the structures and storytelling devices of nineteenth-century ballets, whereas the third work is an example of a new genre of ballet that profoundly engages with, and comments on, the literary source.[4] Although in any non-verbal adaptation of a literary text some aspects of the source will be lost or simplified, other elements are added which can shed new light on the text. The use of dance and music allows choreographers to reveal and emphasize different underlying elements of the source play. It is Neumeier in particular who, by going beyond nineteenth-century storytelling modes, manages to transpose the complexity of Shakespeare's play into his own medium, even as he reimagines some of its characters and situations.

One lens through which these differences can be examined is that of the representation of female protagonists. All three choreographers place particular emphasis on Titania and offer new perspectives on the gender relations in the source. Each choreographer's approach to Shakespeare's play is revealed in the way Titania – and to a lesser extent Hippolyta – corresponds to or deviates from the heroines of nineteenth-century ballets. By examining the different interpretations and placing the three works in their wider ballet-historic context, this article will broaden the perspective of Laura Levine's discussion of Balanchine's *Midsummer Night's Dream*. In her article, Levine argues that the choreographer deliberately erased the history of violence against women, which leads to the seemingly harmonious couplings in the end, as well as the theme of sexual

---

[1] See Alan Brissenden, *Shakespeare and the Dance* (London, 1993), p. 25.

[2] Peter Holland, 'Introduction', in William Shakespeare, *A Midsummer Night's Dream*, ed. Peter Holland (Oxford, 1994), p. 65.

[3] My discussion of Balanchine's *A Midsummer Night's Dream* is based on several performances I watched at the Paris Opera in 2017 and recordings of the ballet with various companies, especially the 1967 film with Suzanne Farrell as Titania and Edward Villella as Oberon. As for Ashton's *The Dream*, my memory of several performances at the Royal Ballet was complemented by the 1970 TV recording with Merle Park and Anthony Dowell and the 2004 DVD with Alessandra Ferri and Ethan Stiefel. My analysis of Neumeier's ballet *A Midsummer Night's Dream* draws on performances I saw in Paris and Hamburg; moreover, I watched various recordings of the ballet at the Deutsches Tanzfilminstitut Bremen.

[4] In my Ph.D. thesis, I have defined this genre at length and called it 'literature ballet'. See Iris Julia Bührle, *Literatur und Tanz: Die choreographische Adaptation literarischer Werke in Deutschland und Frankreich vom 18. Jahrhundert bis heute* (Würzburg, 2014).

coercion in the play. She also points out that by purely visual means ballet has the power to create associations with figures who do not actually appear on stage.[5] This article will demonstrate that the elision of that particular history and the play's darker sides, as well as the association of Titania and Hippolyta with powerful female figures from the history of dance and other arts, is common to all three ballets studied here, and even to most ballet versions of *A Midsummer Night's Dream*. An analysis of the gender dynamics in each ballet will be combined with a broader reflection on each choreographer's transposition of the source. This will reveal how a closer reading of the play, and the creation of individualized figures and new storytelling modes, allow choreographers not only to subtly transpose a very complex text into a visual medium but also to open up new possibilities for the interpretation of the source.

The play form of *A Midsummer Night's Dream* features various examples of female resistance to male domination but also the crushing of this resistance. On the one hand, Helena and Hermia successfully fight to obtain the husband they want, overruling both the will of Hermia's father and, with the help of Puck's flower, that of Demetrius.[6] On the other hand, the play starts with the announcement of a marriage that was brought about by force, and Oberon eventually puts down Titania's rebellion by humiliating her. In spite of the apparent harmony of the weddings and fairy dance in Act 5, the final concord is only achieved by the breaking of both Hippolyta's and Titania's resistance. Skiles Howard has questioned the equality in the concluding dance of the fairy sovereigns in which, according to her, Oberon asserts his 'masculine surveillance and control'.[7] By manipulating the actions and affections of his wife and the human lovers in the wood, and winning the quarrel over the Indian boy, Oberon quickly overcomes his initial defeat and regains his superior position in the fairy realm. As for Theseus, his authority over Athenian society is never questioned in the play.

Ballet versions of *A Midsummer Night's Dream* have painted a rather different picture, and most of them focus on the fairy world. In ballets, this realm is usually dominated by female fairies, and the fairy queen often plays a more important role than her husband. It is no coincidence that the first known adaptation of the play by Marius Petipa was a one-act ballet called *Titania* (Saint Petersburg, 1866).[8] In the nineteenth century, female dancers had definitely overthrown the male supremacy that dated from the days of the court ballet. Due to the evolution of ballet technique and costumes, which had traditionally been long and heavy for women, female dancers acquired a new freedom of movement. The development of the pointe shoe and of flying devices allowed them literally to hover above both the floor and their male colleagues.

---

[5] Thus, Balanchine's Hippolyta and Titania evoke representations of Venus and Diana in Botticelli's paintings and in earlier ballets. See Laura Levine, 'Balanchine and Titania: love and the elision of history in *A Midsummer Night's Dream*', *Shakespeare Survey 65* (Cambridge, 2012), pp. 110–20.

[6] The fact that Demetrius is forced to love a person who previously repelled him usually receives less attention than the violation of Titania's will – one might argue that not only female characters are being manipulated in this play. Worse still, Demetrius remains under the influence of the magic flower and has to marry the maid he so vigorously rejected earlier.

[7] Howard associates Titania and her communal round with an equitable 'popular tradition', Oberon with 'elite culture' and courtly dances in which the gentleman guides and dominates the lady. She argues that Oberon eventually restores 'the hierarchy and authority of the cosmic dance'. See Skiles Howard, *The Politics of Courtly Dancing in Early Modern England* (Amherst, 1998), pp. 71–9.

[8] There was an earlier Italian ballet by Giovanni Casati entitled *Shakespeare, ovvero il Sogno di una notte d'estate* which Rodney Stenning Edgecombe mentions in *The Edinburgh Companion to Shakespeare and the Arts*, ed. Mark Thornton Burnett, Adrian Streete, and Ramona Wray (Edinburgh, 2011). He states that 'next to nothing is known' about it and that '[e]ven its title offers no guarantee of fidelity to its source'. In fact, this ballet was not based on Shakespeare's comedy but on a comic opera entitled *Le Songe d'une nuit d'été* by Ambroise Thomas (libretto by Joseph-Bernard Rosier and Adolphe de Leuven, premiered at the Opéra-Comique in Paris in 1850). The opera and ballet represented a fictional anecdote from Shakespeare's life which included the playwright himself, Queen Elizabeth and a character called Falstaff. See Giovanni Casati, *Shakespeare, ovvero il Sogno di una notte d'estate, ballo in quattro parti* (Naples, 1855).

In the so-called 'Romantic' ballet, the ballerina became the unchallenged centre of attention, and ballets were often named after their heroines.

Many 'Romantic' ballets featured long symmetrical passages performed by a corps de ballet of female dancers who often represented supernatural creatures. These nearly plotless ensemble scenes reappeared in the ballets that Marius Petipa authored and co-authored at the Russian court in the late nineteenth century, such as *La Bayadère*, *The Sleeping Beauty*, *The Nutcracker* and *Swan Lake*. Petipa also choreographed a *Midsummer Night's Dream* ballet in 1876. In the early twentieth century, the renowned Ballets Russes choreographer Michel Fokine created both a version of *A Midsummer Night's Dream* and a plotless ballet entitled *Les Elfes* (New York, 1924), which focused exclusively on the fairies.

Fokine's *Les Sylphides*, a neo-Romantic ballet which featured a group of female spirits in white gauze skirts and one male 'poet' (Paris, 1909), was one of the first plotless ballets of the twentieth century. This genre was brought to a peak with the works of George Balanchine. The Russian-born choreographer, who had danced in Petipa's ballets in Saint Petersburg and created works for the Ballets Russes, subsequently became the co-founder of the New York City Ballet. Among the extensive corpus of Balanchine's creations, most of which were plotless ballets, his *Midsummer Night's Dream* is a rare example of a ballet based on a literary source.

Balanchine claimed that the main inspiration for his ballet was the incidental music which Felix Mendelssohn wrote for a production of the play in 1843 before the King of Prussia, and which included the *Midsummer Night's Dream* overture Mendelssohn had composed in 1826.[9] The availability of this music, which features in most ballet versions of *A Midsummer Night's Dream*, is doubtless a major reason why a large number of choreographers have chosen to adapt this play. Since the incidental score is not sufficient to accompany a full-length ballet, Balanchine added more music by Mendelssohn, which was not written for the play.

In his score for *A Midsummer Night's Dream*, Mendelssohn focused chiefly on the fairy world, and so did Balanchine. The first half of the ballet is set in the fairy wood, the second half in a pavilion erected in that same wood. The choreographer cuts the first act of the play, which takes place in Theseus's palace. He begins directly with the opening scene in the wood, followed by Oberon and Titania's quarrel over the Indian boy in Act 2, scene 1 of the play. Unlike in the play, the boy is visible, but the motives behind the struggle and Titania's unwillingness to part with him are not. Since ballet knows no reported actions, it is rather complicated to represent past events – such as Titania's friendship with the dead mother of the Indian boy – in this genre.[10] In Balanchine's quarrel scene, the quick gestures of the fairy sovereigns are based on traditional ballet mime. Oberon and Titania remain graceful and dignified, and they strike various majestic poses. After a brief interruption by three of the mechanicals, the same scene is repeated in even faster motion. The repetition, acceleration and stylization of the mime scene create an alienation effect which sets the spirits apart from the human lovers.

The ballet's structure, which consists of brief mime scenes and long non-narrative dance passages, remains close to the way nineteenth-century ballets are presented today (although the mime passages were originally much longer).[11] Challenging soli and dances for two, three or four dancers alternate with predominantly female, mostly symmetrical, corps de ballet (ensemble) scenes. If it were not for the children, the fluttering arms and the wings in the first act that identify the dancers as fairies or insects, these scenes could be parts of Balanchine's plotless works. The soloists' displays of bravura technique are only vaguely related to the characters that perform them – if they are identified at all. Various unnamed figures, such as Titania's 'Cavalier', appear out of nowhere and seem to have no other function than to carry

---

9 See www.nycballet.com/Ballets/M/A-Midsummer-Night%E2%80%99s-Dream.aspx.

10 See Levine, 'Balanchine and Titania', p. 114.

11 Marian Smith has argued, for example, that around half of the Paris Opera's 1841 ballet *Giselle* consisted of mime passages. See Marian Smith, *Ballet and Opera in the Age of 'Giselle'* (Princeton, 2000), p. 175.

a woman or perform an elaborate pas de deux. The second act is a long divertissement which is very loosely linked to the first act. In the opening scene, the three ballerinas and the women in the corps de ballet are dressed almost identically in tutus; the plot context is eclipsed. The main pas de deux, which supposedly embodies 'ideal, untroubled love',[12] is executed by an unidentified couple. Apart from the brief final scene in the wood, the second act, which resembles Balanchine's own plotless ballets, could stand on its own as a work of 'pure' dance.

It has been stated that it is precisely this lack of narrative logic which constitutes Balanchine's genius as a choreographer of story ballets,[13] and that his *Midsummer Night's Dream* is 'possibly the greatest narrative ballet of all time'.[14] This seems questionable, considering how little Balanchine engaged with the themes or even the action of Shakespeare's play, which he greatly simplified. Rodney Edgecombe states: 'Balanchine lets the exigencies of dance triumph over plot. What on earth is one to make of the ad hoc cavalier who steps into Oberon's slippers after the quarrel beyond the fact that Balanchine hasn't properly understood the play and needs a partner, come hell or high water, for his *pas de deux*?'[15] For Balanchine, the architecture of his danced scenes was doubtlessly more important than the coherence of the action. Like many nineteenth-century choreographers, he bent the play to his choreographic needs and habits instead of creating a structure and choreography that spring from the play's protagonists and situations. This approach informs the way the characters are represented and relate to each other in his *Midsummer Night's Dream*.

Balanchine seems little interested in giving depth to his protagonists, most of whom remain close to ballet stereotypes. The Amazon Queen Hippolyta, for instance, darts through the woods with soaring *grands jetés* (jumps) and turns series of *fouettés* (pirouettes) in a way which recalls ballet classics such as *Sylvia* and the *Diana and Actaeon* pas de deux. Her hounds make menacing bull-like gestures and rather resemble the fighting mice in *The Nutcracker*. Both Titania and Hippolyta evoke the dominant but non-individualized ballerina figures in nineteenth-century ballets. Oberon and Titania do not dance

a pas de deux together and their changing emotions are expressed through basic traditional ballet mime; their dance style remains lofty and controlled throughout the ballet. Oberon sends Puck off to fetch the flower, but it only occurs to him when he has it in his hands that he could use it to punish Titania (he taps his finger against his temple, which means 'idea' in traditional ballet mime). The relationships between the humans are sketched in broad brushstrokes, with fairly conventional gestures of sadness, despair, love, rejection and confusion. The mechanicals get only as much stage time as necessary to introduce Bottom and make him disappear when he is no longer needed. In most productions, the lovers are identified through the

---

[12] http://balanchine.com/a-midsummer-nights-dream. 'Ideal' probably means remote from too literal human feelings, and free from any link to the play's named characters, since the first pas de deux between Hermia and Lysander expresses harmonious human love in a more emotional way. Robert Garis discusses some of Balanchine's pas de deux 'deeper inside the idiom of classical ballet, in which the male dancer makes no expressive gestures toward the ballerina but is virtually invisible. He appears to be – and Balanchine has said as much – only the instrument by means of which the woman can dance on a larger scale than she could by herself. Yet these abstract pas de deux generate great emotional power in Balanchine's hands, and they are the locus of his highest art': Robert Garis, *Following Balanchine* (New Haven, 1995), p. 45. For Garis, the second-act pas de deux of *Midsummer Night's Dream* is an example of this type; the other examples he mentions are taken from plotless ballets. The emotion created by the beauty of these pieces of choreography is unrelated to action or character.

[13] Anita Finkel proclaims that the pas de deux of the two unnamed figures in the second act 'represents the harmonious and complete reconciliation of all the lovers [...]. Everything that was disjunction in the other couplings – height, spirit, nobility, devotion – is clarified and corrected here. Not only are the ballerina and her partner enlightened, they have never been confused': Anita Finkel, 'A Midsummer Night's Dream', in *Reading Dance*, ed. Robert Gottlieb (New York, 2008), p. 172. Nothing, however, distinguishes this pas de deux from numerous others in Balanchine's plotless works.

[14] Finkel, 'A Midsummer Night's Dream', p. 168.

[15] Rodney Stenning Edgecombe, 'Shakespeare, ballet and dance', in Thornton Burnett et al., eds., *The Edinburgh Companion to Shakespeare and the Arts*, p. 212.

colours of their costumes which reveal from the beginning who should be together. We do not get any insight into the relationship between Theseus and Hippolyta: their only contribution to the action consists of two short appearances in the first act. Theseus briefly witnesses the initial dispute of the four lovers, which here takes place in the wood, and leaves with a gesture of impatience. At the end of the act, he blesses the reconciled lovers, seems to have an idea (as his finger tapping at his temple indicates), falls on his knees and proposes to Hippolyta. Unlike in the play, the wedding is not planned from the beginning, but it suddenly occurs to Theseus that, if everyone else wants to marry, he should maybe do the same. All three couples appear in the second act as interchangeable leads of the divertissement.

The ballet concludes with a short scene in the wood where harmony seems restored and which echoes the opening scene. After Oberon and Titania's exit at opposite sides of the stage, Puck sweeps the floor – as in the play, where he explains: 'I am sent with broom before / To sweep the dust behind the door' (5.2.19–20)[16] – and flies away.[17] Thus, special emphasis is placed on Puck, who opens and closes the ballet.[18]

Balanchine does not explore the darker sides of the play, and his work is as well behaved as a nineteenth-century ballet or Victorian productions of the play in the theatre. He eliminates the potential eroticism of Titania's affair with Bottom: the ass-headed young man, who remains rather cute as he follows Titania on all fours, is more interested in a handful of ferns than in the fairy queen. After making him dance with her, she eventually goes to bed alone while Bottom sits on the floor. The conflicts between the generations and the sexes are hardly visible. After Titania wakes up and quickly pushes Bottom away, she immediately hands the boy over to Oberon, who does not even seem to ask for him. Hippolyta delightedly accepts Theseus's spontaneous marriage proposal – there is no trace of her being 'wooed . . . with [his] sword' (1.1.16).[19] In the ballet, the excessive rudeness of the two men towards the unloved women who pursue them and their sudden murderous hatred in the wood are more amusing than

threatening. The comedy in Shakespeare's play also finds echoes in Balanchine's portrayal of Bottom and Puck, for whom he creates particularly original movement vocabulary.

Balanchine's ballet is a sophisticated danced fairy tale. The choreographer invented impressive tableaux of the fairy wood and the ducal wedding but did not try to dig below the surface of Shakespeare's play. Balanchine doubtless put most of his creative effort into the long sequences of 'pure' dancing, in which he could display his choreographic skill and showcase his dancers' technique. He eliminated numerous elements from Shakespeare's play and related his ballet to other works in the history of dance and art, as Levine has suggested: 'this is one of the tensions of Balanchine, that while the ballets' "stories" may eclipse various elements in their sources, the forms themselves are virtually citational, acknowledging the various traditions they quote'.[20] Balanchine's use of traditional storytelling devices and character constellations influences his depiction of the gender relations in the ballet.

---

[16] Shakespeare's works are quoted from William Shakespeare, *The Complete Works*, ed. Stanley Wells and Gary Taylor, 2nd edn (Oxford, 2005).

[17] Rodney Edgecombe suggests that, in the play, Robin clears the floor for the dance of the fairies but, in the ballet, his sweeping occurs only after the end of the dancing and apparently corresponds to the play's epilogue. See Edgecombe, 'Shakespeare, ballet and dance', p. 201.

[18] He is the first named character to appear in the ballet. In Shakespeare's work, he opens the action in the fairy wood and closes the play.

[19] One might argue that, in Shakespeare's play, Hippolyta is completely reconciled with her fate by the time the action begins, but, since Theseus conquered her by force, his name was linked to the betrayal of numerous women, and their son, Hippolytus, was doomed to die tragically following a curse from his own father, Shakespeare's choice of that mythological couple was probably not supposed to imply cloudless harmony. The unhappy outcome of Theseus and Hippolyta's marriage jars somewhat with the idea that the play was written for an aristocratic wedding. On the dark elements of the Theseus myth which overshadow the comedy, see Peter Holland, 'Theseus' shadows in *A Midsummer Night's Dream*', *Shakespeare Survey 47* (Cambridge, 1994), pp. 139–52.

[20] See Levine, 'Balanchine and Titania', p. 119.

As in the majority of nineteenth-century ballets and Balanchine's own works, the female dancers are very important in *A Midsummer Night's Dream*. All the fairies are women and children, and, in the second act, the female group dancers outnumber the men. In the pas de deux, the ballerinas are set off by their partners. The all-male scenes between the mechanicals are reduced to a minimum. Therefore, the visual presence of women is far greater than in Shakespeare's play. Titania is never really humiliated or subdued, and the scenes in her bower are key passages of the first act.[21] Oberon's dancing is almost limited to one scene in the wood in which he performs a number of short, highly virtuosic soli among a group of female butterflies and children. Theseus only appears very briefly in the first act and he does not dance. Hippolyta is shown triumphant in the woods, even though she is later integrated into the symmetrical male–female pattern of the courtly divertissement: instead of soaring independently among her hounds, she now relies on the support of Theseus. However, her husband kneels before her and lifts her, thus allowing her to attain even greater heights in her jumps, a symbol of a harmonic marriage or ballet partnership in which the woman sparkles by using the strength of a self-effacing man. This is a constellation which, if it may not apply to Hippolyta's marriage in the play, is echoed in various couples in Shakespeare's comedies, perhaps including the relationship of Demetrius and Lysander with their strong-willed brides.

Three years after Balanchine, Frederick Ashton created his ballet *The Dream* for the celebration of Shakespeare's 400th birthday in 1964. Ashton was inspired by Tyrone Guthrie's 1937 production of the play at the Old Vic, which featured the dancer/choreographer/actor Robert Helpmann as Oberon, Vivien Leigh as Titania, and choreography by Ninette de Valois, the founder of the Royal Ballet. *The Dream* evokes Victorian productions of the play, in which the fairies often appeared as 'a full-scale female *corps de ballet* dressed in white',[22] and nineteenth-century fairy drawings. Ashton focused even more on the fairy world than

Balanchine: he condensed Shakespeare's play into one act which is set in the wood, using only the incidental music which Mendelssohn wrote for the play. He eliminated Theseus and Hippolyta and kept only the four lovers from the human sphere. Ashton's fairies are exclusively female, like the spirits in many Romantic ballets.

Like Balanchine, Ashton starts with a brief corps de ballet scene, followed by Titania and Oberon's quarrel over the Indian boy. If Balanchine's fairy king and queen remain aloof and show little emotional interest in the boy – Oberon wants him as a cape-carrier that will allow him to appear even more regal – Ashton's couple looks like a pair of human parents fighting over their child. They physically struggle over the boy, whom Titania embraces like a protective mother, and both try to draw him to their side until he falls on the floor and cries. Ashton's scene is less stylized and more choreographed than Balanchine's: the fairy sovereigns kick their legs in the air and confront each other with opposed *arabesques* (a pose in which the dancer stands on one leg and lifts the other up behind him or her) and *battements* (the dancer stands on one leg and kicks the other forward) while they shift forwards and backwards, which visualizes their changing position in the argument. The passage is a mixture of dancing and specifically composed mime. Ashton repeatedly uses mime – for instance, when Oberon puts his hands to his heart to comment on Hermia and Lysander's love or when Puck imagines the bull or 'meddling monkey' (2.1.181) Titania might fall in love with.

Ashton's work, which contains various divertissements, is anchored in the tradition of nineteenth-century ballet. The symmetrical corps de ballet scenes of fairies recall the second acts of *La Sylphide* (1832) and *Giselle* (1841), as well as Petipa's

---

[21] According to Nancy Dalva, the description of Titania's bower was one of Balanchine's favourite passages of the play. Nancy Dalva, 'We can dream, can't we?' *danceviewtimes* 4.17 (1 May 2006), on http://archives.danceviewtimes.com/2006/Spring/05/nycb1.html.

[22] Peter Holland, 'Introduction', in *Midsummer Night's Dream*, p. 25.

female ensembles. Ashton also quotes a pose from Jules Perrot's 1845 *Pas de quatre*. However, Ashton places special emphasis on the characterization of his figures, especially Oberon and Titania. If Balanchine chooses not to give a pas de deux to his fairy sovereigns, Ashton's duet for them becomes the centrepiece of the ballet. It has been suggested that this passage marks the reconciliation of the fairy sovereigns through Titania's submission,[23] but it rather expresses harmony and companionship, as becomes apparent in the parallel and mirrored movements. On the one hand, the fairy queen repeatedly affirms her independence: she strives and bends in the opposite direction, ducks away from Oberon in a supported arabesque or hops away from him, obliging him to follow her. On the other hand, Titania sinks into Oberon's arms and lays her head on his shoulder, but he also lifts her high above his head. Supported by Oberon, Titania draws perfect circles on the floor with her foot, which might allude to her association with communal round-dances and to the link between circular forms and harmony in the play.[24] In one of the most emblematic poses of the pas de deux, they execute an *arabesque penchée* (both dancers stand on one leg and lean forward, lifting the other leg up high behind them) in which they rely on each other for their precarious balance. They hold hands in this position, which evokes Titania's suggestion that they bless the wedded couples 'Hand in hand with fairy grace' (5.2.29) – in the ballet, however, their own relationship is the centre of attention. In the final moments of the duo, Oberon, who previously disturbed Titania's slumber, cradles and protects his sleeping wife. The ballet ends with the fairy sovereigns' tender embrace.

The portrayal and confusion of the lovers in Ashton's *Dream* is highly comical and spiced with parodies of conventional ballet mime – for instance, Lysander's gesture of despair when Hermia forbids him to lie down next to her. Unlike Balanchine, who merely sends his Lysander offstage to pick flowers for his beloved, Ashton takes up the implicit threat to Hermia's chastity in this scene, but he transforms it into an

innocuous and funny moment. As in the play, the humans and their quarrels are a spectacle for the fairies, who watch their surprising behaviour with amazement.

The brief appearance of the mechanicals with their ungraceful jumps and running movements in the fairy wood is a welcome entertainment for Puck, even though there is no sign that they are rehearsing a play. Ashton makes his transformed Bottom dance en pointe, an idea that, according to Alan Brissenden, inspired Peter Brook to put his Bottom into rather clunky hoof-like boots with flat tips in his seminal 1970 Royal Shakespeare Company production of the play.[25] Ashton's Bottom performs a pounding solo which turns ballet conventions of light-footed nineteenth-century sylphs on their head. He also dances a pas de deux with Titania which comically juxtaposes her daintiness and his clumsiness. The fairies adorn him with flowers under Oberon's amused gaze; however, Bottom seems little interested in Titania's charms. Puck, who is characterized by his airy jumps, both is comic himself – for instance, when he imitates the foolish humans – and creates comic confusion, which, as in Balanchine, is punished by a kick in the pants from Oberon.

Like Balanchine, Ashton establishes a strong visual presence of women in the exclusively female ensemble scenes and in the bower scene, which lends itself perfectly to a balletic transposition. Titania's relationship with Oberon is at the centre

---

[23] See David Vaughan, *Frederick Ashton and his Ballets* (London, 1999), p. 341.

[24] Thus, for instance, the fairy queen invites Oberon to 'patiently dance in our round' (2.1.140).

[25] See Alan Brissenden, 'Shakespeare and dance: dissolving boundaries', in *Shakespeare Without Boundaries: Essays in Honor of Dieter Mehl*, ed. Christa Jansohn, Lena Cowen Orlin, and Stanley Wells (Newark, 2011), p. 102. A recording of the production in the Shakespeare Centre in Stratford-upon-Avon reveals that Bottom did indeed tap, hop and stamp around in his shoes in a way which rather evokes Widow Simone's clog dance in Ashton's *La Fille mal gardée* (1960), a role that was also created for a man. Brook's Bottom walks with his feet turned outward like a ballet dancer, but never attempts to rise 'on pointe'.

of the ballet, and they both have extensive danced passages, first individually or with other protagonists, and then together. In their final pas de deux, Oberon uses partnering techniques that evolved from the nineteenth century onwards in order to lift Titania and make her fly. This evokes her kinship with the female spirits dominating Romantic ballets who hovered weightlessly across the stage, hardly seeming to touch the floor with the tips of their toes.

In 1977, John Neumeier chose a different approach to the source in his *Midsummer Night's Dream* for the Hamburg Ballet. Neumeier's two-act ballet represents almost the entire action of Shakespeare's play, thus giving more weight to its human protagonists. The ballet is set in two places – Theseus's court and the fairy wood – which are peopled by courtiers, fairies and the mechanicals. For each group, Neumeier created specific movement styles, and the spheres are further differentiated through the sets, costumes, lighting and music. This corresponds to the different linguistic styles of the groups in the play. The court scenes take place in the nineteenth century to Mendelssohn's incidental music. The passages in the fairy wood, with their glittering silver costumes, stylized sets, and music by György Ligeti, have a more modern aspect. The mechanicals appear in both the aristocratic and the supernatural spheres, accompanied by their down-to-earth street organ. Possibly inspired by Peter Brook, Neumeier doubled Hippolyta and Titania, Theseus and Oberon, and Philostrate and Puck. Thus, the choreographer emphasized the parallels between the different worlds which are implicit in the play.

Like Balanchine's and Ashton's adaptations, Neumeier's work evokes nineteenth-century ballet history, especially in the wedding divertissement. However, the grotesque antimasque of the mechanicals breaks the solemn atmosphere of the Petipa-like *grand pas* (a number of dances that showcase the technical skill of the main performers). Unlike in Balanchine, Neumeier's three couples retain their individuality, and their diverse personalities remain clearly recognizable in this scene. The fairies are no sylphs clad in fluttering gauze skirts, and there are no children. They are adult men and women wearing skin-tight overalls and caps that recall Ashton's *Monotones* (1965), and they quote a pose from Balanchine's *Apollo* (1928). The cross-dressed Thisbe resembles the women in Vaslav Nijinsky's *Sacre du Printemps* (1913).

If the nineteenth century belonged to the women, the twentieth century saw a new rise of the male dancers, a development that began with celebrities like Vaslav Nijinsky. Moreover, Brook's 1970 production of the play set a precedent for introducing androgynous fairies of both sexes. In Neumeier's *Midsummer Night's Dream*, the gender imbalance in the ensemble scenes of the earlier ballets is reduced: his fairies are danced by men and women, and he gives ample space to the scenes at Theseus's court and among the mechanicals. However, Neumeier was also influenced by the works of choreographers such as John Cranko, who, in his innovative 'literature ballets', focused on the psyche and the evolution of the characters, especially the female protagonists.[26] Neumeier's *Midsummer Night's Dream* is one of a large number of psychological 'literature ballets' he has created in the course of his career.

Neumeier characterizes his protagonists essentially in choreographic terms. Unlike in Balanchine's version, it is not the dress of the four lovers but their style of movement which indicates affinities in personality and shows who should be together. Thus, Neumeier questions the assumption of their interchangeability.[27] There is some mild comedy in Neumeier's portrayal of the lovers, especially the bespectacled Helena who desperately

---

[26] During his time as a dancer with the Stuttgart Ballet from 1963 to 1969, Neumeier witnessed the creation of John Cranko's *Onegin* (1965/7) and *The Taming of the Shrew* (1969). In both ballets, the choreographer devotes special attention to the psyche of the female characters. For a definition of the 'literature ballet', see Bührle, *Literatur und Tanz*, pp. 202–3.

[27] Joan Stansbury challenges this widespread view in her article 'Characterization of the four young lovers in A Midsummer Night's Dream', *Shakespeare Survey* 35 (Cambridge, 1982), pp. 57–64.

tries to charm the stiff Demetrius. All the main couples follow a similar trajectory from confusion and discord to harmony (although the conflict between Lysander and Hermia arises only after Puck's intervention), and their struggles and reconciliation form the centre of the ballet. Neumeier minimizes the mime sequences in his ballet: the Indian boy is not visible, and the quarrel between Titania and Oberon is visualized through kicks and confrontational body language in their first pas de deux. Their reconciliation is expressed in a brief final pas de deux with a harmonious entwined lift.

Neumeier focuses more on Hippolyta's evolution than does Shakespeare. He picks up the hint in the source that Hippolyta might not willingly marry Theseus: in the ballet, her attitude towards him seems reserved, and she expresses no joy about her planned wedding. However, Neumeier makes her a very feminine nineteenth-century lady without any of the Amazon's rebellious spirit. She falls asleep in the first act after smelling the magic flower she received as a gift from Theseus. As she wakes up after the events in the fairy wood, she apparently falls in love with him, and they dance a harmonious pas de deux which celebrates their union. Thus, the flower's magic seems to act on her as well, even though nobody sprinkles the juice on her eyelids. Through the doubling, parallels in the movement language, and certain repeated poses, Neumeier makes Titania and Oberon's relationship directly reflect that of Hippolyta and Theseus, as if the development of one couple influenced that of the other. His focus lies on Hippolyta and Titania who, unlike their male partners, seem to evolve in the course of the ballet.

By giving a significant place to the mechanicals, Neumeier not only increases the weight of the male characters, in comparison to Balanchine and Ashton, but also engages with some of the play's potential eroticism and comedy that had been neglected by his predecessors. The mechanicals first appear in Theseus's palace, where they submit their play to Philostrate, a scene which is not in the play. This allows Neumeier to stage an encounter between Hippolyta and Bottom during which she looks at him with marked interest, a moment that already foreshadows Bottom and Titania's love affair in the forest. The relationship between the ass-eared Bottom and the fairy queen is depicted as clearly erotic but, even though Oberon laughs at 'this sweet sight' (4.1.45), he does not confront Titania with Bottom after her awakening, and she never seems ashamed.

When the mechanicals irrupt into the fairy wood, their jerky movements form a comic contrast with the fairies' elegant, floating style. As in Ashton's ballet, one of the mechanicals dances in pointe shoes, but the cross-dressed Thisbe is significantly less in command of this emblem of graceful and feminine ballerinas than Ashton's Bottom.

Finally, Neumeier is the only one of the three choreographers to show the unwillingly satirical performance of *Pyramus and Thisbe*. As in Shakespeare, the grotesque spectacle comments on the previously troubled relationships of the three couples. Neumeier also depicts the dangers for Helena's and Hermia's virtue in the wood – on the one hand, Hermia and Helena have to fight off Lysander, who almost assaults Helena while he is under the effect of the magic flower. On the other hand, Helena throws herself at Demetrius's feet after ripping open her bodice, which is opposed to his threat of violence in the play where he says:

> You do impeach your modesty too much,
> To leave the city and commit yourself
> Into the hands of one that loves you not;
> To trust the opportunity of night,
> And the ill counsel of a desert place,
> With the rich worth of your virginity.
>
> (2.1.214–19)

In the ballet, the mood remains comical or even farcical during these scenes.

The lovers' entanglements and the rehearsal of the mechanicals are watched by a delighted Puck, who wears Helena's spectacles like a pair of opera glasses. His enjoyment of their efforts evokes the verses in the play: 'Then will two at once woo one. / That must needs be sport alone' (3.2.118–19); and 'Shall we their fond pageant see? / Lord, what fools these mortals be!' (3.2.114–15). Puck, who (mis)employs the magic flower and manipulates the humans, and Puck's alter ego Philostrate, who arranges the wedding divertissement, temporarily assume the role of choreographers of the action. However, Puck's choreography does not suit Oberon's taste, and the fairy king soundly thrashes his mischievous ballet master.

In Neumeier's ballet, characters repeatedly fall asleep on stage and wake up in a world in which nothing is as it was before. There are several distancing frames: Hippolyta awakes just before her wedding, and Titania arises at the very end of the ballet. The parallel world could therefore be a dream of either Hippolyta or Titania, or the sovereigns might lead a double life.

Neumeier's innovative work demonstrates his intense interest in literary sources and his desire to interpret them and shed new light on them through his literature ballets. Although he adjusts the gender imbalance in the previous versions, he places special emphasis on Titania's and Hippolyta's psyche, and he choreographically visualizes and accentuates the connections between the two worlds which are implied in the play.

Balanchine, Ashton and Neumeier had different priorities in creating their ballets, and these become obvious in their adaptations of *A Midsummer Night's Dream*. None of the three choreographers goes very far in the depiction of the play's darker sides, such as the cruel choice Egeus gives his daughter – either to marry a man she does not love or to die – or the gender conflict, which is resolved in Theseus's case by the sword, and in Oberon's case by dubious means.

All three choreographers focus on the main female character(s), and evoke nineteenth-century ballet structures, but they deal with these traditions in very diverse ways. Balanchine remains fairly close to the storytelling devices and character types of late-nineteenth-century ballets. He shows Titania and Hippolyta triumphant, even though the latter is eventually transformed from a solitary and powerful Amazon into a leading participant in a mixed-gender divertissement. As in nineteenth-century ballets, the ballerinas dance more than the men and are showcased like jewels.

Ashton's fairies evoke the all-female ensembles in mid-nineteenth-century ballets and Victorian productions of the play. The choreographer humanizes and individualizes his figures and creates specific mime to characterize them, especially Oberon and Titania, whose relationship is at the centre of the ballet. Nonetheless, he was certainly more interested in exploring the possibilities of choreography than in interpreting the source.[28] For both Balanchine and Ashton, Shakespeare's *A Midsummer Night's Dream* is an inspiration which defines the atmosphere, the settings, the characters, the action, and the music of their ballet, and, starting from these elements, they let their choreographic imagination soar freely.

Neumeier quotes nineteenth-century ballet structures such as the *grand pas* in Petipa's ballets, but goes beyond them in his aim to choreograph between the lines[29] in order to reveal underlying elements in the play. Neumeier's *Midsummer Night's Dream* blurs the boundaries between the different worlds, and between dream and reality, even more than the play does. Like Balanchine and Ashton, he is particularly interested in Titania, but he also emphasizes her kinship with Hippolyta and opens up the possibility that the whole ballet could be Titania's dream.

If the fairy world in Shakespeare's play might seem to be a mirror of the patriarchal Athenian sphere,[30] this is not the case in the ballets discussed

---

[28] Ashton once stated: 'Consciously, all through my career, I have been working to make the ballet independent of literary and pictorial motives … it is the dance that must be paramount'. He also declared: 'It's always the music that starts me off. The story doesn't count at all.' Ashton doubted that very complex stories should be translated into dance. See Ashton in Zoë Dominic and John Selwyn Gilbert, *Frederick Ashton* (Chicago, 1971), pp. 164 and 168, and Vaughan, *Frederick Ashton*, p. 427. Alastair Macaulay even claims that Ashton began an 'overt struggle against "literary" ballets' in the 1940s: Alastair Macaulay, 'Frederick Ashton's Illuminations: dance and literature as parallel universes', in *Sur quel pied danser? Danse et littérature*, ed. Hélène Stafford and Edward Nye (Amsterdam, 2005), p. 251.

[29] John Neumeier, *In Bewegung* (Munich, 2008), p. 79.

[30] Levine, 'Balanchine and Titania', p. 112.

here. Another indicator would be Puck, who plays an important role in all three ballets. With his airy jumps and comic potential, he almost steals the show from the authoritarian Oberon. As a commentator, he comes close to the narrator figure which ballet does not normally have. By the (mis)use of his magic powers, he 'choreographs' parts of the action. Although he serves the fairy king, he often acts contrary to his orders and delights in the confusion he creates, thus eroding Oberon's authority. By focusing more on the play's most balletic figures – both of whom are not patriarchal rulers[31] – the three choreographers shift the power balance in the play and show a parallel world that the characters in Shakespeare's comedy can only dream of, a sphere in which the Athenian law is suspended and in which the lightest foot sometimes has the greatest weight.

---

[31] Puck's lightness brings him close to female dancers: in Balanchine's work, he flies away by using stage machinery like a nineteenth-century sylph; in Neumeier's ballet, he is repeatedly lifted by Oberon.

SHAKESPEARE ON SCREENS: CLOSE WATCHING, CLOSE LISTENING

PETER HOLLAND

Though it is of the nature of my topic – and that of the panel at the World Shakespeare Congress for which it was originally conceived[1] – that most of my attention will be close to detail, thinking about how such close reading of the filmed-text[2] functions and might construct meaning, it seems to me necessary and not simply perverse to begin with some ridiculously broad generalizations. And since it is of the nature of the brevity of short articles like this one, especially ones derived from panel papers at a conference, to be unable to substantiate such statements properly, they take on an air of aggressive imprecision, floating high above the materials with which I shall be concerned, even more so since I shall be focusing thereafter on a six-minute segment of a film, because this seems to me an essential part of the process of analysis, of working on film in close-up, to use the obvious and fundamentally imprecise cliché.

There are three such generalizations that frame and constitute my argument.

1. I think of this as a form of paradox peculiarly applicable to an academic discipline. The more a discipline yearns for a technological advance to transform the possibility of its work, both research and pedagogy, the less it will make use of that advance when it is achieved. This is not, I hasten to say, a paradox that is applicable to Shakespeare studies, but it is applicable to film studies – or, as we tend now to call it, screen studies, given the enormous range of screens – from Imax to iPhone in size, and ranging from celluloid to streaming in distribution – on which the materials of its study are now watched. Go back, as I searingly remember, to how one taught

film decades ago and it involved renting a 16-mm print, running it on a projector, usually on to an inadequate pull-down screen normally used for showing slides, with the soundtrack of the film competing with the sound of the projector. If one had time, the film could be set up to show one segment during class – but only one, for it took ages to run the film (or to cut and splice it) to reach the segment one wanted. For academic research, a few places had copies of a few films that could be run again and again but most research was done from public cinema viewings and with a good memory.

Video made possible the creation of one's own library, bought or taped off-air, and hence a pedagogy of close analysis emerged more fully formed (fast forward to DVD, blu-ray, streaming, etc.), but, at exactly this time, film studies moved

---

away from close analysis of the film image towards that area of contextualized analysis in which it has flourished. When Russ McDonald, in the introduction to *Shakespeare Up Close*, states that 'The critical culture of the past four decades has so insistently privileged context over text that many instructors are no more familiar with the tools and *topoi* of close reading than are the students they teach',[3] he is knowingly overstating in the way that I am now. Those 'many', of course, exclude ourselves – *others* may be unfamiliar but of course one never thinks that applies to oneself.

Since the study of film as semiotic system in the 1960s – say, in the work of Christian Metz and others – looked so closely at the processes of signification in the film image (and it is time we went back to such work and re-examined what it can do without the imperialist framework of a discipline – semiotics – seeking to dominate all humanities, the framework in which it was formed), one will be hard put to it to find research that looks as closely at film as most of us and most of McDonald's 'many' are used to doing in literary/Shakespeare studies. Even when a volume in film studies ostensibly announces close reading, as in Barry Keith Grant and Jeannette Sloniowski's rightly well-regarded collection *Documenting the Documentary: Close Readings of Documentary Film and Video*,[4] there is virtually nothing that constitutes the kind of closeness of close reading that we expect in our own discipline confronted with text (Shakespeare's) that so self-evidently demands close attention to make any kind of worthwhile sense of it.

2. If close watching has been so substantially lost in film research, it is preserved in other areas of timed performance event: for example, in theatre analysis, especially strikingly so, for our purposes, in the work on Shakespeare performance, which so often seeks to record as it analyses and does so with an attention to detail (how this line was voiced, how that move was made) that film has abandoned. *Shakespeare Survey* has, almost throughout its life-span, sought to review Shakespeare performance within the context of academic study – so very different from, say, newspaper theatre-reviewing. And its best exponents have always been outstanding at making the moment

available to the reader. The concern with putting the performance on record for future academic study was for long a feature of *Shakespeare Quarterly* and is a dominant concern now of *Shakespeare Bulletin*, whose reviewers deliberately seek to cover the kinds of productions (local, campus, etc.) that most academic study ignores, but which deepens the availability and presence of the breadth of Shakespeare performance.

If some theatre studies are strikingly like film studies in a certain reluctance, or even refusal, to read the event closely, we might compare what has been argued as needing to be normative elsewhere – for instance, outside our own field, in the brilliant work on the performance of poetry in Charles Bernstein's extraordinary 1998 collection of articles on, as its subtitle puts it, *Poetry and the Performed Word*, called so deliberately *Close Listening*.[5]

And yet close watching, abandoned as a research activity, is still centrally part of the pedagogy of film – this is the core of my second provocative premise. Look, for instance, at a classroom textbook as popular as James Monaco's *How to Read a Film*, first published in 1977, currently in its 2009 4th edition, proudly described as 'completely revised and expanded', and you will find a lengthy 80-page chapter still firmly outlining 'The language of film: signs and syntax' in terms derived from film semiotics (and a chapter on film theory that stops with Metz – so it is not all that 'completely revised' then). Is there then a problem about how to write the close analysis that the means of transmission and consumption of film now makes possible? *We* know how to write about a passage, not least because we can put it on the page as we write about it. But film studies cannot, at least in

---

[3] Russ McDonald, 'Introduction', in *Shakespeare Up Close*, ed. Russ McDonald, Nicholas D. Nance and Travis D. Williams (London, 2013), p. xxxi – though, characteristically, Russ ensured that all three editors were apparently the co-authors of the Introduction, the style is unmistakably his.

[4] *Documenting the Documentary: Close Readings of Documentary Film and Video* (Detroit, 1998, revised and expanded edition in 2014).

[5] C. Bernstein, *Close Listening: Poetry and the Performed Word* (New York, 1988).

print – and I recall how excited I was when a piece of mine appeared in the online journal *Borrowers and Lenders*, precisely because it could include film clips.[6] My students can quote film in their papers through multi-media referencing, but usually I cannot. How could one write about close watching when the object is not present within the analysis or even always easily accessed elsewhere by the reader? There is a gap then between pedagogy and research here that does not confront Shakespeare studies in anything like the same way, except for the study of performance – and even there the theatre performance is assumed to be absent where the film is assumed to be putatively available.

When, in 2013, I created an online 'Shakespeare and Film' course for a 'Semester Online' initiative, I needed to run most clips twice, once without any intervention and with only minimal framing and again with a voice-over and the sound-track turned down, exactly what this article would benefit from my being able to do, not because I conceive of my readers as a class in need of instruction (perish the thought) nor because I want to demonstrate my pedagogy (I'm not that arrogant), but because it is the best way I know to share the object of close watching effectively – to do what is always comparatively easy with non-temporally based texts. How else do we bring the object into our readers'/listeners' purview? (I note, parenthetically, that musicology does not face this problem since the object of study is, at root, usually the score, not the performance.)

3. To focus now on the particularities of the close watching of Shakespeare on screens, it seems astonishing to me – and this is my third and, I suspect, most provocative point – that the study of adaptation has not recognized and understood the curious position Shakespeare has come to occupy within its field of attention, curious because of the degree of Shakespeare's isolation. It is not simply that Shakespeare stands as the major exemplar of the adaptation of play to film but that he has become the *only* dramatist whose work is studied in the transition to narrative film, whether as direct transition (broadly, using Shakespeare's text) or spin-off (using

the narrative as visible or barely allusive basis). Much as I admire the materials in the outstanding collections that Deborah Cartmell has so superbly put together (*Adaptations: From Text to Screen, Screen to Text*, with Imelda Whelehan (London, 1999); the 2007 *Cambridge Companion to Literature on Screen*, also co-edited with Whelehan; and the Wiley-Blackwell *Companion to Literature, Film, and Adaptation* (Chichester, 2012)), there is not a single mention, even in passing, of, say, Ibsen, Tennessee Williams, Eugene O'Neill, Wilde or John Osborne in any of them – though Harold Pinter appears twice in the *Cambridge Companion*, once briefly mentioned for the 1983 film of his play *Betrayal* (p. 22) and its reverse time-sequence, and once, equally passingly, because of his work on *The Proust Screenplay* (p. 100). In adaptation studies, drama equals Shakespeare completely and utterly, to an extent that we would resist in any other context. For all the excellence in these collections of pieces by Douglas Lanier, Richard Burt, Lisa Hopkins, Deborah Cartmell herself,[7] and for all the equally fine work by M. J. Kidnie in her *Shakespeare and the Problem of Adaptation* (Abingdon, 2009) – all research which I return to again and again – there is no sustained attention to the differences between adapting novels and adapting plays. Shakespeare is part of 'literature', and what that might mean for the analysis of, say, voice or location or character or scenic form is ignored.

Yet there is a fundamental difference, to take just my first example, between dialogue in drama and

---

6 Peter Holland, 'Shakespeare, humanities indicators and the seven deadly sins', *Borrowers and Lenders: The Journal of Shakespeare and Appropriation* 7.1 (2012), www.borrowers.uga.edu/783091/show.

7 Douglas Lanier, 'William Shakespeare, film-maker', in Cartmell and Whelehan, eds., *Cambridge Companion*, pp. 61–74; Douglas Lanier, 'Murdering Othello', in Cartmell, ed., *A Companion to Literature, Film and Adaptation*, pp. 198–215; Richard Burt, 'Hamlet's hauntographology', in Cartmell, ed., *A Companion to Literature, Film and Adaptation*, pp. 216–40; Lisa Hopkins, 'Shakespeare to Austen on screen', in Cartmell, ed., *A Companion to Literature, Film and Adaptation*, pp. 241–55; Deborah Cartmell, 'Sound adaptation: Sam Taylor's The Taming of the Shrew', in Cartmell, ed., *A Companion to Literature, Film and Adaptation*, pp. 70–84.

in novel, the former written to be voiced, the latter to be read, and the status of the transference of such passages into film occupies a different relationship in the functioning of the specific modes of adaptation. Just as we have begun to pay attention to the sound of Shakespeare film, so we need to hear what the voices are doing – and, let me be clear, nothing of such work connects to old-fashioned critical positions of fidelity or authenticity. One major part, then, of close watching is not watching at all but close listening, hearing the film, not seeing it – and, if the debate about early modern concepts of hearing a play or seeing a play is now more or less resolved, thanks to Gabriel Egan's fine 2001 article,[8] no one ever speaks of going to hear a film.

The result can be moments of marvellously comic error caused by a Shakespeare film's failing to notice what the characters are actually saying. Take, for example, a moment in the 2015 *Macbeth* directed by Justin Kurzel, with a screenplay by Jacob Koskoff and others. As the film transitions to the scene we know as the Lady's sleep-walking scene (though here there is no suggestion that she is sleep-walking, and there are no observers), she rides, with her gentlewoman, across the bleak, supposedly Scottish, landscapes towards the chapel used earlier for 1.5 (the letter scene), and now apparently deserted and abandoned. By the way, I do find it odd that the film is heavily promoted by Visit Scotland, a.k.a. the Scottish Tourist Board, when the landscapes are almost always shrouded in thick mists, bleached of colour and distinctly unwelcoming – the label on the DVD sleeve 'Win a break to Macbeth country' is the least appealing prize I can imagine.[9] She has been seen, just before, unwrapping the still bloody daggers used to murder Duncan, and washing them to try to remove the blood. Arriving at the place, she apparently leaves her horse and her companion and walks, alone and in close-up, towards something. Cut to a shot of the chapel, the first that clearly identifies it with the one from an hour of film-time earlier. Across the establishing shot, we hear her voice-over (thought rather than speech, perhaps), and then a cut to her sitting on the ground inside, its dark interior lit by bright light through the open door and from the cross-

shaped window above her. The lines here are 'Yet here's a spot ... Out, damned spot; out, I say' (5.1.30, 33). But the first sentence is that voice-over across the shot of the chapel, and it seems therefore to be describing where she is: 'yet here's a spot' for my mad scene or a picnic or whatever (like Quince's 'here's a marvellous convenient place for our rehearsal' (*A Midsummer Night's Dream*, 3.1. 2–3)), the *spot* becoming displaced from the daggers and spots of blood, an effect magnified when the rest of the passage has her immobile, with no indication of washing her hands or even of looking at them, so that the referent for 'spot', damned or not, is never clearly defined. The voice-over is necessarily, through the conventions of film, connected with what we see as we hear it, and the ease with which it can make that connection interferes with the (for lack of a better word) correct or intended referent.

I want to work for the remainder of this article on a segment from the same film, not because I admire it – I don't – but because, if close watching is significant, it ought to be equally effective with poor as well as good films. I have chosen the film in part because it is recent, with a wide range of mostly favourable reviews, and because its treatment of text is striking, not least in its displacements. I shall be concentrating on sound, precisely because of the difficulty of capturing it in print. The sequence starts, arbitrarily, in the second encounter with the weird sisters.

8 Gabriel Egan, 'Hearing or seeing a play? Evidence of early modern theatrical terminology', *Ben Jonson Journal* 8 (2001), 327–47.

9 But see also the Macbeth Trail, 'Macbeth: the man, myth & legend', on the *Visit Scotland* website, http://static.visitscotland .com/pdf/macbeth_map.pdf, which also forms the insert for the DVD box ('This trail brings together the stunning film locations of *Macbeth* (2015), the real-life places immortalised in the play, and many other historic sites and dramatic landscapes connected to the story of the real Macbeth'). The website also includes Macbeth as one of its 'Famous Scots': https://www .visitscotland.com/about/famous-scots/macbeth.

Here, in effect, is the dialogue script for this sequence:[10]

[86] MACBETH.   I conjure you, by that which you profess,
Howe'er you come to know it, answer me!
Speak, I charge you!
OLDER WITCH.   Be lion-mettled, proud, and take no care
Who chafes, who frets, or where conspirers are:
YOUNGER WITCH.   Macbeth shall never vanquish'd be.
MIDDLE WITCH.   Until Great Birnam wood to high
Dunsinane hill Shall come against him.

[87] GHOST SOLDIER.   Beware Macduff.
ANOTHER GHOST SOLDIER.   Beware the Thane of Fife.
Dismiss me. Enough.
A THIRD GHOST SOLDIER.   Beware Macduff.
YOUNG BOY SOLDIER.   Be bloody, bold, and resolute:
laugh to scorn
The power of man, for none of woman born
Shall harm Macbeth.

[89] MACBETH. Saw you the Weird Sisters?
LENNOX.   No, my Lord.
MACBETH. Came they not by you?
LENNOX.   No, indeed, my Lord.
MACBETH. Infected be the air whereon they ride;
And damn'd all those that trust them!

[92] MACBETH.   Who was't came by?
LENNOX.   'Tis two or three, my Lord, that bring you
word,
Macduff is fled to England.
MACBETH.   Fled to England?
LENNOX.   Ay, my good Lord.
MACBETH.   Time, thou anticipat'st my dread exploits.
The flighty purpose never is o'ertook.
Unless the deed go with it. From this moment,
The very firstlings of my heart shall be
The very firstlings of my hand. Be it thought and done:
LADY MACBETH. Hell is murky. What's done cannot be
undone.
MACBETH.   Send out more horses, skirr the country
round;
Hang those that talk of fear.
The castle of Macduff I will surprise,
Seize upon Fife, give to th' edge o' th' sword
His wife, his babes, and all unfortunate souls
That trace him in his line. No boasting like a fool.
This deed I'll do before this purpose cool.

[93] LADY MACDUFF.   Murder! Murder! I have done no
harm.
[My baby. No.][11]

Shorn of its context, both the extensive descriptions in the 'shooting script' and the visual translations of that language, the dialogue looks more than usually bereft. The last line, 'I have done no harm', derives from Lady Macduff's question just before the Murderers' entrance, 'Why then, alas, / Do I put up that womanly defence / To say I have done no harm?' (4.2.78–80). And that act of transposition connects with three other lines in this sequence: Lady Macbeth's line comes from the sleep-walking scene (5.1.34, 65), and the first two lines of Macbeth's last speech in 92 ('Send out ... fear') come from 5.3.37–8. It is a frequent strategy in this part of the film, leaving, for us but not for its designed audience, strange moments of disturbance, as we mark the displacement and risk trying to understand its purposes – 'risk' because that would be to see in it something complexly allusive to its previous contexts where it is, rather, the inevitable consequence of the reshaping of large expanses of text into astonishing brevity.

We cannot but be struck by what is apparent within the dialogue of the screenplay: simply how little text is left. From the end of the scene for the Macbeths before he goes to see the weird sisters (3.4) to the beginning of the English scene (4.3),

---

[10] The dialogue and the speech-headings come from the unpublished 'Shooting script', made briefly available for download in 2015, pp. 63–7. I have cut the lengthy descriptions in the script and not added simple stage-directions. The numbering is the scene-count in the script.

[11] The words are repeated – I have not transcribed the repetitions. Overall, the script represents the following lines: 4.1. 66–7, 106–10, 87–8, 95–7, 152–65; 5.1.34, 65; 5.3.37–8; 4.1. 166–70; 4.2.80, 86 SD. The last line has no Shakespeare equivalent and does not appear in the shooting script.

there are 382 lines of text.[12] This reduces 382 lines to about 35, barely 9 per cent of the text,[13] including the three lines which have been displaced from elsewhere in the play. We are used to the fact that film cuts Shakespeare texts heavily (except for Branagh's 1996 *Hamlet*). But here the *very* heavy cutting is offset by the extraordinarily slow pace of delivery: it takes Scot Greenan, the actor playing the Young Boy Soldier, a full 12 seconds to say 'Be bloody, bold, and resolute' – the director's decision of course, not the actor's. And the sequence within which these 35 lines exist lasts some 8 minutes of screen-time in a film whose total length, discounting opening titles and end-credits, is barely 102 minutes.

Macbeth is short, but slow delivery necessitates exceptionally heavy cutting. The length of pauses between speeches is so substantial – as we hang on for the next word or the answer – that it suggests that the space is placed to enable the audience to absorb, replay, make sense of the speech before, for it is not simply a matter of actors being told to be portentously slow on cue. And the need for this air around lines is exacerbated by two aspects of the actors' work, of the mode of the performance rather than the writing/cutting, and, again, something that is directorial rather than within the actors' choice. The first is the comparative lack of inflection and shaping to the language, and, incidentally, the lack of sensitivity to verse rhythm (though the script reads 'the flighty purpose never is o'ertook', Michael Fassbender, playing Macbeth, says 'overtook' which disrupts the metre, a tiny difference but one that suggests the pulse of the blank verse line is not being felt).[14] As all actors know, the more you shout, the less colour the line is given, but here the monotone is present whether shouting or not.

The second is the choice of strong Scots accents that recall and repeat Orson Welles's choice in his 1948 film. Then, the studio intervened and rerecorded the voices, and here too it is rumoured that there may have been redubbing after previewing. Quite why *Macbeth* needs Scots accents where *Hamlet* doesn't need Danish ones or *Othello* Italian ones is beyond me, but plainly it functions within

a notion of naturalism, something intensified by the incessant drones in the musical underscore that suggest bagpipes, a soundscape analogous to and perhaps derived from the Third Ear Band's similar sounds in Polanski's 1971 version. And that goes with the repeated comments of Nick Swain, the film's dialect coach, Justin Kurzel as the film's director, and others about wanting intimacy and immediacy: Kurzel said in interview, 'There is a certain way in which the verse is done in this film that is very intimate, that is very confessional', and that when 'you're bringing the text into the cinema you can play it [in a] very personal, one-on-one way', while Fassbender remarked that 'The idea Justin had from the beginning was a lot more intimate with the text.'[15] In effect, it seems that the naturalism of sound is supposed to produce immediacy, where it actually generates uncomprehending distancing for all but a Scottish audience.

Vocal sound may, of course, extend beyond what play-text or film-script represents as dialogue. After 'damn'd all those that trust them!', Fassbender lets out what I can only describe as a whoop. My first assumption about the moment was that it was an unscripted actor's invention, possibly in post-production dubbing, an assumption based, not least, on the awkward editing around the absence of a shot of Macbeth saying it so that the sound is matched to a shot of the back of Macbeth's legs as he faces Lennox. But, in fact, it is in the shooting script: 'He lets out a WHOOP, exhilarated by the prophecy he's heard' (p. 66). Yet the sound cannot help but be unmistakably modern, and hence in tension with the language of the

---

[12] My count comes from the Wells–Taylor Oxford text (1986), which prints the Middleton song in 3.5 complete.

[13] The Hecate scenes are, of course, usually cut in performance and, without them, the count would be 11.5 per cent.

[14] In 1.1, the response to 'Where the place?' becomes not 'Upon the heath' (1.1.6) but 'Upon the battlefield' ('Shooting script', p. 1), abandoning the speed of the sisters' rhythms for something more realistically accurate and helpfully anticipatory, albeit disturbing in the change of metre.

[15] The comments come from extras on the DVD release: 'Interview with director Justin Kurzel' and 'Reimagining a classic'.

dialogue, a disruption of the early-modern-ness of Shakespeare's language.

Such a disruption is different from the effect of the transposition of lines from one moment to the other, such as the examples quoted above. This transposition is even more marked when the lines appear in a wholly new scene. After Lady Macduff and her children have been chased through a forest by the murderers – scene 93, quoted above – any viewer who knows *Macbeth* must assume that the family has been killed and that, thank goodness, we do not have to endure the sight of their murders, a relief especially strong after the harrowing filming of the event in Polanski's film. But the next scene, 94, opens with Lady Macbeth, revealed as looking up at what we soon see to be Lady Macduff and her children tied to stakes and surrounded with wood for burning, with a crowd – sullenly, it seems to me – watching as Macbeth 'brandishes a fiery torch', shouting, at no-one in particular,

Bring me no more reports; let them fly all:
Till Birnam wood remove to Dunsinane,
I cannot taint with fear? What's the boy Malcolm?
Was he not born of woman? The spirits that know
All mortal consequence have pronounc'd me thus:
'Fear not, Macbeth; no man that's born of woman
Shall e'er have power upon thee.' Then fly, false
    Thanes,
And mingle with the English epicures.

The passage, 5.3.1–8, has been displaced to go with the imminent threat of an act beyond even the brutality of Shakespeare's play. But it becomes even more confusing when Macbeth's next line, 'Why are you silent?', is addressed at his wife, who is silent in response, except that, of course, it both is and is not Macbeth's line – Macbeth's here but Malcolm's to Macduff in Shakespeare's text, a line from the 'English' scene (4.3.138), his noting of a gap in Macduff's response to Malcolm's enthusiasm, the silence broken by Macduff's equivocating 'such welcome and unwelcome things at once / 'Tis hard to reconcile' (139–40). This scene was clearly on the screenplay writers' minds: they borrow from it again in giving to the bound, about-to-be-executed but 'defiant' (p. 68) Lady Macduff Malcolm's 'This tyrant, whose sole

name blisters our tongues, / Was once thought honest' (4.3.12–13).

It is not in any way that I am complaining of the displacement, for there is no reason not to reattribute lines, but 'why are you silent?' as a line to Lady Macbeth is mysterious, for the question provokes our thought: what does Macbeth see his wife as failing to say? What words or sounds does he think that she ought to be making? Given that her previous lines, displaced now from the sleep-walking scene, had been to him 'Hell is murky. What's done cannot be undone' (scene 92), signs of her incipient madness more than a piece of sage advice, what lack is it that his noting her silence would constitute? In other words, the shifting of the line produces only enigma, not meaning, for me at least, and an enigma that I cannot leave, as it were, deliberately unresolved, unlike Macduff's response to Malcolm's question. The screenplay becomes, at this point, simply elusive in its intentions since I read the effect solely in terms of its writing, not of the functioning of the scene. And, while moving Malcolm on Macbeth as tyrant to Lady Macduff gives her a victim's voice, we then hit the problem of the actor who cannot make the line clear, playing the desperate emotion in this brutal intervention in the play rather than the words (by the by, anyone heading to Scotland, lured by Visit Scotland's enthusiasm for the play, the film and the historical Macbeth, and hoping to see the castle in front of which this scene has been filmed, will have missed it on the way: it is Bamburgh Castle in Northumberland). In any case, the transposition of 'Bring me no more reports' to here from 5.3 makes little sense when shouted in the vague direction of the passive onlookers to the fiery murders, but, the scene being invention, sense is what it needs to make, and any language ought to be working hard and effectively; yet here the shouting reduces concentration on the what by focusing on the how, the shout becoming more important than what is shouted.

Central to Lady Macbeth's presence in the scene is that the editing shows her looking with immense sadness at the Macduff children. The film had opened with the funeral pyre of the Macbeths' son, apparently a victim of plague. It emphasizes Macbeth's sense of loss in his concern for the Young Boy Soldier, one of Duncan's last reserves, killed in the battle but reappearing with the 'air-drawn dagger' (3.4.61), and again in the second encounter with the weird sisters. Now it returns to Lady Macbeth's loss, something it will re-emphasize in the child who appears to her in her mad scene. There is no sound for her in this scene, only the marking of her silence.

For all this, the most memorable moment in the scene is what follows: a shot of the loch-side at night, a long, slow pan that moves from the distant shore towards the crowd, catching sight of embers swirling in the air and then the light from something that they are watching, and finally the revelation of the pyre in full flame, Lady Macduff and her children invisible in the roaring fire. It is the second of the film's three pyres, the last being the burning of Birnam Wood, the wood coming to Dunsinane not because 'every soldier [has] hew[ed] him down a bough' (5.4.4) but because the English soldiers have started a forest fire and the embers are being blown to the castle:

We follow ONE OF THE EMBERS as it dances in the wind and eventually comes to find ... MACBETH'S PALM, held out in the air. He brings it back in. And we notice: his hand entirely still now. Under control.

MACBETH   *(hushed, to himself)*
And now a wood
Comes toward Dunsinane.[16]

As so often occurs, film analysis cannot stop itself from moving away from the sound to the sight, but the activity of trying to close-listen to the sequence has helped me to enable threads of thinking about the whole work to emerge from the detail here. For the pleasures of close reading / close watching / close listening lie in unravelling the weaving of the text, an abundantly unending process, with threads that emerge precisely because of how long it takes to explicate a passage with anything approaching the intensity the analysis demands. And, even so, it seems to me that the surface of this sequence of Kurzel's *Macbeth* has barely been scratched. Whatever we hear and see in the course of this scratching only reminds us how much else there is to hear and to consider.

---

[16] 'Shooting script', scene 110, pp. 79–80 (= 5.5.43–4).

FROM TABLE BOOKS TO TUMBLR: RECOLLECTING THE MICROGENRES OF THE EARLY MODERN STAGE IN SOCIAL MEDIA

CYRUS MULREADY

What is Shakespeare's dirtiest joke? Over a million readers sought the answer to that question when they clicked through to humour website Cracked.com's feature '7 filthy jokes you didn't notice in Shakespeare'.[1] BuzzFeed's readers also widely shared its '21 tattoos only Shakespeare fans will really understand', with images gathered from around social media depicting verse lines as body art.[2] And, each week, hundreds of followers of the BBC's *Hollow Crown* television series (@HollowCrownFans) share their favourite lines, images and video clips through the popular #ShakespeareSunday hashtag. On Sunday, 10 September 2017 (and in the days following), #ShakespeareSunday generated nearly 2,000 Tweets and retweets from over 300 users; these Tweets reached over 2 million readers.[3] To celebrate the 400th anniversary of Shakespeare's death in 2016, and perhaps to tap into this user base, Twitter sponsored its own #ShakespeareLives social media campaign, which included the introduction of a special Shakespeare emoji (first tweeted by Patrick Stewart) and live streaming of pop-up performances around London that were broadcast through the company's Periscope app. Although unlikely to rise to the attention of most Shakespearians, 'listicles' and Twitter communities like these have in recent years become increasingly popular channels for the dissemination of the Bard's work. At first glance, these look like novel textualities: Shakespeare's plays and poetry finding new audiences through the latest technologies.

But these methods and reading experiences bring us remarkably close to the practices and interests of some – perhaps many – seventeenth-century viewers and readers. As Tiffany Stern and Simon Palfrey have shown, early modern playwrights and readers often understood drama as emerging from 'parts' and 'fragments' rather than the 'literary' wholes that have been the object of critical attention for over 200 years.[4] If the work of putting together a play involved a series of 'patches', a stitching together of these parts (as Stern has argued elsewhere), then reading and viewing plays could likewise be understood as a pulling apart of these varied pieces.[5] '[E]arly modern reading and viewing audiences', Laura Estill has argued recently, 'did not see plays solely as cohesive wholes, but rather, as texts that could be fragmented and changed'.[6] An important technology generated by this fragmentary writing milieu is the commonplace book, as scholars of the early modern theatre have long recognized.[7] In his

---

1 Grace McCarthy, '7 filthy jokes you didn't notice in Shakespeare', Cracked.com, www.cracked.com/article_20501_7-filthy-jokes-you-didnt-notice-in-Shakespeare.html.

2 Keely Flaherty, '21 tattoos only Shakespeare fans will really understand', BuzzFeed, www.buzzfeed.com/keelyflaherty/tattoos-only-Shakespeare-fans-will-really-understand.

3 These statistics were generated using the hashtag tracking tools socialalert.net and tweetbinder.com.

4 Simon Palfrey and Tiffany Stern, *Shakespeare in Parts* (Oxford, 2007), p. 6.

5 Tiffany Stern, *Documents of Performance in Early Modern England* (Cambridge, 2009), pp. 1–5.

6 Laura Estill, *Dramatic Extracts in Seventeenth-Century English Manuscripts: Watching, Reading, Changing Plays* (Newark, 2015), p. xxv.

7 The scholarship on Renaissance commonplace books is well summarized in Victoria E. Burke, 'Recent studies in

work on 'commonplace book culture', Adam Smyth notes, among sixteen defining characteristics of these practices, 'the collection and deployment of fragments, not wholes; a conception of "coherent" texts as collections of fragments ... an interest in crumbling texts into parts, and in the production of new texts out of old parts'.[8]

No character exemplifies the early popularity of these fragments – aphorisms, sentences, jokes and jests among them – better than Shakespeare's Falstaff. In his first lines in *2 Henry IV*, the character even touts his own renown: 'The brain of this foolish-compounded clay, man, is not able to invent anything that tends to laughter more than I invent, or is invented on me. I am not only witty in myself, but the cause that wit is in other men' (1.2.6–10). Falstaff has a point: this character and his lines were alluded to in the seventeenth century more than any other of Shakespeare's parts. In fact, Falstaff was mentioned more often than all of Shakespeare's *plays* except *Hamlet* – he is the only character to receive his own index entry alongside play titles in *The Shakspere Allusion Book*.[9] These allusions are diverse in kind: many are notes about the historical Sir John Oldcastle, others are echoes of speech phrases such as 'grinning honor', which one seventeenth-century writer calls 'a very good jest because so ingenious an Author repeats it so often'.[10] The character is, as Falstaff claims above, a remarkable compendium of wit and the source of further invention – a fact recognized early on by John Dryden, who called Falstaff 'a *Miscellany of Humours or Images*'.[11] By any of these measures, and even acknowledged within his own words, Falstaff was perhaps Shakespeare's most popular creation.

In this article, I examine the writing and performance traditions that register both the causes and effects of Falstaff's prominence. Chiefly, I am interested in what I will call 'microgenres', extractable dramatic materials that were arguably as popular and important to early modern audiences as the larger works from which they were taken. When Hemmings and Condell gathered Shakespeare's plays for the 1623 Folio, they established a division of genres ('Comedies, Histories, and Tragedies') that today remains more or less

intact.[12] Within each of these plays, however, was a separate system little recognized in contemporary criticism: a collection of fragmentary but nonetheless coherent materials that included songs, jokes, set pieces, jests and aphorisms. More organized than the word 'fragment' would imply, yet not as long or fully developed as the dramatic genres of comedy or tragedy, these pieces were recognizable to Shakespeare's earliest audiences, a source of imitation and inspiration to authors, and even potential commodities for booksellers. Indeed, this last feature of the microgenre, its portability and vendibility, made this kind of play material particularly apt for distribution, both then and now. Through Falstaff, Shakespeare thus demonstrated a wide mastery of the microgenres of the early modern stage. Read this way, Shakespeare's knight looks less like the sentimentally cast buffoonish hero he has become in modern criticism, and more like a composite of the choicest 'play scraps', as they were sometimes called.

With this evidence in view, I shed new light on a well-worn editorial problem: the First Folio's quizzical description of Falstaff's death. This crux might be better discernible to us today because we live in an age when Shakespeare's writing has come partially unmoored from forms of textuality that have defined its study

---

commonplace books', *English Literary Renaissance*, 43 (Winter 2013), 153–77.

[8] Adam Smyth, *Autobiography in Early Modern England* (New York and Cambridge, 2010), p. 128.

[9] C. M. Ingleby, Lucy Toulmin Smith and Frederick James Furnivall, eds., *The Shakspere Allusion-Book: A Collection of Allusions to Shakspere from 1591 to 1700* (London, 1932).

[10] William Eyre, *A Vindication of the Letter out of the North Concerning Bishop Lake's Declaration of His Dying in the Belief of the Doctrine of Passive Obedience, &c. : In Answer to a Late Pamphlet, Called, The Defence of the Profession, &c. of the Said Bishop : As Far as It Concerns the Person of Quality* (London, 1690), p. 30.

[11] Ingleby *et al.*, eds., *The Shakspere Allusion-Book*, p. 146.

[12] On the importance of disrupting the traditional triad established in the Folio, see Jean E. Howard, 'Shakespeare and genre', in *A Companion to Shakespeare*, ed. David Scott Kastan (Malden, 1999), pp. 297–310.

for so long: collected works, edited editions of the plays, and performances that aim to be comprehensive presentations of the text. Today's readers and viewers of Shakespeare, through platforms like YouTube, Vine, Twitter and Facebook, can experience Shakespeare in fragments by watching small scenes, amateur performances, and sharing favourite quotations with friends and followers. These acts, I will argue, are part of a larger trajectory of genre formation and reformation within the early modern corpus that connects the commonplacing practices of early modern readers with the digital editing and sharing of our contemporaries. By looking at the ways in which language is distributed in digital networks, we can re-discover the systems of fragmentary textual dissemination used by communities of readers and viewers in Shakespeare's time.

The microgenres of the twenty-first century bear a striking resemblance to those of the earlier period: listicles, GIFs, memes, Tweets, and video shorts are cognate with (and in some instances directly reproduce) the aphorism, commonplace, jest or 'play scrap' that were familiar to earlier audiences. Twitter's Media Partnership Manager made a similar observation in the company's press release announcing the #Shakespeare400 events: '[W]e'll be imagining what Shakespeare would Tweet if he were alive. Because he would totally be on Twitter and probably love a GIF.'[13] Beyond simple analogy, though, the recurrence of these genres within contemporary media derives from fundamental structures within the Shakespearian text. Read historically, these adaptations are not so much innovations – Shakespeare's proleptic, anachronistic mastery over yet another media form – as they are a reinscription of early practices.[14] Today's media, this article argues, in which passages are marked, abridged, remixed and shared, in fact unlocks features of the Shakespearian text that have been obscured by centuries of performance and print history.[15]

FLOWERS, FINGERS, AND HASHTAGS

The material link that bridges information technologies of the twenty-first and seventeenth centuries is the hashtag, the now ubiquitous marker of online irony, commerce, and social trends. Originally ordained the 'octothorpe' by early telecommunications engineers, the 'hashtag' or pound sign has a history that predates the advent of Twitter or even the telephone. According to the *OED*, the term probably originated with the distinctive 'hashing' or 'hatching' pattern that engravers and artists used to shade in darker areas of their images.[16] The hashtag originated within the culture of Twitter as a method of subject sorting and indexing. An early Twitter user named Chris Messina first suggested the use of the pound sign, as he called it, as a means for organizing groups around events or topics.

Messina developed this idea on his blog, and eventually started calling his categories 'tag

---

[13] Julia White, 'Is this an emoji I see before me? Twitter plays its part in #Shakespeare400', Twitter.com, https://blog.twitter.com/en-gb/2016/is-this-an-emoji-i-see-before-me-twitter-plays-its-part-in-Shakespeare400.

[14] This historical approach is inspired by N. Katherine Hayles's suggestion that new media allows us to cast new light on the old: 'digital media have given us an opportunity we have not had for the last several hundred years: the chance to see print with new eyes and, with that chance, the possibility of understanding how deeply literary theory and criticism have been imbued with assumptions specific to print'. See N. Katherine Hayles, 'Print is flat, code is deep: the importance of media-specific analysis', *Poetics Today* 25 (2004), 67–90; p. 87.

[15] While scholars of the early modern period have keenly observed the technologies and traditions of early modern textual extraction, there has been less attention to the legacy of 'commonplace book culture' within contemporary media. It has been mainly new media scholars and writers in the popular press who have explored the parallels between these technologies. See, for instance, Nicholas G. Carr, *The Shallows: What the Internet Is Doing to Our Brains* (New York, 2010), who views the commonplace book as a divergent technology from today's social media and, therefore, one that better cultivates thinking and memory. A more historical and compelling treatment of the associations between commonplace culture and social media can be found in Katie Day Good, 'From scrapbook to Facebook: a history of personal media assemblage and archives', *New Media & Society* 15.4 (1 June 2013), 557–73.

[16] 'hatch, v.2, def. 1.' *OED Online*, December 2015, www.oed.com/view/Entry/84525.

Chris Messina™
@chrismessina

how do you feel about using # (pound) for groups. As in #barcamp [msg]?

↩ Reply ⇄ Retweet ★ Favorite ••• More

RETWEETS	FAVORITES	
429	753	

12:25 PM - 23 Aug 2007

34. Twitter post now accepted as the origin of the Internet 'hashtag'. Printed by permission.

channels', that are 'simply used by prefixing one or more words with the hash (#) character'.[17] In the example from this initial post (see Illustration 34), 'BarCamp' becomes the organizing tag for a series of technology conferences, enabling Twitter expressions like 'I'm coming to #barcamp later today.' Attendees of BarCamp could then track their comments through this 'tag channel' as a way of enabling conversation, as well as cyber eavesdropping on the event. As the practice of tagging has grown more diversified since these early efforts, users now employ the marking for a range of purposes, from the utilitarian – of the kind imagined for BarCamp – to figurative uses, as when the hashtag stands in for a kind of irony mark, or introduces subtext: 'Who is going to #barcamp? #threat5'. Messina and the early users of Twitter were attempting to solve an old and familiar problem, that of information overload. With the growth of the service and the number of messages flowing through the Twittosphere (as Messina called it), the vast digital text created in this space could only become usable through a system of marking and collecting.

Whether they knew it or not, Twitter users were adapting much older forms of organizational technologies in their choices. As Ann Blair has demonstrated, strategies of textual categorization and annotation emerged on a wide-scale basis in the early days of print. 'In the main ... early modern annotations in the margins and flyleaves', Blair writes, 'were reading notes – not personal responses of the kind found in more recent periods, but notes primarily designed to facilitate retrieval and retention of interesting passages'.[18] Early annotators, like these Twitter users, did their work with a purpose, one beyond recording personal thoughts: 'predominantly they flagged passages of interest, either non-verbally (through underlining or various kinds of marginal marks) or by high-lighting with keywords the topics treated or the examples or authorities cited in the passages deemed of special interest'.[19] For centuries, William Sherman has powerfully shown in *Used Books*, 'many readers found some method of

---

[17] 'Groups for Twitter; or a proposal for Twitter tag channels', http://factoryjoe.com/blog/2007/08/25/groups-for-twitter-or-a-proposal-for-twitter-tag-channels. Lexicographers Benjamin Zimmer and Charles Carson attribute the creation of 'hash tag', originally separated, now widely used as a compound noun, to another early Twitter user, Stowe Boyd. See 'Among the new words', *American Speech* 88 (2014), pp. 81–99.

[18] Ann M. Blair, *Too Much to Know: Managing Scholarly Information Before the Modern Age* (New Haven, 2010), p. 71.

[19] Blair, *Too Much to Know*, p. 71.

annotation an indispensable practice for digesting and mobilizing the text'.[20] Marks such as the manicule, flower, asterisk or even a simple x were, and still are, used, as Sherman puts it, as 'a visual shorthand for breaking texts down into manageable sections or signaling key subjects and claims at a glance' (see Illustration 35).[21]

Just as the community of Twitter users sought ways to make their Tweets sortable by subject and keyword for others to track and use, readers in earlier periods employed their tagging or marking for the benefit of later discussion, use and artistic inspiration. Once an expression or even image is tagged, it can circulate in the proper channels and become the basis for further adaptation.

A fascinating example of the intersection of Internet technology and Shakespearian fandom is the microgenre of the verse tattoo (see Illustration 36). In May 2015, BuzzFeed featured a collection of '21 tattoos only Shakespeare fans will really understand'. Such a collection is enabled by the marking practice of the hashtag, whereby the aggregator of the story, BuzzFeed staff writer Keely Flaherty, could cull together posts from Instagram, Tumblr, and Twitter with the aid of topics like #Shakespearetattoo (over 375 Instagram images). The verse tattoo expresses the copiousness of the Shakespearian text, quite literally, as 'corpus', a fitting return for the commonplace tradition in contemporary culture.

The digitized image of a Shakespeare tattoo, once shared in social networks, exemplifies a paradox about body art observed by Juliet Fleming. As a surface that 'cannot be reproduced', what makes the tattoo a mode of artistic expression, Fleming firstly observes, is its 'irreducible authenticity', the singular unity of tattoo and surface.[22] Yet the placement of the text on the body also suggests, contrarily, 'that there is nothing about the body or the person in it that is more unique than itself'.[23] The nearly infinite reproducibility of the digital image emphasizes this latter point; written on the body, digitized, re-marked and shared, the textuality of the verse tattoo is an extension of the commonplace tradition. Indeed, a popular choice for a #Shakespearetattoo is Polonius's

gnomic statement 'to thine own self be true', a passage set out in Q1 *Hamlet* with inverted quotation marks that were used to indicate commonplace material. 'Commas and inverted commas, single and double', Margreta de Grazia notes, ' ... were used interchangeably with the pointing index finger that directed the reader's eye to passages of special note, pointing the reader to a special point'.[24] Marked and shared now with a hashtag instead of commonplace markers, Shakespeare's words circulate again as extractable property for inspiration and reuse.

FALSTAFF'S TABLE OF GREEN FIELDS

In the seventeenth century, it was the copious theatrical body of Shakespeare's Falstaff that was marked by the recirculation of commonplace language. Based on the accounting of R. W. Dent in *Shakespeare's Proverbial Language*, there are 187 instances of proverbs in *1 Henry IV* alone – nearly the same number as in *Hamlet* (185) and second only in Shakespeare's canon to *Lear* (197). The two tragedies are longer plays, of course, making the frequency of proverbs in the two history plays much higher and, in Dent's words, 'infinitely more interesting with regard to Shakespeare's use of proverbial language' (Index 3).[25] *2 Henry IV*

[20] William H. Sherman, *Used Books: Marking Readers in Renaissance England* (Philadelphia, 2008), p. 76.

[21] Sherman, *Used Books*, p. 25. My thanks to Sarah Werner for sharing images from Jonson's copy of Martial's *Epigrams*: see her 'O Rare! Wynken de Worde', http://sarahwerner.net /blog/2011/03/o-rare.

[22] Juliet Fleming, *Graffiti and the Writing Arts of Early Modern England* (London, 2001), pp. 84–5.

[23] Fleming, *Graffiti*, p. 85.

[24] Margreta de Grazia, 'Shakespeare in quotation marks', in *The Appropriation of Shakespeare: Post-Renaissance Reconstructions of the Works and the Myth*, ed. Jean I. Martin (New York, 1992), p. 58. For further discussion of the Q1 *Hamlet* and the use of commonplace markers in printed plays, see Zachary Lesser and Peter Stallybrass, 'The first literary *Hamlet* and the commonplacing of professional plays', *Shakespeare Quarterly* 59 (2008), pp. 371–420.

[25] Robert William Dent, *Shakespeare's Proverbial Language: An Index* (Berkeley, Los Angeles, and London, 1981).

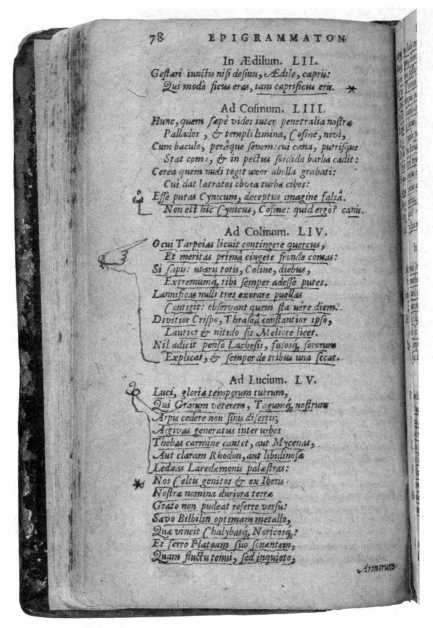

35. Ben Jonson's marginalia in his copy of Martial's *Epigrams*. *[Epigrammata] M. Val. Martialis nova editio: ex museo Petri Scriverij* (Leiden, 1619), E7 v (p. 78). Shelfmark: PA6501.A2 1619 Cage. Used by permission of the Folger Shakespeare Library.

includes some 169 instances, and *The Merry Wives of Windsor* 136. Falstaff, too, speaks a significant number of these proverbial lines in the plays in which he appears: 59 proverbs (32 per cent of the total) in *1 Henry IV*, 48 proverbs (28 per cent) in *2 Henry IV*, and 31 (23 per cent)

36. Instagram post tagged with #Shakespearetattoo. Printed by permission of the author.

in *Merry Wives*.[26] Across the three plays in which he appears, Falstaff speaks slightly less than one-third of the proverbs. Falstaff's language subsequently stood as a source of imitation throughout the seventeenth century: phrases such as 'Grinning honor', 'Reasons as rife as blackberries' and 'there is no faith in villainous man' regularly appear attributed to Falstaff in *The Shakespeare Allusion Book*, along with other scraps of language.

Appropriately, when the Hostess describes Falstaff on his deathbed in *Henry V*, she employs a gathering of gnomic statements about death: 'He'll yield the crow a pudding one of these days' (2.1. 83–4); 'He's in Arthur's bosom' (2.3.9–10); 'A made a finer end, and went away it had been any christom child' (2.3.10–12); 'A parted ev'n just between twelve and one, ev'n at the turning o' th' tide' (2.3.12–13); 'I knew there was but one way' (2.3.15); and that his feet were 'were as cold as any stone' (2.3.23, 25) – statements all identified by

Morris Tilley in his *Dictionary of Proverbs*.[27] The aphoristic nature of the speech was apparent early on, for instance in Henry Bold's mock elegy for Oliver Cromwell: 'Nor went he hence away like Lamb so mild / Or Falstaf-wise, like any Chrisome-Child / In *Arthur's* Bosom'.[28]

It is a separate part of this speech that has spurred a still-unresolved textual dilemma: 'for after I saw him fumble with the sheets, and play with flowers, and smile upon his finger's end, I knew there was but one way. For his nose was as sharp as a pen, and

---

[26] I am grateful to my research assistant, Nicole Hitner, for her help in compiling these statistics.

[27] Morris Palmer Tilley, *A Dictionary of the Proverbs in England in the Sixteenth and Seventeenth Centuries: A Collection of the Proverbs Found in English Literature and the Dictionaries of the Period* (Ann Arbor, 1950).

[28] Ingleby *et al.*, eds., *The Shakspere Allusion-Book*, p. 308. Originally published in Henry Bold, *Latine Songs, With their English: and Poems* (London, 1685), p. 159.

a babbled of green fields' (2.3.13–17). That Falstaff died babbling of green fields is the ingenious solution to what is perhaps the most well-known crux in the First Folio. Faced with the seemingly inexplicable conceit of Hostess Quickly, 'for his Nose was as sharpe as a Pen, and a Table of greene fields' (TLN 838–9), editors and critics have dutifully championed a dizzying array of explanations, excisions and conjectural emendations intended to make sense of the apparently senseless. What distinguishes the many solutions to this textual crux is their notable ingenuity: Quickly speaks of a portrait (first suggested by Edmond Malone, defended by others); she speaks of a famous sea captain; his 'table' is a backgammon board; his described symptoms point to a number of possible medical diagnoses; and, more recently and compelling, that he recalls the words of the twenty-third Psalm.[29]

Despite these attempts, it is still Lewis Theobald's 1733 conjectural emendation ('a babbled of green fields') that today holds the page. Even those who implicitly acknowledge the eighteenth-century editor's intrusion on Shakespeare's text are swayed by the beauty of a solution that is now also backed by centuries of editorial tradition. The note provided by the 1875 New Shakespeare Society Edition of the play sums up what remains a current critical attitude: 'Theobald's emendation – whether it be the true one or not – has for more than a century deservedly retained the favour of Shakespeare's readers. It harmonizes with the tone of pathetic irony which runs through the account of Falstaff's death.'[30] Theobald's gloss was and remains, undeniably, a product of his own time and sensibilities in the reading of Shakespeare. He asserted his reading as a riposte to Pope, who had excised the line 'and a Table of green fields' in his 1725 edition because he saw it as 'nonsense', the result of a 'pleasant mistake of the Stage-editors, who printed from the common piecemeal-written parts'. Mr. Greenfields, Pope speculated, was the theatre's 'property man', and this a direction for a piece of tavern scenery to be brought in.[31] Theobald dismantled his rival's account, and found it unlikely

that a piece of stage property would be brought on mid-scene: 'Greenfield's Table can be of no Use to us for this Scene.'[32]

From their study of Renaissance 'table books', Peter Stallybrass, Roger Chartier, Heather Wolfe, and J. Franklin Mowery make available a different

---

[29] The readings summarized here are to be found in Robert F. Fleissner, 'Allegorical physiology', *American Notes and Queries* 7 (1969), 73; Fleissner, '"A table of greene fields", grasse-greene/table, and balladry', *Shakespeare Jahrbuch* (1976), 143–9; Fleissner, 'Sir John's flesh was grass: a necrological note on Falstaff and the Book of Isaiah', *American Notes and Queries* 23 (1985), 97–8; Fleissner, 'Theobald tabled: more on the picture of Falstaff's death', *Notes and Queries* 39 (1992), 326–8; Ephim G. Fogel, '"A table of green fields": a defense of the Folio reading', *Shakespeare Quarterly* 9 (1958), 485–92; Leslie Hotson, 'Falstaff's death and Greenfield's', *TLS*, 6 April 1956, p. 212; S. F. Johnson, '"A table of green fields" once more', *Shakespeare Quarterly* 10 (1959), 450–1; Michael Platt, 'Falstaff in the valley of the shadow of death', *Interpretation: A Journal of Political Philosophy* 8 (1979), 5–29; Duncan Salkeld, 'Falstaff's nose', *Notes and Queries* 51 (2004), 284–5; and George Walton Williams, 'Still babbling of green fields: Mr. Greenfields and the twenty-third Psalm', in *Shakespeare, Text and Theater: Essays in Honor of Jay L. Halio*, ed. Lois Potter and Arthur F. Kinney (Newark, 1999), pp. 45–61. Gary Taylor offers a useful discussion of the crux's history in Appendix B, Section 2 of his Oxford edition: *Henry V*, ed. Gary Taylor, The Oxford Shakespeare (Oxford, 1982), pp. 292–5. In my response to the crux, I follow the sensible suggestion of Ephim Fogel, who argued, 'If one can show that the original reading makes good sense in its context, then burden of proof rests with anyone who would revise it' (p. 486).

[30] *The Chronicle History of Henry the Fifth: Reprint of First Quarto, 1600*, ed. Brinsley Nicholson, Series II (London, 1875), p. 127 n. 23. As Linda Charnes has rightly argued, Theobald's 'a babbled' gloss poses a sentimentalized tragic hero: 'Reading for the wormholes: micro-periods from the future', *Early Modern Culture*, 6 (2007), http://emc.eserver.org/1–6/charnes.html (para. 11). My reading of the crux differs from that of Charnes, however, who finds 'textual wreckage' in the Hostess's comments.

[31] William Shakespeare, *The Works of Mr. William Shakespear*, ed. Alexander Pope, 6 vols. (London, 1723), vol. 3, p. 422.

[32] Lewis Theobald, *Shakespeare Restored, Or, A Specimen of the Many Errors, as Well Committed, as Unamended, by Mr. Pope in His Late Edition of This Poet: Designed Not Only to Correct the Said Edition, but to Restore the True Reading of Shakespeare in All the Editions Ever yet Publish'd* (London, 1726), p. 138.

reading of 'table' that may help to justify the Folio's rendering of these lines. A writing technology used for a range of purposes, from taking down recipes and jokes to recording legal proceedings and sermons, table books included pages that were prepared with a special surface that allowed the writer to erase entries and reuse the pages.[33] With the historical orientation of this work at hand, the Hostess's language becomes coherent: Falstaff's final moments are materialized in 'sheets', 'flowers', and 'fingersends' (Q), a series of references resonant with the practice of gathering commonplace materials described earlier by Sherman and Blair. Read this way, the Hostess's vocabulary renders intelligible the metaphor of the pen and table in the final clause as a table book, the popular early modern writing apparatus that enabled short compositions without quill and ink.

The idea that Falstaff's table might be a 'table book' was in fact first mooted shortly after Theobald's 'a-babbled' insertion, and frequently included in eighteenth-century variorum editions of the play. In Zachary Grey's *Critical, Historical, and Explanatory Notes on Shakespeare* (1754), William Smith, responding to the alterations of Pope and Theobald, notes: 'had they been appriz'd that *(a) table* in our author signifies a pocket book, I believe they would have retained it . . . On *table-books*, silver, or steel pens, very sharp-pointed, were formerly, and are still fix'd either to the backs or covers.'[34] The line 'his nose was as sharp as a pen, and a table of green fields', could thus be read as elliptical, with 'his nose was as sharp as' the antecedent for 'a table of greene fields . . . ', a suggestion made by Gary Taylor in a note to his Oxford Edition.[35] The Hostess is thus remarking upon the sharpness of Falstaff's nose as signalling the acuity of his wit. For while a sharp nose, as many commentators have offered, was indeed a proverbial symbol of impending death in the sixteenth and seventeenth centuries, this physiognomic trait was also cited frequently as a characteristic mark of a choleric wit and disposition. Sir Nathanial in *Love's Labour's Lost* compliments Holofernes: 'your reasons at dinner have been sharp and sententious, pleasant without

scurrility, witty without affection, audacious without impudency, learned without opinion, and strange without heresy', a compliment he bestows just before, according to the stage direction, he '*draws out his table-book*' and jots down a 'choice epithet' (5.1.2–6, 15). Falstaff's sharp nose might also be a metaphor of taste and discernment, one that aligns with the frequent figurative use in the period of the 'Table' as an offering of verbal delicacies. Finally, the possibility that a sharp nose was another kind of reader's mark is suggested by this singular example: an image of a thirteenth-century manuscript in which brackets have been transformed into faces with unusually sharp noses (see Illustration 37).

Importantly, William Smith's note indicates that the tablebook, or pocket-book, was recognizable to eighteenth-century readers, a fact confirmed by Stallybrass, Chartier, Wolfe and Mowery. Editors had the choice, in other words, of Theobald's version and the more historical account, and chose the former over the latter. That decision is not surprising; this, after all, was the period in which the material traces of reading encoded by the Hostess's 'flowers' and 'fingers end[s]' were systematically erased or scratched out of the margins of books and Shakespeare's language was being abstracted for its 'beauties', and the singularity of his language emphasized over its allusive qualities.[36] The very existence of this crux therefore reveals to us a turning point in Shakespearian criticism, a moment in which emerging ideas of

---

[33] Peter Stallybrass *et al.*, 'Hamlet's tables and the technologies of writing in Renaissance England', *Shakespeare Quarterly* 55 (2004), 379–419.

[34] Zachary Grey, *Critical, Historical, and Explanatory Notes on Shakespeare: With Emendations of the Text and Metre*, 2 vols. (London, 1754), vol. I, p. 381.

[35] Fogel also observed the elliptical structure of the sentence, noting Shakespeare's frequent use of that syntactic structure.

[36] For further discussion of these practices, see Sherman's chapter in *Used Books*: 'Dirty books?', pp. 151–78; Margreta de Grazia notes that the attention to 'beauties and faults' in the eighteenth century 'served the broader cultural ambition of purifying English language, taste, and manners': *Shakespeare Verbatim: The Reproduction of Authenticity and the 1790 Apparatus* (Oxford, 1991), p. 63.

37. Detail showing reader's marks from Leiden University Library MS BPL 6 C. Image courtesy of Erik Kwakkel.

personhood and authorship replaced a more textual and material understanding of character. It is this earlier form of textuality that our contemporary media allow us to see again, with more clarity, once we are attuned to the fragmentary nature of seventeenth-century Shakespeare.

SCRAPS, ENDS, AND BOTTOMS

The 'table of green fields' that accompanies his death thus could be read as the copious record of Falstaff's wit and sententiae. This collection is biblical, poetic and aphoristic, to be sure, but also includes more popular forms of discourse not necessarily encompassed as 'proverbial' – jokes, jests, songs and (broadly speaking) 'balductum' and 'play-scraps', derisive terms sometimes applied to theatrical speeches and set-pieces that hearers and readers of plays extracted for their own uses. Thus, while I see Falstaff's commonplace language as a parallel tradition to the kind of reading and writing practices associated with humanistic 'florilegia', opening the tables of Falstaff also exposes modes of commonplace discourse that have received less attention. This popular discourse is even more hidden from us than the learned – and thus culturally sanctioned – traditions of commonplacing. But traces of it do, indeed, remain, and offer us a wider understanding of how theatre-goers used the material that they heard and read.

More than a simple copying of this language, though, Falstaff's character shows a complicated engagement with the commonplace tradition. The Hostess's conceit comparing Falstaff's sharp nose to a 'table of green fields' speaks to this through its jumbled simile – how could a table hold a green field? The juxtaposition of these images undoubtedly spurred the confusion that produced the crux. But such uncertainty is appropriate to the moment. The Hostess, after all, is characterized by her malapropisms and general infelicity with language. On further analysis, the mixing of metaphor here is illuminating, as the Hostess combines two of the period's dominant tropes for the gathering of sententious language: a 'table' of verbal delicacies and a verdant 'field' or garden of gnomic 'flowers'. These figures of speech connoted different registers of meaning: one that pointed to a more refined and classically inflected form of imitation (flowers, green fields), and the other to crass copying or theft (table 'scraps').

Indeed, many writers allude to the practices of commonplacing as acts of hoarding 'scraps' from another's 'tables'. Thomas Dekker uses such language in *The Belman of London* (1608) to lambast 'decayed Poets', 'whose wits like a fools Land holds out but a twelve month, and then they liue upon the scraps of other mens invention'.[37] The popularity of writing tables among the non-elite is widely suggested in plays and references to the theatre. John Fletcher and Francis Beaumont address such theatre-goers in a prologue to *The Woman Hater*, 'if there bee any lurking amongst you in corners, with Table bookes, who have some hope to find fit matter to feed his mallice on, let them clasp them up, and slinke away, or stay and be conuerted'.[38] Writers of the period commonly allude to the practice of copying lines, especially those that were bawdy or centred on a jest. In this induction from John Marston's *Malcontent* (ascribed there to John Webster), a character named Sly tells an actor that he knows his play so well that he could give notes to the members of the company:

SLY. . . . Where's Harry Cundale, D: Burbidge, and W: Sly, let me speake with some of them.

TYRE.   An't please you to go in sir, you may.

SLY. *I* tell you no; I am one that hath seene this play often, & can give them intelligence for their action: I have most of the ieasts heere in my tablebooke.[39]

This passage poses two important points about theatrical viewing and the use of table books. First, Sly associates roles with particular actors (Henry Condell, Richard Burbage, and William Sly). Moreover, he connects these actors and their characters with particular 'action', the

---

[37] Thomas Dekker, *The Belman of London: Bringing to Light the Most Notoriovs Villanies that are now practised in the Kingdome* (London, 1608), Cr.

[38] John Fletcher and Francis Beaumont, *The Woman Hater* (London, 1607), A2r.

[39] *The Malcontent* (London, 1604), A3r.

series of jests that he has recorded in his table book. We know from the history of the Chamberlain's Men's Will Kemp that jests, jigs and 'merriments' were commodifiable products: four separate editions of Kemp's feats were published in his lifetime, two in German. Sly's commentary here suggests that the extraction of such materials into a table book was a common theatrical practice.

Marston seems to have held particular scorn for this kind of appropriation. In his collection of satires *The Scourge of Villanie* (1598), a number of his targets are men who poach material from plays. There is Luscus, from whose lips 'doth flow / Naught but pure *Iuliat* and *Romeo*' and who 'H'ath made a common-place book out of plaies, / And speaks in print'.[40] Marston further writes about this self-gathered collection of writings: 'He writes, he railes, he iests, he courts, what not, / And all from out his huge long scraped stock / Of well penn'd playes.'[41] There is also Tuscus, 'that jest-mounging youth'. Here the commercial dimensions of the jest and scrap come into focus, as does the sense that these amateurs are stealing from those who wrote the 'well penn'd playes'. Tuscus, the 'monger' of these jests, 'traffics' in them, a metaphor further developed by Marston: '[He] nere did ope his Apish greening mouth / But to retail and broke anothers wit.' This Tuscus is, metaphorically, an 'ill-stuft truncke of iests, whose very soul / Is but a heap of libes'.[42] And, in a final metaphor resonant with the discourse of the 'table', this Tuscus feeds on 'offall scrapes, that sometimes fal / From liberal wits, in their large festiuall'.[43] Just such a character appears in Marston's *What you Will* (1607) quoting from *Richard III* ('A horse, a horse, my kingdom for a horse') before quipping: 'Look the[e] I speak play scrapes.'[44]

In the Q1 text of *Hamlet*, Hamlet's instructions to the Players records yet another allusion to jests being jotted down in table books:

And then you haue some agen, that keeps one sute
Of ieasts, as a man is knowne by one sute of
Apparell, and Gentlemen quotes his ieasts downe
In their tables, before they come to the play, as thus:

'Cannot you stay till I eate my poorige' and, you owe me
A quarters wages: and, my coate wants a cullison;
And, your beere is sowre ...[45]

Like Marston, Shakespeare, through Hamlet, expresses contempt for those who cop their jokes from plays or stale jestbooks; this time, however, it is both the 'gentlemen' in the audience and the inept 'clown' who are objects of scorn. Hamlet casts the performer as ineloquent, 'blabbering' his jokes and inaptly 'keeping in his cinkapase of ieasts', perhaps using crass physical comedy in place of more skilled verbal jesting. Ironically, and maybe ignoring Hamlet's dismissal of the jokes, an early reader of the British Library's copy of Q1 *Hamlet* still saw fit to mark the speech with brackets and manicules. Even cast as parody, 'your beer is sour' may have been a scrap worthy of gathering. As a means of comparison, Hamlet's lines offer some insight to the first performances of Falstaff, a character probably played by one of the Chamberlain's Men's clowns, Will Kemp or Thomas Pope.[46] Falstaff's skill at jesting derives from his adherence to Shakespeare's quotable verbal formations. It is not the personality or 'character' of Falstaff that generates the humour (blabbering and cinquepacing), but the written material itself. Unlike Hamlet's clown, who 'cannot make a iest / Vnlesse by chance, as the blinde man catcheth a hare', Falstaff thrives because the

---

40 John Marston, *The Scovrge of Villanie, Three Bookes of Satyres* (London, 1598), H4r.
41 Marston, *The Scovrge of Villanie*, H4r.
42 Marston, *The Scovrge of Villanie*, H6v.
43 Marston, *The Scovrge of Villanie*, H6v.
44 John Marston, *What You Will* (London, 1607), C1r–v.
45 *The Tragicall Historie of Hamlet Prince of Denmark* (London, 1603), F2r–v. These lines appear only in the earlier Q1 version of the play, as the speech is substantially revised in both Q2 and F.
46 For further discussion of the actors who may have originated the role, see David Scott Kastan's Arden edition of *1 Henry IV* (London, 2002), pp. 78–9. On Will Kemp's connection to the role, see also David Wiles, *Shakespeare's Clown* (Cambridge, 1987), pp. 116–35.

character is a conduit for Shakespeare's scripted wit.

There are witnesses outside of theatrical culture to this practice of gathering scraps from the writings of playwrights. A 1598 religious polemic attacks its adversary for 'transplanting' a variety of 'Puns, Quibbles, Jests, Drolleries and Sarcasms' from stage plays to 'graft' on his books and lectures. The author derisively comments that these phrases 'only serve to proclaim him a pitiful *Jack-Pudding* ... who hath neither Grace nor good manners' (emphasis in the original).[47] Both Marston's satire and the ecclesiastical tract trope on the language of commonplacing in their invocations of food ('offall scrapes', 'Jack-Pudding'). These descriptions are notably resonant with language used to describe Falstaff, for instance in the moment Prince Hal play-acts the role of his father ridiculing the prince's companion: 'Why dost thou converse with that trunk of humours, that bolting-hutch of beastliness, that swollen parcel of dropsies, that huge bombard of sack, that stuffed cloak-bag of guts, that roasted Manningtree ox with the pudding in his belly, that reverend Vice, that grey Iniquity, that father Ruffian, that Vanity in years?' (*1 Henry IV*, 2.5.454–9).

Following on these descriptions of the collector or hoarder of witticisms as being stuffed full of others' words, the similarities with Jack Falstaff emerge with more clarity. The bodily presence of Falstaff on stage remains one of the character's more notable traits. Writers in the seventeenth century frequently summoned the body of Falstaff – one of the most extensive topics of allusion is his corpulence, as this anonymous song humorously illustrates:

> Wilt thou be Fatt, Ile tell thee how,
> Thou Shalt quickly do the Feat;
> And that so plump a thing as thou
> Was never yet made up of meat:
> Drink off thy Sack, 'twas onely that
> Made *Bacchus* and *Jack Falstafe* Fatt, Fatt.[48]

Allusions from earlier in the period also indicate how quickly Falstaff's size became proverbial: an English traveller in Hamburg relates the size of

a German hangman to Falstaff in 1617, and Ben Jonson plays on Falstaff's size in *Every Man Out of his Humor* (1600): 'you may (in time make leane *Macilente* as fat as *Sir John Fall-staffe*)'.[49] These references speak to the physical presence of the actor on stage, the legacy of memorable performances. But these descriptions, even within the plays themselves, are consistently metaphorical as well. Falstaff is 'out of all compass', his excesses extend beyond the physical to his verbal presence within these plays (*1 Henry IV*, 3.3.19). That Shakespeare would eulogize Falstaff's sententiousness in describing his passing is thus fitting, as is the corporeal nature (fingers, feet, nose) of the final description.

A GOOD JEST FOREVER

One of the more curious allusions to Falstaff in the seventeenth century comes from a 1681 political pamphlet, *Heraclitus Ridens: A Dialogue between Jest and Earnest, concerning the Times*. The two-page document stages a discussion between the characters from the title, who remark upon the religious and political issues of the day. 'Jest' sums up their pronouncements in the following: 'Then here are a world of Irons in the fire, 'tis well if some of 'em do not burn, and some-body do not burn their fingers, but let the Bees look to that, as honest *Sir John Falstaff* says.'[50] The oddity of the reference is that nowhere in Shakespeare's plays does Falstaff mention bees, or say anything resembling the quoted statement – nor do any other characters in Shakespeare. A reader in 1875, noting the

---

[47] *A View of an Ecclesiastick in his Socks & Buskins: or, a Just Reprimand given to Mr. Alsop, for his Foppish, Pedantick, Detractive and Petulant Way of Writing* (London, 1698), p. 72.

[48] Ingleby *et al.*, eds., *The Shakspere Allusion-Book*, p. 106. Originally published in *An Antidote against Melancholy: Made up in Pills. Compounded of Witty Ballads, Jovial Songs, and Merry Catches* (London, 1661), p. 72.

[49] Ben Jonson, *Every Man Out of his Humor* (London, 1600), Q1v–r.

[50] Ingleby *et al.*, eds., *The Shakspere Allusion-Book*, p. 276. Originally published in *Heraclitus Ridens; a Dialogue between Jest and Earnest, concerning the Times* (London, 1681), B1v.

pamphlet for an article in *The Athenaeum*, put forth the plausible suggestion that the lines recall a performance from one of the 'Drolls' that were popular during the Interregnum and Restoration, a possibility made more plausible by the use of the suggestive name 'Jest' for one of the interlocutors.[51] As we have seen already, these jests were a significant microgenre within the early modern theatre. Sly, the character from Marston's *Malcontent* quoted above, says that he no longer needs to see a play because he has collected all the jests in his table book.

Interestingly, the most frequently echoed lines and cited episode associated with Falstaff through the seventeenth century come from a 'jest': the robbery at Gad's Hill and the buckram-cloth disguises Prince Harry and Poins use to deceive Falstaff in the first part of *Henry IV*. I have identified nineteen different allusions to or retellings of the incident through the seventeenth century, including a scrap of dialogue recently recovered in a binding that dates to the early seventeenth century.[52] The Gad's Hill ploy involves Poins and Harry robbing Falstaff immediately after he and his confederates have held up a group of travellers. Poins tells the Prince of this plan, 'I have a jest to execute that I cannot manage alone' (1.2.159–60). It is a prank, Prince Harry imagines, that 'would be an argument for a week, laughter for a month, and a good jest for ever' (2.3.3–4).

Shakespeare thus clearly sets out this episode using the language of the jest; in Hal's imagining, the trick promises to live on in the retelling. Like the proverb or commonplace, a jest was a generic and extractable episode to be reused in various circumstances. Ian Munro and Anne Lake Prescott have observed that 'Books of jokes seem to be an inherently reproductive genre; in almost all cases, the wit they publish is coded as coming from somewhere else.'[53] The details of the buckram ruse are mostly of Shakespeare's imagining, yet it shares the general shape and character of other popular jests. The duping of pilgrims at Gad's Hill, for instance, resonates with the religious figures that often figured prominently in the stories.

Falstaff's size and corporeality further accord with early modern traditions and discourses on wit at jesting. Robert Armin's widely popular *Foole upon Foole* (1600, 1605) includes in its archetypes of fooling 'the fat fool', played in his narrative by the Scot Jamy Camber. Jamy is described in terms similar to Falstaff: he is 'Two yardes in compasse … and he did come of gentle bloud'.[54] These details resonate with Shakespeare's characterization: 'Indeed, I am in the waist two yards about', Falstaff tells Poins in *The Merry Wives of Windsor* (1.3.36–7). Falstaff and Armin's Jamy are not so much models for one another as characters drawn from stock figures of a shared tradition. In the seventeenth-century theatre, playwrights made significant use of the jestbook genre, both in copying actual characters and scenarios and also, more broadly, in imitating the tropes and strategies of the genre. Armin again provides an apt example. His Jamy, 'whose very presence made the King much sport', is frequently the target of practical jokes, jests that the king concocts with his other servants.

Later in the seventeenth century, the Gad's Hill episode formed the basis for a dramatic set piece in Francis Kirkman's collection of drolls, *The Wits*, which includes the frequently reproduced image of Falstaff in its frontispiece. This assembly of scenes taken from popular plays of the sixteenth and seventeenth centuries includes 'The Bouncing Knight, or, the Robers Rob'd', a thinly veiled version of the Eastcheap scenes from the *Henry IV* plays that centres on the episode at Gad's Hill. Kirkman's book emulates the format of the jestbook by turning the specific plots of plays into microgeneric material that could be acted in other

---

51 C. Elliot Browne, 'Early allusions to Shakspeare', *The Athenaeum* 2507 (13 November 1875), 640–1.

52 Arthur Freeman, 'The "Tapster Manuscript": an analogue of Shakespeare's *Henry the Fourth Part One*', *English Manuscript Studies* 6 (1997), 93–105.

53 Ian Munro and Anne Lake Prescott, 'Jest books', in *The Oxford Handbook of English Prose, 1500–1640*, ed. Andrew Hadfield (Oxford, 2013), p. 353.

54 *Foole vpon Fool, or, Six Sortes of Sottes* (London, 1605), B2r.

circumstances, or even told as a joke. Looking at the table of contents, we can see that what Kirkman valued about the plays he uses was their extractability. The titles of the entries, too, emphasize their episodic generic nature: 'The Testy Lord', 'The Three Merry boys', 'The Grave-makers', and, of course, 'The Bouncing Knight'. The title page indicates the plays from which these come, but indicates neither authorship nor specific character names. Explaining his rationale for extraction, Kirkman explains, 'He that knows a Play, knows that Humours have no such *fixedness* and indissoluble *connexion* to the Design, but that without *injury* or *forcible revulsion* they may be *removed* to an *advantage*' (emphasis in the original).[55] Rather than diminishing the plays from which he is extracting his materials, Kirkman claims he is adding value – 'removed to an advantage'. By the late seventeenth century, Falstaff had exceeded the generic parameters of the canon.

Early modern theatre-goers and printers thus consumed and reproduced dramatic writing in a variety of forms other than traditional theatrical performance and book publication (the two most widely known and studied today). Indeed, the cultural practices that encouraged the taking down and recounting of play scraps, jests, and other microgenres may have had a more significant role in the perpetuation of theatrical culture than has been realized. In his *Drolls*, first assembled in the 1640s, Kirkman advertises that they were produced at the Red Bull during the closure of the theatres. This evidence suggests that one reason for the survival of pre-revolution dramatic tradition was the enterprise of extracting selections of plays for private production and public circulation. Even into the eighteenth century, as Theobald imagined

a quaintly babbling Sweet Jack, others were reviving Falstaff for a different purpose. An eighteenth-century collection of witticisms, for instance, *Falstaff Alive Again!* (1794), calls forth a Falstaff who lives not as a singular character, but as a textual miscellany of 'jests, witticisms, and anecdotes'.

Because of video services like YouTube, students and readers today are more likely to watch just their favourite scenes from a play, rather than its entirety. This practice has not replaced their reading of the full text, any more than the performance of Kirkman's 'Bouncing Knight' superseded the *Henry IV* plays. Nonetheless, the Hostess's speech as printed in the Folio seems to mark Shakespeare's acknowledgement that Falstaff had already, even before Kirkman's drolls or the Internet age, become such a collection of microgeneric material. And, contrary to the biographical and psychological completeness that later came to define his character, this Falstaff only had a life, or afterlife, insofar as his words could be scrapped, scraped, shared, and collected, once again, into a table of sharp jests, flowers, and fingers' ends.[56]

---

[55] 'To the Reader', in *The Wits, or, Sport upon sport. Part I in select pieces of drollery, digested into scenes by way of dialogue: together with variety of humors of several nations, fitted for the pleasure and content of all persons, either in court, city, countrey, or camp* (London, 1662).

[56] I gratefully acknowledge several readers for their insightful suggestions on drafts of this article: Jane Degenhardt, Tom Festa, Matt Kozusko, Jared Richman and Kurt Schreyer. I also owe special thanks to Margreta de Grazia, whose work on cruxes and the editorial tradition has been a key source of inspiration, and to Peter Stallybrass, who first pointed out the curiosity of Falstaff's early popularity to me.

UNLEARNING SHAKESPEARE STUDIES: SPECULATIVE CRITICISM AND THE PLACE OF FAN ACTIVISM

LOUISE GEDDES

In his 2014 address to the Shakespeare Association of America, Jonathan Dollimore challenged Shakespearians – who are, he noted, pressed with their back against the wall, 'in a marketplace pretty indifferent to what they do'[1] – to engage in a scholarship that maintains a more robust connection with the problems of the 21st-century world. Dollimore's critique offers the opportunity to reflect on the current academic environment, which includes ongoing administrative demands to demonstrate a quantifiable relevance to humanities scholarship and has resulted in the yoking of education funding to generic assessment structures. The output of such constraints is institutionally sanctioned discourse that is too often intellectually and economically fortified against those outside of the profession. Cultural materialism's own evolution from radical discourse to benign staple of the theory classroom is an example of how Marxist thought has been historicized and theorized to the point of inaccessibility to all but the most devoted students. As the models of academic publishing expand, however, bringing challenges and opportunities in equal measure, academe is better positioned than ever to resist the accusation of insularity. The assumption that 'campus intellectual culture seems to reflect all of our worst political debates and has little to offer anyone who isn't already a dedicated partisan'[2] is a characterization that reveals more about the structures of scholarship than it does about the vibrant and multi-modal pedagogical practices today. How, then, in the increasingly privatized avenue of knowledge dissemination might we resist a system of commercialized intellectual goods? The answer can perhaps be found outside of academe in the radical new ways that a generation of users are shaping Shakespeare according to the priorities of their own intellectual and aesthetic communities.

As the rich histories of performed and/or appropriated Shakespeares illustrate, the shift in definition from Shakespeare (singular, text-based, stable) to Shakespeares (pluralized, multi-platform, transforming) is helpful, but limited as long as it is rooted in an ethos of fidelity, offering scholars the challenge of reconciling the presence of a historically identifiable 'Shakespeare' text with a more wide-ranging study of cultural, linguistic and content-based networks. Certainly, while the affective reading practices that drive Shakespeare scholarship hide behind a veneer of objectivity, we cannot hope to produce the pertinent and pithy scholarship that would reaffirm Shakespeare's capacity to speak to the increasingly polarized communities of the 21st-century world.

This article was first presented as part of a seminar at the World Shakespeare Congress at Stratford-Upon-Avon in 2016. My thanks to my seminar participants for the helpful questions and comments. Special thanks to Valerie Fazel and Mario Di Gangi for their thoughtful critiques of the article during the revision process.

[1] Jonathan Dollimore, 'Then and now', Address to the Shakespeare Association of America Conference, Friday, 11 April 2014.

[2] Frederik De Boer, 'Why we should fear University, Inc.: against the corporate taming of the American college', *New York Times Magazine*, 13 September 2015, www .nytimes.com/2015/09/13/magazine/why-we-should-fear-university-inc.html.

Aranye Fradenberg and Eileen Joy assert the need for a neuroscientific approach to learning that recognizes a greater complexity in thought, one that accounts for sentient experience – 'old' knowledge – and new processes in the networks that build education. Joy argues for the place of affect even in the methodologies we term 'academic', asserting affect's importance as a driving force for the detached reading that scholarship celebrates, noting that 'if we keep in mind the role of affect in the formation of memories, the question of why we cling or adhere to "tradition" is a matter of affective investments, of cathexis and de-cathexis'.[3] Shakespeare studies perhaps needs to unlearn not its heritage and the subsequent body of thought that has emerged but the practices that have bound us to institutional capitalist pressures and that are now manifest in a crippling intellectual decorum. Instead, Shakespeare studies might adapt, as the works themselves do, to new practices, new models of reading and new ontologies – in particular, examining ways we might transverse the current creative/critical binary that is used to separate affective reading from the fallacy of scholarly objectivity. Such reading would affirm the value of transformative and transformed Shakespeares,[4] constructed in accordance with Mercutio's observation to Romeo that 'now / art thou what thou art by art as well as by nature' (*Romeo and Juliet*, 2.3.82–3).

Although still tethered to a dichotomy that separates fictional acts of criticism from formal scholarship, the unlearning of traditional models of scholarship has already begun to occur in our field: Will Stockton and Elizabeth Rivlin's leadership at the open-access *Upstart* has seen the journal embrace a robust mixture of 'traditional' essay-based scholarship and creative criticism,[5] and Punctum's online journal *Lunch* offers 'askew reviews'.[6] Graham Holderness affirms the value of 'creative collisions'[7] – novels, short stories and poetical reflections that explore critical questions. Shakespeare scholarship also benefits from an expansion of critical form beyond the creative/critical binary. Rob Conkie's recent book, *Writing Performative Shakespeares*, stylistically rejects the 'front and centre'[8] placement of the theatre critic,

instead embracing a fluid critical form that reflects the 'provisionality, contingency, indefiniteness and indeterminacy'[9] that embodies the experience of Shakespeare in performance. Conkie's work mirrors a re-mapping of critical thought already evident in fan practices, and might offer a more self-conscious assessment of form that recognizes not only the difference between past and present but also the transcultural and transhistorical networks that continue to inform our reading and shape our practices. Creative criticism, which uses abstraction to 'temporarily stabilise the constantly collapsing and mutating energies of the universe into an evanescent but beautiful coherence',[10] occupies a fecund place between appropriation and a speculative textual analysis that creates a new literary topography, emerging out of a philosophy that Joy has termed 'weird' reading. Weird reading is an approach to a text that 'might pay more attention to the ways in which any given unit of a text has its own propensities and relations that pull against the system and open it to productive errancy'.[11] Such reading is playful, exploratory, foregrounding the potentiality of a text as a means of articulating one's experience of literature,[12] and

---

[3] Aranye Fradenberg and Eileen Joy, 'Unlearning: a duologue', in *The Pedagogics of Unlearning*, ed. Éamonn Dunne and Aidan Seery (New York, 2016), pp. 155–81; p. 163.

[4] See Sujata Iyengar, 'Shakespeare transformed: copyright, copyleft, and Shakespeare after Shakespeare', *Actes des congrès de la Société française Shakespeare*, February 2017, http://Shakespeare.revues.org/3852.

[5] https://upstart.sites.clemson.edu/index.html.

[6] www.lunchreview.org/about.

[7] See Graham Holderness, *Creative Collisions: Tales by Shakespeare* (Cambridge, 2014).

[8] Rob Conkie, *Writing Performative Shakespeares* (Cambridge and New York, 2016), p. 12.

[9] Conkie, *Writing*, p. 5. [10] Holderness, *Creative*, p. 19.

[11] Eileen Joy, 'Weird Reading', *Speculations* 4 (2015), 19–31; p. 29.

[12] See Matthew Harrison and Michael Lutz, 'South of Elsinore: actions a man might play', in *The Shakespeare User: Creative and Critical Appropriations in the Twenty-First Century*, ed. Valerie Fazel and Louise Geddes (New York, 2017), pp. 23–40.

is frequently manifest in the aforementioned 'askew' critical engagements. In this article, I aim to loop the collisions manifest in fan practices back to more traditional models of scholarship and ask what is to be gained by integrating such capricious thought into Shakespeare scholarship at large. A more speculative critical approach allows for a broad application of weird reading that encompasses literary criticism, creative and performative critical approaches to a text, and both academic and non-academic discourse. In practice, speculative criticism and weird reading both eschew a linear logic in favour of a networked set of intellectual, critical, creative and cultural associations, and offer a counter-knowledge to the traditional models of scholarship, promoting instead a 'form of resistance to the idea that the only good movement is forward'.[13] Speculative criticism exists in a space between textual analysis and performance studies, capturing a text at the very cusp of play.

The coalescence here between Shakespeare and both creative and speculative criticism directly correlates with the relative global ubiquity of digital culture, the spread of knowledge economies and, in particular, the rise of fandoms as makers of cultural matter. The threat of a third wave of capitalism, termed cognitive capitalism, 'which is founded on the accumulation of immaterial capital, the dissemination of knowledge and the driving role of the knowledge economy',[14] is, in many ways, what is at stake for both the circulation of intellectual Shakespeare goods and the increasingly troublesome economics of higher education. For Yann Moulier Boutang, this new capitalism seeks to curtail and utilize the innovation and creativity that arise from networks of communal spaces and shared information, which Shakespeare scholars can see in practice through paywall-protected journals, steadily increasing conference fees and for-profit file-sharing sites, such as academia.edu. In contemporary online culture, we witness not just an expansion of global knowledge but ongoing acts of de-territorialization and re-territorialization as intellectual communities construct themselves both inside and outside of capitalist archival institutions that would harvest this work.[15] As such, a radical intellectual stance comes

from the scholarly recognition of the relationship of 'outsider', or non-academic, discourse to our own methodologies. Joy is clear about the value that speculative, or weird, ontologies carry, but maddeningly opaque about the sources of such knowledge. I would like explicitly to link outsider reading to the practices of fandoms and argue for a speculative Shakespeare criticism that might utilize close reading, historicism, creative writing, performance theory, affective reading and presentism as a literary practice. Speculative reading practices might encompass creative criticism (in all its varied iterations), as well as more traditionally constructed critical acts that lead directly back to a direct engagement with the text under analysis. Such reading is informed by fannish textual participation and is predicated on the assumption that Shakespeare is essentially transformative, and reading practices that balance an aesthetic critique of Shakespeare with a mining of the text for articulations of contemporary socio-economic concerns. Fan production is a direct material response to the latent power of the palimpsest, manifesting itself as the visible accumulation of textual referents, and, as such, it mirrors the process of consumption-as-production by the academic critical industry. To recognize this common ground is to claim the opportunity to acknowledge and use the affective networks that shape intellectual inquiry.

Fandom is a network of self-identifying aficionados, audiences who knowingly create 'their own cultural environment from the cultural resources that are available to them',[16] gravitating towards a fan object or artefact representative of affective experience. Prior to the advent of Web 2.0, fandoms were concretely tied to more carefully constructed cultural productions of pleasure – socially sanctioned, consumer-oriented spaces of release

---

[13] Fradenberg and Joy, *Unlearning*, p. 169.
[14] Yann Moulier Boutang, *Cognitive Capitalism* (London, 2012), p. 50.
[15] Boutang, *Cognitive*, p. 49.
[16] Lawrence Grossberg, 'Is there a fan in the house? The affective sensibility of fandom', in *The Adoring Audience: Fan Culture and Popular Media*, ed. Lisa A. Lewis (London, 1992), pp. 50–65; p. 53.

manifest in affective pleasure, protest or subcultural group identity.[17] The rise of what Henry Jenkins has famously termed a participatory culture as the model of online interaction has changed the nature of fandoms in two significant ways. Firstly, the Internet has facilitated the collapse of spatial-temporal order – simply put, time is flattened when material is made indiscriminately accessible. Secondly, the participatory shift in Internet behaviour has changed pleasure's reliance on manufactured offerings; with such infinite variety available, consumers of cultural goods are rewarded for actively seeking out their own affective pleasures – no matter what a fan is searching for, there is a good chance that they can either find, commission or create it themselves online. Jenkins's definition of participatory culture is one that carves a space for the latent power of fan activism through a variety of means, embracing 'the values of diversity and democracy through every aspect of our interactions with each other – one which assumes that we are capable of making decisions, collectively and individually, and that we should have the capacity to express ourselves through a broad range of different forms and practices'.[18]

The relocation of fandoms online has also had the effect of bringing fannishness into common parlance – fandom is no longer the underground realm of obsessive consumers of a cultural product but a carefully articulated communal identity that affirms a creative engagement with a particular object. For example, the Shakespeare fandom encompasses the many academics who proudly brandish their Shakespeare-themed conference swag, the online bloggers Shakespeare Geek or Good Tickle Brain, and the teenage Whovian, who follows David Tennant as he forges his career as a classical actor on the RSC stages. Fandom is a carefully constructed 'space between media production and consumption',[19] where affective experience networks with cultural products and intellectual debate, and creates a discourse community around a particular fan object. Undeniably, Jenkins's definition is idealistic – as we know, political structures inhibit access on a daily basis. And yet, at the very least, Jenkins's participatory

space can be seen as productively aspirational. The emergence of fans as agents of social change suggests a space for optimism about how Shakespeare may be used. Joy notes that 'networks of material relationships always under construction that affect our circumstances (whether at unimaginable distances of time and space or not) are still relationships that have implications for all affective experience',[20] and the rise of fandom as an autonomous creative force, increasingly visible through the auspices of the web, posits consumers as active agents who can drive the content and orientation of the culture they adore.

Participatory fandom has already made its presence felt in entertainment, using its power as a body of consumers, and this energy is spreading beyond the fan objects themselves, making explicit the link between reading practices, fan communities and social engagement. Fandom has also become a model for the organizing principles of political activism and, in some cases, the impetus for change itself. The Harry Potter Alliance, for example, is a formidable activist organization that uses the values promoted in the Harry Potter book series, as well as the recognizable bonds of fan communities, to take on real-life issues, positioning itself as a proactive user of literature. Its mission declares that 'we know fantasy is not only an escape from our world, but an invitation to go deeper into it',[21] and, at the time of publishing, the organization had donated over 250,000 books to libraries across America, partnered with Public Knowledge in support of net neutrality, and it continues to support small 'Granger Grants' to assist local chapters with grassroots service projects. Like academia,

---

[17] See Dick Hebdige, *Subcultures: The Substance of Style* (London, 1979).

[18] Henry Jenkins, *Textual Poachers: Television Fans and Participatory Culture* (London, 1992), p. 2.

[19] Cornel Sandvoss, 'Toward an understanding of political enthusiasm as media fandom: blogging, fan productivity and affect in American politics', *Participations: A Journal of Audience and Reception Studies* 10.1 (May 2003), 252–96; p. 262.

[20] Fradenberg and Joy, 'Unlearning: a duologue', p. 164.

[21] www.thehpalliance.org.

fandom offers an opportunity to form discourse communities around a shared subject, and, because of the self-reflexive nature of affective fandoms, participants demonstrate a sophisticated interplay of life experience, ideology and close study of the fannish object, practices that literary critics might term cultural materialist, presentist, feminist, queer, post-colonial and so forth, were they performed in an institutional academic setting. In May 2016, one Tumblr user built a visual guide to non-traditional casting, based on a note given in a lecture by their Shakespeare professor at the University of Southern California. Linked to various fandoms through use of hashtags, this brief discursive note has been reblogged thousands of times, demonstrating the visible network through which fan discourse reaches out.[22]

For many fans, fandoms and socio-political identity are inextricably bound. Since the late 1950s, concurrent with the rise of television and the displacement of theatre as mass media, Shakespeare has become an increasingly protected cultural commodity, and, under these conditions, access to Shakespeare becomes a political act. The primary passage to Shakespeare education is increasingly barricaded by paywalls, often excluding students and scholars alike. The claim of 'alternative' Shakespeare has emerged as a counter-cultural response to his elite status. As we progress (or regress), what constitutes alterity is constantly in flux, but the continued resistance to the values of fan networks stubbornly upholds a binary between the passionate fan and the objective scholar. Digital fan cultures, in particular, have continued to resist the value placed on the distinction between enthusiasm and objectivity and, in doing so, offer new ways to think about how we encounter a text. Instead of a high–low spectrum, we now locate intellectual enquiry in a network of use that accommodates an ever-moving arrangement of associations, forcing recognition of the common ground that scholarship shares with fandom. Elsewhere, Valerie M. Fazel and I have argued for this new construction of Shakespearian as a Shakespeare user.[23] Users can include academics, artists, bored teenagers, their parents, general enthusiasts, proclaimed Shakespeare fans, and members of alternative fandoms who have been drawn in through curiosity, cross-interests or simply through hashtag association. As well as advancing discourses on topics of current interest, the users who exist in fan communities engage in weird reading that strives to understand their relationship to a given text, enmeshed as it is in linguistic, aesthetic, and socio-political networks of its own.

In fandoms, there exists a phenomenon known as 'fanon', a portmanteau of 'fan' and 'canon' that affirms the value of communal shared interpretation. Fanon is an interpretive practice rooted in close reading, and I wish to spend some time considering the accumulation of Mercutio fanon as a source for new critical readings of *Romeo and Juliet*. Fanon is fan-generated ontology that is largely accepted as essential to the fannish object, albeit something that exists out of the 'canon' – in this case, 'canon' is the multimedia composite of *Romeo and Juliet*. That is to say that, in the twenty-first century, *Romeo and Juliet* refers to not only Shakespeare's play but also the extensive cultural associations it has accrued, and fanon, when accepted widely enough, becomes absorbed into the topography of the text. Fan culture's use of Mercutio exemplifies this point: the fanon that has built up around Mercutio as a site of difference is informed not only by the experience of reading *Romeo and Juliet* but also by both the pedagogical setting in which most students first encounter the text and an amalgamation of Harold Perrineau's scenery-chewing performance in the 1996 film *William Shakespeare's Romeo + Juliet*, a 2010

---

[22] Because of the uncertainty of the identity, and age, of the user, I am choosing not to cite user names of fans who offer personal narratives or speak directly to lived experience. For further elaboration on the ethical use of social media, see Valerie Fazel, 'Researching YouTube Shakespeare: literary scholars and the ethical challenges of social media', *Borrowers and Lenders: The Journal of Shakespeare and Appropriation* 10.1 (Spring/Summer 2016), www.borrowers.uga.edu/1755/show.

[23] Valerie M. Fazel and Louise Geddes, *The Shakespeare User: Creative and Critical Appropriations in a Networked Culture* (New York, 2017).

production of Gérard Presgurvic's 2001 French musical entitled *Romeo et Juliette, Les enfants de Vérone*,[24] and its subsequent 2012 Hungarian operatic version by Magyar Színhás, *Rómeó es Júlia*,[25] as well as discourses on male sexuality from contemporary culture. As is entirely typical with fannish production, the hierarchy and time-line of influence are at best convoluted, and work is littered with partial citations and incorrect references, making apparent the messy circulation of influence. And yet, in many ways, this lack of accountability is what has endowed the Mercutio fandom with such potency and created fanon knowledge that is consistent with much academic criticism. By tracing these connections, a scholar rooted in weird reading practices can advance a speculative critical reading of *Romeo and Juliet* in different ways. For example, weird reading makes visible the dialogic relationship a reader has with their text and materializes the cognitive process that drives affective reading. Weird reading manifests a two-way reading process through which personal narratives use Shakespeare as a means of articulating experience, and, on the level of media, it enacts activism through community discourse. From a literary perspective, weird reading carves a space to read radical politics back into the play.

In fan cultures, Mercutio has emerged as a voice of non-conformity in an otherwise culturally conservative, heteronormative Verona. Drawing from the aforementioned appropriative representations, Mercutio fanon identifies him as gay, ethnically Eastern European or African American, sexually sadomasochist, occasionally transvestite, and both sexually and verbally unfettered. The robust corpus of fan fiction that exists for Mercutio is almost always erotic, coupling him with Tybalt (known as 'Tycutio'), Benvolio ('Bencutio'), or Romeo ('Rocutio'). These sexual scenarios are frequently masochistic co-dependent relationships – for example in Tycutio fanon, Tybalt can only respond to Mercutio's linguistic excess with sex and violence. Such reading draws attention to the play's exploration of the social impact of sex and death, but is nonetheless rooted in literalizing Mercutio's recommendation to 'beat love down' (*Romeo and*

Juliet, 1.4.28) and his Queen Mab speech, which 'personifies imagination and performs precisely the task of providing imagined objects of desire for a panoply of social agents'.[26] For the play to kill Mercutio, as constructed through fanon and canon, is to silence the voice of open dissent. Fanon alignment of Mercutio with queer sexuality and non-white racial identity also draws attention to class, as Mercutio exists as part of a lower stratum of Veronese citizen who labours his body in service of an aristocracy that attempts to enact self-affirming social rituals using his blood as a sacrifice. This pointless feud is only resolved when faced with the loss of the final Montague and Capulet bodies that are capable of producing heirs. Keeping Mercutio alive, keeping him weird and keeping him subversive then becomes a political statement against the enforced participation in a hierarchy of corporeal uses at work in the play.

Hugh Grady's recent work on the text suggests that 'the harmony between sex and death described by Friar Lawrence becomes the rupture in the social fabric brought about first by Romeo and Juliet's transgressive, mutual passion, and then by the deaths Romeo becomes involved in',[27] a not altogether atypical assessment of the challenge to patriarchy, homosociality and heteronormativity that Romeo and Juliet's passion represents. Fannish work such as the digital erotica publisher Slipshine's pornographic comic strip *Mercutio* (Illustration 38),[28] and the wealth of erotic fan art that highlights Mercutio's sadomasochistic pleasures (Illustration 39),[29] however, apply that critique to Mercutio, by offering the character ownership of the

[24] https://www.youtube.com/watch?v=xi21XHWVoD4&list=PLPgm3mMUaT-cHz-daTX_vRhSLUhO_kt1x.

[25] https://www.youtube.com/watch?v=0kItGmJQaQM.

[26] Hugh Grady, *Shakespeare and Impure Aesthetics* (Cambridge, 2012), p. 207.

[27] Grady, *Impure*, p. 214.

[28] Slipshine, 'Mercutio', http://slipshine.net.

[29] http://crow821.deviantart.com/art/Teahouse-Fanart-Mercutio-175651760.

38. 'Mercutio'. Slipshine.net.

39. 'Mercutio'. Teahouse Fan Art.

'Tragedy without a soul',[30] imagines Mercutio alongside Jay Gatsby, as part of a body of characters who 'expanded knowledge / And added imagination'. Such a fan-generated analogy suggests a hedonism that drives Verona, and identifies either Juliet, or (more likely) Romeo, with the hedonistic and selfish Daisy Buchanan, opening up a reading that pits the idle pursuit of aristocratic leisure – in this case, manifest in both the families' uncontextualized feud and the romantic and sexual satisfaction of the two noble teens – against all the bodies employed in a larger economy of grudge-holding that appears to serve no other purpose than to bind the lower-class citizens of Verona to a self-sacrificial loyalty. Such a reading might focus, for example, on the Nurse's incredulity at Juliet's response to Mercutio's and Tybalt's death. The Nurse's request that Juliet fulfil her obligation to the family by joining the communal lament is met with an astounding lack of empathy for the larger loss at hand. When framed as part of a Shakespeare/ Fitzgerald network, Juliet's response, 'come nurse; I'll to my wedding bed, / And death, not Romeo, take my maidenhead!' (*Romeo and Juliet*, 3.2.136–7), becomes a microcosm of her family's own insularity and self-regard.

Fan readings that accentuate Mercutio's own perceived masochistic leanings, evidenced in the S&M imagery that circulates around him in fan art and fictions such as Ryouhei Akane's 'You speak in tongues I don't understand',[31] draws attention to a perversity that arguably drives *Romeo and Juliet*, and is suggested by the language of piety that surrounds their rhetoric of sex and death. By embodying the sexual potency bubbling underneath the homoerotic violence that runs throughout the play, Mercutio also implicates Romeo and Juliet's own fascination with the corporeal that is masked by their effusive romantic hyperbole and that must be displaced for the sake of tragedy.

hyper-sexuality that characterizes his language, assuming that his words are aimed at the primary sexualized male of the play, Romeo. Fanon's own assumption of Mercutio's lack of discrimination (evidenced by the equal production of Rocutio, Bencutio, and Tycutio slash fiction and art) sets Mercutio apart from Romeo through his conscious disengagement from not only monogamy but the compulsory heterosexuality at work within the text. This self-awareness of his own sexual appetite without requiring the self-placating myth of love as a justification for hedonistic impulses makes him a realist in relation to his friend. Moreover, Mercutio's seduction of his audience, his wit and charm, his pleasure in his own liberty (both linguistic and sexual), is then presented as violently curtailed by his unwilling involvement in the play's blood-feud.

Often, fan readings build a network between multiple texts. Thamina Laska's poem, for example,

30 http://thaminalaskar-tina.tumblr.com/post/144520971339/ tragedy-without-a-soul.
31 Ryouhei Akane, 'You speak in tongues I don't understand', *An Archive of Our Own*, 25 May 2015, https://archiveofour own.org/works/6979555?view_adult=true.

To foreground Mercutio is to complicate further the notion that 'adolescent desire becomes itself the object of ambivalent desire'[32] by giving space to Mercutio's thwarted longing. Moreover, Mercutio's centrality demands that the reader take stock of the collateral damage that occurs, in spite of the play's dramaturgical resistance to lingering on Mercutio's death, and offers a way to circle back to his central critique: 'a plague o' both your houses' (*Romeo and Juliet*, 3.1.91). As well as exploration through creative critical acts, such a reading could be manifest in traditional, critical scholarship, and would no doubt echo the work done by cultural materialists and queer theorists, for example expanding Carla Freccero's critique of 'the text's seemingly endless infernal ability to breed new iterations of the myth of heterosexual love'.[33] The speculations that draw together aspects such as race and sexuality are the work of an interpretive community and eventually morph into fanon, consolidated through the various reference material available and the communal issues that concern the fans. Together, this practice reframes traditional critical discourse in a new model of knowledge distribution. Moreover, circulations of fan art and the accompanying meta-critical commentary suggest that fan work is often knowingly produced for a self-identified fannish community, and offered up with the expectation that it will generate further discussion and offshoots. Such evolutions are rooted in affect and, as an object of fannish devotion, Mercutio can simultaneously represent an erotic fantasy of dangerous and joyful liberation in an otherwise structured world, an affirmation of omni-sexual hedonism, a conscious commitment to an ideology of equality, and a statement of the diminished value of black male bodies in a violent, white society – in explorations that follow Perrineau's performance and accentuate race, Mercutio's blackness condemns him as an outsider as much as his sexuality does. Speculative critical practices embrace the affective experience that shapes such readings, and welcomes the new ontologies founded in the playful and erratic associations that Shakespeare facilitates.

From an activist standpoint, weird readings of the play allow speculative reconstructions of the Shakespearian narrative that foreground the outsider, linking such work to Dollimore and Sinfield's own cultural materialist agenda. Returning to the position of the text as an affective billboard[34] for the consumerist, socio-economic and cultural investments of a particular generation allows us to see the radical ways in which Shakespeare is being used as a conduit for exploring affective experience. Fan fiction, for example (particularly, for this instance, the slash fiction that circulates around Mercutio), queers Romeo by the 'contra-normative positioning of sexuality within media texts'[35] – in this case, *Romeo and Juliet*. Shakespeare, then, becomes a vehicle for change as the works are used to reflect personal narrative, explore ideas, and engage in ideological discourse. Through weird reading, Shakespeare becomes a safe, imaginary space to push the boundaries of class, race, sexuality and gender. Typical of a methodology that consciously abandons the pretence of objectivity, speculative identification also manifests itself through confessional, which is supported and affirmed by the reading community. On Tumblr, one anonymous user revealed that 'mercutio being gay af[36] is so important to me. i remember bringing it up in english and my teacher just looked at me from where she was perched on her stool and i could FEEL her JUDGEMENT like whoa excuse u but he gay. anywho that's my story for the day thanks for reblogging the gay r+j fix-it post'. Likewise, another tumblr user described Mercutio as 'just basically me in fancier tights' – an identification that is a common response to Mercutio, and whether it be true or aspirational is irrelevant. What matters is that readers, or users, are not only finding Shakespeare and

[32] Jonathan Dollimore, *Death, Desire, and Loss in Western Culture* (London and New York, 2012), p. 112.

[33] Carla Freccero, 'Romeo Juliet Love Death', in *Shakesqueer: A Queer Companion to the Complete Works of Shakespeare*, ed. Madhavi Menon (Durham, 2011), pp. 302–9; p. 307.

[34] Grossberg, 'Fan', p. 585.

[35] Stephen Booth, *Close Reading without Readings: Essays on Shakespeare and Others* (Teaneck, 2016), p. 5.

[36] 'af' is common fan parlance and stands for 'as fuck'.

processing life experience through his creations but up-ending the gender expectations of 'heteronormative mainstream media texts',[37] by foregrounding Mercutio's emotional and homoerotic life as a source of potency and authority. This is, of course, not to say that we ought to ground academic work in such potentially self-indulgent perspectives, but an honest reassessment of our own reading practices might well engender a new literary criticism that more vigorously asserts its place in the 21st-century world and more aggressively seeks out a discourse network that makes use of Shakespeare's capacity to speak with both the dead and the living. Although fans are under no obligation to provide a context for their readings, scholarship bears some broader responsibility for sustained close reading practices, even if the delivery of such critical thought alters its methodologies and form.

The obvious concern about orienting scholarship in affect is its potential for solipsistic reading, a risk of losing one's self-awareness and ultimately losing sight of Shakespeare in the critique. A critical approach led by fandom's acknowledgement of fannish object differs from appropriative theories, such as the rhizome and presentist literary approaches, in that it recognizes the gravitational pull of the fan object at the heart of the reading practice. For that reason, a fan-oriented speculative criticism makes more sense than an approach that offers undue weight to the cultural processes, often at the expense of what has attracted the reader-participant in the first place. Moreover, speculative criticism, rooted in a conflation of sentient experience and weird reading that is in this case filtered through fan communities, is a meta-critical act that recognizes the transformable and networked text at the core of the intellectual process. It affirms erratically constructed interpretive groups and communal readings that disrupt the forward-moving trajectory of the more explicitly Marxist presentism. Speculative critical methodologies are informed by the active collapse of temporal–spatial and geopolitical notions of culture that our digital environment has engendered. That is to say, speculative reading rejects the need to approach the past

ontologically, undercutting the universality implicit in many presentist readings in favour of an affirmation of difference. These practices do not imagine a future that progresses out of a disrupted continuum of past and present, but instead participate in ongoing acts of future creation and re-creation, recognizing the play itself as a site of participation. In pushing back at the boundaries of perceived authority (even when it is complementary, fandom challenges the author/creator's decision to say 'this ends here'), fan cultures are utopian in practice, pledging multiple allegiances simultaneously and enacting the future identities of a text that are galvanized through reading. Fannish practices and speculative criticism's resistance to linear history are both textual exegesis and a moment of archival inclusion, affirming the intellectual resonance of Shakespeare in our contemporary world.

Such critical practices are as aesthetic as they are socio-political. John Drakakis suggests that one of the limits of a presentist approach is that it affirms the value of theme at the expense of form,[38] and, again, this offers the opportunity to think through the differences between presentism and fan-inspired speculative criticism. Fanon is rooted in canon – it has to be, as fanon emerges from the universal agreement of a diverse body of readers. Unlike, say, a rhizomatic approach, a critical network that integrates affective experience necessarily orients itself back towards the fan object, moving in a field of gravity around it.[39] Speculative reading, as literary criticism, must represent 'an exchange that involves both sharing and contested ownership',[40] by understanding that

---

[37] Booth, *Close*, p. 7.

[38] John Drakakis, 'Shakespeare as presentist', *Shakespeare Survey* 66 (Cambridge, 2013), pp. 177–87; p. 186.

[39] See Cornel Sandvoss, 'The death of the reader? Literary theory and the study of texts in popular culture', in Jonathan C. Gray, Lee Harrington, and Cornel Sandvoss, eds., *Fandom: Identities and Communities in a Mediated World* (New York, 2007), pp. 19–33.

[40] Christy Desmet, 'Recognizing Shakespeare, rethinking fidelity: a rhetoric and ethics of appropriation', in Alexa Huang [Joubin] and Elizabeth Rivlin, eds., *Shakespeare and the Ethics of Appropriation* (New York, 2014), pp. 41–57; p. 43.

fan passion builds its iterations around an enthusiasm for Shakespeare, even as it expands the definition of what Shakespeare is. Erik Didriksen's Tumblr-born pop sonnets are an example of form-based fandom that positions text as an agential network in its own right. Pop sonnets are metrical experiments that re-imagine classic rock, rap, pop songs and other popular cultural ephemera as Shakespearian sonnets, such as the R&B singer Drake's 2016 hit 'Hotline bling':

> In the dead of night, thou would me missives send –
> sweet words of love thy sleepless envoys bore.
> Those late-night calls have lately met their end,
> for now thou dost a manner new explore.
> E'er since I left the city, thou hast rous'd
> coarse rumors 'round thy honor, once pristine.
> 'Tis said thou champagne quaffed and long carous'd
> with womenfolk I had ne'er before seen.
> O dost thou seek out countries far and strange
> or merely to attract thy newest beau?
> Thou dost not need thy character to change;
> I beg thee, stay the woman that I know.
> –A new dispatch could only mean one thing:
> 'Tis only love late couriers can bring.[41]

The pop sonnet enacts the potentiality of form, returning the reader to the intricacies of metre and verse by a very carefully networked juxtaposition. Both the sonnet and Drake's song are picked apart, parsed and reassembled, becoming performative through this process of reassemblage. A speculative approach would position form as object, recognizing that M. J. Kidnie's missive on the adaptive process[42] is also applicable to other forms of consumption, such as reading. The sonnet 'Hotline bling' stands as a self-referential network: it deconstructs the authority of Elizabethan form as distanced by creating a network that draws in, via the R&B connection, electric blues, gospel and dance. The sonnet deliberately invokes musicality by its use of an extremely popular song, encouraging an affective reading that prioritizes scansion and an emphasis on the metre and rhyme. Moreover, the choice of Drake's lamentation over an indifferent woman evokes the Sonnets's own Dark Lady and a stricken poet-lover, struggling to process the disinterest of his

beloved. Didriksen's choice to use this particular song activates the form through its invocation of the context that sonnets are traditionally read in, offering us the choice to read Drake through Shakespeare, or Shakespeare through Drake. Drake's own deconstructed blazon of what constitutes a 'good girl' in his song is an opportunity to explore the ways in which the sonnet's form plays with male-authored constructions of femininity. Didriksen's own decision to elide the more problematic gender assumptions that underpin the R&B song – ameliorating Drake's own definitions of female behaviour as 'good' or 'nasty'[43] – to 'the woman I know', not only offers an opportunity to discuss the tropes of gender and sexuality in the Sonnets or the larger early modern canon of erotic verse, but also to build a discourse network that intersects formal early modern poetry with contemporary music culture.

Likewise, Mercutio fanon is predicated on a careful character study, drawing heavily on his penchant for lightness in the face of the seriousness of Benvolio or Tybalt, or his mockery of Romeo's 'too great oppression' (*Romeo and Juliet*, 1.4.24). Perhaps fanon might take a little too literally Mercutio's recommendation to 'be rough with love' (*Romeo and Juliet*, 1.4.27), but, nonetheless, it makes careful note of the formal stylistic elements that construct character and relationships. Moreover, social media interweave memes, gifs and Shakespeare jokes alongside more formally structured inquiries, such as Fandomsandfeminism's blog post that uses a close reading to speculate on the colour of Hermia's skin,[44] or Goodreads's 2,000-member-

---

[41] Erik Didriksen, 'Hotline bling,' *Pop Sonnets*, http://popson net.tumblr.com/post/132623847584/hotline-bling.

[42] See M. J. Kidnie, *Shakespeare and the Problem of Adaptation* (London, 2009).

[43] Drake, 'Hotline bling' (Cash Money Records, Inc., 2015).

[44] I am tentatively citing this discussion as located at http://fandomsandfeminism.tumblr.com/post/151983707749/so-can-we-talk-about-how-maybe-hermia-in-a. It may have originated with another Tumblr user, Ineffable Hufflepuff, but the clarity of origin points for Tumblr notes is obscure, at best, which again insists on a careful citational methodology.

strong Shakespeare Fan Group, which hosts monthly synchronous online reading groups to discuss various plays. The point at issue is that these discussions parallel academic output, and offer microcosms of the close reading that Shakespeare scholarship values, which is why we would do well not to dismiss fandom's more radical or flippant reading practices out of hand.

Fan-inspired or weird readings, speculative and creative criticisms are democratizing practices, but not because they adhere to the fallacy of universal access that digital culture promises but rarely delivers. Fan activism stems from a desire to use the subjective experience of literary reading and channel the enthusiasm for knowledge acquisition and the circulation of ideas into a public, 'real life' sphere.

Digital culture has already reorganized the parameters of fan activism to include academic discourse, and Shakespeare studies would benefit from networking scholarly work with the more explicitly subjective practices of fandom. A speculative critical practice that unlearns the 'traditional frames of critical-historical reference'[45] generates new processes of meaning that are shaped less by the 'slit-eyed armchair interpreter'[46] and more by the complex interplay of human and non-human agencies that shape what we call 'text'.

---

[45] Joy, *Weird*, 32.

[46] Harry Berger, *A Fury in the Words: Love and Embarrassment in Shakespeare's Venice* (New York, 2013), p. 2.

TITUS ANDRONICUS AND TRAPDOORS AT THE ROSE AND NEWINGTON BUTTS

MARK HUTCHINGS

The first playhouse constructed on the Bankside, and another, built a decade earlier about a mile south of London Bridge at Newington Butts, stand at opposite ends of the knowledge spectrum for theatre historians.[1] Three invaluable kinds of evidence exist for the Rose, erected by Philip Henslowe and John Cholmley in 1587: the *Diary* and associated documents held by Dulwich College; the archaeological site excavated in 1989; and printed texts of a number of the plays known to have been staged there.[2] But for the playhouse at Newington Butts, which may have been London's first purpose-built theatre, even its name, if it had one, has not survived.[3] Thanks to William Ingram and most recently Laurie Johnson, we now know rather more than we did, but it remains on the periphery of the playhouse landscape – not only geographically but quite literally – its relative obscurity in the historical record taken to reflect its apparent failure.[4] It may be that 'the tediousnes of the waie', as a Privy Council memorandum described it when an order instructing Strange's Men to play there rather than at the Rose was rescinded, and distance from the populated areas on which the Shoreditch and Bankside playhouses drew disadvantaged it, though Johnson challenges this traditional view.[5] We do know that this playhouse was active in 1594: even if it was out of use sometime before the end of the century, it operated for a not inconsiderable period, as

[1] Earlier versions of this article were presented at the Sederi conference in Oviedo in May 2014, the Henslowe Symposium at Shakespeare's Globe in June 2016, and at the University of Lisbon in December 2016. I would like to thank the organizers of these events and participants for their helpful comments – in particular, Grace Ioppolo, Julian Bowsher, Brian Vickers, Berta Cano Echevarría and Roger Clegg.

[2] For the documents and relevant recent scholarship, see *Henslowe's Diary*, ed. R. A. Foakes, 2nd edn (Cambridge, 2002), and R. A. Foakes, 'The discovery of the Rose Theatre: some implications', *Shakespeare Survey 43* (Cambridge, 1990), pp. 141–8; Christine Eccles, *The Rose Theatre* (London, 1990); Julian M. C. Bowsher, *The Rose Theatre: An Archaeological Discovery* (London, 1998); Julian M. C. Bowsher and Patricia Miller, *The Rose and the Globe – Playhouses of Tudor Bankside, Southwark: Excavations 1988–91* (London, 2009); Julian M. C. Bowsher, *Shakespeare's London Theatreland: Archaeology, History and Drama* (London, 2012); and Grace Ioppolo's Henslowe Digitalization Project, www.henslowe-alleyn.org.uk. Cholmley appears nowhere in the *Diary*; the most thorough examination of this figure is William Ingram's 'John Cholmley on the Bankside', *Early Theatre* 15.2 (2012), 43–65. On Cholmley's absence from the *Diary*, see Laurie Johnson, *Shakespeare's Lost Playhouse: Eleven Days at Newington Butts* (London, 2017), pp. 18–23.

[3] William Ingram, *The Purpose of Playing: The Beginnings of the Adult Professional Theater in Elizabethan London* (Ithaca and London, 1992), pp. 150, 152. In addition, see Laurie Johnson, 'The Two Names of Newington Butts', *Shakespeare Quarterly* (forthcoming).

[4] William Ingram has assembled all the known data in *The Purpose of Playing*, 150–81; see also Johnson, *Shakespeare's Lost Playhouse*, 46, who suggests that 'the venue was a converted interior space rather than an outdoor stage': the evidence for this conclusion is set out in Chapter 2.

[5] Cited in Edmund Chambers, *The Elizabethan Stage*, 4 vols. (Oxford, 1923), vol. 4, p. 313; the relevant Privy Council memorandum is probably from 1592: see *Henslowe Papers: Being Documents Supplementary to the Diary*, ed. W. W. Greg (London, 1907), p. 43. For a reappraisal, see Johnson, *Shakepeare's Lost Playhouse*, pp. 86–90.

Ingram shows.[6] Scholars have regarded the 1594 episode, when the newly formed Admiral's Men and Chamberlain's Men were based together there for a short time, as something of a puzzle. Yet the fact that *Titus Andronicus* was staged successively at the Rose and at Newington Butts may well be significant, given its particular staging requirements, which, this article will argue, were atypical. While it is sensible to conclude that '[w]e have no grounds for assuming that the Newington structure looked like the Theater or Curtain',[7] the other two playhouses constructed in the 1570s, there are grounds to suppose that it shared several features in common with the Rose.

Until recently, theatre historians have tended to assume that the playhouses between which companies moved, and upon which later impresarios drew for experience-based knowledge and inspiration when constructing their own venues, were in essence similar. The *frons scenae* may not have been universally flat, as apparently was the case at the Swan (at least according to the not unproblematic drawing discovered in the late nineteenth century): the Rose excavations revealed that its *frons* was angled. But most theatre historians concur in the view that playhouses featured a tiring house with a stage, onto which two flanking doors and a discovery space opened, while, above, an upper stage was accessible to actors and musicians, and, below, a trapdoor gave alternative access for ghosts and such and the introduction of elaborate stage properties.[8] Few would contest the validity of this schema, but the assumptions underpinning the last of these features are worth excavating further. The use of the trap in *Titus Andronicus* is unexceptional, according to the prevailing view that this facility was readily available as a staple component of purpose-built venues, and thus featured widely in performance. Yet this view is open to challenge, and in the wake of such a re-evaluation, the use of the trap in this play assumes a new significance.

The most famous scene in the entire corpus of English drama features the device. The graveyard scene in *Hamlet* resonates far beyond the theatre, serving as an icon of the 'Shakespearian' stage in the history of modern revivals, cinematic treatments and visual art.[9] But its (unconscious?) influence on theatre historians, over four centuries of theatrical and other forms of cultural production, is worth probing. Just how frequently was a trap used – or indeed available? This is a question as much about how scholars reconstruct the 'timbers' of theatre history as it is about the weighing of evidence. With the (possible) exception of the title-page illustration for Nathanial Richards's *Messalina* (1640), there is no surviving visual evidence for the existence of a trap.[10] The Arend van Buchell copy of a lost original sketch by Johannes de Witt does not feature one (the foreground of the Swan stage taken up by two figures and a bench).[11] The design for an indoor playhouse held in Worcester College, Oxford, details the flanking doors, central opening and upper stage but there is

[6] Ingram concludes that the playhouse was no longer extant by 1596 and may have been dismantled as early as the summer of 1594, for at this time the lords of the manor, the dean and chapter of Christ Church, Canterbury, decreed that the playhouse should be taken down; *The Purpose of Playing*, pp. 157, 176.

[7] Ingram, *The Purpose of Playing*, p. 180.

[8] The principal challenge to the assumption that playhouses provided – and plays required – a discovery space has been made by Tim Fitzpatrick; see his *Playwrights, Space, and Place in Early Modern Performance: Shakespeare and Company* (Farnham, 2011).

[9] See Alan R. Young, 'Eighteenth- and nineteenth-century visual representations of the graveyard scene in *Hamlet*', in *Stage Directions in 'Hamlet': New Essays and New Directions*, ed. Hardin L. Aasand (London, 2003), pp. 189–213.

[10] For the possibility, see Glynne Wickham, *Early English Stages*, 4 vols. (London, 1959–81), vol. 2, p. 88; R. A. Foakes, *Illustrations of the English Stage 1580–1642* (London, 1985), p. 81, is more cautious, and John H. Astington, 'The origins of the Roxana and Messalina illustrations', *Shakespeare Survey 43* (1990), pp. 149–69, argues that the title page is derivative and impressionistic, and thus has no independent authority as evidence of an actual theatre trap.

[11] R. A. Foakes expresses considerable scepticism about van Buchell's drawing skills, and consequently cautions against our relying on the sketch as evidence; see his 'Henslowe's Rose / Shakespeare's Globe', in *From Script to Stage in Early Modern England*, ed. Peter Holland and Stephen Orgel (Basingstoke, 2004), pp. 11–31.

no indication of a trap.[12] And perhaps most surprisingly and disappointingly for theatre historians, the surviving contracts for the Fortune (1600) and Hope (1614) playhouses provide scant information about the stages themselves: again, there is no mention of a trap.[13] Nonetheless, its existence is taken for granted, in part because the evidential trace has not been subjected to sustained analysis.[14]

One of the established narratives of the early modern English theatre depends on a sociological–theological model that interprets playhouse design as reflecting and articulating a stratified social hierarchy and shared religious belief system. The audience surrounding the stage was placed in what Andrew Gurr has described as a kind of 'vertical sociology', ranging from the poorer spectators, who stood, to the more wealthy, seated in the galleries, of which the lords' rooms were the most prestigious.[15] This socially demarcated auditory in turn saw in front of it (whatever its vantage point) another kind of vertical symbolism that neatly replicated the governing theological paradigm of the early modern world – heaven above, hell below, and humankind playing out their lives on the stage suspended in between. A well-known poem widely attributed (on not altogether secure grounds) to Sir Walter Ralegh neatly captures this conceit:

> What is *our* life? it is a play of passion
> what is *our* mirthe? the musicke of diuision
> Our mothers they the tyringe howses be
> wheare we are drest for times short tragedye
> Earthe is the stage, heauen the spectator is
> who dothe behould who heare dothe act amisse.
> The graues which keepe vs from the parching sunne
> are as drawne curtaynes till the play be done.[16]

But perhaps theatre historians have taken too literally – or interpreted too absolutely – the theological modelling as expressed in witty analogies such as this. Tiffany Stern, for example, remarks that 'the trap-door in the centre of the stage was the entrance from hell': a reasonable enough remark, on the surface, but prescriptive in its use of the definite article – '*the* entrance' implying that it was the sole entry point for characters so

condemned – and generalizing in its supposition that this device was common to all playhouses.[17] If it was, this has yet to be proven. Such a statement is based on an accretion of assumptions that ought to be re-evaluated in light of the actual evidence that has survived. Our knowledge of the trap rests on very slim grounds and a great deal of conjecture – poor foundations indeed for such a widely voiced belief.

Once we investigate further, a considerable gap opens up between assertion and grounds. For example, stage directions in surviving texts yield little direct evidence for the use of the trap. According to Alan C. Dessen and Leslie Thomson, a mere three instances indicate unambiguously when a trap was employed.[18] They cite rather more examples that refer to fictional places in the play-world where a trap (if available) could

---

[12] Long considered to be associated with Inigo Jones, this design is now thought to postdate 1642. On this re-dating, see Gordon Higgott's unpublished paper, 'Two theatre designs by Jon Webb in 1660', cited in Francis Teague, 'The Phoenix and the Cockpit-in-Court playhouses', in *The Oxford Handbook of Early Modern Theatre*, ed. Richard Dutton (Oxford, 2009), pp. 240–59; p. 244.

[13] For the respective documents see, Foakes, ed., *Henslowe's Diary*, pp. 306–10, and Greg, ed., *Henslowe Papers*, pp. 19–22.

[14] Mariko Ichikawa devotes a chapter to each of the other areas of the stage in *Shakespearean Entrances* (Basingstoke, 2002), but not to the trap; in Ichikawa, *The Shakespearean Stage Space* (Cambridge, 2013), the device is discussed briefly in a chapter on the logistical issues arising from the disposal of corpses, pp. 141–4.

[15] See Andrew Gurr, 'Traps and discoveries at the Globe', *Proceedings of the British Academy 94* (Oxford, 1997), pp. 85–101; p. 101.

[16] There are a number of versions of the poem; this is the text that appears in the Marsh Manuscript, held in Dublin, and is quoted in Peter Stallybrass, 'Afterword', in *Renaissance Paratexts*, ed. Helen Smith and Louise Wilson (Cambridge, 2011), pp. 204–19. Stallybrass challenges the attribution, based on the inclusion of 'Rawley' at the head of the transcription, which is omitted here (pp. 214–18).

[17] Tiffany Stern, *Making Shakespeare: From Stage to Page* (London, 2004), p. 25.

[18] Alan C. Dessen and Leslie Thomson, *A Dictionary of Stage Directions in English Drama* (Cambridge, 1999), p. 235. These are: the MS of *Believe As You List*; *The Fatal Contract*; and *Queen's Exchange* – the last of which is less secure than the other two.

have come into play – for example, where a 'cave', 'grave', 'tomb', or 'vault' features, as we infer in *Titus Andronicus* and *Hamlet*. In addition, stage directions sometimes signal the position or movement of a character or stage property, such as in the descriptors 'arise', 'below', and 'beneath'; however, none of these offers conclusive proof, and often there are plausible alternative possibilities available, such as the central opening. This is a stark indication of the problem, the lack of *conclusive* evidence on a scale that would justify theatre historians in their confidence that the trap was an integral feature of London playmaking. Thus, we encounter a chicken-and-egg problem. If theatre-builders did go to the trouble of constructing traps, this effort and expense was surely embarked upon because of anticipated need based on existing practice and expectation of future use. So scholars are left with a choice: to assume that this second group of stage directions *does* indicate the presence and use of a trap, a supposition that sustains, if only in general terms, the view that this device was widely – if not necessarily universally – available; or to doubt that the trap was so used, except in specific instances, and yet at the same time acknowledge that it was a staple feature of purpose-built and converted playhouses. But, even with the first option, we find that use was rather low. T. J. King's survey suggests that, of the surviving plays composed between 1599 and 1642, a mere forty-two plays required the trap – a figure that might be revised downwards significantly if the second option is taken, since King does not discriminate between the kinds of evidence documented in Dessen and Thomson's survey.[19] Another example offers a useful snapshot of the problem. Half a century ago, Glynne Wickham pointed out that 'in none of Marlowe's plays do any stage-directions exist authorizing us to assume the existence of a stage-trap at floor level'.[20] And yet scholars habitually assume that the devils who visit Faustus do so via the trap, and that it is there that Barabas meets his end.[21] Such statements about apparent practice reinforce the belief that such a device was available and employed for specific purposes. But Leslie Thomson is surely right in

finding another solution to explain how this kind of business could be staged: 'while none of the stage directions we can safely attribute to Marlowe requires the stage trap, he often made repeated use of the tiring-house wall and its openings'.[22] Part of the problem lies in our recognition of the Senecan influence on late sixteenth-century drama and the stage logic that implies a hellish 'underworld' beneath the stage;[23] and yet few critics would argue that the trap was used for supernatural events on *every* occasion. Even the question of how the entrances of the Ghost of King Hamlet were staged provokes debate, and it is surely unlikely that the eleven ghosts who invade Richard III's dreams on the eve of the Battle of Bosworth do so via the trap.[24] Here, in a nutshell, we have the central point of tension: the clash between the theological model on the one hand and the practicalities of stagecraft on the other. The bigger question is whether the use of a trap was a matter of choice at all.

If we make a counter-assumption and suppose that not all playhouses had traps, that the trap was not necessarily a staple feature – if we remind ourselves, too, that the recent archaeological work on early modern London's theatres suggests difference rather than sameness – it may prove

---

[19] T. J. King, *Shakespearean Staging, 1599–1642* (Cambridge, MA, 1971), pp. 79–96.

[20] Glynne Wickham, '"Exeunt to the cave": notes on the staging of Marlowe's plays', *The Tulane Drama Review* 8.4 (1964), 184–94; p. 189.

[21] For a conjectural exploration of how the *dénouement* in *The Jew of Malta* was staged, see Mark Hutchings, 'Barabas's Fall', *Theatre Notebook* 69.1 (2015), pp. 2–16.

[22] Leslie Thomson, 'Marlowe's staging of meaning', *Medieval and Renaissance Drama in England* 18 (2005), 19–36; p. 21.

[23] See Andrew J. Power, 'What the hell is under the stage? Trapdoor use in the English Senecan tradition', *English* 60 (2011), 276–96.

[24] On the ghost's entrances and exits in *Hamlet*, see Stanley Wells, 'Staging Shakespeare's Ghosts', in *The Arts of Performance in Elizabethan and Early Stuart Drama: Essays for George Hunter*, ed. Murray Biggs *et al.* (Edinburgh, 1991), pp. 50–69, and Gurr, 'Traps and discoveries', pp. 96–9; Wells follows recent critics in arguing against the use of the trap for the procession of ghosts on the eve of the Battle of Bosworth in *Richard III*.

useful to examine afresh instances where there *is* firm evidence of its use. In this way, what appears to be a familiar aspect of playmaking takes on a new significance. *Hamlet* has long been taken to 'prove' that the Globe had a trap, and it is difficult to imagine how the graveyard scene could have been performed without such a device – though actors were adept at fitting their plays to a range of conditions when they went into the country or played at court.[25] It is similarly difficult to conceive how the sequential scenes in *Titus Andronicus* where Bassianus's body is thrown into the 'pit' and Quintus and Martius successively fall into it could have been staged using any other part of the stage, or how the play could work without this business.[26] If such use was exceptional, relative to the varying evidence in the surviving corpus, then perhaps the repertorial trace this play has left may be significant. In other words, matching a play which must have required a trap to a playhouse or playhouses where it is known it was performed may thus lead to reasonable conclusions about the facilities available at such venues – facilities, in the case of the trap, that very possibly were less common than is conventionally supposed. This, it will be proposed, is the case with *Titus Androncius* in 1594.

Whether the play was relatively old in 1594, dating from the late 1580s as is often argued, or comparatively recent, it will be maintained here that Q1 (1594) probably best represents (or at least approximates to) the text that was staged that year: if an earlier date in the range *c.* 1588–94 is preferred, and if it is supposed that Q1 represents that performance trajectory, then it is a nice (further) question as to what the text might lead us to deduce about the playhouse(s) it was performed at before it came to the Rose; but in the absence of new, concrete evidence about this earlier period we could do no more than speculate.[27] What we do know is that. Henslowe's *Diary* tells us that Shakespeare and Peele's play was staged on several occasions in 1594, initially at the Rose and subsequently at Newington Butts.[28] Henslowe first marks the appearance of *Titus Andronicus* in January 1594, where it appears under the colours of Sussex's Men, who enjoyed a brief sojourn at the Bankside playhouse between 27 December 1593 and 6 February 1594. Like other theatres, the Rose had been closed for most of 1593 due to plague. The first company Henslowe identifies as operating there, Strange's Men, had enjoyed a long run in 1592, but then had subsequently gone to the country while London's playhouses remained closed. When Henslowe was permitted to reopen, it was the Sussex's who benefitted from the Strange's absence, until another visitation of the plague shut the Rose once more. According to the title page of the quarto published that year, the play seems to have passed through the hands of Derby's Men (as Strange's had become when Ferdinando Stanley, Lord Strange, became the fifth earl of Derby in September 1593) and Pembroke's Men before reaching Sussex's; what this may tell us about its staging history prior to this, the earliest record, has been a matter for debate.[29] Henslowe marks it as 'ne', which is

---

[25] Both Q1 and F (but not Q2) indicate that Laertes leaps into the grave; only Q1 gives 'Hamlet leapes in after Lertes', but, as G. R. Hibbard points out, further support is evidenced in an anonymous elegy for Richard Burbage which includes the line, 'Oft have I seen him leap into the grave.' See *Hamlet*, ed. G. R. Hibberd (Oxford, 1987), p. 15. The fullest discussion of this crux is S. P. Zitner, 'Four feet in the grave: some stage directions in Hamlet, V.i', *Text* 2 (1985), 139–48. For a conjectural staging of the scene, see Andrew Gurr and Mariko Ichikawa, *Staging in Shakespeare's Theatres* (Oxford, 2000), p. 153.

[26] On the staging of this scene, see Alan C. Dessen, 'Two falls and a trap: Shakespeare and the spectacles of realism', *English Literary Renaissance* 5 (1975), 291–307.

[27] Alan Hughes, ed., *Titus Andronicus* rev. edn (Cambridge, 2006), 6, judiciously weighs the evidence and inclines to a date of around 1588, principally on the grounds of the play's similarities to the plays of Marlowe and Kyd. Eugene M. Waith, ed., *Titus Andronicus* (Oxford, 1984), 20, concludes that the play was 'first perfomed in the years 1590–2, and was revised for the first recorded performance [in Henslowe's *Diary*] in January 1594'. Jonathan Bate, ed., *Titus Andronicus* (London, 1995), 78, argues that the play 'was written in late 1593 and first performed in January 1594'.

[28] See Foakes, ed., *Henslowe's Diary*, pp. 21–2.

[29] See Scott McMillin, 'Sussex's Men in 1594: the evidence of *Titus Andronicus* and *The Jew of Malta*', *Theatre Survey* 32 (1991), 214–23; *Titus Andronicus*, ed. Jonathan Bate (London, 1995), pp. 69–79; and Martin Wiggins in association with

taken to indicate that it was new in 1594 or that it was 'new' to the Rose.[30] At any rate, Sussex's put it on three times during their run of thirty performances, using a total of thirteen titles, as follows:

Ne – Rd at titus & ondronicus the 23 of Jenewary [1594] ... iij[s] viij s
    Rd at titus & ondronicus the 28 of Jeneway [1594] ... xxxx[s]
    Rd at tittus & ondronicus the 6 of febery 1593 [sic] ...... xxxx[s][31]

As Jonathan Bate conjectures, '[i]t must have taken some preparation, for it was not until four weeks of the season had passed that Henslowe recorded' the first entry for the play, the twenty-fifth of the troupe's run;[32] whether or not this preparation was related to its complex stagecraft, this, it will be argued, was a factor in its next appearance in the *Diary*. Following further closure due to plague deaths, Sussex's then combined with the Queen's Men, 'begininge at easter', to give eight performances (1–8 April), but *Titus Andronicus* did not feature, perhaps by design or because the run was cut short; nor was it staged when the newly constituted Admiral's Men first played at the Rose for a mere three days (which also suggests curtailment) in mid-May. But, in the next, rather puzzling, sequence, since it pertains not to the Rose at all and implies some sort of collaborative arrangement between the Admiral's Men and the Chamberlain's Men, Henslowe records two entries for the play (out of a total of ten) at Newington Butts. The puzzle is that we know of no other link between Henslowe and this playhouse. At this point, Henslowe introduces a new form of notation he would carry forward into the subsequent Rose entries; spanning the period 3–13 June, the relevant entries are as follows:

5 of June 1594   Rd at andronicous .... xij s
12 of June 1594   Rd at andronicous .... vij s

Theatre historians are sceptical of the idea that these two newly formed companies *performed* together, and the identity/ownership of the plays entered may support this.[33] It seems that, whatever the nature of the arrangement, each troupe contributed plays which were presumably fresh from their recent scheduling in the respective repertories. The full sequence runs:

3 of June 1594   Rd at heaster & asheweros .... viij s
4 of June 1594   Rd at the Jewe of malta ....x s
5 of June 1594   Rd at andronicous .... xij s
6 of June 1594   Rd at cvtlacke .... xj s
8 of June 1594 ne – Rd at bellendon .... x .... xvij s
9 of June 1594   Rd at hamlet .... viij s
10 of June 1594   Rd at heaster .... v s
11 of June 1594   Rd at the tamynge of A shrowe .... ix s
12 of June 1594   Rd at andronicous ....vij s
13 of June 1594   Rd at the Jewe ....iiij s[34]

(A horizontal line divides this sequence from the next entry, beginning two days later, which theatre historians agree indicates that at this point the Admiral's Men returned to the Rose.) *Titus Andronicus*, *The Jew of Malta*, 'cvtlacke', and 'bellendon' were clearly 'Rose plays': the two extant plays had been staged there, Shakespeare and Peele's by Sussex's, and Marlowe's by all the company configurations known to have performed for Henslowe up to this date (Strange's, Sussex's, Queen's and Sussex's, and Admiral's); 'cvtlacke' had been performed by the Admiral's at the Rose on 16 May 1594 (Henslowe does not mark it 'ne', which suggests it was an old play that had previously been staged prior to the entry-keeping that began on 19 February 1592) and it would be the second play put on at the Rose when the Admiral's returned there following this sojourn at Newington Butts, 'bellendon' being the first.

Catherine Richardson, *British Drama 1533–1642: A Catalogue. Volume 3, 1590–97* (Oxford, 2013), p. 180.

[30] For the first possibility, see Bate, ed., *Titus Andronicus*, 78; for the second, see Hughes, ed., *Titus Andronicus*, 1–6.

[31] Foakes, ed., *Henslowe's Diary*, pp. 20–1.

[32] Bate, ed., *Titus Andronicus*; all subsequent references to the play are to this edition.

[33] See, for example, Carol Chillington Rutter, *Documents of the Rose Playhouse*, 2nd edn (Manchester, 1999), p. 82, who remarks, 'Neither company would have been happy with the arrangement.' However, in *Shakespare's Lost Playhouse*, Laurie Johnson argues that the choice of plays was thematically consonant with a collaborative enterprise, the Admiral's 'cvtlacke' and Chamberlain's 'hamlet'. for example, sharing complementary subject matter; see especially 169–90.

[34] Foakes, ed., *Henslowe's Diary*, pp.21–22; the 'x' in middle of the entry for 8 June has not been explained.

Together with *The Jew of Malta*, these two lost plays would feature frequently in their repertory for the remainder of the year; since one of these plays is marked 'ne', it is likely it had been in rehearsal at the Rose immediately prior to the company's departure south to Newington. Of the remaining plays, given that they do not feature elsewhere in the *Diary*, scholars confidently ascribe them to the Chamberlain's Men: the lost 'hamlet', a precursor to Shakespeare's extant play of that name; *The Taming of a Shrew* (also a possible influence on, or derivative of, Shakespeare's play); and 'heaster & asheweros', the only play this company put on for a second time – unless, of course, they had some involvement in the staging of *Titus Andronicus*, which would follow them to the Theatre.[35]

Shakespeare and Peele's play disrupts this neat division between Admiral's and Chamberlain's offerings and may well complicate our reading of this curious episode, specifically the nature of the inter-company collaboration. Carol Chillington Rutter points out that it might be considered unlikely that a 'ne[w]' play, 'bellendon', was offered by a combination of actors from both troupes when only a week later the Admiral's would perform it at the Rose;[36] yet, similarly, we ought to caution against automatically allocating *Titus Andronicus* to the Chamberlain's Men at this juncture on the grounds that it would migrate with them to the Theatre: this play, after all, had appeared at the Rose in February. However, *who* staged the play in June 1594 – perhaps including members of the Sussex's Men behind its production at the Rose four months previously (particularly if they had joined the Chamberlain's Men in the interim)[37] – is less important here than what this performance record might suggest about the play's staging requirements, and hence the facilities available at these playhouses.

Titus Andronicus calls for sophisticated staging resources. In addition to a trap, it requires an upper playing area and three doors.[38] Of course, not all of these facilities were available outside London, when companies toured, in which case adjustments must have been made. In 1596, when

the play was staged at a private house in Rutland (company unknown), presumably the action involving the trap and the upper stage was modified accordingly, though quite how such integral action was carried out brings with it its own questions, and we know nothing for certain about the resources available on that occasion.[39] But on the London stages for which plays were principally designed and realized, it is logical to assume that there was *some* correlation between the plays and the resources available, a correlation that the printed texts, albeit imperfectly and incompletely, record. The extent to which playwrights were conscious of writing for specific venues remains a matter of debate, and raises once again the thorny issue of theatre design and whether the earliest playhouses were similar or significantly distinctive in terms of playmaking conditions and staging

---

[35] On these lost plays, see the relevant entries in the *Lost Plays Database*, www.lostplays.org, ed. Roslyn L. Knutson, David McInnis and Matthew Steggle (University of Melbourne, 2009). The fullest discussion of this sequence to date is in Johnson, *Shakespeare's Lost Playhouse*, 135–204.

[36] Rutter, *Documents of the Rose Playhouse*, p. 83.

[37] Andrew Gurr, *The Shakespearian Playing Companies* (Oxford, 1996), p. 174, notes that 'some of [Sussex's Men] may have joined the new Chamberlain's Men'. This would go some way to explaining the absence of *Titus Andronicus* from the Rose stage when Sussex's subsequently combined with Queen's.

[38] See G. Harold Metz, 'The early staging of *Titus Andronicus*', *Shakespeare Studies* 14 (1981), 99–109, and 'Stage history of *Titus Andronicus*', *Shakespeare Quarterly* 28 (1977), 154–69. Tim Fitzpatrick, *Playwrights, Space, and Place in Early Modern Performance*, pp. 282–3, challenges the view that the play requires three doors, arguing that, since the opening stage direction in Q1 does not specify that Saturninus and Bassianus enter by separate doors, only one door is needed, rather than two as maintained by Mariko Ichikawa, *Shakespearean Entrances* (Basingstoke, 2002), p. 79. However, Fitzpatrick does not consider the relevance of the staging of the tomb to this question later in the scene – for which, see Metz, 'The early staging of *Titus Andronicus*', p. 104.

[39] The relevant documentary material was uncovered by Gustav Ungerer; see his 'An unrecorded Elizabethan performance of *Titus Andronicus*', *Shakespeare Survey* 14 (Cambridge, 1961), pp. 102–9.

options.[40] This question is further complicated by the fact that we know comparatively little about company–playhouse affiliation prior to 1592; moreover, if our understanding of the characteristics of purpose-built theatres is largely speculative, we know even less about the facilities at the four London inns where plays were staged during this period.[41] Quite what the impenetrably vague 'shewed upon Stages in the Citie of London' proclaimed on the 1590 octavo title page of the *Tamburlaine* plays actually means is indicative of the problems theatre historians face. Scholars tend to assume that the 1594 reorganization meant that, in the second half of the 1590s, (some) playwrights composed with the Rose or Theatre (and, after 1599, the Globe) respectively in mind, but before that date our understanding of the relationship between play composition and theatre space is largely speculative. Moreover, those playwrights who eked out a living by selling their work to more than one company must have recognized the need to be flexible rather than specific in their stagecraft.

Where surviving evidence makes it possible to match a play to a venue or venues, however, specific elements of the play – as indicated in the earliest witness – invite particular consideration. If the stage directions of Q1, published in the year with which this discussion is principally concerned, lead us to conclude that a trap (as well as upper stage and probably a discovery space) was essential for the play to work – and *perhaps* that it was specifically scripted with these stage spaces envisaged – then we may draw some conclusions about the Rose stage in 1594 and the playhouse at Newington Butts. Given the reevaluation proposed here that reads firm evidence of trapdoor use as exceptional rather than commonplace, positing the existence of a trap at these venues takes on a new importance. We do not know when the two newly constituted companies learned they were to play at Newington Butts, but we may assume that, the choice of repertory being their own (there is no evidence to the contrary), they selected plays they could mount readily. Marlowe's play was a mainstay at the Rose, and perhaps an obvious

choice – not least because it was a popular draw – and *Titus Andronicus* would surely not have been nominated had the staging resources at Newington Butts presented any kind of logistical challenge. The two lost Admiral's plays, 'cvtlacke' and 'bellendon', similarly fall into that category; we may assume that the same logic obtained for the Chamberlain's contributions, 'heaster & asheweros', 'hamlet', and *The Taming of a Shrew*, though for this we must rely on inference rather than evidence.

From this, the following may be proposed. In 1594, a trap (as well as an upper stage, together with two and very probably three doors) was available at both the Rose and the Newington Butts playhouses. If 'hamlet' required such a device, as Shakespeare's *Hamlet* does – and it has been argued that the later allusion to Richard Burbage as Hamlet leaping into the 'grave' after Laertes (stage business recorded in Q1 but not Q2 or F) is in fact to the lost play, rather than to the later extant *Hamlet* – then we have further support for there being a trap available at Newington Butts.[42] An unanswerable question is when such a device might have been installed: at the outset or later; but we can speculate that Henslowe and Cholmley may not have included a trap at the Rose in 1587.[43] We do know that, in spring 1592,

---

[40] The uncovering of the archaeological remains of the Rose and Globe in 1989, and more recently Museum of London Archaeology digs at the sites of the Hope and Curtain, provide firm evidence that stage construction and design did not conform to a particular model, as had long been assumed. This development gives renewed impetus to repertory-focused studies, especially where, as in the present article, specific plays can be mapped on to particular performance spaces.

[41] On the importance of recognizing the role played by London's inns, see David Kathman, 'Inn-yard playhouses', in *The Oxford Handbook of Early Modern Theatre*, pp. 153–67.

[42] See John C. Meagher, 'The stage directions, overt and covert, of *Hamlet* 5.1', in Aasand, ed., *Stage Directions in 'Hamlet'*, pp. 140–57; pp. 146–9.

[43] For an alternative view, arguing that the Rose had a trap facility from 1587, see Andrew Gurr, 'The Rose repertory: what the plays might tell us about the stage', in *New Issues in*

Henslowe (Cholmley having disappeared from the record) recorded making renovations to the Rose, and three years later made further alterations. In the second of these works, the *Diary* is quite specific, recording for example 'Itm pd for carpenters work & mackinge the / throne In the heauens the 4 of June 1595'.[44] This certainly indicates a technological development, presumably invested in because of a perceived need, as perhaps expressed by the actors. The 1989 excavations shed considerable light on the *Diary*'s otherwise rather opaque itemizing, headed 'A note of suche carges as I haue layd owt a bowte / my playe howsse in the yeare of o^r lord 1592'.[45] Until the archaeology revealed that Henslowe had enlarged the Rose, increasing audience capacity in the yard and of necessity moving the stage back, while marginally increasing its size, the *Diary* information was considered too general to allow specific conclusions to be drawn. Matching the 'story' told by the archaeology to the payments in the *Diary* revealed that the alternations were far from cosmetic. Henslowe paid out a total of £108: as Carol Chillington Rutter points out, this amounted to a quarter of the total cost of the Fortune he would build at the end of the decade.[46] Yet audience capacity (and Henslowe's share in receipts) did not increase significantly: given that the stage was moved and rebuilt, might it be that the original Rose did not have a trap, but that one was installed in 1591–2,[47] and, like the 'throne In the heauens' introduced three years later, was a sign that Henslowe knew his playhouse needed considerable modernizing, to the extent that in 1600 (and almost certainly before) he reached the conclusion that a wholly new theatre was required?[48]

The performance records Henslowe began to keep in 1592 would appear to have coincided with or followed closely on the heels of the completion of the renovations. The scheduling of *Titus Andronicus* in January and February 1594 is the best evidence we have that a trap was available at the Rose at this time, although, because of the absence of pre-1592 records, we cannot be certain that the facility was a recent innovation. That the Strange's Men repertory featured a distinctive (though not necessarily unique) penchant for staging pyrotechnics, as Lawrence Manley has shown, might point in the direction of a trap, but in fact only in the play *Looking Glass for London and England* (performed on four occasions during the company's interrupted run, the first on 8 March) is there a *possible* indication that a trap featured: '*a flame of fire appeareth from beneath and RADAGON is swallowed*',[49] which Dessen and Thomson gloss, reasonably enough, as signifying 'under the stage';[50] perhaps more persuasive, from the same play, is '*The Magi with their rods beat the ground, and from under the same riseth a brave arbor*'.[51] The absence of more qualitative, as well as quantitative, evidence is not evidence of absence, of course, and if Henslowe did introduce a trap to the Rose stage by 1592, we might reasonably expect that playwrights and actors made use of it; whether the printed texts of the plays that survive from this decade register that is a difficult question: the earliest quarto of *Titus Andronicus* may be the exception that proves the rule. Of the Strange's Men's plays staged at the Rose in 1592–3 that survive, the evidence they offer is not helpful either way. *Friar Bacon, The Battle of Alcazar* ['Mully Molocco'?], *Orlando Furioso, The Jew of Malta, 1*

---

the *Reconstruction of Shakespeare's Theatre*, ed. Franklin J. Hildy (New York, 1990), pp. 119–34; pp. 129–32.

[44] Foakes, ed., *Henslowe's Diary*, p. 7.

[45] Foakes, ed., *Henslowe's Diary*, p. 9; for the entire list of costs of labour and materials, see pp. 9–13.

[46] Rutter, *Documents of the Rose Playhouse*, p. xiii.

[47] Neil Carson, *A Companion to Henslowe's Diary* (Cambridge, 1988), p. 15, considers that the alterations were completed before the Strange's Men are recorded playing at the Rose in February 1592: the 'receipts are for large bills which were probably presented some months after the work was completed'.

[48] As Andrew Gurr points out, 'a possible redesign of the stage' is one explanation for the 1592 changes: 'Why else choose that end of the polygon for the rebuilding?' See his 'The Rose repertory', p. 119.

[49] Lawrence Manley, 'Playing with fire: immolation in the repertory of Strange's Men', *Early Theatre* 4 (2001), 115–29; *Looking Glass for London and England*, 3.2.166, quoted in Manley, p. 117.

[50] Dessen and Thomson, *A Dictionary of Stage Directions*, p. 29.

[51] Cited in Dessen and Thomson, *A Dictionary of Stage Directions*, p. 105.

Henry VI, The Spanish Tragedy, The Massacre at Paris ['Gyves'?], A Knack to Know a Knave, and John of Bordeaux: none of them required a trap – but, perhaps, if a trap had been installed by 1592, and there was occasion for it, it was used when these plays were revived.[52]

Yet in the absence of secure evidence, we can draw on the surviving repertorial record. If Titus Andronicus could not have been staged at the Rose without a trap, it surely would not have been chosen for the Newington Butts repertory had not that playhouse also had such a facility.[53] But if the Rose in 1594 offered the facilities needed to put Shakespeare and Peele's play on – including an upper stage and probably a discovery space – then presumably so too did the theatre at Newington Butts. This neglected playhouse may therefore have been rather more sophisticated than is sometimes assumed, and, if so, this may partly explain why these two newly established companies elected to perform there in June 1594, if it was their choice to make. Although theatre historians have been reluctant to countenance the possibility of a collaboration between the Chamberlain's and Admiral's Men – particularly when the Privy Council's reorganization of the London companies has been read as the official endorsement of a 'duopoly' that would tidy up a messy entertainment environment – this episode provides evidence of precisely such a scenario, muddily opaque though it is. To recap: actors who may have been involved in the production of Titus Andronicus at the Rose in January and February 1594 may have contributed to its production at the Newington Butts performances four months later. But, more significantly, since Shakespeare and Peele's play required a trap, as the 1594 quarto and subsequent quarto and folio texts indicate, it is contended that both playhouses must have had one in 1594.

If the installation of a trap was part of Henslowe's plan in 1591–2, which he augmented in 1595 with a device in the heavens, then this raises several questions about theatre technology and construction at this time. The archaeology and Diary show that Henslowe drastically remodelled his

playhouse, and we know that in 1600 he embarked on a new venture with the Fortune, the Rose's long-term replacement. Might this suggest that the Rose – about which we know the most, from an archaeological/historical perspective – was a poor relation of the already-established theatres in Shoreditch and at Newington, though it was built a decade later? We know now that the Rose was small, compared to the Globe, and Henslowe seems to have identified this as a problem – the Fortune contract stipulating that the contracted carpenter, Peter Street, follow the Globe design in essentials; and we know that, only a few years after constructing it, Henslowe thought it wise to make rather drastic changes, which nevertheless in 1595 were apparently deemed insufficient for his (and the Admiral's Men's) purposes, since further alterations still were made. We know little about the Newington Butts theatre, but if we cannot assume that it was similar to the Shoreditch playhouses the Curtain and the Theatre, we might venture that it was at least equivalent in facilities and appeal to the Rose, despite the theatre narrative its obscurity has engendered. Although commentators have posited a model of 'progression' in theatre design, 'a sequence of development, in which old forms and construction methods were adapted, new elements prototyped and refined',[54] we ought not to assume that the Rose was an

---

[52] Queries over attributions are indicated in brackets.

[53] While the play requires a trap for the pit scene, it may also have been used for the tomb of the Andronici – as, for example, Power assumes; 'What the hell is under the stage?', p. 294. However, it is also possible the discovery space was used. It is difficult to see how the trap could be used as 'the bloody hole in which Lavinia is raped', as Tiffany Stern asserts in Making Shakespeare, p. 25 (quoted in Power, 'What the hell is under the stage?', p. 277). There is no textual evidence to support this view: the rape takes place offstage – at the same time, as it were, as Quintus and then Martius fall into the pit into which Bassianus's body has been thrown at 2.3.186 ('This is the hole where Aaron bid us hide him').

[54] Jon Greenfield, 'Reconstructing the Rose: development of the playhouse building between 1587 and 1592', Shakespeare Survey 60 (Cambridge, 2007), pp. 23–35; p. 23. For a divergent reading of the archaeological evidence, see

improvement on playhouses constructed a decade earlier. Henslowe recognized its shortcomings, in terms of both audience capacity (and hence revenue) and acting facilities. Though much more celebrated and documented than the Newington Butts playhouse, the Rose may originally have been inferior to it: for whatever reason, it may be that Henslowe (and Cholmley, at the outset) not only were unable to improve on the 'first wave' of construction of permanent theatres in 1576–7 but in fact erected an inferior playing space.

Much more work is needed on the trap in early modern playhouses, and what this may tell us about both construction and use, and the relationship between these elements. It is convenient to speak in the singular, as if all traps were the same. How such assumptions have hamstrung theatre historians is beyond the scope of this article, but it is worth considering that, unlike other forms of entry/exit, the trap facility may have varied across the theatre landscape – in both form and function. Ironically, in the light of the common assumption, identified in this article, that the trap was common to most or all playhouses, analysis of the Rose archaeology has cast some doubt on whether less than 4 feet of headroom under the new, post-1592 stage was sufficient for actors to access the stage through a trap.[55] But perhaps this view should be revisited. In point of fact, *Titus Andronicus* does not require movement between the trap and tiring house – the principal objection, it seems, to the feasibility of a trap when there is apparently little under-stage space: Quintius and Martius are hauled out of the 'pit' into which they have fallen and on to the stage, according to Saturninus's order, and it is surely the case that Bassanius's body is brought up from the trap and removed from the stage for burial;[56] it remains a matter of conjecture whether the trap

was also used for the tomb – rather than, say, the discovery space. But, given the apparently low frequency with which traps were used, perhaps we ought not to lay so much emphasis on the seeming difficulty of accessing the trap from the tiring house. And as we ponder that 'there is much evidence to suggest that the playhouses were significantly different from one another',[57] and even when 'similar' and *not* the 'same', we may find that our modelling of theatre characteristics requires nuance rather than categorical certainty. The example of *Titus Andronicus* suggests that the stage architecture at Newington Butts – trap, upper stage, and probably three entrances – was sufficiently similar to that at the Rose (and the Theatre and perhaps Curtain also) to make the plays selected by the Admiral's Men and Chamberlain's Men viable; but this does not mean that in both playhouses the traps, for example, were identical, or indeed used in the same way. At any rate, on the evidence of the repertory scheduling of *Titus Andronicus* in June 1594, the Newington Butts playhouse was no less sophisticated than the Rose, and may have been superior to it; it is by chance that so little information about it has survived, rather than a value judgement that confirms the comparative significance of the richly documented Rose and the deserved obscurity of a playhouse that lasted at least as long as Henslowe's first venture.

Julian M. C. Bowsher, 'The Rose and its stages', *Shakespeare Survey 60* (Cambridge, 2007), pp. 36–48.

[55] Rutter, *Documents of the Rose Playhouse*, p. xxii n.; Rutter cites Bowsher, *The Rose Theatre*, p. 61.

[56] See Bate, ed., *Titus Andronicus*: 'Sirs, drag them from the pit unto the prison' (2.3.283).

[57] Greenfield, 'Reconstructing the Rose', p. 25.

SHAKESPEARE'S BEWITCHING LINE

ROBERT STAGG

In the prefatory material to the First Folio (1623), Ben Jonson praised Shakespeare with a phrase too fitting to be fitting. Shakespeare's lines, he wrote, were 'richly spun, and woven so fit' (l. 49).[1] This makes Shakespeare into, or out to be, a labourer warping and wefting in a tapestry workshop – a description perhaps too artisanal and banal for an encomium (of sorts). Jonson moves over his own verse line to arrive at a more evocative criticism: that Shakespeare writes a 'living line' (59), transforming 'spun' from the tedious routines of a weaver into the alacritous activity of a spider or bug. The textile Shakespeare, weaving 'so fit', becomes a textual Shakespeare. Jonson's line even picks up a thread from Shakespeare's, since in *Henry VIII, or All is True* (1613) the Cardinal Wolsey thrives in 'his self-drawing web' (1.1.63), forever creating the contours of his own power and abundance, at once an act of imaginative range and limitation.

Hugh Holland connected Shakespeare's 'lines' with 'life' in another poem for the Folio, 'Upon the Lines and Life of the Famous Scenic Poet, Master William Shakespeare' concluding 'For though his line of life went soon about, / The life yet of his lines shall never out' (lines 13–14). In some respects, this language is conventional. Poems (or verse) are referred to as 'lines' throughout the English Renaissance and beyond. Like Jonson's poem, Holland's can be an endearing tribute to Shakespeare's enduring work (or, like Jonson's poem, it can have a sharper edge). Yet it also hints at an undead Shakespeare who cannot or will not perish because, somehow, of his prosodic aptitude. It is as though the versification of Shakespeare's lines will keep him alive, fending off death with supernatural tenacity; the lines assume an apotropaic quality rather than simply shuttling information from one location to another. These verse lines become strange participants in their meaning.

When Macbeth asks, 'Is this a dagger which I see before me, / The handle toward my hand? Come, let me clutch thee' (2.1.33–4), the relationship between the dagger, Macbeth's hand and Macbeth's verse lines is thickly imbricated. Does Macbeth reach for the dagger and the verse line reach with him, much as the '*hand*le' of the dagger and the 'hand' of Macbeth seem snugly, dangerously identical? Or is it the other way around: does the verse line reach Macbeth's hand out for him? Is the dagger a metaphor for the verse line, part of Wallace Stevens's 'strange rhetoric' of analogy between 'nature and the imagination'?[2] Actors often encounter the final two syllables of the line as extraneously physical, pushing at the edge of the pentameter with the possibility of a feminine ending. Both Ian McKellen (1978–9) and Patrick Stewart (2010) only properly reached for the dagger on the words 'clutch thee', taking this as

---

[1] All references to prefatory material in the First Folio correspond to *The Norton Facsimile of the First Folio of Shakespeare*, ed. Charlton Hinman and Peter W. M. Blayney, 2nd edn (New York, 1996).
[2] Wallace Stevens, 'Effects of analogy', in *The Necessary Angel: Essays on Reality and the Imagination* (London, 1960), pp. 107–30; p. 118.

Shakespeare's imperative instruction to the players. Once we start thinking about the verse line's contribution to its own meaning, it is difficult not to find Shakespeare's prosody somewhat eerie, as the Victorians often did, fearing it 'a form that could control you without your knowledge'.[3]

Renaissance prosodists were also uneasy about certain kinds of verse. They seem especially disturbed by lines with an odd number of syllables. These lines appeared to them to have incomplete prosodic feet, as though anatomically mangled. Ben Jonson and Thomas Nashe compare seven-syllable lines to a hobbling brewer's cart and a butterwoman's 'rank' to market, phrases Rosalind and Celia invoke or pre-empt when discussing Orlando's seven-syllable love poetry in *As You Like It* (3.2.92–4, 160–1).[4] If we see or hear Orlando's seven-syllable lines ending with an incomplete foot (rather than regarding them as headless or catalectic), then they can easily be figured as stumbling, lame and deformed. The line is not just numerically or syllabically uneven; for the Renaissance prosodists, at least, it is physically unstable too.

One of those prosodists, George Puttenham, reckoned that seven-syllable lines could be excused if 'slid away with a flat accent' (i.e. if the stress falls on the penultimate syllable of the line) – so that the lines move like limbless reptiles, unable to walk on their metrical feet.[5] Although he preferred 'even-footed verse', William Scott thought that odd-syllabled lines could be remedied if 'pressed down' (stressed), since thereby the reader could imagine the line rectified with a closing unstress and a full foot.[6] In a language which relies upon disyllabic feet (if English relies upon feet at all), odd-syllabled metres leave a syllable dangling redundant, sometimes disturbingly, at the end of a verse line.

As one of Raymond Williams's 'key words', 'form' was 'a visible or outward shape, with a strong sense of the physical body' – of what we call 'the human form'.[7] Prosodic forms have always had kinship with the body – a verse line is made up of feet, fingers (the etymology of 'dactyl'), and the 'breathing space' of caesura.[8] These anatomical attributes afford the verse line, in Puttenham's terminology, an *energia* (vividness) as well as a more static *enargeia* (grace).[9] Odd-syllabled lines provoke Renaissance unease because of their deformed form, but also because that physical deformation might deform the meaning a verse line can be said not only to transport but to constitute.

If they can countenance the possibility of an odd-syllabled line (George Gascoigne, among others, doesn't), then Renaissance prosodists read them with their senses in revolt. William Webbe briefly contemplated an odd-syllabled verse (a nine-syllable metre) before dismissing it as synaesthetically 'rough'.[10] Puttenham's palate could 'find no savour in a metre of three syllables nor in effect in any odd'.[11] Shakespeare may have known about the prosodists' disdain. As we have seen, Orlando's execrable love poetry – so wooden as to be indistinguishable from the trees it garlands – is almost entirely in seven-syllable lines, as is Claudio's dubious epitaph for Hero at the start of *Much Ado About Nothing*, 5.3. 'The Phoenix and Turtle', a poem that makes much of its 'defunctive music' (14), is also rendered in seven-syllable lines.

---

[3] Meredith Martin, *The Rise and Fall of Meter: Poetry and English National Culture, 1860–1930* (Princeton, 2012), p. 20.

[4] Thomas Nashe, *Strange Newes* (London, 1592), D2v. For discussion of Shakespeare's local debt to Nashe, see *As You Like It*, ed. H. J. Oliver (London, 1968), p. 168. Ben Jonson, *Ben Jonson's Timber or Discoveries*, ed. Ralph S. Walker (Westport, 1976), p. 102.

[5] George Puttenham, *The Art of English Poesy* (1588), ed. Frank Whigham and Wayne Rebhorn (New York, 2007), p. 160.

[6] William Scott, *The Model of Poesy* (1599), ed. Gavin Alexander (Cambridge, 2013), p. 60.

[7] Raymond Williams, *Keywords: A Vocabulary of Culture and Society* (London, 1983), p. 138.

[8] Puttenham, *Art*, pp. 163–5; the phrase is originally Philip Sidney's – see *The Defence of Poesy* (1595), in *Sir Philip Sidney: The Major Works*, ed. Katherine Duncan-Jones (Oxford, 2002), pp. 212–50; p. 248.

[9] Puttenham, *Art*, p. 227.

[10] William Webbe, *A Discourse of English Poetrie* (1586), ed. Edmund Arber (London, 1870), p. 59.

[11] Puttenham, *Art*, p. 160.

Shakespeare's witches are forever speaking in seven-syllable lines, in which the final, half-formed feet strike the ear like thunder and lightning: 'When shall we three meet again?' (1.1.1), 'When the hurly-burly's done / When the battle's lost and won' (3–4), 'Fair is foul and foul is fair' (10). Critics are always attempting to resolve the lines – in Hamlet's sense of 'melt, / Thaw, and resolve itself into a dew' (1.2.129–30) – by reading them as trochaic tetrameter, perhaps because a seven-syllable line still perturbs us. 'The speeches of the three weird sisters are prevailingly tetrameter', writes D. L. Chambers.[12] George T. Wright finds tetrameter the 'signal' verse line of Shakespeare's witches and fairies.[13] While not entirely untrue – there is a trochaic beat through some of the lines, so it is possible to read them as headless – it is not their 'prevailing' or 'signal' feature. If it were, we could reasonably expect the lines to have eight syllables most of the time. Yet the witches speak more seven-syllable lines than all other lengths of line put together, and more than double the number of octosyllabic lines (most of which are under authorial dispute – see p. 239). These critical resolutions tend to 'supplement' the seven-syllable line – not only to afford it an extra syllable, to 'resolve' it in the sense given above, but also, in Derrida's notion of 'the supplement', to 'add only to replace': to add a syllable in order to replace the seven-syllable line with a markedly different kind of verse (tetrameter).[14] In his seven-syllable lines, as opposed to his tetrameter lines, Shakespeare stresses the length of the line above the stresses of the line; he here prioritizes a syllabic above an accentual prosody. What matters most, in the seven-syllable line, at least, is its form and shape – or, rather, its putative formlessness and shapelessness.

The seven-syllable lines in Macbeth are a metrical version of the deformity they render, where syllable counting is less important than the gruesome shape made during (and by) the counting. These lines are not 'about something' (as Beckett wrote of Joyce); they almost are 'that something itself'.[15] For all Renaissance observers – from the sceptical Reginald Scot (witches are 'lean and deformed')[16] to the assured accusers ('upon her left side near her

arm was a little lump like a wart')[17] – agreed that the witch was deformed. Witches not only were deformed in themselves, they were the cause of deformation in others. Children's hands were 'turned where the backs should be, and the back in the place of the palms'.[18] Witches 'pinch' and 'pull [into] pieces'.[19] In one account, they fold the tongue of their victim.[20] It seems fitting, then, to communicate the deformation and deformations of the witches through a supposedly deformed verse line, a verse line that never seemed to 'fit'. In the seven-syllable lines of Macbeth, we sense (what Walter Pater called) 'the great, irregular art of Shakespeare'.[21] We sense, too, what he can do with verse form when he is nudging or yanking at its edges, or challenging it altogether.

Why should Macbeth be so full of seven-syllable lines, lines that are a little empty, one syllable short of a disyllabic foot? Or, looked at the other way around, why should Macbeth be full of

[12] David Chambers, The Metre of Macbeth: Its Relation to Shakespeare's Earlier and Later Work (Princeton, 1903), p. 11.

[13] George T. Wright, Shakespeare's Metrical Art (Berkeley, 1988), p. 114.

[14] Jacques Derrida, Of Grammatology, trans. Gayatri Chakravorty Spivak (Baltimore, 1976), p. 144.

[15] Samuel Beckett, 'Dante ... Bruno ... Vico ... Joyce' (1929), in Disjecta: Miscellaneous Writings and a Dramatic Fragment, ed. Ruby Cohn (London, 1983), pp. 26–7.

[16] Reginald Scot, The Discoverie of Witchcraft (London, 1584), p. 5.

[17] Unknown authors, Depositions from The Castle of York, Relating to Offences Committed in the Northern Counties in the Seventeenth Century, ed. James Raine (London, 1861), p. 30.

[18] Unknown author, 'A true and just Recorde, of the Information, Examination and Confession of all the Witches, taken at S. Osses in the countie of Essex; whereof some were executed, and other some entreated according to the determination of lawe. Wherein all men may see what a pestilent people Witches are, and how unworthy to lyue in a Christian Commonwealth. Written orderly, as the courses were tryed by evidence, By W.W. 1582' and 'A most Wicked worke of a wretched Witch' (1592–3), in Witchcraft in England 1558–1618, ed. Barbara Rosen (Amherst, 1969), p. 107.

[19] Depositions, p. 82. [20] Depositions, p. 82.

[21] Walter Pater, Studies in the History of the Renaissance (1873), ed. Adam Phillips (Oxford, 1986), p. 72.

supererogatory lines, with one syllable too many, as though suffering from a syllabic abscess? The answer originates in the play's patronage. *Macbeth* is generally thought to have been performed before King James, where Shakespeare struck an uneasy congruence between his seven-syllable line and the Stuarts' dynastic line. In 1584, aged 18, James had written a dialect treatise about prosody: *Ane Schort Treatise, conteining some reulis and cautelis to be obseruit and eschewit in Scottis Poesie.* The treatise was reissued with other of James's works when he came to the English throne in 1603. In it, he warned poets about odd-syllabled lines. 'Always take heed', he cautions, 'that the number of your feet [syllables] in every line, be even, and not odd: as four, six, eight or ten and not three, five, seven or nine.'[22] He excepts the use of odd-syllabled lines for what he calls 'broken verse', which is 'daily invented by diverse poets'.[23] He sustained his prosodical interests; we have records of James pronouncing on psalmody at the 1601 General Assembly of the Kirk and discussing poetic metre in a private audience with William Alexander in 1617.[24]

Despite his exclusion from Gavin Alexander's anthology of Renaissance literary criticism, King James is one of the few Renaissance prosodists we can reasonably suppose Shakespeare and other writers might have read (if only through obligation or opportunism). John Donne wrote for many (as well as himself) when he claimed that James was entering into 'a conversation' with his writer-subjects.[25] Gabriel Harvey 'praised James as a David-like figure'.[26] A couplet attributed to Richard Barnfield celebrates how 'The King of Scots now living is a Poet.'[27] There is evidence that English Renaissance writers knew of, or knew, the *Schort Treatise*. Francis Meres calls the king a 'favourer of poets',[28] Francis Bacon flatters James's literary knowledge in *The Advancement of Learning* (1605),[29] and Samuel Daniel, who binds and presents his *Defence of Rhyme* (1603) with a panegyric to the king, praises James's 'happy inclination' to discuss poetics and the place of 'rhyme in this kingdom'.[30] In a recent study Jane Rickard has demonstrated the wide range of allusive engagement between James and Shakespeare – from Shakespeare's references to James's poem *The Lepanto* (1591, reprinted 1603) in *Othello*, to a meditation upon *2 Henry IV* in James's *Meditation upon Saint Matthew* (1620).[31] Given all this, it seems at least plausible that Shakespeare knew (something of) James's *Schort Treatise.*

James's interest in witchcraft is much better known; Joyce called him a 'Scotch philosophaster with a turn for witch-roasting'.[32] In 1597, James published the *Daemonologie* (inspired by 'The fearful abounding at this time in this country of these detestable slaves of the Devil, the witches or enchanters') and introduced legislation to address English witchcraft in 1604. Shakespeare clearly responds to the king's interest in witchcraft with *Macbeth* (1606): some lines in the play indicate Shakespeare's close knowledge of the *Daemonologie.*[33]

The seven-syllable line does double service to Shakespeare's king-patron by combining two of his preoccupations or pedantries. Macbeth

---

[22] King James VI of Scotland, *Ane Schort Treatise, conteining some reulis and cautelis to be observit and eschewit in Scottis Poesie* in *Ancient Critical Essays upon English Poets and Poesy*, 2 vols., vol. 2, ed. Joseph Haslewood (London, 1815), p. 106.

[23] James VI, *Ane Schort Treatise*, vol. 2, p. 106.

[24] Alan Stewart, *The Cradle King: A Life of James VI & I* (London, 2004), p. 203; Jane Rickard, *Writing the Monarch in Jacobean England: Jonson, Donne, Shakespeare and the Works of King James* (Cambridge, 2015), p. 41.

[25] John Donne, *Pseudo-Martyr* (London, 1610), sig. A3r.

[26] Rickard, *Writing the Monarch*, p. 25. See Gabriel Harvey, *Pierces Supererogation* (London, 1593), p. 53.

[27] Francis Meres, *Palladis Tamia. Wits Treasury* (London, 1598), sig. Oo4v.

[28] Meres, *Palladis Tamia*, p. 284.

[29] Francis Bacon, *The Advancement of Learning*, ed. William Aldis Wright (Oxford, 1963), p. 3.

[30] Samuel Daniel, *Selected Poetry and A Defense of Rhyme*, ed. Geoffrey G. Hiller and Peter L. Groves (Asheville, 1998), pp. 198–9.

[31] Rickard, *Writing the Monarch*, pp. 209–49.

[32] James Joyce, *Ulysses: The 1922 Text*, ed. Declan Kiberd (Oxford, 2008), 9.751–2.

[33] John Kerrigan, *Archipelagic English: Literature, History, and Politics 1603–1707* (Oxford, 2008), pp. 16–17.

straightaway refers to the witches as 'imperfect speakers' (1.3.68). The *OED* furnishes this instance within its fourth definition of 'imperfect': 'of persons in respect of imperfect or defective action or accomplishment'. This is correct: Macbeth thinks their speech defective because they stop speaking, and make him want to hear 'more' (68). But it is an imperfect example, too, since the speech of the witches is imperfect in two other senses. In a now obsolete implication, it is 'positively faulty, vicious, evil' (first usage 1377). It is also 'wanting some part or adjunct usually present ... not fully formed, made, or done; unfinished, incomplete; of less than the full amount' (first usage 1340). Like King James, Macbeth complains that the numerical unevenness of the witches' lines is part of their 'broken' physical deformity – they need one more or one fewer syllable to end on a full metrical foot. Just before Macbeth speaks, Banquo points out the witches' 'withered' bodies or attire (38), their 'choppy' fingers (42) and 'skinny lips' (43), as physical accompaniments to or reflections of their verse lines.

Shakespeare most often uses his seven-syllable lines in scenes of spoken supernatural action: the casting of spells, the application of curses, and the incantation of magic. In *Macbeth*, for example, the witches use seven-syllable lines when plaguing the shipman's card (1.3.14–24), going about and about the sea and land (30–5), adding ingredients to the cauldron (4.1.1–38), opening locks without contact (61–3), and conjuring the show of kings (126–7). The seven-syllable line's deformity is also, therefore, its efficacy: by refusing the normalities or normativities of the body and the verse line, it attempts to be free of the line's physical constraints and move into movement (not an illusion of movement but 'the thing itself' (*King Lear*, 3.4.97)). Strictly speaking, the attempt fails. Yet the seven-syllable line provokes these reflections in a way that other lines could not – that is, certain kinds of thought and association can only occur in and with certain lengths of verse line.

The seven-syllable lines are additionally eerie for their relationship to other verse lines, other bodies, other types of form. If verse lines are a little like our

bodies, these deformed verse lines must be in a perverse proximity to us too. Since verse lines are also unlike our bodies, lacking some of the attributes that bodies have, it ought to follow that seven-syllable lines can be kept at the safe distance proffered by such analogy. However, one of the ways Shakespeare's seven-syllable lines test their audience is by being at or in the hinterland of other verse lines; they are always close to both trimeter and tetrameter, only ever an elision or expansion away. When Picasso looked at Cézanne's painted apples, he saw 'the weight of space on that circular form' rather than fruit 'as such'.[34] Picasso noticed how forms, including the forms of verse lines, are always drawn or motivated by other, surrounding forms. Indeed, in *As You Like It*, Touchstone calls Orlando's seven-syllable love poetry infectious (*As You Like It*, 3.2.111–12). It is as if deformity is catching; as if the chant of the seven-syllable lines could also en-chant – as if the witches speak with a 'socially poisonous tongue'.[35]

If *Macbeth* is threatened with deformation by the witches' seven-syllable lines, Malcolm's accession to the throne offers some respite to, and through, the play's prosody.

> this, and what needful else
> That calls upon us, by the grace of grace
> We will perform in measure, time, and place.
> So thanks to all at once, and to each one,
> Whom we invite to see us crowned at Scone.
>
> (5.11.37–41)

In fairly smooth iambic pentameter, Malcolm brings some 'measure' back to Scotland, the word partly meaning 'metrical order' (*OED* 16a).

We can imagine a few of James's possible responses to Shakespeare's witches. He may have been flattered and interested. Here was the chief writer of the King's Men connecting two of

---

[34] Pablo Picasso, qtd in Franklin R. Rogers, *Painting and Poetry: Form, Metaphor, and the Language of Literature* (London, 1985), p. 152.

[35] Jonathan Gil Harris, *Foreign Bodies and the Body Politic: Discourses of Social Pathology in Early Modern England* (Cambridge, 1988), p. 107.

James's published interests: witchcraft and prosody. James may not have responded at all, because he may not have noticed at all – although people sometimes wrote of going to *hear* rather than *see* a play in Renaissance England, and although James's ear seems to have been metrically sensitive, it can be difficult to register the exact prosodic arrangement of verse lines in performance (which could in turn mean that Shakespeare smuggled offence past James). James thought that he had been the subject of assassination attempts by witches, so Shakespeare's grating stumbling prosody may have been eerie to the kingly ear. James might have been angry: the play's conclusion contains a series of hints – think of the witchy hailings by the thanes in 5.11 – that Malcolm's (and therefore James's) unification of the two kingdoms has the witches' endorsement (or worse). All of these possible reactions are accommodated within a court performance – 'treason's license' says Supervacuo in *The Revenger's Tragedy* (5.1.173) – in which the king's ability to react to Shakespeare's provocations was girdled by ceremony. Though the play's prosody is born out of patronage, *Macbeth* is 'aware of the fact of [its] compromise' while being 'in no sense compromised'.[36]

Perhaps *Macbeth*'s verse lines have been infected by those in *A Midsummer Night's Dream* (*c.* 1594), another play dark with supernatural menace. The fairies of the *Dream* speak in seven-syllable lines too; to adapt Stephen Greenblatt, they are not exactly witches but they are not exactly *not* witches either.[37] The witches 'hail' Banquo thrice (1.3.60–2) and the fairies 'hail' Bottom four times (3.1.167–70). In Simon Forman's account of seeing *Macbeth* in April 1611, he describes the witches as '3 women fairies or nymphs' (perhaps recalling Holinshed, in which the supernatural characters are more fairy than witch).[38]

At first, Shakespeare emphasizes the fairies' benevolence – they are like the Clean Fairy of folklore, tidying up the stage:

> You spotted snakes with double tongue,
> Thorny hedgehogs, be not seen.

> Newts and blindworms, do no wrong,
> Come not near our Fairy Queen . . .
> Weaving spiders, come not here;
> Hence, you long-legged spinners, hence;
> Beetles black, approach not near,
> Worm nor snail, do no offence.
>
> (2.2.9–12, 20–3)

This fairy song is in seven-syllable lines (apart from line 9) but there is little sense of danger. The fairies clear the stage of any witchy familiars. In banishing newts and blindworms, they get rid of two ingredients from the witches' cauldron (4.1.14–16); in banishing 'Weaving spiders' they get rid of the 'creeping, venom'd things' that menace Lady Anne in *Richard III* (1.2.19–20). Yet the clearing-away of witch-like 'offence' also creates space for Oberon to enter and to cast the first of the play's morally dubious spells – crucially, in seven-syllable lines (2.2.33–40). By ending the spell 'Wake when some vile thing is near', Oberon both contradicts and counteracts the fairy song that has taken place ten lines earlier. Nor is Oberon's the only ethically suspect spell: Puck's spell on Lysander (2.2.72–89), Oberon's spell on Demetrius (3.2.102–9), and Puck's invocation to lead the mortals 'up and down' (3.2.397–400) are all, with the exception of two lines, conducted in seven syllables. By their metre shall we know them: the fairies are less benevolent than they seem.

The supernatural seven-syllable line appears to be Shakespeare's invention. Between 1594/5 and 1606, there are no seven-syllable lines in (surviving) supernatural drama. Before 1594/5, there is a little seven-syllable verse in John Lyly's *Endymion* (*c.* 1588), a play that Shakespeare may

---

[36] Geoffrey Hill, '"The true conduct of human judgment": some observations on *Cymbeline*', in Hill, *Collected Critical Writings*, ed. Kenneth Haynes (Oxford, 2008), pp. 58–71; p. 60.

[37] Stephen Greenblatt, *Hamlet in Purgatory* (Oxford, 2002), p. 162.

[38] Raphael Holinshed, *Shakespeare's Holinshed: The Chronicle and the Historical Plays Compared*, ed. Walter Boswell-Stone (London, 1907), p. 124.

have drawn upon when writing *A Midsummer Night's Dream*. Lyly's fairies fitfully speak in a seven-syllable metre when chanting supernaturally:

> Pinch him, pinch him, black and blue.
> Saucy mortals must not view
> What the Queen of Stars is doing,
> Nor pry into our Fairy wooing.
>
> (*Endymion*, 4.3.29–32)

(There is another bundle of seven-syllable lines at 4.3.42–5.) The way the fairies 'pinch' Corsites has witchiness hovering about it, a witchiness Shakespeare developed in *A Midsummer Night's Dream* and in the molested Herne/Falstaff of *The Merry Wives of Windsor* (*c.* 1597). However, Lyly takes the pinching to a safer destination – although Tellus causes Corsites 'to be pinched with Fairies', he punningly forgives her since 'her fairness hath pinched [his] heart more deeply' (5.3.249–50).

Slightly later than *Macbeth*, from 1608, other writers find themselves similarly provoked by the seven-syllable line. Ben Jonson's masques are able, more so than Shakespeare's theatre, to realize the manifold, multiform potential of the seven-syllable line. *The Masque of Queens* (1609), for example, stresses deformity in all its forms – physically, musically, metrically. The masque's witches enter 'with a kind of hollow and infernal music' while 'making a confused noise with strange gestures' (20–1). The court audience would have seen them dance, 'making their circles backward, to their left hand, with strange phantastic motions of their heads and bodies' (349–51). Such sinister (Latin: 'left, or left hand', *OED*) action reverses the normal patterns of movement. It was accompanied by music 'metrically unstable . . . unable to sustain metrical coherence', in which the time signature changes four times in rapid succession.[39] The rhythmically regular first section of the dance is blared over by two protracted blasts, and the restoration of convention (in the form of a triple metre) is soon shocked by a bombardment of eight notes. The first words spoken by a witch are in uneven seven-syllable lines ('Sisters, stay, we want our Dame; / Call

upon her, by her name' (47–8)) and there are bursts of seven-syllable lines, as well as eleven-syllable lines, throughout the witches' speech. Like the music, like the movement or dance, this is a verse which will 'loose the whole hinge of things' (148). Jonson's masque is the seven-syllable line's *Gesamtkunstwerk* 'in which partial contributions of the related and collaborating arts [dance, movement, music, prosody] blend together, disappear, and, in disappearing, somehow form a new world' for which the seven-syllable line could be thought the prosodic *leitmotif*.[40]

When Heroic Virtue and the other personifications of fame arrive, they subvert the witches – which is to say, they correct the witches' subversions and bring the masque to a new kind of order. As the witches have familiars, so the allegorical worthies have fame-iliars: eagles 'to note Fame's sharp eye' (467), griffins 'that design / Swiftness and strength' (468–9), and lions that 'imply / The top of graces' (470–1). Heroic Virtue enters and disperses the hags in heroic couplets: 'So should, at Fame's loud sound and Virtue's sight, / All poor and envious witchcraft fly the light' (367–8). Her iambic pentameter performs a restoration, with its only abruption the double stress at the centre of line 367 – meaning that 'Fame's *loud sound*' is heard all the more clearly, supplying additional emphasis to the line's proclamation.

Jonson's witches were perhaps more offensive to James than Shakespeare's. They form the masque's 'political unconscious' to the extent that, at one point, they are called 'Erinyes' (367) – invoking Aeschylus's tragedy of Orestes, pursued by Furies when he has killed his mother.[41] This may be a dim allusion to James's complicity in the execution of

---

[39] Amanda Winkler, *O Let Us Howle Some Heavy Note: Music for Witches, The Melancholic, and the Mad on the Seventeenth Century English Stage* (Bloomington, 2006), pp. 31–2.

[40] Carl Maria von Weber, review of Undine (1816), in *Source Readings in Music History: The Romantic Era*, ed. Oliver Strunk (New York, 1965), p. 63.

[41] Martin Butler, *The Stuart Court Masque and Political Culture* (Cambridge, 2008), p. 138.

his mother Mary Queen of Scots – the kind of dim allusion (or 'dark conceit') that James noticed, to Spenser's disadvantage, in Book 5 of the *Faerie Queene*.[42] Even here though, amid the offence, Jonson's 'independent image' could make him 'a more valuable and attractive dependent': in the space of a few months, for example, Jonson was imprisoned for part-authorship of *Eastward Ho!* before being commissioned to write his second court masque *Hymenae*.[43]

When Thomas Middleton wrote *The Witch* (1616), he took much from Jonson's *Masque of Queens*, but he did not take the masque's seven-syllable lines. Middleton's witches speak in heroic and tetrameter couplets. Even in Hecate's metrically shifting address, there are only three seven-syllable lines distributed through her speech. This suggests that if Middleton revised *Macbeth*, he did not contribute the play's seven-syllable lines. There is an irony of influence here. Some of Jonson's masques use the seven-syllable line more consistently than *The Masque of Queens*. *The Masque of Blackness* and *The Haddington Masque* (both 1608) feature moments of seven-syllable verse – in the former, the song from the sea (295–300) and a song beginning 'Come away' (283–8) that bears a few resemblances to *Macbeth*; in the latter, the speeches of the Three Graces and of Cupid (85–156, 165–82). Jonson's later masques incorporate even more seven-syllable lines. *A Masque of Her Majesties Love Freed From Ignorance and Folly* (1611) contains a Sphinx speaking in seven-syllable lines (6–231). *Oberon, The Faery Prince* (also 1611) has satyrs speaking in seven-syllable lines (6–290), with their 'crooked legs' (106) a visual accompaniment to their crooked metrical feet. When the satyrs turn to James, however, they conduct themselves in numerically even lines (300–13), perhaps as an appropriate deference to the author of the *Schort Treatise*.

It is possible that Jonson took the seven-syllable line from *A Midsummer Night's Dream* and/or *Macbeth*, using it in his masques for supernatural characters much as Shakespeare does in his plays. (Note that *The Alchemist*'s Doll Tearsheet speaks only in pentameters when playing Doll Queen of Fairy; her pretence does not warrant Jonson's

authentically supernatural seven-syllable line. So in Shakespeare, when the unsupernatural Edgar uses words that will later appear in *Macbeth* – 'aroint thee, witch' (*Macbeth*, 1.3.5) – he is given an additional monosyllable at the start of his verse line to create an unsupernatural tetrameter: '*And* aroint thee, witch, aroint thee' (*Lear*, 3.4.113).) Middleton, though borrowing from *The Masque of Queens* for *The Witch*, did not borrow the masque's crucial Shakespearian component: the seven-syllable line. Then, if he revised *Macbeth*, Middleton supplied the witches with tetrameter couplets and pentameter lines, diluting the presence of the seven-syllable line in the play. In so doing, he put into *Macbeth* the opposite of what Jonson might have taken from it: a set of numerically even lines. If this is a wheel of influence, it has not come full circle.

In 1611, Shakespeare wrote two plays that seem to mitigate the supernatural seven-syllable line.[44] When Paulina casts her spell at the end of *The Winter's Tale*, she does so in carefully constructed pentameter:

> 'Tis time. Descend. Be stone no more. Approach;
> Strike all that look upon with marvel. Come,
> I'll fill your grave up. Stir. Nay, come away.
> Bequeath to death your numbness, for from him
> Dear life redeems you. You perceive she stirs.
>
> (5.3.99–103)

---

[42] By 1611, Spenser's allegory was so transparent that Jonson could tell Drummond 'That in that paper S.W. Raleigh had of the Allegories of his *Faerie Queene*, by the Blatant Beast the Puritans were understood, by the false Duessa the Queen of Scots' (Jonson, *Timber*, p. 17).

[43] Robert C. Evans, *Ben Jonson and the Poetics of Patronage* (London, 1989), p. 61.

[44] After 1611, in collaboration with John Fletcher, Shakespeare returned to the line in two brief songs – one in *Henry VIII, or All Is True* (3.1.3–14) and one in *The Two Noble Kinsmen* (1.1. 1–14), although only the scene in *The Two Noble Kinsmen* is usually attributed to Shakespeare – but its status as a supernatural line ends with Shakespeare and Jonson. When Fletcher writes *The Faithful Shepherdess* (1608), for example, his seven-syllable lines are distributed between a range of characters (from priests to satyrs) with no obvious purpose.

As in 5.3.101, Paulina fills up the grave, so Shakespeare fills up the line. In filling it up, the line becomes busy and vivacious – 'Stir. Nay, come away' implies a dialogue with someone (Hermione?) refusing to co-operate, implies life outside the line. We also see life outside the borders of 5.3.102. In order to escape the numbness of 'death', we have to move over the line, enjamb into 'Dear life' and be redeemed. Pauses balance the verse. 5.3.99 is divided almost into its component feet: ''Tis time / Descend / Be stone no more / Approach' (in Folio this is done by a profusion of colons). Caesuras fall exactly halfway through 5.3.101 and 5.3.103. It does not seem an accident of punctuation; rather, Paulina's claim to legality and morality in her spellcasting – 'You hear my spell is *lawful*' (105) – is vindicated by her even-syllabled verse. Leontes agrees: 'If this be magic, let it be an art / *Lawful* as eating' (110–11).

In *The Tempest* (1611), Prospero's renunciation of magic involves a renunciation of the seven-syllable line, a line Ariel had used to cast spells under Prospero's command.

> Now I want
> Spirits to enforce, art to enchant;
> And my ending is despair
> Unless I be relieved by prayer,
> Which pierces so, that it assaults
> Mercy itself, and frees all faults.
> As you from crimes would pardoned be,
> Let your indulgence set me free.
>
> (Epilogue 13–20)

There is a struggle here, most noticeable in Prospero's 'want': is this 'want' the lack of spirits or the desire for spirits, or both? The epilogue wobbles between the two. The lack of spirits is mimicked in the catalectic (or headless) line 14, as though Shakespeare's metrical art cannot make up for Prospero's magical art. 'And my ending is despair' is a seven-syllable line (one in which the trochaic pulse distinctly flickers) but there is little risk that Prospero will renege on his renunciation – for 'despair' is relieved by the rhyme with 'prayer' over the line, 'prayer' being the syllable which makes line 16 an even tetrameter (although if

'prayer' is treated as disyllabic, the line could tip into nine syllables). Prospero's appeal to the audience ('As you from crimes would pardoned be / Let your indulgence set me free') is paced iambically across tetrameter lines, with a slight accentual hesitation over whether his imperative ('Let') or the audience's presence ('your') should sport a stress. His final evenness, his refusal to despair and descend to the seven-syllable line, makes Prospero 'most profound in his art and yet not damnable' (*As You Like It*, 5.2.59).

The seven-syllable line is never absent from these plays. Prospero slips into it, as though momentarily yielding to his tyrannical magic, and Ariel's speeches buzz with it. Paulina risks it, by perpetrating a 'lawful' spell that must, like all Renaissance spellcasting, be always on the cusp of illegality. If Shakespeare's blank verse gradually bleaches out the seven-syllable line, then it does so by becoming more and more akin to it. Shakespeare's blanks increasingly possess a feminine ending – by the time of these later plays, every third or fourth verse line has an uneven eleven syllables. At these points, in these plays, the seven-syllable line is a ghost form (or a 'ghost in the shell' of Shakespeare's blank verse).[45] It is the kind of undead verse line that Jonson and Holland would nervously celebrate – indeed, it has become the kind of supernatural entity it was previously spoken by.

When Jonson wrote of Shakespeare's 'living line', he pre-empted the metaphor of a later classicist. In the *Essay on Man*, Alexander Pope's spider 'Feels at each thread, and lives along the line' (7.12). We hear the truth of that statement in the alliterative, assonant reach from 'lives' to 'line', where the sound is not so much a divisible echo of Pope's sense as the spider's experiential confirmation of it. Like Pope's, Shakespeare's self-

---

45 Gavin Alexander, 'On the reuse of poetic form: the ghost in the shell', in *The Work of Form: Poetics and Materiality in Early Modern Culture*, ed. Ben Burton and Elizabeth Scott-Baumann (Oxford, 2014), pp. 123–43.

drawing web is forever drawing and never finally 'drawn' (Nicholas Rowe's deadening emendation to *Henry VIII*, 1.1.63). The web is scuttling with life: with, in the remit of this article alone, a seven-syllable verse that twists and gurns and contorts; that, in its putative deformities, is bound to the breadth of human experience, moving, thinking, shaping, and feeling 'Till the bridge you will need, be form'd – till the ductile anchor hold' and 'Till the gossamer thread you fling, catch somewhere, O my Soul'.[46]

---

[46] Walt Whitman, 'A Noiseless Patient Spider' (lines 9–10), in *Leaves of Grass: The Original 1855 Edition*, ed. Bliss Perry (New York, 2007).

AT THE SIGN OF THE ANGEL: THE INFLUENCE OF ANDREW WISE ON SHAKESPEARE IN PRINT

AMY LIDSTER

In his address to the 'Gentlemen Readers', prefacing the first edition of *Tamburlaine* (Parts 1 and 2) in 1590, stationer Richard Jones positions himself as an active reader and editor, drawing attention to the ways in which he has transformed Marlowe's plays as they were performed on stage, and adapted them to suit a projected image of his reading public:

> I haue (purposely) omitted and left out some fond and friuolous Jestures, digressing (and in my poore opinion) far vnmeet for the matter, which I thought, might seeme more tedious vnto the wise, than any way els to be regarded, though (happily) they haue bene of some vaine conceited fondlings greatly gaped at, what times they were shewed vpon the stage.[1]

This preface, which was the first paratextual address to be attached to a professional playbook, points to the significant role stationers could have in selecting works for publication, controlling their transmission as editors, expressing interpretations of the texts, and reshaping the plays that were performed on stage.[2] Prior to 1590, plays from the commercial theatre were rarely published. The small number of dramatic texts reaching print during the 1580s was dominated by translations, academic plays, closet plays and accounts of royal entertainments – with, however, the plays of John Lyly forming the most notable exception.[3] In many ways, Richard Jones's publication of Marlowe's *Tamburlaine* and Robert Wilson's *Three Lords and Three Ladies of London* in 1590 can be seen as a significant turning point in the emerging market for printed

playbooks. The prefatory address in *Tamburlaine* positions professional plays as worthy of attention from 'Gentlemen Readers', while also suggesting a separation between the play in performance and as a printed text, effected by the intervention of stationers. Even at this nascent stage in the development of a market for commercial playbooks, stationers display and assert their agency, as opposed to assuming a functional role of impartial transmission from stage to page, and often prioritize, as suggested by Jones's marketing strategy, the play's new status as a book for readers, as distinct from its theatrical existence.

One of the most important early publishers of Shakespeare's plays was Andrew Wise, who was responsible for eleven separate play editions between 1597 and 1602. Starting in 1597 with the first editions of *Richard II* and *Richard III*, Wise's quartos usher in the first notable publication concentration of plays by Shakespeare. From his bookshop location at the Sign of the Angel in Paul's Churchyard, Wise published and distributed

---

[1] Christopher Marlowe, *Tamburlaine* (1590), A2r.

[2] The terms 'professional' and 'commercial' are used throughout this article to refer to plays that were performed by adult and boys' companies in front of paying audiences.

[3] The first plays from the professional stage were published in 1584: Robert Wilson's *Three Ladies of London* from Leicester's Men, George Peele's *The Arraignment of Paris* from the Children of the Chapel, and several of John Lyly's plays for the Children of the Chapel and the Children of Paul's, including two editions of *Sappho and Phao*, and three editions of *Campaspe*. These first playbooks were followed by the anonymous *Rare Triumphs of Love and Fortune* in 1589.

editions of *Richard II*, *Richard III*, *1 Henry IV*, *2 Henry IV* and *Much Ado About Nothing* (the last two published jointly with William Aspley): he invested in the plays, entered all of them in the Stationers' Register, and hired printers, including Peter Short, Valentine Simmes, Simon Stafford and Thomas Creede, to manufacture the physical texts.[4] Judging by the number of second and subsequent editions, Wise's quartos proved phenomenally successful with early readers – indeed, they were the first of Shakespeare's plays to be reprinted.[5] Between 1597 and 1602, *Richard II*, *Richard III* and *1 Henry IV* were each published three times, and *2 Henry IV* and *Much Ado About Nothing* were printed once, making a total of eleven editions in under five years.[6] By the end of the sixteenth century, largely as a result of these quartos, Shakespeare was the most published professional dramatist, having approximately twenty-two play editions in circulation, and about half of which had been published by Wise.[7]

The importance of these editions to Shakespeare studies and early modern drama has been regularly acknowledged, especially as these quartos are often used as the copy-texts for modern editions. However, the significance of Andrew Wise and his publishing strategies and connections are frequently overlooked.[8] This article aims to suggest that Wise contributed both to the selection of these plays for publication and to their printed presentation, specifically in relation to paratextual attributions, which are included on his title pages from 1598 onwards. Both of these aspects are particularly significant: the process of selection has considerably defined the corpus of extant plays from the commercial theatres, as well as our understanding of wider theatrical repertories, and the introduction of authorial attribution helped to elevate Shakespeare's status and reputation as a professional dramatist at the end of the sixteenth century, influencing later publishing ventures, such as the First Folio. Profiling Wise's involvement in play selection and presentation, this discussion will draw attention to two contributing factors: the influence of the geography of London's book trade, specifically Wise's business location at the Sign of the Angel in St Paul's Churchyard, and

the role of patronage associations in the publication of Shakespeare's plays. An assessment of commercial and patronal agendas will serve to break down the separation that is often maintained between these two areas of influence, both of which can be seen as fashioning Shakespeare's position as a published dramatist at the end of the sixteenth century.[9]

Having a wider degree of application, the practices and connections of Andrew Wise will help to

---

4 Wise is unique in entering all of his plays in the Stationers' Register prior to publication: *Richard II* was entered on 29 August 1597, *Richard III* on 20 October 1597, *1 Henry IV* on 25 February 1598, and *2 Henry IV* and *Much Ado About Nothing* were entered jointly to Wise and William Aspley on 23 August 1600.

5 This is true if Q2 of *The Taming of a Shrew* in 1596 is not considered as part of Shakespeare's oeuvre.

6 Wise published *Richard II* in 1597 (Q1), 1598 (Q2), and 1598 (Q3); *Richard III* in 1597 (Q1), 1598 (Q2), and 1602 (Q3); *1 Henry IV* in 1598 (Q0, for which only one sheet survives, hence this quarto designation), 1598 (Q1), and 1599 (Q2); *2 Henry IV* in 1600 (Q1); and *Much Ado About Nothing* in 1600 (Q1).

7 The twenty-two editions of plays by Shakespeare exclude, in this count, *The Troublesome Reign of King John* (1591), *The Taming of a Shrew* (1594, 1596), *Arden of Faversham* (1594), *Locrine* (1595), and *Edward III* (1596, 1599). In comparison, plays from Shakespeare's contemporaries had achieved significantly fewer editions by the end of the sixteenth century. As Lukas Erne has shown, John Lyly was the next most published dramatist on the basis of edition numbers, with thirteen separate editions printed by 1600, followed by George Peele and Robert Greene with eight editions each, Marlowe with seven, and Kyd with six. See Lukas Erne, *Shakespeare and the Book Trade* (Cambridge, 2013), p. 44.

8 For recent studies that highlight Wise's importance, see Sonia Massai's chapter on 'The Wise Quartos', in *Shakespeare and the Rise of the Editor* (Cambridge, 2007), pp. 91–105, and Adam Hooks's discussion of Wise and Thomas Playfere in *Selling Shakespeare: Biography, Bibliography and the Book Trade* (Cambridge, 2016), pp. 66–98.

9 Critics who have drawn attention to the interconnections between aristocratic and commercial agents include Kathleen McLuskie, Helen Smith and Adam Hooks. In particular, see Adam Hooks, 'Shakespeare at the White Greyhound', *Shakespeare Survey 64* (Cambridge, 2011), pp. 260–75.

demonstrate that the publication of professional plays was not arbitrary, but involved a highly motivated process of selection; it was not representative, but focused on narrow groupings of plays that supported a variety of literary and political agendas; and the plays themselves were not simply transmitted, but transformed through their publication.[10] With this approach, the printed playbook is not a record of a performance event but a text displaying traces of multiple producers that point to the literary, theatrical and political contexts which mediate our access to the plays that were once performed on the early modern stage.

'TAKING PLEASURE IN READING HISTORIES': THE SELECTION OF SHAKESPEARE'S PLAYS FOR PUBLICATION

Jones's prefatory address in *Tamburlaine* highlights his understanding of readers' interests, or at least constitutes an attempt to generate them, describing his prospective buyers as 'taking pleasure in reading Histories' (A2r). While the fluidity of the term 'history' precludes specific identification in subject matter, as the term suggests both material related to an acknowledged 'past' (including chronicle sources), and the more expansive application of retelling a 'story' or account, its use here is chiefly interesting for what it indicates about a publisher's concentration and effort to select material that will appeal to readers. As the individuals carrying the financial risk of their ventures, publishers actively chose which texts to invest in, and while the availability of plays from the professional theatres inevitably shaped print opportunities and patterns, publishers still asserted a considerable degree of influence in positively selecting which available plays to pursue in anticipation of finding a responsive readerly market.[11]

Andrew Wise's playbooks form a remarkably unified group: all of his dramatic publications consist of plays by Shakespeare that were part of the repertory of the Chamberlain's Men and focus on the lives of fourteenth- and fifteenth-century English monarchs, with the exception of *Much Ado About Nothing* (one of Wise's last publications which, in collaboration with William Aspley, perhaps indicates a change in publishing strategy that accords more closely with Aspley's interests).[12] All of these plays reached the bookstalls in their first editions between 1597 and 1600, a rapidity that heightens Wise's concentration in both dramatist and subject matter. Such an emphasis is unusual at this stage in the publication of professional plays, suggesting Wise occupies a unique position in the London book trade and warrants more sustained critical attention. Other stationers were investing in plays at this time but none privileged historical subject matter in their selection of texts, and none displayed the same focus on one dramatist or company. Cuthbert Burby, for example, published Lyly's *Mother Bombie* from the Children of Paul's in 1594 and 1598, Shakespeare's *Love's Labour's Lost* from the Chamberlain's Men in 1598, and Greene's *Orlando Furioso* in 1599 (which had probably been independently performed by the Queen's Men, the Admiral's Men and Lord Strange's Men), demonstrating a publishing interest in plays from a range of dramatists and companies.

---

[10] On the transformative nature of publication and its politics, see Zachary Lesser, *Renaissance Drama and the Politics of Publication* (Cambridge, 2004).

[11] As critics such as Peter Blayney have demonstrated, stationers purchased play scripts from manuscript owners and, while such owners could seek out a particular stationer, the decision to invest remained with the publisher, who would make choices based on their wider publishing strategies and output. While some writers developed close relationships with certain stationers (as with Samuel Daniel and Simon Waterson), and occasionally invested in the publication of their texts themselves, this pattern is not especially widespread, particularly not in relation to the early stages of playbook publication. Instead, it is the agency of the stationer that is centralized in the final selection of texts. See Peter Blayney, 'The publication of playbooks', in *A New History of Early English Drama*, ed. John Cox and David Scott Kastan (New York, 1993), pp. 383–422.

[12] Aspley would go on to publish several comedies, notably those from the boys' companies, including Marston's *The Malcontent* (1604) and Chapman, Jonson and Marston's *Eastward Ho* (1605).

Wise's specialism in plays dramatizing the lives of medieval English monarchs may be connected to the location of his bookshop in Paul's Cross at the Sign of the Angel, an area in the north-east corner of St Paul's Churchyard which witnessed a concentration of publications dealing with medieval English history during the late 1590s – perhaps most significantly, Samuel Daniel's *Civil Wars* (1595). Focusing on the reigns of Richard II to Edward IV (in its later continuations), and the conflicts between the 'houses of Lancaster and Yorke', *The Civil Wars* was immensely influential, and its impact, as John Pitcher argues, 'was felt throughout the literary scene at once'.[13] Stationer Simon Waterson published the majority of Daniel's works (including *The Civil Wars*), and the location of his bookshop at the Sign of the Crown was in the same part of the churchyard as Wise's business (with less than 200 feet separating them).[14] Given the proximity of the bookshops and the frequency of Waterson's influential editions, Wise would have been aware of the success of Daniel's works. In 1595, Waterson had published two editions of *The Civil Wars*, containing the 'First Fowre Bookes'; a fifth book was then printed separately in an undated edition, but was also bound as an attachment to the four books; and in 1599, Waterson published the five books as part of *The Poeticall Essayes of Samuel Daniel*. Judging by his dramatic rendering of similar material in *Richard II*, Shakespeare was one of the early readers of Daniel's *Civil Wars*, likely drawing on the first four books within weeks of their publication, probably in November 1595.[15] The depth, subtlety and inwardness of Daniel's historical characters, the added significance and maturity of Queen Isabel that departs from the chronicle sources, and the emphasis on the two central competitors, Richard and Bolingbroke, can be seen as informing Shakespeare's treatment of the same material. This connection between Shakespeare's dramatic representations and Daniel's *Civil Wars* possibly encouraged Wise's interest in these particular plays by Shakespeare, as he attempted to capitalize on the position of *The Civil Wars* as one of the most reprinted and

influential works published in this part of Paul's Churchyard during the late 1590s.

Moreover, the ensuing success of Wise's quartos (with nine editions by 1600) may have, reciprocally, motivated the expansions to *The Civil Wars*. Waterson was instrumental in the development of *The Civil Wars*, and it was at his request, in about 1600, that Daniel provided him with another continuation: in 1601, Waterson published *The Works of Samuel Daniel*, containing six books of *The Civil Wars*.[16] Waterson was clearly aware of the consumer demand for Daniel's narrative poem and the reading public's wider interests in medieval English monarchs and their battles (as featured in Wise's editions), while also recognizing Daniel's literary reputation and connections to the Sidney circle, which could benefit his own position as a publisher and make the continuations profitable. Other texts dealing with similar subject matter were also published during this time, including Michael Drayton's *Mortimeriados* (1596, later published as *The Barrons Wars* in 1603) and *Englands Heroicall Epistles* (1597), Richard Crompton's *The Mansion of Magnanimitie* (1599), John Hayward's *The First Part of the Life and Raigne of King Henrie IIII* (1599), the anonymous *First Booke of the Preservation of King Henry VII* (1599), and John Speed's *A Description of the Civill Warres of England* (1601), which indicate the emergence of a minor literary trend in late-medieval monarchical history at the end of the sixteenth century, with Wise's numerous editions occupying a significant position within these publication patterns.

While the close proximity of Wise's and Waterson's bookshops and the connection of Shakespeare's plays to Daniel's *Civil Wars* may

---

[13] John Pitcher, 'Daniel, Samuel (1562/3–1619)', in *Oxford Dictionary of National Biography* (Oxford, 2004), para. 7 (www .oxforddnb.com/view/article/7120).

[14] See Peter Blayney, *The Bookshops in Paul's Cross Churchyard*, Occasional Papers of the Bibliographical Society, No. 5 (London, 1990), p. 76.

[15] Pitcher, 'Daniel, Samuel', para. 7.

[16] Pitcher, 'Daniel, Samuel', para. 11.

have appealed to Wise's business strategies, the question of the availability of these plays must be addressed. Publishers were limited to the texts they were able to access, which necessarily shaped their output. Interestingly, in the case of Andrew Wise, evidence from his publication patterns points to a possible patronage network between Wise as a publisher, George Carey, second Baron Hunsdon, as a literary and theatrical patron, and the Chamberlain's Men as a repertory company that was patronized by George Carey from 1596 to 1603.[17] As Sonia Massai has shown, Wise almost exclusively published texts by three writers under the direct patronage of George Carey, namely Thomas Nashe, Thomas Playfere and Shakespeare, as the leading dramatist of the Chamberlain's Men.[18] This kind of patronage link is relatively rare in publishers' outputs suggesting a connection between Wise, George Carey and the Chamberlain's Men that may have motivated Wise's selection of texts for publication and determined their availability to him as a publisher.

Wise's unique position as the only Elizabethan publisher to specialize exclusively in plays by Shakespeare (in addition to his non-dramatic publications) and to prioritize historical dramatizations had possible implications for the publication of other plays dealing with medieval monarchical history, therefore shaping the corpus of extant texts from the commercial theatres. Thomas Millington published second editions of *The First Part of the Contention* and *The True Tragedy of Richard Duke of York* in 1600, potentially to capitalize on the phenomenal success of Wise's quartos with readers. Similarly, Thomas Creede published *The Famous Victories of Henry V* and *The Scottish History of James IV* in 1598 (both of which had been previously entered in the Stationers' Register in 1594 but not printed), and John Oxenbridge released editions of *1* and *2 Edward IV* in both 1599 and 1600. While the treatment of historical subjects varies considerably between the texts, with a play such as *James IV* having only a slight connection to any historical accounts, it is notable that the titles and title-page descriptions of these editions emphasize their depiction of historical events and

battles, establishing a marketing parallel with the Wise editions.[19]

Focusing on the active selection of plays for publication, according to the specialisms, connections and strategies of stationers, reveals the influences that have shaped the survival of plays from the professional stages, complicating any sense of this process being either arbitrary or representative. Largely owing to Wise's publications, Shakespeare was the most published commercial dramatist by 1600, and a majority of his printed plays demonstrate a preference for the conflicts and debates surrounding the Wars of the Roses. However, these patterns are not reflected in the wider performance repertories of either the Chamberlain's Men or other theatrical companies. Evidence for plays in performance reveals a wider range of subject matter and greater variety in approach. As opposed to centring on medieval English history, as in Shakespeare's printed plays and other non-dramatic texts published at this time, the commercial stage witnessed a profusion of historical dramatizations that are not clearly related to print patterns and the narrower historiographical focus of published works, a significant factor in understanding the range and definition of 'history' in relation to early modern plays. Henslowe's *Diary* indicates a considerable number

---

[17] George Carey became the patron of the Chamberlain's Men in July 1596, upon the death of his father, Henry Carey, first Baron Hunsdon and Lord Chamberlain, who had been the company's patron since its formation in 1594. For the first year of George's patronage, the company's name reverted to Lord Hunsdon's Men, as the office of the Lord Chamberlain had passed to William Brooke, Baron Cobham. Following George's later investiture with the chamberlainship in April 1597, the company regained its title as the Chamberlain's Men.

[18] Sonia Massai, 'Shakespeare, text and paratext', *Shakespeare Survey 62* (Cambridge 2009), pp. 1–11; p. 6.

[19] For example, the title page for *1* and *2 Edward IV* embellishes the plays' description as it was recorded in the Stationers' Register on 28 August 1599, with the addition 'Likewise the besiedging of London, by the bastarde Falconbridge, and the valiant defence of the same by the Lord Maior and the Cittizens': Thomas Heywood, *The First and Second partes of King Edward the Fourth* (1599), A1r.

of now 'lost' plays that, from the evidence of their titles and records, dramatized legendary British history, classical history, biblical history and foreign history – all of which are either unrepresented or under-represented in print at this time.[20] These lost plays have been overlooked by dominant critical narratives of the 'history play', which tend to define the genre and chart its development in parallel with Shakespeare's extant dramatic output and, in particular, by Wise's quartos.[21]

Supposing a direct correlation between stage and print success ignores the fact that these two environments had different audiences and agendas. Although prominent on the London bookstalls, the plays Wise published represent only a small fraction of what would have been performed on stage and, as Holger Syme points out in relation to archival absences, 'the danger lies in assuming that everything that was valued and broadly influential has survived and that the literary development of early modern drama was largely a print phenomenon, with trajectories of influence dominated by published plays'.[22] While focusing on extant texts is inevitable and justifiable to a certain degree, evidence from performance accounts and records points to a significant difference between published plays and theatrical repertories, and, in considering the dramatization of historical subject matter, a more expansive range of histories was prominently (and profitably) featured in the commercial theatres. As opposed to playbook publication being representative of theatrical patterns, it can be seen, instead, as a motivated process of careful selection that connects with wider literary trends, becoming a signifier of the plays' literary identity, as distinct from their performance existence. Far from being a self-contained example of a successful publishing venture, the Wise quartos highlight the importance of exploring the strategies and influences, including non-dramatic publication patterns and patronal connections, that underlie the selection of certain plays for publication and the effect this selection can have on wider issues of play survival and repertory studies.

BETWEEN THE SIGNS OF THE ANGEL AND THE WHITE GREYHOUND: THE SIGNIFICANCE OF PARATEXTUAL ATTRIBUTION

During the 1590s, as Lukas Erne observes, the majority of professional plays were published anonymously, with paratextual attributions to authors appearing infrequently.[23] In 1598, Shakespeare's name was first presented – unambiguously – on the title pages of playbooks, in the second editions of *Richard II* and *Richard III*, published by Wise, and the first extant edition of *Love's Labour's Lost*, published by Cuthbert Burby.[24] Within one year, Shakespeare was the most attributed professional dramatist in print,

---

[20] Consider, for example, the references in Henslowe's *Diary* to lost plays that, from the evidence of their titles, dramatized early British history, none of which were published – 'Chinon of England' (January 1596; fols. 14r–15v, 21v, 25r); 'Vortigern' (December 1596; fols. 22v, 25v, 26r, 95r); 'Uther Pendragon' (April 1597; fols. 26v–27r); 'The Conquest of Brute' by Chettle and Day (July 1598; fols. 49r–52v); 'Arthur King of England' by Hathaway (April 1598; fols. 45v–46r); 'Mulmutius Dunwallow' by William Rankins (October 1598; fol. 50r); 'Brute Greenshield' (March 1599; fol. 54r); and 'Ferrex and Porrex' by Haughton (March 1600; fols. 68r–69r): *Henslowe's Diary*, ed. R. A. Foakes, 2nd edn (Cambridge, 2002). For a discussion of lost plays from the late 1590s featuring the legend of Brutus, see Misha Teramura, 'Brute parts: from Troy to Britain at the Rose, 1595–1600', in *Lost Plays in Shakespeare's England*, ed. David McInnis and Matthew Steggle (Basingstoke, 2014), pp. 127–47.

[21] See, for example, Phyllis Rackin, *Stages of History: Shakespeare's English Chronicles* (London, 1990), and Ralf Hertel, *Staging England in the Elizabethan History Play: Performing National Identity* (Farnham, 2014).

[22] Holger Syme, 'The meaning of success: stories of 1594 and its aftermath', *Shakespeare Quarterly* 61.4 (2010), 490–525; pp. 519, 524.

[23] Lukas Erne, 'The popularity of Shakespeare in print', *Shakespeare Survey 62* (Cambridge, 2009), pp. 12–29; pp. 26–7.

[24] *Locrine*, published in 1595, contains a title-page attribution to 'W.S.', which could be taken to suggest Shakespeare, although the ascription is far from unambiguous and does not convey or advertise the same clarity of authorship as the editions from 1598.

with five title-page references to his authorship by 1599, and nine by 1600.[25] While *Love's Labour's Lost* may appear to warrant greater attention as the first extant edition of a play with a Shakespearian attribution, the reprinted quartos published by Wise point to a more developed, consistent and specific strategy in their paratexts. This concentration in attribution again relates to Wise's business location in Paul's Churchyard, and can be seen as part of an effort to elevate the status of commercial drama and advertise Shakespeare's connection to a powerful literary and theatrical patron.

While Burby was one of the main stationers involved in the publication of commercial plays during the 1590s, responsible for playbooks such as *Orlando Furioso* (Q1 1594, Q2 1599), *Mother Bombie* (Q1 1594, Q2 1598), *The Cobbler's Prophecy* (Q1 1594), *The Taming of a Shrew* (Q1 1594, Q2 1596), and *Romeo and Juliet* (Q2 1599), his dramatic publications do not prioritize authorial attributions, unlike Wise's quartos. Aside from *Love's Labour's Lost*, Burby's only other play to contain a title-page attribution is *The Cobbler's Prophecy* (to 'Robert Wilson, Gent.'), and, significantly, the full attribution in *Love's Labour's Lost* reads 'Newly corrected and augmented / By W. Shakespeare', which implicitly aligns Shakespeare's name, through the spacing and phrasing of the attribution, with the processes of correction and expansion rather than initial authorship.[26]

Wise, on the other hand, exclusively published plays by Shakespeare, which, from 1598 onwards, carried title-page attributions. Regardless of whether it was Burby's edition of *Love's Labour's Lost* (or its antecedent) or one of Wise's reprints that first appeared on bookstalls with a paratextual attribution in 1598, it is Wise's publication practices that are especially significant, owing to their relative consistency, which also distinguishes Wise from the other individuals who may have influenced the inclusion of paratextual attributions. Tiffany Stern has suggested that title pages resembled the playbills that were used to advertise theatrical performances, as the construction of title pages drew on their content, phrasing and layout,

therefore raising the possibility that dramatists and companies could have encouraged the inclusion of authorial paratexts through a parallel usage on the playbills.[27] Indeed, the title pages of playbooks were a site of collaborative writing, with a play's title usually deriving from the manuscript, the imprint details coming from the publisher, and the other title-page descriptions (including attributions) occupying a more ambiguous space in terms of agency (and possibly reflecting the influence of playbills in their composition). However, in the case of the Shakespearian attributions at the end of the sixteenth century, the greatest consistency appears when Wise is involved as the publisher. As discussed in connection to Burby, other plays by Shakespeare that were published by different stationers do not contain the same regularity in attribution, suggesting that Wise occupies a key role in its inclusion and that the patronage connection between Shakespeare, Wise and George Carey points towards a synergetic relationship between these agents in the incorporation of authorial attributions.

While Wise's first editions of *Richard II* and *Richard III* in 1597 do not contain any attributions, suggesting that the marketability of Shakespeare's name was not immediately apparent, and corresponding to the inconsistent appearance of other dramatists' names on playbook title pages, Wise's editions from 1598 onwards regularly carry the attribution 'By William Shakespeare'.[28] This development marks a shift in the status and importance of Shakespeare's name in relation to his dramatic works, which is further signalled by the first appearance of his name in the Stationers' Register on 23 August 1600. Wise was again involved in this

---

[25] Erne, '*The popularity of Shakespeare in print*', pp. 26–7.

[26] Robert Wilson, *The Cobbler's Prophecy* (1594), A2r; *Love's Labour's Lost* (1598), A1r.

[27] Tiffany Stern, *Documents of Performance in Early Modern England* (Cambridge, 2009), pp. 36–62.

[28] Of Wise's play editions, *Richard II* Q2 (1598) and Q3 (1598), *Richard III* Q2 (1598) and Q3 (1602), *1 Henry IV* Q2 (1599), *2 Henry IV* Q1 (1600), and *Much Ado About Nothing* Q1 (1600) contain attributions to Shakespeare.

introduction, with the inclusion of Shakespeare's name being part of Wise and Aspley's joint entry for *2 Henry IV* and *Much Ado About Nothing*, and containing a clear declaration of Shakespeare's authorship: 'Wrytten by mr Shakespere'.[29]

The one exception in relation to Wise's attribution practices concerns the publication of *1 Henry IV*. Wise probably published the (undated) first edition in 1598, as he entered the play in the Stationers' Register on 25 February 1598 (providing the *terminus a quo*) and published the second edition later in 1598 (giving the *terminus ad quem*). The first edition survives in one sheet only (C1–4 v), with the title page no longer extant, which makes it impossible to determine conclusively the play's original history of attribution. The title page of the second edition contains no reference to Shakespeare or the Chamberlain's Men, while the third edition, published by Wise in 1599, claims the play was 'Newly corrected by W. Shake-speare'.[30] Although it is possible that the first two editions of *1 Henry IV* were actually printed earlier in 1598 than the second quartos of *Richard II* and *Richard III* (containing the first attributions), and therefore not constituting an exception to the overarching patterns described, the phrasing on the 1599 title page of *1 Henry IV* and the absence of any references to the Chamberlain's Men on subsequent editions potentially indicate a connection to the Oldcastle controversy. While the title pages of all the extant editions encourage recollection of the association between Falstaff and the Cobham family, notably by drawing attention to this character in their paratexts, the 1598 title page, perhaps strategically, refrains from mentioning those involved in the offence – namely, Shakespeare and George Carey's company. The 1599 title page introduces Shakespeare as a corrector, in contrast to the more assertive claims of authorship on the other Wise quartos, suggesting an effort to curtail attributive claims and emphasize the play's 'corrected' state. Indeed, this new incorporation of Shakespeare as a corrector in the third edition is particularly striking, as the changes to the play – specifically the renaming of the character Sir John

Oldcastle as Falstaff – were made in the copy for the first edition (see C3v–4 v). *1 Henry IV*'s sequence of publication displays a continuing negotiation of the Oldcastle debacle, with the first edition containing the renamed character, the second edition eschewing any reference to Shakespeare or the company, and the third edition belatedly introducing Shakespeare as a corrector.

This possible marketing sensitivity in relation to an incident of play censorship supports the previously proposed connection between Wise and the Chamberlain's Men. Moreover, Wise's other title pages after 1598 consistently align Shakespeare's name with attributions to the Chamberlain's Men and, by extension, to the company's patron, George Carey. This title-page link between dramatist, theatrical company and patron was relatively uncommon at this stage in the publication of professional plays. The earliest examples come from 1594, in Robert Greene's *Friar Bacon and Friar Bungay*, Thomas Lodge's *Wounds of Civil War*, Marlowe and Nashe's *Dido, Queen of Carthage* and Marlowe's *Edward II*. In *Friar Bacon and Friar Bungay*, for example, the title page contains the attribution 'As it was plaid by her Maiesties seruants' and 'Made by Robert Greene Maister of Arts', linking, through the *mise en page*, Greene with Queen Elizabeth's Men, and, by extension, with Elizabeth I as the company's titular theatrical patron.[31] All of these title pages also

---

29 The full entry, made out to Wise and Aspley, reads 'Two bookes. the one called: Muche a Doo about nothinge. Th[e] other the second p[ar]te of the history of kinge Henry the iiijth w[i]th the humours of S[i]r John Ffallstaff: Wrytten by mr Shakespere': The Worshipful Company of Stationers and Newspaper Makers: Liber C, fol. 63v. Available through *Shakespeare Documented*, www.Shakespearedocumented.org.

30 William Shakespeare, *The Historie of Henrie the Fovrth* (1599), A1r.

31 Robert Greene, *The Honorable Historie of Frier Bacon and Frier Bongay* (1594), A2r. See Scott McMillin and Sally-Beth MacLean's *The Queen's Men and their Plays* (Cambridge, 1998), pp. 25–9 for a discussion of how the Queen's Men, through their name, patron and court connections, presented an opportunity for carrying royal influence throughout the country.

contain assertions of their dramatists' gentlemanly standing or university education, suggesting an attempt to elevate the status and marketability of commercial playbooks through these connections. With his second editions of *Richard II* and *Richard III* in 1598, Wise was the first publisher to connect Shakespeare's name with a theatrical company in print, and, in doing so, to advertise an association with an influential aristocratic patron. Burby's 1598 edition of *Love's Labour's Lost* does not reference the Chamberlain's Men, and, after the 1594 texts (all of which were published by different stationers), Wise's playbooks are the first to draw attention to a dramatist and patron in their paratexts, suggesting a marketing and positioning strategy that aligns the plays with the interests and cachet of George Carey.[32]

The presentation of the Wise quartos and their title-page attributions highlight the overlap between patronal and commercial considerations in the transmission of plays, pointing to a synergetic relationship between these two factors, which is further highlighted by Wise's bookshop location at the Sign of the Angel and the publication patterns of his neighbouring stationers at the White Greyhound in Paul's Cross Churchyard. During the late 1590s, this area witnessed the greatest concentration of Shakespearian wholesale in London and emerged as the locus for Shakespearian paratextual attribution, which in all cases connected Shakespeare with an aristocratic patron.

Before 1598, Shakespeare's name had only been associated in print with his two narrative poems, *Venus and Adonis* and *The Rape of Lucrece*, first published in 1593 and 1594 respectively, and containing signed dedications by Shakespeare to his patron, Henry Wriothesley, third Earl of Southampton. These editions were printed by Richard Field for John Harrison and, later, William Leake, and proved hugely successful with readers, judging by the scarcity of extant copies (suggesting they were, quite literally, read to destruction by their early readers) and their numerous subsequent editions.[33] Harrison published reprints of *Venus and Adonis* in 1594, 1595(?) and 1596, and *Lucrece* in 1598 and twice in

1600.[34] Leake was responsible for two further editions of *Venus and Adonis* in 1599.[35] Significantly, all of these editions (with the exception of Harrison's 1598 and 1600 reprints of *Lucrece*) were offered for wholesale at the Sign of the White Greyhound, just three doors (or about 20 feet) away from Wise's shop in Paul's Cross.[36] With the editions of the narrative poems and seven of Wise's playbooks displaying authorial attributions and patronal associations, this small section of Paul's Churchyard between the signs of the Angel and the White Greyhound became a focal point for Shakespearian wholesale and paratextual attribution in London at the end of the sixteenth century. Wise's exclusive focus on Shakespeare's plays and his later inclusion of authorial attributions in the second editions of *Richard II* and *Richard III* were possibly shaped by the earlier strategies of the narrative poems and their ongoing success with readers. Indeed, this area of London could

---

[32] A considerable number of the wider publications dedicated to George Carey involve military or historical subject matter, suggesting contemporaries associated him with these interests, and making Wise's investment in Shakespeare's English histories appear attuned to Carey's reputation. See the dedications in Thomas Churchyard's *A pleasant discourse of court and wars* (1596), Marin Barleti's *Historie of George Castriot* (1596), and Giles Fletcher's *Policy of the Turkish Empire* (1597).

[33] Colin Burrow suggests there were further editions of *Venus and Adonis*, which were 'completely destroyed by their eager consumers'. See William Shakespeare, *The Complete Sonnets and Poems*, ed. Colin Burrow (Oxford, 2002), p. 7.

[34] The title page of the third edition of *Venus and Adonis* is no longer extant. Conjectured date of publication is taken from the ESTC.

[35] Richard Field initially entered *Venus and Adonis* in the Stationers' Register on 18 April 1593, before he transferred his rights to John Harrison on 25 June 1594, who then published a further three editions between 1594 and 1596, before transferring ownership to William Leake on 25 June 1596. *Lucrece* was first entered to Harrison on 9 May 1594 but, unlike for *Venus and Adonis*, Harrison retained his rights to the poem.

[36] Leake took over Harrison's premises at the White Greyhound in 1596, and Harrison moved to the nearby Greyhound on Paternoster Row, taking with him the publication rights to *Lucrece*. For a map of the area, see Blayney, *The Bookshops in Paul's Cross Churchyard*, p. 76.

well have been associated in the minds of stationers and readers with the publication of Shakespeare's dramatic and non-dramatic works, with no other part of London exhibiting a similar concentration at this time.

This claim of a reciprocal connection between Shakespeare's dramatic and non-dramatic texts is further supported by the publication of *The Passionate Pilgrim* in 1599. Until this time, Shakespeare's name had only appeared on the title pages of his printed *playbooks*, with the narrative poems containing signed dedications, which was common practice with poetic collections.[37] However, in 1599, the second edition of *The Passionate Pilgrim* became the first non-dramatic text attributed to Shakespeare on its title page, which describes the collection as 'By W. Shakespeare'.[38] Interestingly, this octavo collection of poems (only five of which are by Shakespeare) was printed for William Jaggard and William Leake, and offered for wholesale, along with Shakespeare's narrative poems, at the White Greyhound.[39] Given the geographical proximity of the bookshops, *The Passionate Pilgrim*'s title-page attribution was probably influenced by the Wise quartos and their success with readers, thus furthering the link between these two bookshops and their stationers. While Wise's investments can be primarily associated with the evidence for a publication network between Wise, George Carey and the Chamberlain's Men, the surrounding bookshops also shaped his venture, and, reciprocally, Wise's editions impacted neighbouring publishers, particularly in relation to title-page attributions.

The importance of bookshop locations becomes even more apparent when considering, as Stern has argued, that printed title pages were used as advertisements and were posted around the bookstalls in London.[40] These extracted title pages announced the availability of specific works for individual or wholesale purchase from a given stationer, and Paul's Churchyard, as the centre of the London book trade, was a prominent place in which to view these advertisements, as described by Thomas Campion in his address 'The Writer to his Booke'

from *Observations in the Art of English Poesie* (also published by Wise in 1602):[41]

> Whether thus hasts my little booke so fast?
> To Paules Churchyard; what in those cels to stand,
> With one leafe like a riders cloke put vp
> To catch a termer?

The title page 'leafe like a riders cloke put vp' was designed to attract prospective buyers and appeal to their literary interests, and the inclusion of Shakespeare's name on Wise's editions represents, as Joseph Loewenstein describes, 'the process by which authorship was converted into a new form of economic agency', investing Shakespeare's position as a dramatist for the professional stage with increasing importance.[42] During the late 1590s, the area between the signs of the Angel and the White Greyhound regularly featured a considerable number of title pages advertising works by 'Shakespeare' (including *Richard II*, *Richard III*, *1* and *2 Henry IV*, and *The Passionate Pilgrim*, all with Shakespearian attributions), as well as the advertisements for *Venus and Adonis* and *Lucrece*, which did not contain Shakespeare's name but which were connected to Shakespeare through the signed dedications that were part of the complete texts. This geographical concentration would

---

[37] Colin Burrow observes that (in relation to the narrative poems) 'it was quite usual in this period for authors' names to be attached to the dedicatory epistles rather than appearing on the title-pages'. See Shakespeare, *The Complete Sonnets and Poems*, p. 6.

[38] *The Passionate Pilgrime* (1599), A2r. No copies of the title page for the first edition of *The Passionate Pilgrim* are extant. This edition was probably also published in 1599, or possibly in late 1598, after the printer of the volume, Thomas Judson, set up his press in September 1598. See Shakespeare, *The Complete Sonnets and Poems*, p. 74.

[39] Of the twenty poems in *The Passionate Pilgrim*, those attributable to Shakespeare are numbers 1, 2, 3, 5, and 16. See Shakespeare, *The Complete Sonnets and Poems*, p. 76.

[40] Stern, *Documents of Performance*, pp. 36–62.

[41] Thomas Campion, *Observations in the Art of English Poesie* (1602), B4v.

[42] Joseph Loewenstein, *Ben Jonson and Possessive Authorship* (Cambridge, 2002), p. 25.

have encouraged an association between Shakespeare as a poet and as a dramatist for the stage, shaping the literary reputation and characteristics of this part of Paul's Churchyard.

By 1600, the impact of Wise's paratexts, made more significant through the success of these editions with readers, can be seen through the widespread incorporation of Shakespearian title-page attributions, as they start to appear more regularly in playbooks published by other stationers. *A Midsummer Night's Dream* (published in 1600 for Thomas Fisher), *The Merchant of Venice* (published in 1600 for Thomas Hayes), *The Merry Wives of Windsor* (published in 1602 for Arthur Johnson), and *Hamlet* (published in 1603 for Nicholas Ling and John Trundle) all contain the title-page attribution 'By William Shakespeare'.[43] Along with being the most published commercial dramatist at the end of the sixteenth century (based on edition numbers), Shakespeare was also the most attributed, with nine playbook editions advertising his authorship on their title pages by 1600. In comparison, as Erne points out, Robert Greene was the second most attributed dramatist at this time, with only five playbook editions displaying his name on their title pages.[44]

Suggesting that readers and publishers were associating Shakespeare's plays with works of a more established 'literary' status, compilers of poetic miscellanies and commonplace books started to extract quotations from Shakespeare's plays and poetry, presenting them alongside passages from writers such as Spenser and Daniel.[45] William Scott's manuscript treatise *The Model of Poesy* (c. 1599) incorporates references to *Lucrece* and *Richard II*, together with extracts from classical and English authors, such as Philip Sidney, pointing to a development in Shakespeare's literary status, which Gavin Alexander describes as 'unprecedented'.[46] Other readers and collectors singled out Shakespeare's plays from amongst other dramatists, as shown by an inventory list (1627) from the library of Lady Frances Egerton, Countess of Bridgewater, which references a bound volume containing 'Diuers Playes by

Shakespeare 1602', while other play volumes recorded in the collection have no authorial designations.[47]

Similarly, the miscellanies published under the auspices of John Bodenham, specifically *Belvedere, or The Garden of the Muses* (1600), and *Englands Parnassus* (1600), contain a significant number of extracts from Shakespeare's plays, with the majority of these quotations coming from Wise's quarto editions.[48] *Englands Parnassus* identifies authors throughout (although not always correctly), placing, for example, a quotation from *Richard II* ('If Angels fight / Weake men must fall, for heauen stil gards the right') immediately before an extract from Daniel's closet play, *Cleopatra* (first published in 1594), with such juxtapositions encouraging interpretative and literary

---

[43] The Stationers' Register entries for *A Midsummer Night's Dream* (8 October 1600) and *The Merchant of Venice* (28 October 1600, following its initial entry on 22 July 1598) were recorded shortly after Wise and Aspley's joint entry on 23 August 1600, which contained the first reference to Shakespeare in the Register. Interestingly, these later entries do not reference Shakespeare, further suggesting the singularity and significance of Wise's attribution project.

[44] Erne, 'The popularity of Shakespeare in print', p. 27.

[45] For defining Shakespeare as a 'literary' dramatist and the implications of that definition, see Lukas Erne, *Shakespeare as Literary Dramatist* (Cambridge, 2007).

[46] William Scott, *The Model of Poesy*, ed. Gavin Alexander (Cambridge, 2013), p. lxi.

[47] As discussed by Erne in 'The popularity of Shakespeare in print', p. 15.

[48] *Bel-vedere* contains forty-seven quotations from *Richard II*, thirteen from *Richard III*, thirteen from *Romeo and Juliet*, ten from *The True Tragedy*, five from *Love's Labour's Lost*, and one from *1 Henry IV*. *Englands Parnassus* includes thirteen quotations from *Romeo and Juliet*, seven from *Richard II*, five from *Richard III*, three from *Love's Labour's Lost*, and two from *1 Henry IV*. Between the two texts, sixty-one quotations are extracted from Wise's editions, while forty-four are taken from plays published by other stationers. Quotation statistics are drawn from Zachary Lesser and Peter Stallybrass, 'The first literary *Hamlet* and the commonplacing of professional plays', *Shakespeare Quarterly* 59.4 (2008), 371–420; p. 395. See also Peter Stallybrass and Roger Chartier, 'Reading and authorship: the circulation of Shakespeare, 1590–1619', in *A Concise Companion to Shakespeare and the Text*, ed. Andrew Murphy (Oxford, 2007), pp. 35–56.

connections between the writers.[49] *Bel-vedere* presents shorter quotations without identifying the authors or texts, but the prefatory address, 'To the Reader', lists Shakespeare alongside other prominent English poets, including Spenser and Daniel, as well as 'Honourable' and 'noble personages', including Mary Sidney, Countess of Pembroke, Philip Sidney, and Walter Ralegh.[50] Similarly, Francis Meres's *Palladis Tamia* (1598) favourably compares English writers to Greek, Latin and Italian poets, describing the 'English tongue [as] mightily enriched and gorgeouslie inuested in rare ornaments and resplendent abiliments by Sir Philip Sidney, Spencer, Daniel, Drayton, Warner, Shakespeare, Marlow, and Chapman'. Meres identifies Shakespeare as the best for comedy and tragedy, specifically referencing 'his Richard the 2, Richard the 3, Henry the 4, King Iohn, Titus Andronicus, and his Romeo and Juliet'.[51] The wider significance of Wise's quartos, with their authorial and paratextual concentration, can be partly traced in these miscellanies and collections, which often prioritize the Wise editions and, in doing so, place Shakespeare as a professional dramatist alongside celebrated classical and English poets.

While Shakespeare's position as a published and marketable writer perhaps seemed assured at the beginning of the seventeenth century, it has regularly puzzled critics that patterns in Shakespearian playbook publication decline significantly after 1603. Between 1604 and 1623, only four first editions of plays by Shakespeare were printed, a considerable reduction in frequency from Elizabethan publication patterns.[52] Changes in the literary landscape of Paul's Cross and the patronage network between Wise, George Carey and the Chamberlain's Men offer a possible explanation, again drawing attention to the importance of looking collectively at commercial and patronal influences in publication. In 1603, Andrew Wise stopped publishing and disappeared from historical records; George Carey, patron of the Chamberlain's Men and Wise's writers, died; and the geographical centre for Shakespearian wholesale between the Angel and the White Greyhound

dissipated. Matthew Law at the Sign of the Fox near St Austin's Gate (in the southeast corner of St Paul's) received the rights to Shakespeare's history plays from Wise, while John Harrison had moved to Paternoster Row in 1596. Only William Leake, who retained the rights to *Lucrece* and *The Passionate Pilgrim*, remained in Paul's Cross, after moving premises to the Sign of the Holy Ghost in 1602. This prior concentration of Shakespearian publication and wholesale within a spatial range of approximately 20 feet was ultimately a short-lived (yet highly significant) enterprise that did not continue into the Jacobean period.[53] With James I's patronage of the renamed King's Men, and different stationers taking over the publication of Shakespeare's plays, the previously prominent patronal and geographical connections that may have encouraged rapid playbook publication in the late 1590s were no longer in play.

CONCLUSIONS

Far from having either limited consequential agency in the publication of plays, or merely contributing ineptly or destructively to the process (a view that continues to prevail), publishers, such as Wise, were actively involved in selecting plays for publication and influencing their presentation as printed playbooks. Wise is particularly significant as the first publisher to concentrate exclusively on plays by Shakespeare and incorporate regular paratextual attributions, as well as specializing in a narrow group of plays that dramatize similar historical material. Largely as a result of these editions, Shakespeare was the most published and

---

[49] Robert Allott, *Englands Parnassus: or the choysest flowers of our moderne poets* (1600), B2r.

[50] John Bodenham and Anthony Munday, *Bel-vedere, or The Garden of the Muses* (1600), A4v–A5v.

[51] Francis Meres, *Palladis Tamia: Wits treasury being the second part of Wits common wealth* (1598), Nn4r, Oo2r.

[52] Of Shakespeare's plays, only *King Lear* (1608), *Troilus and Cressida* (1609), *Pericles* (1609), and *Othello* (1622) were published in single-text first editions between 1604 and 1623.

[53] Blayney, *The Bookshops in Paul's Cross Churchyard*, p. 18.

most attributed professional dramatist by the end of the sixteenth century, shaping his reputation as a poet and playwright for the stage, and possibly paving the way for other dramatists to establish a prominent and distinctive identity in print. Ben Jonson's *Every Man Out of His Humour*, for example, was published by William Holme in 1600 'As it was first composed by the Author B.I. / Containing more than hath been Publickely Spoken or Acted', and marking the beginning of Jonson's regular claims of authorship and ownership of his dramatic texts.[54]

This article has suggested that, in the selection of plays and incorporation of paratextual attributions, Wise was influenced by both a patronal connection to George Carey and the Chamberlain's Men, and the position of his business within the London book trade, with the non-dramatic publication patterns of neighbouring stationers (including Waterson's editions of Daniel's *Civil Wars*, and Harrison's editions of *Venus and Adonis* and *Lucrece*) encouraging his investment in Shakespeare's history plays. While the nature of extant records and texts, and the multiplicity of agents involved in the transmission process, inevitably make it impossible to assert conclusively the factors controlling the selection and presentation of playbooks, exploring these questions and recognizing the important role that was played by stationers are nevertheless critical in furthering our understanding of play survival and reception, as well as the wider performance repertories of theatrical companies.[55]

---

[54] Ben Jonson, *The Comicall Satyre of Every Man Out of His Humour* (1600), A1r. As Zachary Lesser and Peter Stallybrass point out, this was also the first professional play to be printed with commonplace markers. See Lesser and Stallybrass, 'The first literary *Hamlet* and the commonplacing of professional plays', p. 395.

[55] This article originated as a paper for the seminar 'Notions of Influence in Shakespeare's Work' at the World Shakespeare Congress. I would like to thank the seminar organizers, Christy Desmet, Donatella Pallotti, Paola Pugliatti, Robert Sawyer, for their support of this article, as well as John Jowett and Sonia Massai for their later feedback.

SHAKESPEARE AND HARDY:
THE TRAGI-COMIC NEXUS

TOM McALINDON

'... an antagonistic glare that had begun as a smile'
(Thomas Hardy, *The Mayor of Casterbridge*)[1]

In the first three of his major tragic novels, *The Return of the Native*, *The Mayor of Casterbridge* and *Tess of the D'Urbervilles*, Thomas Hardy exploited his natural gift for comedy, no doubt for commercial as well as artistic reasons. There is, moreover, a high degree of self-consciousness in his mixing of the two genres; this is manifest in explicit references to tragedy and comedy (used either as metaphors for contrary attitudes to the human condition or as indices of character), and in accounts of dramatic, ritual or ceremonial events, signalled as a reprehensible confusion of levity and gravity. This self-consciousness indicates a profound and fruitful relationship with Shakespeare, though not one which deflected Hardy from his gloomier sense of the tragic.[2]

I

It is noteworthy that genre self-consciousness is already apparent in *Far from the Madding Crowd* (1874), which immediately precedes *The Return of the Native* (1878), almost as if Hardy was gearing himself up for an ambitious experiment to come. The earlier novel is not, as has been suggested, an undeveloped tragedy,[3] but rather a pastoral romance loosely but deliberately shaped as a tragi-comedy, arguably with *The Winter's Tale* in mind, a play to which (as we shall see) Hardy had earlier given close attention in his narrative

[1] Thomas Hardy, *The Mayor of Casterbridge*, Wessex Edition (London, 1920), p. 128. Subsequent references to this novel are included in the body of the text.

[2] J. K. Lloyd Jones, *Thomas Hardy and the Comic Muse* (Newcastle upon Tyne, 2009), pp. 202–5, comments perceptively on the combination of comedy and tragedy in Hardy. Ronald Knowles's Bakhtinian essay 'Carnival and Tragedy in Thomas Hardy's Novels' (*The Thomas Hardy Journal*, 21 (2004), 109–24) does not consider Shakespearian affinities. Neither does Jakob Lothe in 'Variants on genre: *The Return of the Native*, *The Mayor of Casterbridge*, *The Hand of Ethelberta*', in *The Cambridge Companion to Thomas Hardy*, ed. Dale Kramer (Cambridge, 1999), pp. 112–29; nor Richard Nemesvari in '"Genres are not to be mixed ... I will not mix them": Discourse, Ideology, and Generic Hybridity in Hardy's Fiction', in *A Companion to Thomas Hardy*, ed. Keith Wilson (Oxford, 2009), pp. 102–15. These two critics emphasize Hardy's commitment to genre blending but touch only lightly on that of comedy and tragedy. Nemesvari interprets Hardy's 'genre hybridity' as ideologically subversive and a challenge to 'cultural proprieties'. In his study of Hardy's relationship, both temperamental and artistic, to Shakespeare ('Hardy', in *Scott, Dickens. Eliot, Hardy. Great Shakespeareans*, vol. 5, ed. Adrian Poole and Peter Holland [London, 2011], pp. 139–83), Peter Holbrook stresses the 'impure multiplicity' of their art: their love of the grotesque and a cognate attraction to 'mongrel tragi-comedy', these having ethical as well as aesthetic significance, being symptomatic of an empirical, non-doctrinaire, pluralistic morality. In these respects, Shakespeare 'helped Hardy to become Hardy' (pp. 174–6). In a series of articles based mainly on Hardy's marginal comments in Singer's edition of the plays, Dennis Taylor shows conclusively that the influence of Shakespeare on Hardy was 'early, continuing, and pervasive': Dennis Taylor, 'Hardy's copy of *Hamlet*', *The Thomas Hardy Journal*, 20 (2004), 38–54; 'Hardy and Hamlet', in *Thomas Hardy Reappraised: Essays in Honour of Michael Millgate* (Toronto, 2006), 38–54; 'From Stratford to Casterbridge: the Influence of Shakespeare', in *The Ashgate Companion to Thomas Hardy*, ed. Rosemary Morgan (Farnham, Surrey, and Burlington, VT, 2010), pp. 124–43.

[3] Dale Kramer, *Thomas Hardy: The Forms of Tragedy* (Detroit, 1975), p. 47.

TOM McALINDON

poem 'Life and death at sunrise' (1867). Introduced as an amiable young farmer with a smile as expansive as the rising sun, the hero of *Far from the Madding Crowd* is obviously destined to overcome obstacles and win the beautiful, coquettish heroine, Bathsheba. Being of a moderate and patient disposition, Gabriel Oak is not greatly troubled by the show of teasing indifference with which she terminates their first encounter; instead, he returns to his work 'With an air between that of Tragedy and Comedy', more bemused than amused by her 'antics' on horseback.[4] By contrast, his rival in love, Farmer Boldwood, is a man whose 'equilibrium disturbed, he was in extremity at once' (137); he is the novel's chief source of 'tragic intensity' (58), bringing to the plot its powerful ingredients of insane jealousy and murder. Invariably stern, he 'was not quite companionable in the eyes of merry men and scoffers'; but he was tolerable to 'those acquainted with grief. Being a man who read all the dramas of life seriously, if he failed to please when they were comedies, there was no frivolous treatment to reproach him for when they chanced to end tragically' (138).

Just such a reproach is directed by Gabriel at Joseph Poorgrass, the waggoner given the unhappy task of conveying the coffin of Fanny Robin in a makeshift funeral cart from the Casterbury Poorhouse to the corner of a graveyard reserved for 'reprobates'. Joseph is oppressed by 'the unfathomable gloom' of the night and by the proximity of his 'very pale companion' and 'the grim Leveller'; and although anxiously aware that the parish would disapprove, he breaks his 'melancholy errand' at a wayside inn, where he succumbs to the spirit of bibulous friends. These friends never 'trouble or worry … about doctrines', celebrate 'the merry old ways of good life', and offer a persuasive argument in his defence when Gabriel arrives to reproach him for effectively ensuring that the abused maiden's funeral will not be 'performed with proper decency' (332–9). With this rebuke and defence of mirth in funeral, Hardy's genre-consciousness translates into metafictionality; the scene invites us to reflect on his

own bold mixing of the two modes, albeit in a novel that is primarily comic rather than tragic.[5]

Although classical objections to mingling tragedy and comedy may no longer have held sway, the difficulty of injecting comedy into a primarily tragic work in an aesthetically satisfying manner remained. And, since Shakespeare more than anyone else had succeeded in this, it was to his example that Hardy looked for inspiration and reassurance. The first of *Far from the Madding Crowd*'s abundant literary allusions is a humorously intended quotation from *Macbeth*; far more significant, however, is the extent to which the interment of Fanny Robin, love's tragic victim, echoes that of Ophelia, where the clown-sexton's insensitivity ('Has this fellow no feeling of his business that a sings at gravemaking?') and Laertes' anger at the burial's 'maimèd rites',[6] call attention to what Ben Jonson and his like would have seen as 'the proper decency' of high tragedy. But even more illuminating, perhaps, is the allusion, signalled in Joseph's 'very pale companion' on that 'melancholy journey', to *A Midsummer Night's Dream*, a play in

---

[4] *Far from the Madding Crowd*, Wessex Edition (London, 1922), pp. 1, 21. Subsequent references in the text.

[5] Reference should be made here also to *A Pair of Blue Eyes* (1873), written one year before *Far from the Madding Crowd*. It shows Hardy's awareness that the rigid canons of dramatic and social decorum were part and parcel of the same deadening conservatism. This notion is powerfully (almost allegorically) projected in the character of Henry Knight, the reviewer and literary critic who rejects and effectively kills his beloved when he learns that she once attempted an elopement. He is appalled by the fact that – the phrasing is finely ironic – 'the proprieties must be a dead letter to her'. The 'untouched and orderly' volumes on his shelves, he feels, rebuke him for having fallen so deeply in love with an 'unstable' young woman with so much 'indifference to decorum'. This contrasts ironically with the cheerful irreverence of the workmen in Lady Luxellian's vault, an obvious allusion to the grave-digger clown whose unfeeling behaviour shocks and amuses Hamlet in a scene that would have offended many 'correct' sensibilities well beyond the eighteenth century (Thomas Hardy, *A Pair of Blue Eyes*, Wessex Edition (London, 1927), pp. 406–7, 293–4).

[6] *William Shakespeare: The Complete Works*, ed. Stanley Wells, Gary Taylor, John Jowett, and William Montgomery (Oxford, 1986), 5.1.65–6, p. 214.

256

which the mingling of the two genres is a question so explicitly foregrounded.

In *A Midsummer Night's Dream*, and in *Romeo and Juliet*, Shakespeare provided a theoretical and practical response to Sidney's aristocratic sneer at 'our mongrel tragi-comedy'.[7] Written at approximately the same time (we don't know which came first), each of these two plays, as has often been remarked, is potentially the other, one being a comedy which hovers on tragedy throughout, the other a romantic comedy in the making which suddenly becomes tragic with the killing of its great joker, Mercutio. A key notion in both plays is the need not only to acknowledge opposites as such, but also the rewards and the dangers of trying to unite them in an orderly fashion. In the *Dream*'s opening scene, Theseus presents himself as the master of socio-aesthetic order, determined to ensure that the spirit of merriment appropriate to his marriage revels is not disturbed by sad thoughts: 'Turn melancholy forth to funerals – / The pale companion is not for our pomp' (1.1.14–15). He is banishing memories of his war with Hippolyta, the Queen whose love he won by doing her injuries; their relationship will now be one of pure harmony: 'I will wed thee in another key' (1.1.17–18). But discord immediately erupts in this scene when he is called upon to arbitrate in a matrimonial dispute. And in the next scene, unbeknown to him, a clownish plan is under way to celebrate his wedding with the performance of a tragedy, and one which its bumbling performers describe as '*A Lamentable Comedy*' (1.2.11). When later he learns what the mechanicals have in store for him, he exclaims: '"Merry" *and* "tragical"? . . . How shall we find the concord of this discord?' (5.1.58–60). However, the phrasing of his question, which recalls the concept of *concordia discors* (or *discordia concors*), contains the answer to his problem: such discords are intrinsic to the functioning of the natural order – and can even be seen as harmonious. In fact, he and Hippolyta have already shown an intuitive understanding of universal nature's system of concordant discord in their declared enthusiasm for the sounds of the hunt: 'musical confusion' when all of nature, 'The skies, the fountains, every region near /

Seemed all one mutual cry . . . So musical a discord, such sweet thunder' (4.1.115–17). Oxymora and paradox are abundant in both plays. However, they can signify not only the delightful harmony of the opposites, 'an union in partition' (3.2.211) – like the friendship of mild, tall Helena and sparky, short Hermia – but also their bewildering confusion or violent mutual antagonism: conditions which temporally overwhelm these two friends, and will – in time hereafter – ruin the splendid marriage of Theseus and Hippolyta, making it the subject of a grim Senecan tragedy: 'So quick [do] bright things come to confusion' (1.1.149) when 'all things change them to the contrary' (*Romeo*, 4.4.117) in the natural order of precariously united opposites.

In *Romeo and Juliet*, Shakespeare expands this indirect justification for the generic mix in the philosophical Friar's discourse on nature's dialectical order (2.2.1–30). The earth is Mother Nature's womb and her tomb; it provides precious flowers and baleful weeds; but within both 'Poison hath residence, and medicine power' (2.2.24). Thus, the early comic scenes provide not only anticipatory parallels to the tragic action but causal, genetic connections and so serve to bind the play into a profound imaginative unity. For example, the merry duel of wits between Romeo and Mercutio, apropos Romeo's Petrarchan affectations, not only prefigures a duel which is fatal rather than funny, it also contains a precondition: Mercutio's temperamental dislike of affectation shifts from friendly banter at Romeo's expense into mocking sarcasm when he thinks of Tybalt's duelling lingo (2.3.12–33), and later, when he encounters Tybalt, into uncontrollable hatred – 'look to hear nothing but discords' (3.1.46–7). Verbal echo brilliantly establishes the oneness of comic and tragic Mercutio. Romeo's huffy 'He jests at scars that never felt a wound' (2.1.43) later

---

[7] See T. McAlindon, *Shakespeare's Tragic Cosmos* (Cambridge, 1991), p. 61; 'What is a Shakespearean Tragedy?' in *The Cambridge Companion to Shakespearean Tragedy* (Cambridge, 2004), p. 5.

becomes his dying friend's response to his assurance that the wound 'cannot be much': ''tis enough. 'Twill serve. Ask for me tomorrow, and you shall find me a grave man' (3.1.95–8). The punning jest encapsulates generic confusion and crystallizes a view of life as terrifyingly unstable. With its dangerously irrepressible joker, this tragedy is holding the mirror up to Nature's fragile harmony.

II

One of Hardy's biographers, Claire Tomalin, has remarked that *The Return of the Native* is full of echoes of *A Midsummer Night's Dream*, mainly in its symbolic use of dream, moonlight and magic.[8] She does not observe, however, Hardy's framing of the tragedy in 'nature's contrarious inconsistencies', nor his often conspicuous combination of the tragic and the comic: 'two distinct moods in close contiguity'.[9] The comic mood is associated from start to finish with Grandfer Cantle, a 'wrinkled reveller' whose respect for his own versatility ('I am up for anything') and sublime confidence in his leadership role, are strongly reminiscent of Bully Bottom (19, 29, 37). Remarks to the effect that his 'well-known merry way' and his 'jerks of juvenility' are inappropriate in 'so venerable' a man leave him unflustered (20, 164). Nor do they deter him from initiating an impromptu choral welcome for Tamsin and Wildeve on the night of their intended wedding. Since (unknown to him and his friends) the wedding was awkwardly postponed and the presumed bride is miserable, the singing is most unwelcome: 'Blundering fools!' mutters Wildeve (51). Moreover, the singing is literally, as well as metaphorically, discordant, being dominated by two voices, of which 'one was a very strong bass, the other a wheezy piping' (50). Nevertheless, like Bottom's entertainment (reflecting the perilously poised relationships of the four lovers and the ducal pair), it is ironically appropriate in context, since it matches the impending, ill-made and doomed marriage it celebrates.

Grandfer Cantle is later criticized by his emasculate son, Christian, for an unseemly eagerness to join in the dancing that attends the mummers' play celebrating Clym's return from Paris (163; cf. 473). Itself an instance of contrarious role-confusion, this criticism anticipates a more vivid instance of the same in the mummers' play, where, as in Bottom's entertainment, 'There is not ... one player fitted' (*Dream*, 5.1.65). The haughty and beautiful Eustacia has secretly appropriated the peasant actor's part of the Valiant Knight. And because of the amateur costumiers' decorative extravagance, the visual distinction between the principal characters is lost: 'the Valiant Soldier, of the Christian army, was distinguished by no peculiarity of accoutrement from the Turkish Knight, and what was worse ... St George himself might be mistaken for his deadly enemy, the Saracen' (145). Eustacia's grandfather laughs heartily at this, but again there is tragedy's precondition and meaningful parallelism. The confused play is the very means by which Eustacia begins to ensnare Clym in a relationship of profoundly incompatible opposites. Clym loves the heath, which is identified with permanence, and despises fashionable Paris – Eustacia yearns for Paris and hates the heath; he is a natural optimist and believes that their love will be eternal, she a pessimist who believes that, despite – indeed because of – its intensity, it will 'evaporate like a spirit', so that her infatuation with him is 'a fearful joy' (166, 232). The genesis of misery in revelling and play, of tragedy in comedy, is echoed in the

---

[8] Claire Tomalin, *Thomas Hardy: The Time-Torn Man* (London, 2006), p. 165. The epigraph to the first chapter of *A Pair of Blue Eyes* (1873) is a quotation from the *Dream* ('A fair vestal thronèd by the west' (2.1.158)). This may be designed to enhance the stature of Elfride as a love-smitten maid, but there are more significant allusions – to Ophelia (in the title-page quotation from *Hamlet* 1.3.7) and to Juliet (in the name of the steamer, the *'Juliet'*, and in the final chapter, when Elfride's grieving lovers visit her vault); Wessex Edition (London, 1906), pp. 336, 338, 445–53. On the aptness of the Ophelia allusion, see Marlene Springer, *Hardy's Use of Allusion* (London, 1983), p. 41. Pertinent to this article is the fact that most of Hardy's Shakespeare allusions in the novels are to *Hamlet* and *Romeo and Juliet*.

[9] *The Mayor of Casterbridge*, p. 387; *The Return of the Native*, Wessex Edition (London, 1929), p. 44. Subsequent references appear in the text.

oxymora that mark the disintegration of their marriage. To escape from domestic boredom and conflict, Eustacia rushes off defiantly to join the dancers on the green, declaring: 'I'll be bitterly merry and ironically gay, and I'll laugh in derision!' (303). In her hectic enjoyment of the dance, she succumbs to her old lover, Wildeve, and seals her fate.

Hardy intimated in the steady character of (well-named) Gabriel Oak that the avoidance of tragedy lies in a harmonious balancing and distinguishing of opposites – what in *The Mayor of Casterbridge* is called 'a careful equipoise between imminent extremes' (69). In Hardy's tragic perspective, however, events seldom allow what nature demands: nature seems deeply and irremediably conflicted. Clym Yeobright's 'natural cheerfulness striving against depression from without' (162) is undone by his moonlight encounters with the passionate young woman who anticipates the worst in life and love: 'It is my nature to feel like that. It was born in my blood, I suppose' (71); he and she are 'Ill met by moonlight' (*Dream*, 2.1.60). The tragedy of his marriage is defined symbolically by contrast with the musicianship of his long-dead father, whose astonishing ability to switch unerringly from the clarinet to the bass-viol in the same musical event is intensely recalled by his fellow bandsmen as a Utopian marvel: "Twas a wonderful thing that one body could hold it all and never mix the fingering' (53).

A notable feature of the novel is the way in which Hardy negotiates between the genres towards the end, by which time the shocking death of his mother and Eustacia's suicide have convinced Clym of 'the grimness of the general human situation' and 'the horror' of his own existence (227, 447). A singularly dark phase in the narrative, the terrible suffering of Mrs Yeobright, and Clym's and Eustacia's belief that they are responsible for her death, is lightened by the reappearance of Grandfer Cantle, bragging about his time in uniform when he was 'always first in the gallantest scrapes'. But this otherwise conventional piece of comic relief is accommodated to the pattern of significant discord by means of Timothy Wise's response to Grandfer: 'I suppose that was because they always used to put the biggest fool afore ... 'Tis very nonsense of an old man to prattle so when life and death's in mangling' (349). An analogous clash of opposites – specifically of matrimonial merriment and mourning – is indicated and tactfully evaded at the end when Clym declines to join in the feasting and dancing on the evening of Tamsin and Diggory's wedding, telling the bride that he 'might be too much like the skull at the banquet' (476). He does not die, but his status as a tragic figure is confirmed by his melancholy departure from the festive house in the company of a fellow mourner, young Charley, his dead wife's humble idolater. Charley looks back through the window and tells him (uncomprehending or incredulous), 'they all be laughing again as if nothing had happened' (479). Clym's near-blindness, and his earnest wish that he too were dead, seem intended to recall Oedipus. More obviously, however, his alienation recalls Hamlet, mourning alone in a revelling court that mixes mirth and funeral, marriage and dirge. So potent in Hardy's imagination is the image of Hamlet's mournful isolation in a matrimonially festive court that he repeats this strategy at the end of *The Mayor of Casterbridge*, where Henchard, 'poorly dressed in the midst of such resplendency', finds that the 'gaiety' of the marriage revellers 'jarred upon [his] spirits', and is disillusioned to discover that the serious-minded bride, Elizabeth-Jane, 'should have had zest for this revelry' – she 'who knew ... that marriage was as a rule no dancing matter' (393–4).

As is apparent in 'In Tenebris II',[10] where he broods on the misfortune of being 'one born out of due time', incapable of concurring with 'the many and the strong' who 'breezily' insist that 'Our times are blessed times', Hardy had something of a Hamlet complex. He projected a touch of this on to these two tragic heroes, and especially Clym, who is conceived specifically as 'a modern type',

---

[10] Thomas *Hardy: The Complete Poems*, edited by James Gibson (London, 2001), no. 137. References to the poems in my text follow the numbers given them in this edition.

'an anachronism' in his time and place, the final product of 'a long line of disillusive centuries' and therefore 'a tragical figure' (197–8).

III

In *The Mayor of Casterbridge*, Hardy's description of the threads in Farfrae's life as 'intertwisted yet not mingling' (192) refers to the commercial and romantic aspects of his life before it takes a disastrous turn. However, the image is also a clue to the difference in character between himself and Henchard, the close friend who becomes his bitter rival in commerce and love, confounding the twin threads in both their lives. Impulsive and extreme in his emotions, the antithesis of equable, balanced Farfrae, Henchard is a man whose tragic fate unfolds in a psychological arena where levity and gravity, amiability and malevolence, mingle disastrously. Strongly indicative of this syndrome in the novel is the proliferation of smiles, laughs, and grins that are variously characterized as mocking, sardonic, grim, grotesque, distressed, bitter, even terrified. At the level of action, the syndrome is apparent in practical jokes, tricks, games and entertainments that are mischievous or malign in effect, if not also in intention. They are almost all designated as jocular, but the most important have a distinctly theatrical character, reminding us perhaps, like the Play of St George, of Hardy's Shakespearian starting point in handling the genre mix. Richly symbolic, therefore, of the conflicts and confusion at the heart of this tragedy, giving it a transhistorical dimension, is the old Roman Amphitheatre, the most conspicuous sign of a moral affinity with ancient Rome that is otherwise 'announced … in every street, alley, and precinct' of Casterbridge (83). This now 'secluded arena' is one where spectators once enjoyed 'gladiatorial combat' and other 'sanguinary games', and in later times were entertained by 'public hangings' and 'pugilistic encounters almost to the death'; where latterly, too, some boys tried 'to impart gaiety to the ruin' by turning it into a cricket pitch, an attempt that 'languished' in the shadow of 'these old tragedies' (84–5). A place of pleasure,

rivalry and cruelty, the Amphitheatre is Hardy's version of the world-stage metaphor. It constitutes an appropriate symbolic backdrop for the professionally and physically combative Henchard: at the end, in defeat and despair, he figures as a dying gladiator, one who has 'no wish to make an arena a second time of a world that had become a mere painted scene to him' (388).

Henchard's original tragic error, emanating from the sourness of marital and professional disappointment, is the practical joke in which he offers to auction his wife to the highest bidder ('I am a fearful practical joker when I choose', he remarks much later (283)). Staged impromptu in a fairground tent and watched by a tipsily appreciative audience, this cruel confusion of love and business perfectly exemplifies the morphing of comedy into tragedy. Henchard spots and responds to the old furmity woman's sly 'game' (7) of offering to lace her wholesome family drink with rum secretly; thus inebriated, he puts Susan up for sale. Newson's offer to buy her is received with 'a laugh of appreciation' by all present (9). They suppose they are merely watching 'a piece of mirthful irony carried to extremes'; but when the transaction is completed in earnest, 'the jovial frivolity of the scene departed. A lurid colour seemed to fill the tent, and change the aspect of all therein. The mirth-wrinkle left the listeners' faces.' Moreover, the wife who had warned him that this was a joke he had practised too often exits 'sobbing bitterly' (12–13). This eclipse of jocularity by tragedy is poignantly and succinctly echoed eighteen years later when Susan re-visits the furmity woman's tent and is made the same sly offer that her husband had accepted: she 'smiled bitterly at the survival of the old trick' (24).

Tragi-comical, too, and even more theatrical, is the central scene that marks 'the edge or turn in the incline of Henchard's fortunes' (262) after his ascent to wealth and the mayoralty. In this police-court incident, where he acts as a proxy judge, the accused, the old furmity woman, 'with a twinkle in her eye', ensures that his 'mad freak' of twenty-four years ago becomes public knowledge, acquiring the character of a recent crime (262). Initially, the trial is rendered farcical by the performance of the bumbling, malapropian constable who arrested her ('on the night of the fifth instinct, Hannah Dominy'), a clown of purest Shakespearian pedigree. Farcical, too, are the old woman's complacently obstructive legalisms (reminiscent of Hamlet's grave-digger), which baffle the magistrates and delight the slum-dwellers whom she had mobilized in advance of the performance (240–1). But the effect of her mischief is the immediate shattering of Henchard's reputation and his loss of the wavering Lucetta, who decides to marry Farfrae instead.

The character of Lucetta has already been neatly integrated to the tragi-comic design in a quasi-theatrical manner. Her coquetry, by means of which she stage-manages Henchard's step-daughter, Elizabeth-Jane, as well as her two suitors, is conceived by herself and accepted by Henchard as delightful playfulness; but it contributes substantially to his unhappiness and continuing decline. His 'gloomy soul' brightens when she writes to tell him that her secret employment of Elizabeth-Jane as a companion was just 'a practical joke (in all affection)' intended to give him an excuse to come visiting (and courting). She writes that she expects him to laugh at this joke, and indeed he almost does: '"The artful little woman!", he said, smiling to himself (with reference to Lucetta's adroit and pleasant manoeuvre)' (178). The clever card tricks with which she entertains Elizabeth-Jane, and 'kills time' when alone (context converts this cliché into an omen), and the recumbent poses on the sofa (à la Titian's *Venus and the Lute Player*) which she rehearses in advance of her suitor's visit (180, 186), anticipate and lay the ground for the playful theatricality that will literally kill her and spread misery to all concerned. The genre implications of her narrative are spelt out with reference to the tense little tea-party in which she entertains her rival suitors – and 'which Elizabeth-Jane, being out of the game, and out of the group, could observe from afar': '"Oh – I am so sorry!" cried Lucetta, with a nervous titter. Farfrae tried to laugh; but he was too much in love to see the incident in any but a tragic light' (217–18).

The single event which gives the novel its decisively tragic character is not, as we might have expected, the wrestling bout to which Henchard challenges Farfrae while the rest of the town is at play, celebrating a royal visit. His plan is to tip Farfrae over '*the dizzy edge*' (287; emphasis added) of the Granary's top floor to his death 40 feet below (the italicized phrase being a fine metaphor for the genre nexus). This plan is abruptly abandoned in an emotional turnabout that is indicative of the humane Henchard's tragic stature: the 'womanliness' of sudden remorse at wanting to kill a man he once loved 'sat tragically on so stern a piece of virility' (331). The death that betokens tragedy comes, rather, as a result of 'the great jocular plot' (324), the 'satirical mummery' (335) of the skimmington ride which occurs later on the same day of general celebration and entertainment. Ironically, it is due in part to Henchard's magnanimous decision to return to Lucetta her old love-letters, unwisely sending them to her by means of the disgruntled Jopp, who allies himself with the Casterbridge slum-dwellers intent on 'a good laugh' (311) by publicly shaming her as a recently wed, upper-class woman with a shady sexual past. The incompetence and cowardice of the constables in their attempts to restrain these wily revellers injects a touch of simple comedy into the episode, but it serves merely to emphasize the closeness of malicious comedy to its opposite. Solomon Longway's wise remark that the traditional skimmington is 'too rough a joke and apt to wake riots in towns' (323) not only anchors the event in the concatenation of jokey actions that go back to the protagonist's initiating tragic error; it also anticipates the pregnant Lucetta's horrified outburst and correct prediction when she sees the paraded caricatures of herself and Farfrae, tied back to back on an ass, and hears the cacophonous 'roars of sarcastic laughter': 'it will kill – kill me!' (337–8). Hardy's reference to the wild mummery as a 'Demoniac Sabbath', and his subsequent allusion to the morning star as 'Lucifer', associates the novel's comic element with the kind of mocking laughter that goes back through villain heroes and villains like Richard III, Iago, Edmond and Middleton's

Vindice to the demonic characters of medieval legend and drama.[11] And his theatrical conception of the tragi-comic nexus is reinforced by Henchard's comment: 'That performance of theirs killed her' (361).

J. K. Lloyd Jones remarks that Hardy's combination of the two genres is based on the idea that they are complementary and symbiotic, reflections of the totality of experience.[12] That idea is undoubtedly present in this novel; and yet Hardy goes beyond it – and beyond Shakespeare – to suggest that comedy is not just one part or half of reality but in effect – and because of time, chance, and change – unreal and delusive. 'Tragedy is true guise, / Comedy lies', says Time, the speaker in Hardy's poem, 'He did not know me' (no. 854). Early in this novel, Elizabeth-Jane voices the same idea: 'she felt that life and its surroundings were a tragical, rather than a comical, thing; that though one could be gay on occasion, moments of gaiety were interludes, and no part of the actual drama' (65). Although fortune eventually smiles on her, she is allowed to end the novel expressing the same conviction: 'happiness was but the occasional episode in a general drama of pain' (406).[13]

The delusive, even malign, nature of comedy is reinforced in the novel by the notion that the mocking jocularity and smiling malevolence with which mortals too often treat one another match the behaviour of the invisible forces that seem to govern our lives.[14] Henchard is intensely of this conviction when he chances to find the letter which reveals that, just when he and Elizabeth-Jane have begun to love each other as father and daughter, they are not related at all, so that he has no claim on her affections, of which he is desperately in need: 'This ironical sequence of things angered him like an impish trick from a fellow creature' – but much more like that of the 'infernal harpies' of legend who spread the table for Prester John only to snatch it away suddenly (151). Hardy has a number of mythic names for the force or forces responsible for life's tragic ironies – the Gods, Fate, Destiny, Providence; but these are mere tokens for the entirely natural and virtually synonymous forces, referred to above, mentioned

at the start of the novel, and evident in the unfolding of events: 'Time and Chance', at whose hands anything is possible, 'except, perhaps, fair play' (3). (Henchard had invoked just that notion when he offered to wrestle one-armed with the slightly built Farfrae, while intending to kill him (329).)

As in *The Return of the Native*, but more forcefully, music plays an important symbolic role in delineating the conflicts affecting the tragic hero: we begin to see how Hardy's life-long love of music and music-making attracted him to Shakespeare's seminal idea. The extraordinary relationship, as both friends and business partners, which develops between Henchard and Farfrae – 'strength and bustle' and excitability on the one side, and 'judgement and knowledge' (57) and calmness on the other – is a perfect but doomed 'union in partition', a *discordia concors*. With his beautiful voice and repertoire of Scottish songs, rendered with intense feeling, Farfrae enchants everyone in The Three Mariners, featuring in that vividly described scene as a kind of Orpheus, winning from rough-spoken men 'a burst of applause, and a deep silence which was even more eloquent than applause', having 'completely taken possession of the hearts' of all, tough Henchard included (61, 63). When his love for Farfrae turns to hatred and murderous intent after

---

[11] Tom McAlindon, 'Comedy and Terror in Middle-English Literature: the Diabolical Game', *MLR* 60 (1965), 323–32; 'The evil of play and the play of evil', in *Shakespeare's Universe: Renaissance Ideas and Conventions. Essays in Honor of W. R. Elton*, ed. John M. Mucciolo (Aldershot, and Brookfield, Vermont, 1996), pp. 148–54.

[12] *Thomas Hardy and the Comic Muse*, p. 204.

[13] Compare Hardy's oft-quoted remarks: 'All comedy is tragedy, if you only look deep enough into it' (*The Collected Letters of Thomas Hardy*, 7 vols., ed. Michael Millgate and R. L. Purdy (Oxford, 1977–88), vol. 1, p. 190); 'If you look beneath the surface of any farce you see tragedy; and on the contrary, if you blind yourself to the deeper issues of a tragedy you see a farce' (Florence Emily Hardy, *The Life of Thomas Hardy* (London, 1962), p. 215).

[14] Says Lloyd Jones (*Thomas Hardy and the Comic Muse*, p. 133): 'Nearly all the novels have as their backdrop a satirical and mocking presence that makes laughingstocks of the lovers and their attempts to be united and to live happily together.'

the failure of his athletic and pugilistic entertainments to win the townspeople away from Farfrae's offering of music and dance, Henchard bitterly complains: 'As for him, it was partly by his songs that he got one over me and heaved me out' (282). The violence in his feelings of antagonism for the friend he has begun to see simply as 'my enemy' (138) figures as a horrible perversion of music when, brandishing a poker, he coerces the church choir into singing biblical curses aimed at Farfrae and his new bride (278–82). At the end, the tragedy of lost love in his relationship with both Farfrae and Elizabeth-Jane is imaged in the pathetic wedding gift he leaves them in token of remorse and reconciliation: lying unnoticed for days, a victim of time and chance, it is discovered too late, 'a new bird cage, shrouded in newspaper, and at the bottom of the cage a little ball of feathers – the dead body of a goldfinch' (399).

IV

In chapter 2 of *Tess of the D'Urbervilles*, Tess experiences 'the jar of contrast' when she returns from 'the holiday gaieties' of the May Day dance to the 'unspeakable dreariness' of her parents' cottage.[15] However, in this novel, too, the relationship between levity and misery is one of causality and confusion, as well as stark contrast. Tess's friends make jokes at her drunken father's acting the part he thinks is properly his, that of Sir John Durbeyfield, a man of noble lineage; but her parents' fantasy of rising high in the world, although truly comical, is precisely what sends her to meet her nemesis in Trantbridge, Alec d'Urberville. The 'marked levity of the younger women' in that village is said to be symptomatic of the ruling spirit of the place, so that, on their weekly trip to the fair in a nearby market town, Tess finds 'the hilariousness of the others ... quite contagious' (76–7). But at the start of the return journey by night, she makes the mistake of joining in the laughter of the others at Car Darch's mishap: 'How dar'st th' laugh at me hussy!', shouts that virago, challenging her to a fight; all the 'contentious revellers' then turn on her, and, excluded

thus, she falls back reluctantly on the protection of Alec on the lonely return journey. 'Heu, heu, heu!' laughs Car's mother, 'Out of the frying pan into the fire!' (83–5).

Alec d'Urberville shares in the levity that characterizes Trantbridge, and his levity is at the expense of his intended victim. He laughs often at and about her, amused by her shy vulnerability. After their first encounter, relishing already the prospect of seduction or worse, 'he broke into a loud laugh. "Well I'm damned! What a funny thing! Ha-ha-ha! And what a crumby [i.e. shapely] girl!"' (50). An emotional eternity separates this pre-tragic phase of Tess's history from the period of total desolation when she is rejected by her husband, Angel Clare, and Alec reappears, more sinister than ever: his disguise 'had a ghastly comicality that chilled her', as did his 'low, long laugh'. Hardy labours the point that mocking laughter, being the ultimate in falsity and perversion, is Satanic: Alec jokes to the effect that some might see him here as the tempter in Milton's *Paradise Lost* (450).

Satan, however, was a fallen angel, and so is Tess's adored husband, Angel Clare. Her moment of absolute misery occurs when she tells him about her sexual past and asks his forgiveness. He 'broke into horrible laughter, as unnatural and ghastly as a laugh in hell' (295). She offers to commit suicide for his sake (to save him from 'disgrace'), but he tells her bitterly that 'the case is rather one for satirical laughter than for tragedy. It would be viewed in the light of a joke by nine-tenths of the world were it known' (300–1). In other words, she is no Juliet.

My allusion is not forced. The narrator has imputed to her the feeling that her idolatry of Angel was 'ill-omened', and 'the notion expressed by Friar Laurence: "These violent delights have violent ends"', adding, 'It might be too desperate for human conditions – too rank, too wild, too

---

[15] Thomas Hardy, *Tess of the d'Urbervilles*, Wessex Edition (London, 1916), p. 20. Subsequent page references appear in the text.

deadly' (276), a verbal trinity which echoes Juliet's fear that her love-contract is 'too rash, too unadvised, too sudden' (*Romeo*, 2.5.9, 2.1.159–60). But the allusion not only associates Tess with Juliet (she might at this point in the narrative repeat Juliet's cry: 'Is there no pity sitting in the clouds / That sees into the bottom of my grief?' (3.5.196–7)), it indirectly confirms the Shakespearian affinity evident also in the role of Time. As in Shakespeare's sonnets, as well as *Romeo and Juliet*, Time, mocking Time, is here designated as the great enemy. And so, when 'the terrible and total change' in Angel takes place, 'Time', says the narrator, 'was chanting his satiric psalm at her' (298); this anticipates the identification – in one edition of the novel – of Time (and not 'the President of the Immortals') as 'the arch-satirist' who 'ended his sport with Tess' by sending her to the gallows.[16]

At the end of *The Mayor of Casterbridge*, the amiable Newsom treats as 'a good joke' (383) the impulsive lie that turned Susan so bitterly and fatally against Henchard. The notion that what is comedy or farce to some people is the opposite to others (who by implication see things correctly) is manifest elsewhere in *Tess*. During her idyllic time in Var Vale, where 'maids and men lived on comfortably, placidly, even merrily' (167), she listened with her friends to the dairyman's story about Jack Dollop, who got a young woman pregnant, was bullied by her mother into marriage, and then was furious when he discovered that his wife was not financially what he thought she was. The dairyman's manner of narration makes this story a very funny one, and his audience respond accordingly. But Tess sees the double parallel with her own story, so 'What was comedy to them was tragedy to her; and she could hardly bear their mirth.' But, for 'form's sake', she registers 'a sorry smile' (233), another one of Hardy's numerous tragi-comic oxymora. Her pathetic counterpart in the novel, Izzy Huett, echoes this experience when Angel, whom she worships, asks her to forget 'the levity' of his impulsive proposal that she become his mistress, and she sadly replies: 'O, it was no levity to me' (346). Again, the burden of the novel is not that tragic and comic views of life are both

subjective, or of equal merit, or complementary, but that the comic, optimistic view is delusive.

V

Hardy's pessimism, of course, was not unqualified and even gave way at times to a qualified optimism. In Shakespeare's tragedies, the bleakness of the conclusion is modified by the cessation of civil conflict and the restoration of social order; the same effect is obtained in *The Return of the Native* and *The Mayor of Casterbridge* by the weddings which augur a provisional happiness and a sense of restored normality. Functionally comparable in *Tess*, but specifically attuned to a major symbolic element in the novel, is the final pairing of Angel and Tess's sister, Liza-Lu, 'a tall *budding* creature – half-girl, half woman – a spiritualized image of Tess, slighter than she, but with the same beautiful eyes' (515–16; emphasis added).

The suggestion, most delicately implied, and barely affecting the impression of a singularly cruel fate, is that Tess, although dead, is not dead, or has in some sense returned to life. This suggestion relates to her association with the myth of the earth goddess, Ceres (Demeter), and her beautiful daughter, Proserpina (Persephone), who, as Ovid records (*Metamorphoses*, Book V), was kidnapped by Pluto (god of death, funerals, and the underworld) while gathering flowers, and later allowed by Jupiter, because of her grieving mother's pleas, to return yearly to earth for a period of six months.

---

[16] Kenneth Marsden, *The Poems of Thomas Hardy: a Critical Introduction* (London, 1969), p. 50, citing A. P. Elliott on the American edition of *Tess*. Hardy said that he once planned 'a novel entitled *Time against Two* in which the antagonism of the parents of a Romeo and Juliet *does* succeed in separating couples and stamping out their love' (Florence Emily Hardy, *The Life of Thomas Hardy*, p. 164). Although he never wrote that novel, the poems, as well as the three novels considered here, stress the successful hostility of Time to love and lovers: see Tom McAlindon, 'Time and Mutability in the Poetry of Thomas Hardy', *English Studies* 97 (2016), 22–41. So heavy (or heavy-handed) is Hardy's emphasis on Time in *The Return of the Native* that Eustacia even carries an hourglass in her moonlight encounters with Clym.

The embeddedness of this myth in the texture of the novel has been much commented on.[17] Its special significance in this context is its binary essence. Being an aetiological myth explaining the cycle of the seasons – Ovid's 'circling year' – it projects a dualistic vision of Time and the natural order as both cruel and kind, a fact reflected in Proserpina's response to Jupiter's decree: 'Her expression and her temperament change instantly; at one moment she is so melancholy ... the next, she appears with radiant face, as when the sun breaks through and disperses the watery clouds that have previously concealed him'.[18] Nature, the myth implies (and as Friar Lawrence perceived), is a system of dynamic permanence, a dialectical order subject to strict temporal limits in which neither gain nor loss, 'comedy' nor 'tragedy', is permanent. As Time the Chorus says in *The Winter's Tale* (4.1.1), he brings 'both joy and terror'.

That the final pairing of Angel and Liza-Lu, Tess's spiritual twin, can be interpreted, because of Tess's identification with Proserpina, as a gentle corrective to tragic finality might be inferred from Hardy's tersely eloquent lyric prompted by the tragedy of World War I, 'In Time of "The Breaking of Nations"' (no. 500). Its proleptic pun on the word 'breaking', which anticipates the image of the ploughman 'harrowing' the earth; the essentially paradoxical significance of the word 'harrowing'; the final image of 'a maid and her wight' who 'go whispering by'; and the assurance that 'war's annals will fade into night ere their story die': these combine to offer a positive vision of permanence in a cycle of destruction and renewal.

Hardy's association of Tess with Proserpina echoes, and was probably inspired by, *The Winter's Tale*, where the myth is concisely invoked by Perdita (4.4.116) and where the barrenness of Leontes' tragic world gives way to the budding future of Florizel and the maiden who has been restored from presumed death to her grieving mother. Expressing the same hopeful dialectic is Hardy's funny but profoundly serious narrative poem 'Life and death at sunrise' (no. 698). Here the dawn encounter of two acquaintances in a pastoral setting, one carting a coffin for a man who lived till his nineties, the other bearing news of a successful childbirth, quite consciously echoes *The Winter's Tale* and its focused conjunction of the two genres in the meeting of the Old Shepherd (carrying the infant Perdita) and his son, the Clown, terrified after seeing a man torn to pieces by a bear: 'Heavy matters, heavy matters. But look thee here, boy. Now bless thyself. Thou metst with things dying, I with things new-born' (3.3. 109–11). In the poem, Hardy ingeniously confirms his Shakespearian discipleship, tying the dialectic of natural order to the philosophy of *discordia concors* by means of binary structure and a couplet which perfectly mimes the ancient concept: 'While woodlarks, finches, sparrows, try to entune at one time, / And cocks and hens and cows and bulls take up the chime' (11–12).

Hardy, however, was at pains to point out in the preface to the collection in which this poem appears (*Human Shows*) that 'no harmonious philosophy' could be found in them. As if to demonstrate the point, he includes a little later in the same volume a poem in which his temperamental pessimism trenchantly speaks out. The Latin title of 'Genetrix Laesa' (no. 736), meaning 'Wounded Nature', prepares us for a Latin phrase in line 13. He now accuses nature of constructing a 'world work', a 'dream' of rhythmic chiming and tuneful chording – 'This "concordia discors"!' – that experience contradicts: nothing can gainsay or compensate for the tragic fact that we, and the earth we inhabit, are doomed in time, or by Time, to final extinction, 'all is sinking / To dissolubility'.

Although he might have recalled that just such an idea can be found in Prospero's melancholy reflection that 'the great globe itself', and all our beautiful constructions, 'shall dissolve' and 'Leave

---

[17] See, for example, Glen W. Wickens, 'Hardy and the Aesthetic Mythographers: the Myth of Demeter and Persephone in *Tess of the D'Urbervilles*', *University of Toronto Quarterly* 53 (1983–4), 85–106.

[18] *The Metamorphoses of Ovid*, trans. Mary M. Innes (London, 1955), p. 142.

not a rack behind' (*The Tempest*, 4.1.153–6), the fact remains that *'Genetrix Laesa'* is a rejection of *concordia discors* as a valid, all-encompassing philosophy of nature – or 'world view'. On the other hand, the tragic novels examined here are vivid proof – in so much of their conception and design – of his awareness that it is an entirely fruitful *aesthetic* philosophy: an ideal conceptual scheme for bringing the contradictions, complexities and instabilities of life into a coherent and harmonious – and enduring – work of art: 'something of great constancy' (*Dream*, 5.1.26). That, I suggest, is implied in his 1916 tercentenary tribute 'To Shakespeare.

After three hundred years' (no. 370). Showing his appreciation of Shakespeare's dialectic art, and modifying his obsession with the destructive action of Time, he here applauds the 'bright baffling soul' whose 'discourse today ... throbs on / In harmonies that cow oblivion'.[19]

---

[19] Another great novelist and short-story writer who looked to Shakespeare for inspiration and assurance in boldly combining the tragic and the comic is the late William Trevor. See Tom McAlindon, 'Comedy and Tragedy in the Fiction of William Trevor', *MLR* 112 (2017), 82–101.

QUEER IAGO: A BRIEF HISTORY

JONATHAN CREWE

Some Shakespearians may be surprised, as I was, to discover that the queer Iago has a critical history dating back at least to 1950. By this, I mean that Iago was diagnosed as a 'latent homosexual' in a series of essays beginning with one published by the psychoanalyst Martin Waugh in *Psychoanalytic Quarterly* and continuing at least through the 1970 essay by Stanley Edgar Hyman titled 'Iago psychoanalytically motivated'.[1] Other contributors included Feldman (1952), Emery (1959), Smith (1959), Lesser (1962), Shapiro (1964), and Rogers (1969).[2] The initial diagnosis having been made, it was elaborated in these successive essays, admittedly subject to the vagaries of individual critics, but nevertheless in a systematic, substantial fashion.

Not to beg the question of a 'queer Iago', the essays mentioned above, all of which are psychoanalytic – perhaps necessarily so – diagnose Iago as a paranoid (latent) homosexual in 'classic' Freudian terms. These essays are decidedly old-school Freudian. With only one exception, they predate Stonewall (1969) and hence gay rights or gay liberation. They all predate Michel Foucault's *History of Sexuality*, vol. 1 (French, 1976; English, 1978), and the consequent launching of the discourse of 'sodomy'. They predate the Lacanian turn in psychoanalysis and its subsequent inflection of queer theory. They predate the depathologization of same-sex relationships that began in 1973 in the DSM-II and ended in 1987. Finally, they predate the publication of *Between Men*,[3] which introduced the complicating factor of homosociality into the male same-sex equation.

The essays thus belong to a pathologizing psychoanalysis that invokes the *ipso facto* woman-hating male homosexual as a transhistorical character-type (Iago thus becomes the scapegoat for the

---

[1] See Martin Waugh, '*Othello*: the tragedy of Iago', *Psychoanalytic Quarterly* 19 (1950), 202–12, and Stanley Edgar Hyman, 'Iago psychoanalytically motivated', *The Centennial Review* 14 (1970), 369–84. The queer Iago appears even earlier in the theatre than in Shakespeare criticism. Both Hyman and Stephen Orgel ('*Othello* and the end of comedy', in *Spectacular Performances* (Manchester, 2011), 83–100) refer to Sir Laurence Olivier's 'flirtatious and "campy"' (Hyman, 'Iago psychoanalytically motivated', p. 382) performance as Iago in Tyrone Guthrie's 1937 production of the play. Hyman writes that '[Ernest] Jones told Sir Laurence, according to Rosenberg, that to his mind the clue to the play was not Iago's hatred for Othello, but his deep affection for him . . . he possessed a subconscious [*sic*] affection for the Moor, the homosexual foundation of which he did not understand'. Gordon Ross Smith ('Iago the paranoiac', *American Imago* 16 (1959), 155–67; p. 163) and others refer to a nineteenth-century performance by Edwin Booth, in which Iago held Othello's hand during the dream speech, before Othello 'drew [it] with disgust from his grasp'. Notwithstanding which, they joined hands during the parodic marriage speech that unites them.

[2] A. B. Feldman, 'Othello's obsessions', *American Imago* 9 (June 1952), 147–64; John P. Emery, 'Othello's epilepsy', *Psychoanalysis and the Psychoanalytic Review* 46 (Winter 1959), 30–5; Smith, 'Iago the paranoiac'; Simon O. Lesser, 'The nature of psychoanalytic criticism', *Literature and Psychology* 12 (1962), 5–9; Stephen Shapiro, 'Othello's Desdemona', *Literature and Psychology* 14 (Spring 1964), 56–61; Robert Rogers, 'Endopsychic drama in Othello,' *Shakespeare Quarterly* 20.2 (Spring 1969), 205–15.

[3] Eve Kosofsky Sedgwick, *Between Men: English Literature and Male Homosocial Desire* (New York, 1985).

play's pervasive misogyny, in which Othello also participates).[4]

What is more, the essays belong to a Cold War formation in which paranoia regarding homosexuality was rife.[5] While the essays are all written from a standpoint of appropriate clinical detachment, giving no countenance to Cold War scaremongering, Iago as a homosexual enters psychoanalytic consciousness having already been demonized (even self-demonized) in the play and in a large body of Shakespeare criticism:

> Divinity of hell!
> When devils will the blackest sins put on,
> They do suggest at first with heavenly shows,
> As I do now.
>
> (*Othello* 2.3.338–41)[6]

All the psychoanalytic critics perceive demonization as a bad *alternative* to analytic understanding. Rogers goes so far as to coin the term 'Diabolist' for the critical tradition that begins with Coleridge's 'motiveless malignity' and continues through various constructions of the satanic, including what F. R. Leavis mockingly called 'diabolical intellect'.[7] Iago's parodic inversion of the divine 'I am that I am' – i.e., 'I am not what I am' –supplies grist to the satanic mill. Iago is Evil itself.

For Rogers, psychoanalysis belongs to a Realist critical tradition distinct from the Diabolist one. Nevertheless, the psychoanalytic outing of Iago tends to make the 'hidden' homosexual threateningly demonic by association, in a way to which psychoanalytic denials and disclaimers draw attention. Moreover, the critics' insistence on homosexual paranoia makes Iago the sole exemplar of that condition. The paranoia arises, we are told, from the unfulfilled lover's sense of being 'persecuted' by the love-object, and from being negatively positioned in the Oedipus Complex, at once desiring and fearing violation by the father. Yet every diagnosis, as we know, has a context, and the cultural one in which this diagnosis originated was hardly free of ambient paranoia regarding the 'latent' homosexual. Where Iago's 'paranoia' ends and the projected paranoia of the critics begins is a fair

question. More recent critics may have refrained from pursuing the 'latent homosexual' thesis for fear of participating in homophobic stigmatization.

My point in referring to developments that postdate the initial moment of psychoanalytic discovery is that it may seem questionable to posit a critical history of the 'queer Iago' reaching all the way back to 1950. Properly speaking, the critical history of a *queer* Iago may begin only with essays like those more recently written by, for example, Matz and Orgel, in which the anachronistic 'homosexual' no longer features.[8] Nevertheless, I shall continue to posit this history of a queer Iago going back to psychoanalytic beginnings. I do so partly because psychoanalytic and queer understandings of Iago remain interconnected, and certain arguments recur throughout *Othello*'s critical history. Same-sex desire as the primary explanation of Iago's motivation and of his interaction with Othello is the psychoanalytic innovation from which there has been no going back. Iago's fake dream of being in bed with Cassio/Othello/Desdemona remains key evidence throughout the entire queer history I am positing. Moreover, the dream continues to reauthorize the psychoanalytic unconscious and Freudian dream-interpretation. Without psychoanalysis, we are back to 'motiveless malignity', to the blank incomprehension of the entire community within the

---

[4] Rather than being the tragedy of Iago as male homosexual, *Othello* could be viewed as an episode in the continuing tragedy of male misogyny, one consequence of the cultural construction of masculinity in Shakespeare's time. For psychoanalysis, the question might therefore be 'Who is not a latent homosexual?'

[5] See Robert J. Corber, *Homosexuality in Cold War America* (Durham, NC, 1997).

[6] Line numbers refer to William Shakespeare, *Othello*, ed. Edward Pechter (New York, 2004).

[7] Rogers, 'Endopsychic drama in Othello'; F. R. Leavis, 'Diabolical intellect and the noble hero: a note on *Othello*', *Scrutiny* 6 (December 1937), 259–83.

[8] Robert Matz, 'Slander, Renaissance discourses of sodomy, and *Othello*', *ELH* 66.2 (Summer 1999), 261–76; Orgel, '*Othello* and the end of comedy'.

play, and to similar incomprehension throughout much of critical and stage history.[9] When Iago says at the end of the play, 'What you know, you know' (5.2.308), the phrase may imply 'what you know all too well but won't admit to consciousness'. Well may Lodovico say at the end of the play, 'The object poisons sight. / Let it be hid' (5.2.369–70).

In this article, I shall critically survey the history of the queer Iago and conclude by projecting a future – or, rather, no future – for that history. I will not suggest that psychoanalytic dealings with the play are necessarily over, or, indeed, that psychoanalysis itself is now 'history'. It does seem to me improbable, however, that any psychoanalytic approach to the play would now focus diagnostically on Iago as an isolated figure, let alone feel that something had been accomplished by outing him. I am bound by my topic to remain focused on the queer Iago, and I shall also maintain that focus through the conclusion of this article, pushing beyond the point at which the actual history I relate breaks off. In other words, I shall posit what I take to be at once a possible trajectory of that history *and* the final turn of the screw of psychoanalytic interpretation.

I began by describing myself as surprised to discover a critical history of the queer Iago dating back to 1950 and speculating that other Shakespearians might similarly be surprised. In comparison with the Oedipal Hamlet, the queer Iago remains a fairly well-kept secret, even now. It is entirely possible for critical editions of *Othello* not to mention that history. One example is Pechter's excellent Norton critical edition, in which the queer/homosexual Iago is unrepresented (the edition is, however, currently under revision). The same applies to Orlin's essay collection.[10] In *Othello* criticism, questions of race and gender typically take precedence over ones of sexual desire and orientation.[11] This situation was anticipated early in the psychoanalytic history. Smith wrote that: 'Aside from automatic listing in the standard annual Shakespearean bibliographies, Dr. Waugh's article has gone unnoticed or at least uncommented upon by Shakespearean scholars.'

Smith speculates about the meaning of this neglect, adducing, among other things, 'the disinclination of most literary historians to acquaint themselves with psychoanalytic theory'.[12] It should additionally be noted that the earlier essays were all published in psychoanalytic journals, not in Shakespearian ones. We could speculate about what additional forms of resistance or disinclination may have been at work: what we, individually or collectively, do or do not want to know – cannot afford to know – and why, is certainly one line of questioning opened up by the play. Othello asks the onlookers at the end of the play to 'demand that demi-devil / Why he hath thus ensnared my soul and body' (5.2.306–7), and Gratiano believes that 'Torments will ope your lips' (5.2.310), but in the dream speech Iago has already as good as told

---

9 There are, of course, influential discussions of Iago that do not seek the 'key' to his psychology or seek to understand him, either as a character or a character-type. Like the discovery of Hamlet's Oedipus Complex, the discovery of Iago's homosexuality represents the psychoanalytic solution to the problems he is understood to pose. Indeed, this discovery can be tracked back to Ernest Jones (see n. 1), who had already cut his teeth on Hamlet's Oedipus Complex. As Orgel recalls in 'Othello and the end of comedy', p. 95, Greenblatt ('The improvisation of power', in *Renaissance Self-Fashioning* (Chicago, 1984), pp. 222–54) identified the demonic principle in Iago with theatricality itself, Iago being the ultimate shape-shifter and theatrical manipulator. Indeed, Greenblatt went so far as to identify Shakespeare, disturbingly, with Iago as theatricality incarnate, an identification that might help to account for Iago's creative–destructive power and exhilaration.

10 Lena Cowen Orlin, ed., *Othello: New Casebooks* (New York, 2004).

11 See, for example, Karen Newman, '"And wash the Ethiop white": femininity and the monstrous in Othello', in *Essaying Shakespeare* (Minneapolis, 2009), pp. 38–58 (first published in 1987); Emily C. Bartels, 'Making more of the Moor: Aaron, Othello and Renaissance refashionings of race', *Shakespeare Quarterly* 41 (1990), 433–54; Kim Hall, *Things of Darkness: Economies of Race and Gender in Early Modern England* (Ithaca, 1995); Lynda Boose, '"Let it be hid": the pornographic aesthetic of Othello', in Orlin, ed., *Othello: New Casebooks*, pp. 22–48; Ania Loomba, '"Delicious traffick": alterity and exchange on early modern stages', *Shakespeare Survey 52* (Cambridge, 1999), pp. 201–14.

12 Smith, 'Iago the paranoiac', p. 155.

Othello (and the audience) the implicating truth in the guise of a lie.

Smith begins his essay by summarizing:

Some years ago, Dr. Martin Waugh discussed Shakespeare's Iago as a paranoiac who disdains women, who loathes Desdemona for usurping the place he coveted in Othello's affections, and who rationalizes with incompatible excuses his conscious hatred (unconscious love) for Othello and Cassio. Waugh suggested homosexual panic in Iago precipitated by Othello's marriage, pointed out how three times Iago interrupts what he believes to be Othello's connubial proceedings, and showed how Iago's behavior illustrates two of the four masks of homosexuality described by Freud.[13]

In attributing 'delusional jealousy' to Iago, Waugh cites Freud, who views that form of jealousy as the manifestation of an 'acidulated homosexuality' that rightly takes its position among the classical forms of paranoia.[14] As an attempt at defence against an unduly strong homosexual impulse, it may, in a man, be described in the formula: 'Indeed, I do not love him; she loves him.' The principal forms of paranoia can all be represented as contradictions of a single proposition: 'I (a man) love him (a man).' The first contradiction is: 'I do not love him; I hate him.' A second contradiction may be: 'It is not I who love the man; she loves him.'

Such, shorn of its elaborations in the essays, is the psychoanalytic thesis. The power its proponents claim for it includes its ability to engage in considerable detail with Iago's frequent changes of ground and self-contradiction; with the lack of conviction and plausibility with which he says that 'I do suspect the lusty Moor / Hath leaped into my seat' (2.1.289–90) (nevertheless, quite a suggestive way of putting it); with his multiplying explanations of his antipathy towards Othello where one explanation would do better; with the fact that he is not satisfied once Cassio is dismissed and he has taken his place; with his ambivalence regarding Cassio, who 'hath a daily beauty in his life / That makes mine ugly' (Othello, 5.1.19–20), and Othello, who 'is of a free and open nature' (1.3.390); with his marked antipathy towards women; with his simultaneously deceptive and

revealing fictional dream. The psychoanalytic critics are perfectly well aware that internal consistency alone is not enough to verify an interpretation, and that they may ultimately be unable to satisfy the criterion of evidential sufficiency. Moreover, they recognize an obligation to consider evidence contradicting, rather than confirming, their interpretation. Nevertheless, at the time of writing, there was little in the field to compete with their interpretation, or even count as an interpretation. They could additionally claim to answer a question that most critics had not even thought to ask: *why* jealousy? Why, in other words, is jealousy Iago's chosen instrument for the destruction of Othello? The psychoanalytic answer is that no one knows jealousy better than Iago, and no one has more reason to project it away from himself and implant it in Othello (when claiming anguish at having been cuckolded by Othello, Iago may say more than he intends about his own experience of jealousy in the lines 'the thought whereof / Doth, like a poisonous mineral, gnaw my inwards' (2.1. 290–1)). It is his own jealousy that makes him capable of identifying and sympathizing with the hated Othello, even while savouring his torture:

Look, where he comes! Not poppy nor mandragora
Nor all the drowsy syrups of the world,
Shall ever medicine thee to that sweet sleep
Which thou owedst yesterday.

(3.3.331–4)

Well may Iago declare 'I did say so' (3.3.330).

How, then, does gay/queer criticism pick up where the early psychoanalytic criticism left off? While discounting the Freud–Jones version of repression, Orgel, nevertheless, imagined a production of the play with an appealing 'gay'

---

[13] Smith, 'Iago the paranoiac', p. 155. I simply note that, in Waugh's psychoanalytic terminology, 'homosexual panic' means something different from what it means when Sedgwick uses the term in *Between Men*. For Waugh, the panic arises for the homosexual when a female rival displaces him; for Sedgwick, the panic arises from being suspected as, or suspecting oneself to be, a homosexual under social surveillance.

[14] Waugh, '*Othello*: The tragedy of Iago', p. 4.

Iago (the gay charm of this imagined Iago would help to explain his ability to seduce and persuade Othello).[15] The introduction of that gay figure is enough to dispel any remaining perception that the play is a tragedy of heterosexual love only, and it also implicitly takes account of the erotic appeal of the black man in a white, gay male imaginary. Discussion of race in *Othello* has focused more on fear and loathing of the other than on this intense and disturbing attraction. Yet, as Matz remarks, 'everyone loves Othello'.[16]

Orgel spells out the implications of his thought-experiment in short order. Noting that Iago and Othello are inseparable, he adds: 'Their bond can be construed as a love-relationship, with Iago's resentment that of a scorned lover, rejected in favor of Cassio on one hand and Desdemona on the other ... the jealousy, then, in the first instance would be Iago's' (92). Cassio is the suitor he in turn displaces, however, along with Desdemona, in the famous 'marriage scene' between him and Othello (Di Gangi notes that displacement[17]):

OTHELLO :   Now, by yond marble heaven,
      In the due reverence of a sacred vow
      I here engage my words.
IAGO : Do not rise yet. [*Iago kneels*]
      Witness, you ever-burning lights above,
      You elements that clip us round about,
      Witness that here Iago doth give up,
      The execution of his wit, hands, heart,
      To wronged Othello's service.

                (3.3.460–7)

The failure of critics or theatre audiences to 'see' what is going on here may indeed result partly from Iago's endlessly reiterated assertion that he 'hate[s] the Moor'. Yet Orgel pertinently quotes Romeo's line from *Romeo and Juliet*: 'Here's much to do with hate, but more with love.'[18] Iago's strangely circuitous expression of hatred early in the play implies as much:

        Now, sir, be judge yourself
  Whether I in any just term am affined
  To love the Moor.

                (1.1.35–7)

Certainly not in any just – i.e. rational – terms, yet apparently the irrational bond holds; Iago merely doesn't understand it, or cannot acknowledge it.

At the heart of Matz's 'sodomitical' reading of the play, as it is of Orgel's 'gay' one and those of prior psychoanalytic critics, is Iago's dream speech. Since it has supplied key evidence throughout the critical history of the queer Iago, I shall quote it in full:

          There are a kind of men
  So loose of soul that in their sleeps will mutter
  Their affairs; one of this kind is Cassio.
  In sleep I heard him say, 'Sweet Desdemona,
  Let us be wary, let us hide our loves!'
  And then, sir, would he gripe and wring my hand,
  Cry, 'O sweet creature!' and then kiss me hard,
  As if he plucked up kisses by the roots
  That grew upon my lips, then laid his leg o'er my
     thigh,
  And sigh, and kiss, and then cry 'Cursèd fate
  That gave thee to the Moor!'

                (3.3.416–26)

About this dream, Hyman writes: 'Iago has turned himself into a Desdemona for Cassio's sexual enjoyment on the surface of the spurious dream, and for Othello's in the latent content.'[19] That pretty well says it for classic psychoanalysis. In Matz's later reading, however, same- – and other – sex fantasies overlap and intersect, with all parties simultaneously occupying their own and others' positions. Matz heeds one of Foucault's primary contentions – namely that the operative early modern term covering, but not restricted to, same-sex relations was 'sodomy', not 'homosexuality'. As Bray elaborated, 'sodomy' was understood as a category of sexual disorder rather than

---

[15] Orgel, '*Othello* and the end of comedy'.
[16] Matz, 'Slander, Renaissance discourses of sodomy, and *Othello*', p. 266.
[17] Mario Di Gangi, *The Homoerotics of Early Modern Drama* (New York, 1997), p. 83.
[18] Orgel, '*Othello* and the end of comedy', p. 93.
[19] Hyman, 'Iago psychoanalytically motivated', p. 376.

exclusively of same-sex object choice; because it signified disorder, it was frequently linked to treason in legal indictments. Bray also noted that the boundary between love and friendship in male same-sex relations was precarious.[20]

Matz situates the homoerotics of *Othello*, discussed above, within a discourse of sodomy in which those erotics are not categorically distinct from heteroerotic ones: identifications are unstable and axes crisscross between what would now be regarded as homo- – and hetero- – sexual, but also between love and friendship, public and private. In this context, it could be misleading to speak of a 'gay' Iago, since that would tend to imply a homosexual *identity* rather than a more indeterminate 'sodomy'. Matz emphasizes, in fact, that both heterosexual love and male friendship were subject to affective regulation in the interests of order; male same-sex relations did not necessarily pose a unique or distinct threat.[21]

Matz's reading of the dream highlights the implosive tendency of sodomy, in which gendered identities and trajectories of desire overlap and intermingle in a scene of 'disorder'. We might therefore describe the dream as queer with a vengeance, rather than as homosexual. Indeed, the figure of the 'homosexual' tends to dissolve in Matz's reading, as it has typically done in criticism after Foucault. Yet we need to proceed with caution here. A significant element of the threat to 'order' is undeniably the dream's graphic bodily encounter between men. Perhaps there is no modern 'homosexual' present, but the male same-sex encounter is nevertheless explosively charged. Moreover, rather than being a bedroom free-for-all, the dream presents successive and distinct heterosexual and homosexual scenarios, the speech thus marking a switch-point between them. The switch puts Iago in the place of Desdemona. When Othello responds 'monstrous! monstrous!' (3.3.427) we cannot know precisely what, or what combination of things, elicits that reaction. Or, for that matter, what combination of desire and disgust the imaginary experience of 'grossly gap[ing] on' (3.3.396) arouses in him. In any event, the breakdown of order shortly precipitates a breakdown of

linguistic order in him, as if all his defences have been overwhelmed.

Perhaps it is necessary to add the caveat that nowhere in Shakespeare's work, or Marlowe's, or that of most of his leading theatrical and literary contemporaries, does the term 'sodomy' appear. Its absence does not necessarily negate the possibility that Shakespeare's writings are situated within a formative, hegemonic discourse of sodomy. Yet the use of the term in Shakespeare's time was primarily legal, polemical and religious. One of its polemical contexts was that of antitheatrical writing, perhaps reason enough for Shakespeare and his theatrical contemporaries to refuse it. Summary imposition of the term in readings of Elizabethan drama may thus beg the question. Different affective charges, social constructions and legal liabilities obviously still attached to the respective 'behaviours' constituting heterosexual adultery and male sodomy.[22] Furthermore, over-reading of Foucault's thesis regarding the 'invention' of the homosexual by nineteenth-century sexologists (i.e. the invention of a homosexual 'identity') has sometimes obscured the fact that male same-sex stereotypes date back at least to classical antiquity, sometimes in the guise of what would now be regarded as intolerably homophobic caricatures. Examples of the latter are to be found in the fiction of late antiquity, for example – notably in Longus' *Daphnis and Chloe* and Apuleius' *The Golden Ass (Metamorphoses)*. In the latter particularly, a coterie

---

[20] Alan Bray, *Homosexuality in Renaissance England* (New York, 1996), pp. 22–5.

[21] Matz notes as well that, as a mobile signifier, 'sodomy' was also open to exploitation for a variety of political purposes, including policing of the boundary between the indigenous and the exotic: 'sodomy' as male homosexuality was more often attributed to foreign cultures than acknowledged at home.

[22] In *Thinking Sex with the Early Moderns* (Philadelphia, 2016), pp. 283–8, Valerie Traub notes the lesbian's continuing invisibility and failure to signify, both in the historical, heteronormative scheme of things and in the contemporary domain of queer theory.

of what the English translator calls 'old queens' hijacks Lucius in his guise as an ass and puts him to work, along with some well-endowed slave-boys, as their sex slave. Such social stereotyping did not have to wait for the invention of homosexuality.

There is no indication, however, that Shakespeare had recourse to this kind of stereotyping in *Othello*. Pertinent stereotypes for Iago, as perceived by psychoanalytic and Shakespearian critics alike, include the New Comedy slave, the medieval Vice, the Machiavel. If male same-sex stereotypes are irrelevant, it is because they are *overt* social stereotypes. The point about Iago is that he is the prototype of the *hidden* 'homosexual', hidden even from himself. He 'passes' throughout the play, and his very unconsciousness powers his limitless destructiveness. In the view of the psychoanalytic critics, this is where Shakespeare seems to be doing some inventing of his own. Practically nothing in the play that belongs to their conception of the paranoid latent homosexual comes from Shakespeare's source-text, Giraldo Cinthio's *Hecatommithi*, 'Una Capitano Moro' [A Moorish Captain] (1565). It is as if we are again left with a Shakespeare anticipating psychoanalysis, producing a configuration under the name of Iago that will not become intelligible until the arrival of Freud (who, in turn, credits Shakespeare among other great authors with intuitive understanding of unconscious motivation that will eventually be formalized in psychoanalysis). It is hard to do other than leave it at that.

Yet perhaps that is not all Shakespeare anticipates in Iago, if 'anticipation' is the right term. Shakespeare has not only been credited on occasion with uncanny foreknowledge, but entertains that possibility himself in, for example, the sonnets and *Macbeth*. Such 'foreknowledge' would unfold in readings over time, an unfolding in which, among other things, a myriad of cultural desires and fantasies could successively become manifest. Under that premise, what is already latent, so to speak, in *Othello* appears to be the modern (twentieth-century) demonizing fantasy of the solitary, male homosexual as the inveterate hidden enemy

of the heterosexual couple, of marriage and, *a fortiori*, of heteronormative order. Boose aptly describes the bedroom murder in *Othello* as an 'anti-epithalamion'.[23] In other words, Iago prefigures the imagined homosexual of a certain paranoid modernity, the covert antagonist of the conjugal, reproductive norm.

To my mind, a clue to the latter development can be found in Kenneth Branagh's film of *Much Ado About Nothing* (1993). The play includes a villain who, using theatrical means, incites Claudio's jealousy in such a way as to forestall his marriage to Hero, and, in the process, subjects Hero to public humiliation. Don John explicitly resents his invidious position as a bastard, but precisely why that resentment translates into a marriage-wrecking plot – and into the incitement of jealousy in Claudio – is hardly better explained than it is in the case of Iago. In the film, Keanu Reeves was cast as Don John, to the surprise and amusement of most viewers familiar with his abilities as an actor. Yet Reeves's well-established public character as a gay icon separated him from the 'straight' performers in the cast and served as an explanation in itself for his malice. Reeves's

---

[23] See Boose, "'Let it be hid": the pornographic aesthetic of *Othello*', p. 26. For Boose, the marriage bed as the site of murder becomes the point at which all pathways in the play converge. This convergence, with practically the entire community of the play finally present in the bedroom, is the culmination in her view of a prurient, pornographic curiosity, in the play and in the audience, about what transpires in the privacy of that room, the woman always being the object of the male pornographic gaze. According to Boose, what is presented in the bedroom, and in Desdemona's last moments, is an orgasmic grand finale in which the two different early modern English senses of the term 'death' collapse into each other. In more than one sense, this is the pornographic climax of the play. The scene may indeed include this voyeuristic element, yet the bedroom remains a more complex 'text' than that, since it includes Othello and Iago as well as the dying woman, and it is on Othello and Iago that the wondering gaze of the community is finally fixed. Whatever the text of that bedroom may signify, it is text the community patently cannot, or does not wish to, read. Or, more specifically, doesn't want to 'see', whatever its voyeuristic desire.

amiable appeal seems consistent with Orgel's ima-gining of the charming gay man as villain, yet, as in the case of Iago, the charm belies destructive mal-ice. Faced with the opacity of both Don John and Iago, the communities of the plays have no recourse other than that of self-incriminating torture.

Paranoid perception of the homosexual – which is to say perception of the homosexual in the dominant culture and ideology, not exclusively perception of the homosexual by straight people – may seem incompatible with the thesis of cultural repression, yet evidence abounds of their ability to coexist during, for example, the Cold War period in America. The paranoid perception (projection) depends on an almost hallucinatory othering of the homosexual, while the inner homosexual, so to speak, continues to be repressed. That may be an individual repression, but the critical history and audience reception of Iago more interestingly sug-gest the existence of widespread collective repres-sion. One might almost add 'massive' repression, attested by the reception-history of the play.

From the paranoid standpoint, the motivations of the hidden homosexual are ones of limitlessly destructive antipathy to the heterosexual norm: he becomes, so to speak, the invisible enemy within. Without overt homosexual identity, this figure will, in fact, typically be a figure of non-identity. As Goldberg writes regarding the film-maker Todd Haynes's constructions of (non-)identity: 'there is no me, no ego ... identification without an I: *I'm not there*' (Iago: 'I am not what I am' (1.1.62)). Quoting Oscar Wilde, Goldberg continues: 'Each Man Kills the Thing he Loves.' Finally, invoking Edelman, Goldberg writes that Haynes 'delivers his queer and now by way of the death drive'.[24] I am not aware of any psychoanalytic essays that deliver the queer Iago 'by way of the death drive', but that does seem like a plausible trajectory, and perhaps the terminus, of the history I have been relating.

The figure of the homosexual antagonist will almost inevitably be 'woman-hating', especially insofar as a woman may appear to be the successful rival for his own object of desire. This anti-romance antagonist will also *ipso facto* be the enemy of reproductive futurity; the murder of Othello and Desdemona will 'stop posterity' – per-haps incidentally, or even fundamentally, catering to a cultural horror of miscegenation – flagged by Karen Newman, to which Iago gives voice when inflaming Brabantio (that horror appears upper-most in Cinthio's text). Reproductive futurity is the implied *telos* of Shakespearian romantic comedy, a genre that has certainly 'gone wrong' in *Othello*.

All of this brings us to the homosexual in the guise of Edelman's *sinthomosexual*, the queer expo-nent of the Freudian death drive implacably opposed to the sentimental, reproductive futurism of heteronormative ideology. This demonized fig-ure of the homosexual is, in the first instance, a figment of the dominant, reproductive culture's paranoia, yet he is also a figure capable of being reclaimed for an anti-normative queer politics at odds with the ideology of reproductive futurism.[25] As a figment of Alfred Hitchcock's Cold War cinematic imaginary, Edelman's *sinthomosexual* verifies rather than refutes Cold War paranoia. If Iago has any bearing here, it is because of the unique virulence he evinces as a prototypical *sinthomosexual*. Furthermore, the only 'birth' the otherwise sterile Iago allows is that of his own conception:[26]

---

[24] Jonathan Goldberg, *Melodrama: An Aesthetics of Impossibility* (Durham, NC, 2015), p. 107; and Lee Edelman, *No Future: Queer Theory and the Death Drive* (Durham, NC, 2004).

[25] A number of queer theorists have pushed back against Edelman's negativity, while Traub (*Thinking Sex*, pp. 321–4) as an early modernist has produced a substantial critique of his uncompromisingly anti-historicist Lacanianism. Traub justly questions whether an all-encompassing futurist ideology invested in the Child pre-vailed in the early modern period, yet at the very least the anticipated perpetuation of an aristocratic lineage constitutes a form of reproductive futurism, as in Shakespeare's young man sonnets. In contrast, the death-driven, non-procreative dark lady sonnets project no salvific future.

[26] Here Iago displays the 'childbirth envy' of many male writers of the period, whose intellectual artefacts become their own 'progeny'. None of the psychoanalytic critics links this form of envy to Iago's homosexuality, although that would be consistent with their reading.

I have't! It is engendered! Hell and night
Must bring this monstrous birth to the world's light.

(1.3.394–5)

By invoking the Lacanian *sinthome*, Edelman obviously moves beyond the kind of psychoanalysis with which my article began. If the death drive does not feature in the psychoanalytic essays I have reviewed, perhaps it is because the concept was not always accepted in psychoanalytic interpretation, but perhaps also because it does not yield the endlessly rich intricacies for analysis that the pleasure principle does. On the contrary, the death drive threatens to close down such analysis.[27]

For critics like Edelman and Goldberg, what we might call the Iago type has a role to play, either in opposition to the ideology of heteronormative futurism or as an exemplar of radical non-identity as a fundamental condition, belied by the coercive identitarianism of normative ideologies. For Shakespeare, these political justifications were presumably not available. What *was* available to Shakespeare and/or his audiences is obviously a matter of continuing historical, theological, political, dramaturgical and other construction, but it seems reasonable to infer, as Greenblatt did long ago, that Shakespeare's thematics of non-identity belong to his self-reflexive immersion in theatre and performance. The phrase 'I am not what I am' is first spoken by Viola in *Twelfth Night* (3.1.139), in danger of losing 'her' gendered identity in her cross-dressing performance; her phrase radicalizes her earlier one, 'I am not that I play' (1.5.177). She also fears that 'disguise [is] a wickedness / Wherein the pregnant enemy does much' (2.2.27–8). Iago evidently realizes those fears. Any distinction

between being and seeming, truth and dissimulation, seems to have eroded completely, leaving only endless destructive simulation without identity, emanating from an 'I' who is 'not there'. Such is the condition of radical *inhumanity* that both onlookers in the play and so many subsequent readers and audiences have been unable to comprehend. If there is an ideology against which one can imagine Iago being critically mobilized – gleefully mobilized – what can we call it but humanism?

To conclude, then, it appears to me that the only psychoanalytic discourse capable of engaging with Iago as the figure of radical non-identity is a poststructuralist, Lacanian one, for which the work of Goldberg and Edelman offers us some hints. This approach 'delivers' Iago as exponent of the death drive, not an Iago to whom psychoanalysis attributes the *identity* of the paranoid homosexual. Following Edelman's logic, Iago would then emerge not as the villain of the play but, in a telling paradox, as its single culture-hero. I do not believe most Shakespearians, myself included, would have the nerve to take that leap, but the play does bring us to that threshold. Whether psychoanalysis has anything more than this to offer remains to be seen, but this point of arrival comes at the end of an interesting and consequential history in psychoanalytic criticism – one that remains, I believe, insufficiently appreciated.

---

[27] Which is not to deny that the death drive has its own interpretive or therapeutic application, especially as regards trauma and compulsive repetition.

GLOBAL SHAKESPEARE AND THE CENSOR: ADAPTATION, CONTEXT AND *SHAKESPEARE MUST DIE*, A THAI FILM ADAPTATION OF *MACBETH*

MARK THORNTON BURNETT

The relationship between censorship and stagings of Shakespearian drama is usually discussed in exclusively early modern terms.[1] Annabel Patterson has established that playwrights during the period were obliged to develop specific 'codes of communication ... to protect themselves from ... dangerous readings of their work' and, as a consequence, they wrote with the Master of the Revels or Lord Chamberlain in mind.[2] Post-Renaissance, and isolated examples notwithstanding, the general consensus in Shakespeare studies is that censorship – defined by Francesca Billiani as an 'act, often coercive and forceful, that ... blocks, manipulates and controls ... communication' – is no longer relevant to critical discussion.[3] But can the same confidently be said for the burgeoning field of global Shakespeare? While critics have occasionally recognised that local productions have incurred a censor's interference, there has been no sustained engagement with censorship as a backdrop to regimes of adaptation world-wide.[4]

This is despite the fact that, since the turn of the twenty-first century, several Shakespearian films, explicitly and implicitly, have been linked to censorship controversies. The most recent example, Vishal Bhardwaj's *Hamlet* adaptation, *Haider* (2014), set in Kashmir, has been banned in Pakistan, the censors stating that the film runs counter to the country's 'ideology'.[5] Perhaps more suggestively, in interview, film directors have cited censorship anxieties as a factor in their choice of the Shakespearian text.[6] As Mario Kuperman, director of a Brazilian

adaptation of *Hamlet*, *O Jogo da Vida e da Morte* (1971), explains: 'I feared having my work banned or mutilated (I had an earlier play cut by the

---

[1] See Richard Burt, *Licensed by Authority: Ben Jonson and the Discourses of Censorship* (Ithaca and New York, 1993); Janet Clare, '*Art made tongue-tied by authority': Elizabethan and Jacobean Censorship* (Manchester and New York, 1990); Richard Dutton, *Mastering the Revels: The Regulation and Censorship of English Renaissance Drama* (Basingstoke, 1991); Annabel Patterson, *Censorship and Interpretation: The Conditions of Writing and Reading in Early Modern England* (Madison and London, 1984).

[2] Patterson, *Censorship and Interpretation*, p. 11.

[3] Francesca Billiani, 'Assessing boundaries – censorship and translation', in *Modes of Censorship and Translation: National Contexts and Diverse Media*, ed. Francesca Billiani (Manchester and Kinderhook, 2007), pp. 1–25, esp. p. 3. For examples of the censorship of Shakespeare, see Jean I. Marsden, *The Re-Imagined Text: Shakespeare, Adaptation, and Eighteenth-Century Literary Theory* (Lexington, 1995), pp. 41, 45.

[4] See Wilhelm Hortmann, *Shakespeare on the German Stage* (Cambridge, 1998), p. 420; Alexa Huang [Joubin], *Chinese Shakespeares: Two Centuries of Cultural Exchange* (New York, 2009), pp. 130, 188–9; Dennis Kennedy, 'Introduction: Shakespeare without his language', in *Foreign Shakespeare*, ed. Dennis Kennedy (Cambridge, 1993), pp. 1–18, esp. pp. 3–4; Margaret Litvin, *Hamlet's Arab Journey: Shakespeare's Prince and Nasser's Ghost* (Princeton and Oxford, 2011), pp. 131, 141, 227; Zdeněk Stříbrný, *Shakespeare and Eastern Europe* (Oxford, 2000), pp. 45, 90.

[5] Vaibhav Vats, 'Bollywood takes on the agony of Kashmir, through Shakespeare', *New York Times*, 27 October 2014, www.nytimes.com/2014/10/28/arts/international.

[6] See Mark Thornton Burnett, *Shakespeare and World Cinema* (Cambridge, 2013), p. 140.

censors), so I ended up deciding to film a classic.'[7] Darlene J. Sadlier, a critic working on the Brazilian imaginary, argues that the choice to adapt is often contingent: 'Film adaptations, especially of the classics, tended to be ignored by the military regime, which regarded the process as simply the transposition of a literary work onto celluloid.'[8] Such examples remind us that film censorship thrives in war-torn locales, is often adopted as the default position by short-term governments, is quick to assert itself at times of military rule, and is a staple of systems underpinned by forms of religious orthodoxy.[9] This article contends that censorship – and the possibility of censorship – needs to be recognized as a crucial factor in the production and dissemination of Shakespeare film throughout the world. But it also argues that censorship is complicatedly contextual in the operation of its mechanisms and processes. Critics interested in the relationship between Shakespeare and censorship, then, are obliged to take seriously the historically particular and locally situated restrictions shaping a particular appropriation. As Pierre Bourdieu summarizes, censorship is always 'constituted by the . . . structure of the field in which . . . discourse is produced'.[10]

As its case study, this article explores a sensational example of contemporary censorship – the 2012 controversy surrounding *Shakespeare Tong Tai / Shakespeare Must Die*, a Thai film adaptation of *Macbeth* (Illustration 40). *Shakespeare Must Die* translates Shakespeare into local modalities and imagery, adapting *Macbeth* to suit the conventions of Thai theatre and culture. The film comprises two 'Macbeth' narratives – a theatrical production of *Macbeth* is intercut with a second *Macbeth* unfolding in the external world – which, in a tumultuous *dénouement*, merge as one. A double first, the film is the first Thai Shakespeare film and the first full-length feature by a female Thai director (Ing Kanjanavanit – or Ing K., as she is more popularly known). Judged in juxtaposition with a Thai industry dominated by action films, lightweight romances, melodramas, popular comedies and Hollywood fare, *Shakespeare Must Die* occupies

a unique place as an 'art-house' filmic experiment. Yet the film has attracted interest not because of its interpretive complexities but because of its censored status: all public screenings have been banned due to the Thai Film Censorship Board's ruling (3 April 2012) which identified 'content' in *Shakespeare Must Die* 'that creates divisiveness among the people of the nation'.[11] On 11 May 2012, a reinforcement of the ban issued in the wake of an unsuccessful appeal additionally noted that, although the film 'has been adapted to take place in a fictitious country, it has elements that communicate the understanding that it is referring to Thai society. Furthermore, some scenes have contents that are in conflict with social order or good public morality, or may adversely affect the security of the state and the patriotic dignity of the nation.'[12] Inside a system in which film is vulnerable to censorship (the 1930 Film Act in Thailand remains the first point of legal reference), this version of *Macbeth* is deemed dangerous; its narrative is perceived as fomenting discontent, undermining the country's pride, opposing the public good and jeopardizing national stability.

How might this judgement – and the Shakespeare film that has given rise to it – be explained? For Thailand, a nation that has never been directly colonized, Shakespeare is neither an educational import nor a signifier of the appurtenances of imperialism. In this sense, it is set apart from some other Asian countries in which adaptations of Shakespeare are deployed to address issues

---

[7] Interview between the author and Mario Kuperman, 20 November 2012.

[8] Darlene J. Sadlier, *Brazil Imagined: 1500 to the Present* (Austin, 2008), p. 247.

[9] Daniel Biltereyst and Roel Van de Winkel, eds., *Silencing Cinema: Film Censorship Around the World* (New York, 2013).

[10] Pierre Bourdieu, *Language and Symbolic Power*, trans. Gino Raymond and Matthew Adamson (Cambridge, MA, 1991), p. 137.

[11] 'Press release', www.Shakespearemustdie.com.

[12] 'Press release', www.Shakespearemustdie.com. The ban was upheld by the Thai Administrative Court on 11 August 2017. See Ing K., 'Undertow', http://bangkokloveletter.blogspot.com.

40. Poster for *Shakespeare Tong Tai* / *Shakespeare Must Die* (directed by Ing K., 2012). Courtesy of Jai Singh Films.

of post-colonial inheritance. As this article argues, part of the process of understanding this censorship involves appreciating the extent to which *Shakespeare Must Die* is moulded by the to-and-fro of political vicissitude and ideological disputes characteristic of Thailand in the late twentieth and early twenty-first centuries. The first part of the article explores the particular interpretive decisions afforded by *Shakespeare Must Die*, concentrating on Thailand's political situation, issues of funding and language, and the film's use of nomenclature. Attention is paid to the ways in which, in a culture sensitized to acts of *lèse majesté*, all filmic and theatrical acts of representation potentially run the censorial gauntlet. *Shakespeare Must Die*, notwithstanding a strategic deployment of translation, triggers the censorship apparatus because of the political uses to which Shakespeare is put. Via the trajectory of Macbeth, the film constructs the Presidency of Thaksin Shinawatra as morally and institutionally corrupt, offering up a critical vision bolstered by a representational allegiance between Thai theatre and radical comment. The particular politics of the film's construction – currently in exile, Thaksin hopes for a political return – are played out in a self-conscious mode of delivery that betrays an adversarial orientation. The second section focuses on the film's concern with audiences, spectators, and viewers, who are generally seen as actants, whether in the auditorium or on the street. Imagining a variety of crowds, *Shakespeare Must Die* demonstrates its immersion in the contemporary by confronting a series of episodes from political history, including recent protests and the notorious Thammasat University Massacre of 6 October 1976. These substitutions – undoubtedly the most contentious sequences – sit easily within a *Macbeth* that is highly charged in the specificity of its range of reference. Any act of censorship carries repercussions in its wake, and the final part of this article charts the fortunes of *Shakespeare Must Die* after the ban. *Shakespeare Must Die* enjoys a subsequent existence in the documentary, *Censor Must Die*, released in 2013, and in a number of high-profile protests, in which forms of theatre are again mobilized for critical ends. Efforts directed at the reversal of the censors' ruling point out how censorship can work to bring into greater visibility that which it would ostensibly occlude. In the afterlives of *Shakespeare Must Die* can be seen the film's broader symbolic implications, the means whereby it is not only constrained but also opened out by the systems it positions itself against. Thinking about censorship and *Shakespeare Must Die*, we confront some of the conflicting ways in which Shakespeare plays out in the global marketplace today.

I

Known for her ecological campaigns and political protests, Ing K. – an investigative journalist, activist, environmentalist and artist born in Thailand but educated in England – is no stranger to controversy. *My Teacher Eats Biscuits* (1998), for example, her documentary study of superstition, worship, belief and the commodification of religion, was banned on the grounds of social depravity and as an offence to Buddhism (a private screening was raided by police).[13] Forms of censorship, then, have cut across the director's career in ways that have defined her imaginative endeavour. Such professional experiences of censorship are, of course, intimately related to Thailand's troubled political history. Since 1932 (when the country adopted a constitutional form of monarchy and an elected legislature), there have been nineteen successful and attempted coups and nineteen constitutions. Throughout this history of instability, states of emergency have been declared, bringing to mind Giorgio Agamben's notion of the 'state of exception' in which 'emergency has … become the rule' and is, further, '*confused with juridical rule itself*'.[14] Presiding over the banning of *Shakespeare Must Die* was the coalition government of Prime Minister Yingluck Shinawatra. Yingluck, democratically elected in 2011, is the sister and

---

[13] See Graiwoot Chulphongsathorn, '*To Khon Grab Maa / My Teacher Eats Biscuits*', *Criticine: Elevating Discourse on Southeast Asian Cinema*, www.criticine.com/feature; Wise Kwai, 'Giving birth to Citizen Juling', *Wise Kwai's Thai Film Journal: News and Views on Thai Cinema*, http://thaifilm journal.blogspot.com. Ing K.'s other documentaries include: *Thailand For Sale* (1991) and *Green Menace: The Untold Story of Golf* (1993), both concerned with the ecological effects of tourism; *Casino Cambodia* (1994), which examines the aftermath of military conflict; *Citizen Juling* (2008), which centres on the abduction of a children's art teacher in the context of civil unrest; and *Bangkok Joyride, Part One* (2016) and *Bangkok Joyride, Part Two* (2017), which deploy footage of Bangkok demonstrations and strikes in reflections on political protest.

[14] Giorgio Agamben, *Homo Sacer: Sovereign Power and Bare Life*, trans. Daniel Heller-Roazen (Stanford, 1998), pp. 12, 15, 168.

supporter of Thaksin Shinawatra, the leader of the Thai Rak Thai (Thais Love Thais) Party and democratically elected Prime Minister from 2001 to 2006. A populist politician who marshalled unprecedented working-class and rural support, Thaksin has nevertheless attracted accusations of corruption, cronyism, authoritarianism and human rights abuses.[15] Using as justification Thaksin's undermining of constitutionally mandated institutions, the military (traditionally associated in Thailand with old-guard loyalties, the royal family and the urban business community) overthrew Thaksin in a 19 September 2006 coup, annulling the constitution, dissolving Parliament and announcing a state of martial law: democratic elections were only re-established the following year.[16] Two further governments ensued, in a period plagued by accusations of electoral fraud, conflicts of interest and judicial malpractice, before Abhisit Vejjajiva, the leader of the Democrat Party, became Prime Minister in 2008. It was during the premiership of the Democrat Party that *Shakespeare Must Die* was green-lighted. The film was funded by the Office of Contemporary Art, part of the Ministry of Culture, under the 2010 Thai Kem Khaeng (Creative Thai Film Fund) stimulus scheme, which, encouraging all manner of film work – including script development, distribution and educational schemes – had as its ostensible aim the highlighting of Thai cultural products.[17] However, this government was also itself riddled with irregularities (charges included political favouritism, bribery and a repressive response to civil unrest), and it is possible that the *ressentiment* of *Shakespeare Must Die* and, in particular, its antipathetic construction of Thaksin, appealed to a new regime anxious to distinguish itself and bolster a claim to legitimacy.[18] If this is the case, the current ban, then, marks a return to an earlier dispensation. Under the government of Yingluck, funding for film projects was shelved against a Bangkok backdrop of anti-government unrest, shootings, the attempted cancellation of a disputed general election, and, following the overthrow of Yingluck

in 2014, the seizure of power once again by the military.[19]

Michael Kelly Connors notes that, in response to a series of recent regime changes in Thailand, the crime of *lèse majesté* (an action, such as a verbal defamation or a written libel, that insults the sovereign) has 'moved from being an offence against the monarchy to being an offence against national security', resulting in exponential numbers of prosecutions.[20] Coupled with the introduction of emergency measures, the rise in applications of *lèse majesté* legislation has had far-reaching effects on freedom of speech. Particularly contentious would seem to be any commentary that reflects back on the historical past. Writing on Thailand, David Streckfuss suggests that 'history has gone into

[15] Marc Askew, 'Introduction', in *Legitimacy Crisis in Thailand*, ed. Marc Askew (Chiang Mai, 2010), pp. 1–29, esp. p. 2. For a less pejorative assessment of Thaksin's reformist policies in relation to micro-credit, health care, and agriculture, see Michael Kelly Connors, *Democracy and National Identity in Thailand* (Copenhagen, 2007), pp. 171, 229, 249; Federico Ferrara, *Thailand Unhinged: The Death of Thai-Style Democracy* (Jakarta and Kuala Lumpur, 2011), p. 38; Richard Lloyd Parry, 'The story of Thaksin Shinawatra', *London Review of Books* 36.12 (2014), 11–12.
[16] Askew, 'Introduction', p. 2; Pavin Chachavalpongpun, 'Temple of doom: hysteria about the Preah Vihear Temple in the Thai nationalist discourse', in Askew, ed., *Legitimacy*, pp. 83–117, esp. p. 91. For links between the royal family and the military, see Nick Nostitz, *Red vs. Yellow: Thailand's Crisis of Identity* (Bangkok, 2009), p. 39; Barend J. Terwiel, *Thailand's Political History: From the 13th Century to Recent Times*, 2nd edn (Bangkok, 2011), pp. 297, 301, 309.
[17] See Colleen Kennedy, 'Interview of Ing K., Director of *Shakespeare Must Die*', http://globalShakespeares.mit.edu/blog/2013.
[18] See Ferrara, *Thailand*, pp. 49, 52, 55, 61, 69, 91, 111, 146–9, 163; Parry, 'Story', p. 12; Claudio Sopranzetti, *Red Journeys: Inside the Thai Red-Shirt Movement* (Chiang Mai, 2012), pp. 16, 23.
[19] Kate Hodal, 'Riot police use tear gas as Thai protesters attack barricades', *Observer*, 25 November 2012, p. 25; Kate Hodal, 'Thai army imposes martial law', *Guardian*, 21 May 2014, p. 19; Simon Tisdall, 'Thailand is heading for crisis – and it's not alone', *Guardian*, 28 January 2014, p. 17; Udon Thani, 'Thai "red shirt" leader shot and wounded as conflict grows', *Guardian*, 23 January 2014, p. 23.
[20] Connors, *Democracy*, p. 133.

suspended animation ... [and] verifiable historical events are erased or obscured'.[21] In such a climate, memory becomes a fraught and conflicted category. What one constituency seeks to remember may become controversial or questionable when set alongside a state-approved version of the historical record. In this process, even acts of adaptation find themselves under a critical spotlight.

As adaptation, *Shakespeare Must Die* is immediately marked by its fidelity to Shakespearian dialogue; as the director affirms, 'I [chose] to stick to Shakespeare word for word.'[22] Cuts to the 'original text' are sparse, and vernacular additions (although significant, as will be seen, when they occur) are few in number. *Shakespeare Must Die* eschews versification to employ a literal but nevertheless poetically suggestive translation. Examples of incidental richness abound. However, as befits the idea of a literal translation, the subtitles to *Shakespeare Must Die* are almost wholly Shakespearian, and this often belies the inventiveness with which the play's language is made accessible to a local imaginary. For example, Macbeth is Mekhdeth – the Thai translates as 'one who would grasp at the clouds', wonderfully suggesting overreaching and an impossible trajectory of greed. Similarly, substituting for the 'raven' of 1.5.37 (as Ing K. reflects, in Thailand, there are no ravens, only 'scruffy fun crows') is 'Ega Payayom Aiang' or 'The crowing Death Lord himself', a stock figure from Thai fairy-tales that succinctly encapsulates notions of foreboding.[23] In such resonant translations, a gap opens up between what is heard aurally and what is seen in the subtitle. Shakespeare's language here occupies the status of a supplementary text; it functions in contradistinction to conventional subtitles, which, as Atom Egoyan and Ian Balfour note, typically represent 'charged markers of ... difference'.[24] By contrast, subtitles in *Shakespeare Must Die* operate as an indication of the integrity of the translation process, as a reminder of sameness, and as an on-screen announcement of adherence to 'source'. It is tempting to suggest that stressing authenticity is part of a pre-emptive strike against censorship. As one cast member, asked for his response to the censorship

verdict, states, 'The script is *Macbeth* ... So I'm stunned ... Unbelievable!'[25] Shakespearian authenticity becomes both defence and displacing device – if the script is a literal translation of Shakespeare's words, how, then, can it be controversial? In its linguistically respectful approach, *Shakespeare Must Die* showcases the extent to which 'euphemization' – to adapt Pierre Bourdieu's discussion of 'the structure of the field' of censorship – 'uses' Shakespearian 'language ... to conceal repressed elements by integrating them into a network of relations which modify their value'.[26] The means whereby the translation is effected take on an oppositional dimension, mediating the film's political interstices.

If translation suggests the film's conjuration of the censor, then so too does nomenclature. *Shakespeare Must Die* demonstrates a surrogate terminology – 'Xanadu' takes the place of England and 'Shangrilla' stands in for Ireland – that steers Thailand towards the territory of fabled ancient civilizations. In addition, drawing on romantic associations, the film gestures to locations linked with what is variously lost, inaccessible, paradisiacal and exotic. Scotland itself becomes 'Atlantis', an example both of the 'dislocated "Scotland" that figures so prominently in ... media adaptations of Shakespeare's *Macbeth*' and of a society that overreached itself and disappeared into the 'wild and

---

21 David Streckfuss, *Truth on Trial in Thailand: Defamation, Treason and Lèse Majesté* (London and New York, 2011), pp. 304, 305, 312.

22 Interviews between Ing K. and the author, 14 April, 4 May, 12 August, and 19 September (2012). Unless otherwise stated, all quotations from Ing K. are taken from these interviews and appear in the text.

23 Quotations from *Macbeth* are taken from William Shakespeare, *The Complete Works*, ed. Stanley Wells, Gary Taylor, John Jowett, and William Montgomery (Oxford, 1986).

24 Atom Egoyan and Ian Balfour, 'Introduction', in *Subtitles: On the Foreignness of Film*, ed. Atom Egoyan and Ian Balfour (Cambridge, MA, 2004), pp. 21-30, esp. p. 21.

25 The comment is recorded in the documentary *Censor Must Die* (directed by Ing K. and Manit Sriwanichpoom, 2013).

26 Bourdieu, *Language*, pp. 139, 142.

violent sea' (4.2.21).[27] Such associations are of a piece with *Shakespeare Must Die*'s water-centred aesthetic. For, referencing the ways in which *Macbeth* is haunted by the confounding properties of 'yeasty waves' (4.1.69), *Shakespeare Must Die* echoes the effects of the tsunami that ravaged Thailand in 2004, bringing to mind the fate – engulfment by water – of the mythical Atlantis / filmic Scotland. Water is everywhere in *Shakespeare Must Die*, from the ornamental pond on the golf course in which Bangkho/Banquo's body is dumped to the swimming pool in which the Lady Macbeth figure hallucinates, and it invariably connotes the arbitrary operations of power. Such episodes bolster a universalizing notion of *Macbeth*'s 'multitudinous seas incarnadine' (2.2.60). Notably, the film's water features are uncontrolled, suggesting, in their visceral visual impact, a country whose plight is registered in the physical appearances of its liquid landscape.

An impression of crisis is confirmed by the film's opening, in which *Macbeth*'s 'fog and filthy air' (1.1.11) are summoned via a sinister *mise-en-scène* dominated by incense and smoke (failure and futility are intimated by the scene, an abandoned *san phra phum*, or spirit-house, littered with broken clay votive symbols). The opening privileges recognizably performative gestures as a worried-looking young woman progresses to a painted representation of the Hindu 'war goddess', Durga, astride a tiger and bearing a necklace of skulls.[28] Propitiating Durga with a platter of food and drink, the woman enacts a ritual that recalls the ways in which, at the start of a traditional theatrical performance in south-east Asia, actors 'pay obeisance to the gods who preside over theatre . . . [and seek] . . . self-protection'.[29] Theatre is also prepared for in the camera's movement through the empty void of Durga's face to a presidential-looking individual. At once, the penchant of Thaksin, the previous Prime Minister, for white shirts, a black tie and sleek black business suits are replicated in *Shakespeare Must Die*'s complementary costuming of Dear Leader.[30] Seated at table in a mansion's gloomy ballroom, he listens to the sounds of a street protest, with heavy plasterwork and oppressive

chandeliers indicating a decadent figure. *Shakespeare Must Die* continually invites its audience to identify Dear Leader as having failed in his leadership responsibilities. Germane here is the singular reading of 5.5: an external scene discovers a group of protesters waving a sea of placards on which Dear Leader is pictured as a Führer-like demagogue (*Macbeth* is purposefully reworked, the inspiration for the episode being the reference to the 'rabble's curse' (5.10.29) on a monster 'Painted upon a pole' (5.10.26)). The derelictions placed at his door – 'Murder/Corruption/Greed/Lies' – appear on the placards in crudely rendered letters, while the consignment of an effigy of Dear Leader to a bonfire provides testimony of anti-authoritarian sentiment. Fascistic images (a skull in a storm-trooper's helmet) and sounds (the thud of jackboots) both indict Dear Leader as a modern tyrant and suggest the extent and range of an oppressive regime. Later, Dear Leader is imaged as a water-monitor in insets, the association with the meanings enshrined in the Thai term for the reptile, *hia* (evil persons and/or deeds), embracing both filmic and extra-filmic realms of suggestion.

Immediately after our introduction to Dear Leader, the scene shifts to the opening of a theatrical production of *Macbeth* in which a histrionic mode of delivery and ritualistic gestures recall *likay* (or Thai folk opera).[31] The theatrical space is characterized by dark presentiments and unnerving images. Based on Caravaggio's famous painting, a Medusa head adorning the theatrical

---

[27] Courtney Lehmann, '"Out damned Scot": dislocating Macbeth in transnational film and media culture', in *Shakespeare, the Movie, II: Popularizing the Plays on Film, TV, Video and DVD*, ed. Richard Burt and Lynda E. Boose (London and New York, 2003), pp. 231–51, esp. p. 231.

[28] See Nilima Chitgopekar, *The Book of Durga* (New Delhi, 2003), p. 5.

[29] James R. Brandon, *Theatre in Southeast Asia* (Cambridge, MA, 1967), p. 223.

[30] The term 'Dear Leader' recalls both Kim Jong-il and Kim Jong-un, leaders of North Korea and bywords, in the West, for totalitarianism.

[31] On *likay*, see Jukka O. Miettinen, *Classical Dance and Theatre in South-East Asia* (Oxford and New York, 1992), pp. 73–4.

production's curtains represents a monstrous replacement for the *rishi* head, or symbol of the divine spirits, traditionally placed on the back wall of the *likay* stage.[32] Creatures of ill omen are deployed in narrative patterns, as when a shot of flapping bats spiralling outwards from a cave is recalled in the twirling black leaves of the painting *Exploding Flowers*, which is seen in the background as Khunying Mekhdeth / Lady Macbeth begins her incantation to the infernal 'spirits' (1.5.39); the impression is of an imminent release of malign forces. In many cases, such interpolations can be traced to Thai practices and beliefs. Hence, the theatrical production is dominated by a 'Tree of Spirits' (or *Bodhi* tree of Buddhist enlightenment) on which is placed a doll-like, garlanded figure; this is the so-called *kumarn thong* or 'golden boy', the 'ghost' of 'sacrificed foetuses' (Illustration 41)[33] Not only does the figure establish arcane, black magic rituals as a motif of the theatrical production, it also surrogates for the 'birth-strangled babe' (4.1.30) of *Macbeth* and the larger Shakespearian preoccupation with abortion, child murder and projected infanticide. On stage, extravagantly dressed and elaborately coiffured witches exemplify the ways in which this film combines theatrical action with a *Macbeth* narrative external to the playhouse locale. Thus, scenes including Bangkho/ Banquo's feast, the sleep-walking, and the murder of Lady Macduff are split between theatrical and external perspectives, suggesting the fundamental coherence of the film's two worlds: the tale of Shakespeare's *Macbeth* is seamlessly pertinent in both.

Topically charged references link to the broader critique mounted in the theatrical production's version of 3.5, Hecate's address to the witches.[34] In this instance, the 'spirits' are envisioned as uniformed schoolchildren (they are led on by a skeleton playing the role of a pied-piper) who, as they march about the stage, chant in unison: 'Dear Leader leads to Nation's Glory ... Dear Leader born to lift the masses ... Dear Leader brings happy-ocracy'. The children, it is suggested, have been brain-washed and fallen victim to the 'strength of ... illusion' (3.5.28). The episode

functions, in part because of the witches' excited applause (they are present on stage approving their youthful charges), to critique a blind subscription to the state apparatus. But it also suggests a misplaced patriotism that reduces a country's subjects to unthinking automatons; the elevation theme of the song's banal lyrics is countered by the spectacle of the children moving in a series of ever-diminishing circles. If the children's demonstration for Hecate points up an anaesthetized response, other moments in the film aim to provoke, via recollection, specific controversies of the Thaksin era. For instance, the 'War on Drugs' in 2003, which resulted in widespread extra-judicial killings, is alluded to in the ways in which *Shakespeare Must Die* realizes the killing of Lady Macduff. At an improvised roadside checkpoint, Lady Macduff and her daughter are stopped by the 'Safari Suit Man' (a Thai government agent identified by his threatening mien and dark blue fatigues), pulled from the car, assaulted and murdered.[35] Slow-motion camera work, a scream, a shattered window and final silence are the chilling accompaniments to a murder whose identifying features evoke one episode in Thailand's unpalatable human rights record.

Behind the episode, of course, lies the spectre of Mekhdeth/Macbeth, and, if *Shakespeare Must Die* is provocative in hinting at Dear Leader / Thaksin comparisons, it is no less attentive in drawing attention to unflattering correlations between Dear Leader and the central theatrical protagonist. Bryan Adams Hampton notes that *Macbeth* comprises a 'series of "mirroring" moments, insistent doublings', and it is this principle that the film uses

---

[32] For the *rishi* head, see Ghulam-Sarwar Yousof, *Dictionary of Traditional South-East Asian Theatre* (Kuala Lumpur, 1994), p. 142.

[33] See Philip Cornwel-Smith, *Very Thai: Everyday Popular Culture* (Bangkok, 2005), p. 181.

[34] Hecate appears as the cardboard representation of the goddess Durga, her empty face now filled by the female supplicant of the start.

[35] For the 'War on Drugs', see Thak Chaloemtiarana, *Thailand: The Politics of Despotic Paternalism*, 2nd edn (Ithaca and New York, 2007), p. xvii.

41. Mekhdeth/Macbeth, Bangkho/Banquo, the 'Tree of Spirits', and the witches. Courtesy of Jai Singh Films.

as its *modus operandi*.[36] All of the major cast members are doubled, with each actor undertaking a part in the film's two environments (Dear Leader and Mekhdeth/Macbeth are played by the same actor, Pissarn Pattanapeeradej). Not only does the doubling method encourage audience comparison, it also stresses how the two enjoy twin-like relations. For example, at the moment when he honours and accepts Duncan's blessing, Mekhdeth/Macbeth is represented as simultaneously coveting the monarch's golden slippers. His will to power is juxtaposed with an inset in which a newly elected Dear Leader waves to supporters; the effect is to suggest ulterior motives and hypocrisy on both counts. More generally, *Shakespeare Must Die* vigorously eschews opportunities to allow an empathetic or even ambiguous reading of Shakespeare's protagonist. Rather, Thai supernatural motifs and generic horror imagery serve to limn Mekhdeth/Macbeth primarily as

the 'butcher' (5.11.35) of theatrical tradition who brings a 'poor country' (4.3.165) to ruin. Part of that figuration involves discovering Mekhdeth/Macbeth as variously oily, wild-eyed, fearful, easily led, self-satisfied, hectoring and cowardly: in addition, notable soliloquies, such as 'My way of life / Is fall'n into the sere' (5.3.24–5), are presented as terror-racked voice-overs that insist on audience alienation. At the same time, this Mekhdeth/Macbeth very much chimes with the 'usurper' (5.11.21) designation of Macduff's final address. Elderly, smiling indulgently, and speaking slowly, Duncan is *par excellence* a divinely conceived sovereign, and here the film avails itself of the deep reverence that the Thai monarchy has traditionally been accorded. *Shakespeare Must Die* emphasizes

---

[36] Bryan Adams Hampton, 'Purgation, exorcism, and the civilizing process in Macbeth', *SEL* 51.2 (2011), 327–47; p. 328.

Duncan's role – his splendid robes and golden *chada* or crown are of a piece with the dignity of his performance – so as to stress Mekhdeth/Macbeth's flaws as a subject. Additional insets of the murdered sovereign – one shows him as a vision with his wife and children – reinforce a sense of a familial crime of sacrilegious proportions. Characteristic of *Shakespeare Must Die*, then, is an elaboration of Macbeth that, via a chain of associations, calls into question Thai political leaders beyond the film's narrative.

II

Particularly picked out for critique in *Shakespeare Must Die* is Dear Leader's cultivation of media visibility (television broadcasts and public actions are repeatedly staged before a camera). In these respects, the meta-theatricality of the film is vital, allowing for an interrogative treatment of the mediatized forms through which national debate is conducted. In this regard, it is notable that Thaksin, a director of his own telecommunications company, was able, for the first time in the Thai political arena, skillfully to use online and televisual electoral platforms. The film's suggestion that television viewers are misled by 'spin' stands in stark contradistinction to the identification of the theatre audience as a discerning interpretive constituency. Hence, in the parts centred on the theatrical production, the camera continually pans to the faces of the spectators; via a doubled perspective, we watch the performance in the knowledge that it, too, is being separately appreciated. Russell Jackson identifies 'theatre audiences on film' as sites where 'important social and emotional transactions take place' and, indeed, in *Shakespeare Must Die*, reaction shots construct the audience as positively sentient – a moral barometer.[37] At various points, an actor – notably, the porter – delivers a speech by descending from the stage, thereby drawing attention to the significance attached to audience response. Audiences are also visualized on-stage, as in the scene with Boonrod/Ross and the Old Man in which the latter wheels on a mobile coffee-stall, his vendor status establishing him as a witness

and 'man-on-the-street'. Highlighting what is at stake in audience engagement, *Shakespeare Must Die* reifies Brecht's notion of a 'political theatre' that can 'amaze its public' and 'provoke with its representations', but it simultaneously – to adopt a formulation of Fredric Jameson – imagines theatre as 'a figure for the social more generally', showing how drama, in raising consciousness and contributing ideologically, might function as a catalyst for change.[38]

If it is suggested that theatre can work in these instrumental capacities, then this is realized in the film's explicit paralleling of the audience in the auditorium and the protesters on the street. Both, responding to the representation of Mekhdeth/Macbeth and the presence of Dear Leader respectively, chant 'Get Out!' and participate in imitative practices that confirm the theatrical production's interventionist potential. Herbert Blau sees 'the crowd as the consummation of the audience', and *Shakespeare Must Die* exemplifies the notion in showing how a response to despotism within the theatre is replicated in popular actions outside.[39] In particular, the movement of the forest of Dunsinane is visualized in the street protesters; their to-and-fro motion suggests the sway of uprooted trees, and their green headscarves reference new growth and the resurrection of the natural order. In these non-cast protesters, then, we see sketched the combined forces of Munkam/Malcolm and Mekhdub/Macduff's 'power' (4.3.238). Judged in the light of the pseudo-newscast format of the protesters' scene, it is possible to suggest that *Shakespeare Must Die* draws at this point upon communal memories of the massive street upheavals which, in the wake of the 2006 coup, brought Thailand to a standstill. That the

---

[37] Russell Jackson, *Theatres on Film: How the Cinema Imagines the Stage* (Manchester and New York, 2013), pp. 15-16.

[38] Bertolt Brecht, *Brecht on Theatre: The Development of an Aesthetic*, ed. and trans. John Willett, 2nd edn (London, 1974), p. 192; Fredric Jameson, *Brecht and Method* (London and New York, 2000), p. 72.

[39] Herbert Blau, *The Audience* (Baltimore and London, 1990), p. 18.

42. Mekhdeth/Macbeth and Khunying Mekhdeth / Lady Macbeth steeped in gore. Courtesy of Jai Singh Films.

film explicitly references this period is confirmed in one of the early appearances of the witches. As they greedily tear apart and eat a heart-shaped sponge cake, footage from the disturbances accompanying the coup flashes up in the background: their excess and appetitiveness, it is implied, are played out in the political arena. *Shakespeare Must Die* is also sensitive to the coup's violent aftermath. Between 2008 and 2010, there were sustained clashes between the 'Yellow Shirts' (street supporters of the People's Alliance for Democracy Party and its association with the military) and the 'Red Shirts' (now disenfranchised supporters of the pro-Thaksin United Front for Democracy against Dictatorship party).[40] *Shakespeare Must Die*, taking its cue from the play's own colour scheme, indexes these events by privileging strategic flashes of red. Illustrative are the red mist that surrounds a distracted Mekhdeth/Macbeth and the red scarf worn by one of the hired murderers; these, it is suggested, are the identifying hues of the protagonist's regime, as well as a 'poor country' (4.3.165) racked by 'violent sorrow' (4.3.170). In this connection, it is revealing that, shortly before the ban, on 26 March 2012, the producer of *Shakespeare*

Must Die, Manit Sriwanichpoom, was summoned by the Film Censorship Board to answer a series of questions about the film's distinctive use of colour. One member of the board noted that 'the "Red Shirts" will say the film causes people to misunderstand them and perceive them as being prone to violence'.[41] In a culture where remembering is a contested activity, *Shakespeare Must Die*'s colours are read as provocative, as stirring up unwelcome memories of the all too recent political maelstrom.

Arguably the most forceful connection between the theatre and the street is reserved for the film's realization of 5.11, during which a plaster model of 'Th'usurper's cursèd head' (5.11.21) is kicked about the theatre by an excited audience. Brutally dramatic in a way that ruptures traditional stage interpretations of the scene, the moment prioritizes audience involvement, as the laughing, cheering spectators attack the effigy with a sense of joyful

[40] Askew, 'Afterword', in Askew, ed., *Legitimacy*, pp. 303–18, esp. p. 303; Terwiel, *Thailand's Political History*, p. 301. On links between the 'Yellow Shirts' and the military, see Askew, 'Introduction', p. 14; Connors, *Democracy*, p. 272.

[41] 'Censor News 28 March 2012' http://shakespearemustdie .com.

release. In short, *Macbeth*, as it unfolds in the theatre, provides a narrative for an audience rising up, taking power into their own hands, and symbolically beheading a tyrant. Previous external insets of Dear Leader in his mansion now make sense; he has been forced into hiding, it is suggested, by the implications of the drama in his midst. Earlier, the radical potentiality of the drama is recognized on screen by the arrival in the theatre of pro-government supporters. After 2.4, the scene with Boonrod/Ross and the Old Man, the theatrical production cuts to an interval during which the 'Safari Suit Man' (he reappears later as the murderer of Lady Macduff) approaches the fictional director, played by Chatchai Puipia, a Thai artist, who is in conversation at the bar with Ing K., the film's actual director. The intertextuality of the casting is indicative of the extent to which *Shakespeare Must Die* invests in self-referential registers, presumably reflecting traditional alliances between the People's Alliance for Democracy Party, intellectuals, and academics.[42] Iconic for his anti-materialist stance, as expressed in experimental sculptures, still-lifes and self-portraits, Chatchai Puipia stands in for Thai artists in general, sensitizing us both to the significance of his creations in the film (many of the paintings that appear are his own work) and to a 'real-life' community of creative practitioners. Exposing the doubling conceit, the 'Safari Suit Man' demands, 'Your actor looks like our Dear Leader ... Is this intentional?', to which the theatrical director replies, 'My job is to create the work; what you the audience may think is up to you.' Privileging audience reaction over authorial intention, the answer highlights exactly the politics of reception that the film has made visible. Impelled to seek reinforcements, the 'Safari Suit Man' leaves the theatre at the line 'And damned be him that first cries "Hold, enough!"' (5.10.34), and ironically reappears at the line 'The time is free' (5.11.21) – on this occasion accompanied by a gang of red-scarfed thugs who assault the spectators, beat up the theatrical director, drag him away and subject him to an extended lynching. Through a final paradox of doubling, 'Th'usurper's cursèd head' is mirrored in the theatrical director's hanged corpse,

'this most bloody piece of work' (2.3.127). With such connections, the title of the film acquires its meaning, the charge thrown at the theatrical director by his executioner being that, as a representative of 'Shakespeare', he must 'die'.

Recalling disturbances in Thailand of the mid-1970s, the lynching episode directly images one event in particular: the Thammasat University Massacre. On 5 October 1976, students protesting against the return to Thailand of a former military leader staged a satirical play which, detractors claimed, showed the Crown Prince in a mock-hanging pose (photographs of the production were, in fact, falsified).[43] In response to the perceived act of *lèse majesté*, armed groups supporting the military entered the campus of Thammasat University on 6 October and fired on, raped, mutilated and burned alive unarmed students suspected of communist sympathies.[44] Over 300 students were killed (there have been no prosecutions), and a military junta assumed power soon afterwards. An index of the significance of the episode to *Shakespeare Must Die* lies in the ways in which it is prefigured at several points, not least when the camera glimpses the doll of a yellow gibbon (an offering for monks) hanging from the 'Tree of Spirits'. The black heart-shaped face of the gibbon is replicated in the heart-shaped cake consumed by the witches, making of the theatrical production's theatrical director a sacrificial figure, a totemic focus for the film as a whole.

The lynching episode casts a light back on previous censorship regimes. Although the Thammasat University Massacre was made internationally infamous by the work of Pulitzer Prize-winning photographer Neil Ulevich (who pictured a student hanging from a rope and being

---

[42] On support for the People's Alliance for Democracy Party, see Terwiel, *Thailand's Political History*, p. 291; Giles Ji Ungpakorn, *A Coup for the Rich: Thailand's Political Crisis* (Bangkok, 2007), p. 20.

[43] *Political Repression in Thailand* (London, 1978), pp. 18, 33; Terwiel, *Thailand's Political History*, p. 281.

[44] *Political*, p. 12; Ungpakorn, *Coup*, p. 83; David K. Wyatt, *Thailand: A Short History* (New Haven, 1984), p. 302.

43. Mekhdeth/Macbeth and Khunying Mekhdeth / Lady Macbeth during the banquet scene. Courtesy of Jai Singh Films.

beaten with a chair), inside Thailand the massacre, to cite Patsorn Sungsri, has 'not been recorded . . . at any level'.[45] Interestingly, at the core of Ing K.'s address (on 5 July 2012) to the Foreign Correspondents' Club of Thailand was an objection to the ways in which 'stories' in Thailand are dictated to by 'law'; she makes the point that 'we are not allowed to examine ourselves: our cultures, our wounds of history, our very soul'.[46] Here, *Shakespeare Must Die*'s consistent disregard for those who stay silent seems relevant. As discussed earlier, subtitles generally respect Shakespearian dialogue, but there is an exception when, in the porter's address, taking the place of the 'farmer' (2.3.4) and the 'tailor' (2.3.13), 'whore academics' and 'journalists for sale' are addressed. These shapers of public opinion are represented as failing to exercise independence of judgement: cowed or paid off, they have not honoured their professional integrity. *Shakespeare Must Die* endeavours to play a recuperative role in these respects, finding in Shakespearian language mechanisms for making evident what has been occluded. In this way, the film works as mnemonic practice. The memory work performed by *Shakespeare Must Die* suggests its function as 'trauma cinema', a species of

representation that, as Susannah Radstone writes, has 'come to be understood as a substitute, supplement, or support for modern memory's atrophy, failure, or vicissitudes'.[47] *Macbeth*, too, of course, is a drama of ghosts; the protagonist is himself haunted and, as the appearance of Banquo at the banquet discovers, massacres of the past return to plague the present (Illustration 43). And, because *Shakespeare Must Die* occurs at a juncture where history is fought over, its choice of *Macbeth* as the play to privilege is timely, if not politic.

The lynching episode is immediately followed by the emergence from hiding of Dear Leader; indeed, the montage suggests that the latter is facilitated by the former. Such incendiary relations between art and politics are confirmed when Dear Leader's television broadcast places restrictions on artistic practice. 'Brothers and sisters', he

[45] Patsorn Sungsri, *Thai National Cinema* (Saarbrücken, 2008), p. 151.
[46] 'Address to the Foreign Correspondents' Club of Thailand', www.Shakespearemustdie.com.
[47] Susannah Radstone, 'Cinema and memory', in *Memory: Histories, Theories, Debates*, ed. Susannah Radstone and Bill Schwarz (New York, 2010), pp. 325–42, esp. p. 333.

proclaims, 'ill-intentioned people seek to create hatred and social division ... I am forced to announce emergency rule ... all publication, mass media and the arts, including public performance and exhibition, must be passed by the Public Relations Department'. In these formulations, not only is censorship tied to a 'state of exception', echoing the default position of a succession of governments, but anodyne versions of the arts are presented as key to the restoration of the status quo. As the witches watch the broadcast, the camera swirls giddily to a backdrop of the tangled carcass of Bangkok's famous Siam Theatre, burned to the ground in 2010 by 'Red-Shirt' agitators.[48] A dissolve to a prison cell (where the actors languish, having been forcibly removed from the theatre before the ending of the play proper) links the historical desecration of this Thai landmark with the break-up of *Macbeth*. Lying on the ground, clinging to the vestiges of theatricality (bloodied and torn costumes) and showing clear signs of having been beaten (bruised faces), Boonrod/Ross and Mekhdub/Macduff greet Munkam/Malcolm by his new title, openly referencing 'Scotland' for the first time and finding in the continuation of the production a newly resistant force. Eschewing the cuts often reserved for this scene, *Shakespeare Must Die* plays it in full, making of Munkam/Malcolm an afflicted hero who will not relinquish his Shakespearian responsibility, even in the most oppressive of conditions.

In part here, *Shakespeare Must Die* recalls the prologue-like cemetery ceremony, and realizes Munkam/Malcolm as agitating to bestow the actor's traditional blessing on the audience. His line 'So thanks to all at once, and to each one, / Prosperity and joy', adapted from 5.11.40–1, is extended into and played as a kind of epilogue, replicating how, in the theatre traditions of southeast Asia, a performance is concluded with a prayer.[49] And yet, given its embittered tone, this is no traditional act of devotion. Instead, the pledge 'We will perform in measure, time, and place' (5.11.39), with its emphasis on a performance still to ensue, is a defiant one: Munkam/Malcolm's voice rises to a scream, and his hands shake the

grille of his cage-like cell, pointing out a will to make Shakespeare heard. This is despite the fact that Munkam/Malcolm's language is almost drowned out by the whirr of a helicopter and the wail of a siren, sounds of a 'real' protest that, taking place on the day of filming, Ing K. chose not to edit out; these are the diegetic supplements to *Shakespeare Must Die* that indicate the continuing 'emergency' situation that is the condition of the film's possibility. And it is with the state of the country that we close in the soundtrack, a musical realization of Ross's lament, 'Alas, poor country, / Almost afraid to know itself. It cannot / Be called our mother, but our grave' (4.3.165–67), complete with dark piano notes and minor chord changes. The code of 'Atlantis' having been abandoned, we confront 'Scotland', for which we read Thailand, and are invited to recognize *Macbeth*'s relevancies to a deeply entrenched and divided nation-state.

III

If *Shakespeare Must Die* ends by reifying a refusal to capitulate, this impulse is sustained in subsequent 'real-life' events. In the wake of the Film Censorship Board ban, there were concerted attempts by cast, crew, and production team to reverse the ruling. A 17 April 2012 'Letter to the National Board of Film and Video' argued that the film had been disallowed from 'working its truthful magic ... [because] truth threatens the foundations of a tyrannical power'; it was signed by 514 co-complainants (academics, journalists, artists, dramaturgs).[50] Formal proceedings ensued on 30 May 2012, Ing K. and Manit Sriwanichpoom filing a petition with the Citizens' Rights, Political Rights and Media Rights section of the National

---

48 In addition to the destruction of the Siam Theatre, 37 buildings were set alight, including the Central World shopping complex, over 90 died and 1,500 were injured. See Askew, 'Afterword', p. 315; Terwiel, *Thailand's Political History*, pp. 311, 312.
49 Brandon, *Theatre*, p. 222.
50 'Letter of Appeal to the National Board of Film and Video', www.Shakespearemustdie.com.

Human Rights Commission, and this was followed up on 31 May 2012 with a petition to the Senate House Committee on Human Rights, Freedom and Consumer Protection. Although the latter two bodies have not been entirely unsympathetic (suggesting that amendments need to be made to accommodate greater freedom and expression in the spheres of film and media), to date, none of the appeals has been successful.

In addition to legal proceedings, resistance to the ruling took the form of staged public events, all of which had Shakespeare and *Macbeth* at their core. To mark the occasion of the delivery of the 'Letter to the National Board of Film and Video' on 17 April 2012, cast and crew staged a street protest outside Bangkok's Government House. Assuming the role of Shakespeare in a pseudo-Elizabethan ruff, Boonrod/Ross proclaims the key 'Alas, poor country' (4.3.165) lament. Highlighting provenance and authorship through play, the protest showcases a kind of resurrection, the Bard coming back from the grave to castigate modern officialdom. Other cast members revive their filmic roles, appropriating lines from *Macbeth* that speak loudly to the current injustice. Khunying Mekhdeth / Lady Macbeth recites her 'Out, damned spot' (5.1.33) speech, resituating the 'spot' of the imaginary in the material praxis of censorship, while Mekhdeth/Macbeth cries 'The devil damn thee black' (5.3.11), impugning the banning of the film via site-specific theatre variations. Similarly playing with citation and double meaning are the formulations emblazoned on the placards, 'To Ban or Not to Ban: That is the Freedom Question' and 'Shakespeare Must Live'. The protest uses Hamlet's philosophical question as a rallying call, repeatedly name-checking Shakespeare to keep at the forefront the paradox of Bardic repression. In this way, the treatment meted out to a Shakespeare film becomes the rationale for launching a broader critique. A 'Free Thai Cinema' placard, in particular, demonstrates how Shakespeare stands in for political debate: the limbo-like situation of *Shakespeare Must Die* works as a test-case that reflects back on the state of Thai society as a whole.

The most sustained opposition to the censors' verdict came in the form of *Censor Must Die* (directed by Ing K. and Manit Sriwanichpoom, 2013), a lengthy documentary that constitutes not so much a companion piece to the film as a riposte to the ban. Described as 'part of our campaign to free *Shakespeare Must Die*', the documentary intends 'to influence attitudes, increase understanding, [and] persuade to action'.[51] It follows the producer, Manit Sriwanichpoom, through a series of increasingly frustrating institutional encounters. The documentary shifts among various registers – black-and-white, half-tone and full-colour – whose effect is to suggest a journey through different realms of experience, none of which accords with each other or amounts to a coherent whole. Along the way, *Shakespeare Must Die* surfaces in extracts, the surrounding commentary feeding into those fragments and creating a defensive meta-narrative. In a typically impassioned inset, Sakul Boonyatat, who plays Boonrod/Ross in *Shakespeare Must Die*, speaks despairingly of 'work of worth which is stepped on as worthless' and of how the 'artistic discipline' in Thailand is always beholden to 'propaganda', shaped, as it is, by a condition of 'fear' and dictated to by 'cultural fascism'. This affective set-piece gains credence from Sakul Boonyatat's positions as a professor of drama and festival panel judge in 'real life'.

Notably, *Censor Must Die* illuminates the extent to which the ban placed upon the film is shaped by a climate of political uncertainty. In the background of several shots, election broadcasts play out on television monitors, and unrest is thrown into sharp relief when the focus shifts to a rally objecting to the Reconciliation Bill – which would have allowed the exiled Thaksin to return to Thailand – being held outside Senate House. 'You hold the people in contempt: we're forced to resort to other measures', a speaker exclaims, her complaint both echoing the situation of the film-

---

51 Steve Blandford, Barry Keith Grant, and Jim Hillier, *The Film Studies Dictionary* (London, 2001), p. 74.

44. Cast and crew protest in *Censor Must Die*, directed by Ing K. and Manit Sriwanichpoom, 2013. Courtesy of Jai Singh Films / Kamikaze Productions.

makers and making the point that, in contemporary Thailand, the dissatisfaction aroused by the verdict brought to bear on *Shakespeare Must Die* indicates a more expansive network of factions and grievances.

Because of the rally, Sriwanichpoom, confined within the parliamentary compound, finds his every attempted effort at escape blocked, his body becoming a cipher for *Shakespeare Must Die*'s own stalled momentum. Although on occasions we see the threatening undercurrent of governmental inertia (when the camera lingers on police shields thrown down on the pavement, for instance), dominating *Censor Must Die* are sequences which highlight the experience of delay. As Sriwanichpoom wanders through a series of vast internal architectural environs, it is easy to see how complainants lose their verve. Expressed in such visuals is the bureaucratic illogic of Thailand's internal operations. The movement motif is given a particularly depressive turn when the producer is glimpsed wandering disconsolately past piles of papers – material manifestations of deadlock. Later, during one of his many journeys to lodge counter-

arguments and appeals, Sriwanichpoom ironically finds himself stuck in a traffic jam next to Bangkok's Democracy Monument. Giorgio Agamben notes that 'He who has been banned is not ... simply set outside the law ... but rather abandoned by it ... exposed and threatened on the threshold in which life and law, outside and inside, become indistinguishable', an observation that *Censor Must Die* is consistently at pains to illustrate.[52]

At the close, in a serendipitous stroke of filmmaking, an elderly man, like the producer who has come before him, chafes at the chains of an institutional order. 'I wish to see the Chief Judge', he asks at the Administrative Court, adding, 'Three years and still no judgment'. We do not know the nature of his grievance, although his blindness and disability hint at a history of Gloucester-like mistreatment. *Censor Must Die* finds in the figure of the unheeded, waiting citizen an emblematic everyman, a proxy for the predicament of

---

[52] Agamben, *Homo*, p. 58.

45. Poster for *Censor Must Die* (directed by Ing K. and Manit Sriwanichpoom, 2013). Courtesy of Jai Singh Films / Kamikaze Productions.

postponement. His echoing question – 'How many more years?' – stands as the epitaph for the documentary, encapsulating in its weary repetition the perils of attempting reform, and underscoring the ways in which delay functions as a covert mechanism with which to quell dissent. In this way, the documentary works as critique, indicting in its very length the inability – or unwillingness – of the system to reconsider the Shakespearian adaptation in its midst.

Although *Censor Must Die* might seem to offer a particular challenge in its cynical *exposé* of the workings of Thai institutions, the documentary – unlike *Shakespeare Must Die* – was passed for exhibition, the rationale being, according to the statement issued by the Film Censorship Board, that the 'events' represented within it 'really happened'.[53] The distinction is an intriguing one: the Board is able to affirm the 'real-life' events that followed

Shakespeare Must Die but not the dramatization to which the film gives voice. Fictional projection, it seems, is more destabilizing. *Censor Must Die* has been shown at the Bangkok Arts and Cultural Centre and the RMA Institute, educational environments open to debating censorship judgements. Given that it contains extracts, afforded in such showings are other means of experiencing *Shakespeare Must Die*, local ways of accessing a film that, through the ban, has acquired an underground Bangkok following.

The ban has also precipitated international attention, granting to *Shakespeare Must Die* a certain aura and *caché*. A Western press seized on the censorship of an adaptation of Shakespeare as exceptional. Typical are headlines such as 'Shakespeare est mort à Bangkok', 'Thai censors ban *Macbeth*', and 'Thailand's Battle of the Bard', which centre on the extraordinary disjunction between the fate visited on the film and Shakespeare's standing as a revered playwright.[54] And, in the wake of the controversy, *Shakespeare Must Die* is beginning to be screened outside Thailand (for instance, at the Cindi Film Festival, Seoul, in 2013; at the Asian Shakespeare Association Conference, Taipei, in 2014; and as part of a retrospective of all of Ing K.'s films at the Pompidou Centre, Paris, in 2017) to considerable acclaim.[55] At the 2013 Tripoli International Film Festival in Libya, the film was awarded both the Prix du Meilleur Film de Fiction and the NETPAC Prize for the Best Asian Picture. Via the act of denying the film public screenings in Thailand, the Film Censorship Board has created

53 See 'Censor Must Die' won't be censored', http://mekhdeth-cmd.blogspot.co.uk.

54 Andrew Dickson, 'Thailand's Battle of the Bard', *G2: Film and Music*, 6 June 2014, pp. 12–13; Bruno Philip, 'Shakespeare est mort à Bangkok', *Le Monde*, 14 April 2012, p. 23; 'Thai censors ban Macbeth as too political', *Guardian*, 5 April 2012, p. 29.

55 For the retrospective, see Nicole Brenez, 'Rétrospective: Ing K., la "Démocratie cinématographique en action"', *De Ligne / En Ligne: Centre Pompidou, Bibliothèque Publique d'Information* 22 (2017), 5-7. At the time of writing, the film has been screened most recently at the Close-Up Film Centre, London (31 March 2017).

the conditions for other kinds of visibility, stimulating interest not only in *Shakespeare Must Die*'s own ideological investments but also in the critical state of Thailand's political milieu.

In a recent overview, Alexa Huang [Joubin] calls for the need for global Shakespeare studies to develop from 'a catalogue of exotic objects into a critical methodology'.[56] Available theories and current discourses of globalization, she comments, cannot 'adequately deal with the issues of multiculturalism, multilingualism, diaspora, and identity raised by' Shakespeare in his world-wide manifestations.[57] In part, the lack of methodology is linked to the ways in which easy assumptions are made about the field; all too often, it is suggested, an adaptation is judged according to 'deterministic, linear, teleological histories ... oriented towards preconceived end points', the effect of which is to homogenize the example and to flatten the unique features of time and place.[58] Censorship disrupts the narrative of Shakespeare in particular national contexts, revealing how his plays might function in strategic, but not straightforward, applications. As a paradigm of understanding, censorship is marked by a restless mix of impulses and effects: a phenomenon that is resolutely of the contemporary, it lies behind the production, or non-production, of global Shakespeares at multiple levels and colours categories of 'Shakespeare' and the 'global' in the process. Films such as *Shakespeare Must Die* are important, for they stimulate thinking about existing mechanisms of scholarly engagement and remind us how Shakespeare – and particularly *Macbeth* – retains a radical edge and a power to upset.

Indeed, *Shakespeare Must Die* follows in the footsteps of a number of recent adaptations, suggesting that *Macbeth* has become the play of choice in nation-states where questions of artistic freedom and cultural entitlement are actively debated. A film such as *Sangrador* (directed by Leonardo Henríquez, 2000), for instance, a Venezuelan adaptation of the play, implies via popular images of despotism an allegory of Hugo Chávez and his association with human rights abuses. Similarly, although working in different registers, *Macbeth* (directed by Bo Landin and Alex Scherpf, 2004), a Sámi-language adaptation set in the Arctic Circle,

takes its cue from the play's preoccupation with tyranny and absolutism. The film elaborates Sámi culture as in danger of assimilation, finding in the film's linguistic and aesthetic decisions a plea for the preservation of an indigenous cause.[59] As Shakespearian interpreter, Ing K. joins a long – but otherwise exclusively male – list of world filmmakers who have used *Macbeth* to attempt political intervention.[60] Hers is a uniquely gendered position, and it is one that the film wishes to privilege. Included in the soundtrack to *Shakespeare Must Die* are snippets from the Rimsky-Korsakov symphonic suite *Scheherazade*, a musical adaptation of *The Arabian Nights* in which a sultan's new wife avoids execution by entertaining her husband with stories. Aligning herself with a woman who is able to reverse a death sentence, Ing K. turns the spotlight towards her own status as a female artist in what is a 'patriarchal cultural context', invoking, to adopt Geetha Ramanathan's formulation, 'feminist authority' in an effort to 'overwrite [other] forms of cinematic power'.[61]

A salient and significant intervention, *Shakespeare Must Die* invites an audience to loosen the grip of the 'hand accursed' (3.6.50) that has been placed upon it, and to spectate upon a 'Scotland' that has been revivified for Thailand's here-and-now. But responding adequately to this challenge insists upon a scrupulously gradated awareness of the work of adaptation, one which pushes at, and teases out, the

---

[56] Alexa Huang [Joubin], 'Global Shakespeares as methodology', *Shakespeare* 9.3 (2013), 273–90; p. 280.

[57] Huang [Joubin], 'Global', p. 287.

[58] Huang [Joubin], 'Global', p. 287.

[59] See Burnett, *Shakespeare*, pp. 112, 181.

[60] For African and Indian examples of resistant *Macbeth*s in the theatre, see James Gibbs and Christine Matzke, '"Accents yet unknown": examples of Shakespeare from Ghana, Malawi and Eritrea', in *Shakespeare's Legacy: The Appropriation of the Plays in Post-Colonial Drama*, ed. Norbert Schaffeld (Trier, 2005), pp. 15-36, esp. p. 20; Rosa M. García Periago, 'The ambiguities of Bollywood conventions and the reading of transnationalism in Vishal Bhardwaj's *Maqbool*', in *Bollywood Shakespeares*, ed. Craig Dionne and Parmita Kapadia (Basingstoke, 2014), pp. 63-86, esp. p. 76.

[61] Geetha Ramanathan, *Feminist Auteurs: Reading Women's Films* (London and New York, 2008), pp. 1, 3.

complexities and contests introduced when, in Craig Dionne and Parmita Kapadia's words, Shakespeare is 'rewritten, reinscribed, and translated to fit within the local traditions, values, and languages of various communities and cultures around the world'.[62] The act of adaptation, we now have to acknowledge, is not simply confined to aesthetics and translation – rather, it involves a concomitant absorption in issues of articulation and reception. For, to cite Ingo Berensmeyer, 'any theory of cultural mobility needs to acknowledge the asymmetries, dislocations, and discordances that arise from shifting flows of exchange and lines of conflict'.[63] Just recently, the Thai military junta has hit the headlines for censoring showings of *The Hunger Games: Mockingjay, Part I* (directed by Francis Lawrence, 2014), a film that in Thailand has been linked to student protest.[64] The similar fates accorded this film and Ing K.'s adaptation should not blind us to the irony that very different constituencies stand behind the judgements. No one body in Thailand holds a monopoly on the exercise of censorship, and the verdict visited upon *Shakespeare Must Die* represents a salutary example of the nonlinear relations that obtain between a Shakespearian adaptation and its sites of production.[65]

---

[62] Craig Dionne and Parmita Kapadia, 'Native Shakespeares: indigenous appropriations on a global stage', in *Native Shakespeares: Indigenous Appropriations on a Global Stage*, ed. Craig Dionne and Parmita Kapadia (Aldershot, 2008), pp. 1–15, esp. p. 6.

[63] Ingo Berensmeyer, 'Cultural ecology and Chinese Hamlets', *New Literary History* 42.3 (2011), 419–38; p. 428.

[64] Richard Lloyd Parry, 'Thai junta menaces *Hunger Games* rebels', *The Times*, 21 November 2014, p. 56.

[65] There is no DVD of the film commercially available, although extracts are available on the MIT Global Shakespeares Video & Performance Archive website and on YouTube. It is hoped that this situation will change in due course. I would like to thank Ing K. and Manit Sriwanichpoom for the many courtesies and kindnesses extended to me during the writing of this article.

HATHAWAY FARM: COMMEMORATING WARWICKSHIRE WILL BETWEEN THE WARS

KATHERINE WEST SCHEIL

So this is Shakespeareland! After the Birthplace in Henley-street comes Anne Hathaway's cottage at Shottery; and after that Hathaway Farm. That has been the programme of thousands of visitors to Shakespeare's native town during the summer.[1]

This 1929 description of Stratford-upon-Avon includes two familiar locales, but the third, Hathaway Farm, has all but disappeared from accounts of the Stratford tourist circuit. This article examines a particular commemoration of Shakespeare between the two world wars, at Hathaway Farm, a tourist attraction near Anne Hathaway's Cottage. Located at the former Burman's Farm, the home of the long-standing family friends of the Hathaway family, Hathaway Farm was the third stop for visitors to Stratford in the early 1930s, after the Birthplace and Anne Hathaway's Cottage. This site celebrated a version of Shakespeare embedded in rural Warwickshire life, designed for travellers and tourists in search of Shakespeare Country and 'the days of Good Queen Bess'. Run by Midlands solicitor Philip Baker, Hathaway Farm claimed to be an unspoiled, preserved oasis of 'antiquity'.[2] This was far from the truth, however; Hathaway Farm was a carefully curated immersive tourist experience, where visitors could partake of a variety of faux Warwickshire experiences related to rural English life, alongside amenities designed to attract tourists. Baker sought to recreate a period experience, commemorating a version of pastoral England in-between the two world wars, linked to a mythical and idealized rendition of Shakespeare's Warwickshire life. The survival of Hathaway Farm would have changed the landscape of what we think of as 'Shakespeareland' today, but world events intervened to curtail this commemorative project prematurely.

Hathaway Farm occupied the site of Burman's Farm, the home of the Burman family in Shottery, just outside of Stratford, and a few doors down from Anne Hathaway's Cottage. In Shakespeare's day, the land and house were simply called 'Burmans', and the Burman family were tenants of Francis Smyth and his descendants. Connections between the Burmans and Hathaways stretch back to the fifteenth century.[3] Stephen Burman was one of the executors of the will of Richard Hathaway (Anne's father), and Richard Burman was one of the witnesses to the will. Stephen Burman was an executor to the will of Anne's brother Bartholomew Hathaway, and a later Richard Burman borrowed money from Thomas Nash, the husband of Shakespeare's granddaughter Elizabeth.[4] Holy Trinity Church in Stratford has a large memorial tablet in honour of the Burman family, a lasting memorial to their influence and longevity in the

---

[1] J. H. Bloom, 'Shakespeare land: a visit to Hathaway Farm, Shottery', *Evesham Journal and Four Shires Advertiser*, 14 September 1929.

[2] Bloom, 'Shakespeare land'.

[3] C. J. Sisson, 'Shakespeare's friends: Hathaways and Burmans at Shottery', *Shakespeare Survey 12* (Cambridge, 1959), pp. 95–106; p. 102.

[4] Katherine Scheil, 'His wife Anne Shakespeare and the Hathaways', in *The Shakespeare Circle: An Alternative Biography*, ed. Paul Edmondson and Stanley Wells (Cambridge, 2015), pp. 58–9.

Stratford area.[5] The customized stationery for Hathaway Farm played up the connections between the three families, proclaiming that 'The Records indicate a close friendship between the Poet, the Hathaways, and the Burmans from 1582.'[6]

Local solicitor and cattle breeder Philip Baker purchased Burman's Farm in January 1928, intending to turn it into a tourist mecca.[7] One of Baker's first actions was to rename Burman's Farm to signal a particular connection with Shakespeare, through his wife Anne and the Hathaway family name. Baker's decision to rename Burman's Farm as Hathaway Farm is significant. While it would have been more logical to rebrand it with Shakespeare in the title, we might surmise that he intended to call to mind the pastoral Warwickshire associations of Anne Hathaway in the early twentieth century through the Hathaway family name, and the Farm was almost always advertised with a note about its proximity to Anne Hathaway's Cottage (see Illustration 46). In a booklet outlining the attractions of Hathaway Farm, Anne Hathaway figures prominently in the memorialization. The opening illustration features a bust of Shakespeare, with his comments: 'Let me thank you one and all for The New Memorial Theatre, and also for Preserving Hathaway Farm, as a Memorial for Anne, the life partner of my joys and sorrows.'[8]

Baker tapped into the desire to get closer to Shakespeare by inviting visitors physically to inhabit the spaces where Shakespeare was thought to have trod, especially areas where guests could envision a romantic courtship taking place. A writer in the *Queenslander* paper from Australia noted that, in order to know 'Stratford as Shakespeare knew it', one had to go beyond the Birthplace, New Place and Holy Trinity Church, in search of the 'green and leafy Warwickshire of ancient beauty and peace', which is 'very largely what it was hundreds of years ago'. With Philip Baker's recent purchase of Burman's Farm, this writer notes that visitors can now 'walk in the shadow of its walls, through its courtyards and foldyards and greens, and feel that what one sees is very much what the young Shakespeare saw when he came over the fields to

Shottery to woo his Anne, whose cottage stands neighbor to the friendly farm'.[9] Other visitors corroborated the appeal of getting in touch with Shakespeare's romantic life. As one visitor put it, the homestead 'has been restored to a condition very much as it was when young Shakespeare skipped across the fields to Shottery to woo Anne, whose cottage, be it noted, is but a few yards away'.[10] A postcard advertising the Farm (Illustration 47) features a naked Shakespeare and his wife sunbathing en route to Hathaway Farm, suggesting a vision that travellers could only hope to encounter. Hathaway Farm was publicized in Burrow's guide books to Stratford in the 1930s, giving it legitimacy as a travel destination.[11]

Baker evokes the pastoral Warwickshire associations of Shakespeare's wife and her family's cottage nearby, also imbuing the renamed Hathaway Farm with associations of Shakespeare, of his plays, and of a nostalgic Renaissance culture from 'the good old days' in what was promoted as a 'shrine' to Tudor England.[12] Baker advertised Hathaway Farm as 'a Place of Rare Charm and Antiquity which thro' Ancient Oversight, for Centuries has slept in strange Oblivion' (see Illustration 46), suggesting that this space not only commemorated an earlier period of history but also celebrated a place

---

[5] Val Horsler, *Shakespeare's Church: A Parish for the World* (London, 2010), p. 49.

[6] Shakespeare Birthplace Trust, PR353.

[7] Abstract of Title, Shakespeare Birthplace Trust DR165/113. Baker had apparently been buying up property in the area; in 1919, he purchased Hansell's Farm and two cottages in Shottery (Shakespeare Birthplace Trust DR469/13). Baker was described in the *Holstein Breeder and Dairyman* as: 'besides being a lover of Shakespeare, . . . also an enthusiastic breeder of purebred black-and-white cattle' (22 October 1928, p. 613).

[8] *Rules and Regulations of Hathaway Farm Club*, Shakespeare Birthplace Trust P87.3.

[9] 'Hathaway Farm', *The Queenslander* (Brisbane), 29 November 1928.

[10] Bloom, 'Shakespeare land'.

[11] I am grateful to Roger Pringle for this detail.

[12] Percival Chamberlain, 'A camping holiday in Shakespeare's country', *Country Homes and Estates* (April 1932).

46. Advertisement for Hathaway Farm. © Shakespeare Birthplace Trust.

untouched by the recent global and local turmoil of World War I.

Given the circumstances in Stratford in the 1920s, it is easy to understand Baker's plans for Hathaway Farm. Levi Fox records that 'the decade of the 1920s saw a remarkable increase in the number of visitors, due to the return to peace-time conditions, associated with improved transport and the growing attraction of Stratford's annual Shakespeare Theatre Festival'.[13] In February of 1922, the memorial to World War I was unveiled in Stratford at the top of Bridge Street, but was later moved in 1926 to Bancroft Gardens. In discussing the plans to revive the Shakespeare Festival in 1922, a writer for the Stratford *Herald* remarked, 'People were weary of the War – weary of the peace negotiations dragging themselves so languidly along – and they wanted something that would take them out of the morbid state into which they were rapidly drifting. It was felt that amusement was the best cure to effect this object.'[14]

Baker's plans clearly tapped into this perceived desire for amusement among visitors to the Stratford area. One traveller, Percival Chamberlain, wrote in 1932 that Hathaway Farm was 'an unqualified success, and the demand for accommodation in the seventeen rooms of the Guest House and the Holiday Camp is well sustained throughout the season'. Chamberlain's description highlights the fact that Baker designed his amusement centre to allow visitors to escape by going back in time, with a guest house 'that remains much as it was centuries ago', where 'the visitor nowadays can rest in the utmost comfort in an atmosphere that has all the serenity and charm of

---

[13] Levi Fox, *The Shakespeare Birthplace Trust: A Personal Memoir* (Norwich, 1997), p. 49.
[14] Nicholas Fogg, *Stratford: A Town at War, 1914–1945* (Stroud, Glos., 2008), pp. 59–60.

"TUDOR CLOSE," Alcester Road, Stratford-upon-Avon (1 mile G.W.Ry)

Who knows? Shakespeare and Anne Hathaway, may have been Sun-Bathers !
" Well, sit you out : ....adieu ! "   Love's Labour's Lost. 1.1.110.

47. Postcard advertising Hathaway Farm. © Shakespeare Birthplace Trust.

bygone days', with features of the house designed 'so as not to spoil the old-world effect'.[15] Another visitor corroborated the immersive qualities and the large-scale possibilities of Hathaway Farm: 'It has been said that Stratford-on-Avon would do well to provide more active amusements for visitors – this injunction must have been taken very much to heart when the amenities of Hathaway Farm were outlined and effected. The opportunities to give pleasure and wholesome recreation to large numbers of people are almost without limit.'[16]

A brief summary of Hathaway Farm reveals the impressive extent of Baker's plans, and the elaborate machinations he undertook to construct this escapist fantasy. The layout of Hathaway Farm included two courtyards, Plough Court and Harrow Court, designed to host outdoor plays, with timbered outbuildings – Poet's Parlour and Hathaway Shelter – on either side. No evidence

survives of play performances, but at least the infrastructure was there. Baker offered lodgings in a seventeen-room guest house or in a camping area. A barn ('Ye Olde Barn') was converted to a restaurant with food catered by a Stratford café, and a green hosted dancing and a maypole. A maze 'similar in design to the one at Hampton Court' was part of his plan.[17] The stable rooms were converted to a museum and library 'in which local curios and Shakespearean books are accommodated'.[18] Birmingham antiques dealer Ernest Etheridge sold furniture on the estate, and

---

[15] Chamberlain, 'A camping holiday'.
[16] Bloom, 'Shakespeare land'.
[17] 'Hathaway Farm', *Stratford-on-Avon Herald*, 17 August 1928. The Heather Café of 21 High Street in Stratford catered food for the restaurant.
[18] The article in the *Queenslander* (29 November 1928) provides the details of the layout of Hathaway Farm.

a sports stadium could facilitate 'track racing, flower shows, or an Old World Faire'.[19] Baker encouraged large groups by pointing out that 'the Spacious Grounds, Sheltered Orchards, and Sports' Fields ... are ideal for large and select Parties, also for Camping'. The house itself featured a brewhouse, a dining hall, and wool room. Baker added various amenities, such as a dancing hall, tennis, miniature golf, bathing in the river, plays, Morris dancers, and a rifle range which is 'much esteemed by scoutmasters and others'.[20] Baker also included a museum with antiques, and a store called the Old Curiosity Shop. The advertisement for the Farm promoted tea, dancing and proximity to Anne Hathaway's Cottage, as well as 'Health from Sunshine', noting that 'in the Grounds are nooks and corners, where Sun Baths may be enjoyed, with a Picnic Basket, a Book, or a Congenial Companion' (Illustration 46). The site featured a 'more active amusement for visitors', including grounds of 30 acres with modern amenities of a golf course, café, and motor and aviation park. In the early 1930s, Baker fervently collected items for his museum, as evidenced by surviving letters in the Shakespeare Birthplace Trust, and commissioned a sun-dial with the 'Seven Ages of Man' passage from *As You Like It*.

Baker promoted Hathaway Farm's 'old world atmosphere' through period displays, notably a scold's bridle, ducking stool, whipping post, pillory, and stocks inscribed with quotations from Shakespeare's plays, which 'remind one of the "good old days"'.[21] One visitor, upon observing the scold's bridle, noted that 'a notice on this one-time implement of torture assured us that ladies of Hathaway lanes no longer require such drastic measures to enforce moderate speech'.[22]

The idea of commemorating 'the good old days' recurs throughout descriptions of Hathaway Farm, both in its advertising, and in accounts of visitors to the site. This sentiment offers a clue as to Baker's agenda, as well as to what visitors sought in their journeys to this Shottery locale. Nicola J. Watson has pointed out that, as the tourist trade developed, 'Stratford increasingly strove to become more like the Stratford of the imagination, stripping off its modern façades to become more "Tudor"'.[23] When the 100 members of the Birmingham Rotary Club visited Hathaway Farm in 1929, they expressed just such a reaction, and were 'greatly impressed by the old-world atmosphere and the holiday facilities'. Members remarked that they were reminded 'of the days of Good Queen Bess'.[24]

Baker also intended Hathaway Farm to be an agricultural collection; an early announcement in the *Connoisseur* magazine of 1927 noted:

> The house is to be furnished in such a manner as to give some impression of the domestic life of that period ... on the walls, rafters, and floors of the farm-buildings will be displayed cider and cheese presses, ploughs, flails, horse-brasses, and various other agricultural and rural relics, augmented by pictures, prints, and many items directly or indirectly related to husbandry.

The overall aim was to provide a 'stimulating record of the habits and methods of our farming ancestry'.[25] Baker included a cock-fighting pit, which one visitor described as 'reminiscent of the pastimes of a bygone generation'.[26] The Tudor cock-fighting pit was a functional museum to the sport, with old prints dating from the 1770s illustrating the sport adorning nearby walls. Visitors could thus combine escape to the country, dining, imaginary connections to Shakespeare's romantic life, and a close look at pastimes like cock-fighting. A poem included in a guide to Hathaway Farm praised its atmosphere, whereby visitors could experience 'natural charms' which 'whisper love's romance, or deeds more bold / Of tilt and tourney in the days of old'.[27]

[19] Chamberlain, 'A camping holiday'.
[20] Chamberlain, 'A camping holiday'. [21] 'Hathaway Farm'.
[22] Bloom, 'Shakespeare land'.
[23] Nicola J. Watson, 'Shakespeare on the tourist trail', in *The Cambridge Companion to Shakespeare and Popular Culture*, ed. Robert Shaughnessy (Cambridge, 2007), p. 213.
[24] Bloom, 'Shakespeare land'.
[25] *The Connoisseur* 79 (November 1927), p. 190.
[26] 'Hathaway Farm'.
[27] Undated brochure for Hathaway Farm, Shakespeare Birthplace Trust.

Baker's place also functioned as a museum, and he displayed artwork, antiques and other Shakespeariana. Surviving photos of the interior show works of art on the walls of the tea room, and, according to one account, these pictures 'are reminiscent of past generations in every walk of life'.[28] After Baker's death, the auction catalogue for Hathaway Farm listed over 500 pictures, including 79 plaster masks and skulls of 'Notorious Murderers', 12 Shakespeare scenes and another 12 prints of Shakespeare characters. Even the artwork contributed to the overall goal of commemorating Shakespeare and an unspoiled bygone era.

In its heyday, Hathaway Farm had a substantial place in the tourist landscape of Warwickshire. A map of Hathaway Farm places it at the heart of 'Shakespeare Country', noting that 'all roads lead to Hathaway Farm' (Illustration 48). The Birthplace on Henley Street and Holy Trinity Church are peripheral figures on the illustration, with Shakespeare symbolically enclosed in a heart in the centre. The second illustration on the map also commemorates the Memorial Theatre, built in 1879 and destroyed by fire in 1926. This symbolic map positions Hathaway Farm in the centre, amid the other, more established Shakespeare locales, luring visitors outside the circuit of the Birthplace on Henley Street and Holy Trinity Church, both only marginally included in 'The Heart of Shakespeareland'.

As part of Baker's commemoration of 'the good old days', he not only imbued his locale with faux Tudor aspects, he also enlisted the most famous Shakespeare promoter of Stratford, actor-manager David Garrick. A postcard sold at the Farm superimposes a picture of the eighteenth-century actor leaning on a bust of Shakespeare (Illustration 49) in front of the Burman home.

The inclusion of Garrick at Hathaway Farm was an attempt to create long-term historical Shakespearian associations with this newly created space. By placing Garrick on-site, Baker aimed to fashion a history of Shakespeare memorialization as part of his creation of this new commemorative space, linking it to more famous celebrations of Shakespeare in Stratford, notably the 1769 Jubilee.

Clara Calvo has discussed the ways Shakespeare was commemorated at the 1916 Tercentenary and during World War I, when 'commemoration of Shakespeare's life and works was often linked to the war effort'.[29] At Hathaway Farm, the object of commemorating Shakespeare was not to link Shakespeare with the war, but instead to escape the war effort, to be part of a larger history of memorializing Shakespeare dating back to the time of Garrick, and to retreat into a faux Tudor world. A poem called 'For tired souls' included in an undated tourist pamphlet suggests that Hathaway Farm (and its various commemorations) could serve as a remedy for the instability and turmoil of modern life:

> When life looks extra rotten,
> And all the World goes ill,
> When 'Snags,' and sorrows seem to throng,
> Too thick to be endured,
> It means that you have worked too long
> On earthy things, your grip is wrong
> Go out—and get it cured.

According to this account, Hathaway Farm provided a place 'where jaded nerves may get a rest'.[30]

Although most accounts of Stratford omit mention of Hathaway Farm, in the early 1930s it held a central position in the commemorative landscape of Stratford. In 1935, it was the site of Jubilee Celebrations of King George, adding a further layer of memorialization to its roster – to Shakespeare, to his wife, to a bygone Warwickshire life, but also to the English monarchy itself. A surviving photo from the celebration shows the mayor surrounded by children in front of the house (Illustration 50).

Hathaway Farm offers a fascinating example of how Shakespeare was commemorated between the wars, and how various components of his life and his afterlife were marketed to visitors in the interwar

---

[28] Undated brochure for Hathaway Farm, Shakespeare Birthplace Trust.

[29] Clara Calvo, 'Shakespeare as war memorial: remembrance and commemoration in the Great War', *Shakespeare Survey 63* (Cambridge, 2010), p. 199.

[30] Undated brochure for Hathaway Farm, Shakespeare Birthplace Trust.

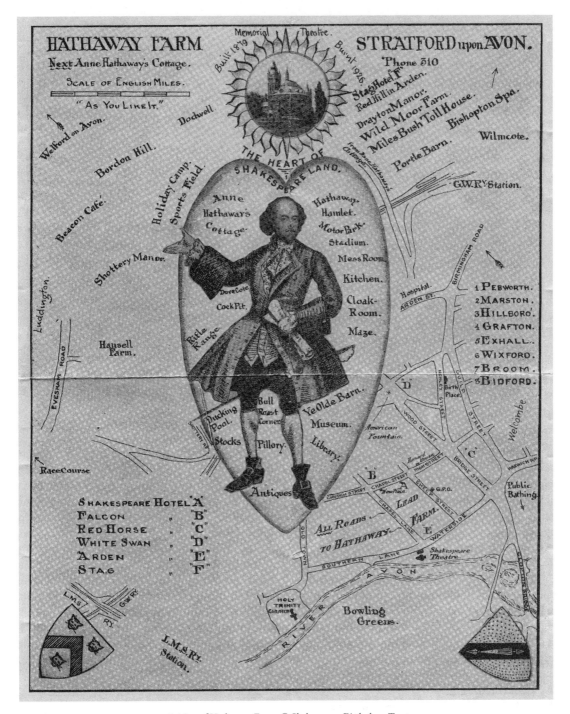

48. Map of Hathaway Farm. © Shakespeare Birthplace Trust.

Note :—David Garrick, the Actor, (b. 1716 d.1779) affectionately reclining on the bust of the Bard.

Hathaway Farm (formerly Burman's Farm) Shottery, Stratford-upon-Avon. ('Phone 310) **next** Anne Hathaway's Cottage

49. David Garrick at Hathaway Farm. © Shakespeare Birthplace Trust.

years. Philip Baker optimistically believed that school groups, campers, antiquers, diners, and overnight guests would partake of offerings at Hathaway Farm, but these potential visitors probably became preoccupied with the growing war efforts.

It is unclear exactly what happened to Hathaway Farm. Philip Baker died in April of 1938, but the Farm seems to have ebbed before that. It is possible that the potential for Hathaway Farm to commemorate Shakespeare and draw a crowd to support the enterprise was cut short by world affairs and by Baker's untimely death. The Depression of the 1930s brought decreased attendance to all of the Birthplace properties in and around Stratford, and the events leading up to World War II further diminished tourist travel in the area. In 1931, 'the Birthplace Trust's receipts were down by

30 percent', and by 1932, 'hunger marchers became a familiar sight' in Stratford.[31] Other activities related to World War II further encroached on leisure time. Plans for constructing air-raid shelters were made available at the Town Hall, and ten public air-raid shelters were put up around the town by 1937. Residents were measured for gas masks, and in early 1939 plans were made to host evacuee children around Stratford. By fall of 1938, Hathaway Farm's contents had been sold.[32] Nicholas Fogg notes that, by 1939 in Stratford, 'war fears increased dramatically' and 'the world crisis was affecting the Shakespeare industry'. Later

---

[31] Nicholas Fogg, *Stratford-upon-Avon: The Biography* (Stroud, Glos., 2014), p. 308.

[32] Fogg, *Stratford-upon-Avon*, p. 309.

50. The Mayor with children at Hathaway Farm, 1935. © Shakespeare Birthplace Trust.

that year, railway excursions from Stratford were cancelled due to the arrival of evacuee children.[33] Stratford hotels were requisitioned for government personnel, and were 'stripped of their furniture in favour of more functional office equipment; walls were reinforced, communication systems were installed, and coded notices signaling (to these that could interpret them) the accommodation's new significance were posted'.[34] Simon Barker points out that the new influx of military and government personnel attended productions at the Memorial Theatre, but venturing out to the Shottery countryside seemed to be beyond the purview of wartime entertainments in Stratford. Levi Fox observes that 'when war broke out in 1939, visitors [to Anne Hathaway's Cottage] decreased steeply and it was only in 1944, when

service personnel were admitted free', that attendance increased.[35] By then, Hathaway Farm was gone.

Despite the fact that Hathaway Farm had only a brief life-span, visitors to the Shakespeare sites around Stratford in the 1930s would be surprised to learn that Hathaway Farm is rarely mentioned, if at all, in most later accounts of the area. A brief history of the Burman estate written in 1946 by John Burman makes no mention of Baker's enterprise for Hathaway Farm

---

[33] Fogg, *Stratford: A Town at War*, pp. 64–5.

[34] Simon Barker, 'Shakespeare, Stratford, and the Second World War', in *Shakespeare and the Second World War*, ed. Irena R. Makaryk and Marissa McHugh (Toronto, 2012), p. 205.

[35] Fox, *The Shakespeare Birthplace Trust*, p. 59.

merely a decade before.[36] Baker's project seems to have disappeared from the Burman family account, as well as from other histories of the Stratford tourist scene. Yet Hathaway Farm was a central commemorative site to Shakespeare's wife, to the Warwickshire countryside and to an imagined Tudor way of life untouched by recent world events.

Today, the site of Hathaway Farm has come full circle, with the family name of 'Burmans' displayed at the entrance. It is now a privately owned home, with no evidence of its former life as a central stop on the tourist circuit throughout the 1930s. In 1946, Hathaway Farm was renamed Shottery Grange. As of 1951, it was listed as a Grade II historical building, with the name Burman's Farmhouse, and has been the residence of textile exporter Arthur Leslie Miller, and Conservative MP (1970–4) and Birmingham businessman Derek Michael Coombs. In the 1990s, it was secretly used as the Midlands location for BBC's long-running TV programme *Gardeners' World*, presented by Monty Don.[37]

The recent controversy over a housing complex to be built near Anne Hathaway's Cottage, and the sale of nearby land by the Shakespeare Birthplace Trust, begs the question of how the physical spaces of Shakespeare Country would be different if Hathaway Farm had survived. This independently run memorial to Shakespeare's wife and to a bygone way of life in Warwickshire would have added an immersive Tudor experience to Stratford. Visitors to the Shakespeare Birthplace Trust properties have been enticed by similar hands-on features, including the Dig for Shakespeare at the site of New Place, farming activities at Mary Arden's Farm and the like at Anne Hathaway's Cottage. One could easily imagine the busloads of tourists at the Shakespeare Birthplace Trust properties adding Hathaway Farm to their itineraries.

A small marginal comment on the stationery designed for Hathaway Farm hints at Baker's long-term plans for the project, advertising 'Hathaway Lands: Choice Building Sites, price £36, instalments, National Electric Power'. A brochure for Hathaway Farm gives further details of the plan for houses at Hathaway Lands, which were designed for 'those wishing to reside within easy reach of the "Shrine of the Bard"'.[38] Had Baker's plan succeeded, Anne Hathaway's Cottage would have had adjoining homes in the 1930s and 1940s, presumably occupied by residents who sought the commemorative pleasures of Shakespeare as a daily feature of their own lives.

---

[36] John Burman, 'The Hathaways of Shottery', *Stratford-upon-Avon Scene* (1946), p. 69.

[37] I am grateful to Roger Pringle for this information and for feedback on the larger argument.

[38] Undated brochure for Hathaway Farm, Shakespeare Birthplace Trust.

SHAKESPEARE PERFORMANCES
IN ENGLAND, 2017

STEPHEN PURCELL

BEHAVING VERY BADLY

It's the 17th of March 2017, and I'm sitting in the middle of row M in the Barbican Theatre listening to a recording of Bob Dylan's 'The times they are a-changin''. I'm about to watch Ivo van Hove's Roman Tragedies, *a six-hour adaptation of* Coriolanus, Julius Caesar, *and* Antony and Cleopatra, *for the second time (I first encountered this Toneelgroep Amsterdam production back in 2008). Its set looks like a huge conference centre, composed of clusters of sofas around numerous TV screens. Around the edges of the stage are a make-up and hair station, a couple of bars, and a sandwich stall. At the rear of the set, a row of clocks display the time in various global cities, among them New York, Rome, Tokyo, and Sydney. Above the stage, a scrolling ticker relays information about the show alongside real-world news stories: Donald Trump says North Korea is 'behaving very badly'; Theresa May has been granted the Queen's permission to invoke Brexit (at this, the spectator next to me makes a sudden movement, looking around for somebody with whom to share her reaction). As the performance starts, a woman who will turn out to be Virgilia sits on a sofa at the front of the stage watching footage of Trump's inauguration.*

The Barbican hosted four internationally touring Shakespearian productions this year, all of them dealing in various ways with capricious, morally compromised leaders. Thomas Ostermeier's *Richard III*, on tour from the Berlin Schaubühne, was edited and directed in order to focus our attention on the title character, many of the supporting roles losing key speeches and even whole scenes. Lars Eidinger's Richard was heavily disabled, with a club foot, a hunchback and a jaw strap. In the centre of the stage, a microphone dangled from the fly loft by a long elastic cable; its own electrical cord was coiled untidily around the cable, a visual echo of Richard's crooked spine. Richard used this microphone for most of his soliloquies, fostering a feeling of intimacy that is otherwise difficult to achieve in the cavernous space of the Barbican. Inside the microphone was a bright LED light, which illuminated his face with a cold glow; towards the end of the play, it became clear that the microphone also contained a small video camera, allowing Richard's anguish to be projected in extreme close-up onto the wall behind him. At the start of the performance, a burst of music and a blaze of glitter heralded the arrival of a raucous bunch of finely dressed aristocrats celebrating the coronation of Edward IV. Eidinger's T-shirt-wearing Richard remained visibly detached from this group. He delivered sections of his opening soliloquy softly into the microphone, his speech interrupted at intervals by blasts of noisy dance music and intrusions from the increasingly debauched revellers.

Eidinger's Richard was a compelling performance, a riot of outrageous, provocative showmanship. He was unpredictable and exciting, occasionally breaking from the German dialogue to interact in English with spectators in the front row; in a moment of breathtaking theatrical danger, he used the microphone cable to swing himself over their heads. He was something of a rock star, returning to the stage in a series of showy outfits, even launching into an expletive-laden rap (Tyler the Creator's 'Yonkers') in which he declared himself 'a fucking walking paradox'. But this was also a Richard who was self-conscious about his theatricality. He stripped naked in order to woo Lady Anne (Jenny König), a gesture of self-exposure that paradoxically exposed the non-disabled body of Eidinger: his hump was shown to be made of black fabric and held on with a strap, while the removal of his large shoe revealed a non-disabled foot. When Anne spat on him, he moved away from her to weep, gaining a sympathetic 'aah' from some sections of the audience despite the fact that this was clearly a ruse. Left alone at the end of the scene, he looked up at us and grinned, gloating at his own theatrical abilities: still naked over his closing soliloquy, his nudity was no longer a sign of vulnerability, but of exhibitionism.

As the play went on, his pain became more apparent. Having achieved the crown, Richard switched to a costume that emphasized his deep-seated desire to conform to a normative body image, constricting his body with a corset and a neck brace (Illustration 51). His power was based on humiliating others as he had himself felt humiliated: in 4.2, he co-opted the audience into

taunting Moritz Gottwald's Buckingham, inviting us to chant 'You look like shit!' as he smeared food into his erstwhile accomplice's face. Buckingham directed his angry, tearful response partly at us (4.2. 122–5), before disappearing from the play entirely (his death and subsequent appearance in the ghost scene were cut). Towards the end of the play, Richard's impulsiveness became a weakness rather than a strength: bothered by a high-pitched chirruping sound that would not stop, he asked the audience, in English, if we could hear it too. He began to talk increasingly to the camera hidden inside the microphone, the projected close-up of his face echoing the claustrophobic discomfort of his costume. His face, smeared with some kind of creamy white food, was starting to flake and peel as if he were decaying. The final battle, for which Richmond remained merely an offstage presence, gave us the picture of an increasingly frantic, conscience-stricken Richard slowly breaking down, alone onstage, physically fighting himself and the set. He repeated the line 'There is no creature loves me' (5.5.154) in English, almost as a challenge to

51. *Richard III*, Schaubühne Berlin, Barbican Theatre, directed by Thomas Ostermeier. Lars Eidinger as Richard. Photograph by Arno Declair.

the audience to rediscover the sympathy that they had earlier expressed. For this spectator, at least, it was too late: the production had pushed to its limits and finally severed the theatricality that had made Richard temporarily, diabolically, appealing.

Declan Donnellan's *The Winter's Tale* for Cheek by Jowl made several stops in the UK as part of its world tour. In what has become Cheek by Jowl's signature style, the production opted for a pared-down, starkly symbolic staging, combining full-bodied emotional realism with stylized ensemble choreography. Donnellan and his cast made brilliant use of silence and movement throughout the production, and this was especially evident in its opening scene. 1.1 was replaced with a wordless sequence between Leontes (Orlando James) and Polixenes (Edward Sayer), who sat in awkward silence at either end of a bench as if they had just been arguing; Leontes then broke the ice by instigating a childish game – albeit one tinged with real, half-buried emotion – in which he chased Polixenes around the stage before wrestling him to the ground. When Polixenes recalled their childhood friendship during the dialogue that followed, a snap change in the lighting and the sudden incursion of musical underscoring suggested that Leontes was somehow obsessed with this early moment in his adolescence: he joined in with Polixenes to declare his childhood self 'not guilty' of any subsequent 'ill doing' (1.2. 72–6), and fidgeted uncomfortably as Hermione (Natalie Radmall-Quirke) started to allude to his sexual awakening (1.2.83–8). Leontes' 'Too hot, too hot' (1.2.110) came out of the blue; there was nothing remotely 'hot' about Hermione and Polixenes' interactions, and the two were sitting several feet apart from one another. Leontes moulded their bodies during his soliloquy, lifting their arms so that they were 'paddling palms and pinching fingers' (1.2.117). He manoeuvred them into a comically implausible sexual embrace, simultaneously graphic and mechanical, and they remained on stage like this during his subsequent exchange with Camillo, frozen in a grotesque parody of an extramarital affair. As Leontes resolved to 'seem friendly' to them (1.2.351), he broke apart the tableau into which he had arranged their bodies,

inserting himself between them so that Polixenes' hand was on his own knee, and his own hands were on both Hermione's and Polixenes'. The scene thus suggested, largely through movement, that Leontes' jealousy stemmed in part from a repressed desire for sexual closeness with his friend.

The production took literally Hermione's complaint that Mamillius 'so troubles me, / 'Tis past enduring' (2.1.1–2). Despite appearing to be a child of around 11 or 12 (actor Tom Cawte himself, of course, was significantly older), Mamillius erupted into the kind of screaming tantrum more commonly seen in toddlers when he was removed from Hermione by her ladies-in-waiting. This was a child with a serious behavioural disorder, and Hermione alone seemed capable of calming him, fondling his hair and face in the same way she did her husband's. He seemed distressed by the thought of his mother's pregnancy – jealous, perhaps, of the imminent arrival of a competitor for her affection. When Leontes entered the scene in a similar jealous rage and kicked his wife in the belly, bringing on an early labour, it became clear that the king suffered from a similar disorder to his son. Hermione's tolerance of this horrific mistreatment thus read as her understanding that it was not her husband but his illness that was causing it. In a lengthy pause after her innocence was proclaimed, Leontes began to weep hysterically; she crossed over to him, making efforts to comfort him as he flinched and struggled against her before finally accepting her embrace. Momentarily reconciled, the couple hugged and wept, until the Officer read out the last part of the oracle: 'and the King shall live without an heir if that which is lost be not found' (3.2.134–5). It was his puzzlement at this pronouncement that led Leontes to conclude that there was 'no truth at all i'th' oracle' (3.2.139) – indeed, the production added a new line in which he objected, 'my son lives still, / A promising and worthy prince'. The news of Mamillius' death was shouted from the back of the auditorium – the first such use of the space in the performance, and thrillingly effective – and the panels of the set collapsed simultaneously to reveal the boy's corpse, laid out on a bed.

The moments bookending the interval emphasized the transition from death to life. The first half finished with the Old Shepherd's discovery of the abandoned Perdita, his lines heavily rewritten to recall the parable of the lost sheep. The act stopped mid-scene, the line 'Thou metst with things dying, I with things new-born' (3.3.110–11) functioning both as the final line of the first half and as the opening line of the second. But, as it turned out, the production made interesting attempts to draw parallels between the two halves. Bohemia was darker than usual, blighted by flashes of irrational rage: Polixenes sexually assaulted Perdita (Eleanor McLoughlin), and even the Young Shepherd (Sam McArdle) was unable to control his temper. The sheep-shearing festival took place in an indoor location as characters hurried in from the rain outside, and was overshadowed by grief: the Old Shepherd (Peter Moreton) fought back tears as he recalled the way his late wife used to play the hostess, and most of his guests gave vocal affirmation to his fond recollections. New lines were added to suggest that she had died only recently, and the Shepherd's evocation of her as a figure who 'welcomed all, served all' (4.4.57) contrasted powerfully with the Young Shepherd's topically hostile attitude towards 'strangers' ('We won't take it any longer! ... No one's stickin' up for the little person any more!'). Later, in a sharp-edged satire on border control, Autolycus' 'courtier cap-à-pie' persona (4.4.736) became an immigration official, demanding a bizarre sequence of immigration papers, bribes and arcane forms. When the Young Shepherd failed to provide the last of these, Autolycus (Ryan Donaldson) whipped out his baton and brutally beat him, silencing the audience's laughter. As the Old Shepherd left the stage supporting his bloodied and nearly unconscious son, insisting 'We are blest to have known this man ... he was provided to do us good' (adapted from 4.4.828–31), it was hard not to read the moment as a pointed commentary on the phobias about immigration that had led to the various recent political upheavals in Europe and the USA.

Yukio Ninagawa's *Macbeth* stopped off in London for a week in October. This revival of Ninagawa's influential 1980 production was mounted, in part, as a tribute to the director, who died in 2016. It was an especially fitting production in this respect, since much of its power came from its reflections on mortality. Kappa Senoh's set was designed to evoke a *butsudan*, a Japanese household shrine especially associated with family ancestors. At the start of the show, two elderly women (Yoko Haneda and Yoko Kato) prayed in front of it, before retreating to positions at either side of the stage to watch the performance as if they were encountering an ancient tale from their own ancestral histories. The central motif, with which the production has become almost synonymous, was its use of cherry blossom, a potent symbol in Japan for the transience of life. Cherry blossom petals fell like gently falling snow during the witches' scenes, and again during some of Macbeth's soliloquies as he contemplated his destiny; his throne room had a painted frieze of a cherry-blossom tree as its backdrop. A full-size cherry-blossom tree made its first appearance in the scene of Banquo's murder, and reappeared during the climactic battle; Malcolm's army carried cherry-blossom boughs, moving around like dancers. In 4.3, Malcolm (Hayata Tateyama) carried a small stem of cherry blossom as he listed his vices to Macduff (Keita Oishi), dropping it when he dropped his act. This last example suggested that the production's use of the symbol was not merely a reminder of life's ephemerality; it appeared during all the production's scenes of temptation, recalling Lady Macbeth's injunction to her husband to 'look like the innocent flower' (1.5.64) in order to mask their evil intentions. The witches were not obviously wicked as they are in many productions: here, they were ethereally beautiful in silky kimonos, played by male actors as *onnagata* in the Kabuki style. It was easy to see how Macbeth might be seduced by their prophecies.

This sense of moral neutrality was emphasized by the production's use of music. Ninagawa drew heavily on Western classical music for the production's score, making repeated and prominent use of

Barber's 'Adagio for Strings' and Fauré's 'Requiem'. The production did not attempt to hide from the temporal and cultural anachronism of its music: indeed, Lady Macbeth (Yuko Tanaka) played a cello (unknown in Japan in the Azuchi-Momoyama period, the time of the production's setting) just before the messenger brought news of Macbeth's imminent arrival. To me, the mismatch between the serene, relatively modern music and the violent historical story seemed to suggest a kind of tragic inevitability to proceedings. The murder of Macduff's family took place to the same slow, melancholy piece of music ('Adagio for Strings') as Macbeth's own journey towards his death. This underscoring was alienating but not, perhaps, in the Brechtian sense, since the disjunction allowed Masachika Ichimura's Macbeth to seem almost as innocent as his victims, as if these characters, all of whom died long ago, were fulfilling their allotted roles in a preordained pattern. There was a haunting, balletic quality to Macbeth's final battle: surrounded by enemy soldiers, he picked them off in slow motion, one by one, even as reinforcements entered. Accompanied once again by the strains of Barber's 'Adagio', Macbeth seemed almost heroic, certainly superhuman. As he was dealt the *coup de grâce* by Macduff, the music suddenly cut out, the production's weirdly amoral spell broken.

Both of the leads were played by older actors, a fact that added something to the production's meditations on ephemerality. The gong that heralded Duncan's impending death at the end of 2.1 returned at the end of the banquet scene, interrupting the orchestral music: it seemed to terrify Macbeth and his wife, who cowered upon hearing it, as if it exposed the self-delusion implicit in Macbeth's observation 'We are yet but young in deed' (3.4.143) and confronted them with their own mortalities. Macbeth surrounded himself with a circle of flickering candles just before he heard of his wife's death, a visual emblem of the dying light of their lives; the old women watching at the sides started to cry audibly as he reacted to the news of his wife's death. The final sounds of the play itself were the funereal gongs, and, during the

curtain call, a large photograph of the late director standing before the play's cherry-blossom tree was displayed in pride of place. It became, inevitably, a resonant part of the production itself.

ROMAN TRAGEDIES

About 18 minutes into Roman Tragedies, *we get the first three-minute break. We are invited by an onstage announcer to move to a different part of the space, including anywhere on the stage itself. Like many of my fellow spectators, I take up the invitation to move to the stage, and I loiter at the back near the drinks stall to watch the next section of* Coriolanus. *Martius (Gijs Scholten van Aschat) is a grizzled, scruffy politician of the old school; the Tribunes (Eelco Smits and Alwin Pulinckx) are younger and better groomed. This conflict is not about aristocratic privilege versus the power of the people – it's about the professionalization of modern politics, in which a dinosaur like Martius threatens the stability of his own political class with his politically incorrect speech and indifference to causing offence. In the onstage surtitles, Martius accuses Sicinius of being a 'populist'; this is a painfully topical word at the moment, in Britain and abroad. Just this week, Toneelgroep Amsterdam's home country narrowly avoided electing Geert Wilders' hard-right Party for Freedom into government.*

Roman Tragedies was not the only production this year to make parallels between Shakespeare's Roman plays and modern politics. The link became inescapable in June, when Oskar Eustis's New York production of *Julius Caesar* provoked fierce right-wing protests against its presentation of the title character as a Trump-like demagogue.[1] In the UK, numerous productions drew similar analogies. Robert Hastie's modern-dress *Julius Caesar*, his inaugural production as artistic director of Sheffield Theatres, was a chillingly timely portrait of democracy descending into fascism. The production made use of the Crucible's thrust stage to evoke various kinds of public spaces, an

---

[1] See Michael Paulson and Sopan Deb, 'How outrage built over a Shakespearean depiction of Trump', *New York Times*, 12 June 2017.

ensemble of twenty-three community actors aug-menting the professional cast of sixteen to create a lively and diverse onstage 'public'. In 1.2, they formed the kind of crowd often seen at modern political rallies, penned in behind temporary bar-riers and carrying placards that deliberately recalled the design and typeface of the 2016 Trump/Pence campaign and the iconic 'Hope' portrait of Obama from 2008. In the context of this play, these pla-cards functioned as reminders of the dangers of personality politics; later, two young people in informal clothes passed two older politicians in suits, each pair acknowledging the other with a 'Hail Caesar' and a casual salute. The layout of the senate building in 3.1 suggested an uneasy ten-sion between democracy and authoritarianism – the swivel chairs, desk lights, and microphones around the stage's perimeter evoking a modern parliament building, while Caesar sat in the middle of the stage on a kind of throne, a dictator at the centre of a personality cult. The production's rais-ing of the house lights during this scene implied that the audience, too, were senators in the scene, simultaneously empowered to intervene and pre-vented, of course, from doing so. The incursion of violence into this ordered space was strongly remi-niscent of the footage of the recent brawl in the Turkish Parliament, a photograph of which was reproduced in the programme.

Women were very much part of the public sphere in this production. With a 50:50 gender split in the cast, several major roles were re-gendered, among them Cassius, Casca and Octavius (a pattern similar to *Roman Tragedies*). These casting decisions also spoke directly to mod-ern politics. When Zoë Waites' Cassius told Samuel West's Brutus that she could not tell 'what you and other *men* / Think of this life' (1.2. 95–6), she was speaking as a woman who did not share Brutus' male privilege. Jonathan Hyde's Caesar was a very modern kind of sexist, with a clear preference for masculine company and a distrust of powerful, intelligent women. As he complained that Cassius 'thinks too much' and observed 'such women are dangerous' (1.2.196), the implication was that it was precisely her status

as a woman in a male-dominated world that made her subversive:

> She is a great observer, and she looks
> Quite through the deeds of men.
>
> (1.2.203–4)

'Let me have women about me that are fat' (1.2.193) was exactly the kind of casual sexism one might expect to hear on a leaked Trump recording; it was perhaps significant that four of the five conspirators who came to visit Brutus were women.

The fact that the conspirators were largely coded as frustrated progressives, and their opponents as fascists, exacerbated the bleak mood of the play's final acts. The second half opened with an emblem of the wreck of democracy, the Parliament set strewn with littered papers and a barricade made of office furniture, the senate building itself ruined and converted into a site of war. Three hooded bodies hung from the ceiling, unmistakably those of Ligarius, Metellus and Casca. The role of Lucilius was merged with that of Cinna the con-spirator (Mark Holgate), so that it was he who claimed to be Brutus in 5.4; rather than sparing his life as he does in the text, Antony (Elliot Cowan) summarily executed him by shooting him in the head. The play's final scene took place not on the plains of Philippi but in the ruined shell of the senate building: Brutus cleared some papers off a desk and spoke ironically into the micro-phone: 'The senate recognises Marcus Junius Brutus.' Then he found the giant laurel wreath that had previously adorned the balcony, and threw it to the stage, and we heard the echo of a flock of roosting birds being scared off as it clattered to the ground. The symbolism was clear: the descent into fascism and violence had left civi-lization in tatters. Left alone with Brutus' body in the closing moments, Antony turned him over, looked at him dispassionately, and then straigh-tened up with the air of a man who had just successfully finished a difficult job.

In Stratford, the Royal Shakespeare Company's Rome season suggested similar parallels. Four major productions in the Royal Shakespeare

Theatre shared the same designer, Robert Innes Hopkins, and the first two, which opened together, had an almost identical set: Season Director Angus Jackson's *Julius Caesar* and Iqbal Khan's *Antony and Cleopatra* were both played in front of a stepped platform with towering columns, behind which a vast cyclorama swirled with increasingly portentous-looking clouds. In both plays, the Roman set fell into ruins over the course of the performance, being pulled apart into rocky crags for the war scenes of *Julius Caesar*, and its columns becoming derelict quayside posts for the naval battles of *Antony and Cleopatra*. Both designs prominently featured a copy of Rome's *Lion Attacking a Horse* sculpture, an emblem of Roman might that reappeared in the season's subsequent productions of *Titus Andronicus* and *Coriolanus*.

There were no explicit Trump parallels in Jackson's production of the play, which was set in the historical Julius Caesar's Rome, but it did not need to update the setting to resonate with current events. Andrew Woodall's Caesar was strongly reminiscent of the US President, repeatedly tilting his chin upward and frowning in a self-conscious (and not entirely convincing) performance of thoughtfulness. This Caesar treated his followers as little more than pets, publicly ruffling Antony's and Brutus' hair in displays of affection, having no compunctions about grabbing Decius Brutus by the throat when he displeased him, and tapping him on the nose to indicate his approval. But Cassius' description of Caesar as weak and infirm was also true: he repeatedly doubled over, as if about to faint. Calpurnia's 'say he is sick' was not, as Caesar insisted, 'a lie' (2.2.65) – he was evidently ill, and pretending not to be. He was deeply distrustful of Cassius, greeting him in 2.2 with a curt 'Mm-hm' as he verbalized his greetings for everyone else onstage. The impression was, perhaps, that, since Cassius had witnessed his infirmity at first hand, Caesar could no longer bear his company, as it risked exposing the weakness behind his façade of strength.

The production was the twin tragedy of Brutus and Cassius. In contrast to the Sheffield production's tortured intellectual, Alex Waldmann's Brutus was young, arrogant and aggressive, only occasionally troubled by his conscience. Following Caesar's assassination, he started to present himself almost as a new Caesar, ordering his fellow conspirators around, as if that were the only model of leadership he could think to emulate. He was smug and self-satisfied as he anticipated his funeral oration and, when the crowd started to chant his name during the speech, he gestured for them to continue. When he insisted upon their staying to listen to Antony, it was the action of a man so drunk on power that he was blind to the obvious danger that Antony posed. Later, as he pretended not to know of Portia's death so that he could feign stoicism upon being told the news, it seemed like the empty posturing of a naive leader who had a fatal misconception of what leadership actually entails. Martin Hutson's Cassius, meanwhile, was a fervent revolutionary. It was clear from his first soliloquy that he was deeply conflicted about the morality of his plot: when he asked the audience, 'For who so firm that cannot be seduced?' (1.2.312), he looked suddenly ashamed of himself. In the next scene, Casca found him running through the streets of Rome, bare-chested and howling against the storm, submitting himself 'unto the perilous night' (1.3.47) as a kind of pre-emptive penance (Illustration 52). There was no doubt in Hutson's performance that, on some level, this Cassius actively wanted the 'thunder-stone' to strike him (1.3.49); I had never noticed before how frequently Cassius offers to commit suicide, and Hutson's Cassius really seemed to mean it.

These interpretations made sense of both Brutus' and Cassius' suicides as the culminations of their respective tragic arcs. Cassius, so eager to punish himself for his role in Caesar's murder, found an excuse to commit the self-slaughter with which he had been toying in virtually every one of his appearances throughout the play. Brutus, meanwhile, came to a realization that he had become the very thing against which he had rebelled. When he saw Caesar's ghost on the battlefield, the ghost picked up the victory wreath from Cassius' corpse and waved it tauntingly, shaking his head – not just a sign that Brutus would be

52. *Julius Caesar*, 1.3, RSC, Royal Shakespeare Theatre, directed by Angus Jackson. Martin Hutson as Cassius. Photograph by Helen Maybanks © RSC.

denied victory, I think, but a pointed comment on Brutus' own imperial ambitions. In this interpretation, Antony's concluding speech therefore seemed a completely inaccurate assessment of Brutus' character – of all the conspirators, Brutus had been the *least* noble and *most* envious of Caesar. But in this production, we had also learned not to trust a word Antony said; James Corrigan's canny political operator had calmly ripped what he had claimed was Caesar's will in half after the mutinous crowd left the stage in 3.2, and his attempt to assert moral authority at the end had been fatally undermined by his soldiers' conduct during the battle. In the moment for which the production will probably be best remembered, one of Antony's soldiers encountered Brutus' boy servant on the battlefield, and – to gasps and howls of

outrage from the audience – suddenly and sickeningly snapped the child's neck.[2]

Iqbal Khan's *Antony and Cleopatra* was built on a familiar binary: while the colonnaded Rome represented austerity and discipline, Egypt was a space of luxury (Illustration 53). Both Antony (Antony Byrne) and Enobarbus (Andrew Woodall) were under its spell: while Antony seemed almost resentful of the hold it had over him, Enobarbus was evidently enjoying a fling with Iras (Kristin Atherton), and he wore an Egyptian scarf around his neck from start to finish. A huge red and gold curtain descended to partially obscure the Roman set for many of the Egyptian scenes, and the latter made particular use of a central platform which could be raised and lowered to present human tableaux (and to remove them). The title characters were thus revealed on their first appearance frolicking under bedsheets; at the ends of their scenes, Cleopatra (Josette Simon) and her handmaidens would regularly pose into frozen images as they descended into the bowels of the stage. The impression this gave of Cleopatra and her attendants as human sculptures, objects to be looked at, was augmented by the fact that their ascents onto the stage were often accompanied by the simultaneous descent of statues of Egyptian gods. Egypt, then, was cast as a space of mysterious otherness, a counterpoint to the white, male space of Rome: nearly all the production's non-white actors, and most of its women, were cast in Egyptian roles. While it was good to see a production responding to Cleopatra's description of herself as 'black' (1.5.28), then, the production did not entirely avoid an exoticized reading of the character.

Egypt was a space for play-acting, and Cleopatra its most consummate performer. In her first speech, she did a mocking impersonation of 'the scarce-bearded Caesar' as a shrill-voiced child (1.1.22–5); later, she pushed Charmian (Amber James) to the floor to play Antony's horse, taking the role of Antony upon herself as she mounted her

---

[2] Some reviews identified the soldier who killed the boy as Antony himself, but this was not clear to me as I watched it.

53. *Antony and Cleopatra*, 1.5, RSC, Royal Shakespeare Theatre, directed by Iqbal Khan. Kristin Atherton as Iras, Josette Simon as Cleopatra, Joseph Adelakun as Mardian, and Amber James as Charmian. Photograph by Helen Maybanks © RSC.

handmaiden. Simon's Cleopatra was capricious and self-consciously theatrical, dancing around the stage on tiptoes, extending her arms to their full length in grand gestures, and appearing in a variety of spectacular costumes (not least a golden, sphinx-like helmet in 3.7). This was a Cleopatra of 'infinite variety' (2.2.242), switching moods at the drop of a hat; even in her death scene, she sobbed at Caesar's feet, wailing audibly until he had left the stage and then looking up to reveal that her sobs had been nothing but a sham. If it was hard to empathize with this Cleopatra, it was because it was hard to know whether we were seeing the 'real' woman or yet another act. Significantly, the only part of the performance that felt fully sincere to me was a moment entirely without speech, as the grief-stricken queen held her lover's corpse and contorted her face into a long, silent scream.

Rome was constructed as a homosocial, masculine space in contrast to the feminized world of Egypt. The first scene in Rome was relocated to a steam bath, allowing Patrick Drury's Lepidus to be established as a drunk, lounging around with a jug of wine; it seemed strange, though, to introduce us to Octavius (Ben Allen), a character who condemns Antony's luxurious lifestyle from his first speech, in a space associated with Roman decadence, especially since the subsequent scenes emphasized Rome's coldness and formality. Perhaps this was an attempt to suggest that the men of Rome were projecting onto Egypt something they wished to deny about their own culture. Later, in the barge scene, Octavius got very drunk and sang his own solo verse of the song: the implication, perhaps, was that this frustrated young man was secretly envious of Antony's libertinism.

Hopkins's set was used again for Blanche McIntyre's *Titus Andronicus*, transformed this time into the glass-fronted colonnade of a modern civic building. This was, it seemed, a modern society that modelled itself on the Rome of the first two plays. The opening scene was reframed as a tense stand-off between the forces of the state and a group of protesters. Dharmesh Patel's Bassianus, wearing a plain hoodie, was the leader of the demonstration: he had popular support, and made it clear that he expected the mandate of 'pure election' (1.1.16), his followers chanting this last word after him. Martin Hutson's Saturninus, on the other hand, was the consummate post-ideological professional politician, wearing a sharp blue suit and appealing not to the onstage crowd but to the audience in the stalls, pointedly addressing the RSC's highest-paying customers as 'Noble patricians' (1.1.1). Later, he accepted the role of Emperor with honeyed tones and a saccharine smile, prompting a laugh of cynical recognition from the audience. As he thanked Titus 'for thy favours done / To us in our *election* this day' (1.1. 234–5), he over-emphasized the word 'election',

insistently reclaiming (and by implication redefining) the word that his rival and the protesters had used against him.

Generally speaking, the first half did not play for laughs. David Troughton's Titus was clearly traumatized by the war that had claimed the lives of so many of his sons. He attempted to hide a trembling hand as he solemnly saluted the people of Rome, and remained resolutely unemotional as he and Lucius stage-managed the brutal sacrifice of Alarbus. The most terrifying thing about this sequence was the impassivity of the surrounding politicians, soldiers and civil servants: a functionary whispered blandly into his head-mounted microphone in order to facilitate the smooth running of this act of state-sanctioned murder. Stefan Adegbola's Aaron was unusually serious, a clinical and efficient manipulator rather than a wickedly appealing prankster; he seemed to be driven by a sense of injustice at the racism to which he was relentlessly subjected. Where some productions find a seam of dark humour in the scene in which Aaron tricks Titus into chopping off his hand, this was noticeably muted here: indeed, the moment itself was not sudden and brutal, as it usually is, but tense and drawn out. Aaron called out a couple of nurses, who pushed a wheeled apparatus that had clearly been designed specifically for punitive amputations of this sort: once again, the production emphasized that it was set in a state that had an established infrastructure for institutionalized violence. Titus was invited to choose which hand to sacrifice, and a cleaver was passed from one nurse to the other in horrible silence before the amputation was performed. In this context, perhaps, it was no surprise that Aaron's diabolical aside after promising Titus that he could now 'Look by and by to have thy sons with thee' – 'Their heads, I mean' (3.1.200–1) – was met not with an audience laugh, as it has been at every other performance of the play I can remember, but with a shocked silence. Both this scene and Lavinia's rape in 2.3 were presented in such a graphic fashion that multiple audience members left the auditorium during the performance; in the interval, an usher told me that this happened at every show.

It was perhaps surprising, then, that the production opted for a definite change in mood in its second half, moving the play much more towards black comedy. Perhaps this is inevitable – while the atrocities of the first half can seem like the sorts of things that a modern state might credibly sanction, the wild excesses of the second half tip into absurdity. This part of the production contained an increased amount of audience interaction, Titus asking spectators in the front row whether they could lend him some money to pay the Clown, while, in 5.1, Lucius press-ganged another front-row audience member into holding Aaron's baby as he decided whether or not to execute it (cue uneasy audience laughter). Titus spent most of 5.2 hiding in a large, body-sized cardboard box, his feet poking comically out at the bottom. In the final scene, his pie was especially gruesome, a huge sloppy thing with blood spilling down its sides; as he revealed the still-recognizable but half-smashed heads of Tamora's sons within it, there was much delighted laughter from the audience. I could not help but feel there was a problem here: the production had worked so hard to construct the violence of the first half as plausible depths to which modern human beings could descend that to culminate with cartoonish excess of this sort seemed to let the audience off the hook, to wriggle out of the moral discomfort the production had earlier provoked. This was mitigated, however, by another aspect of the staging. Throughout the second half, the ghosts of murdered characters had haunted the stage: in 4.3, for example, the bloody ghosts of Quintus and Martius appeared behind the gates of Saturninus' residence, climbing them from inside. For the final scene, the ghosts of numerous characters, including the nurse and the Clown (now with a noose around his neck), appeared behind the glass of the colonnade. During the play's closing moments, as Lucius descended once again into vindictive rage against the dead Tamora, the ghost of Alarbus appeared downstage, pacing up to a terrified Lucius and grabbing him as the lights blacked out.

Angus Jackson's *Coriolanus* was the concluding Shakespearian production of the Rome season. Like *Titus*, it was set in a modern-day Rome in which a patrician world had shut itself off from an angry working class: its pre-show depicted a huge automated shutter coming down, separating stacks of grain-sacks from a rioting mob. When Menenius (Paul Jesson) came out to dispute with the protesters, he was wearing evening dress; Sope Dirisu's Martius emerged moments later in the same formal wear, his smart suit and cool amusement creating the impression of a rather less martial Martius than we might usually see at this point in the play. The lines of this scene were slightly redistributed so that Menenius' diatribe was directed not at the first citizen who had stoked the mob's anger, but at the more ambivalent and thoughtful second citizen (Justine Marriott). Menenius attacked her for impatience and for being a troublemaker, both rather unfair charges given her earlier appearance in the scene as a restraining force on the rioting plebeians; it was hard to avoid the conclusion that he was attacking her because he felt affronted at being challenged by an outspoken woman.

This theme emerged more strongly with the introduction of the Tribunes (Jackie Morrison and Martina Laird), both of whom were played as female characters. Menenius seemed to relish telling them how they 'are censured here in the city' (2.1.22), spitting insults at them; this was a character who hid his deep-seated hatred of powerful women with attempts at humour. The exchange felt ugly and uncomfortably current. This was a world in which leadership was virtually synonymous with machismo; the Tribunes could be seen stifling laughter and rolling their eyes as Cominius (Charles Aitken) recounted the tale of a battle in which the young Martius might have played 'the woman in the scene' but 'proved best man i'th' field' (2.2.96–7). It was noticeable that all the military officers and patricians were played by men, making the Tribunes the only public female figures in Rome's political world. Whilst they were evidently manipulating public opinion against Coriolanus, the suggestion seemed to be that they saw him – not unreasonably – as representing a political order that was stacked against women.

The women in Martius' domestic life were presented rather differently. The set for Martius' home had as its centrepiece a statue of Aphrodite inside a glass display case. Hannah Morrish's Virgilia made her first appearance on a sofa right in front of it, the image visually linking her with another venerated but trapped and objectified female figure. Martius' relationship with Volumnia (Haydn Gwynne) was interestingly nuanced: when he returned to Rome wearing the oaken garland, he took it off and presented it to his mother immediately, and she cradled it proudly for the rest of the scene. Everything he did, it seemed, he did for her approval. Much was made of his closeness to her – she took him into a long embrace upon his return to Rome, and seemed almost embarrassed to remind him afterwards that he had not yet acknowledged his wife (2.1.172). His capitulation to her plea at the play's climax thus had an air of inevitability: he held back from showing any emotion for as long as he could, but when she disclaimed him as a son ('This fellow had a Volscian to his mother', 5.3.179), he could not hold himself together for much longer. After a charged silence, he burst into child-like sobs, his macho persona falling into ruins as he held her hand to his face, begging to be parented once again.

Dirisu's Coriolanus also seemed to be in denial over his homoerotic desire for James Corrigan's Aufidius. His single combat with Aufidius in 1.8 was a highlight of the production, both for the fight choreography, which was fast and thrilling, and for the character insights it offered. As Martius challenged his rival, drawing attention to the blood that covered his body, Aufidius responded with a purr of pleasure; after a breathless, frenetic swordfight, Martius suddenly relinquished his weapons, throwing them to the ground and inviting Aufidius to do the same. Aufidius did not hesitate to do so, evidently hungry for this physical contact with his rival. Their fight was underscored by the slow, harmonious drone one might more usually expect to accompany a love scene. When Aufidius' officers came in to break up the fight, he howled with frustration at being interrupted. Following this encounter, Martius – now Coriolanus – seemed distracted and unsettled. Upon their reunion in 4.5, Aufidius' claim that 'more dances

my rapt heart / Than when I first my wedded mistress saw / Bestride my threshold' (4.5.117–19) seemed no exaggeration, and Coriolanus appeared to be somewhat taken aback by Aufidius' candour in admitting that he had dreamed nightly 'of encounters 'twixt thyself and me' (4.5.124). In the final scene, Aufidius strangled his rival with a chain in a fit of animal rage: a consummation of sorts, perhaps, but a strangely ambivalent culmination of the thread that had until this moment been so well foregrounded.

The Rome season extended beyond these four Shakespearian productions, encompassing Phil Porter's comedy *Vice Versa*, based on the plays of Plautus, and *Imperium*, Mike Poulton's six-play adaptation of Robert Harris's Cicero trilogy. It also provided the RSC with a welcome opportunity to revive Gregory Doran's 2004 production of *Venus and Adonis*, a collaboration with the Little Angel Theatre. About an hour long, this puppet adaptation saw Shakespeare's poem read in full by an onstage narrator (Suzanne Burden) and accompanied live by a guitarist (Nick Lee) as a team of six puppeteers (Louisa Ashton, Ailsa Dalling, Edie Edmundson, Rachel Leonard, Avye Leventis, and Toby Olié) brought it to life in and around a miniature proscenium-arch stage. The two main puppets, each of which took two or three puppeteers at a time to operate them, seemed to be made from different materials: Venus from something soft and pliable, maybe leather, costumed in a white gown that wafted as she moved; Adonis from wood. Her movement was liquid, sensuous, defying gravity as only a puppet can. She floated into the air as she explained that 'Love is a spirit all compact of fire, / Not gross to sink, but light, and will aspire' (149–50), hovering weightlessly with her gown hanging down around her; she fell to earth with a thud as she observed that Adonis felt love 'heavy' (156). Adonis was more stilted in his movements, occasionally melting into a more fluid sensuality as Venus kissed or caressed him. During their climactic embrace, her legs slowly floated up into the air behind her, and she pulled the earthbound Adonis up into the sky (Illustration 54). As in Forced Entertainment's *Table Top Shakespeare* last year, it

54. *Venus and Adonis*, RSC, Swan Theatre, directed by Gregory Doran. Venus, Adonis, and puppeteers. Photograph by Lucy Barriball © RSC.

was astonishing how much space the combination of narration and puppetry allowed for the creation of the subtlest performance details in the imagination. Adonis's face seemed bashful one moment, angry the next, though the facial features of the puppet had not altered in the least; at one point, Venus's face seemed to follow the momentum of her body and break out into a sob.

As the poem continued, the production's inventiveness came to the fore. There was a lovely anthropomorphic wooing scene between Adonis' horse and the mare, every flick of the tail crammed with subtext. Shadow puppetry was used to illustrate the hounds and to introduce the boar, his 'brawny sides with hairy bristles armed' horribly apparent (625). Upon the entry of Death into the narrative, the golden globe at the top of the miniature theatre swivelled to reveal a skull, and the curtained edges of the stage suddenly detached to

become skeletal arms. This gigantic figure of Death cradled Venus in his bony hands as she chided him; abandoned by his puppeteers, the lifeless Adonis was more completely dead than any actor can be.

CORRUPTERS OF GENDER

An hour and a half in, and I'm back in the stalls, a little farther towards the front. No sooner has Coriolanus died than Julius Caesar *starts, without a break. We start with Brutus (Eelco Smits), Cassius (Marieke Heebink), and Casca (Chris Nietvelt); Brutus and Cassius are brisk and professional, Casca amusingly awkward. They are backstage political players, anxious about the charisma and ambition of a political leader whom we have not yet had a chance to assess for ourselves (and whom, indeed, we barely see in his public capacity in this production). In this adaptation, Cassius and Casca are female characters, meaning that it's one woman speaking to another who complains that 'Our yoke and sufferance show us womanish' (1.3.83, re-translated from the Dutch on the subtitles as 'Our patience under the yoke makes us womanish'). This seems to be saying something about the de-feminization that modern female politicians often seem to feel compelled to perform.*

Numerous productions this year put gender under the microscope, many of them continuing the momentum of 2016 in cross-casting major roles. One such production was Ellen McDougall's *Othello*, which opened at the Sam Wanamaker Playhouse (SWP) in February. Here, Cassio was reinvented as a woman: as the cast sang a close-harmony rendition of Lana Del Rey's 'Video Games', we watched Othello's new lieutenant Michelle Cassio (Joanna Horton) put on a leather jacket and tie back her hair. If there was some audience laughter at the anachronism of this sequence in the 'original practices' space of the SWP, there was more as it concluded: the candles were all extinguished, and suddenly the double bed that stood in the middle of the stage – now piled with the corpses it would carry at the end of the play – was illuminated by the flash of a smartphone camera. I got the feeling that this production was uncomfortable with the heritage trappings of its building, that it wanted to subvert its context and ironize its relationship with the space. This tension was evident in other Globe productions this season, following the announcement of artistic director Emma Rice's departure and her public disagreement with the Board over her use of modern lighting and sound equipment (the same season's adaptation of *The Little Matchgirl*, for example, contained sardonic references to 'boring old electricity' and a 'delivery of codpieces'). But there was also a strong sense that the production wanted to distance itself from the play. Rice's introduction to the programme expressed 'concerns about the brutal racism and sexism', while a note by McDougall and her dramaturg Joel Horwood emphasized the imperative they felt to 'take responsibility for the racism, misogyny and sexual violence in both the language and dramatic action of the play'.

As a result, the female characters were presented as unambiguous victims of patriarchy. Natalie Klamar's Desdemona was on edge from her first appearance, physically tense around Othello as if she had suspected all along that their romance was built on shaky foundations. She was tightly bound into a white corset, an image of both repression and oppression. Thalissa Teixeira's Emilia was evidently the victim of an abusive relationship, flinching as she interacted with her husband. These women were not passive in their victimhood, however: Desdemona fought back violently as Othello murdered her, her dying words becoming a full-throated scream of '*Get off me!*', and the moment at which Emilia finally found her voice and let rip at Iago was, for me, the highlight of the production. The play ended with another close-harmony song, as the two surviving women – Cassio and Bianca (Nadia Albina) – ripped up the bloodstained mattress in a symbol of the women's defiance against the system in which they were trapped.

The production seemed less interested in generating sympathy for its male protagonists. The presentation of Othello himself was ambivalent. McDougall and Horwood had rewritten numerous lines to exacerbate the play's racism: Brabantio's assertion that his son-in-law was 'a practiser / Of arts inhibited and out of warrant' became one of 'voodoo magic' (1.2.79–80), and he accused Othello of having sourced his 'spells and medicines' not from 'mountebanks' but 'witch doctors' (1.3.61). That Kurt Egyiawan's Othello had internalized this racism was evident from his final speech, in which his reference to 'the base Indian' became 'the base Negro' (5.2.356), and the 'turbaned Turk' not a 'circumcisèd dog' but a 'black, black dog' (362–4), the text's images of threatening otherness becoming points of self-loathing identification for the character. His jealousy, however, seemed to come out of nowhere: he flipped from reserved control to noisy rage over the course of a single scene, covering most of this arc over a single exit and re-entrance in 3.3. Egyiawan was not aided in this by the fact that much of his first soliloquy ('This fellow's of exceeding honesty', 3.2.262–83) had been cut, as if perhaps the production team were concerned that it would make the character seem too credulous, but the effect of the cut was to render his behaviour inexplicable. Sam Spruell's Iago, meanwhile, was a thoroughly nasty piece of work: he snarled and grimaced at the audience during his soliloquies, speaking with a rasping voice, so there was no danger that he might co-opt us into his perspective. I could not help but feel that this insistence on Iago's unpleasantness – surely something we can take for granted – rather threw away the play's potential to unsettle.

The production's attempts to problematize the play's sexism and racism were somewhat undermined by the decision to set it in a kind of ironic nowhere-time. At once both early modern and 21st-century, it was never entirely clear what sort of society was under scrutiny: the costumes tended to suggest the play's Jacobean origins but almost as parody, with elaborate ruffs and oversized codpieces, and anachronistic modern intrusions such as Cassio's leather jacket. The fact that Cassio was a female soldier was itself an anachronism in the semi-Jacobean world of the play, but nobody commented on her gender in this respect or with reference to her supposed affair with Desdemona. All of the other female characters are called 'whore' at some point in the play, often for the slightest social and sexual transgressions: what was it, then, that enabled the female Cassio to be so open about her lesbian affair with Bianca, even to 'lie with' Iago (3.3.418), without becoming a victim of the same sort of verbal abuse from her male colleagues? Prejudices and inequalities of the sort to which the production team quite rightly object are socially specific, taking different forms in different cultures and different historical periods. The production seemed to acknowledge that sexism now is different from its Jacobean antecedents – Iago's misogynistic rhyme (2.1.151–63), for example, was completely rewritten to express current sexist ideals. But, elsewhere, it was not really clear whether we were being asked to condemn a Jacobean misogyny from which we are separate, or a modern version in which our own society is complicit.

There were four major productions of *Twelfth Night* in 2017 (one of them considered in the section below). The first to open was Simon Godwin's at the National Theatre. This was a broad, comic production in the mould of *One Man, Two Guvnors*, but it was also attempting a more nuanced exploration of gender and sexuality. Oliver Chris's Orsino was an overgrown schoolboy, attempting to woo Olivia in 1.1 with a bunch of flowers and a gigantic teddy bear. He was approaching his fortieth birthday (which he celebrated in 2.4), but surrounded himself with much younger men. He seemed to want to prove his masculinity, sparring with Cesario in a boxing match in 1.4; he would get carried away with affectionate horseplay, even kissing Cesario on the lips at one point, before finding himself troubled by his growing attraction to his attendant. Upon his discovery of Viola's female identity in the final scene, he exclaimed with relief. Tamara Lawrance's Viola was a confident, swaggering presence in her guise as Cesario; she wooed Olivia with gusto, singing Orsino's embassy and accompanying herself on guitar. Later in the scene, she hugged Olivia from behind, caressed her with her voice, and literally swept her off her feet – it was no wonder that Olivia fell in love with this charmingly flirtatious Cesario, but a little odd that Viola seemed at all surprised that her actions had had this effect. Phoebe Fox's Olivia was played in a similarly comic register, only casually committed to her mourning. Her first outfit was a lacy black party dress, her hair in girlish bunches and her 'veil' a pair of sunglasses; left alone, we saw her dancing up the staircase, and she threw caution to the winds in 3.1 with an unsubtle attempt to seduce Cesario in her hot tub. These central performances were warm and appealing, but sometimes rather overlooked the play's melancholy undertones: there was little sense, for example, that Lawrence's air-punching Viola was pining away, 'Smiling at grief' (2.4.115), or that Fox's exuberant Olivia was battling against any self-imposed restraint.

The performance for which this production will be best remembered was Tamsin Greig's as a re-gendered Malvolia. Malvolia was a sort of Mrs Danvers figure, her face framed by a severe black bob, her body literally buttoned up in a formal black blouse. She was devoted to Olivia, creeping up to her sleeping mistress in 2.3 in order to deliver a hot drink without waking her (and anticipating, perhaps, her later fantasy about the daybed upon which she would leave Olivia sleeping). Greig developed a wonderfully layered relationship with the audience, sneering at us as examples of 'these wise men that crow so at these set kind of fools' (1.5.84–5) and glaring at us with disapproval whenever we laughed at suggestive wordplay (a trick, of course, that would provoke more audience laughter and yet another withering glance from Malvolia). Following her discovery of the letter, she warmed to the audience, seeking spectators' advice on the pronunciation of 'slough' (2.5.144 and again at 3.4.66) and sharing her emotional vulnerability. At the start of the gulling scene, the odd-job woman Fabia (Imogen Doel) was in the process of fixing a fountain in Olivia's garden; this faulty water feature provided not only some predictably enjoyable moments of physical comedy, but also a lovely symbol of repression giving way to liberation as it exploded into full flow at the scene's climax, and Malvolia, worked up into a state of extreme physical passion, jumped into the water, joyful and unconcerned. She appeared in 3.4 in not just yellow stockings, but a huge Pierrot blouse, which she threw off midway through a Cole Porter-style musical number to reveal a showgirl outfit complete with revolving nipple tassels. Perhaps this Malvolia had always been repressing an exhibitionist tendency: she gave an unrestrained performance with a showy finish, before doubling over in a moment of amusing vulnerability as she admitted, 'this does make some obstruction in the blood, this cross-gartering' (3.4.19–20). By the time she had been confined to the 'dark house', bound and blindfolded, she was a deeply pitiable figure, her treatment all the more cruel since this was now the story of a closeted lesbian coming out only to be met with rejection and punishment. In the final scene, her plea for an explanation of her treatment was pained and confused; 'I'll be revenged on the whole pack of you' (5.1.374) was directed at the whole auditorium, as if she felt we had befriended her only to betray her.

The production's final moments made use of the Olivier's revolving stage for a montage of the conclusions to the characters' stories. Many of them were sad: we saw Antonio (Adam Best) leaving alone, Sir Toby (Tim McMullan) swigging from a bottle of vodka and Maria (Niky Wardley) trying to wrest it from him, and Sir Andrew (Daniel Rigby) waiting in the rain with his suitcase, patting Orsino's abandoned teddy as if he were comforting a crying baby. A glimpse of Olivia and Sebastian (Daniel Ezra) flirting by her hot tub suggested that at least those two had a potentially happy future in store. As the sequence ended, the dishevelled Malvolia climbed the set's giant staircase, her hands reaching up towards the rain, in an ambiguous gesture somewhere between yearning and emancipation. Throughout the show, Greig's Malvolia had been paired visually with Doon Mackichan's Feste, a cabaret performer in glittery boots, snake headdress, and feather boa (Illustration 55). Played by an actress who physically resembled Greig, Feste regularly stood in symmetrical opposition to Malvolia: at first equal and opposite, wild abandon versus Puritan restraint, and then later, in these final moments, as a sort of mirror version of the newly-liberated character, looking up at her counterpart from the opposite side of the stage.

In Jo Davies's *Twelfth Night* for the Royal Exchange Theatre, Manchester, Kate O'Donnell's Feste was a wry, detached figure on Illyria's margins. O'Donnell, a trans performer, wrote in the programme that her version of the character was not just a 'corrupter of words' (3.1.35) but a 'corrupter of gender'. She appeared at both the beginning and the end in a long, androgynous coat, throwing it off during 2.3's party scene to reveal a brilliant-blue floor-length feathered dress. As in Godwin's production, this was a character representing the uninhibited half of *Twelfth Night*'s binary between restraint and liberation: with her gown, her headdress of blue feathers, and a miniature Christmas tree made of silver tinsel, she looked like a carnival version of the Statue of Liberty (Illustration 56). Feste interacted with the audience towards the end of the interval, striking up a warm rapport, and she built on this in a short bit of stand-up as the second half

55. *Twelfth Night*, 1.5, National Theatre, Olivier Theatre, directed by Simon Godwin. Doon Mackichan as Feste and Tamsin Greig as Malvolia. Photograph by Marc Brenner.

opened, advising the parents in the audience not to let their children go into fooling ('very much a minimum wage occupation ... very reliant on tips'), reporting back on her interval chats, and telling us about her drunken night out with the boys.

The 'restraint' half of the binary was evident in the black and grey costumes on display everywhere else in Illyria, and in the almost Chekhovian sense of relentlessly passing time and underlying grief that haunted the production. As it opened, Faith Omole's Viola was carried on by six sailors as if she were a corpse being carried by pall bearers. Libby Watson's set featured a simple pile of sand in the middle of the in-the-round stage, and as Kevin Harvey's Orsino stood upon it to reflect upon the transient effects of music, more sand rained down upon him as though he were standing in an hourglass. Later, as he listened to Viola sing 'Come Away, Death' – a sad, haunting ballad – he looked

pained, as though he had been struck by the cruel pace of a life that was slipping by faster than he had realized.

A production with Feste as its heroine leaves little space for a sympathetic Malvolio, and this one was happy to let us enjoy Malvolio's humiliation. In the gulling scene, Anthony Calf's Malvolio was not aware of the audience's presence in the way Tamsin Greig's Malvolia had been; Sir Toby (Simon Armstrong) and Sir Andrew (Harry Attwell) hid amongst the audience to watch him read the letter, implicitly casting us as their accomplices, anticipating that we, like them, would be looking forward to his comeuppance. Malvolio was a rather obsessive figure, repeatedly whipping out a bottle of hand sanitizer. He appeared in 2.2 riding a bike, his trousers tied back with yellow bicycle clips: this was the setup for his 'yellow stockings' and 'cross gartering', reinterpreted here

56. *Twelfth Night*, 2.3, Royal Exchange Theatre, directed by Jo Davies. Kate O'Donnell as Feste. Photograph by Jonathan Keenan.

as a full-body yellow-and-black Lycra cycling suit. When he was imprisoned beneath a conical construction of interlocked sticks in 4.2, the appeal of the scene was through Feste, who dressed up as an Orthodox Priest to play Sir Topas, an inverted top hat for her headwear and a teapot as her censer.

The production ended on a note of melancholy, with Feste watching as the stage emptied. Sebastian (Daniel Francis-Swaby) returned Antonio's (Aaron Anthony) purse to him, sharing a moment of apologetic eye contact before going off to join his new wife (Kate Kennedy). When Feste sang the words 'When that I was a little boy' (adapted from 5.1.385), she was singing as a trans woman remembering a more difficult time, and this was emphasized by having her repeat the line at the end of the song. But this downbeat, thoughtful ending was

subverted almost immediately with another eruption of carnival: the whole cast re-entered to dance a celebratory jig, the play's couples dancing together, Sir Andrew showing off his leaps once more, and Malvolio, presumably having been successfully 'entreated to a peace' (5.1.376), back to his old ways trying to stop everyone from having fun. The ending seemed to suggest that this back-and-forth between restraint and release would be ongoing forever.

All four *Twelfth Night*s I saw this year cast BME actors as Viola and Sebastian. While none of these productions was 'colour-blind' – the actors playing the twins shared a similar ethnicity to their stage-siblings in each – the National Theatre and Royal Exchange productions did not seem to be exploring racial or cultural difference as a central concern. However, all four productions opened either with a depiction of Viola's shipwreck or her arrival in Illyria, so, on some level, all four were framed as stories about displacement and immigration; the fact that all four Violas and Sebastians were played by non-white actors, and the Illyrians largely (though not exclusively) by white actors, is therefore significant. Of the four, the production in which issues of cultural difference were most foregrounded was Christopher Luscombe's for the RSC, in which Viola and Sebastian were Indian castaways making their way in an Illyria that was clearly a version of nineteenth-century England. Dinita Gohil's Viola found a place as an exoticized boy servant to Duke Orsino (Nicholas Bishop), a Wildean aesthete who appeared in 1.1 in an art-filled attic room completing a painting of a nearly naked Curio (Luke Latchman), another Indian attendant. Curio was listed in the programme as Orsino's 'muse', and there was a distinctly erotic dimension to their relationship; later, as the disguised Viola asked Valentine whether the Duke was inconstant in his 'favours', Curio interjected 'No, believe *me*' (1.4.7–8), with a knowing chuckle. This Orsino seemed to love Olivia as a kind of romantic ideal; while the pursuit of heterosexual love allowed him to adopt a heroic posture, he was clearly more interested in male companionship. Drawn in by Cesario's description

57. *Twelfth Night*, 2.4, RSC, Royal Shakespeare Theatre, directed by Christopher Luscombe. Nicholas Bishop as Orsino and Dinita Gohil as Viola. Photograph by Manuel Harlan © RSC.

of unrequited love in 2.4 – perhaps even recognizing that it referred to him – he leaned in for a long and passionate kiss, a moment of such transgressive emotional intensity that when I saw it there were audible gasps from spectators (Illustration 57). Cesario's immediate response to the kiss was to ask 'Sir, shall I to this lady?' (2.4.122) – evidently Viola wanted to know whether this encounter had alleviated Orsino's desire for Olivia, and the fact that it had not left her visibly crestfallen. The production also alluded to Victorian attitudes towards homosexuality in its presentation of Antonio (Giles Taylor), who was refigured here as an English dandy with a green carnation in his lapel. When the police officer attested 'I know your favour well' (3.4.322), he flicked at the carnation with disgust, implying that it was Antonio's sexual orientation rather than his naval service that had made him a social outcast in Illyria.

In another Wildean allusion, the programme divided the play's characters into 'Town' and 'Country' (with Viola and Sebastian as 'Visitors'). The characters who traversed these spaces – Viola, Sebastian and Antonio – took trains between locations, meaning that some scenes were set either in the quaint regional station nearest to Olivia's country estate or in the busy city station of the 'Town' (3.3). 'Town' was evidently London – a large map of the late Victorian-era Underground occupied the central spot during 3.3, and when Antonio arranged to meet Sebastian 'In the south suburbs at the Elephant' (3.3.39), he pointed directly at Elephant & Castle. Olivia's country home formed a kind of mirror space to Orsino's townhouse attic: in a parallel with the Duke's erotic art, the Countess's garden was filled with classical-style nude statues, suggesting perhaps that, whereas his sexual desires had been hidden away, hers had somehow become ossified. Indeed, Kara Tointon's Olivia spoke and moved with a kind of glacial elegance, coming alive only as Cesario's passion ignited her own.

At the end, there was a suggestion that none of the lovers had really got what they wanted. As Sebastian (Esh Alladi) laughingly informed Olivia that she had been 'betrothed both to a maid and man' (5.1.261), her pained reaction indicated that she found nothing funny about the situation. Orsino, congratulating himself that 'I shall have share in this most happy wreck', took Sebastian's hands and declared 'Boy, thou hast said to me a thousand times / Thou never shouldst love woman like to me' (5.1.264–6), before awkwardly realizing that it was Viola who had made those promises. Antonio left the stage, heartbroken, as Sebastian stared off after him. The final speech was reassigned to Olivia, so that it was she, not Orsino, who urged

> Cesario, come –
> For so you shall be, while you are a man;
> But when in other habits you are seen,
> Orsino's mistress and his fancy's queen.
>
> (5.1.381–4)

In Olivia's voice, the speech was sorrowful, as if she were enjoying one last moment with the fictional boy she loved before relinquishing him to somebody else. In the closing moments, Olivia reached for Viola, Viola for Orsino, and Orsino for Sebastian.

While the main plot was played for emotional intensity and sexual ambiguity, the Malvolio subplot employed a much broader register, all comic double-takes and unified ensemble movement. Occasionally, it burst into full-blown musical theatre, with a catchy, feel-good musical score by Nigel Hess. Malvolio's soliloquy in 3.4 was augmented with a Gilbert-and-Sullivan style patter song based on the lyrics to the Elizabethan ballad 'Please one and please all'; Adrian Edmondson's Malvolio seemed suddenly to notice the audience in this scene, playing up to their appreciation of his new-found musical abilities. In 2.3, Feste (Beruce Khan) played 'O mistress mine' and (repositioned from the end) 'The wind and the rain' on a Polyphon,

a mechanical disc-playing music box, prompting the characters to caper around the drawing room in a sequence reminiscent of 'The rain in Spain' from *My Fair Lady*. In 4.2, his 'Jolly Robin' song was expanded into a set-piece musical number, performed under a spotlight.

Like Luscombe's previous productions for the RSC, this *Twelfth Night* was underpinned by nostalgia. As in his 2014 productions of *Love's Labour's Lost* and *Much Ado About Nothing*, the play was transplanted into a period setting during the heyday of the British Empire, with an ornate set by Simon Higlett based on a real-life English stately home. Here, this fond depiction of the recent English past extended to a questionable allegory of British colonialism: Viola was a devoted servant to Orsino, her 'Indianness' making her an object of fascination for him, while the identically costumed Sebastian appeared to have a similar relationship with Antonio. Feste, meanwhile, was reinvented as Olivia's 'munshi' or Indian secretary, in a nod to the relationship between Queen Victoria and her attendant Abdul Karim, depicted in the 2017 film *Victoria and Abdul*. Like that film, the production thus participated in a nostalgic construction of the relationship between Britain and India during the Raj as that between a benevolent aristocratic patron and a contented and willing colonial subject.

Kate Saxon's *As You Like It* (Illustration 58), a touring co-production between the Theatre by the Lake in Keswick and Shared Experience, seemed to be in dialogue with these *Twelfth Nights*. Opening in a kind of iron-clad vault, the production constructed Duke Frederick's court as an exclusive, oppressive space (made all the more oppressive, somehow, by the coffee machine and water cooler that bookended it). It was a shallow, corridor-like set, with barely enough space for the characters to navigate the long black conference table that extended across it, let alone the wrestling scene. Nathan Hamilton's Orlando was literally an intruder in this space, breaking in during the opening moments; wearing a T-shirt with the slogan 'The Last Rebel', he was a visual contrast with the smart-suited lackeys of the Duke's court. Duke Frederick was played by Alex Parry as a modern

58. *As You Like It*, 5.4, Theatre by the Lake and Shared Experience, touring, directed by Kate Saxon. Alex Parry as Duke Senior, Nathan Hamilton as Orlando, Layo-Christina Akinlude as Celia, Jessica Hayles as Rosalind, Matthew Darcy as Oliver, Josie Dunn as Phebe, and Adam Buchanan as Silvius. Photograph by Keith Pattison.

right-wing populist, a purple rosette attached to his pinstripe suit, his cockney man-of-the-people demeanour masking an underlying penchant for violence and authoritarianism. It was not quite clear how he had 'usurped' his brother – the programme suggested he was the 'newly elected Head of State', which would imply his assumption of power was legitimate – but it was evident that he was now abusing it.

His court was also a space of sexual inequality, its female characters craving freedom from its constraints. Rosalind (Jessica Hayles) and Celia (Layo-Christina Akinlude) made their first appearances in tight-fitting dresses and high-heeled shoes. Left alone just after having met Orlando, Rosalind caressed the hard surface of the table as if willing it to melt; she seemed to be about to begin an expressive dance sequence before she was interrupted. At the end of the scene, she and Celia took off their shoes to herald the transition into 'liberty, and not to banishment' (1.3.137), and then pulled at the hard metal plates of the Duke's vault, parting them down the middle to reveal the Forest of Arden. The stage was large, white, and lit from the back to show silhouettes of a large tree, a telephone box with a clarinettist sat on top of it, and a puppet deer and dancers surrounding them like a pastoral scene from classical myth.

The good Duke's court in Arden was an ultra-liberal commune. He and his followers all wore

Nepal shirts and harem pants and played guitars; books were communal property here, to be read and shared (the use of the telephone box as a makeshift library was presumably a reference to the real-life phenomenon that has happened in decommissioned phone boxes across the UK since 2009). The Duke, Amiens and Jaques were animal rights activists, deeply upset at the hunting of deer and sharing only vegetarian foods at their forest picnic. The 'What shall he have that killed the deer?' song in 4.2 was played as an anti-hunting protest anthem, the Duke and his followers carrying hand-painted placards with slogans like 'All Stags Have Rights' and (interestingly, given the UKIP overtones of the bad Duke's court) 'Deers for Remain'. This Arden was a space where people could shed oppressive identities and embrace social freedoms: Celia, played by a black actress, changed out of her tight dress and into a loose-fitting kaftan, and released her hair from its tied-back, constrained style to set free its natural volume. At one point, she could be seen in the phone box engrossed in a copy of Zadie Smith's *White Teeth*, the suggestion being, perhaps, that she had space in Arden to explore her identity as a modern black woman in a way that would have been taboo in Duke Frederick's court.

The production's attempts to extend this emancipatory outlook to gender politics were mixed. Audrey was played here as a transvestite, a male actor (Matthew Darcy) dressed as a kind of super-kitsch Bo Peep. With her blonde bob, frilly petticoats and knee-length dress, this Audrey was clearly a version of the artist Grayson Perry – though, whereas Perry identifies as a transvestite and uses male pronouns, this Audrey was presumably transgender, the female pronouns of the text retained. The implication was that Arden was welcoming of people who wished to express non-traditional gender identities, but this felt problematic to me: Audrey is a grotesque figure of fun and the joke is generally at her expense. Rosalind, of course, found a freedom in playing Ganymede that had been unavailable to her in her female guise. Interestingly, though, her male persona also seemed to be a weight to her towards the end of the play. As she was left alone onstage, she celebrated Orlando's love for her by taking off her masculine jacket to reveal an androgynous T-shirt, and danced around the space, finally expressing herself in movement in the way that the production had earlier gestured towards in her scene at Duke Frederick's table. But at the end of the sequence, as she picked up the jacket in order to resume her Ganymede role, she seemed suddenly sad, almost defeated. This role, too, came with its constraints.

WHAT IS THIS, SOME KIND OF COMMUNITY THEATRE?

There's another short break around 2½ hours into the show. I bump into a fellow Shakespearian academic, and we get sandwiches and drinks from one of the onstage kiosks. Running out of time to find a good spot for the next section, we sit on the nearest available sofa. It's facing away from all the action, towards the wings, but right in front of a large TV screen. We are both, I think, aware that the funeral orations must be coming up. My colleague comments that it feels a bit wrong to have our backs to the actors in order to watch a TV. As it happens, ours turns out to be a brilliant, albeit accidental, choice of viewing location. We watch Brutus' oration on the screen. We crane our necks occasionally to watch the live action but, since this is uncomfortable and the actor is facing towards the auditorium, it's much better watching the TV. Antony's oration follows. He pauses for a long time at the start, and later disappears from the screen (I think he's slumped beneath the podium). I'm frustrated – the interesting stuff is happening off-camera, and I can't see it. But as the oration goes on, the conspirators gather one by one right next to our sofa, muttering to one another, shaking their heads, conferring with increasing urgency (I assume they are trying to determine whether or not they can stop him). I'm reminded of the footage of the pro-EU and Clinton campaigners during those pivotal moments last year when it became clear that the polls had been wrong and that the elections were, unthinkably, not going their way. I'm so transfixed by this live, semi-private show taking place so close to me that I don't pay enough attention to Antony's televised speech, something I regret when there is a big audience laugh and a round of applause and I pivot to try to work out what I missed. I can't work it out, but on the TV screen he is addressing his speech at two audience members in the front row of the stalls. (I learn afterwards that they walked across the stage at a key moment, and Antony chased them in mock outrage.) I think somebody in the stalls shouts 'Read the will!' in English, and he replies 'I can't', before continuing in Dutch, but I could be wrong – there's so much going on that I can't keep track of it. It's all thrillingly live.

A similar combination of politics, playfulness, and anarchic interactivity marked Emma Rice's 'Summer of Love' season, her last summer season as artistic director of Shakespeare's Globe. Like her inaugural season in 2016, this one presented the Globe as a festival space, filling the piazza once again with silver trees, and adding fairy lights and a big sign that spelled out 'LOVE'. Once again, the productions were irreverent, tongue-in-cheek, unafraid of iconoclasm; Rice was clearly signalling that, despite the circumstances of her departure from the Globe, she would not be deterred from her artistic vision. Lines were rewritten for accessibility in all four Shakespearian productions (Viola's suggestion that Sebastian was 'in Elysium', for example, becoming 'in a watery grave'). Electric lighting and sound played a major part across the season: as in 2016, modern pop songs were incorporated into the productions, and musical underscoring and coloured lighting helped to generate (and sometimes impose) mood. Much has been made of Rice's decision to abandon the Globe's use of 'shared light', but there were undoubted advantages here: in *Romeo and Juliet* and *Much Ado About Nothing*, for example, it seemed fitting that the environment got darker as the plays did. In keeping with Rice's admirable policy of aiming for a 50:50 gender split in every cast (which most, but not all, of the productions achieved), major roles were re-gendered in every production. In that sense, this section of my article should be considered a continuation of the one above.

Rice's own valedictory production in the Globe itself was another *Twelfth Night*. It was a good example of many of the features that have characterized her artistic directorship: an exuberant riot of a production, filled with music, its cast drawn from the world of musical theatre and cabaret as much as classical drama. An extended opening sequence

aboard the 'SS *Unity*' set the tone for what was to follow: a joyful celebration of diversity and an almost defiantly hopeful statement of faith in the future. In the context of the recent terrorist attacks in the UK, including one just metres from the Globe at London Bridge, it was moving to observe that the ship's life-rings spelled out 'In Love We Trust'. With its dancing sailors, disco soundtrack and a bearded drag queen leading a chorus of Sister Sledge's 'We are family', the sequence was gloriously camp, and its message of inclusivity chimed with 2017's fiftieth-anniversary celebrations of the partial decriminalization of homosexuality in the UK.

One of the production's greatest strengths was its inventive use of sea imagery. During the opening sequence, Antonio (Pieter Lawman) sailed into the yard to rescue the shipwrecked Sebastian (John Pfumojena) on a lifeboat called *Bewitched*, and the shifting heads of the spectators that surrounded him brilliantly evoked the surge of the sea and the slipstream of the boat. The groundlings remained in this role for the rest of the production: Orsino (Joshua Lacey) and Viola (Anita-Joy Uwajeh) fished into them from the edge of the stage, and Antonio's lifeboat returned through the yard for his arrival in Illyria. The onstage ensemble also evoked the ebb and flow of the tide, surging forward as a group to pull characters offstage and simultaneously bringing other characters on with them, depositing them onstage like washed-up driftwood. Several characters were brought on- and off-stage in this fashion, including Viola, Olivia and Antonio, as if they were being propelled by forces over which they had no control: a metaphor for sexual desire, maybe, or even fate itself. If this was on the verge of seeming like a slightly highbrow concept in an otherwise rambunctious production, it was neatly subverted by Katy Owen's Malvolio, who stopped as he was washed onto the stage by the ensemble and turned to ask: 'What is this, some kind of community theatre? Next you'll all be playing "Zip Zap Boing"!'

Rice had clearly attempted to repeat the magic of last year's casting of a cabaret star – Meow Meow's brilliant turn as Titania – by inviting the drag performer Le Gateau Chocolat to play Feste. Unfortunately, the gambit was not quite as successful this time. Feste was reinvented here as a kind of transcendent representative of fate or 'the whirligig of time' (5.1.373), hovering over the events of the play on the balcony, invisibly manipulating the characters, and providing musical interludes, largely adapted from Feste's own text, as the action unfolded below him. Only occasionally did characters interact with him directly, and this was often in cryptic, non-Shakespearian exchanges: both Olivia (Annette McLaughlin) and Malvolio asked him, at different moments, 'Are you here to save me?', to which Feste replied he could save nobody, 'Not even myself'. Feste's Shakespearian dialogue was cut almost entirely, and what little remained was mostly reassigned to Nandi Bhebhe's Fabian. This had the effect of rendering Feste a more remote and mysterious figure than usual, blunting his wit, effacing his insight into his fellow characters, and raising questions about what his connection with the events of the play actually were. The only Feste scene that was retained more or less in full was his taunting of the imprisoned Malvolio, who referred to him throughout as 'Soul' rather than 'Fool'. Quite why this god-like figure chose to descend from the heavens to dress up as a nun called 'Sister Topas' and wind up an already thoroughly humiliated steward was not entirely clear.

There were striking stylistic overlaps between the four *Twelfth Nights* this year, and some direct borrowings between productions. Three of them featured Viola participating in a boxing match; two of them, a man-child Orsino sending his servants to woo Olivia with silly presents; three of them, a re-gendered Fabian (and the other, no Fabian at all); all four of them, a teddy bear, a symbol of childishness and (recalling *Brideshead Revisited*) aristocratic privilege (two of the teddies were a gift from Orsino to Olivia, two of them Sir Andrew Aguecheek's). The most obvious point of comparison between Godwin's production and Rice's, of course, was the casting of a female actor as Malvolio. Much like Greig's, Katy Owen's Malvolio was the star of the show (Illustration 59). Played as a male character

59. *Twelfth Night*, Shakespeare's Globe, Globe Theatre, directed by Emma Rice. Katy Owen as Malvolio. Photograph by Hugo Glendinning.

with moustache, glasses and a tweedy suit, he appeared initially like a cross between Captain Mainwaring and a tiny Basil Fawlty, a control freak who policed the propriety of his household's behaviour and attire, and often announced his presence with a whistle. He was, nonetheless, suppressing a deeply playful spirit, skipping on- and off-stage and interacting with the audience much more than anybody else in the play: in a moment reminiscent of her performance last year as Puck, Owen goaded a groundling into stroking her yellow stockings and shouting 'I love it!' By the time Malvolio presented himself to Olivia in his new outfit, he was irrepressible, jumping into her arms, repeatedly thrusting his groin at her and swooping around the stage like a little bird ('I'm a canary!'). With Tony Jayawardena's Sir Toby an unlikeable bully, Marc

Antolin's Sir Andrew a lisping caricature, and Feste virtually absent from the comic scenes, Malvolio's effervescence created a strange dynamic in which the killjoy was a more enjoyable theatrical presence than the clowns, the carnival spirit most fully embodied by its supposed opponent. More puzzlingly, this Malvolio was given the bleakest of endings. At the start of the show, Feste had emptied a bucket, laying down a number of stones at the front of the stage. The payoff came at the conclusion, as the humiliated Malvolio came to the edge of the yard and filled the pockets of his dressing gown with the stones, before being helped into the yard by Feste. Since the yard had been coded as the sea throughout the production, the implication was clear: Malvolio was not planning revenge but drowning himself. I'm not sure the production noticed, let alone some of the spectators, because another high-octane disco number started up just as this was happening, sending the audience off on a wave of optimism that felt, to me, rather jarring.

Daniel Kramer's *Romeo and Juliet* was an archly ironic deconstruction of the play. Like the amateur dramatic production parodically depicted in Edgar Wright's film *Hot Fuzz* (2007), it seemed at times to be attempting a stage reconstruction of the famous 1996 Baz Luhrmann film. Our introduction to Kirsty Bushell's Juliet was accompanied by a screechy, highly strung Lady Capulet (Martina Laird) yelling for her daughter from offstage, coming on with her hair in a net and a wig in her hand ready to don a costume for the masked ball. The ball itself was accompanied by a disco classic ('YMCA' here, 'Young hearts run free' in the film) and saw the characters adopting ironically appropriate fancy dress: the title characters in Day of the Dead monochrome and skull make-up, Capulet as a dinosaur, Tybalt as a butcher, Paris as a gold-plated C-3PO from *Star Wars*. Edward Hogg's Romeo chased Juliet around in a frenetic party montage, before the music suddenly switched to slow strings and soul for their first exchange ('This bitter earth', strongly reminiscent of the film's 'Kissing you'). Guns replaced the play's swords and rapiers without any accompanying textual alterations; like their *Hot Fuzz* counterparts, the

characters even shouted 'Bang!' as they fired. Friar John returned his undelivered message in a FedEx envelope, transparently a reference to the Luhrmann film's FedEx-like 'Post Post Haste Dispatch'. As in the 1996 film, the seemingly dead Juliet woke up as Romeo cradled her, and he realized moments too late.

The production also carried echoes of past *Romeo and Juliet*s at the Globe. Like the Grupo Galpão production that visited the theatre in 2000 and 2012, it featured age-blind casting (including lead actors significantly older than their characters) and pretty much the whole company in clownish whiteface (Illustration 60); as in that production, the gang warfare was sketched in through sequences of comic movement. Like Dominic Dromgoole and Tim Hoare's Globe Touring production of 2015, it edited the text so that two (and in one case, three) scenes played onstage simultaneously, creating a sense of uncontrolled momentum. Like that production, it merged the two 'banished' scenes (3.2 and 3.3). But it also made inventive use of juxtaposition: Romeo and Juliet's marriage was ingeniously intercut with Mercutio and Tybalt's altercation, emphasizing surprising verbal parallels between the scenes and suggesting, perhaps, that the never-ending grudge between the factions was itself a form of marriage. Juliet's 'Gallop apace' soliloquy (3.2.1–31) was delivered onstage as Romeo and Tybalt fought to the death, Romeo pinning Tybalt down on the bed and 'shooting' him repeatedly in an unambiguous parallel to the forthcoming consummation of his marriage to Juliet (indeed, he seemed to be consummating his relationship with Tybalt at the *expense* of his relationship with Juliet). The Nurse's discovery of Juliet's apparent death, Balthasar's delivery of the news of the same to Romeo, and Friar John's revelation that he could not deliver the message all happened onstage at once, unfolding at a nightmarish pace.

But, unlike its various *Romeo and Juliet* intertexts, Kramer's production seemed to be actively working to generate detachment from its characters. Whereas most productions play the balcony scene for its emotional impact, for example, here it was all ironic

60. *Romeo and Juliet*, Shakespeare's Globe, Globe Theatre, directed by Daniel Kramer. Kirsty Bushell as Juliet and Edward Hogg as Romeo. Photograph by Robert Workman.

chuckles as Romeo parted the audience in the yard to position his stepladder (he cast the audience, brilliantly, as the silver-tipped fruit trees of 2.1.150, which in the electric light of the darkened yard they genuinely resembled). The actors impersonated rather than inhabited their characters, playing cartoonish types who were patently unlike them. As Juliet, Bushell seemed to be doing an impression of a young teenager; Hogg started the show striking various poses to indicate Romeo's attitude, a kind of emo Pierrot. Tybalt (Ricky Champ) was a comic psychopath, gleefully swinging his baton, and he doubled as Capulet's ferocious dog. Paris (Tim Chipping) had a golden face and matching boots to indicate his privilege. Indeed, each character seemed to be played with a Brechtian *gestus*. To keep us thinking about the play's poisonous sexual politics, the song 'Keep young and beautiful' played at moments throughout the performance,

mostly when Juliet was onstage, becoming more distorted and broken-down with each repeated sample. Even the final scene was played with an alienation effect, Juliet's lines about the poisoned cup retained in their entirety as she handled not a cup but the gun with which Romeo had shot himself, and she sought – nonsensically – for poison hanging on his lips. The production had had Juliet drink a vial of potion earlier on; I can only assume that here, as elsewhere, Kramer wanted to pull us out of empathy for the character.

Matthew Dunster's *Much Ado About Nothing* was set during the Mexican Revolution of 1910. Beatrice (Beatriz Romilly) and Hero (Anya Chalotra) were war medics, tending to a seriously wounded revolutionary during the opening moments; Martin Marquez's Leonato was a grizzled veteran with a limp and an eye-patch, and he heard the news of the army's return from a female child soldier. The soldiers returned from war on stilts, carrying wire horse-heads as if they were on horseback. Lines were rewritten to facilitate the shift in location: 'Messina' became 'Monterrey', for example, and 'ducats', 'pesos'. Steve John Shepherd's Don Pedro – based, according to the programme, on the revolutionary leader Pancho Villa – was referred to simply as 'Pedro' and not as 'Prince': a military commander but nobody's social superior. The news that the soldiers had lost 'But few of any sort, and none of name' (1.1.7) was edited down to 'But few': this was a community in which every life was equal. I wondered whether this change rather underestimated the importance of social class in the play: the play's repeated reminders of Hero's status as Leonato's heir, for example, or the re-gendered Doña Juana's anger at her supposedly subordinate position, made less sense in this context. A smattering of casual anti-American gags recalled current tensions between Mexico and the United States in light of Trump's controversial plans to build a border wall: Benedick (Matthew Needham) concluded that if he did not love Beatrice, 'I am no better than an American' (adapted from 2.3.250–1) and, at a later moment, his fellow revolutionaries spat on the floor at the very mention of an American. With its abundance of ponchos and sombreros and characters knocking back tequila shots, I am not sure that the production entirely avoided cultural cliché: indeed, it was noticeable that while several characters were played by Hispanic actors, many of the leads were not.

As in Dunster's *Imogen* last year, most of the characters spoke with working-class London accents. It became apparent as the production went on that the cockney accent was intended to signify the speaking of Spanish: Dogberry was reimagined as American film-maker 'Dog Berry' (Ewan Wardrop), who spoke in an American accent when he was speaking 'English', and a Dick Van Dyke mockney when he was attempting 'Spanish', a conceit that explained his malapropisms (to which various new ones were added) as the errors of a non-native speaker.[3] Verges (Sarah Seggari) was thus reimagined as his translator, continually

correcting his mistakes. The watch scenes were heavily rewritten in order to fit this new concept: Dog Berry's Mexican film crew caught the plot on camera – though, of course, without any sound (there was no explanation as to why Conrad and Borachio failed to notice the floodlight and huge camera being pointed at them). Allowing the film to stand in for the interrogation rather overcomplicated the scene; since this was before the invention of 'talkies', the silent film proved nothing at all, the dialogue placards having been inserted after recording. Why it led Borachio to confess was thus rather puzzling.

Setting the play in a period when female soldiers fought alongside men allowed the production to explore sexual double standards and female emancipation. Chalotra's Hero was unusually fierce: she did not 'Walk in the orchard' (3.1.5) but 'Work in the armoury', and both she and Margaret were excellent shots, firing at lined-up cans. Later, Beatrice appeared in the iconic costume of Mexican *soldaderas* with two bullet-filled bandoliers strapped across her torso. But for all their independence, these women were still judged by old-fashioned sexual standards. Built around one of the pillars was a shrine to the Virgin Mary, a permanent visual reminder of this society's fetishization of female virginity, and the play did not replace the lines that repeatedly insist upon Hero and Beatrice's virginities. Needham's Benedick and Romilly's Beatrice were appealingly equal, their gulling scenes making almost identical uses of the set, and the scene in which they declared their love was pacy and charged with emotion. They sat opposite one another on the floor for 5.2, cross-legged, in a moment of simplicity and equality; the lines of the final scene were reassigned so that it was Beatrice, not Benedick, who led into their kiss with the words 'Peace, I will stop your mouth'

---

[3] I am not sure this rather complicated concept read to the whole audience; the *Daily Telegraph*'s reviewer, for example, referred to Wardrop's 'variable accent' without noting that the bad accent was presumably deliberate (21 July 2017).

(5.4.97). The reinvention of Don Jon as Doña Juana (Jo Dockery), meanwhile, was (according to Dunster's programme interview) meant to foreground issues of gender politics, but it was not clear from the production why she was so keen to slander Hero for sexual transgression.

Nancy Meckler's *King Lear* signalled a confrontational relationship with the Globe space in its opening moments. The theatre's *frons scenae* and pillars were completely covered with dirty white tarpaulins and boarding; scrawled across the centre-stage boards were the words 'KEEP OUT' (a nod, perhaps, to the debates around Shakespeare's cultural inaccessibility that Rice's departure from the Globe had prompted). The cast entered from the yard in scruffy anoraks and woolly hats, invading the stage, literally assaulting the tiring house as they pulled down some of the sheets and used a metal luggage trolley to batter down the board that was blocking one of the doors. They all carried suitcases, and these props reappeared throughout the play, sometimes non-realistically (for example, as Kent's stocks) but more often than not actually as suitcases, drawing attention to the amount of travelling the characters of this play do. The play was thus framed as a performance-within-a-performance, *King Lear* as performed by a group of squatters. 'A King!' announced one of the ensemble, as Kevin R. McNally had a crown placed on his head and a cape made of silver plastic put over his shoulders; 'Three daughters!', said another, as the three characters stood on wooden crates to present themselves. The play did not remain in this register for long: when the same actors re-entered later in the scene, they appeared in more fully realized character costumes. However, an ensemble in neutral costumes remained onstage for much of the performance, and short, highly stylized dumbshow vignettes displayed some of the offstage action. Swords were represented by wooden sticks, and most of the violence was performed without actual physical contact but with percussive sound effects from the onstage ensemble. This was an effective storytelling technique but seemed rather detached from the boldly metatheatrical opening: *King Lear*

has a lot to say about homelessness but the production seemed to forget its framing device at precisely the moments when this theme came into sharpest focus.

The production came alive in its moments of direct address. Ralph Davis's Edmund seemed genuinely in conversation with the audience: 'Why "bastard"? Wherefore "base"?' (1.2.6) were questions that really troubled him, and he asked them squarely of particular groundlings. In his final soliloquy, he asked 'Which of them shall I take?', clocking a nearby spectator and saying 'Both?' as if reading the man's mind (5.1.48–9). At the end of the speech, he concluded that 'my state / Stands on me to defend, not to debate' (5.1.59–60), spitting the last three words at the audience as if informing us that our conversations with him were now at an end, and he had not found us as helpful as he'd hoped in assuaging his conscience. Lear himself cast members of the audience in the galleries as the 'cataracts and hurricanoes' and 'sulph'rous and thought-executing fires' of the storm (3.2.2–4); this foreshadowed his later scene at Dover, when he cast spectators as the characters of his hallucinations. 'What was thy cause?' he asked a groundling, waiting for an answer, before replying on his behalf: 'Adultery!' (4.5.109–10). 'Yon simp'ring dame' (4.5.116), accused of a voracious sexual appetite, was also a spectator, though the justice and the thief were not (4.5.147–8).

Two key roles were re-gendered in this production. Saskia Reeves's Kent was a high-ranking female advisor who relinquished her ring-binder, the symbol of her status and function within Lear's court, upon being banished. She then adopted a disguise as a man (and a cockney accent) to play Caius, creating a new Shakespearian cross-dressing role. Her reply upon being asked what she was – 'A man, sir' (1.4.10) – thus seemed to be trying a bit too hard, and got a big audience laugh. One thing that made less sense here was her eagerness to start fights in her role as Caius, knowing perfectly well she was not trained with a sword – indeed, she was comically hopeless in her fight with the cowardly Oswald in 2.2, a scene which, played this way, now resembled Viola and Sir Andrew's duel in *Twelfth*

Night. Loren O'Dair's Fool, meanwhile, was an observant, unobtrusive character, frequently lurking on the edges of scenes unnoticed by the other characters. She played violin and accordion, sometimes as part of the action, sometimes standing at the back on the musician's gallery. She was strangely genderless – clearly female, but referred to repeatedly by Lear as 'my boy'. Perhaps this was a figure who transcended the fictional world of the play – indeed, at the end of 3.6, she took off her red clown nose, her ruff and her cap, and went off to join the musicians permanently.

NOT DARK YET

The show is nearing its conclusion, and spectators are asked to return to the auditorium. I return to row M, more or less where I started. Antony (Hans Kesting) and Cleopatra (Chris Nietvelt) dance to Dylan's hauntingly beautiful 'Not dark yet' as they face defeat. Antony announces his military tactics to the onstage camera operator. Enobarbus (Bart Slegers) defects by moving to the sofa on which Caesar (Maria Kraakman) and her followers are sitting, and when Antony learns of his betrayal, he goes over and kisses him. The set is organized around two parallel glass screens: by now, it has become clear that the space between these screens is not traversed by anyone unless they are approaching death, and that, as they die, an overhead camera captures a bird's-eye photograph of each corpse and projects it onto the screens while the ticker gives the character's name and dates of birth and death. Antony goes into this valley of death for his botched suicide, and stays there some time, his freeze-frame failing to come. Cleopatra moves over to the glass for their last conversation; it is now smudged from the white paint that was used earlier to paint maps onto it. There is a barrier, a mist, between them as he dies; the screen finally freezes, and she screams, repeatedly, over the noisy percussion. It sends a shiver down my spine.

This was a great year for taut, gripping productions that made Shakespeare's tragedies feel like newly written plays. Richard Twyman's *Othello* for Shakespeare at the Tobacco Factory in Bristol presented a contemporary world whose divisions and prejudices felt horribly familiar. Much was made of Othello's religious identity. A short preshow allowed us a glimpse of Othello and Desdemona's wedding ceremony: he laid out a small prayer mat upon which the two knelt opposite each other and then recited a prayer in Arabic as he placed his handkerchief over both of their hands. The production implied that Othello (Abraham Popoola) had publicly converted to Christianity for political reasons – he wore a large cross around his neck – but continued to practise his Muslim faith in private. Alan Coveney's Brabantio was evidently deeply prejudiced against his son-in-law's Islamic origins, and indeed Othello seemed at points to retreat from his own attempts at cultural conformity, delivering his reference to 'yon marble heaven' (3.3.463) as '*your* marbled heaven'. It transpired in the final scene that his cross concealed a penknife, and it was with this weapon that he slit his own throat.

Popoola's Othello was young, physically and vocally powerful, while Mark Lockyer's Iago was middle-aged and low-status. The age gap between them really emphasized Iago's resentment at being passed over for promotion, adding a humiliating double meaning to his status as 'Ancient': Piers Hampton's Cassio, also a younger man, was dismissive of Iago, rudely shooing him away as he brought 'a business of some heat' to the general (1.2.40). Unlike his counterpart at the SWP, Lockyer's Iago was a sad, vulnerable figure. Even his racism seemed to be a misguided attempt to fit in: when he made a racist joke in 2.1, everyone onstage cringed in silence, and Iago looked embarrassed for a moment before attempting to continue. He tended to deliver his soliloquies as if he were genuinely trying to impress upon the audience the rightness of his actions. His aside, 'He takes her by the palm' (2.1.170), was played as though he thought he were making a genuine realization that Desdemona and Cassio were having an affair. He showed real emotion as he recounted the rumour that Othello ''twixt my sheets / ... has done my office' (1.3.379–80), leaving us in no doubt that he believed it to be true and, later, his voice wavered and broke as he confessed 'I do suspect the lusty Moor / Hath leapt into my seat' (2.1.294–5). Indeed, his relationship with Katy

Stephens's Emilia was beautifully layered: his nasty joke about her 'tongue' (2.1.104) was a wounded response to Cassio's alpha-male flirtation with her, and he kissed her hands apologetically immediately afterwards as if he knew he had gone too far. Their marriage had evidently been fatally damaged by his jealousy. He shrank from her attempts at physical intimacy following her theft of the handkerchief – a theft that seemed to be motivated here by her desire to repair their relationship. When she referred dismissively to his suspicions of her and Othello (4.2.149–51), his face suddenly fell, and she looked immediately apologetic, as if she had brought up a subject that was a taboo between them. A brief kiss on the lips between Emilia and Othello at the start of 4.2 – their only private exchange together – left it tantalizingly unclear whether or not their evident physical closeness had indeed strayed into infidelity.

Norah Lopez Holden's Desdemona was also a direct contrast from her counterpart in the SWP production: a happy, confident young woman in a warm and playful relationship with her husband. She play-acted throughout, impersonating a moustache-twirling old general, for example, on 'they say, the wars must make example / Out of her best' (3.3.66–7), getting her husband to relent on his hard line against Cassio by making him laugh. The start of 4.3 was played as if it were the end of a meal, many of the cast gathered around a long trestle table covered with empty plates and wine glasses; Desdemona and Emilia were left alone at the table, drunk and giggly. Desdemona told the story of Barbary's death with a strong layer of irony, chuckling and miming suicide with a knife she picked up from the table. She got up onto the table to sing the 'Willow' song, which was here a sensual, rhythmic number sung largely in Arabic – a transgressive, even mischievous act. The mood of this scene was simultaneously lighter and more tense than usual: more tense because it was so at odds with the escalating passion of the surrounding scenes, and because its playful mood was intermittently interrupted (as, for example, when Desdemona thought she heard knocking, 4.3.51). The final

scene was taut, fast and convincing, the earned payoff of a brilliantly paced production that had been building to this moment over 3 hours like a slowly coiling spring.

Kelly Hunter's *Hamlet*, a touring co-production between Flute Theatre and English Touring Theatre originally titled *Hamlet, Who's There?*, was an inventive 90-minute adaptation structured around the title character's soliloquies, with a clear focus on his psychological through-line. Mark Arends's Hamlet started the show curled up on a centre-stage sofa, weeping as he looked through a cardboard box of family photographs; as if haunted by a presence he could not see, he demanded 'Who's there?' (1.1.1). The opening lines of 1.2 and a truncated version of 1.3 were run together so that the rest of the six-strong cast filled the stage behind him, emphasizing his isolation: Claudius (Tom Mannion) and Gertrude (Katy Stephens) celebrating their marriage, while Polonius (David Fielder), Ophelia (Francesca Zoutewelle), and Laertes (Finlay Cormack) said their farewells. The absence of Horatio from this edit made Hamlet an even lonelier figure than usual, and he was confined to the sofa for much of the performance. It was a strenuously physical performance nonetheless, Arends's body wired and restless. This created a slowly accumulating sense of an immense energy being confined within a too-small space, perhaps a metaphor for Hamlet's mental state (this Prince was indeed bounded in a nutshell and haunted by bad dreams). There was a strong suggestion that the Ghost was a product of Hamlet's disturbed mind: at its arrival, Hamlet felt a sudden pang in his forehead, and he voiced and embodied his father's spirit himself. Perhaps this Hamlet had unconsciously recognized the facts of his father's murder, and the struggle to come to terms with this knowledge was what had brought him to his state of psychosis. Later, as the 'Ghost' pointed out that 'amazement on thy mother sits' (3.4.102), Hamlet gazed intently at his mother, before kissing her passionately, fully embodying his father (or an imaginary version of him). Mother and son alike were left shell-shocked by this incestuous, transgressive moment.

The adaptation's reduction in scale allowed for an increased focus on Ophelia and Laertes. Ophelia sought comfort from her brother rather than her father ('Laertes, I have been so affrighted ... ', adapted from 2.1.76), interrupting his dialogue with Claudius (repositioned from 1.2.42–63). The news prompted Claudius to rescind his permission for Laertes to leave for France, and to ask him to stay at court in order to glean the source of Hamlet's affliction. Laertes was thus merged with Rosencrantz and Guildenstern in a dramaturgical sleight of hand that not only facilitated the small cast size but also gave Laertes a new arc. Laertes's conversation with Hamlet in 2.2 indicated a warm and sincere friendship, which was strained by Hamlet's immediate perception that his friend had been put up to it by the King. No Players arrived in this production: in their stead, Laertes set out three plastic tubs and performed a drum solo on them. The solo got faster and more desperate, until – evidently still profoundly upset by Hamlet's 'What a piece of work is a man' speech (2.2. 295–312), which had moved him to tears earlier in the scene – Laertes let out a cry of pain and left the stage. It was this outburst, and not a Player's speech, that prompted Hamlet's (slightly adapted) third soliloquy. Hamlet also seemed to have a genuine love for Ophelia. When she said that Hamlet had made her 'believe' he loved her (3.1.118), he picked up on the word 'believe' as if he were affronted by it: 'You should not have *believed* me', he replied, implying that she should have *known* (3.1.119). Ophelia, like Hamlet, was deeply physical in her distress, tense and contorted. The production took a turn for the surreal as she delivered the news of her own drowning, pulling at a long grey sheet (Gertrude held the other end). Drowning, like the sofa, seemed to function here as a metaphor for mental illness – another image of being fatally enclosed, engulfed by forces beyond one's control.

The final scene was radically altered so that Hamlet and Laertes's fatal duel broke out spontaneously at Ophelia's funeral, rather than as a premeditated act. The two men fought to the death as they competed to claim Ophelia's corpse,

their three bodies physically entangled. The change rendered Hamlet's murder of Laertes more deliberate than usual, and also made him an unambiguous suicide – he stabbed Laertes in the stomach, before turning his knife on himself. This non-naturalistic, nightmarish ending changed the register of the play from a Strindbergian chamber piece to an Artaudian theatre of cruelty. The whole adaptation worked, like Laertes's cry, as a short, sharp burst of pure human anguish – a deeply visceral metaphor for grief and mental illness.

The highest-profile *Hamlet* of the year was Robert Icke's at the Almeida Theatre. It was marked by the influence of *Roman Tragedies*: throughout the show, multiple TV screens across the space relayed both live and recorded footage, sketching in the play's wider political world (Fortinbras, for example, appeared on television news in 4.4). The Ghost (David Rintoul) made his first appearances on CCTV footage in a security office, interference cascading down the screens like an eye blinking. An onstage cameraman recorded Claudius's reactions to *The Murder of Gonzago*, and, after having seen his uncle 'frighted with false fire' (3.2.254), Andrew Scott's Hamlet reviewed the footage, pausing on a close-up of Claudius's almost inscrutable response. The influence of van Hove's production also extended to the music. The show was accompanied by a soundtrack of Bob Dylan songs, many of them with striking *Hamlet* resonances: between 1.5 and 2.1, for example, a live and video montage of Hamlet musing on his encounter with the Ghost played alongside Dylan's 'Up to me' ('Now somebody's got to show their hand, time is an enemy / I know you're long gone, I guess it must be up to me'). The instrumental of 'Not dark yet' played under – and over – much of the final scene, so that as Hamlet's duel with Laertes started, the music drowned out the dialogue entirely. A great amount of important action thus took place in a kind of dumbshow: Gertrude's realization that the cup was poisoned and her decision to drink regardless; Laertes's attack of conscience and his attempt to back out of the fight before changing his mind.

The production reinvented Shakespeare's play, for the most part, as a naturalistic drama. The cast

61. *Hamlet*, 1.2, Almeida Theatre, directed by Robert Icke. Andrew Scott as Hamlet. Photograph by Manuel Harlan.

spoke with realistic cadences, sometimes partially inaudibly, with no real sense that anybody was speaking verse.[4] Each character was a complex human being: Angus Wright's Claudius as much a loving husband as a calculating political player, Rosencrantz (Calum Finlay) and Guildenstern (Amaka Okafor) a couple whose relationship was under strain, Jessica Brown Finlay's Ophelia a source of emotional strength for Hamlet in a new, silent scene just before 1.3. Peter Wight's Polonius was not the usual overbearing old bore but an affectionate father struggling with early signs of dementia: he paused for what felt like an eternity before asking, defeated and scared, 'what was I about to say?' (2.1.50), and his list of dramatic genres ('tragical-comical-historical-pastoral', 2.2. 399–401) was not pedantry but a painful and unsuccessful attempt to remember a fifth term. Icke replaced 4.6 with its equivalent scene from the first quarto, so that Juliet Stevenson's Gertrude

knew of Claudius's duplicity and made a conscious decision to deceive him. Icke re-ordered and amalgamated scenes in order to create an Ibsenesque effect: 1.2, 1.3 and the start of 2.2, for example, were conflated into a single long scene taking place at Claudius and Gertrude's wedding reception. Hildegard Bechtler's set was bisected by a huge glass screen, behind which the reception was still in full flow (Illustration 61); the main part of the stage was a domestic space into which the characters retreated to have more private conversations, though the boundary remained fluid, the noise of the party audible whenever the door opened. Time was moving fast: before the scene was over, Luke Thompson's Laertes had already packed his bags,

---

[4] Icke made it clear in an interview with the *Sunday Times* that this was a central aspect of his approach to Shakespeare (Louis Wise, 'Andrew Scott and Robert Icke: there's method in their madness', 12 March 2017).

despite having only just got Claudius's permission; Rosencrantz and Guildenstern arrived in Elsinore as the party was winding down.

Direct audience address did not fit easily into this naturalistic style, so soliloquies and asides were generally reinvented, either as characters speaking to themselves or as moments of dialogue. Scott's Hamlet had occasional moments of direct contact with the audience but, for the most part, his soliloquies were internal, the speeches of a man thinking aloud. Polonius was wearing a wire in 2.2, and having given Claudius and Gertrude earpieces, he was clearly directing his asides to them; Ophelia was bugged in the same way in 3.1, and there was a suggestion that her soliloquy there was directed, at least in part, at the listening Claudius and Polonius. The most audacious reinvention of a soliloquy came in 3.3, when Claudius spoke the whole of the speech beginning 'O, my offence is rank' (3.3.36–72) directly to Hamlet, as a frank admission of his guilt and a semi-remorseful desire to repent but to retain the 'effects' of the murder. This was not a simple confession, but a masterful piece of manipulation: Hamlet had begun by pointing his gun at his uncle, ready to execute him but, as Claudius knelt to pray, Hamlet started to panic, realizing that he would not be able to kill a praying man. Hamlet spoke his own soliloquy in Claudius's hearing, but to himself, in a manic state; Claudius was evidently listening, responding with a flicker of triumph when Hamlet resolved not to go through with it, and he seemed to taunt his nephew with his final couplet. Infuriated, Hamlet looked ready to shoot him again but, as he wavered, the scene cut to blackout. How Hamlet left this confrontation was unclear – indeed, the sudden ending might even be read as a hint that the whole exchange had been Hamlet's fantasy.

The production repeatedly foregrounded the themes of time and mortality, a motif of wristwatches recurring throughout. In 1.3, Polonius presented Laertes with an expensive watch as a leaving gift; the dumbshow before *The Murder of Gonzago* was adapted to show a similar scene of a father giving his son a wristwatch, in a montage evoking the young Hamlet's childhood and

adolescence before he went off to Wittenberg. Hamlet grabbed his own wrist in exactly the spot where one wears a watch as he wished 'that this too too solid flesh would melt' (1.2.129), and he snatched at Ophelia's wrist in the same way in a silent scene just before 2.1. The payoff came in the play's final moments. Following the deaths of Gertrude, Claudius and Laertes, the curtains obscuring the windows were pulled back to reveal the same balloon-strewn wedding reception that had opened the play, Polonius and Ophelia dancing together beside Rosencrantz and Guildenstern. Ophelia wore a wedding dress and veil, and lifted her veil to welcome her brother into the afterlife. The Ghost stood at the sliding glass doors as a kind of gatekeeper, taking the watches of those who passed him (presumably the afterlife is outside of time), but holding Hamlet back. Hamlet grabbed his wrist in panic, noticing that his watch was missing. He was still alive, still on the outside, as the afterlife disappeared from view. When he died, the space behind the glass was lit up once again to reveal only a black, empty space. 'The rest is silence' (5.2.310) was thus spoken with a chilling realization that his notion that he might be reunited with his loved ones after death had been merely a comforting fantasy, and that all he could look forward to was nothingness: 'not to be'.

Lip-synch performer Dickie Beau's one-man show *Re-Member Me* was performed on the set of Icke's *Hamlet*. Directed by Jan-Willem van den Bosch, the show was billed as – and initially seemed to be – a largely comic production about Beau's own unrealized ambition to play Hamlet. Early in the performance, Beau lip-synched to the speech from the film *Withnail and I* in which pretentious failed thespian Uncle Monty (Richard Griffiths) opines that 'the most shattering experience of a young man's life [is] when one morning he awakes and quite reasonably says to himself, "I will *never* play the Dane"'. The show started as a parody of the Great Hamlet tradition, Beau lip-synching to samples of histrionic Hamlets of the past and making ironic segues into modern music: the 'YMCA' lyric 'Young man, there's no need to feel down' was played here as advice both to Hamlet and to the young actor who feels the part slipping out of his grasp, for example, while Hamlet's encounter with the Ghost transitioned suddenly into Barbra Streisand's rendition of 'Papa, can you hear me?' from *Yentl*. Over the course of the hour-long performance, Beau literally re-membered a series of Hamlets, reassembling a number of dismantled mannequins and dressing them in the costumes of Hamlets past (a pyjama suit, for example, of the sort worn by Mark Rylance at the RSC in 1989) – though the act of remembering was also one of forgetting, the origins of each costume unclear and uncited, the quotations haphazard and literally patched together. Perhaps performances of this play are always haunted by 'ghosts' of this sort: at one point, Beau lip-synched to an interview with John Gielgud in which the actor complained that, in performing the role, one was always 'competing' with one's predecessors.

As the performance continued, it became clear that Beau's intentions went beyond pastiche. Four onstage TV screens showed close-ups of his face, each one lip-synching to a recorded interview with one of four subjects: the agent John Wood, directors Richard Eyre and Sean Mathias, and the actor Ian McKellen. Beneath the screens, the live performer lip-synched to a fifth interview with former National Theatre dresser Stephen Ashby. These five voices recalled (often partially or uncertainly) the story of Eyre's 1989 production of *Hamlet*, dealing first with lead actor Daniel Day Lewis's breakdown and then with the triumphant performance of his terminally ill replacement, Ian Charleson. Charleson died of AIDS shortly after the production closed, and his illness evidently lent his performance a powerful resonance for all of Beau's interviewees. Beau's lip-synching gave the interviews an air of second-hand irony – he exaggerated physical tics, giving visual prominence to every swallow, exhalation, giggle or smack of the lips caught on the recording. But the joke wore thin at just the right moment, the lip-synch form allowing a surprising amount of room for sincerity. The performance soon became just as much about gay politics as it was about *Hamlet*, the story of Charleson's struggle with his disease giving way

to wider points about the impact of AIDS in the 1980s, intercut with accounts of the young Gielgud's career difficulties after his arrest for 'importuning' in 1953.

As the title suggests, this was a performance about memory and impermanence. The voices themselves were ghosts of sorts – Beau's lip-synching gave the recorded voices of deceased actors the same corporeal status as those of living ones. Throughout the show, these voices struggled to remember and admitted to having forgotten, their words echoing the repeated imperatives of Shakespeare's play: 'Remember me' (1.5.91), 'Do not forget' (3.4.100), 'Pray, love, remember' (4.5.175–6). Towards the end, in silhouette, Beau lip-synched an interview with the actor Suzanne Bertish, who recalled Charleson's frustration that, since he had not been playing Hamlet when Eyre's production had opened, his performance would not be immortalized in a review. As it happened, it was: we listened to *Sunday Times* critic John Peter reading his own glowing write-up as the TV screens played slow-motion footage of Charleson running in the film *Chariots of Fire*. But the performance itself, of course, was tantalizingly out of reach, its ephemerality a metaphor here for that of life itself. Early in the show, we heard an interview in which an elderly Gielgud questioned the extent to which his life had really mattered, and Beau performed the speaker as a nervous, fidgety young man. At the performance's climax, Beau picked up a mannequin head and began 'Alas, poor Yorick' (5.1.180) in his own thin, unmediated voice, breaking off after a couple of lines and moving into 'The love song of J. Alfred Prufrock': 'No! I am not Prince Hamlet, nor was meant to be.' In an amusing coda, Ian McKellen (now played by Beau in silhouette) chucklingly acknowledged that his own *Hamlet* was never included in lists of the great performances of the role.

McKellen was the star of Jonathan Munby's *King Lear* in Chichester, the actor's second take on the role following Trevor Nunn's RSC production in 2007. Performed in the intimate Minerva Theatre (rather than the larger Festival Theatre next-door), this was a much more human-scale Lear than McKellen's last. Paul Wills's set emphasized that this was a production about stripping away the signifiers of monarchy, nation, and religion until we are left with 'the thing itself' (3.4.100). For the first half, the low circular stage was covered with a plush red carpet that became more dishevelled as the play progressed: fragments of food thrown by Lear's knights, chalky footprints, a tear (Jonathan Bailey's Edgar scored into the carpet with his knife so that he could smear his arms and face with the chalk beneath it). In the storm sequence, the stage was drenched with rain, creating a puddle in the middle that grew until it eclipsed the stage. 3.6 and 3.7 were run together and set in an abattoir, so that the squelching red surface underfoot seemed as though it was slick with blood: animal carcasses hung in the background, Lear imagined severed animal heads to be those of his daughters, and Danny Webb's Gloucester was blinded with a meat hook. Shedding the veneer of civilization,

the characters of the play were reducing themselves, and others, to animals, butchers, meat. In the second half, the carpet was removed entirely to reveal a chalky floor, and the panelling at the rear of the stage parted to show a large, white, cliff-like surface across the back wall. The whole second half thus seemed to be taking place at 'th'extreme verge' (4.5.26).

The production opened in a world dominated by formality and protocol. The characters wore evening dress and military uniform for the opening scene, and joined in with a bombastic national anthem, their hands on their hearts, for Lear's ceremonial entrance with Tamara Lawrance's Cordelia. A huge painting of the king descended at the back. This was a diplomatic event: on Lear's centre-stage desk stood two small flags and two framed pictures representing the lords of France and Burgundy. Lear sprang the love test on his

62. *King Lear*, 1.1, Chichester Festival Theatre, Minerva Theatre, directed by Jonathan Munby. Ian McKellen as King Lear and Sinéad Cusack as the Countess of Kent. Photograph by Manuel Harlan.

daughters with a chuckle, enjoying their discomfort; pleased with the efforts of his eldest daughters, he pulled out a pair of scissors and cut a large map of Britain into thirds, presenting Scotland to Albany (thus effectively giving his son-in-law only his own dukedom) and Ireland, Wales and Cornwall to Cornwall (thus augmenting his), clearly reserving the majority of England for Cordelia. But Lear himself seemed to be the gravest threat to the order of his kingdom in this scene. Angered by Cordelia's response, he ripped the map of England in half, barely registering which fragment he gave to Albany and which to Cornwall. He threatened Sinéad Cusack's Kent with a chair rather than a sword, being disarmed by those around him (Illustration 62). He took a childish pleasure in clearing away Burgundy's flag and picture when the latter refused to marry Cordelia, scooping them into a drawer and shutting it with a snap.

The gods themselves seemed to disappear over the course of the show. As Lear invoked 'the sacred radiance of the sun' (1.1.109), he held up a hand and put the other to his heart, and everyone else on stage adopted the same gesture: this was a culture with a shared sense of religious propriety, it seemed. When Lear began another prayer later in the scene – 'Now, by Apollo' (1.1.159) – the rest of the assembled company joined in and seemed shocked when Kent interrupted it, blasphemously mocking the king's words. It was fascinating to see how the gesture deconstructed itself through the play. Edmund (Damien Molony) began praying to 'nature' in a similar way (1.2.1), before giving his goddess the finger. Dervla Kirwan's polite and formal Goneril knelt and adopted the gesture even when Lear was cursing her with an appeal to 'nature' (1.4.254); this was a woman whose sense of order was absolute, and she clung to formality even at moments of intense personal pain. Later, when Gloucester and Edgar both knelt and employed the gesture during the 'cliff' scene, it seemed hollowed out, emptied of its power.

McKellen's Lear was a portrait of an erratic, unpredictable mind caught between uncontrolled impulse and self-awareness. He had a tendency to pause in the middle of a sentence, as if reaching for words, before rushing on to the next. He was holding back tears as he railed at his daughters in 2.2; no sooner had he promised 'this heart shall break into a hundred thousand flaws / Or ere I'll weep' (2.2.458–9) than he broke out into an involuntary sob, humiliating himself. His exit line, 'O Fool, I shall go mad!' (2.2.459), was a partial recognition that he was no longer in control of himself, let alone his kingdom. There was a ring of truth to Edgar's description of Lear's behaviour as 'matter and impertinency mixed – / Reason in madness' (4.5.170–1): encountering Gloucester at Dover, the king seemed to be sincerely trying to teach his former subject something about the amorality of power.

Much of the production's tragic impact came from its feeling of incompletion. McKellen delivered 'This feather stirs, she lives' (5.3.240) as though there were an 'If' at the start of the sentence, flourishing a leaf as if it were Lear's last hope. He never got to hold it against Cordelia's mouth, Kent intervening as if to spare him this last painful realization. When the king resisted by brandishing a revolver, Kent tried to disarm and placate him by asking him where Caius was – but Lear could not make this last mental connection, leading Kent to conclude that this was a tragedy without a redeeming realization or lesson: 'All's cheerless, dark, and deadly' (5.3.266). Lear was interrupted even as he died, attempting a sing-song, up-down, 'Never-never, never-never, never-' (5.3.284), cut short by a sensation in his chest before he was able to articulate the final 'never'. Kent seemed to suggest suicide as she held her dead master's gun, but Edgar intervened, playing his final speech as an insistence that she should speak about her grief rather than taking a rash action. Seemingly persuaded – for the time being, at least – she stayed onstage as the lights faded to black.

While not technically a tragedy, Joe Hill-Gibbins's *A Midsummer Night's Dream* at the Young Vic is the last, honorary inclusion in this section, since it was easily the darkest version of this play I have seen. Johannes Schütz's set was a giant semi-circle 'filled up with mud' (2.1.98) and backed by a huge mirror that made the semi-circle look like a full one, reflecting the audience's own image dimly back at us. The actors remained onstage throughout, often (though not always) signifying their character's absence from a scene by turning their backs to the audience and watching the performance in the mirror, their reflected counterparts watching 'our' version of the play from the other side ('everything seems double' indeed; 4.1.189). The mortal characters of 1.1 were oddly unsuited to the muddy field in which they found themselves, Theseus (Michael Gould) in a silky black dressing gown, Hippolyta (Anastasia Hille) a pair of grossly impractical high-heeled shoes. The four lovers were all dressed in white and pale yellow, so it was painfully clear from the off that their pristine costumes would be getting very dirty, very soon: indeed, Jemima Rooper's Hermia planted herself face down in the mud during her first scene. The mud had a particular physical effect on the performance, making the actors stumble as they moved across it: journeying into the forest was hard work. The mechanicals were dressed more practically, most of them in Wellington boots (Leo Bill's hipster Bottom wore rather less practical zip-up leather boots), but they seemed terrified of the forest, pressing themselves up against the mirror during 3.1. Bottom's return from the forest was signified by several exhausting laps of the stage; tripped over by Lloyd Hutchinson's Puck, he did the last lap on his hands and knees.

As all of this indicates, the forest was no benevolent green world in this production but a dark, fearsome place full of danger and cruelty. Puck was a malevolent figure here, low energy and sarcastic: he promised to 'put a girdle round about the earth / In ... forty minutes?' (2.1.175–6) as if he were a contractor reluctantly giving his best quote, before lumbering off in no particular hurry. When he returned with the 'flower', he mimed it almost contemptuously, as if he could not really be bothered to act convincingly and thought the whole storyline rather stupid. He was also prone to violence: on 'Churl, upon thy eyes I throw / All the power this charm doth owe' (2.2.84–5), he

grabbed a plastic water bottle and emptied it over Lysander's head, proceeding to hit the sleeping man with the empty bottle repeatedly. As he led the lovers in 3.2, he smacked Lysander's head violently into the mud, dropped Helena face down, and dragged Hermia by her cardigan.

There were strong hints in this production that the love potion released the already-repressed feelings and desires of its subjects. Demetrius (Oliver Alvin-Wilson) and Helena (Anna Madeley) evidently shared a mutual physical attraction, she pushing him to the ground and straddling him as they entered the forest; during Hermia and Lysander's extended argument in 3.2, Demetrius and Helena resumed this pose in order to share a long, passionate kiss. The potion released something darker in John Dagleish's Lysander. In 2.2, his attempts to persuade Hermia to let him sleep beside her had shifted from flirtatious, to coercive, to downright violent: when she gently pushed him away, he grabbed her wrist, and when she resisted, he grabbed her again, harder, as she repeatedly shouted at him to 'Lie further off' (2.2.63). He stood with his back to her for the rest of her speech, half-ashamed, half-resentful. Once he was under the influence of the potion, his resentment took over, and he spoke his rejection of the sleeping Hermia with his hand clutching her neck (prompting her to grab at it in her sleep and, waking, to imagine it as the 'crawling serpent'; 2.2.152). This disturbing interpretation made a lot of sense – the love potion makes Lysander fall in love with Helena but it does not explain why he suddenly 'hates' Hermia with such vehemence. The lovers' quarrel in 3.2 was funny at times, but it was also dirty, violent, and cruel; when they awoke in 4.1, it seemed they had all been somehow broken by the night's events. Hermia staggered over to Lysander to hug him; he found himself unable to touch her, clenching his fists in anger and then opening them again in what I read as self-hatred.

Oberon and Titania were clearly versions of Theseus and Hippolyta, he taking off his dressing gown and playing Oberon bare-chested, she removing her suit jacket and trousers to reveal a long, flowing black dress. The fairy king and queen were unusually low-status: she was nervous, indecisive, and fidgety with her fairies, and awkward and apologetic with Bottom. When Oberon crept up on her as she slept, he lay down beside her and hugged her gently for a few moments as if he were craving a lost intimacy between them. At the end, he turned suddenly violent, pelting the sleeping Bottom with mud; Oberon and Titania played out the rest of this scene as if they were both traumatized by the irrevocable loss of trust that Oberon's actions had led to.

The final scene blurred the play's layers of reality. Over Theseus's 'lovers and madmen' speech (5.1.2–22), Egeus and Philostrate used rollers to paint over much of the mirror with black – an image, perhaps, of the world of the unconscious disappearing from view. But the dream-world erupted with force during the play-within-the-play. During his death speech as Pyramus, Bottom suddenly noticed Hippolyta, and started to play it directly to her as if it were a love poem; she disrobed, becoming Titania again, they began to fondle one another, as Theseus/Oberon looked on in horror. The performance ended in chaos, Puck delivering his 'hungry lion' monologue at the same time as Theseus's 'iron tongue of midnight' speech, while the mechanicals danced their bergomask, Hippolyta/Titania and Bottom made love, and the four lovers murmured speeches from earlier in the play, Demetrius repeating 'Are you sure that we are awake?' The company joined hands, processing in a spiral, before suddenly running to the blacked-out mirror, reaching upwards towards the unobscured part of the mirror above their heads as if they were being pulled back into the space of the unconscious. Puck delivered the epilogue, cutting its last two lines: this was not an offer of friendship.

THE TIMES THEY ARE A-CHANGIN'

I'm sitting down to write up my thoughts on Roman Tragedies. *I have pages and pages of notes, but it's proving hard to craft them into a review. My experience of the performance was too provisional: there were things I didn't see because I was sitting or standing in the wrong places, nuances I missed because I couldn't see the subtitles. Some of my favourite moments in the production were completely accidental, even unique, the result of a combination of chance and random choice. How can I possibly hope to offer a balanced account?*

My difficulty writing about *Roman Tragedies* is, perhaps, the epitome of the challenge facing the author of an article like this one. It is called 'Shakespeare Performances in England, 2017', but the productions I reviewed this year were, of course, only a small proportion of the Shakespearian theatrical activity in the country. What I saw was partly dictated by the constraints of time and space: I can only see, and write about, so many shows. I have chosen to see some over others on the basis of such hard-to-defend factors as personal taste, geographical location and artistic reputation. Other choices have been made for me: I would have loved to have been able to see Northern Broadsides's *Richard III* or the Liverpool Everyman's *Romeo and Juliet*, but their relatively short runs during the busiest part of my year meant I simply could not fit them in. Where I have reviewed a production, I sometimes find myself shaping my account of it months after the event, cutting out observations that seemed crucial at the time in the interests of a comparison or an organizing through-line that did not occur to me until long afterwards. Things I loved – actors' performances, design features, interpretive insights, particular jokes – remain unmentioned because they fall outside the focus of a paragraph. The snapshot of Shakespeare in England provided by this article, then, is provisional, partial, compromised and contingent. This is an inescapable problem, but one that presents exciting challenges: in the interests of broadening the scope of the article, I will be sharing reviewing duties in 2018 with Paul Prescott. I look forward to reviewing in dialogue with him next year.

At the end of my first year as *Shakespeare Survey's* theatre reviewer in 2015, I took the opportunity to make some observations about the year's trends. Two years later, much has stayed the same: psychological characterization; thrust and in-the-round staging; modern dress; multimedia;

explorations of gender, power, and identity; and strong elements of visual symbolism – all remain central ingredients, it seems, of Shakespeare in England or at least of what I have seen of it. But a great deal has also changed. I observed in 2015 that 'gender-blind casting remains unusual and confined largely to small supporting roles',[5] but in the two years since I wrote that, major productions have cast female actors in such roles as Prospero, King Lear, Henry V and Malvolio. Re-gendering male roles as female ones remains more common than genuinely gender-blind casting, but casting equality initiatives like Emma Rice's 50:50 policy have considerably changed the field, quite rightly rendering cross-casting less remarkable than it was before. Rice's successor at the Globe, Michelle Terry, has promised to continue the policy, and the RSC looks set to stage its first 50:50 Shakespearian production in 2018 with *Troilus and Cressida*.[6] Rice's Globe also championed a more irreverent attitude towards the Shakespearian text. Productions were unafraid of heavy rewrites, and signalled their distance from problematic historical attitudes to race and gender through ironic detachment; it remains to be seen how much of an influence this postmodern, pop-culture-inflected work will have on the rest of the Shakespearian mainstream. As political divisions have sharpened both in Britain and abroad, Shakespeare productions also seem to have become more overtly politicized: Trump and the new right were major presences on Shakespearian stages this year, and I would be surprised if they ceased to be in 2018. We shall see.

---

[5] 'Shakespeare performances in England (and Wales), 2015', *Shakespeare Survey* 69 (Cambridge, 2015), p. 433.

[6] Giverny Masso, 'Gregory Doran: "I won't enforce 50/50 gender casting at RSC"', *The Stage*, 12 September 2017.

PROFESSIONAL SHAKESPEARE PRODUCTIONS IN THE BRITISH ISLES, JANUARY–DECEMBER 2016

JAMES SHAW

Most of the productions listed are by professional companies, but some amateur productions are included. The information is taken from *Touchstone* (www.touchstone.bham.ac.uk), a Shakespeare resource maintained by the Shakespeare Institute Library. *Touchstone* includes a monthly list of current and forthcoming UK Shakespeare productions from listings information. The websites provided for theatre companies were accurate at the time of going to press.

ALL'S WELL THAT ENDS WELL

Shakespeare at the Tobacco Factory. Factory Theatre, Bristol, 31 March–30 April; Derby Theatre, Derby, 25–28 May; Northcott Theatre, Exeter, 15–18 June.
www.tobaccofactorytheatres.com
Director: Andrew Hilton

Bowler Crab Productions. Half House Farm, Three Oaks, East Sussex, 18 June–2 July.
www.bowler-crab.com
Director: Stephen John

Changeling Theatre. UK tour 1 July–21 August.
http://changeling-theatre.com
Director: Robert Forknall

AS YOU LIKE IT

National Theatre. Olivier Theatre, London, 26 October 2015–5 March 2016.
www.nationaltheatre.org.uk
Director: Polly Findlay
Rosalind: Rosalie Craig

OVO. Minack Theatre, Porthcurno, 6–10 June.
www.ovotheatre.org.uk
Director: Adam Nichols
Set in the late '60s with Summer of Love soundtrack.

Watch Your Head. The Savill Garden, Windsor Great Park, 22 June–20 July.
www.watch-your-head.co.uk
Director: Sasha McMurray

GB Theatre Company. UK tour 24 June–27 August.
www.gbtheatrecompany.com
Director: Nancy Medina

Storyhouse Theatre. Grosvenor Park Open Air Theatre, Chester, 13 July–21 August.
www.storyhouse.com
Director: Philip Wilson

Folksy Theatre. Boiling Wells Amphitheatre, Bristol (part of the Bristol Shakespeare Festival), 22–23 July.
www.folksytheatre.co.uk

Cambridge Shakespeare Festival. King's College Gardens, Cambridge, 1–27 August.
www.cambridgeShakespeare.com

THE COMEDY OF ERRORS

Guildford Shakespeare Company. Guildford Castle Gardens, 14 June–2 July.
www.guildford-Shakespeare-company.co.uk

Cambridge Shakespeare Festival. Trinity College Gardens, Cambridge, 1–20 August.
www.cambridgeShakespeare.com

Antic Disposition Theatre Company. Gray's Inn Hall, London, 20 August–1 September.
www.anticdisposition.co.uk
Director: Ben Horslen

PROFESSIONAL SHAKESPEARE PRODUCTIONS

Adaptation

The Comedy of Errors – Primary Shakespeare
Orange Tree Theatre, London, 11 June.
www.orangetreetheatre.co.uk
Director: Imogen Bond
Cast of four. Intended for primary-school children.

CORIOLANUS

Bard in the Botanics. Botanic Gardens, Glasgow, 23 June–9 July.
www.bardinthebotanics.co.uk
Director: Gordon Barr

Cambridge Shakespeare Festival. Robinson College Gardens, Cambridge, 11–30 July.
www.cambridgeShakespeare.com

Adaptation

Coriolanus and Du Liniang
Zhejiang Xiaobaihua Yue Opera Troupe. Peacock Theatre, London, 23–24 July.
All-female production. Adaptation combining *Coriolanus* and Tang Xianzu's story *The Peony Pavilion*.

CYMBELINE

Shakespeare's Globe Theatre. Sam Wanamaker Playhouse. 2 December 2015–21 April.
www.Shakespearesglobe.com
Director: Sam Yates

Royal Shakespeare Company. Royal Shakespeare Theatre, Stratford-upon-Avon, 29 April–12 August; Barbican Theatre, London, 31 October–23 December.
www.rsc.org.uk
Director: Melly Still
Cymbeline played as a woman.

Venture Wolf Productions. London Theatre, 24–25 May.
http://venturewolf.yolasite.com
Director: James Paul Taylor

Adaptation

Imogen
Shakespeare's Globe Theatre, 17 September–16 October.
www.Shakespearesglobe.com
Director: Matthew Dunster

Modernized version subtitled *William Shakespeare's 'Cymbeline' Renamed and Reclaimed*.

HAMLET

Shakespeare at the Tobacco Factory. Factory Theatre, Bristol, 11 February–30 April; Derby Theatre, Derby, 24–28 May; Northcott Theatre, Exeter, 14–18 June.
www.tobaccofactorytheatres.com
Director: Andrew Hilton
Hamlet: Alan Mahon

Royal Shakespeare Company. Royal Shakespeare Theatre, Stratford-upon-Avon, 12 March–13 August.
www.rsc.org.uk
Director: Simon Godwin
Hamlet: Paapa Essiedu

Shakespeare's Globe Theatre. Globe Theatre, London, 23–24 April.
www.Shakespearesglobe.com
Director: Dominic Dromgoole and Bill Buckhurst
The final performances of the world tour.

Creation Theatre Company. University Parks, Oxford, 13 July–13 August.
www.creationtheatre.co.uk
Director: Gari Jones

Black Theatre Live. Watford Palace Theatre, 15–17 September; and tour to 5 November.
http://blacktheatrelive.co.uk
Director: Jeffery Kissoon
Hamlet: Raphael Sowole
Billed as the first all-black production of *Hamlet* in Britain.

Festival Players Theatre Company. Bread and Roses Theatre, London, 27 September–15 October.
www.thefestivalplayers.co.uk
All-male company.

Adaptation

Hamlet Our Brother
Jack Studio Theatre (previously Brockley Studio Theatre), London, 5–9 April.
www.brockleyjack.co.uk
Playwright: Julia Stubbs Hughes
Director: Timothy Stubbs Hughes
Solo performance from the perspective of Horatio.

Ilissos Theatre. Cockpit Theatre, London, 7–30 April.
Director: Charles Ward
First Quarto version.

Something Rotten – Hamlet's Uncle Gets His Say at Last!
Georgian Theatre Royal, Richmond, 20 April and tour.
Playwright and performer: Robert Cohen
Director: Jenny Rowe
Solo performance from the perspective of Claudius.

Ophelia's Zimmer
Royal Court Theatre and Schaubühne Berlin. Jerwood Theatre, London, 17–21 May.
Playwright: Alice Birch
Director: Katie Mitchell
In German with English subtitles.

Gertrude – The Cry
Theatre N16, London, 12–30 June.
Playwright: Howard Barker
Director: Chris Hislop
Premiered at Elsinore Castle in 2002.

Hamlet in Bed
Pleasance, Edinburgh (part of the Edinburgh Fringe), 3–29 August.
Playwright: Michael Laurence
Director: Lisa Peterson
Two-hander. A writer, obsessed with finding his real mother, persuades an actress out of retirement to play Gertrude to his Hamlet.

Remember Me: Horatio's Hamlet
Somesuch Theatre. Greenside @ Nicolson Square (Venue 209), Edinburgh (part of the Edinburgh Fringe), 15–27 August.
www.somesuchtheatre.com
A cast of two.

Fox and Chips. The Pack and Carriage, 162 Eversholt Street, London, 17 October–13 December.
www.foxandchips.com
Director: Vince Gade
Staged in a pub with Polonius as the bar manager and his pub the venue for Claudius and Gertrude's wedding reception.

Hamlet, Who's There?
Flute Theatre Company (in co-production with English Touring Theatre). Trafalgar Studios, London, 6–31 December.
www.flutetheatre.co.uk
Director and Gertrude: Kelly Hunter
Hamlet: Mark Quartley

Played without an interval with a company of six. Horatio, Rosencrantz, and Guildernstern were cut.

Hamlet Part II
Theatre of Heaven and Hell. The Hen and Chickens Theatre, London, 8–10 December.
Playwright: Perry Pontac
Director: Michael Ward
A sequel.

HENRY IV PART I

Royal Shakespeare Company. Barbican Centre, London, 29 November 2015–24 January.
www.rsc.org.uk
Director: Gregory Doran
Falstaff: Antony Sher
Henry IV: Jasper Britton
Prince Hal: Alex Hassell
Played with *Henry IV Part 2*, *Henry V* and *Richard II*, and billed as *King and Country: Shakespeare's Great Cycle of Kings*.

Donmar Warehouse, King's Cross Theatre, London, 17 November–17 December.
www.donmarwarehouse.com
Director: Phyllida Lloyd
King Henry: Harriet Walter
Revival of the 2014 production. Conflation of Parts 1 and 2.

HENRY IV PART 2

Royal Shakespeare Company. Barbican Centre, London, 29 November 2015–24 January.
www.rsc.org.uk
Director: Gregory Doran
Falstaff: Antony Sher
Henry IV: Jasper Britton
Prince Hal: Alex Hassell
Played with *Henry IV Part 1*, *Henry V* and *Richard II*, and billed as *King and Country: Shakespeare's Great Cycle of Kings*.

Donmar Warehouse. King's Cross Theatre, London, 17 November–17 December.
www.donmarwarehouse.com
Director: Phyllida Lloyd
King Henry: Harriet Walter
Revival of the 2014 production. Conflation of Parts 1 and 2.

PROFESSIONAL SHAKESPEARE PRODUCTIONS

HENRY V

Royal Shakespeare Company. Barbican, London, 7 November 2015–24 January.
www.rsc.org.uk
Director: Gregory Doran
Henry V: Alex Hassell
Played with *Henry IV Part 1*, *Henry IV Part 2* and *Richard II*, and billed as *King and Country: Shakespeare's Great Cycle of Kings*.

Merely Theatre. UK tour 2 February–7 May.
http://merelytheatre.co.uk

Antic Disposition Theatre Company. Middle Temple Hall, London, 26 March–6 April and UK tour to 29 April.
www.anticdisposition.co.uk
Director: Ben Horslen and John Risebero

Regent's Park Open Air Theatre. Regent's Park, London, 17 June–9 July.
http://openairtheatre.com
Director: Robert Hastie
Henry V: Michelle Terry

Adaptation

Kings of War
Toneelgroep Amsterdam. Barbican, London, 22 April–1 May.
http://tga.nl
Adaptors: Bart van den Eynde and Peter van Kraaij
A conflation of *Henry V*, *Henry VI* and *Richard III*.

HENRY VI PARTS 1–3

Omidaze Productions. Millennium Centre, Cardiff, 1–20 February.
www.omidaze.co.uk
Director: Yvonne Murphy
All-female cast of eight.

Kings of War

Toneelgroep Amsterdam. Barbican, London, 22 April–1 May.
http://tga.nl
Adaptors: Bart van den Eynde and Peter van Kraaij
A conflation of *Henry V*, *Henry VI* and *Richard III*.

HENRY VI PART 3

Adaptation

The Barded Ladies. Windmill Hill City Farm, Bristol, 21–24 July.
http://bardedladies.com
Part of Bristol Shakespeare Festival. All-female production featuring King Margaret.

JULIUS CAESAR

Donmar Warehouse. King's Cross Theatre, London, 27 October–17 December.
www.donmarwarehouse.com
Director: Phyllida Lloyd
Brutus: Harriet Walter
Revival of the 2012 production.

KING JOHN

Rose Theatre, Kingston, 13 May–5 June.
www.rosetheatrekingston.org
Director: Trevor Nunn

Worcester Repertory Company. Worcester Cathedral, 18–22 October.
www.worcester-rep.co.uk
Director: Chris Jaeger

KING LEAR

Creation Theatre. The Norrington Room, Blackwell's Bookshop, Oxford, 12 February–19 March.
www.creationtheatre.co.uk
Director: Charlotte Conquest

Talawa Theatre Company. Royal Exchange Theatre, Manchester, 1 April–7 May; Birmingham Repertory Theatre, Birmingham, 19–28 May.
www.talawa.com
Director: Michael Buffong
Lear: Don Warrington

Royal & Derngate Theatre, Northampton, 1–23 April; and tour to 2 July.
www.royalandderngate.co.uk
Director: Max Webster
Lear: Michael Pennington

Maddermarket Theatre, Norwich, 22–30 April.
http://maddermarket.co.uk
Director: Chris Bealey

Bristol Old Vic. Bristol Old Vic, Bristol, 18 June–10 July.
www.bristololdvic.org.uk
Director: Tom Morris
Lear: Timothy West

Royal Shakespeare Company. Royal Shakespeare Theatre, Stratford-upon-Avon, 20 August–15 October; Barbican Centre, London, 10 November–23 December.
www.rsc.org.uk
Director: Gregory Doran
Lear: Antony Sher

The Old Vic Theatre, London, 25 October–3 December.
www.oldvictheatre.com
Director: Deborah Warner
Lear: Glenda Jackson

Bowler Crab. St Mildred's Church, Tenterden, 12 November, and Kent and East Sussex tour to 10 December.
www.bowler-crab.com
Director: Stephen John

Adaptation

The Shadow King
Malthouse Theatre Company. Barbican, London, 22 June–2 July.
http://malthousetheatre.com.au
Playwright and director: Michael Kantor
Set in the Aboriginal community in the Australian outback.

King Lear (Alone)
Inamoment. St Paul's Church, Birmingham, 16 July; and tour to 9 August.
Playwright: Frank Bramwell
One-man version.

Queen Lear
Ronnie Dorsey Productions. Assembly Roxy (Venue 139), Edinburgh 4–15, 17–29 August.
Playwright: Ronnie Dorsey
The back story to Lear's queen, Everilda.

Enter Queen Lear
Drayton Arms Theatre, London, 20 September–2 October.
www.thedraytonarmstheatre.co.uk

Playwright: Timeri N. Murani
Director: Simone Vause
An ageing film star takes on the role of Lear.

Queen Lear
The Phil Willmott Company. Union Theatre, London, 20 September–8 October.
Director and Adaptor: Phil Willmott
Queen Lear: Ursula Mohan
Previously played as *Lear* at the Union Theatre in 2014.

Lear/Cordelia
1623 Theatre Company. Attenborough Arts Centre, Leicester, 14–15 October; Derby Theatre Studio, Derby, 18–19 November.
http://1623theatre.co.uk
Director: Ben Spiller and Louie Ingham
Double-bill. One-act reworking of *King Lear* followed by a new play *Cordelia*.

LOVE'S LABOUR'S LOST

Oxford Shakespeare Company. Wadham College, Oxford, 28 June–18 August.
http://oxfordShakespeare.co
Director: Nicholas Green

Royal Shakespeare Company in collaboration with Chichester Festival Theatre. Chichester Festival Theatre, Chichester, 29 September–29 October; Opera House, Manchester, 23 November–3 December; Theatre Royal Haymarket, London, 9 December–18 March 2017.
www.rsc.org.uk
Director: Christopher Luscombe
Berowne: Edward Bennett

MACBETH

Young Vic and Birmingham Repertory Theatre. Young Vic Main House, London, 26 November 2015–23 January and tour.
www.youngvic.org
Director: Carrie Cracknell and Lucy Guerin
Macbeth: John Heffernan
Lady Macbeth: Anna Maxwell Martin

The Broadway Theatre, London, 27 January–21 February.
www.broadwaytheatre.org.uk
Director: Asia Osborne

Arrows and Traps Theatre Company. New Wimbledon Theatre, London, 15 April–9 July.
www.arrowsandtraps.com
Director: Ross McGregor

Insane Root Theatre Company. The Redcliffe Caves, Bristol (part of the Bristol Shakespeare Festival), 8 June–14 July.
www.insaneroot.co.uk
Promenade production in Redcliffe Caves.

Shakespeare's Globe Theatre, London, 18 June–1 October.
www.Shakespearesglobe.com
Director: Iqbal Khan
Macbeth: Ray Fearon
Lady Macbeth: Tara Fitzgerald
Included a midnight performance on 22 July.

Bard in the Botanics. Botanic Gardens, Glasgow, 15–30 July.
www.bardinthebotanics.co.uk
Director: Gordon Barr
Cast of five.

Fluellen Theatre Company. Swansea Grand Theatre, Swansea, 28–30 September; Lyric Theatre, Carmarthen, 5–6 October; Grand Pavilion, Porthcawl, 7 October.
www.fluellentheatre.co.uk

Adaptation

Macbeth: A Tale of Sound and Fury
6Footstories Theatre Company. The Hope Theatre, London, 2–20 February.
www.6footstories.co.uk
Cast of three.

Macbeth – A Two Man Macbeth
Out of Chaos. Midlands Arts Centre Theatre, Birmingham, 11–13 February.
http://macbirmingham.co.uk
Director: Mike Tweddle
80-minute version delivered by a cast of two.

The Devil Speaks True
Goat and Monkey. The Vaults, London, 17–27 February; and tour to 19 March.
Director: Joel Scott
The story from Banquo's perspective delivered through headphones in a pitch-black space.

The Macbeth Curse
Octagon Theatre Bolton and Prime Theatre. Octagon Theatre, Bolton, 19–23 April.
http://octagonbolton.co.uk
Playwright: Terry Deary
Director: Mark Powell
An Edwardian stage production is plagued by catastrophe.

Oddsocks Theatre. Guildhall Theatre, Derby, 15–18 June; and tour to 27 August.
www.oddsocks.co.uk
Musical version.

Lady Macbeth
South West Dance Theatre Company. Colston Hall Lantern Theatre, Bristol, 3 July.
www.southwestdancetheatre.co.uk
Ballet, street, contemporary dance, Latin, poetry, prose and British Sign Language for the deaf.

Macbeths
Golem Theatre. The Hope Theatre, London, 26 July–3 August.
www.golemtheatre.co.uk
Playwright: David Fairs.
Director: Anna Marsland
Two-hander.

Bob
Gin and Tonic Productions. Above the Arts, Arts Theatre West End, London, 26–30 July; and on tour.
https://ginandtonicproductions.wordpress.com
Director: Elske Waite
Parody loosely based on *Macbeth*. Lady Bob takes over Finland in a coup d'état.

MacBain
Dood Paard. Summerhall (Venue 26), Edinburgh (part of the Edinburgh Fringe), 3–14 August.
http://doodpaard.nl
Contrasting stories of Macbeth and Kurt Cobain and Courtney Love.

Fire Burn: The Tragedy of Macbeth
ImmerCity. The Cockpit, London, 2–5 August; theSpace on the Mile (Venue 39), Edinburgh, 15–27 August.
www.immer-city.com
The story retold by three sisters.

Act Three Theatre. Paradise in the Vault (Venue 29), Edinburgh (part of the Edinburgh Fringe), 5–13 August.
http://actthreetheatre.co.uk
60-minute version set in a young offenders' prison.

Screw Your Courage! (or The Bloody Crown!)
Klahr Thorsen / Frozen Light Theatre. Greenside @ Infirmary Street (Venue 236), Edinburgh (part of the Edinburgh Fringe), 5–27 August.
One-woman show about the struggles to play Lady Macbeth.

Blood Will Have Blood
ImmerCity. C venues–C nova, Edinburgh, 9–29 August.
www.immer-city.com
Director: Rosanna Mallinson
Playwright: Clancy Flynn
From the perspective of Fleance and played to a maximum audience of twelve.

Solo Shakespeare, Macbeth: Hecate's Poison
Players Tokyo. Quaker Meeting House (Venue 40), Edinburgh (part of the Edinburgh Fringe), 16–20 August.
A solo version from the perspective of Hecate.

Splendid Productions. Pleasance Theatre, London, 28 September; and tour to February 2017.
www.splendidproductions.co.uk
60-minute version with a cast of three.

Macbeth – Director's Cut
Volcano Theatre Company. The Riverfront Theatre, Newport, 18–20 October; and tour to 22 November.
www.volcanotheatre.co.uk
Director: Paul Davies and Fern Smith
Cast of two. Revival of 1999 production.

Lady Macbeth: Unsex Me Here
Company Chordelia and Solar Bear. The Tron, Glasgow, 1–2 November.
www.chordelia.co.uk
Director: Kally Lloyd-Jones
Contemporary dance version with a cast of three men, all playing Lady Macbeth. Choreography used British Sign Language and billed as reaching deaf and hearing audiences on different levels.

Scratch: Macbeth
The Paper Cinema Theatre Company. BAC (Battersea Arts Centre), London, 15–17 December.
Billed as a showcase for a developing project. The full production is scheduled for 2018.

Opera

A Terrified Soul – Macbeth
China Anhui Opera Institute. the Space @ Surgeons Hall (Venue 53), Edinburgh, 25–27 August.

A mixture of contemporary and classical Chinese opera elements. Presented in Mandarin (with English subtitles).

Welsh National Opera. Wales Millennium Centre, Cardiff, 10–24 September; and tour to 23 November.
www.wno.org.uk
Composer: Giuseppe Verdi

MEASURE FOR MEASURE

Heady Conduct Theatre. The Rose Playhouse, London, 10–20 May.
http://headyconduct.com
Director: Simon Rodda and Rebecca Rogers

Cheek by Jowl Theatre Company. Royal Lyceum Theatre, Edinburgh, 16–20 August.
www.cheekbyjowl.com
Director: Declan Donnellan
In Russian.

The Questors Theatre Company. Questors Theatre, London, 4–12 November.
www.questors.org.uk

Swan Theatre Company. The Place, Bedford, 8–12 November.
www.swantheatrecompany.co.uk

THE MERCHANT OF VENICE

Shakespeare's Globe. Everyman & Playhouse, Liverpool, 30 June–9 July; Shakespeare's Globe, London, 4–15 October.
www.Shakespearesglobe.com
Director: Jonathan Munby
Shylock: Jonathan Pryce
Revival of the 2015 production.

Canterbury Shakespeare Festival. Greyfriar's Garden, Canterbury, 5–7 August.
www.canterburyShakespeare.co.uk

Adaptation

Shit-Faced Shakespeare: The Merchant of Venice
Magnificent Bastards Production. Southbank Centre, London, 17 June–10 July.
Billed as including one genuinely inebriated actor.

Gratiano
Grist to the Mill Productions. Spotlites (Venue 278), Edinburgh (part of the Edinburgh Fringe), 4–28 August.

www.gristtheatre.co.uk
A new look at the play from Gratiano's perspective. Solo performance.

Shylock
Theatre Tours International. Assembly Roxy (Venue 139), Edinburgh (part of the Edinburgh Fringe), 4–28 August.
Playwright: Gareth Armstrong

Opera

Welsh National Opera. Wales Millennium Centre, Cardiff, 16–30 September; and tour to July 2017.
www.wno.org.uk
Composer: André Tchaikowsky

THE MERRY WIVES OF WINDSOR

Northern Broadsides. UK tour 2 February–28 May.
www.northern-broadsides.co.uk
Director and Falstaff: Barrie Rutter

Guildburys Theatre Company. Minack Theatre, Porthcurno, 22–26 August.
www.guildburys.com

A MIDSUMMER NIGHT'S DREAM

Merely Theatre. Old Joint Stock Theatre, Birmingham, 1 February; and UK tour to 7 May.
http://merelytheatre.co.uk/current-productions
90-minute version.

Royal Shakespeare Company. Royal Shakespeare Theatre, Stratford-upon-Avon, 17 February–5 March; and tour to 17 July.
www.rsc.org.uk
Director: Erica Whyman
A touring production with mechanicals' parts played by local community players. Billed as *A Midsummer Night's Dream: A Play for the Nation*.

Garrick Theatre, Stockport, 12–19 March.
www.stockportgarrick.co.uk

Shakespeare's Globe Theatre, London, 30 April–11 September.
www.Shakespearesglobe.com
Director: Emma Rice
Emma Rice's inaugural production as artistic director.

Dream East Theatre. Brixton East 1871, London, 2–5 May.
http://dreameastcompany.wix.com
Director: Mathew McPherson

Rain or Shine Theatre Company. Tour 4 June–29 August.
www.rainorshine.co.uk

Wolsey Theatre, Ipswich, 16 June–9 July.
www.wolseytheatre.co.uk
Director: Trevor Nunn
Fairies played by local children aged 8 to 13.

Chapterhouse Theatre Company. UK tour 17 June–3 September.
www.chapterhouse.org

Illyria Theatre Company. UK tour 21 June–29 August.
www.illyria.uk.com

Wildcard Theatre. Jack Studio Theatre (previously Brockley Studio Theatre), London, 5–23 July.
http://wildcardtheatre.co.uk

Cambridge Shakespeare Festival. King's College Gardens, Cambridge, 11–30 July.
www.cambridgeShakespeare.com

Theatre Royal, Bath, 3–20 August.
www.theatreroyal.org.uk
Director: Laurence Boswell
Bottom: Phil Jupitus

Adaptation

Pocket Dream
Propeller Theatre Company. Christ Church University, Canterbury, 1–2 February; and tour to 12 March.
http://propeller.org.uk
Director: Edward Hall
60-minute version with all-male cast.

The Lyric Hammersmith and Filter Theatre. Lyric Theatre Hammersmith, London, 20 February–19 March.
http://filtertheatre.com
Director: Sean Holmes and Stef O'Driscoll
Revival of 2012 production. In response to an onstage announcement about a sick actor, a noisy heckler volunteers to play Bottom.

Titania – A Solo Cabaret
Greenwich Theatre, London, 22–24 March.
Performer: Anna-Helena McLean

The Play's The Thing
Attic Door Productions. The Midlands Hotel, Morecambe, 23 April.
www.bardbythebeach.co.uk
Part of Bard by the Beach, Morecambe Shakespeare Festival.

Go People and Glass Half Full Productions. Southwark Playhouse, London, 31 May–1 July.
Director: Simon Evans
Madcap comedy performance as an undercast production struggles to cover all seventeen roles.

Shit-faced Shakespeare – A Midsummer Night's Dream
Magnificent Bastards Productions. Leicester Square Theatre, London, 26 April–11 June; Southbank Centre, London, 17 June–10 July.
Director: Lewis Ironside
Billed as having one genuinely inebriated actor.

The Donkey Show – A Midsummer Night's Disco
Proud Camden, London, 9 June–21 August.
http://donkeyshowlondon.com
Set under a glitterball to a disco soundtrack.

To Dream Again
Theatr Emlyn Williams and Polka Theatre. Theatr Clwyd, Mold, 18 June–2 July.
www.theatrclwyd.com
Playwright: Toby Hulse
Director: John Young
A new play featuring Sophie, daughter of Demetrius and Helena.

CandleFire Productions. Waterloo East Theatre, London, 12–23 July.
Director: Joshua Jewkes

Robin Goodfellow's Amazing Travelling Show
Umbrella Arts. Penlee Park Open Air Theatre, Penzance, 24 July.
Performer: John Brolly
The story retold by Puck.

Ballet

The Dream
Birmingham Royal Ballet. Birmingham Hippodrome, Birmingham, 17–20 February.
www.brb.org.uk
Composer: Felix Mendelssohn
Choreography: Frederick Ashton

Opera

Surrey Opera. Minack Theatre, Porthcurno, 18–22 July; and tour.
www.surreyopera.org
Composer: Benjamin Britten

Glyndebourne Opera Company. Glyndebourne Theatre, Lewes, 11–28 August. www.glyndebourne.com
Composer: Benjamin Britten
Director: Peter Hall

MUCH ADO ABOUT NOTHING

Queen's Theatre, Hornchurch, 4–26 March.
www.queens-theatre.co.uk
Director: Douglas Rintoul

Wolf-Sister Productions. The Rose Playhouse, London, 5–29 April.
www.rosetheatre.org.uk

Dundee Rep Ensemble. Dundee Repertory Theatre, Dundee, 9–25 June.
www.dundeerep.co.uk
Director: Irene Macdougall

Theatr Clwyd, Mold, 9 June–2 July.
www.theatrclwyd.com
Director: Tamara Harvey

Fox and Chips. The Pack and Carriage, 162 Eversholt Street, London, 12 June–26 July.
www.foxandchips.com
Director: Vince Gill

Iris Theatre Company. St Paul's Church (The Actors Church), London, 22 June–22 July.
http://iristheatre.com
Director: Amy Draper

Lord Chamberlain's Men. UK tour 1 July–4 September.
www.tlcm.co.uk
Director: Peter Stickney
All-male production.

Guildford Shakespeare Company. University of Law Grounds, Guildford, 15–30 July.
www.guildford-Shakespeare-company.co.uk

The Handlebards. Assembly @ Royal Botanic Garden Edinburgh: West Gate, 6–27 August.
www.handlebards.com
A company that cycles between venues.

Sudden Impulse Theatre Company. Greenside @ Royal Terrace (Venue 231), Edinburgh, 15–20 August; and tour.
www.suddenimpulse.co.uk
Director: Simon Winterman

The Faction. The Refashioned Theatre, Selfridges & Co., London, 23 August–24 September.
www.thefaction.org.uk
Director: Mark Leipacher and Rachel Smith
Performed on a pop-up stage inside Selfridges shop.

Royal Shakespeare Company in collaboration with Chichester Festival Theatre. Chichester Festival Theatre, Chichester, 24 September–29 October; Opera House, Manchester, 25 November–3 December; Theatre Royal Haymarket, London, 9 December–18 March 2017.
www.rsc.org.uk
Director: Christopher Luscombe
Billed as *Love's Labour's Won or Much Ado About Nothing*.

Mercury Theatre, Colchester. 30 September–15 October.
www.mercurytheatre.co.uk
Director: Pia Furtado

Adaptation

Shit-Faced Shakespeare – Much Ado About Nothing
Magnificent Bastards Productions. Leicester Square Theatre, London, 11 April–16 September.
Billed as including one genuinely inebriated actor.

Oddsocks. Belgrade Theatre, Coventry, 21–23 June; and UK tour to 28 July.
www.oddsocks.co.uk
Musical version.

MadCap Theatre Productions. UK tour 1 July–14 August.
www.madcaptheatreproductions.co.uk

Opera

Béatrice et Bénédict
London Philharmonic Orchestra. Glyndebourne Theatre, Lewes, 23 July–27 August.
www.glyndebourne.com
Composer: Hector Berlioz

OTHELLO

Adaptation

Othello's Guilt, A Monologue from William Shakespeare

Calatafimi Segesta Festival. The Rose Theatre, London, 20 September–1 October.
www.calatafimisegestafestival.it
Performer: Marco Gambino
Monologue.

PERICLES

Shakespeare's Globe. Sam Wanamaker Playhouse, London, 19 November 2015–21 April.
www.Shakespearesglobe.com
Director: Dominic Dromgoole
Pericles: James Garnon
Gower: Sheila Reid

RICHARD II

Royal Shakespeare Company. Barbican, London, 7–10 January.
www.barbican.org.uk
Director: Gregory Doran
Richard II: David Tennant
Played with *Henry IV Part 1*, *Henry IV Part 2* and *Henry V*, and billed as *King and Country: Shakespeare's Great Cycle of Kings*.

Dippermouth Productions in assoc. with Arcola Theatre. Members Dining Room, House of Commons, 23 April; Arcola Theatre, London, 3–7 May.
www.arcolatheatre.com
Director: Jack Gamble and Quentin Beroud
Reported as the first Shakespeare performance in the Palace of Westminster.

Adaptation

Hip Hop Shakespeare Company. O2 Academy, Oxford, 29 April.

RICHARD III

The Faction. The New Diorama Theatre, London, 5 January–6 February.
www.thefaction.org.uk
Director: Mark Leipacher
Richard III: Christopher York

Almeida Theatre, London. 7 June–6 August.
www.almeida.co.uk

353

Director: Rupert Goold
Richard: Ralph Fiennes
Queen Margaret: Vanessa Redgrave
A prologue recreated the 2012 Leicester archaeological
dig that unearthed Richard's bones.

The Handlebards. @ Assembly Royal Botanic Garden
Edinburgh: West Gate (Venue 370), Edinburgh (part of
the Edinburgh Fringe), 5–19 August.
www.handlebards.com
A company that cycles between venues.

Schaubühne Theatre Company (Berlin). Royal Lyceum
Theatre, Edinburgh, 24–28 August.
www.schaubuehne.de
Director: Thomas Ostermeier
Richard III: Lars Eidinger

Adaptation

Kings of War
Toneelgroep Amsterdam. Barbican, London, 22 April–1
May.
http://tga.nl
Adaptors: Bart van den Eynde and Peter van Kraaij
A conflation of *Henry V*, *Henry VI* and *Richard III*.

Brite Theater. The Lion and Unicorn Theatre, London,
16–28 May; and tour.
www.lionandunicorntheatre.co.uk
Directors: Kolbrun Bjort Sigfusdottir and Emily Carding
A one-woman show.

My Kingdom for a Horse?
Everyman Theatre, Cheltenham, 13–14 July.
Performer: Richard Derrington
One-man show on the historical figure of *Richard III*.

ROMEO AND JULIET

Blue Orange Theatre, Birmingham, 4–13 February.
www.blueorangetheatre.co.uk
Cast of six.

The Watermill Theatre, Newbury, 25 February–2 April.
www.watermill.org.uk
Director: Paul Hart

Brentwood Shakespeare Company. Brentwood Theatre,
Brentwood, 20–23 April.
www.brentwood-theatre.co.uk
Kenneth Branagh Theatre Company. Garrick Theatre,
London, 12 May–13 August.

Directors: Kenneth Branagh and Rob Ashford
Romeo: Richard Madden
Juliet: Lily James
Mercutio: Derek Jacobi

Tower Theatre Company. Theatro Technis, London,
24–28 May.
www.towertheatre.org.uk
Director: Penny Tuerk

Taking Flight Theatre Company, UK tour 16 June–29
July.
www.takingflighttheatre.co.uk
All performances accompanied by British Sign Language.

GB Theatre Company. Appleby Castle, Appleby-in-
Westmorland, Cumbria, 24–26 June; and UK tour to
27 August.
www.gbtheatrecompany.com

Civil Brawl Theatre Company. The Old Slaughterhouse,
Stratford-upon-Avon, 18 July; Methodist Church Hall,
Stratford-upon-Avon, 21–23 July.
Director: Richard Nunn
Cast of eight.

The Handlebards. Assembly @ Royal Botanic Garden
Edinburgh, Edinburgh, 21–28 August.
www.handlebards.com
A company that cycles between venues.

Isle of Wight Shakespeare Company. Ryde Methodist
Church, 3–4 September.

Adaptation

Rubbish Shakespeare Company. Library, Morecambe,
23 April.
www.rubbishShakespearecompany.com
60-minute comic version mixing improvised dialogue
with Shakespeare's text.

National Youth Theatre of Wales and Frantic Assembly.
Teatr Anthony Hopkins, Teatr Clwyd, Mold,
6 September; New Theatre, Cardiff, 9–10 September.
www.franticassembly.co.uk

The Pantaloons Theatre Company. The Regal Theatre,
Minehead, 5 October; and tour to 5 November.
http://thepantaloons.co.uk
Comic version.

Wolf-Sister Productions and Pepe Pryke. The Rose
Playhouse, London, 15 November–10 December.
www.rosetheatre.org.uk

PROFESSIONAL SHAKESPEARE PRODUCTIONS

Ballet

Birmingham Royal Ballet. Birmingham Hippodrome, Birmingham, 24–27 February; and tour to 16 April.
www.brb.org.uk
Choreographer: Kenneth MacMillan

Northern Ballet. Lyceum Theatre, Sheffield, 14–17 September; and tour to 15 October.
http://northernballet.com
Choreographer: Jean-Christophe Maillot

Ballet Cymru. The Riverfront, Newport, 4–5 November; McMillan Theatre, Bridgewater, 11 November.
http://welshballet.co.uk
Choreographer: Darius James and Amy Doughty

Opera

I Capuleti e i Montecchi
Pop-Up Opera. The Vaults, London, 21 March; and tour to 5 May.
http://popupopera.co.uk
Composer: Vincenzo Bellini
Director: James Hurley

THE TAMING OF THE SHREW

Shakespeare's Globe Theatre, London, 13 May–6 August.
www.Shakespearesglobe.com
Director: Caroline Byrne
Midnight performance 1 July.

Adaptation

Custom/Practice. Arts Theatre, London, 5 April–1 May.
www.custompractice.co.uk
Reverses the gender of every character.

EDP (Korea). C venues – C South (Venue 58), Edinburgh (part of the Edinburgh Fringe), 14–20 August.
Fusion of hip hop dance and traditional Korean theatre.

The Handlebards. Assembly @ Royal Botanic Garden Edinburgh, Edinburgh, 23–27 August.
www.handlebards.com

A company that cycles between venues.

Kiss Me Kate
Welsh National Opera Company / Opera North. UK tour 29 September–10 December.
www.wno.org.uk
Director: Jo Davies

Ballet

Birmingham Royal Ballet. Birmingham Hippodrome, Birmingham, 16–18 June.
www.brb.org.uk
Choreographer: John Cranko

Bolshoi Ballet. Royal Opera House, London, 3–4 August.
Choreographer: Jean-Christophe Maillot

THE TEMPEST

Shakespeare's Globe. Sam Wanamaker Playhouse, London, 17 February–22 April.
www.Shakespearesglobe.com
Director: Dominic Dromgoole
Prospero: Tim McMullan
Dromgoole's final production after eleven years as artistic director.

PerformInternational. Rudolf Steiner House, London, 22 April.
Director: Geoffrey Norris

Attic Door Productions. Winter Gardens, Morecambe, 22–23 April.
www.bardbythebeach.co.uk
Part of Bard by the Beach, Morecambe Shakespeare Festival.

Quantum Theatre. UK tour 19 June–1 September
www.quantumtheatre.co.uk

Cambridge Shakespeare Festival. St John's College Gardens, Cambridge, 11–30 July.
www.cambridgeShakespeare.com

Flute Theatre. Southbank Centre, London, 29–31 July; Orange Tree Theatre, London, 25 October–4 November.
www.flutetheatre.co.uk
Director: Kelly Hunter
Specifically designed for children with autism or other special needs, and their families.

Red Rose Chain. Jimmy's Farm, Ipswich, 29 July–28 August.
Director: Joanna Carrick
Cast of five.

Donmar Warehouse. King's Cross Theatre, London, 23 September–17 December.
www.donmarwarehouse.com
Director: Phyllida Lloyd
Prospero: Harriet Walter

Thick as Thieves Theatre Company. Tacchi-Morris Arts Centre, Taunton, 27 September; and tour to 7 October.
Director: Nicky Diss

Scrawny Cat Theatre Company. The Rose Playhouse, London, 18 October–12 November.
www.rosetheatre.org.uk

Royal Shakespeare Company. Royal Shakespeare Theatre, Stratford-upon-Avon, 8 November–21 January 2017.
www.rsc.org.uk
Director: Gregory Doran
Prospero: Simon Russell Beale

Fluellen Theatre Company. Swansea Grand Theatre, Swansea, 9–11 November.
www.fluellentheatre.co.uk

The Print Room at the Coronet, London, 21 November–17 December.
www.the-print-room.org
Director: Simon Usher

Adaptation

Mirando the Gay Tempest
Theatre North Company. Jermyn Street Theatre, London, 14 February; Lion and the Unicorn Theatre, London, 23 February–5 March.
http://theatrenorth.co.uk
Playwright: Martin Lewton
One-man show with Mirando as Prospero's son.

The Tempest in a Teacup
Umbrella Arts Theatre Company. Minack Theatre, Porthcurno, 17 February; and tour.
www.umbrellaarts.co.uk
Storytelling.

Return to the Forbidden Planet
Romiley Operatic Society. Plaza Theatre, Stockport, 15–19 March.
http://romileyoperatic.co.uk

This Last Tempest

Uninvited Guests Theatre Company. Battersea Arts Centre (BAC), London, 22–24 March.
www.uninvited-guests.net
Sequel featuring Ariel and Caliban.

Sound Affairs. Malvern Theatres, Malvern, 4 May; and tour to 2 December.
www.soundaffairs.co.uk
Musical adaptation.

Royal & Derngate Theatre and The National Youth Theatre. Royal & Derngate Theatre, Northampton, 23 June–2 July.
www.royalandderngate.co.uk
Director: Caroline Steinbeis
Prospero becomes Prosper, older sister to Miranda.

The Young Shakespeare Company. Millfield Arts Centre, London, 7–11 November; Blackpool Grand Theatre, Blackpool, 2–4 March 2017.
http://youngShakespeare.org.uk
90-minute production for primary-school audience.

The Salon Collective. The Cockpit Theatre, London, 11 December–15 January 2017.
http://thesaloncollective.org
Rehearsed with cue scripts to replicate Elizabethan theatre companies.

Ballet

Birmingham Royal Ballet. Empire Theatre, Sunderland, 20–22 October.
www.brb.org.uk
Choreography: David Bintley

TIMON OF ATHENS

Adaptation

Rendered Retina. Theatre Arts Exchange (Venue 116), Edinburgh, 8–13 August.
http://retinatheatre.com
Cast of three.

TITUS ANDRONICUS

Luvas Theatre and Time Zone Theatre. The Rose Theatre, London, 5–29 July.

www.rosetheatre.org.uk
Director: Jung Han Kim

TROILUS AND CRESSIDA

Adaptation

To The Elephant. The Rose Playhouse, London, 5–15 October.
www.rosetheatre.org.uk
75-minute version.

TWELFTH NIGHT

Scena Mundi. The French Protestant Church, Soho Square, London, 22 March–9 April.
www.scenamundi.co.uk

Thick as Thieves Theatre Company. The Hope Theatre, London, 12–30 April.
Director: Nicky Diss
Cast of four.

The Questors Theatre Company. Questors Theatre, London, 20–30 April.
www.questors.org.uk

Grassroots Shakespeare London. Leicester Square Theatre, London, 5–14 May.
www.grassrootsShakespearelondon.com
Viola: Ellie Nunn

Bard in the Botanics. Botanic Gardens, Glasgow, 22 June–9 July.
www.bardinthebotanics.co.uk
Director: Jennifer Dick

Cambridge Shakespeare Festival. Downing College Gardens, Cambridge, 11–30 July.
www.cambridgeShakespeare.com

Canterbury Shakespeare Festival. Canterbury Tales, St Margaret's Street, Canterbury, 12–14 August.
www.canterburyshakespeare.co.uk

Isle of Wight Shakespeare Company. Shorwell Village Hall, 26–27 August.

Adaptation

Kings Cross Theatre, London, 5 January.

One-night-only charity event with a cast of twelve comedians.

I, Malvolio
Orange Tree Theatre, London, 25 February.
Playwright: Tim Crouch
Director: Karl James and Andy Smith
One-man show from Malvolio's perspective.

Playing Shakespeare with Deutsche Bank
The Globe Theatre, London, 12–19 March.
www.Shakespearesglobe.com
A Globe Education project for younger audiences.

Filter Theatre Company. Clwyd Theatr Cymru, Mold, 29 March–2 April; and tour to 21 May.
www.filtertheatre.com
Director: Sean Holmes
Loose adaptation concentrating on knockabout comedy.

12 Nights
Manchester Shakespeare Company. Winter Gardens, Morecambe, 22 April.
www.bardbythebeach.co.uk
Part of Bard by the Beach, Morecambe Shakespeare Festival.
Playwrights and Directors: John Topliff and Gina T. Frost
Set in a farcical future with Jamie Oliver as Prime Minister of the Former United Kingdom which has rebuilt Hadrian's Wall and closed the Channel Tunnel.

Shake
Eat a Crocodile Theatre Company. Royal Lyceum Theatre, Edinburgh, 11–13 August.
Director: Dan Jemmett
Seaside resort adaptation with a cast of five.

THE TWO GENTLEMEN OF VERONA

Shakespeare's Globe and Liverpool Everyman & Playhouse. UK tour 20 May–29 October.
www.Shakespearesglobe.com
Director: Nick Bagnall

THE TWO NOBLE KINSMEN

Royal Shakespeare Company. Swan Theatre, Stratford-upon-Avon, 17 August–7 February 2017.
www.rsc.org.uk

Director: Blanche McIntyre
A production marking the thirtieth anniversary of the
Swan Theatre.

THE WINTER'S TALE

Kenneth Branagh Theatre Company. Garrick Theatre,
London, 17 October 2015–16 January.
Directors: Rob Ashford and Kenneth Branagh
Leontes: Kenneth Branagh
Paulina: Judi Dench

Shakespeare's Globe. Sam Wanamaker Playhouse,
London, 28 January–22 April.
www.Shakespearesglobe.com
Director: Michael Longhurst

Guildford Shakespeare Company. Holy Trinity Church,
Guildford, 8–27 February.
www.guildford-Shakespeare-company.co.uk

Cambridge Shakespeare Festival. Robinson College
Gardens, Cambridge, 1–27 August.
www.cambridgeShakespeare.com

Octagon Theatre Bolton and University of Bolton.
Octagon Theatre, Bolton, 21 October–5 November.
www.octagonbolton.co.uk
Director: David Thacker

Adaptation

Moving Stories. Minack Theatre, Porthcurno, 11–15 July.
www.movingstories.org.uk
Director: Emma Gersch
Mamillius represented by a puppet.

The Hermes Experiment. Cockpit Theatre, London,
13 December.
Director: Nina Brazier
The Hermes Experiment musical quartet join a group of
actors in a 60-minute version.

Ballet

The Royal Ballet. The Royal Opera House, London,
12 April–7 June.
www.roh.org.uk
Composer: Joby Talbot
Choreographer: Christopher Wheeldon

POEMS AND APOCRYPHA

The Mystery of the Sonnets

King's Arms Players and The Children of the Midnight
Chimes. Fusion Arts, East Oxford Community Centre,
30 April.
A selection of sonnets with a musical soundtrack.

Venus and Adonis

Fake Escape. We Are: Proud in partnership with the
Bristol Shakespeare Festival. The Wardrobe Theatre,
Bristol, 6 July.
www.fakeescape.com
Director: David Shopland
All-male company.

At War with Love

Chiaroscuro Theatre. Greenside at Nicolson Square,
Edinburgh Fringe Festival, 8–20 August.
www.chiaroscurotheatre.com
Director: Gail Sawyer
Adaptation of the sonnets.

MISCELLANEOUS
(IN ALPHABETICAL ORDER)

Analyse Thou

Ruff Trade. The Cellar, Oxford, 23–24 April.
Counselling sessions with Shakespeare characters.

Bardolph's Box

Up The Road Theatre, UK tour 1 March–3 April.
www.uptheroadtheatre.co.uk
Shakespeare's stories adapted for ages 8–12.

Best Intentions

Shark Eat Muffin Theatre Company. Mint Studio,
Edinburgh Fringe Festival, 8–13 August; and on tour.
www.sharkeatmuffin.com
Playwright: Catie O'Keefe

Based on female characters from *Othello* and *Romeo and Juliet*.

The Complete Deaths

Spymonkey. Theatre Royal, Brighton, 11–15 May.
Playwright: Tim Crouch
Comedy depicting all seventy-five onstage deaths.

The Complete Works: Table Top Shakespeare

Forced Entertainment. The Pit, Barbican, London, 3–6 March.
www.forcedentertainment.com
Director: Tim Etchells
King John: Potato Masher
Rosalind: Shampoo Bottle
The complete works played out over six days with rotating solo performers. A single table serves as the stage, with the characters portrayed by kitchen utensils and household objects.

The Complete Works of William Shakespeare (Abridged)

The Reduced Shakespeare Company. Playhouse Theatre, Salisbury, 15 January; Playhouse Theatre, Nottingham, 28 January.
www.reducedShakespeare.com

Dedication – Shakespeare and Southampton

Nuffield Theatre Southampton, 9 September–8 October.
www.nuffieldtheatre.co.uk
Playwright: Nick Dear
Director: Sam Hodges
New drama exploring the relationship between Shakespeare and Henry Wriothesley.

Digging for Shakespeare

R.I.P.E. Roedale Allotments, 7–22 May.
Playwright: Marc Rees
Promenade piece charting the story of James Orchard Halliwell-Phillipps.

Ellen Terry with Eileen Atkins

Sam Wanamaker Playhouse, London, 11 January–13 February.
Playwright and Performer: Eileen Atkins
Revival of 2014 production.

The Female Question

Z Theatre Company. the Space @ Surgeons Hall (Venue 53), Edinburgh (part of the Edinburgh Fringe), 8–18 August.
An elderly Shakespeare, with the help of his younger self, looks back on how he portrayed female characters.

A Fool's Paradise

Valiant Flea Productions. Venue 13, Edinburgh (part of the Edinburgh Fringe), 6–12 August.
Thirty Shakespeare scenes in 60 minutes.

The Herbal Bed

English Touring Theatre and Rose Theatre Kingston, UK tour 5 February–7 May.
www.ett.org.uk
Playwright: Peter Whelan
Director: James Dacre

Impromptu Shakespeare

KPS Productions and Get Lost & Found. Just the Tonic at the Caves (Venue 88), Edinburgh (part of the Edinburgh Fringe), 4–28 August.
A completely improvised Shakespeare play inspired by audience suggestions.

Lady Shakespeare

WhoareyouWilliam Company. Paradise in the Vault (Venue 29), Edinburgh (part of the Edinburgh Fringe), 15–28 August.

Love's Labour's Won

Avaunt Theatre Company. The Willow Globe, Powys, 6 July; and tour to 28 July.
Playwright: Ryan J. W. Smith

Director: Katie Harris
A modern love story billed as written in Shakespearian style.

Love's Labour's Wonne

Riverside Drama Company. Duchess Theatre, Long Eaton, 3–5 November.
Playwright: Liz Turner
A modern love story visited by the ghost of Shakespeare.

Red Velvet

Garrick Theatre, London, 23 January–27 February. Revival of 2012 Tricycle Theatre production.
Playwright: Lolita Chakrabarti
Director: Rob Ashford
Ira Aldridge: Adrian Lester

R.I.P. Mr. Shakespeare

Hand-In-Hand Theatre. Treasure House Theatre, the World Museum, Liverpool, 10 April; and tour.
www.handinhandtheatreproductions.co.uk
April 1616 and a company of clowns pay homage to Shakespeare.

Scottish Falsetto Sock Puppets Do Shakespeare

Scottish Falsetto Sock Puppet Theatre. Edinburgh Festival Fringe, Gilded Balloon Teviot, Edinburgh, 3–28 August.
Puppet show featuring selections from Shakespeare.

The Second Best Bed

Square Chapel Arts Centre, Halifax, 22 January.
Playwright: Avril Rowland
One-woman show from the perspective of Anne Hathaway. First performed at the Swan Theatre Worcester in 2012.

Shakespeare 400

Clwyd Theatr Cymru, Mold, 3 June.
www.theatrclwyd.com

A selection of songs, sonnets, speeches, and scenes.

Shakespeare, His Wife and The Dog

Bated Breath Theatre Company. Mercury Theatre, Colchester, 16–18 November; Birmingham Repertory Theatre, Birmingham, 21–23 November.
www.batedbreaththeatre.org
Playwright: Philip Whitchurch
Director: Julia St John
Shakespeare in his retirement at Stratford.

Shakespeare Dream Bill

Birmingham Royal Ballet. Theatre Royal, York, 13–14 May; The Lowry, Salford, 15–17 September; Theatre Royal, Plymouth, 25–26 October.
Including Wink (Sonnets), Romeo and Juliet, The Dream, The Taming of the Shrew, and The Moor's Pavane.

Shakespeare Multi-room Murder Mystery

After Dark Murder Mystery Events. Library, Morecambe, 24 April.
www.bardbythebeach.co.uk
Part of Bard by the Beach, Morecambe Shakespeare Festival.

Shakespeare Mus'd

The Rose Playhouse, London, 7 March.
Playwright: Mark Irvine

The Shakespeare Revue

Kenny Wax Ltd, Cambridge Arts Theatre, 9–20 August; and tour to 3 December.
Director: Malcolm McKee
First performed by the RSC in 1994.

Shakespeare Show

Royal Shakespeare Company. Royal Shakespeare Theatre, Stratford-upon-Avon, 23 April.
Director: Gregory Doran
Broadcast live on BBC 2 and to cinemas around the world.

PROFESSIONAL SHAKESPEARE PRODUCTIONS

The Shakespeare Slam

The Fish90 Production Company. Winter Gardens, Morecambe, 24 April.
www.bardbythebeach.co.uk
Part of Bard by the Beach, Morecambe Shakespeare Festival. Performance poets delivering a poem or speech in a slam poetry style.

Shakespeare Tonight

Cheeky Productions. Paradise in Augustines (Venue 152), Edinburgh (part of the Edinburgh Fringe), 22–27 August.
Set at the time of *Hamlet*'s first performance.

Shakespeare Untold

Shakespeare's Globe and Seabright Productions. Camberley Theatre, Camberley, 4 March.
Playwrights: Harper Ray and Adam Sibbald
A double bill: *Romeo Untold* from the perspective of the Capulet ball's party planner; *Titus Untold* from the view of Titus's piemaker.

Shakin' Shakespeare

Captivate Theatre. Edinburgh Festival Fringe, Gilded Balloon at the Museum, Edinburgh, 19–28 August.
www.captivatetheatre.com
Adaptation for children featuring 'Brave Macbeth', 'Romantic Romeo', and 'Cheer Up, Hamlet!'

Will and Anne

Manchester Shakespeare Company. Three Minute Theatre, 21–24 April.
Playwright: John Topliff
Present-day setting with Shakespeare as a successful television writer.

William Shakespeare's Long Lost First Play (Abridged)

Reduced Shakespeare Company. UK tour 3 August–25 May 2017.
www.reducedShakespeare.com
Performance of a 'new' work discovered in a Leicester car park.

1. CRITICAL STUDIES
reviewed by CHARLOTTE SCOTT

JEWELL'S BOX AND THE BODILY TURN

In September 2017, the Royal Shakespeare Company held a jumble sale to sell over 10,000 items from its wardrobe – from crinoline cloaks, ball gowns, fairy wings to pig suits; hundreds of people queued up to buy when the doors opened. According to the *New York Times*'s coverage, 'theatre history was for sale'. This was a veritable jewel box which told the history of the great theatre's evolution and its surviving material worlds. In Evelyn Tribble's *Early Modern Actors and Shakespeare's Theatre: Thinking with the Body*, another form of theatre history is offered for sale. Beginning with the mysterious box of Simon Jewell, a sharer in the Queen's Men, who bequeathed 'all my playing things in a box and my black velvet shoes' to Robert Nicholls, Tribble sets out her project as one in search of what might have been in that box – both literally and figuratively – and what such objects might reveal about the early modern actor, 'their experience, their training, the past roles that they have played, the physical and mental preparations, as well as specialised knowledge'. For the great many people who queued all night for costumes in Stratford-Upon-Avon, a similar endeavour was at stake: the quest not only for knowledge of the past, the theatre and those who inhabited the now-discarded clothes and objects but also for the traces of the actors themselves. Patrick Stewart, who covered the event for the BBC, coveted a modern-day grey suit worn by his late friend and colleague, Tim Pigott-Smith. This was the stuff from which dreams were made, and everybody wanted what was left of the melted illusions. Tribble is less sentimental and more forensic in her imaginative reconstruction of that box, because it becomes a symbolic storehouse for the actor's craft. Central to Tribble's project is an exploration of the physical body of the actor, not just beneath or inhabiting their costumes but the specific skills learned and developed in performance, all of which demand both agility and precision. Tribble reveals the extent to which models of cognition were embedded in 'physical, social and material smart structures'. This approach, which she calls 'thinking with the body' enables Tribble to 'take account of complex interactions' between the body and its environment to 'ask how skill is inculcated, appraised, transmitted, valued, and evaluated'. Drawing on a range of theoretical models, Tribble emphasizes the importance of voluntary skill and engagement in the development of the body in social context. Attending to different forms of expertise and their treatment in social as well as cultural contexts, Tribble analyses the performative body as skill on display. Exploring a range of plays and playwrights, her focus is less on the literary status of texts and more on the ways in which the plays reveal, allude to and animate the moving body. Over the course of the book, she examines the 'art of action', including gesture, gait and posture; the theatrical displays of martial combat, including fencing and the social implications of 'draw', 'stand' and 'strike'; dancing, grace and the 'fantasma' of a state between dream and waking, in which dance can become a powerful liminal state between noise and silence, transitional and transformative. Many of the terms that Tribble uses to describe both early modern and theoretical responses to the moving body are networked to feeling and imagination. Terms such as 'enthral', 'entrance', 'charm' and 'bewitch' follow many of the experiences that she describes of the body in action. Most compellingly, however, Tribble demonstrates the deeply embedded structures of interpretation that attend on the actor's body, so that we learn to read movement beyond the synthetic assemblies of gesture towards a much more nuanced and complex – kinaesthetic – dynamic between body and environment. Many of these readings are informed by early modern attitudes to the body – medical, philosophical, humoral, performative and skill-based – but they are also accompanied by sophisticated applications of theories of cognition and movement, the poetics of space and Bourdieu's *habitus*. *Early Modern Actors and Shakespeare's Theatre* is a fine assimilation and development of much of the best work on this subject and Tribble's ability to animate the text visually and performatively makes it a brilliant contribution to the way we think about the art of performance, on- and off-stage.

The Oxford Handbook of Shakespeare and Embodiment, edited by Valerie Traub, provides a range of incisive and varied attitudes to the concept of embodiment. A fashionable term in current criticism, the word has been conventionally used to explore the relationship between body and text, with a particular focus on performance. The diversity of recent theoretical work has supported the mobilizing of terms usually associated with psychology, phenomenology and cognition to take shape across a wide range of interpretations, manifestations and texts. In this collection, the idea of embodiment extends beyond the corporeal to an exploration of how abstract ideas emerge and are given form across the plays. Traub's introduction situates the book within the context of revitalizing some of the major preoccupations of feminist studies, which she believes have been neglected by an 'ambivalent academic institutionalization' of the subject. To that end, feminist studies converges with other approaches through a shared belief in the interrogation of identities, both early and modern. The 'current state of incoherence regarding feminism in Shakespeare' is, for Traub, a productive place from which to begin to address the subject in a 'post' environment of critical complacency where the subject itself needs some redefining. Traub provides an extremely helpful introduction to each section, in which she surveys the critical fields as well as situating the various essays within their traditions and divergences. The focus on feminism shows how it can intersect, at each level, with multiple interests and approaches. The prevailing argument is that ideas of embodiment bring together a vast range of approaches which allow the body and the subject to be explored as 'transformative' and 'transitive' agencies – collective, individual, material and esoteric. The book is divided into sections which loosely correspond to subjects (including biography), historical contexts, race, sexuality, bodies (animal and human, imagined and manifest), the material text, and performativity. The eclectic and copious range of the essays is corralled by Traub's subsections which regroup the essays according to genre. The first essay, by Lena Orlin, addresses Anne Hathaway and her 'unstable' identity in biographies of Shakespeare, as well as the 'myth of ... marital misery'. Addressing a range of archival evidence, Orlin shows the instability and potential inaccuracy in the recording of not only which Anne (or indeed Joan or Agnes) Shakespeare did marry but how he felt about her. Returning to the thorny subject of the second-best bed, Orlin examines Shakespeare's will in the contexts of its revisions during the period in which he was attempting to secure a living for Judith following her marriage to Thomas Quiney. She also makes the very strong case that Anne did not contest the will nor did she invoke her 'dower' rights. Equally sensitive to the discrepancies between official law and lived practice, Orlin attends to the commonly held view that Shakespeare and Anne were socially compelled to marry because she was pregnant, and that the marriage was a stricture rather than a celebration: 'the marriage may not have been one from which Shakespeare had to break free but instead the means by which he was able to break free'. Orlin's revisionism defines many of the best essays in this collection, which seek to read existing evidence in new ways. Alan Stewart picks up this approach in a shrewd and witty essay on the 'undocumented' lives of Shakespeare, by which he means the (surprisingly) large amount of seventeenth-century references which, because they do not tally with the creative impulses of the works, tend to be undeveloped in the prevailing narratives of Shakespeare's life. Returning to the remarks of John Manningham, Ben Jonson, Charles Gildon, Nicholas L'Estrange and Thomas Fuller, for example, Stewart weaves a compassionate and compelling story of layers, in which Shakespeare is dressed not by the patriarchal institutional impulses of 'documentary fact' but by the 'homosocial conviviality' of 'table-talk, chamber-talk and tavern-talk', as a worthy and rivalrous 'man of the theatre'. The attention to gender continues through the second part of the collection, which addresses the physical and socio-political lives of women. Bernadette Andrea's essay explores the complexities of female agency through a focus on Islamic women living in subordination in London and 'their neglected, albeit constitutive role in its literature', while Stephen Speiss attends to the different representations of the gendered body of Jeanne la Pucelle as both Joan of Arc and Joan de Puzel. Developing the tensions between the female body and power, Susan Frye explores the temporality of the female body, while Wendy Wall examines 'recipe cultures of knowledge' as both culinary and philosophical transactions. Subsequent sections

deal with broader questions of identity through a wide-ranging focus on ethnicity and racialism. In this section, M. Lindsay Kaplan explores the physical and spiritual power relations between Christians and Jews, images of subordination and physical barriers, while Ian Smith provides a lucid essay on the materiality of early modern performances of race in 'shadowed livery' and the 'conceptual and commercial conditions for the emergence of a dehumanized subjectivity whereby black bodies are construed as material objects'. Continuing the focus on the body, essays which concentrate on *The Comedy of Errors*, *Hamlet*, *Henry V* and *Cymbeline* explore questions of racialism, not as explicit modes of segregation but as the multivalent and subtle assertions of belonging, assimilation, hybridity and sexual difference through the plays' various transnational optics and encounters. The following section, which includes essays from Julie Crawford, Karen Raber and Carol Thomas Neely, seeks to re-adjust the critical focus on the family away from heterosexual coupledom to a much more diverse and 'perverse' exploration of erotic pleasure, freedom, bodily conflation and agency. Many of these essays, driven it seems by a critical impulse to reconcile the relationships between presentism and historicism, approach the idea of embodiment as a dynamic process between stage and page, as well as subject and object. Some of the best essays bring the terms of embodiment to bear on the incorporeal or ethereal as well as the one-dimensional. Gina Bloom's chapter on the game of chess in *The Tempest* examines the motif 'as a material analogy for an alternate conception of history'. Showing us how to read the game through its interruptions, progressions and models of winning, Bloom re-reads this moment as a critique of Prospero's conception of history as progressive. Understood as a 'prosthesis', the game of chess links this section's concern with the body in relation to social environment and Shakespeare's treatment of disability. Tobin Siebers and Vin Nardizzi explore the interrelations between body and environment through complex and mobile networks of 'disablement' that extend to the inward as well as outward models of conformity. Nardizzi provides an especially compelling reading of the 'crutch' and its historical antecedents. Moving beyond the 'human', and through clever re-readings of many of the key terms of plays such as *Richard III* and *The Winter's Tale*, this section examines political agency, disintegration and hybridity. Some of the most engaging essays appear in the last two sections of the collection, which deal with textual production and cultural performance. Attending to the word in space, as Walter Ong suggested, Valerie Wayne, Laurie Maguire and Jeffrey Masten focus on editing, glossing and vacancies or blanks. Examining the editorial process, both Masten and Wayne exert pressure on the terms through which meaning is mediated by the printed text, as well as unpacking the ideological assumptions behind many of those editorial interventions. Maguire's essay on 'etcetera' focuses on the gestures towards something not said and the apparently complicit ways in which meaning is made in the blanks. Here, embodiment extends to the textual absences that invite the reader to 'break off' as well as complete the sentence: 'the ghost character of early modern writing, the site of perpetual exchange between the potential and the actual in knowledge'. It is this elliptical 'ghost character' that brings many of these essays together: the past and the present, the actual and the imagined, the physical and the ethereal, unity and disintegration. All provide the spectral spaces for forms of embodiment to take shape across the words and spaces of the plays as historical and continuous records of being. The final sections on performance produce some very helpful insights into the culturally powerful ways in which production encodes meaning, as well as how specific theatrical techniques must be reinvented across the plays' histories: on this point, Jennifer Waldon's section on the bed trick in *All's Well* is especially good. Holly Dugan's analysis of the history of sexual violence on stage is particularly interesting for its engagement with gender, the erotics of assault, and the politics of concealment. Evelyn Tribble's essay develops her work on the training of boy actors and the 'skill

environment' through which the body is both exploited and trained. Diana Henderson examines the manipulation of material objects to disrupt gender hierarchies, as well as their role in mediating forms of cultural information across political and temporal divisions. Denise Albanese's essay, the last in the collection, provides an insightful and engaging analysis of how performance enlists sensation through representation in the production of cultural value. Here, she explores how we identify pleasure in Shakespeare, as well as the forms through which we access the phenomena of performance and 'the problem of value'.

Moving into the specific spaces of performance, Sarah Dustagheer's *Shakespeare's Two Playhouses: Repertory and Theatre Space at the Globe and the Blackfriars 1599–1613*, sets out to explore the influence of the playhouse on the play. Beginning from the context of the new Sam Wanamaker Playhouse, 'an archetypal reimagining of an early modern indoor playhouse', next to The Globe on London's Bankside, Dustagheer focuses on one of Webster's most arresting lines on the death of his heroine: 'Cover her face. Mine eyes dazzle, she died young.' This captivating synthesis of a brother's guilt, love, fear and absolution becomes for Dustagheer a way into the poetics of the playing space, where the word 'dazzle' shines out of the glow of candlelight to 'illuminate the stage for key dramatic moments'. Concentrating on the language of light and luminescence in the indoor theatre, Dustagheer introduces her book as concerned with the 'connections between theatre space and text'. Central to her thesis is a comparative model of two theatres, the Globe and the Blackfriars, and how plays produced during this time for two different playing spaces record the variable expectations and exploitations of the indoor and amphitheatres. Utilizing theories of space, environment and aesthetics, Dustagheer attempts to analyse various plays through the embedded structures of social and imaginative contexts produced by the formative theatres of the late sixteenth and early seventeenth centuries. Her focus is on repertory and on the variety of plays being produced in these theatres, alongside the works of their company's playwrights. In examining the 'two-venue arrangement', Dustagheer hopes to redress the more conventional treatment of these theatres as binary. Instead, she suggests, there was more of an exchange between these spaces, adapting to, but also reproducing, certain effects and allusions for the benefit of both audiences. Despite Dustagheer's proclaimed resistance, her work is heavily influenced by contemporary theatrical practice, but she attempts to navigate the waters of anachronism through a focus on perception and projection rather than authentic rehabilitation. To this end, the book provides an accessible and straightforward appraisal of the theatrical spaces, their architecture and environment, their culturally inscribed legacies, and the changing structures of Elizabethan and Jacobean spatial awareness. Dustagheer's concern with the implications of socially organized spaces, their political and cultural hierarchies, as well as the way in which terms such as 'public' and 'private' are used, shapes her discussion of the interconnectedness of these theatrical spaces, as well as their differing 'urban' contexts. The final chapter attends to the 'haunted' space, which, the book suggests, was a way of using the past to inhabit the spaces of the present and thus stand as a dominant spectre of what remains of history as well as individual memories. She makes a particular case for the staging of *Henry VIII* at Blackfriars, rather than – or as well as – at the Globe, because of how 'it is haunted by the unique cultural memories of that site'. Haunting becomes a resonant metaphor in this chapter since it allows Dustagheer to exploit the interconnectedness between space and place: 'The entire plot of *Cupid's Revenge* is a provocative piece of haunting at the Blackfriars, as it concerns the dismantling and destruction of a religion.' Some of these readings seem a little over-determined, but the book as a whole offers a helpful introduction to the theatres of early modern London and how spaces are shaped, legitimized, disturbed and re-imagined by the art that authorizes them.

SEEING IT FEELINGLY

The focus on the visual language of the theatre continues in John H. Astington's *Stage and Picture in the English Renaissance: the Mirror up to Nature*, which examines the interrelations between pictorial art and drama. Concentrating on patterns of pictorial meaning as they are produced by drama as well as art, Astington examines the wide contexts of visual meaning within this period. From fine art, woodcuts, illustrations, design, tapestries and emblems to the ways in which images of theatres were reproduced and circulated, he establishes the extraordinary range and depth of Tudor and Stuart visual culture. Exploring the different forms and temporalities through which stories were told, the book identifies the constructive ways in which audiences are gathered by images to experience certain narratives within the context of both animate and inanimate art. Central to Astington's thesis is the interweaving between story and history and the powerfully visual ways in which biblical, historical or mythological narratives are shaped by the reproduction of certain images in static and dramatic art. The book is concerned not just with the applied and craft arts of tapestries, churches, progresses and processions but also with the graphic art of the city, including trade and house signs, 'which identified business and houses pictorially, before the days of street numbering'. Much of Astington's focus is on the ways in which certain systems of signs produced embodied meanings, virtues or qualities in heraldry; social networks in livery or sumptuary; and emblems which present the visual as heuristic. In all such cases, the visual power is developed through the interpretative networks produced by object culture and context, which become a resonant analogy for the place and development of early modern theatre. Exploring the capacities of both mediums, Astington asserts: 'The stage, then, unites the intellectual and interpretative powers of the Poet with the instant visual impressiveness at the command of the Painter.' The book's chapters are organized thematically according to the stories told through certain themes within the visual and sensory experiences. The first begins with Rome and its various incarnations across Shakespeare's plays, including the *Antiques*, or seven tapestry panels, acquired by Henry VIII. Focusing on the striking visual resemblances between one of the panels, *The Triumph of Venus*, and North's translation of Plutarch, Astington examines the impact of the visual networks that would produce Enobarbus's now famous story of Cleopatra's appearance on a barge. Astington assumes that Shakespeare would have seen the tapestries during his visits to court and that he replayed many of their images in his work, not only as visual effects but also as emotional registers of feeling. Particularly fascinating within this context is Astington's reading of another tapestry, the Madrid Panel, alongside the moment when Coriolanus meets his mother outside the gates of Rome. Astington does not claim that Shakespeare ever saw this extraordinary piece, but that the story of Coriolanus – and this moment, especially – was taken up through this image and reproduced across various different forms. Chapter 2 attends to the fall of Troy and its frequent retellings in contemporary literature, while Chapter 3 turns to scripture. Here, the focus on tapestries continues through the popular retellings of biblical stories and the various traditions through which they were reimagined. Central to the dynamic between pictorial and stage stories is the sense of the uncanny, where both the familiar and the arresting can be exploited. The second half of the book turns to graphic art and the printed picture. Beginning with mockery, Astington sets out to explore the relationship between genre and image through a focus on printed material. Mapping the relation between moral drama and visual art, the book extends its focus to the history play, iconography and ritual display. The final chapter focuses on the theatre 'as a pictorial subject', both in what it represents and how it is represented itself; here, Astington makes a case for the interrelationships between scene and scenic, and the role of the visual sign in placing and displacing audience response. Images of theatres and theatrical images of narrative moments, as well as allegory and emblems, support the book's enthralling exploration of the powerful dynamic between visual and performative arts. The book is beautifully illustrated for an academic monograph, and there are over fifty-two illustrations, as well as colour plates. Astington's

compassionate and perceptive analysis of the deep pleasures and intricacies of the visual, both embodied and imagined, is a powerful and brilliant testimony to the vibrancy of the theatre and its imaginative legacies. Putting the aesthetic contexts in place, whether direct or networked, reveals the intricate and captivating ways in which stories are told not only across time and place but also across mediums and genres. This is a wonderful book which brings together many of the most fruitful and important currents in literary criticism of the period.

Keir Elam continues the presence of the visual arts in his book *Shakespeare's Pictures: Visual Objects in the Drama*. Like Astington, Elam understands that 'Shakespeare's pictures ... open up dramatic discourse and theatrical performance to the variegated world of visual culture and to the interrelations between the arts that was so vital a part of early modern poetics.' But where Astington's focus moves between the images and narratives that forge Shakespeare's relationship with the worlds of early modern visual culture, Elam's focus is more precisely on how visual objects perform onstage. Although Elam is primarily concerned with pictorial images (painting, portraits, and visual emblems), he also considers the various ways in which material objects can become visual signifiers. Beginning with the portrait – which, according to Elam, 'Shakespeare elects as his main iconographic paradigm' – we can observe the 'affinity between dramatic dialogue and portraiture in the emergence of the early modern subject'. Moving through an analysis of how Shakespeare plays with the relationships between static and animate art, Elam examines the interplay between the real and the counterfeit, the living and the plastic, and the remarkable ways in which visual forms interrupt and interfere with the narrative dimensions of the plays. Noticing the ways in which the pictorial can function to suggest a destiny, a moment of interpretation, a theme or an allegorical network, Elam examines the multivalent and powerful stories of the picture in play. Beginning with the performance of art, Elam explores the picture in *Pericles*, *Timon of Athens*, *The Two Gentleman of Verona* and

The Two Noble Kinsmen. In each play, the picture functions slightly differently – as trophy, evidence, ceremony or seduction. Imagining the 'wanton pictures' of *The Taming of the Shrew*, how they might be referenced and read, as well as their suggestive relationships to the play as a whole, Elam opens up the play's interest in imagination as well as objectification. The chapter on *The Merchant of Venice* explores the play's exploitation of the proxy powers that images may hold and the contexts in which Venice becomes a 'privileged site of the gaze'. A chapter on *Hamlet*, who 'thinks in pictures', explores the unsettled place of the visual image as both refuge and betrayal. The final chapter deals with *Twelfth Night* and the question of perspective, 'natural' and otherwise. In an 'Afterimage', Elam turns to Hermione's statue to reaffirm the spectacular power of the speaking picture, in both its silence and its courage.

Although not assertively dedicated to the visual arts, Jonathan Post's *Very Short Introduction* to *Shakespeare's Sonnets and Poems* is similarly fascinated by the interrelationships between the visually static and the animate as it is expressed in Shakespeare's work. Beginning with the narrative poems, Post addresses the dominant range of visual signifiers in *Venus and Adonis* and the exemplary way they engage the pictorial as well as dramatic imagination. Studying some of the most famous aspects of this poem, Post explores Shakespeare's foremost reputation as a poet and his unique ability to combine conventional Renaissance subjects and idioms with vivid renegotiations of provocative subjects, including sexually aggressive goddesses, death and sex, and reluctant heroes. On *The Rape of Lucrece*, Post traces its literary heritage, the powerful use of visual narratives and the variant readings of suicide and will, as well as the narrative representation of rape. The latter section of the book turns to the Sonnets and gives a general introduction to the emergence of the collection, having noted in the introduction that 'few books have left, initially, so small a trail'. Acknowledging the relative disinterest in Shakespeare's sonnets, despite his foremost reputation as a poet for the narratives, Post rehearses a brief history of the conventions of the sonnet and how Shakespeare adapts and develops the form. Adumbrating some of the major themes of the collection, Post goes on to offer some useful readings of particular sonnets which will help students of the form understand the basics of wordplay, punning, antithesis, argument and imagery. Using some of these sonnets as platforms for wider discussions about sexuality and desire, subjectivity and revelation, Post explores some of the major concerns of the Sonnets as well as the plays, in terms of both their poetic textures and their reception history. As with many of Oxford University Press's *Very Short Introductions* this is a very accessible, elegant and thoughtful introduction to the subject, which productively raises as many questions as it hopes to answer.

CRY FREEDOM

In *Shakespeare for Freedom: Why the Plays Matter*, Ewan Fernie appears to address the frequently subversive and whimsical question of why we read, study or bother with Shakespeare at all. Only Shakespeare, it seems, provokes such questions, as he appears year after year on syllabi, in media and in the public domain. Part of Fernie's thesis is a defence of the arts more generally, but the most important and persuasive argument of this book is the vibrant claim that 'Shakespeare means freedom.' Breaking open the culturally contingent shackles of language and aesthetics, Fernie addresses the value of freedom, and how it is explored and expounded, confounded and conjured by the plays in which 'freedom is richly various'. Within these terms, the cornucopian liberty of the Shakespearian text ranges across the existential impulses of characters who break the bounds of their own bodily or lived limits, for pleasure, performance or punishment. Such unpredictability is part of the rich tapestry of what freedom can mean within the play worlds and the individuals who inhabit them. Sometimes, this variety leads Fernie into value judgements of his own, where various states of liberty are described as 'glamorous' or 'wicked' but resolutely 'triumph-[ant]', whether 'as a blessing or grace'. Fernie's approach is ambitious and capacious and attempts to engage with the moral complexities of freedom, as well as its culturally contingent definitions. Exploring the differential impulses towards individual and collective freedoms, the tensions they produce and the narratives they promote, many of the chapters attend to freedom as a struggle, not a god-given right or an individual expectation but a constant state of moving from one state to another and often reconstructing the boundaries of entrapment in the process. One of the most engaging aspects of Fernie's argument is that Shakespeare is not interested in myth-making or producing an over-arching narrative of progression or redemption; rather, he is absorbed by the vagaries of belonging and not belonging and the ethics of the ties that bind. Fernie dodges the ethical bullets by taking refuge in interpretation: 'the thing I am', 'the thing itself', become powerful pledges to individual interpolations of humanity, which he also recognizes as potentially bathetic (and certainly so in his scathing review of Shakespeare's role in the opening ceremony for the London Olympics in 2012). Fernie's project seems to encompass two major aims. One is to re-politicize Shakespeare, while the other is to obfuscate the ethical implications of such politicization. Thus, the neo-liberal Shakespeare can accommodate multiple freedoms for multiple ends, which means also that it often does not really matter how the play ends because, in comedy at least, the idea of 'mutual happiness' is untenable. Fernie is a very astute reader of other writer's sensitivities and offers some lovely connections between 'the wondrous knowledge of the heart', as Chartist Thomas Cooper puts it, and 'a subtle openness to that human complexity which is inalienable from freedom'. What brings many of these different moments together, from Garrick to Mandela, Cooper to Kossuth, is Shakespeare's characterization as both a powerful 'inspiration and an existential mandate for a pluralist politics even as they exemplify the promise of such politics in their own vividly Shakespearean self-realisation'. Fernie's examination of Shakespeare's contexts for freedom is predominantly mapped by

white men, which tells only one version of what his freedoms come to mean, and, despite the many great moments in this book, the fascinating connections and anecdotes, the explorations of ceremony, pageantry, godlessness, defiance and savagery, and the powerful history of those who made Shakespeare meaningful, the book runs the risk of creating the very myths that Fernie so carefully shows Shakespeare resisting.

Shakespeare and the Politics of Commoners: Digesting the New Social History, edited by Chris Fitter, provides a series of very accomplished essays on a range of Shakespeare's plays, including history, romance and tragedy. Beginning with the effects, producers and manifestations of poverty as that 'which plungeth the English into rebellion', Fitter's introduction establishes the book's interest in dissent and the communities who produced as well as expressed it. As a remarkable history of protest, the book brings together some of the most eloquent historicist scholars in the field to examine and digest the interrelations between social classes, economic and political conditions, and the representations – allegorical, naturalistic, historical and contemporary – of the voices who want change. Over the course of the essays, anger, resistance, complacency, violence and authority come under scrutiny for how they record and suppress some of the most urgent questions of monarchical rule. Establishing the extraordinary contexts of suppression, in which 'no fewer than sixty-eight Treason Acts' were passed in the sixteenth century in order to criminalize actions, writings and 'casual speech critical of royal policy', Fitter establishes the various humanist, liberal, totalitarian and strategic attitudes to popular insurrection. Assimilating history's complex and often contradictory attitude to the voices of the populace, Fitter sets out the various contexts through which insurrection could be presented as either constructive or debilitating for the stability of power. Many of these essays produce new ways of addressing familiar writers and contemporary discourses: Machiavelli's support of 'the populace', and a more cogent understanding that what troubled the annals of power was not the spectre of the ignorant multitude but the many who were 'more prudent, more stable, and of sounder judgement than the prince'. Essays by both Peter Lake and Steven Pincus demonstrate the creation of an 'early modern public sphere' through the large-scale organization of popular protest-turned-process. Central to the book's focus is a revision of how we understand the class-laden hierarchies of early modern England and the changing perceptions of the common people: 'The national regime was inescapably dependent on popular compliance for regulation operation.' In this way, 'class conflict' becomes, in Andy Wood's phrase, a 'constant, trans-historical friction'. As Shakespearians are well aware, forms of dissent haunt the drama – and not just in the history plays – but the particular focus that these plays place on the interrelations between monarch and subjects, empires and islands (including Ireland), as well as the pervasive discourses on the nature of good government, make them extraordinarily resonant documents of dissent. The most striking and brilliant aspect of this collection, however, is its refusal to shrink the 'definition of politics to the clubbable discoursing of a privileged elite'. Working away from 'the upbeat consensualist school of interpretation', which 'calmly occludes 'the domain of daily suffering and contention for the masses', to quote Fitter, the book establishes the importance of social history that does not seek to find glib narratives of subversion and containment, but contradiction, 'popular disaffection' and 'graphic class critique'. What follows is a series of superb essays devoted to the 'destabilising boldness' of 'oppositional motifs' and 'broken individuals'; the book attends to, as Fitter says of *Measure for Measure*, 'the unquenchability of demotic irreverence and subcultural independence'. The first half of the book focuses on Shakespeare's history plays and offers terrific essays by Peter Lake, David Rollison, Andy Wood, Thomas Cartelli and Stephen Longstaffe, ranging over the circulation and representation of 'popularity politics', who put the common into 'commonwealth', plebeian protest, the representation of the citizenry, and social protest. Paola Pugliatti's essay on military developments explores the changing culture of war, which looks both forwards and backwards to skills, theories and weapons of conflict. Markku Peltonen reconsiders *Julius Caesar* within the contexts of *ars rhetorica*, not from an elitist model of oratorical conformity but as a divisive and destructive exploration of eloquence and rebellion. David Norbrook provides a brilliant essay on *Coriolanus* through Machiavelli's reading of Livy, and the emergence of a political language of belonging and division. Norbrook's investigation of the 'discourses of the plebeian' reveals an ambiguous, multivalent play in which Shakespeare confounds the binaries between 'elite and popular . . . citizenship and subjecthood'. *Shakespeare and the Politics of Commoners* is a superb collection of essays which brings together trenchant readings of the plays alongside a vigorous reengagement with social history, a sensitive appreciation of the modulations across variant texts, a highly attuned ear for the vagaries of political discourses, and a sharp focus on the non-conformist worlds of Shakespeare's dissenters, as well as the reactionary figures who confound them.

Another excellent book this year is Tanya Pollard's highly perceptive and scrupulously argued book *Greek Tragic Women on Shakespearean Stages*. Her absorbing account of the role of Greek tragedy in the development of early modern theatre establishes the extraordinarily diverse ways in which plays by Euripides, in particular, took hold of the dramatic imagination to support and develop a productive network for the exploration of tragic women, notably deranged mothers and sacrificed daughters. Embedded in these representations of tragic women was an emotional shorthand through which other writers of the period could develop their tragic range: 'Surfacing in both explicit and subtle allusions, they suggest uncanny and capacious forms of literary influence, challenging traditional intertextual models.' She demonstrates how the use of 'Greek words, genres and authors' reflected a 'widespread identification of the new dramatic forms with their Greek roots', as well as 'unlocking a lost realm of theatrical origins and authority'. Concentrating on character and genre, Pollard traces the ways in which Greek plays were received and transmitted in the period, the quantifiable impact this had on the advancement of theatrical affect, and the prominence of female protagonists, as well as the evolution of tragicomedy. Examining sympathy and the privileged status that the maternal body holds as a 'conductor for a kind of affective electricity', Pollard addresses questions of empathy and 'the ability to make listeners share their feelings'. Centralizing the transmission of, and interest in, Greek drama, Pollard provides a new focus on the 'substantial literary consequences', including translation and collaboration, of these models. The book moves chronologically through a series of case studies which demonstrate and explore the complex and foundational ways in which Greek drama supported the development of English theatre. Beginning with Lumley's *Iphigenia* and Gascoigne and Kinwelmersh's *Jocasta*, Pollard ranges across questions of female authority, counsel and secession. Exploring mother–daughter dyads, in chapter 2, Pollard addresses the spectre of the tragic Greek mother and her role in garnering and expressing forms of emotion, not least of all sympathy. A chapter on Hecuba specifically focuses on Hamlet's invoked relation to the figure of suffering, and the extents to which the play consciously challenges the conventions of revenge tragedy. Chapter 4 turns to comedy and examines the manifestation of female tragic figures in a different genre, in order to contest generic boundaries as well as supply forms of mediation and reconciliation through the virgin and the mother. Later chapters develop the question of generic intermingling through the figure of the veiled woman and the ghost of Euripides' Alcestis. In the final chapter, Pollard turns to Ben Jonson to argue that 'in playful homage to Shakespeare's just-ended career, Jonson not only acknowledges the pleasures of Shakespeare's Greek-inflected plots, but also discovers how he can profit from this himself'. This is a highly articulate and thoughtful book that produces some fascinating insights not only into the transmission of ideas and figures through stage and page but also for the dramatic grammar that Greek drama provided for the development of highly sophisticated networks of engagement through the memories, contexts, genres, and motifs of the most maligned and revered women on the early modern stage.

Maintaining the tragic focus is Michael Neill and David Schalkwyk's edited collection, *The Oxford Handbook of Shakespearean Tragedy*. This weighty survey offers a comprehensive range of essays which seek to explore the genre, concept, language, effects and performance of tragedy in its multiple directions in Shakespeare's drama. There are fifty-four essays, about half of which are on reception and performance, both modern and early modern, with a focus on Global Shakespeare as cultural artefact and political appropriation. Unlike Traub's *Oxford Handbook of Shakespeare and Embodiment*, there is no introduction here nor helpful summary of how the book builds on or fits into the history of Shakespeare's tragedy. (The only interjection by one of the editors is the witty inclusion of a quote from an email to David Hillman which prefaces his essay.) Instead, the collection appears to be structured according to a narrative arc in which we start with the classical definitions, character and catharsis, and move unflinchingly through an eclectic range of essays on genre, textualities, language and theme. Tracing the 'inheritance' of tragedy through its classical, medieval and romantic legacies, essays by Richard Halpern, Rory Loughnane and Edward Pechter establish the permeable boundaries between forms and experiences of tragedies. Emma Smith concentrates on the 'particular focus and particular history' of character criticism, which produces historically contingent binaries between the inscrutable interior and the theatrical display. Shifting the focus to embodiment, and the context of character in plot, Smith examines individuality within the contexts of 'an epistemology of the human'. Locating tragic character within the realms of a 'shared human subjectivity', she explores how characters inhabit their play worlds and how we, as readers or audiences, attempt to abstract them in order to make sense of the inevitability of tragic process, as well as the 'fantasy of human agency'. Essays on the tragic textures and environments of the plays follow, including a very eloquent piece on lament by

Lynne Magnusson; David Hillman on 'affect', 'the very stuff of tragedy'; Steven Mullaney on the dialectics of tragedy; and Peter Lake on religion and revenge. Richard Sugg provides an existential focus on tragic deaths, including bodily decay and why Yorick's skull is so iconic. The focus on genre continues through some thoughtful explorations of 'mixing' and the 'middle phase', including Subha Mukherji on tragi-comedy, Lee Edelman and Madhavi Menon on queer tragedy and Paul Werstine on authorial revision. The middle section on 'Reading the Tragedies' offers incisive perspectives on tragic (including ethical) visions, structures, and 'local effects' − in Michael Neill's phrase − and the 'sacrifices' of *Romeo and Juliet*, as Crystal Bartolovich explores. Catherine Belsey takes on the question in Hamlet and the many and various manifestations of enquiry that the play proposes. *Hamlet, Lear, Antony and Cleopatra, Macbeth, Coriolanus* and *Othello* all receive chapters of their own through some clever re-workings of dominant themes, like doubt, nihilism, the geographical imagination, fear, political language and race. The latter sections of the book move towards performance, beginning with the early modern and Tiffany Stern's essay on the development of a tragic dramaturgy; Peter Holland on post-Restoration performances of four major tragedies, *Romeo and Juliet, Hamlet, Macbeth* and *King Lear*, and the spaces through which production allows affect to erupt. Russell Jackson's essay on nineteenth-century productions of tragedy focuses on a theatrical emphasis on character, scenery and the drives towards a 'unified scenic picture'. Attending to this unified approach through both critical and theatrical perspectives, Jackson explores the Victorian impulse towards character rather than play world, and 'a lack of attention to social context in line with twenty-first-century notions of class, status, and relations between the sexes'. Bridget Escolme takes us into the twentieth and twenty-first century through a focus on *Hamlet* and *King Lear* and the changing structures of emphasis which produce what she calls a 'politics of intimacy'. The following sections of the *Handbook* focus more specifically on film, and include essays by

Courtney Lehmann, Douglas Lanier, Macdonald P. Jackson, Katherine Rowe, and Sarah Hatchuel and Nathalie Vienne-Guerrin, variously covering *Romeo and Juliet, Lear, Macbeth, Othello, Hamlet* and the Roman plays. Peter Byrne and William Germano explore cinematic adaptation and opera, respectively. The latter sections of the collection are geographically invested in the cultural and political appropriations of Shakespearian tragedy across the developed world. These essays range throughout Europe and Eastern Europe − described by Pavel Drabek as a 'political and cultural concept rather than a geographical description of a region'. Many of these essays focus on the 'cultural footprint' of Shakespeare through both national and transnational agendas. *Hamlet* is the prominent play to be addressed throughout, and affirms its extraordinarily enduring power. *Othello* and *Romeo and Juliet* are also heavily featured in these sections but, as we move away from Europe to South Africa, the Caribbean, India, North Africa, Latin America and East Asia, the range of tragedies becomes both more fluid and more fascinating. Many of these essays are interested in the treatment and appropriation of Shakespeare during periods of conflict, the 'snare of racial history', and the development of 'generic hybridization, intra-regional and trans-historical allusions'. Foremost, we can trace the cross-cultural movement of tragedy, how it is absorbed and the marks it leaves, the appetites for revolution it can produce and the discourse of repression it can support. Many of these essays deal frankly and elegantly with the spectre of imperialism that haunts Shakespeare, and one of the many strengths of the collection is its understanding of reception and rehearsal and the many vibrant and powerful ways in which Shakespearian tragedy zeroes in on the times, then and now, which are out of joint. *Titus, Hamlet, Romeo and Juliet, Coriolanus* and *Lear* are probably the most frequently discussed plays, but there are essays on some of the history and problem plays − most notably, of course, when tragedy intersects with other genres. Some of the most interesting work across many of this year's books is on *Coriolanus*: Smith on character and the assertion of a discernible self, Schalkwyk on language and Norbrook on the plebs.

Maintaining the focus on cultural appropriations of Shakespeare, Shaul Bassi's *Shakespeare's Italy and Italy's Shakespeare* revisits the country's role in shaping Shakespeare's dramatic imagination, as well as his reception. Considering 'the role of Shakespeare in the Italian processes of national self-fashioning', Bassi explores 'Fascist and racist appropriations of' the plays, as well as 'more recent Italian transactions with Shakespeare in the age of globalization'. Beginning with *Othello*, and the 'genealogy of Shakespeare "race" studies', the book is divided into three sections: race, politics and place. Each one attempts to reread the history of those terms as they have been used in Shakespeare criticism, and the extent to which they provide historically sensitive and contextually relevant frameworks. Bassi confronts the category of 'race' as both misleading and revealing in its attempts to homogenize multivalent discourses, whilst also admitting 'Shakespeare as an ally in the building of a real transnational and cross-cultural consciousness'. Following Paul Gilroy, Bassi adopts 'ethnicity' as the more critically productive term, through which he analyses the ethnic identities of main characters beyond the terms of black or white. Despite this focus, however, Bassi has less on *The Merchant of Venice* than one might expect, given the book's interest in Italian cultural identities. Recalling the 2015 production of the play in the Ghetto, however, Bassi considers: 'Can the *Merchant* add another narrative, a new critical layer to the Ghetto of Venice? Is the project violating or infringing a sacred space? . . . Is it forcing a global project on a local site?' Such questions reveal the book's fascination with the political memories of the plays, as well as their futures. Concentrating on the cultural politics of fascism, the geopolitics of ethnicity and Shakespeare's relation to Italian political theory, Bassi offers a fluently argued survey of socio-political responses to Shakespeare's plays. His Italian connection is not exclusively based on setting and source, but also on appropriation and performance. In the chapter, 'Hamlet in Venice', Bassi asserts that 'the Danish prince becomes a

special guide to contemporary Italian theory', as *King Lear* does to 'political succession strategies'. Addressing the imaginative spaces of Italy through which Shakespeare continues to exert fascination, Bassi explores the Italian locations which are haunted by Shakespeare's characters. A section on Giordano Bruno examines the 'hermetic', in counter-argument to much of Frances Yates's work, to establish the potential of Shakespeare's politically subversive ideas and the 'secret of nature'. The chapter on 'fixed figures' is especially clever since Bassi looks at the 'Mori' in relation to images, shapes, artefacts and the shifting historical legibility of these terms. The final chapter, on Taviani's 2012 film *Caesar Must Die*, reconsiders the play within the context of a neo-liberal Italy where the 'stark reality of Rebibbia prison is a counterpoint to the Rome of tourist clichés and Roman centurions posing for the visitors' selfies . . . and the reality show.' It is the dynamic between Italy and Shakespeare as both reality and cliché that provides some of the most intriguing and original aspects of this book. Bassi largely maintains his focus on *Othello* and a selection of other plays with Italian connections, including *Romeo and Juliet* and *Antony and Cleopatra*.

In *Wrestling with Shylock*, edited by Edna Nahshon and Michael Shapiro, however, the focus is exclusively on *The Merchant of Venice*. Subtitled *Jewish Responses to The Merchant of Venice*, the collection seeks to examine the character of Shylock through its multiple representations and adaptations, in which the figure of the Jew is scrutinized by Jews themselves. Recognizing the complex and often devastating ways in which Shylock has been configured in the Jewish imagination, the essays engage with the contexts in which Shylock was created, interpreted and sustained. Shapiro opens the collection with an essay on the emergence and development of Jewish villainy in late medieval theatre. Describing the more secular impulses of early modern drama, Shapiro then examines how Marlowe's Barabas and Shakespeare's Shylock arrived on the Elizabethan stage, and how they were subsequently developed and appropriated through cultural narratives of race, nationality and religion. Writing on the 'Anti-Shylock campaign in America', Nahshon examines how Shylock became incorporated into American culture as a byword for terms of hatred, and practices including 'predatory financial' ones (still current until their ban in 2009). Focusing on the 'ill effects' of Shylock, the essay traces how Shakespeare's character supported anti-Jewish sentiments that provoked narratives and counter-narratives of oppression and revision. Nahshon establishes how, despite the vicissitudes of the play's performance history, it remains the constant marker of anti-Semitic feelings, but nevertheless continues to be a 'Jewish play' for 'it is largely Jews who care about it, write on it, talk about it, and are the first to buy tickets for its revivals'. Continuing the focus on reception, Abigail Gillman explores a key text within German-Jewish historiography, Heinrich Graetz's essay, 'Shylock in legend, in drama, and in history'. Some of the most fascinating threads of this collection reveal the extraordinary and unprecedented ways in which the fictional character has slipped in and out of his own historical reality, so that the 'problem of Shylock' is also the problem of history and the ways in which fiction has become, albeit unwittingly, complicit in redefining the ethics of memory, responsibility and agency. Reflecting on two late nineteenth- and early twentieth-century German-Jewish historians, Gillman observes how Shylock moves from 'a stereotyped Stage Jew into a symbol of hope and redemption'. The presence of these two Shylocks dominates the layered and complex history of Jewish responses to the play, in which the dominant impulses are to show a character who only 'happened to be Jewish', whilst also refusing to erase oppression from the play's performance history – as Alexander Granach said of the character he portrayed on the German stage in 1934: 'Socially, Shakespeare was anti-Semitic, but the genius in him defended Jews as they had never been defended before.' Unsurprisingly, the majority of the essays here focus on the twentieth century and variously explore the development of Yiddish theatre, including a fascinating essay by Nina Warnke and Jeffrey Shandler, which examines the cultural concerns produced by the interaction of Yiddish and Shylock, the expansion of interest from legally trained critics and the staging of mock trials, in which Antonio's case is re-examined through a public interrogation of the law, as well as the protagonists. The second half of the book is more specifically shaped by the stage and the play's performance history. Some of these essays examine specific productions: Mark Hodin on David Belasco's 1922 direction of the play; Nahshon on three different versions of the play performed in New York in 1947; and Shelly Zer-Zion on Israeli productions in Hebrew (of which there have been only six on mainstream stages). Central to her chapter is an analysis of Jessner's 1936 Habima production which showed a 'willingness to grapple with a deep-seated contradiction between its aspirations to universalism and its commitment to Zionist and Jewish concerns'. Sabine Schülting considers George Tabori's adaptation of the play within the 'complex issue of Holocaust remembrance'; Gad Kaynar-Kissinger writes on the 'Buchenwald' production in Weimar; Efraim Sicher on the play in a 'post-colonial' context; and Miriam Gilbert on Jewish actors and directors. The final section of the collection moves towards adaptation and re-workings in a variety of genres: Michael Shapiro on Ludwig Lewisohn's *The Last Days of Shylock*; Michelle Ephraim on feminist adaptations of the play; Susan Chevlowe on Christian iconography and Maurycy Gottlieb's 1876 painting *Shylock and Jessica*, a powerfully emotive testimony to the ethically ambiguous assimilation of this father and daughter into wider European culture; and Judah M. Cohen on Shylock in opera from the nineteenth to the twenty-first century. The book concludes with Edna Nahshon's chapter on Shylock in the Arab–Israeli conflict. This is a superb and fascinating collection of essays that produces new thinking on the play, in terms not only of its complex and provocative history but also of the ways in which the 'problem of Shylock' continues to reinvent and reinvigorate questions about the relationship between history and story, performance and complicity. It is a very important collection for any

Shakespearian who understands the power of the play, and the legacies, as well as spectres, of theatrical history. As Tabori said, 'I think it is wrong to see Shakespeare without the fairy-tale, but also to see Shakespeare without the horror.' *Wrestling with Shylock* understands the importance of keeping both the horror and the fairy-tale in view.

WHAT'S LOVE GOT TO DO WITH IT?

The thorny questions of justice and mercy, so important to *The Merchant of Venice*, are taken on a different journey in Regina Mara Schwartz's *Loving Justice, Living Shakespeare*. Here, love is the central motif through which Schwartz examines what justice means in Shakespeare's play-worlds; as a debt, obligation, entitlement and gift, love becomes a powerful arbitrator in the instigation and regulation of social law. Looking at what she calls 'love commands', Schwartz interrogates canon and biblical law as a legislative structure of care, in which kinship, community, reciprocity and affection are distinguished from political justice, where 'fairness' is a response to inadequate supply or inequality. Love, on the other hand, is boundless: 'the more I give to thee / The more I have, for both are infinite'. Understanding 'the power of love to create justice', Schwartz advances her argument through a focus on the Bible, as well as the Book of Common Prayer, and the dominant impulses to 'love your neighbour', 'love the stranger' and 'love your enemy', in which love seeks to unite rather than distinguish. Against the infinite capacities of love, Schwartz examines the 'dark anthropology' of political thought which pitches human imperatives as counter-intuitive to the 'logic of love'. The complexities of human justice emerge in the multiple ways in which it is both sought and expressed. For Shakespeare, the multivalent tensions between political, legal, social and emotional justice become central concerns in his drama, not only for the implicit questions they raise about human value and social integrity but also for how they engage with a specific and creative moment in religious history: 'When Reformation theology emphasizes the

necessity of divine and human love and that flowed into a culture already saturated with a belief that loving relations are part of the fibre of the universe in which human beings participate, a world view takes hold, one that also inflects the energetic legal and economic debates about justice.' Tracing the different permutations between love and justice in *King Lear, Romeo and Juliet, The Merchant of Venice, The Tempest* and *Hamlet*, Schwartz creates a remarkable narrative of the human heart, which can resist the divisive strains of political philosophy, whilst also investing in an economics of living in which everything is based upon supply and demand, use value and scarcity. Advocating the irrational power of love to push reason off its post-Enlightenment pedestal, Schwartz looks through a lens of love, in which the 'ethical challenge becomes not so much how to avoid co-opting another but to find the resources within and without to respond to another's need'. And to that end, we should 'reason not the need'.

And finally, two short books from The Arden Shakespeare Series, which deal with critical approaches. In the first, *Shakespeare and Ecofeminist Theory*, Rebecca Laroche and Jennifer Munroe approach the field as offering, in Noel Sturgeon's words, 'a double political intervention; of environmentalism into feminism and feminism into environmentalism'. Such a productive approach allows the authors to explore 'multiple and related forms of subjugation' written deep into the history of exploited resources and peoples. Working from a vantage point through which competing discourses can be 'untangled', away from 'either–or propositions', to show 'how neither a flight from nor a flight to nature provides a full picture of early modern life or thinking'. Organized through approaches that allow the authors to apprehend the interrelations between women and nature, as a non-essentialist construct, the various and thoughtful chapters animate and collect nuanced historical and theoretical binaries in order to explore and explode their differences. Through chapters on household practice, 'the discourse of pest control', the etymology of 'cat', the inanimate, the garden and craft, Laroche and Munroe reveal that the 'cultural exercises that seek to obliterate the enemy invader to find someone to blame also look to deny our shared and finite place in our environment', and that 'the "human" is always already part of an active, often unpredictable, material world'. In *Shakespeare and Cultural Materialist Theory*, Christopher Marlow produces a very cogent and clear exploration of some of the major tenets of historicism – old and new – and cultural materialism. Beginning with the fundamental question 'what is the relationship between a text and the human culture that produced it?', Marlow sets out to explore 'the point of literary criticism' within the critical traditions that focused on power and the socio-political agencies that promoted it. Structured according to a dialectic between the positions of historicism and materialism, Marlow sets out some of the major doctrines and critics of these approaches and sets them in motion within the politically charged moments in which they appeared. The book is laced with reflections on the nature of power and politics, the contemporary climate, and the role that Shakespeare can play in shaping the interrelations between ideology and imagination. The final chapter looks at *Julius Caesar* through the conventional powers of *ars rhetorica*, but Marlow specifically sets Antony's speech over Caesar's body against Trump's speech at the Republican National Convention, when he accepted his presidential nomination with a speech that began 'Friends, delegates, and fellow Americans'. The comparisons are apposite, if also odious. But Marlow's book engages with the many brilliant minds who changed the face of Shakespeare criticism in the 1980s and 1990s, and the political imperatives that we all share in remaining alert to the opportunities we render possible through the language of persuasion and the belief in the imagination.

WORKS REVIEWED

Astington, John H., *Stage and Picture in the English Renaissance: the Mirror up to Nature* (Cambridge, 2017)

Bassi, Shaul, *Shakespeare's Italy and Italy's Shakespeare: Place, 'Race', Politics* (Basingstoke: Palgrave Macmillan, 2017)

Dustagheer, Sarah, *Shakespeare's Two Playhouses: Repertory and Theatre Space at the Globe and the Blackfriars 1599–1613* (Cambridge, 2017)

Elam, Keir, *Shakespeare's Pictures: Visual Objects in the Drama* (London, 2017)

Fernie, Ewan, *Shakespeare for Freedom: Why the Plays Matter* (Cambridge, 2017)

Fitter, Chris, ed., *Shakespeare and the Politics of Commoners: Digesting the New Social History* (Oxford, 2017)

Laroche, Rebecca, and Jennifer Munroe, *Shakespeare and Ecofeminist Theory* (London, 2017)

Marlow, Christopher, *Shakespeare and Cultural Materialist Theory* (London, 2017)

Nahshon, Edna, and Michael Shapiro, eds., *Wrestling with Shylock: Jewish Responses to the Merchant of Venice* (Cambridge, 2017)

Neill, Michael, and David Schalkwyk, eds., *The Oxford Handbook of Shakespearean Tragedy* (Oxford, 2017)

Pollard, Tanya, *Greek Tragic Women on Shakespearean Stages* (Oxford, 2017)

Post, Jonathan F. S., *Shakespeare's Sonnets and Poems: A Very Short Introduction* (Oxford, 2017)

Schwartz, Regina Mara, *Loving Justice, Living Shakespeare* (Oxford: 2017)

Traub, Valerie, *The Oxford Handbook of Shakespeare and Embodiment* (Oxford, 2017)

Tribble, Evelyn, *Early Modern Actors and Shakespeare's Theatre: Thinking with the Body* (London, 2017)

By happenstance, or perhaps by the intervention of the theatrical wing of the organization run by Clio the Muse of History, the voices of actors resound in most of the works reviewed this year. The voices of directors are heard to good effect in many of the books discussed in this year's review, but in two cases actors also speak through and with them. One directorial voice is that of Peter Brook, whose *Tip of the Tongue: Reflections on Language and Meaning* is in the same meditative vein as *The Quality of Mercy: Reflections on Shakespeare*, published in 2014. Brook is always engaging and thought-provoking, whether he is commenting on the subtleties of the French language or recalling incidents from his career. Among the most striking and, for a director, humbling but also stimulating, is the response of Paul Scofield, 'who never soiled his mind with theory or philosophy', to Brook's attempt to start a discussion with him during the rehearsals of *King Lear*: 'No no, I have to play this' (93). Brook is constantly enthralled but never daunted by contemplation of the art he serves, as this short work – effectively a pamphlet – shows with grace and eloquence.

In Nicholas Hytner's *Balancing Acts*, the voice of the director is necessarily dominant, but room is made for the perceptions of the actors with whom he collaborates. Often the actor's intuition is read through their performance: when Michael Gambon as Falstaff spoke to the audience, 'he worked on the assumption that they were all wannabe Falstaffs' (157). As Hamlet, Rory Kinnear 'believed "I did love you once" so we believed him', so that 'In five words he told us what would have taken Tolstoy four chapters' (170). Hytner's generous memoir is full of such moments of clarification arising from the actor's thinking, their creative 'voice', which he as a director helps to support as much as he pursues his own sense of meanings in the plays, the motor that powers his directorial self-expression.

He promises glimpses 'Behind the Scenes at the National Theatre', where he was artistic director from 2003 to 2015, but, although there are indeed occasional glimpses of tensions and disappointments, Hytner is not dealing here in personalities or settling any scores and is concerned rather to unveil the thinking behind some remarkable productions, including *Henry V*, his first during his tenure as artistic director and a bold assertion of the play's contemporary relevance in a time of controversial military interventions abroad. It was also a way of avoiding *Hamlet* – at least for the time being. Hytner came to the tragedy in 2010, in a modern-dress version with Rory Kinnear as a strikingly grown-up Prince negotiating his way through the dangers of a surveillance regime where the television broadcast by Claudius and, subsequently, Fortinbras, was a means of asserting power. This take on the play was not in itself innovative but Hytner and his cast brought to it a new urgency and clarity. 'Among the reasons to do the classical repertoire', he writes, after his account of the *Hamlet* production, 'are both the discovery that things never change and the discovery that things change completely' (177). Discussing *The Winter's Tale*, Hytner observes that 'every production of Shakespeare asks its audience to make an imaginative leap between what it sees and what the play is asking us to take on trust' (31).

Hytner's voice is also heard to good effect through quotation from interviews and articles in Abigail Rokison's *Shakespeare in the Theatre: Nicholas Hytner*, in a new Arden series, two other titles from which are discussed later in this review. Rokison's thorough collation of reviews and prompt copies underpins illuminating assessments of his productions at Manchester's Royal Exchange Theatre, the RSC, the National Theatre and elsewhere. Hytner's practices as a director in musical theatre (notably *Miss Saigon*) and opera provide an intriguing context for Shakespeare productions whose visual expressiveness has sometimes seemed to dominate the meticulous textual analysis that is one of his trademarks in the rehearsal room. On her first page, Rokison celebrates the 'vitality and relevance' of the Shakespeare stagings and notes that, since his *As You Like It* in Manchester in 1986, although he has tended to choose 'non-specific, modern day settings', he has become 'increasingly assiduous about defining a world for each production, moving away from a fabulistic concept of the plays to a more socially realist one' (25). The distinction serves Rokison's argument well, providing a line through what must necessarily be a chronologically organized survey. Tracing his Shakespearian experience from Manchester Grammar School, through Cambridge – where he read English – and onto the professional stage, Rokison constructs a picture of a notable exponent of a particular British approach to text and theatricality. She quotes a 1992 profile by Stephen Fay in the *Independent on Sunday* that adds another colour to the picture, emphasizing 'the uncanny way [Hytner] regularly identifies what he calls the "centre" of a play or opera, making the work intellectually clear and wildly theatrical' (83).

Rokison echoes the general acclaim for Hytner's achievements: he has 'transformed the National Theatre physically, financially and in terms of its repertoire and audiences' (180), by such measures as the introduction of the Travelex scheme, by which a proportion of tickets were made available for £10 at each performance, and the overdue redesign of performance spaces. After he stepped down, Hytner and the theatre's executive director Nick Starr announced the formation of The London Theatre Company and the intention of opening a theatre in the vicinity of Tower Bridge, a little way downriver from the National itself. The Bridge Theatre opened in 2017 and *Julius Caesar*, its first Shakespeare production, was premiered in January 2018. In the *Guardian* (29 October 2017), Susannah Clapp hailed the company's arrival:

London's newest theatre has landed. Triumphantly. Two hundred tonnes of steel on a sprung concrete slab. A place in which the audience can be wrapped around the performance area, as in an Elizabethan theatre – but which has no pillars to block its view. A space that seats 900 but which feels intimate and intense. No subsidy. Seats from £15 to £65. A construction schedule that would be the envy of anyone who has ever had a new kitchen fitted.

Clapp writes in terms that reflect the ambition of so many twentieth-century theatre professionals for intimacy and accessibility, with the example of the Elizabethan Theatre – replicated further upstream by Shakespeare's Globe – always in view.

Hytner and Starr's project would certainly have been the envy of Sir Philip Ben Greet (1857–1936), although, apart from attention to textual matters, the director's preferred production style would not have accorded in most respects with his own. (He would have been appalled by what he would have seen as the return of the scale, if not exact kind of scenic elaboration, he objected to in the theatre of Tree and Irving.) Greet, one of the dedicated group involved in the establishment of the Old Vic, is remembered chiefly for his touring companies, particularly in the field (sometimes literally) classed by Michael Dobson as 'wet grass Shakespeare'. He was a tireless promoter of Shakespeare as a fundamental right and requirement of popular audiences, and late in his career was engaged by Robert Atkins and Sydney Carroll in the Regent's Park open-air theatre, where he was given the appropriate – if quaint – title of 'Master of the Greensward'.

Shakespeare for Everyman, Ben Greet in Early Twentieth-Century America, by Don-John Dugas, gives a very full account of his formidably extensive transatlantic ventures, particularly interesting not so much for the productions themselves as for the educational contexts in which they were presented. The Ben Greet Players offered 'Shakespeare's Plays as He Wrote Them', as one charming poster (reproduced on the cover) proclaims: Shakespeare, seated at a trestle table on the cramped stage of a rather small-scale 'Globe', holds a sheaf of manuscript in his hand as he admonishes his company to 'hold as 'twere the mirror up to nature'. The galleries of the theatre appear to be populated as if by an audience, and a beefeater lurks in the shadows to one side of the stage. This is 'heritage theatre' and proudly so, and Dugas's account of Greet and his enterprise suggests that the mission to share the heritage was generous in spirit if not invariably profitable. Dugas is under no illusions regarding Greet's limitations: he was 'a third-rate actor, but his second-rate managerial skills and first-rate abilities as a teacher of acting enabled him to make a living as a theatrical professional for fifty-six years' (87), Robert Atkins, who encountered him at the Old Vic in 1915–16, recalled that 'BG knew his Shakespeare and a talk with him about the part one was rehearsing was more interesting and illuminative than his rather slapdash methods of production'.[1]

Dugas's account of his North American tours bears out this impression of an indefatigable devotee of the Shakespearian cause. Among his contemporaries, he was closer to the much more distinguished actor Frank Benson in this respect than to the more scholarly 'Elizabethanist' William Poel. Greet rejected the use of a fit-up Elizabethan stage such as that used by Poel, though he did commission three 'simple fit-ups copied from historic sites in London: the Middle Temple, the courtyard of Clerkenwell Priory and the hall of Christ's Hospital' (97). All represented non-theatrical locations in which plays had been performed, the Clerkenwell set being considered appropriate for *Everyman*, the text that gave Greet his entrée into circles where more secular entertainments might not have been acceptable.

By what was known as the 'Concert Booking System', performances were sold to local organizations – educational or charitable – who would make what profit they could above the costs and an agreed percentage of the take. Because Greet's productions were eminently portable, the 'Elizabethan Manner' of staging the plays with 'a maximum of Shakespearian text and a minimum of stage carpentry' (98) was adaptable to performances outdoors as well as indoors or under canvas. Costuming was conventionally 'in period' and this was the kind of simplified production style that appealed as a contrast to the grander scenic Shakespeare of the established stars and their companies. Universities and colleges, the Chatauqua and 'Circuit Chatauqua' and the 'Lyceum' networks provided attentive and reasonably high-minded audiences across the United States, sufficient to warrant Number 2 and Number 3 companies under the 'Ben Greet' banner. Dugas's estimate of audience numbers between 1912 and 1921 suggests that he and his franchisees 'brought the actor-manager's Shakespearian productions to a conservatively estimated 1,671,000 mostly rural North Americans', in addition to 'the unknown hundreds of thousands . . . who attended campus performances by the Woodland Players during the same period' and the 'unknown tens of thousands of Cincinnatians who attended the 149 performances . . . on the grounds of the Zoological Gardens' (302).

In some venues Greet's companies encountered another aspect of the 'Elizabethan Manner'. Fredrick H. Koch, then an instructor at the University of North Dakota and 'one of the pioneers of dramatic instruction in American higher education' studied the work of the Number 3 company as it toured through the Northeast. Dugas quotes his description of a performance of *Much Ado About Nothing* in 'a crass lumbering town in the Adirondacks', where the audience was 'just such a restless crowd as one might expect to be gathered in this community made up chiefly of French Canadians and Jews, with a sprinkling of immigrants of many nationalities – a considerable number of them actually illiterate'. Contrary to Koch's expectations, the wholehearted involvement and 'unrestrained responses' to the play suggested that this audience was 'genuinely Elizabethan – spontaneous, enthusiastic, versatile in the joyful adventure of life'. When Claudio slandered Hero at the altar, the 'intense silence' was interrupted by 'an excited lumberjack who rose to his feet, eyes flashing and hands clenched; "It's a lie you blaggard! It ain't so! That girl's *right*!"' (288–9; emphasis in the original).

---

[1] Robert Atkins, *An Unfinished Autobiography*, ed. George Rowell, with contributions from J. C. Trewin and A. C. Sprague (London, 1994), p. 91.

Although he may go too far in claiming that 'Greet, not his erstwhile protégé Granville Barker, brought Shakespeare into the twentieth century' (114), Dugas's well-documented study is a valuable addition to the literature on early twentieth-century Shakespearian performance. It complements two studies in the Arden Shakespeare series 'Shakespeare in the Theatre', Paul Menzer's *The American Shakespeare Center* and Stephen Purcell's *Mark Rylance at the Globe*.

The American Shakespeare Center (hereafter ASC), based at the Blackfriars Playhouse in Staunton, Virginia, has its origins in the Shenandoah Shakespeare Express (SSE), a touring company founded by Ralph Alan Cohen and Jim Warren in the early 1990s in answer to the need for accessible Shakespearian performances. Its productions 'adhered loosely to some of the performance conditions of travelling companies in early modern England – casts that employed doubling, "universal lighting," minimal sets and a swift-paced commitment to "two hours' traffic of the stage"' (95–6). An important motivation was the desire to counter the effect of what Cohen describes in an interview as 'the many years of watching students yawn their way through what I would now say is overly-produced proscenium Shakespeare' (195) – notably, the RSC productions available to them during study visits to London. The simplicity of the staging allowed their productions to be easily transported to colleges and other venues, both indoors and in the open air. Comparison with Greet's enterprises seems inevitable, especially as some of the us-and-them rhetoric of the earlier years of the SSE – talk of 'crushed velvet' Shakespeare and the antipathy to men in tights 'spouting' verse – seems to be directed at a 'Victorian' mode of theatre long absent from living experience. The combative spirit may have been modified, or at least applied differently, when in 2001 the 'Express' became a 'Center', with a local habitation in a lovingly reconstructed theatre, but there remains a residue of the need to attack preconceptions about Shakespearian performance rather than actual productions from the mainstream, especially the associations of 'British' stage speech.

Menzer examines the ASC's work in its Blackfriars Playhouse, not only in relation to its participation in the exploration of 'original practices' but also in its local historical context. Any associations with Virginia's early colonial status are overshadowed by the more immediate and troubling era evoked by the building's situation on Market Street between the Stonewall Jackson Hotel and the Dixie theatre. (Efforts by Cohen to have the hotel renamed were unsuccessful: like it or not, the red neon marquee itself is one of Staunton's historical landmarks.) The ASC thus negotiates between two kinds of heritage and, although Menzer's primary concern is that represented by what goes on in the handsome and lovingly crafted theatre, the wider cultural and historical context is also examined.

In its selective use of 'original practices', the ASC participates in what Menzer, with the unavoidable nod to J. L. Styan's seminal work, identifies as 'the permanent revolutions by which the Shakespeare industry invents and reinvents itself' (22). Adopting Robert Weimann's terms, Menzer points out (120) that the stage is 'all *platea*' and has no *locus*, a variation on the 'in-one-room' configuration that differs from most other thrust-stage theatres built during the last half-century. The main Shakespeare seasons are remarkable more for their exploration of the opportunity – or demand – for direct actor–audience contact than for any notable innovation in interpretation. The adoption of 'universal light', sometimes achieved by a sleight of (electrician's) hand, supports this, and the sense of a performance by 'quick comedians' is enhanced by the adoption of some of the rehearsal practices analysed and documented by Tiffany Stern and other scholars. Nevertheless, Menzer points out, 'authenticity' has 'always been low on the ASC's "to do" list'. The company 'engaged in best-guess scholarship but, once the building was opened, they've made their own way' (160).

Touring work with a separate acting company precedes each summer season and then is shown on the Blackfriars stage, together with the 'Actors' Renaissance Season', which offers adventurous workings and re-workings of texts by other dramatists as well as Shakespeare's less popular plays. It is the second of these that 'offers the richest plunder from the ASC's "revolution," an intervention in history that recovers the past, changes the present, and alters the future of Shakespeare and performance (and scholarship and pedagogy) in yet unpredictable ways' (138), In his chapter on this project, Menzer is able to offer accounts of the kind of interpretative work necessarily absent in most of the book, where the emphasis, like that of the company, is on methodology and process in rehearsal and performance, and the effect of the *platea* and 'universal light', rather than the director-led interpretation of texts.

In a spirit of greater tolerance than was felt necessary when SSE/ACS was founded, Jim Warren reflects in an interview on the work done on other thrust stages, including those of the RSC's new theatres and Shakespeare's Globe: 'I don't feel like Shakespeare *has* to be done the way we do it to be great. Most theatre companies for me are hit and miss, in a way that inspires me to try and be more consistent' (191). Menzer's thoughtfully argued study raises questions that arise in what appears, by the coincidence of publication dates, to be almost a companion volume: Purcell's account of Mark Rylance's work at Shakespeare's Globe on London's South Bank.

Purcell is able to draw on the new Globe's thorough documentation of its own work, as well as the voluminous national and international academic and journalistic attention it has attracted. The part played by theatre historians in the realization of Sam Wanamaker's vision has perhaps obscured the importance to him of serving audiences in new ways, and Purcell gives this appropriate credit. The alarm caused by over-enthusiastic and jokily xenophobic audience responses to *Henry V* in 1997 – the theatre's first full season – was a consequence of the Globe's being 'a democratic space, complete with all of the problems that democracy entails' (189). Such behaviour, prompted in part by an injudicious suggestion before the season welcoming lively participation, soon became modified, but it reflected what emerged as a general characteristic of productions in this space. Purcell points out that 'in giving so much artistic and narrative control over to their audiences, [the company] were changing the way in which theatrical meanings were produced' (57). The control of an individual director is heavily qualified in this arena of 'contingent, negotiable, unstable and fragmented' meaning (53), where the sightlines differ so radically from one part of the auditorium to another and the actors have to adjust skillfully to the focus not only of 'direct address' but of all speech and movement.

Purcell argues for the Globe as a radical theatre that 'under Rylance's directorship . . . pioneered a form of directing which was also beginning to emerge elsewhere in the theatre of the 1990s: unmistakably modern in its appropriation of various forms of psychological realism, and yet simultaneously non-naturalistic and deeply responsive to the presence of the audience' (59). Rehearsal methods that strike a balance between attention to the demands of the texts' structures as well as character psychology – 'the desire to create a set of realistic characters in a believable fictional world' (66) – were joined by spontaneity in response to the 'given circumstances' (to borrow Stanislavski's term), not only to those evoked in the play's imagined world but to the real and immediate circumstances of architecture and audience. Kathryn Hunter, directing *The Comedy of Errors* in 1999, 'saw the clarification of character objectives as key to clear storytelling and spontaneous performance' (101). Drawing on the account by Lecoq-trained actor Marcello Magni of the scene (2.2.71–107) in which Antipholus of Syracuse and his Dromio 'share a quickfire exchange of puns about baldness', Purcell highlights the ways in which, for this comedy, 'the Globe practice of changing tactics in order to achieve an objective' became 'wild, mischievous, playful and clown-like' (102).

Of the 'original practices' likely to make most impact on the audience, the imposing but embracing building itself is the strongest, followed by the varieties of direct address and – when it is employed – the playing of female roles by men. Productions that seem most open to the accusation of being antiquarian, such as Tim Carroll's *Twelfth Night*, have proved among the most exciting, and 'mixed gender' casting has opened up new perspectives on not only the gender politics of the plays but also the ways in which power is asserted and excercised by both men and women. Purcell addresses all of these factors in such a way as to provide context as well as detail, and is able to provide vivid accounts of the basic artistic strategies of several productions and the ways in which directors have adjusted to (or taken advantage of) what the theatre offers them, and also of such notable personal performances as Rylance's Hamlet (2000) and Cleopatra (1999), and Janet McTeer's Petruchio (2003). The overall picture that emerges is of a theatre that is not so much dependent on or restricted by a historical reconstruction of its building, as able to explore to radical effect the opportunities it offers.

Argument about the artistic policies and cultural significance of Shakespeare's Globe has moved on from the sometimes rancorous debates of the 1980s, but, far from being a settled matter, it continues to offer challenges as well as opportunities. An especially eloquent reflection on these comes from Rylance himself, in his 'Foreword' to *London Theatres*, a volume of sumptuous colour photographs by Peter Dazeley. with commentary by Michael Coveney. The theatres whose stages, backstage areas and auditoriums are represented range from the Royal Opera House and Drury Lane Theatre to the more intimate West End theatres and such outlying gems as the Wimbledon Theatre, Wilton's Music Hall, and the extraordinary Victorian private theatre in the hospital at Normansfield, near Teddington. The Globe, which Coveney describes as 'arguably the most popular theatre in London' (87), is represented by four two-page spreads, one of them devoted to the new Sam Wanamaker Playhouse, which is also featured on the front cover. The photograph on the back cover is of the ceiling of the London Coliseum, and Rylance's 'Foreword' suggests how the two images complement each other. 'In my experience', he writes, 'the best of these old theatres always have some circular device in their ornate ceiling' (6). His first job was at the

Citizens Theatre, Glasgow, where the director Giles Havergal 'made a true circle of the audience and artists, inspired I propose by the architecture of his old theatre' (7), and in his time at 'the newest old theatre in this book, Shakespeare's Globe', Rylance found a confirmation of his perception that the circle was of vital importance:

Unable to turn off the sun in the daytime I saw my audience for the first time. Saw, for the most part, their innocence and willingness for the play. In the dark I had projected onto them my own criticism and disbelief. Thrust, on the Globe stage, into the middle of the circle of shared light, in an age before steel allowed the architects to throw forward the galleries and push the actors behind a proscenium, I realized the single most important lesson I have ever learnt as an actor. I must play with the audience, for them or to them ... with them, with their imagination, as fellow players. I was amongst them, part of a circle, a storytelling circle. They were at the same table, in the same room, around the same imaginative fire of whatever story we had lit.

(7; points of suspension in the original)

In many of the older theatres, the commandeering of the boxes to hold lighting rigs has broken the circle, and Rylance laments 'the straight lines of rationality creeping into the modern auditoriums of this book' (7). Fittingly, he takes the reader away from arguments about the historical status of the reconstructions to their significance as offering new freedoms for the imagination of actors and audience, while at the same time acknowledging the same qualities in the work of the Victorian and Edwardian architects.

Discussion of reconstructed theatres and 'original practices' in performance inevitably highlights the valuable, if not always harmonious, dialogue between historians and practitioners. Bridges are built between these constituencies and across centuries in *Shakespeare, Music and Performance*, edited by Bill Barclay and David Lindley. The editors' introduction states that the volume 'implicitly asserts the pleasure and creative advantage in understanding music's immense possibility in Shakespeare' (13), a claim fully justified by the essays that follow. The wider topic is further defined in essays by William Lyons on 'theatre bands and their music in Shakespeare's London', and by Simon Smith on the 'performance spaces for music in a Jacobean indoor playhouse'. The first of three 'in practice' sections moves to specifics of the music in Shakespeare's theatres. Claire van Kampen describes the music she prepared for the 'original practices' productions of *Twelfth Night* and *Richard III* at the reconstructed Globe. One intriguing minor insight into the material realities of such practices is afforded by her discovery that, by the time the 2002 *Twelfth Night* was revived in 2012, 'the Globe's acoustics had already changed their nature; during the intervening ten years the green oak had hardened to such an extent that it was possible to explore the use of historical instruments that exhibited a more delicate aural palate and a wider dynamic range' (47). Paul L. Faber, in 'Ophelia's songspace', puts the character's singing into the context indicated by the second part of his title: 'Elite female musical performance and propriety on the Elizabethan and Jacobean stage'. Evidence from accounts of women singing drawn from conduct manuals, travel literature, Puritan polemic, and other sources suggests a new understanding of the contemporary 'model of female musical decorum' (69). Ophelia conjures up both a 'singing courtesan' ('the eminently cultured celebrity courtesan' of Venice) and 'the chaste young gentlewoman displaying her marriageability to a select group of social equals in an exclusive but hardly private place' (62, 63). Other essays in this section examine the nature of the bells heard within and outside the playhouses, the use of music in *The Knight of the Burning Pestle*, and the changes in musical practices between 1620 and 1642.

Section Two moves to aspects of the use of music in post-Restoration theatres, proceeding from Elizabeth Kenny's discussion of *The Tempest, or the Enchanted Island* to John Cunningham's study of the survival in the traditional repertoire of Arne's Shakespeare songs from 1740–1 – their persistent presence being the result of a combination of 'style, popularity and celebrity endorsement' (143) – and Michael Burden's 'Processing with Shakespeare on the eighteenth-century stage'. In this theatrical

culture, songs were, in Cunningham's phrase, 'entertainments within the entertainment, easily divorced from, and replicated beyond, their original context' (135). Val Brodie analyses new evidence for the musical accompaniment of mid-Victorian Shakespeare with a study of the remarkable cache of scores for Charles Kean's *Henry V* now held in the Folger Shakespeare Library. The third 'practice' section deals with film music and popular music in contemporary productions, and the final section consists of two items: Carol Rutter's interview with John Trenchard, music director for five productions by Propeller; and Bill Barclay's account of music in the diverse performances brought to the 2012 Globe-to-Globe festival. The volume is a notable achievement in opening up new ways of appreciating the 'pleasure and creative advantage' offered by music in Shakespeare's plays throughout the centuries.

Film and television adaptations of Shakespeare's plays have been addressed in two very different books: *Shakespeare on Screen: 'The Tempest' and Late Romances*, edited by Sarah Hatchuel and Nathalie Vienne-Guerrin; and Jennifer Barnes's *Shakespearean Star: Laurence Olivier and National Cinema*. Like its predecessors in the series they have edited, Hatchuel and Vienne-Guerrin's volume offers a variety of effectively overlapping essays in which specific plays – or in this case, groups of plays – are examined from different points of view. The comparative rarity of feature film and television versions of the plays discussed in this volume allows for a particularly effective cross-referencing from essay to essay on the well-known films of *The Tempest* by Jarman, Greenaway and Taymor, together with accounts of such relatively less familiar productions as the Royal Ballet's *Winter's Tale* and its broadcast version, and Polish theatrical and television productions of *The Tempest*. *Cymbeline* is featured as produced in the BBC/Time-Life television series and as adapted for the cinema both in the silent era and more recently by Michael Almereyda. John Wyver, in 'Scenes from *Cymbeline* and early television studio drama', explores the BBC's written archive to illustrate the techniques of the medium as they developed and were applied in television drama both before and after World War II, and points the way to further study of the script material that is the only remaining evidence for broadcasts for which no archive recordings exist. Among the chapters dealing with *The Tempest*, Peter J. Smith's '"Something rich and strange": Jarman's defamiliarisation of *The Tempest*' draws on the director's personal archive, as well as giving illuminating readings of the film itself and its background. Together with the other four discussions of the screen adaptations of the play, this suggests new lines of enquiry as well as important sources of information. In 'Almereyda's *Cymbeline*: the end of teen Shakespeare', Douglas Lanier examines the film (shown at the Venice Film Festival in 2014 and released in the UK after some delay as *Anarchy*) in terms of the commercial absorption and neutralizing of American dissident culture, 'now merely a matter of songs of rebellion rather than a dissident perspective on mainstream American culture' (236). The essays are preceded by an introduction by the editors and followed by a 'select film-bibliography' compiled with customary thoroughness by José Ramón Díaz-Fernández.

Shakespearean Star addresses itself to three familiar films and one unmade one: Olivier's *Henry V*, *Hamlet* and *Richard III*, and the projected *Macbeth*, which is represented only by script material and other documents. Elements of each film are analysed in the course of the book, but the productions are treated not as freestanding texts in themselves but as texts alongside others that support the argument concerning Olivier's achievement of representative 'national' status. Barnes traces the development of this in his theatrical and personal career to good effect, with reference to the actor's papers, held in the British Library, as well as to press reports and other sources. Much of the story is familiar to historians of cinema and the theatre, but Barnes is able to produce new material that fleshes it out and clarifies aspects that have previously seemed to be unavoidably a matter of surmise. The interpretation of the *Macbeth* script drafts in terms of Olivier's relationship with Vivien Leigh is persuasive, and 'Olivier' emerges in respect of the completed films as part of a multi-faceted entity that encompasses 'Shakespeare' (the figure and the referent in cultural discourse), as well as 'National' as applied to the cinema and, specifically, to the National Theatre. (It is after all a statue of Olivier's film Hamlet, sword held aloft as he climbs up to meet the Ghost on the battlements, that greets visitors to the National Theatre.)

The commercial significance of *Henry V* receives welcome attention. In the film magnate J. Arthur Rank's pronouncements regarding *Henry V* in 1945, Barnes identifies 'a sense of slippage between the idea of the nation-at-war and the striving post-war British film industry, linking his export drive with an assertion of national culture and/or national community' (48). In the film business, America was still the enemy in a bitter trade war. The patriotic tone of the film, and its effectiveness as morale-boosting propaganda, are given a new spin in such statements as the following, which one hopes was not to be taken literally by Rank's executives: 'I have a property in "Henry" worth more than any other motion picture extant. I propose to sell it or "close the wall up with our English dead"' (48).

The effect of Olivier's bodily presence within and around the film characters is connected with the discourses of personal psychology, as well as national identity and his status as a Shakespearian. In historical terms, Barnes's most intriguing suggestion is probably her claim that, given the direction his career had taken from 1957 and his performance in Osborne's *The Entertainer*, not only was the *Macbeth* film no longer feasible in the context of the film industry, but the failure to finance the project 'enable[d] Olivier's Shakespearean star image to evolve in response and, ultimately, to reach the apex of its national-cultural power by 1963' (125). (In a touch of irony that Barnes does not mention, one outcome of the failure may have been the availability of funding for the lacklustre 1960 *Macbeth* with Maurice Evans and Judith Anderson.)[2]

---

[2] See the account given by the publicist Clayton Hutton in 'Finding the finance', in *Macbeth: The Making of the Film* (London, 1960), Ch.4.

Olivier's physical voice, unmistakable, is still current and much imitated, notably by Peter Sellers in his rendition of the lyric of 'A Hard Day's Night' as if by the actor's Richard III. He found another kind of voice in the autobiographies and life-writing, which were his means of speaking to posterity, so much so that the adjustments and revisions in them are remarkably revealing. This kind of 'voice' can also be recovered through the medium of skillful historical scholarship, such as that provided by Sophie Duncan in *Shakespeare's Women and the Fin de Siècle*. Duncan brings together memoirs and other published accounts (some of them first-person) of personalities and performances and an impressive array of archival materials, letters, annotated promptbooks and newspaper reviews. The strategy brings new clarity to our understanding of a group of celebrated actresses (the historically appropriate noun) including Lily Langtry, Ellen Terry and Mrs Patrick Campbell. Duncan makes exemplary use of the wide spectrum of provincial as well as metropolitan reviews, now available online from the British Library and previously accessible only through laboursome journeys to newspaper collections at Colindale. In the case of Terry, she has collated preparation and rehearsal copies, lectures and letters. She is able to shed new light on (for example) Terry's Lady Macbeth and the 'fascinating nexus of critical gulfs and congruences between Terry's stated intentions and reception in the role' (70). Her performance of Imogen in Irving's 1896 *Cymbeline* and her preparation for it receive close attention, and Duncan explores at fascinating length the likely connection between this Lyceum production and the novel *Dracula*, by Irving's business manager Bram Stoker. It is typical of Duncan's approach that she links this example of somnophilia – assault on sleeping women – to wider issues in later nineteenth-century culture. More important, perhaps, is the confirmation of the actress as a sensitive and original interpreter of plays and roles. The specific attractions of Lily Langtry's 'serpent of old Nile' in her 1890 performance as Cleopatra, and Campbell's unorthodox Ophelia (1897) and Lady

Macbeth (1898), are interpreted in the light of contemporary sexual politics as well as the kind of archetypal representations discussed and illustrated to arresting effect in Bram Dijkstra's *Idols of Perversity: Fantasies of Feminine Evil in Fin-de-Siècle Culture* (1986). Duncan's book is a significant contribution to the historiography of theatre, as well as an enhancement of our access to the thinking of some remarkable interpreters.

Shakespeare on Stage, Volume 2: Twelve Leading Actors on Twelve Key Roles, Julian Curry's second collection of interviews with actors (the first being published in 2010) brings detailed commentary from more recent theatrical interpreters, all highly articulate and penetrating in their analysis of the plays, as well their own work in them. It benefits from the editor's skill as an interviewer and his personal experience as an actor: he knows the plays thoroughly and knows what kind of questions will lead his subjects through a well-structured account of their work on the roles in question.

Throughout the interview on his 2007 Othello at the Donmar, Chiwetel Ejiofor moves between imaginative appreciation of the mentality of Shakespeare's time, as it informs the play, and his understanding of more immediate contemporary perceptions. One striking example is his Othello's demand for ocular proof and the grabbing of Iago by the throat on 'Villain, be sure thou prove my love a whore' (3.3.364). Curry asks 'Would you say that was when Othello starts losing it?' and the answer is in the negative:

I think it's a perfectly rational response to somebody who tells you this, but offers no hard evidence. That's fighting talk where I come from. It's like if you tell a guy his girlfriend's been sleeping around, but offer no explanation. He turns round and says go fuck yourself. It's perfectly reasonable. But it encourages Iago, because it shows him that what he's doing is working.   (91)

As well as the thoughtful step-by-step analyses of rehearsal and performance, the interviews abound in striking perceptions of the plays as a whole, the kind of vision that guided the actors throughout the process of rehearsal and performance. Ejiofor ends with a striking image that expresses a view of the whole play: 'I suppose *Othello* is a kind of beautiful, ornate building, like a palace. It's extraordinary and fine, and so well looked after. And through the course of the play a gigantic wrecking ball smashes it away until there is absolutely nothing left' (102). Zoe Wanamaker (Beatrice in the 2007 National Theatre production, directed by Nicholas Hytner and discussed in his own book) reaches for an extreme topical analogy in reflecting on the interrupted wedding scene (4.1) in *Much Ado About Nothing*. Beatrice is in shock at what happens and cannnot believe what she is hearing: 'I read the other day about these two guys who murdered an officer with knives . . . There was a witness who said she simply stood there and couldn't believe what she was seeing . . . The horror of it means that [Beatrice] can't speak' (295). Ian McKellen (King Lear in Trevor Nunn's 2007 RSC production) rejects the usefulness of Beckett in approaching the play – 'Shakespeare got there first' – and insists that there is more hope than in Jan Kott's perception of the scene between Lear and the blinded Gloucester (Folio text 4.4), 'because it's a man on a journey trying to understand himself and other people. He's not given up. He's still alive, more alive in this scene than perhaps anywhere else' (151). Michael Pennington describes Timon (RSC, 1999), responding offhandedly with his thanks for the offerings of the poet and painter (1.1.247–50), as 'a sort of connoisseur without qualification' who 'seems to find it difficult to concentrate . . . a kind of amoeba of generosity' (170).

This is a remarkably rich collection, ranging from insights such as these into the actor's imaginative processes and the interpretation of specific lines and situations to such immediately practical matters as the placement of the pillars on the stage of Shakespeare's Globe. (Roger Allam, who played Falstaff there in the two parts of *Henry IV* in 2010 'guesses' they should be 'six or eight feet upstage'.) Some of the productions in question date from the 1980s: Fiona Shaw on Katherine in *The Taming of the Shrew*, Alan Rickman revisiting his Jacques in the 1985 RSC production, Harriet Walter on Imogen at the Other Place in 1987. Interviewed

with immediate reference to his performance as Shylock at the RSC in 2011, Patrick Stewart evinces a remarkable degree of intimacy with the play, having appeared in it five times and having 'returned repeatedly to the role since he was twelve years old' (Curry's prefatory note, 233). Sara Kestelman, Hippolyta and Titania in Brook's 1970 *Midsummer Night's Dream*, describes rehearsals in terms that shed new light on the director. Brook had brought in a 'box of tricks, a chest of things to play around with'. She was blowing bubbles from a little pot of soap solution 'and he came behind me and he said you must take this work more seriously'. Curry, somewhat bemused, asks what he wanted the actors to do:

I've no idea. Maybe he thought I wasn't applying myself, that I was enjoying blowing bubbles rather than making use of them, seeing what the bubble might do. He's a very serious man. I don't remember much laughter. On the other hand, he's got his humour. He loves dirty jokes and anything to do with dicks and cocks makes him shriek with laughter, real schoolboy stuff. Not that there's anything wrong with schoolboy humour, but it surprises one for such a fine intellectual. (109)

Somewhere in here, it seems, lies a key to the playful seriousness – or, rather, serious play – that made the production so special, but also sometimes puzzled the actors during rehearsals.

The final word in this review goes to a fine, versatile actor whose recent death was a sad loss to the profession. Tim Pigott-Smith saw his memoir, *Do You Know Who I Am?*, through the press shortly before his death in April 2017. His career encompassed (indeed was transformed by) his performance as Ronald Merrick in the television adaptation of Paul Scott's 'Raj Quartet', *The Jewel in the Crown*, and one of his most recent appearances was in the title role of Mike Bartlett's iambically inflected *Charles III* in London and on Broadway. Shakespeare's plays figured at many points in his career, and there are informative descriptions of his work as Angelo in the 1979 *Measure for Measure*, King Lear at the West Yorkshire Playhouse in 2011, and numerous roles with the RSC at

Stratford-upon-Avon and elsewhere. He describes vividly his earliest experiences of Stratford as a schoolboy, on a summer job in the theatre's paint shop – perching on a ladder to retouch the *periaktoi* in the 1964 *Wars of the Roses* set – and finally as an actor. There are compelling accounts of struggles with Arts Council England over its meagre and intrusive support for Compass Theatre Company, the rigours of directing *Hamlet* in Regent's Park, and the practicalities of working in the changing British theatres of the last fifty years. The engaging anecdotal element of Pigott-Smith's memoir reflects the mutually supportive (or, on rare occasions, mutually destructive) spirit of the acting profession. Some of the stories are handed down to the author from senior colleagues, but are no less illuminating for that. One such concerns Robert Atkins, artistic director of the Shakespeare Memorial Theatre in 1944–5, whose 'notoriously foul language' caused the vicar of Holy Trinity Church to pass him over as a reader of the lesson in the service commemorating Shakespeare's birthday, a privilege that would normally have gone with the director's position: 'Espying the vicar in the street, just after he had received this humiliating news, Atkins hailed him, "My good man!" The vicar turned, inquisitively. Atkins boomed across the road, with full voice, "My dear Vicar, advance me one cogent reason why I shouldn't read the fucking lesson!"' (19). It would be a churlish theatre historian who did not perceive the documentary value of the story and the vital significance of its magisterially profane language in understanding Atkins, the theatre of his time and the milieu of Stratford in the 1940s. For appreciating this and retelling the story, as well as for his performances and his book's perceptive insights, Tim Piggott-Smith deserves our posthumous thanks.

WORKS REVIEWED

Barclay, Bill, and David Lindley, eds., *Shakespeare, Music and Performance* (Cambridge, 2017)

Barnes, Jennifer, *Shakespearean Star: Laurence Olivier and National Cinema* (Cambridge, 2017)

Brook, Peter, *Tip of the Tongue: Reflections on Language and Meaning* (London, 2017)

Coveney, Michael, and Peter Dazeley, *London Theatres*, foreword by Mark Rylance (London, 2017)

Curry, Julian, *Shakespeare on Stage, Volume 2: Twelve Leading Actors on Twelve Key Roles*, with a foreword by Nicholas Hytner (London, 2017)

Dugas, Don-John, *Shakespeare for Everyman: Ben Greet in Early Twentieth-Century America* (London, 2016)

Duncan, Sophie, *Shakespeare's Women and the Fin de Siècle* (Oxford, 2016)

Hatchuel, Sarah, and Nathalie Vienne-Guerrin, eds., *Shakespeare on Screen: 'The Tempest' and Late Romances* (Cambridge, 2017)

Hytner, Nicholas, *Balancing Acts: Behind the Scenes at the National Theatre* (London, 2017)

Menzer, Paul, *Shakespeare in the Theatre: the American Shakespeare Center* (London, 2017)

Pigott-Smith, Tim, *Do You Know Who I Am? A Memoir* (London, 2017)

Purcell, Stephen, *Shakespeare in the Theatre: Mark Rylance* (London, 2017)

Rokison, Abigail, *Shakespeare in the Theatre: Nicholas Hytner* (London, 2017)

3. EDITIONS AND TEXTUAL STUDIES
reviewed by PETER KIRWAN

2017 has been something of a red-letter year for Shakespeare editing, with the arrival of a large number of long-awaited projects, including four brand-new Arden editions and the most substantial new *Complete Works* in thirty years. In order to give these projects due attention, therefore, next year's review will consider new books and articles from 2017 as well as 2018. In this review, I concentrate exclusively on editions: the Arden 3 instalments of *Cymbeline*, *The Comedy of Errors*, *A Midsummer Night's Dream* and *Edward III*; three revised volumes in the New Cambridge Shakespeare; and *The New Oxford Shakespeare* (*NOS*).

NEW ARDEN SHAKESPEARE EDITIONS

Valerie Wayne's sensitive introduction to the new Arden *Cymbeline* offers a complex interweaving of the mythical, historical, and national associations within a play 'so full it almost overflows its own measure' (1). *Cymbeline* operates, in Wayne's view, as something of a best-of compilation, incorporating an uncommon number of plot points from earlier plays (28). The play's breadth of allusiveness in recalling is part of both the play's structure and content, particularly in the magisterial closing scene. Wayne's argument throughout is that *Cymbeline* only falters when measured against the wrong yardsticks, such as the attempts to define it as a tragedy (20), factually oriented history (27), or an ill-defined 'romance' (18). Wayne aims 'to restore the meanings of "romance" to the rich cultural heritage from which Shakespeare's later works arose', linking it to work of the 1580s/1590s as part of the play's 'recapitulatory' mode (29).

Wayne focuses on three aspects: the calumny plot, the influence of Prince Henry, and early modern attitudes to ancient Britain. She argues that the exploration of women's subjectivity was central to medieval romance (6), and offers a careful negotiation of these tropes that acknowledges both the play's misogynistic discourse and the flawed characters who deliver it. Perhaps her most important observation is that Posthumus's speech in 5.1 forgives Innogen while still believing in her infidelity, which Wayne sees as the play's most radical intervention in gender politics (13). Elsewhere, she explores the play's gender fluidity, arguing that the play complicates binaries, including in the presentation of older men in nurturing roles and the intense same-sex/sibling attachments (91–2).

James's court, and Prince Henry in particular, enjoyed several entertainments concerning ancient Britain in 1610, leading up to the first performances of *Cymbeline* in 1610–11. Henry was repeatedly situated within the lineage of ancient British history in entertainments that also celebrated the nation's connections with Europe (35). Henry was also a shareholder in the Virginia Company, and Wayne relates Innogen's encounter with the 'savage' Welsh to early descriptions of native Virginians (59). Wayne reads the play as two twinned narratives of invasive colonialism: Iachimo's invasion of Innogen's bedroom, and the Roman invasion (64). This is complicated by mixed early modern attitudes towards the ancient Britons, characterized as either great forebears or barbarians (54), a paradox manifest in Guiderius and Arviragus. The mixed attitudes are symptomatic of a play that asserts a hybridized British identity, anachronistically invaded by both 'Italian' and 'Roman' visitors (81), and which stages, in Posthumus's vision, a process of ancestral recovery.

Wayne's work on the play's afterlives is a little more unbalanced; a section on allusions to *Cymbeline* in *Mrs Dalloway* gets as much space as all screen and radio productions combined. The strength here is Wayne's identification of recurring patterns, such as the long abandonment of Posthumus's vision for 300 years, leading to the diminution of that role and the brief tradition of Iachimo as the play's male lead (114); and the romantic idealization of Innogen until the late twentieth century (117). Wayne also considers the reclamation of the play in women's writing as part of her treatment of the play as one that interrogates and undermines cultures of misogyny (136).

The text is well presented and justified, and Wayne's textual appendix outlines the primary innovations, many using databases to justify unusual words. 'Frame yourself / To orderly solicity' (2.3.46–7) is a rare retention, as opposed to most editors' preference for F2's 'solicits'; Wayne's discovery of early modern usages of 'solicity' as a synonym for 'concern, carefulness, anxious attention' justifies its presence. Other unusual retentions include 'this imperseverant thing' (4.1.14) meaning 'lacking in perseverance' following contemporary sermons, as opposed to 'imperceiverant' (not perceptive), for which Wayne finds no precedent; and 'Richer than doing nothing for a babe' at 3.3.23, glossed as 'more lucrative than assuming care for a child' – this latter fits with the play's ruminations on care and childhood, as well as having topical resonance to Parliamentary debates over abolishing the Court of Wards (43–4). An equally significant retention is the conclusion of Posthumus's letter in 1.6: 'as you value your trust. Leonatus' (1.6.24–5). Wayne sensibly notes Innogen's emphasis on having read 'so far' and that she is 'warmed by th'rest' (1.6.26–8), making Hanmer's emendation to 'your truest Leonatus' unlikely. More generally, Wayne resists regularizing metre, pointing to the play's general metrical flexibility.

An unusual feature of this edition is the retention of the folio's scene divisions in act 5. A primary pillar of Wayne's reading is the self-contained nature of 5.4 as a dramatic unit, 'a coherent and distinctly antiquated scene that opens with a dumb show and includes a dream vision, theophany and prophecy' (388). This involves some of Wayne's most interventionist work, adding an exit and entrance for Posthumus and his captors, but the effect is to establish the dumb show as a formal and deliberate break in the action before Posthumus is left alone onstage; the effect may divide readers but is worth preserving in a modern edition. Notes throughout the edition are judicious,

justifying standard emendations and tracing word patterns and resonances across the play in line with Wayne's emphasis on the play as one that recaps itself.

On the broader questions of the text's provenance, Wayne is non-committal, staging the debates without offering a firm conclusion. She accepts that a Ralph Crane transcript underlies the folio text, and that the copy behind that may have been prepared by two different scribes, but doesn't try to define the nature of that manuscript. Addressing the folio's unique use of 'Imogen' raises the question of whether Crane copied this from the manuscript or simply imposed his own consistent tidying-up, a question understandably without resolution; Wayne uses 'Innogen' throughout. Similarly, she supports the idea that the play may have gone through a process of authorial revision, which for her is most strongly evidenced by the shift in the use of sources after the second act, but she doesn't pursue the implications of this for what the play may have looked like prior to revision (400).

Kent Cartwright's edition of *The Comedy of Errors* is an unapologetic and refreshingly enthusiastic celebration of a play whose disparagement in the eighteenth and nineteenth centuries has had a lingering effect despite the more recent revival of its fortunes (8). While Cartwright gestures towards the play's triumphant theatrical resurgence, he is most interested in its linguistic and structural complexities, unpacked in a rich introduction.

Cartwright thematizes 'error', noting that this was an obsessive concern of Renaissance humanists (9). Error is understood both as wandering and as a consequence of iteration, building nicely into the play's formal doublings and repetitions. Arguing that Renaissance writers conceived of error as something that 'leaps from a small particular to a vast conclusion and then overwhelms the mind' (13), Cartwright traces the 'dim inwardness' and 'deceptive outwardness' leading to fixed mindsets that compound and solidify positions of error, and he examines the 'emotional intensity' of characters' experience of magic and sorcery (29) that makes rational solution become impossible. The attention to magic brings up the differences in perception that replicate the plays' identity crises, with the Syracusans experiencing as magic and anger what the Ephesians experience as commerce and madness.

The place of the play is fluid, but the economic resonances of market circulation 'reformulate the play's larger question of whether agency is a function of the self or of outside forces' (39). The circulation of objects is central to the play's compounding of errors, and Cartwright is liberal in the addition of stage directions to clarify the movements of purses and the chain. His interest in objects is thematic rather than dramaturgical, aligning with the play's religious imagery in the shared focus on 'redemption', coming after the apocalypse-tinged chaos of the play's middle three acts (44).

The combination of market and magic in Ephesus, however, disrupts normal transactions, leading to the edition's most important guiding principle: that of 'connective repetition' (33). Over a third of the play's lines are taken up by characters recapping their own stories (60), creating farce and initiating crises of identity. This manifests in Cartwright's decision to add speech marks to repetitions such as at 1.2.87–8: 'Thy "mistress' marks"? What "mistress", slave, hast thou?'. The emphasis on repetition also leads to unusual retentions, as in 5.1. 404–6: 'And you, the calendars of their nativity, / Go to a gossip's feast, and go with me; / After so long grief, such nativity!'. Where other editions emend the second 'nativity' to 'festivity', Cartwright argues that the different metrical emphases indicate the Abbess's own use of repetition-with-variation to move from the individual births to a more general rebirth (67). In emphasizing the taking up of words by others, Cartwright effectively distinguishes his edition in light of the play's intricate connections.

The remainder of the introduction concentrates on sources and a brief discussion of performance. Cartwright argues that *Errors* is Shakespeare's most derivative play (75), and details the play's two sources in Plautus, convincingly arguing for the darker angle taken by Shakespeare, particularly in

the introduction of romance material. Perhaps more interesting are the biblical allusions (89) and the attention to Elizabethan urban writings such as Greene's pamphlets, evoking the horror of debtors' prisons (93). The more contemporary Tudor sources (including *Mother Bombie*) feature in an appendix on dating the play, which Cartwright puts in 1593–4, some months before the Gray's Inn performance.

Given the introduction's emphasis on objects, the section on staging is disappointingly cursory. A dedicated discussion of 3.1 (the 'lock-out' scene) is welcome, and Cartwright points to the fluidity required of the *frons scenae* if Adriana is to enter above on the balcony, disrupting the vertical plane by blurring the interior and exterior of the house (100). The complexity of the theatrical resources needed supports Cartwright's argument that the play was not written specifically for the Gray's Inn revels (315). The question of doubling is barely discussed and, while Cartwright suggests that this can cause problems of comprehension while highlighting virtuosity, he doesn't provide any examples (101). Cartwright highlights four significant productions, as well as *The Boys from Syracuse*, but the three-page survey of other recent productions leaves little space for more than brief mentions of the wide variety of interpretations (130).

Cartwright's textual essay draws on Paul Werstine, agreeing that the manuscript underpinning the folio text was close to many scholars' definition of 'foul papers', but that this does not imply the clear distinction from a playbook that it once did (345). Playbook copy is defined here as text that *doesn't* exhibit the classic features of foul papers (for *Errors*, most significantly, shifting speech prefixes and character descriptions). The discussion picks up on textual idiosyncrasies to indicate the provenance of the copytext, but reaches no firm conclusions (though a long section on the seemingly duplicated stage directions *Runne all out* and *Exeunt omnes, as fast as may be, frighted* [Folio, H6ᵛ], might have gone further in considering the action implied if both directions *were* intended: 333–7).

Particular textual innovations include the retention of 'fraughtage' at 4.1.87 and the choice to keep

Emilia as 'Abbess' in order to maintain something of a surprise ending (347). The crux at 2.1.108–12 occasions an original intervention, in which Cartwright constructs a new conditional sub-clause by converting the folio's 'yet the gold bides still' to 'and though gold bides still ... ', an intervention that necessitates further changes to syntax in 110 and 111, but which creates more immediate clarity in this difficult passage. Cartwright claims to prefer long clauses to a practice of end-stopping (348), though in his example – Egeon's long speeches in 1.1 – he doesn't go as far as Sarah Neville's *NOS* edition, which even turns a full stop in the folio (1.1.82) into a semi-colon. The main value of Cartwright's glosses is their attention to rhetorical devices (e.g. Glosses on *antisthecon* at 1.1.157, *palilogia* at 3.2.44, and *anaphora* at 5.1.68) and structural repetitions and similarities, such as the alignment of Dromio's experience of Nell with Antipholus's experience of magical romance as nightmarish grotesque.

Performance history is the launchpad for Sukanta Chaudhuri's fascinating edition of *A Midsummer Night's Dream*. Noting the play's mythic status and that 'postmodern Shakespeare is a socially complex and multicultural construction' (2), Chaudhuri begins his Arden edition by locating *Dream* at a series of cultural crossroads and historical tipping points, from Auschwitz to Lebanon, the Soviet bloc to apartheid South Africa, Australian aboriginal productions to reunified Germany. Chaudhuri insists on 'the formal and thematic versatility of the play' (38) and its 'transhuman dimension' (37) that has allowed it to be continually reappropriated during sea changes in global politics.

Having begun with the contemporary, Chaudhuri's introduction returns to the play's prehistories in sources. The value of this section is the attention to 'rustic popular belief'; Chaudhuri digs deeply into cultural beliefs around fairies, distinguishing the different traditions that align the specific figure of Robin with the more generic Puck. Chaudhuri believes fairies would have been played by child actors, and includes eight boy actors in his casting chart (281). Yet beyond English folklore,

Chaudhuri also picks up interweavings from French romance (the thirteenth-century *Huon of Bordeaux*, he suggests, provides the detail of Oberon and Titania's disruption of nature), the classics and Chaucer. 'Shakespeare turns the syncretic fairy love of his times into a sustained poetic creation mingling classical, medieval and contemporary, remote and proximate, popular and elite' (55).

The introduction is a vociferous defence of the play; Chaudhuri's section on language, in particular, argues for Shakespeare's 'new confidence' in verse and explicates the oral/aural effects that align dramatic verse with action (111). Yet Chaudhuri is also frank about its failings; most notably, he critiques the structural patterning that reduces the lovers to pawns, arguing that none of them is explored in depth. He is critical of readings of the play that over-emphasize the subjugation of Hippolyta, but at the same time asserts that 'the play operates from start to finish within a framework of patriarchy' (82), as evidenced by the silence of Helena and Hermia in the final act and by Oberon 'reducing [Titania] to bestiality' (84).

A pleasing element of Chaudhuri's approach is his attention to the play as one of very few to have ordinary working-class people as main characters. Bottom is both clown and jester, a metaphor for innocence and the 'sheer capacity for unshaken survival' (94). Bakhtin's reading of carnival as formalized disorder is thus central to an understanding of the play's social politics, which leads to Chaudhuri viewing the satire on the players as genial comedy among co-equals (98). Within pastoral, understood here as a courtly form 'controlled by the elite imagination' (71), Shakespeare thematizes theatrical presentation so that the play can gently subvert itself throughout; as he puts it, 'the value-structure supporting the narrative is undermined but never quite toppled' (106), resulting in 'a comedy of compromise'.

Chaudhuri's appendices debunk some popular myths, particularly concerning the play's date. Chaudhuri allows that the play may originally have been staged as part of wedding celebrations, but dismisses any attempts to specify a particular occasion. He is particularly resistant to notions that Elizabeth may have been in the audience, arguing that any identification between Titania and Elizabeth would be too transgressive, and that the play anticipates her cultural rather than literal presence. Chaudhuri shows more sympathy for speculations that explain the play's 'two endings' (291), though a hypothesis about Puck's epilogue implying intended performance by a children's company seems unnecessarily elaborate.

The discussion of the text concentrates on the traditional signs of working copy in Q1, even taking into account Werstine's cautions about the 'features' of 'foul papers' (297). Q1 is Chaudhuri's copy-text, with F probably consulting a new theatrical manuscript but not offering any greater authorial authority. Chaudhuri retains the traditional act/scene divisions, while noting that 2.1 to 4.1 have a single setting and broad continuity of action, with the stage indisputably cleared only once, at the end of 3.1 (321). Much work is done to regularize speech prefixes that, in Q and F, change to avoid confusion (e.g. 'Th' for Theseus and Thisbe in 5.1). For the same reason, Chaudhuri uses the mechanicals' names throughout 5.1 rather than the parts they play, and prints the dialogue from 'Pyramus and Thisbe' in italics. This leads to a nice effect when the italics for '*This lanthorn doth ...* ' (5.1.234, 238) give way to roman for 'All that I have to say' (251), visually depicting Starveling breaking out of his role.

Chaudhuri's liberal emendation leads to some questionable choices. At 5.1.216, he calls for Lion and Moonshine to enter separately, breaking from both Q and F. His rationale is that QF's punctuation of 'Here come two noble beasts, in a man and a lion' (215–16) suggests that the two noble beasts are the man and lion *in one*. This is plausible, but involves a substantive change to an explicit direction and causes a logical problem when Theseus then says 'let us listen to the Moon' (233) before Starveling has entered. Other disruptions include an original reading of 5.1.205–6: 'Now is the more use between the two neighbours', for Q's 'Now is the moon used' or F's 'Now is the moral down'.

Where other editions offer the more practical 'Now is the wall/mural down', Chaudhuri argues that 'moon used' may be a misreading of 'mor use' as 'mon usd' in secretary hand (262); the gloss implies that the wall's departure may lead to more familiar exchanges between the neighbours. The emendation at 5.1.59 of 'wondrous strange snow' (QF) to 'wondrous swarthy snow' (Dyce) seems less persuasive in its attempt to make the image consistent. A much more interesting discussion concerns the modernization of 'ere'; at 3.1.83, Chaudhuri makes the unusual decision to render Puck's line as '... A stranger Pyramus than ere [rather than e'er] played here'. In interventions such as this, Chaudhuri ties together his thematic interests in the play's preposterousness with textual choices that privilege the play's uncanny sense of time.

The debut of *Edward III* in the Arden canon will cause no controversy; the play has already been anthologized in the Oxford Shakespeare and published as a stand-alone edition in the New Cambridge Shakespeare. What Richard Proudfoot and Nicola Bennett's new edition does offer, however, is the fullest and most comprehensive treatment of a neglected play to date, and it is well worth the wait.

The text of *Edward III* presents few difficulties. The editors' most interesting choice is to treat the traditional scenes 1.2 and 2.1 as a single 625-line scene, a decision followed by the *NOS*. Proudfoot and Bennett contend that Lodwick's first speech simply describes the encounter that has just taken place, leading them to bring him on earlier. The reasoning makes sense, though Proudfoot and Bennett provide the more customary scene division and line numbers in square brackets for convenience. More interventionist is the treatment of 12.42–60. Giorgio Melchiori's NCS edition stuck to the line order of the 1596 quarto, attempting to make sense of its contorted lines through punctuation. *NOS* moves a single line, 'Then all the world, and call it but a power', adjusting punctuation to create the exclamatory sentence 'Thy parcelling this power hath made it more / Than all the world!' Proudfoot and Bennett reallocate another eleven-line segment, so that the image of the 'handful of so many sands' is now the penultimate sequence in the passage. Their choice allows the final clauses to follow logically from one another. The intervention is extreme but makes structural sense, and supports the editors' case that the play has undergone revision. They believe new similes were 'interlined or marginally added' (66), and that the printed scene represents the compositor's attempt to make sense of these interlineations.

The argument for revision also explains the play's surprising lack of mention of the Countess subsequent to her appearances. Proudfoot and Bennett suggest that this indicates that scenes 4–18 were already in existence before Shakespeare wrote her scenes, which the editors suggest replaced an earlier version of the Countess scenes 'in which the Countess's honour is never seriously jeopardized and the king gets over his infatuation with her without risk of murder or perjury' (79). They more speculatively suggest that Shakespeare also worked on other scenes in a piecemeal fashion, perhaps specifically bolstering the role of Prince Edward.

The edition rationalizes its choices well, particularly in the handling of speech prefixes and stage directions, including the apportioning of the closing couplet of the first scene to the king ('their tone of authority and experience signal the highest-ranking character onstage', 1.168 n.); the choice to keep Warwick onstage until the end of scene 2, following Q's *Exeunt* ('to leave the Countess alone for her final couplet adds pathos to her predicament, but at some cost to a sense of Warwick's solicitude', 2.624 n.); and the correction of obvious errors such as Villiers for Charles at 13.73 and Philip for Prince Edward at 6.137. The management of stage action is sometimes unnecessary, as in the choreographing of Prince Edward's kneeling and rising during his final speech, but for the most part the action reflects textual cues.

A third of the introduction is devoted to authorship, but refreshingly 'without trying to draw purportedly conclusive lines of demarcation between sharply defined areas of the text' (49). The editors note that few of the linguistic features offer clear distinctions between traditional authorial divisions,

and are keen to avoid shutting down the possibility of shared writing. The discussion of which other authors may be present is short, though the editors show some sympathy for work associating Marlowe with the play and are reluctant to dismiss Kyd from the conversation. For the purposes of this edition, the editors are content to support the circumstantial case for Shakespeare and leave the remainder of the authorship question open.

The editors couch the question in a broader discussion of the play's history and sources. This is an unusual history play in its lack of onstage carnage, the simple structures of opposition and the unbalancing of symmetry (6). They note that, while King Edward's role is more than twice the size of anyone else's, it diminishes to become subsidiary to that of his son by the play's end (93). Proudfoot and Bennett identify the 1590s as a time of nostalgia in which Edward III's victories were celebrated as evidence of England's role as a European power, and, as well as drawing on obvious contexts such as the succession crisis and Spanish Armada, suggest that the civil war in France and the end of the Valois dynasty, whose early years the play dramatizes, may be a major source of inspiration.

A long section on sources confusingly concentrates on later critics' reactions to Froissart, Holinshed, Ocland and Painter without actually describing the content. While this is initially disorienting, the editors devote more than thirty pages of longer notes to line-by-line discussions of parallels. The editors are also keen to note the influence of Marlowe's drama, particularly implying that Tamburlaine provides a model for Edward's vindictive violence (45), and intriguingly suggesting that the play may consciously respond to *Edward II* by showing the son to be everything the father was not.

The final significant contribution made by the edition is the finest stage history of the play yet produced, noting its re-emergence in the 1980s and discussing several prominent British and European productions. The editors have strong opinions about some of the decisions, including the choice by the 2002 RSC production to render

Lodwick a clown (103), but also celebrate what is revealed when the play is performed outside of England, where national concerns give way to questions of oaths and ethics (104). While the RSC production dominates the discussion, the range of performance choices highlighted by Proudfoot and Bennett will no doubt be of encouragement to future producers in its insistence on the play's interpretive possibilities.

UPDATED NEW CAMBRIDGE SHAKESPEARE EDITIONS

The New Cambridge Shakespeare has published three revised editions in the last year, none of which includes changes to the texts. Penny Gay's revision of her 2004 introduction to Elizabeth Story Donno's *Twelfth Night* is the most minimal, mostly tweaking phrasing and filling out the stage history with brief descriptions of productions that create a much more multicultural image of the play. Anthony Dawson and Gretchen E. Minton similarly extend the globalized outlook in their updated introduction to Dawson's 2003 *Troilus and Cressida*, focusing on the ways in which 'theatre has understandably reflected the perilous threats to traditional identifications' (65). Covering recent shifts that focus on the play's politics and presentism, they suggest that the play's 'often corrosive scepticism undermines individual investments in ways that speak to the world we inhabit' (68), and argues that both criticism and performance are increasingly foregrounding the elements that link rather than divide both sides in a conflict.

Jeremy Lopez's brand new introduction to Martin Spevack's 1988 *Julius Caesar* utilizes negative contrast as a means to understanding the play. This informs a brilliant discussion of sources in which, rather than focusing on similarities between Plutarch and Shakespeare, he concentrates on how Shakespeare's account diverges. He argues that almost every other treatment of the Caesar story in the period focused on Pompey (8), suggesting that Shakespeare's strategy is to detach the title character from historical context. By stripping Pompey and the pre-history of the play away,

Shakespeare subtly moves the play's focus away from the external, making the primary drama that which is happening within Brutus. Lopez suggests that Shakespeare set out to write the kind of Caesar-play that people would not expect to see (13). The sixteenth-century cultural idea of Caesar was of someone larger than life, but Shakespeare diminishes Caesar throughout in a way that Lopez imagines may have evoked the aged Elizabeth, 'a royal power that is wilfully unaware of its own mortality' (18). The play uses religious and secular ritual to continually shadow Caesar with the spectre of his own death (22). What ties the play together, Lopez concludes, is the emphasis on how things are seen or things that are not seen, the epitome of which is Cassius and Brutus falling out over the crimes of an unseen official. Lopez notes that the play in performance has rarely been about Caesar, and that the play's shift from Brutus to Antony in its final movements is reflected in oscillations over who is presented as the lead character. Lopez also points out that the scenes that are most frequently cut for their disconnectedness within the episodic structure – such as Portia's suicide or the murder of Cinna the poet – are among those considered most significant by contemporary critics. His interventions in the text are restricted to commentary notes, which retain many of Spevack's notes in substance and form but offer new glosses with an eye to the modern student and cut back on notes relating to textual matters.

THE NEW OXFORD SHAKESPEARE

The *New Oxford Shakespeare*, overseen by Gary Taylor, John Jowett, Terri Bourus and Gabriel Egan, is a monumental piece of scholarship that is far too large to do full justice to in this brief survey. It is also, at the time of writing, incomplete; the edition refers repeatedly to a forthcoming 'Alternative Versions' volume, which will be reviewed when released. Here, I will cover some of the edition's more distinctive features. At present, the edition comprises the *Modern Critical Edition* (*MCE*), a two-Volume *Critical Reference Edition* (*CRE*), an *Authorship Companion* edited by Taylor and Egan, and *The New Oxford Shakespeare* (*NOS*) *Online*, which includes all of the above.

The economic model for *NOS Online* is baffling. While purchasers of *MCE* get a one-year free trial, an individual subscription to *NOS Online* costs £340 *a year*. Given that the four print volumes retail at £295, one might expect a substantial amount of additional online content, but at the time of writing unique online content includes only facsimile images (some of which are open access) and a search function. *NOS Online* will include the 'Alternative Versions', but there is no indication of when this will be available. For those unable to access institutional subscriptions, the new *Norton Shakespeare*, which gives one-off purchasers of the print volume *perpetual* access to a simpler but extremely useful online edition with embedded facsimiles, audio files *and* edited versions of variant texts, offers considerably better value.

The presentation of much of *NOS Online* is deeply disappointing. The *Authorship Companion* is laid out chapter-by-chapter according to the restrictions of the print edition, without even making the effort to move tables to their logical appropriate position in the text (see 9.3–9.5). Features which in the print version of *MCE* look fabulous – such as the opening *bricolage* and timelines to each play – are reduced to plain text. However, the actual works are dynamically rendered. Full line-numbering appears in the left-hand margin when the cursor hovers there; annotations and glosses appear in a column parallel to the text that can be hidden; and notes are indicated by small circles that, when pressed, pleasingly highlight the pertinent text *and* the accompanying note, as well as scrolling the other column to align. Another column includes facsimile pages of early texts, often in multiple copies. The most helpful feature is a 'read with' panel that allows you to call up the associated pages of *MCE* and *CRE* and read the original spelling and modern spelling editions side by side – though, of course, this can be done much more cheaply by simply making a one-off purchase of the print volumes.

The cost of the print edition, however, is thoroughly justified. *CRE* in particular is a much-needed resource; the first fully realized, free-standing original-spelling edition of Shakespeare's complete works ever prepared (xxiii), and *MCE* offers an innovative, freshly considered version of the text for the more general reader. Before getting into finer detail, it is worth noting some of the headlines. This is the first *Complete Works* to include *Arden of Faversham*, the additions to *The Spanish Tragedy*, and *Cardenio* (in various forms). It eschews critical introductions entirely, favouring a *bricolage* of assorted critical quotations along with some key facts and a timeline in *MCE*, and detailed textual introductions in *CRE*. It acknowledges the validity of variant early texts, but both *MCE* and *CRE* offer only one version of each play, based on careful selection of copy-text; the 'Alternative Versions' volume will include all other versions, as well as full texts for *The Spanish Tragedy* and *Sir Thomas More*, represented only by their Shakespearian additions in *MCE*. The edition also offers bold new conclusions about chronology, including a substantial reorganization of the order of the early plays. Taken as a whole, *NOS* offers an extraordinary synthesis of new work that will doubtless set the research agenda for coming years.

Bourus and Taylor's introduction to *MCE* is self-consciously idiosyncratic, indulging in a dizzying array of metaphors best summed up in the preface's reference to 'tapas Shakespeare' (iv). The intention is to avoid a by-the-numbers approach to introductions and create something passionate and inspiring; readers expecting a conventional historical introduction must look elsewhere. The authors celebrate Shakespeare as 'our best, most rewarding read' (1), and make a commendable attempt to include a range of voices, including two whole pages on Lin-Manuel Miranda's *Hamilton* (29–30), repeated reference to Zadie Smith's use of Shakespearian quotations (19), and even an entire section on Shakespearian naysayers (9–16) which, while dismissing the claims of anti-Stratfordians, also acknowledges that 'there are some genres of human experience that [Shakespeare] may have represented badly, or not at all' (16).

The playfulness of the introduction will not be to everyone's tastes, and at times is frustrating. 'Shakespeare's favourite subjects are monarchy, monogamy, and monotheism' (5) is an unexplained soundbite in search of a subject, and there is no apparent irony intended when the editors later assert that once you have read Shakespeare, 'you will also have learned to correct false generalizations' (8). Happily, the introduction settles down into a thoughtful series of reflections on the uses of Shakespeare in contemporary society, from his deployment by marginalized peoples to the value of theatre itself; *Thomas More* is used to illustrate the importance of imaginative work in generating empathy (34). The editors qualify the idea of universality as meaning that 'certain statements or characters or events in Shakespeare's works coincide with our own experiences or prejudices' (35), and draw attention to the ethical, liberal values and responsibilities inherent in working with Shakespeare.

John Jowett's introduction to *CRE* is a more substantial scholarly overview of the edition's textual underpinnings. Jowett surveys the documents that form the basis of modern texts, the cultures of manuscript circulation and the workings of the printing press. Refreshingly, he repeatedly underlines how there is *less* critical confidence in earlier foundational orthodoxies, including the identification of compositors (xxxix) and the category of 'foul papers' (xxvi). Most dramatically, Jowett announces the 'collapse of confidence in the earlier categorization of Shakespeare texts' (xli) and the consequential foregrounding of a 'directly observable criterion' in the selection of copy-texts for *NOS* – length. The edition's interest in completeness 'shifts editorial emphasis away from textual minutiae that reflect proximity or distance from Shakespeare's hand and onto the literally larger issues of structure and content' (xli). Jowett explains that 'length is usually a symptom of proximity to the early state of the play', with honourable exceptions such as *Richard II* (xlii), but that this edition takes a pragmatic rather than absolutist approach to the integrity of textual versions. *Richard II*, for instance, is here based on the quarto

text but includes the folio-only deposition scene 'as an intrinsic part of the play as Shakespeare wrote it', but one that was censored (xliii). The terminology of 'addition' is a source of some confusion in the edition; the general principle in *NOS* is 'to mark off as added text the passages that are not found in the copy text' (2999), but this principle is broken in texts such as *Measure for Measure*, where 1.2.1–67 – present in the copy-text – is bracketed as an addition written by Middleton. The edition is normally clear in its narrative, but the word 'addition' is made to do rather too much work in referring separately to both passages that were *written* later and passages that *appeared in print* later.

Jowett sets out the rationale for emendation in *CRE*, which at a minimum corrects printing errors. His chapter 'Shakespeare and the Kingdom of Error' aims to do for 'error' what Stanley Wells did for 'modernisation' in the 1986 *Oxford Shakespeare*. I am not persuaded that it offers quite the same level of methodological intervention, but Jowett lucidly sets out the historical and theoretical implications of error and its correction. He refutes scholars who would insist on the retention of errors, pointing out that the discourse of correction was an integral part of the early printing industry: 'printers recognized, even as they committed errors, that it would do the reader a significant disservice to keep silent about them' (liii). The principle of *CRE* is to retain the erratics but emend the error (xlix), and he illustrates editorial processes through the case study of *Macbeth* 1.2.14, changed here from 'Fortune on his damned quarry smiling' to 'Fortune on her damned quarry smiling' (rather than earlier emendations of 'quarry' to 'quarrel'). He concludes by articulating the paradox of textual editing: 'to remove error is to misrepresent the textual materials that, in the first instance, are the only Shakespeare that we have. To retain error is to idealize the quartos and folio as untouchable objects embodying the text as though it existed in such an object as a mysteriously pure substance' (lxii). The achievement of *CRE* is to make this paradox and its negotiations as visible as possible.

The *NOS* 'includes all of the music that can be reasonably associated with contemporary performances of Shakespeare's plays' (lxv), and John Cunningham's introduction to early modern theatrical music, divided helpfully into 'formal' and 'impromptu' categories, is a highlight. Cunningham's confident setting-out of the issues of attribution, variation, embellishment and arrangement is a valuable primer for anyone interested in the complex provenances of songs, and his principles for editing and modernizing the reconstructions of the extant fragments are clearly set out. Andrew Power's dramaturgical introduction sets out the principles for the edition's casting charts, for which he prioritizes economy and is conservative about re-returns, generally favouring the 'consecutive scene' rule in which actors may not return as a different character within the same scene (lxxxviii). This means, importantly, that the 'busiest scene' is less important than the 'most congested' group of scenes in determining the minimum number of actors needed. Power provides useful lists of doubling possibilities and property requirements throughout *CRE*.

The final substantial essay is Taylor's extended introduction to the First Folio. He treats the folio as offering a 'double transformation of intertextual space' (xxi), in binding plays together and simultaneously disseminating them, ensuring both their collective identity and survival. The most significant contribution Taylor makes is a lengthy discussion of Edward Blount, who, Taylor argues, has been severely neglected, but whose status as 'the most reliable judge and purveyor of printed literature in London' consolidated the claims of the Shakespeare canon to *be* 'literature' (xlix). Taylor argues that the folio '*revived and expanded* Shakespeare's declining reputation ... by betting on posthumous nostalgia' (lx). Francis Connor offers a brief follow-up introduction to the folio preliminaries, identifying the authors and their connections to the stationers.

NOS Texts

Texts in *MCE* are organized chronologically by date of composition (publication in the case of poems), in *CRE* by order of printing, and alphabetically in *NOS Online*. Plays are divided into scenes or acts/scenes based on copy-text and editorial judgement (*Authorship Companion*, xixff.). Scene divisions are unobtrusive in the printed text, though hugely exaggerated in *NOS Online* where each scene has its own page. Speech prefixes are written in full, and are sensitive to context; in *Richard II*, Richard is 'King Richard' until the end of 3.3, while Bolingbroke becomes King Henry in 5.3; during the deposition scene, neither is 'King'. The print volumes include both marginal notes and footnotes (in *NOS Online*, no distinction is made). Marginal notes in *MCE* open up alternatives and variants, especially concerning staging. For example, Bourus inserts a stage direction at *Two Gentlemen of Verona* 1.2.88 ('[She reaches for the letter, but Lucetta keeps it away]'), but in the margin notes that 'Alternatively, Lucetta can immediately hand it over; if so, Julia reacts to what she reads.' Footnotes in *MCE* provide glosses and brief commentary. The *CRE* marginal notes and footnotes are more complex, offering line-by-line collation and discussion of significant variants that will be invaluable to textual scholars. In what follows, I offer some snapshots of editorial treatments of arbitrarily selected scenes and poems, which illustrate the kinds of work found throughout *NOS*. In general, editorial choices are efficient and well justified, but it is in the combination of *MCE* and *CRE* that the edition breaks important ground, making the decision process as transparent as possible. The clear and cross-referenced presentation makes simultaneous reading extremely convenient.

Sarah Neville's *CRE* introduction to *The Comedy of Errors* offers fascinating detail about the place of Plautine drama in sixteenth-century school curricula (1793) and the influence of printed exegesis of Acts and Ephesians on the master–servant relationship (1794). She discusses the relative evidence for authorial practice (descriptive literary elements in stage directions and permissive stage directions, 1795–6). Neville follows Paul Werstine in disputing distinctions between 'foul papers' and 'playbooks', arguing that the inconsistencies in speech prefixes would cause few difficulties for early actors (1797).

She offers a detailed discussion of the duplicated exit directions at 4.4.141, ultimately rejecting the idea that the exits are duplicated or a splitting of a single instruction by instead emending 'Runne all out' to 'Runne all [about]', which certainly accords with theatrical logic. *MCE* makes several interesting choices in 1.1, especially when compared to Cartwright's Arden text. Neville does not follow Cartwright in the popular emendation of deleting the unmetrical 'to' at 22, but does emend the folio's *Epidamium* to 'Epidamnium' (40), a spelling I have not been able to find anywhere else. Cartwright's longer note (303) sets out the various options and his own reason for preferring 'Epidamium'. The editors fascinatingly diverge at 55 in punctuation: Neville follows the folio in printing 'of such a burden male, twins both alike', while Cartwright repunctuates to 'of such a burden, male twins, both alike'; both readings are plausible. Neville makes 'wished' disyllabic in 'and by the benefit of his wishèd light' (90), while Cartwright treats it as a monosyllable. At 127, Cartwright follows the folio in printing 'that his attendant, so his case was like', but Neville silently accepts F2's emendation of 'so' to 'for', printing 'that his attendant – for his case was like'. The F1/F2 variant is missing from the *CRE* collation. A more substantial emendation occurs at 151, where the folio prints 'to seeke thy helpe by beneficiall helpe'. Neville emends the first 'helpe' to '[hap]' and glosses it as 'luck'; Cartwright follows Collier in emending to 'hope'. Neville's *MCE* edition includes interesting notes on staging possibilities, including noting at 152 that 'in some productions, Egeon appeals to the crowd to help pay his debt, but is rebuffed' (731).

Rory Loughnane's *CRE* introduction to *Cymbeline* covers an impressive array of sources and summarizes the indicators of Ralph Crane's style that characterize *Cymbeline* (3355). The primary interventions made in the text concern act and scene breaks; as with Wayne's Arden edition, the new scene at 1.1.70 is removed, and a new scene is marked at 2.4.152. Loughnane adds new scenes to break up the battle in Act 5; Wayne's eighteen-line 5.2 is three separate scenes in *NOS*, though both editors imply the continuity of the tumult.

By contrast, Loughnane's removal of the scene break during which Posthumus is delivered to Cymbeline (5.5.95) retains the continuity of action implied by the stage direction. Loughnane is much more specific than Wayne about what in the text may indicate revision, suggesting that 3.3.99–107 is a later addition to provide narrative detail, including Belarius's assumed name (3358). He also interestingly suggests that 'say our song' (4.2.256), before 'fear no more', may be a revision to account for the actors' inability to sing the song.

2.3 demonstrates some of *NOS*'s unique features, incorporating Robert Johnson's setting for 'Hark, hark, the lark' within the text, visually illustrating the interruption occasioned by the song. The two editions dispute Cloten's 'it is a vice / voice in her ears' (24). Loughnane corrects 'voyce' to 'vyce' in *CRE*, dismissing it as an 'easy misreading', and *MCE* reads 'vice'. Wayne, conversely, argues that the close pronunciation of 'voice' and 'vice' means that this is a quibble, and retains 'voice'. Wayne's use makes better sense of 'voice in her ears', but Loughnane's emendation makes better sense of the whole. Wayne assumes that the 'Dorothy' referred to at *MCE* 129 is the same as F's 'Lady' who enters at line 76, and emends the speech prefix; Loughnane understandably retains 'Lady'. The Lady's line 'That's more / Than some whose tailors are as dear as yours / Can justly boast of' is turned into an aside by Loughnane, but Wayne argues that 'delivering the lines directly positions her as Innogen's defender' (210), an interesting divergence in interpretation of this character. Loughnane justifiably retains the folio's punctuation of 'Good morrow, fairest. Sister, your sweet hand' (78), whereas Wayne emends to 'Good morrow, fairest sister. Your sweet hand'. She argues that the emendation 'reflects conventional usage and improves the line', but to conclude a first sentence on 'fairest' sounds to me more typical of a suitor, followed by a hasty correction to 'Sister'. Loughnane's marginal notes do excellent work imagining the tone of the scene, including suggesting added emphasis on 'his meanest garment' (2.3.124), which is exaggerated further in *MCE* through the addition of quotation marks around repetitions of the phrase.

John Jowett's textual introduction to *Macbeth* sets out the principle that, as Shakespeare's 'original' is 'lost' (2999), the text of the folio must 'of necessity be edited as the work of two authors'. Jowett makes explicit that the editorial procedure concerning additions is 'to mark off as added text the passages that are not found in the copy text'. Here, this refers to the two songs from *The Witch*, based on Ralph Crane's transcript supplemented by reference to a manuscript music book, a songbook and two versions of Davenant's *Macbeth*. Jowett's notes record substantial variants between these various witnesses. A final feature of note is the recording of Gaelic forms of historical names in commentary notes, though there is no comment on the somewhat unusual form 'MacDuff', as opposed to the folio's 'Macduff'.

Scene 4.1 features one of the songs. The text of the scene is otherwise relatively conventional: Jowett modernizes 'howlet's' to 'owlet's' (17) and 'antique' to 'antic' (128), preserves the 'weyard' sisters of the folio (134), and removes the break in 82, so that Macbeth says he will 'take a bond of fate though shalt not live', rather than speaking 'Thou shalt not live' as a separate clause. He reads the folio's 'witches mummey' as plural 'witches' mummy' (23), which involves the most minimal intervention but makes this item an anomaly in a list of otherwise singular ingredients. A note in *CRE* for line 104 says that the stage direction for '*Hoboyes*' comes 'after "Caldron?" in *Modern*'; in *MCE*, however, the stage direction is moved to *before* 'Why sinks that cauldron?'. Lines 61–2 are rendered as a demand rather than a question ('Say if thoud'st rather hear it from our mouths / Or from our masters'). The big changes come as the song begins, with a seventeen-line addition marked off in a separate box (online, pleasingly, the text is subtly shaded), with separate line numbers. The detailed textual notes in *CRE* give a clear sense of how the text of the song has been constructed.

The *bricolage* for *Venus and Adonis* includes an unusual number of seventeenth-century commentators, giving a pleasing sense of the poem's importance in its own time. Francis Connor's textual introduction gives a detailed account of the early printing history, and notes that the survival of only one copy of the first edition means that the second edition – which may record stop-press readings – is given substantial consideration (*CRE*, 83). Connor's history of the poem's publication includes study of the stationers involved in its production, the poem's influence on miscellanies, and the ongoing history of reprints throughout the early modern period. Connor offers extensive bio-bibliographies of Richard Field and John Harrison. He argues that 'spelling inconstancies in the poem' are at least in part 'a result of long lines' (89), seeing the constraints of the printer's measure as the major obstacle to establishing conventional spellings. Connor sets out the fundamental dilemma – does one emend spelling to 'reproduce the ideal copy of a book Field hoped would result', or 'do we retain the spelling to admit the possibility that the printer's lapses reveal Shakespeare's hand?' (91). He strikes a middle position, emending when a spelling deviates from Field's normal use (rather than Shakespeare's), and where the emendation is justified either by the limitations of typesetting or to preserve a sight rhyme. Connor's diligence results in the decision to bracket incidental as well as substantive emendations in *CRE*, which means that normally silent corrections are made visible: for example, 'somtime' becomes 'sometime' at 658, with Connor pointing out that this is a 'long line where the first "e" in each "sometime" was omitted to save space'; a similar rationale underpins the abbreviation of 'will' to 'wil' (1158). One of the fascinating implications of this is that *CRE* often *de*-modernizes the poem, such as 'frown' to 'frowne' (45). Connor notes that this is the only instance of this spelling, as opposed to two elsewhere of 'frowne', and that the eye-rhyme at line 43 is 'downe'; the odd spelling may be accidental or, again, to save space in a long line.

Taylor's text of *Cardenio* sets out its stall in a curated *bricolage* that concludes with an array of scholars arguing for the importance of attending to *Double Falsehood*, and a final quote from Martin Wiggins that 'the fragments need to be available as discrete items'. Taylor's textual introduction in *CRE* introduces *Double Falsehood* as 'a very good text of a very bad play of 1727' but 'an execrable text of what was almost certainly a very good play of 1612' (3661). As such, rather than providing a good reading text of *Double Falsehood*, Taylor offers two reference resources. The *CRE* text is the primary achievement, offering a complete text of *Double Falsehood*, along with five fragments from early seventeenth-century documents including the title, a stage direction and three songs. Taylor also marks as 'additions' those parts of the text that the editors are sure did *not* appear in the Jacobean play, and places extracts of 'mixed writing' in a different font. The extensive textual notes of *CRE* list parallels to Theobald, Shakespeare, Fletcher, Davenant and, in a new claim for this edition, Colley Cibber, who Taylor believes contributed comic prose to 2.3. The result is a busy *mise-en-page* that dissects the play in granular detail, and shows his best guess for authorship at the local level. By contrast, *MCE* 'has removed from the 1727 text everything demonstrably or probably written, or overwritten, by Theobald, Davenant, or Cibber' (3136). Only the passages that the editors think most likely to have originated in the seventeenth century are printed. The stated assumption is that the reader of *MCE* will not have interest in a 'minor eighteenth-century editor-playwright' (*CRE*, 3665), though Taylor also admits that 'many modern readers will find [this text] alienating and, in places, unintelligible' (*CRE*, 3666). For example, 1.1 includes the first seven lines, and then a series of open-ended square brackets with a marginal note summarizing the action that 'must have' happened in this section (*MCE*, 3137). The fragments of individual words and disconnected phrases are a clear indicator of what the *NOS* thinks may survive from *Cardenio*, but the vast majority of readers will doubtless find *CRE* more useful and readable.

Bourus's *A Midsummer Night's Dream* reduces the play to only eight scenes, conflating 2.2 and 3.1 into Scene 4, and 3.2 and 4.1 into Scene 5, both on the basis that sleeping characters 'remain asleep onstage' (*MCE*, 1118). Bourus's textual introduction concentrates on the relationship between the 1600 and 1623 texts, noting that the quarto appears to have been set from an authoritative, and 'probably autograph', text (*CRE*, 863), and that, while the folio has no independent authority, it does seem to have had 'at least partial access to an independent manuscript'. Andrew Power's dramaturgical notes interestingly argue that there are no doubling options for any of the adult characters without making cuts, and he takes the cue that Flute has 'a beard coming' to categorize the actor as an adult (*CRE*, 867). *NOS* regards the folio *not* as a fully fledged 'alternative version', but will include an edited version of scene 7 in 'Alternative Versions' to explore the more substantive changes in this scene alone. Here, I focus on the second half of Scene 4, with Titania already asleep on stage, which Bourus notes 'creates opportunities for "near-misses" where one of the clowns might seem certain to wake her up' (*MCE*, 1102). A marginal direction in *MCE* notes that Snout's line at 201 'may be spoken by Snug'; this only makes sense with reference to *CRE*, which explains that the speech prefix is the ambiguous '*Sn.*'. The scene preserves the quarto's later entry for Robin, but adds a marginal note to discuss some of the affordances of bringing him on earlier. Unlike Arden, *NOS* retains the quarto's 'or' in 'or let him hold his fingers thus' (214–15) rather than emending to 'and'; Bourus argues that 'holding up the fingers to present the chink is an alternative to the plaster/loam/roughcast'. Where Arden used italics for lines from *Pyramus and Thisbe*, Bourus adds square brackets for '[*as Pyramus*]' etc., and puts Quince's correction of 'odours, odours' into speech marks (226–7). Fascinatingly, at 232, *NOS* preserves the speech prefix 'Quince' to speak the line 'A stranger Pyramus than e'er played here', dismissed by Chaudhuri as 'obviously wrong'. Bourus emends 'brisky' to 'brisly' in *CRE* and 'bristly' in *MCE*, and emends 'Iuuenall' to 'juvenile' to create a piece of comically inappropriate praise at 238. Another significant emendation occurs at 246, which Bourus reads as 'If I were horse, fair Thisbe, I were only thine.' This original emendation makes excellent sense, picking up on Thisbe's use of 'horse' in the preceding line. Bourus suggests that a spelling of 'hors' would be close enough to 'fair' to allow for eye-skip; this is less compelling, but not implausible. In a rare instance of breaking from the copytext when Arden follows it, Bourus adds an 'of' to 'desire you [of] more acquaintance' at 320 and 325, mimicking the similar usage at 314. The further pleasure of Bourus's marginal notes is a sense of production history, noting the various interpretations of historical Titanias and Bottoms.

Anna Pruitt's textual introduction to *Richard II* presents it as 'the first Shakespeare play to become a bestseller in the book trade' (*CRE*, 357), and devotes the majority of its length to explication of the play's status (similar to *Dream*) as a 'lightly annotated text'. This introduction explains the *NOS* convention of naming texts after their printers or publishers – thus, the folio is JAGGARD throughout, while the early quartos of *Richard II* are designated 1SIMMES, 2WISE, etc. (360). Pruitt takes the first quarto as copy-text, with the deposition scene based on the folio, and traces the line of transmission between the various versions. Pruitt notes the difficulty that the folio appears to retain many authoritative variants (367), which are recorded prominently in the right-hand margin of *CRE*. The commendable principle is to make as many of the plausible options available as possible, revealing the different temporal layers of the text 'without overwhelming the reader with the sheer volume of potentially indifferent variants' (368). 4.1 is one of the most typographically complex scenes in *NOS*. In both *CRE* and *MCE*, the eight lines following 52 ('I task the earth ... twenty thousand such as you'), omitted from the folio, are marked as a 'deletion', while the deposition scene is presented as a boxed-off addition of 166 lines. The continuous line numbering of the deletion and addition creates a very busy page, but visually distinguishes the isolated material. Pruitt's marginal annotations note that the staging of the scene may recall the spectator configuration of the trial-by-combat scene, and includes several comments on the use and symmetry of the gages. Her emendations are minimal; Pruitt follows the traditional emendation of 'sinne to sinne' to 'sunne to sunne' at 51.D4 without comment, and the omission of 'it' in the previous line as 'disruptive of both meter and sense'. At line 93, Pruitt follows the earlier Oxford Shakespeare's emendation to read 'Why Bishop [of Carleil] is Norffolke dead?', an expansion that 'gives the line a regular pentameter'. The deposition addition includes a full collation of differences between the episode as printed here and as preserved in the fourth quarto; an edited version of the Q4 version will appear in 'Alternative Versions'.

This brief survey of some of the editorial work hopefully captures the extent of the labour and interventions, and the diligent recording of variants and rationales in *CRE* makes it easy to understand the decisions underpinning the presentation of *MCE*. Both editions have their individual advantages, but the simultaneous consultation of both is highly recommended.

The NOS Authorship Companion

The *Authorship Companion* is a hefty volume of essays that sets out the *NOS* team's position on the constitution, authorship and chronology of the canon, as well as offering a substantial amount of new research on issues of attribution. While it is unlikely to win over those who are still sceptical of the project of attribution research in general, this is a landmark of its branch of scholarship, and makes major overtures to accessibility and readability that will hopefully stimulate further interest in this area.

The first group of essays covers 'methods'. The opening essay is a manifesto in defence of attribution, in which Taylor coins the phrase 'artiginality' to articulate 'the originality proper to artisans ... the labour of transforming already-existing works, already-existing text-things, into recognizably new text-things' (25). Taylor argues for the importance of the *specificity* of the individual artisan's relationship as a cyborg intertwined with these institutions. The ethos of *NOS* is to give those artisans credit for their work, rather than taking the position of 'proprietary capitalists' (20) by according agency to the institution. The *Authorship Companion* represents a range of approaches, predominantly favouring variations on tests involving shared word usage, from n-grams (short collocations) to rare words, although several other methods feature; and the scale of the studies varies from broad patterns across a whole play to 'micro-attribution' of individual phrases. There is thus no one method or process; instead, Egan offers an extremely useful overview of the history of Shakespeare attribution research that extrapolates broad principles from the long historical overview, including making data available for checking, multiple independent tests (distinguishing *plausibility* from *probability*, 47), and adjusting canon sizes to ensure fair comparison.

Other essays outline basic principles, often through negative example. Macdonald P. Jackson focuses on the most common trap into which researchers fall – mistaking mere accumulation of parallels between a favoured candidate and a disputed text for evidence of authorship – while Egan critiques Brian Vickers's failure to make databases and methods available for cross-checking, in keeping with current debates about the 'replication crisis' in social studies research. Both focus on Shakespeare's authorship of *The Spanish Tragedy* additions, shrewdly using an example where they agree with the result but dispute the method. Jackson devotes a second chapter to responding to reviews of his book on *Arden of Faversham* and *A Lover's Complaint*, a chapter that implicitly acknowledges right-of-reply as an integral part of attribution research.

The other chapters in 'Methods' concentrate on case studies. Taylor and Doug Duhaime use shared word-strings to argue that Thomas Middleton wrote the fly scene in *Titus Andronicus*. The essay is a *tour de force* in setting out its initial rationale, its description of method, and its gradual establishment of Middleton as a favoured candidate, and they make a strong case, even if the stylistic inconsistencies demand a hypothesis that Middleton was deliberately trying to match his style to that of the older play (90–1). The quantitative case is supplemented by their subtle consideration of

Middleton's use elsewhere of fly imagery. Anna Pruitt's chapter refines Jackson's LION tests to confirm that Shakespeare wrote Act 4, scene 1 of *Titus*, with the main methodological contribution being the importance of gathering and publishing all hits for any given search, and conducting filtering after. The final chapter concerns the authorship of miscellaneous short poems. Francis Connor demonstrates that 'attribution methods that work for short passages of plays do not work for short poems' (109), owing to the complexity and volume of comparative material. Connor instead shows how LION can be used to establish parameters for narrowing down the list of plausible candidate authors, leading to the exclusion of 'Upon the King' from the present edition.

The individual case study chapters that follow ignore works whose authorship is reasonably well established, though I am surprised that *2 Henry VI* does not feature, given that this is the first edition to publish the attribution to Marlowe and Shakespeare. The essays here instead focus primarily on *Arden of Faversham*, *3 Henry VI*, *The Spanish Tragedy*, *All's Well That Ends Well* and *Double Falsehood*.

Jack Elliott and Brett Greatley-Hirsch's essay on *Arden of Faversham* is exemplary in its explanation of techniques and systematic in its application. The surprising conclusion of their investigation is that all tests 'attribute the majority of *Arden of Faversham* segments to Shakespeare' (179). The indeterminacy of their results for other authors may indicate textual corruption or the presence of other authors who are under- or un-represented in the extant drama. Nonetheless, the sense that Shakespeare is 'responsible for the lion's share' (181) underpins *NOS*'s confident inclusion of the play. Jackson adds supplementary evidence for Shakespeare's presence in the central scenes (190). John Burrows and Hugh Craig meanwhile build on an earlier study of *3 Henry VI*, winnowing out candidates for the parts of the play they had already identified as non-Shakespearian. Marlowe dominates their results, though they argue that the plays 'do everything possible to obscure an authorial signal' (217).

Four essays are devoted to *The Spanish Tragedy*. David L. Gants is uninterested in authorship, but his short essay estimates that William White's work on the 1602 quarto began in autumn 1601, proving that the additions Henslowe paid Jonson for in September 1601 and June 1602 could not be those printed in the quarto. Taylor and John Nance investigate the additions through systematic checking of parallels; while Nance confirms Shakespeare's authorship of the painter scene, Taylor's work leads him to Thomas Heywood as the author of the first addition. I am not persuaded that a single study justifies the confidence Taylor puts in the identification of Heywood and Shakespeare as the additions' authors, but the evidence here will hopefully provoke further research. Craig takes a quick look at the 1610 additions to *Mucedorus*, and his analysis of function words confirms that, unlike the additions to *The Spanish Tragedy* and *Thomas More*, those to *Mucedorus* look nothing like Shakespeare.

The essays on *All's Well* begin *in medias res*, intervening in the dispute between Laurie Maguire and Emma Smith on one side and Brian Vickers and Marcus Dahl on the other, about whether Middleton revised the play. The essays concentrate on micro-attribution of very localized parts of the play; ideally, I would have liked to see an additional essay that gave a broader overview of the play's features (cf. Elliott and Greatley-Hirsch). Loughnane's two-part essay traces the clustering of pre-established Middletonian markers in 4.3, supported by dramaturgical opinion from Bourus and Farah Karim-Cooper about the 'dispensability' of lines 140–238 (the interrogation of Parolles about the Lords Dumaine) that suggests this may be a later addition. Taylor and Nance's essays consolidate the case for Middleton at the level of individual lines. All this is indicative; as Taylor wisely notes, while the evidence here is leading, 'much remains to be done' (365). I prefer to overlook obvious typos, but to help readers who may be confused while following the close detail of Nance's essay, his two references to the passage under investigation as '2.3.118-45' (331, 336) are errors for '2.3.109-36'.

The case studies conclude with Roger Holdsworth's revised chronology for Middleton and Shakespeare's work in 1605–6, a methodological essay by Taylor which points out the rarity of false attribution in manuscript miscellanies of poetry (justifying the edition's inclusion of 'When God was pleas'd' and 'Shall I die'), and chapters by Marina Tarlinskaja and Giuliano Pascucci on *Double Falsehood*. Tarlinskaja's expertly explained versification analysis supports the theory that *Double Falsehood* is based on a post-Restoration adaptation of the original *Cardenio*, while Pascucci uses compression algorithms to argue that Massinger may have contributed to the original manuscript along with Fletcher and Shakespeare.

The most important contribution of the *Authorship Companion* is Loughnane and Taylor's magisterial survey of 'Canon and Chronology', which outlines the rationales for dating (they give both a range and a 'best guess') and attribution for every work included in the edition, though much discussion is deferred to 'Alternative Versions'. Among the more interesting points here are continuing ambivalence about the possible co-authorship and date of *The Taming of the Shrew* (best guess: late 1591); a note that the authorship of the battle sequences of *Edward III* is still in dispute; a later date for Shakespeare's revisions of *1 Henry VI* (best guess: 1595); and a brief survey of arguments by Bourus that Q1 of *Hamlet* represents a 1588 version of the play that was then substantially revised by Shakespeare in 1602/3. There is a long treatment of the debate over *Sejanus*, the editors concluding that Shakespeare is the strongest candidate for the 'second pen' excised by Jonson. A brief section on disputed plays excluded from the edition largely accords with existing work on the 'Shakespeare Apocrypha'. The volume of work here is impressive, and this essay alone will stand alongside Martin Wiggins's *British Drama: A Catalogue* (with which *NOS* often productively disagrees) as an essential reference resource, setting out all sides of the various debates and inviting further exploration. The great work continues.

WORKS REVIEWED

Cartwright, Kent, ed., *The Comedy of Errors*, The Arden Shakespeare (London, 2017)

Chaudhuri, Sukanta, ed., *A Midsummer Night's Dream*, The Arden Shakespeare (London, 2017)

Dawson, Anthony B., ed., *Troilus and Cressida*, 2nd edn (Cambridge, 2017)

Donno, Elizabeth Story, ed., *Twelfth Night*, 3rd edn (Cambridge, 2017)

Proudfoot, Richard, and Nicola Bennett, eds., *King Edward III*, The Arden Shakespeare (London, 2017)

Spevack, Martin, ed., *Julius Caesar*, 3rd edn (Cambridge, 2017)

Taylor, Gary, and Gabriel Egan, eds., *The New Oxford Shakespeare Authorship Companion* (Oxford, 2017)

Taylor, Gary, John Jowett, Terri Bourus, and Gabriel Egan, eds., *The New Oxford Shakespeare: Modern Critical Edition* (Oxford, 2016)

Taylor, Gary, John Jowett, Terri Bourus, and Gabriel Egan, eds., *The New Oxford Shakespeare: Critical Reference Edition*, 2 vols. (Oxford, 2017)

Wayne, Valerie, ed., *Cymbeline*, The Arden Shakespeare (London, 2017)

ABSTRACTS OF ARTICLES
IN *SHAKESPEARE SURVEY 71*

SHAKESPEARE IN PERFORMANCE — AFRICA AND ASIA

SANDRA YOUNG

Shakespeare's Transcolonial Solidarities in the Global South
The article invokes the critical framework of the 'global South' to probe Shakespeare's resonances across an unequal world. A creolized *Tempest*, Dev Virahsawmy's *Toufann*, bears witness to the aftermath of slavery and imagines for the post-colony a just and polyvocal future that resists the ethnocentric logic of colonial modernity.

ASHISH BEESOONDIAL

Shakespeare's Creolized Voices
Shakespeare has found resonance in Mauritius, in particular, in the works of playwright Dev Virahsawmy, who has sought to challenge the bias against Kreol Morisien (Mauritian Creole) by using Shakespeare as his instrument. This article explores how Virahsawmy articulates his social and political vision for a better, unified Mauritius through Shakespeare.

POMPA BANERJEE

'Accents Yet Unknown': *Haider* and *Hamlet* in Kashmir
Vishal Bhardwaj's *Haider* realigns Shakespeare's cultural authority and language in Kashmir, producing a rich afterlife for *Hamlet* in new geopolitical realities. *Haider* destabilizes the role of English in modern, multilingual India. Adapted and revitalized, *Hamlet* reaches unanticipated audiences across linguistic and cultural borders through the global reach of Bollywood.

JUDY CELINE ICK

The Forests of Silence: Global Shakespeare in the Philippines, the Philippines in Global Shakespeare
When does Shakespeare cease to be just 'Shakespeare' and when does it become Global Shakespeare? What are its conditions of existence? This article explores these questions by looking at contemporary Shakespearian productions in the Philippines as they negotiate the evolution of Shakespeare from colonial artefact into an element of contemporary, post-national global culture.

KATHERINE HENNESSEY
AND MARGARET
LITVIN

Arab Shakespeares at the World Shakespeare Congress
A synopsis of the 'Arab Shakespeares' panel at WSC 2016. Presentations examined the first Arab performance of *The Taming of the Shrew*, a television adaptation of *Lear* set in Upper Egypt; an Omani theatrical mash-up of *Othello* and Arab epic;

and the collaborative dialogue that helped shape Sulayman Al-Bassam's Shakespeare adaptations.

HAO LIU

The Dual Tradition of Bardolatry in China
This article discusses the reception of Shakespeare in China in the early twentieth century, and the revival of enthusiasm in Shakespeare since the late 1970s. Shakespeare symbolizes paradoxically both the 'new' and the 'old' in Chinese culture, informing the Chinese discourse of globalization and cultural exchange with dual meaning.

MICHIKO SUEMATSU

A Catalyst for Theatrical Reinvention: Contemporary Travelling Companies at the Tokyo Globe Theatre
Cultural displacement created by travelling companies from overseas can work as a catalyst for reinvention of local Shakespeare. In Japan's case, this happened twice, in the late nineteenth century and in the 1980s. The article assesses how travelling companies at the Tokyo Globe Theatre (1988–2002) transformed today's Japanese Shakespeare performance.

SHAKESPEARE IN PERFORMANCE — THE AMERICAS

ALFREDO MICHEL MODENESSI

'Both Alike in Dignity': Havana and Mexico City Play *Romeo and Juliet*
This article discusses the films *Shakespeare in Avana* (David Riondino, 2011) and *Besos de azúcar* (Carlos Cuarón, 2013), two 'anthropophagic transcreations' of Shakespeare's *Romeo and Juliet* that place as much trust in the dauntless love of their main characters as in the spiritual resilience of their troubled settings.

DONNA WOODFORD-GORMLEY

Cuban Improvisations: Reverse Colonization via Shakespeare
Shakespeare in Havana and *Otello all'improvviso*, film collaborations between Cuban poet Alexis Díaz-Pimienta and Italian director David Riondino, explore Cuban *Repentismo*, or improvisational poetry, inspired by Shakespeare. These documentaries and the tour that followed perform a reverse colonization, using Shakespeare to introduce a Cuban art form to Europe.

ANDREW JAMES HARTLEY

Mixing Memory with Desire: Staging *Hamlet* Q1
This article considers the unique role played by the 'bad' quarto of one of the world's most famous plays, engaging as it does with memory and with forgetting, suggesting that the very things that make a script work as a piece of theatre might be considered its failings as 'Shakespeare'.

CARLA DELLA GATTA

Shakespeare, Race and 'Other' Englishes: The Q Brothers' *Othello: The Remix*
The Q Brothers' *Othello: The Remix* and the OSF's *Play On!* initiative bring forward issues of race and language in English-to-English translations of Shakespeare's plays. *Othello: The Remix*, a hip hop Shakespeare adaptation, used music, AAVE and hip hop performance to reveal assumptions about black culture and American Shakespearian performance.

SHAKESPEARE IN PERFORMANCE — EUROPE

BOIKA SOKOLOVA

'Mingled Yarn': *The Merchant of Venice* East of Berlin and the Legacy of 'Eastern Europe'

The article discusses the dip in the performance of *The Merchant of Venice* during the communist period in Eastern Europe and considers several important post-1989 productions, and issues of anti-Semitism. The directors presented are Zdravko Mitkov, Robert Alföldi, Robert Sturua, Andrey Zhitinkin, Egon Savin and Krzystof Warlikowski. A reflection on André Tchaikowsky's opera ends the overview.

KIRILKA STAVREVA

Ariel's Groans, or, Performing Protean Gender on the Bulgarian Post-Communist Stage

Theatre performances of Ariel's gender during the Bulgarian post-communist transition map a shift in the use of *The Tempest* as part of an emerging artistic vocabulary of cultural change. From melancholic femininity to exuberant and protean gender performativity, Bulgarian Ariels dramatize elusive and resurgent hope in new cultural narratives.

CAROL CHILLINGTON RUTTER

Dressing the History 'Boys': Harry's Masks, Falstaff's Underpants

Observing a recent spate of Shakespeare anniversaries, this article looks at how the Shakespeare theatre industry in England has aligned itself with this national cultural project by putting on view a particular view of 'England' in recent productions of Shakespeare's *Henry IV* plays. If costumes are the stuff of production memory and preserve the material remains of stories told, what does the costume archive tell us about the England on view to England (and the world) of late?

KATE DORNEY

Shopping for the Archives: Fashioning a Costume Collection

This article considers the slippery nature of performance remains and the perils and pleasures of collecting and working with theatrical costumes. In particular, it offers a material reading of performance focusing on the silk costumes from Harley Granville Barker's *Twelfth Night* and Peter Brook's *A Midsummer Night's Dream*.

HOLGER SCHOTT SYME

Pastiche or Archetype? The Sam Wanamaker Playhouse and the Project of Theatrical Reconstruction

This article critiques the Sam Wanamaker Playhouse, the reconstructed indoor theatre at Shakespeare's Globe. The article investigates the project's theoretical and historiographical foundations, explores the relationship between the Wanamaker and actual early modern indoor venues, and asks what we can learn about performance practices of Shakespeare's time from this (re)construction.

RANDALL MARTIN

Evolutionary Naturalism and Embodied Ecology in Shakespearian Performance (with a Scene from *King John*)

Darwin's quotations of Shakespeare in *The Expression of the Emotions in Man and Animals* implied that theatrical performance originates in inherited, reflexive, and non-verbal affective communication. Understanding of this imitable capacity allows spectators to judge natural and artificial character performance, while

Darwinian ethology provides a new epistemological resource for eco-Shakespearian performance.

SHAKESPEARE AND OTHER ART FORMS

JOSEPH CAMPANA

Of Dance and Disarticulation: Juliet Dead and Alive
Choreographic treatments of Juliet tap into *Romeo and Juliet*'s complex meditation on mortality as a problem but also a challenge. How should Juliet move or be moved when she is apparently dead and when actually dead? Does choreographic idiom break down in the face of death? Four distinct patterns of treatment emerge as choreographers grapple with Juliet's body and make of her a sleepwalker, a corpse, a revenant and a survivor.

IRIS JULIA BÜHRLE

Titania's Dream: Three Choreographic *Midsummer Night's Dreams* of the Twentieth Century
This article analyses ballet adaptations of *A Midsummer Night's Dream*, by George Balanchine (1962), Frederick Ashton (1965) and John Neumeier (1977). It argues that the first two works are deeply rooted in the structures and storytelling devices of nineteenth-century ballet, whereas the third work profoundly engages with the literary source.

PETER HOLLAND

Shakespeare on Screens: Close Watching, Close Listening
By closely watching sections of Justin Kurzel's film of *Macbeth* (2015), I set out to test three propositions about Shakespeare film adaptation: the disjunction between technological advances and film studies' methodologies; the close watching of performance; and the place of Shakespeare in adaptation studies.

CYRUS MULREADY

From Table Books to Tumblr: Recollecting the Microgenres of the Early Modern Stage in Social Media
This article analyses Shakespeare's circulation in new media to illuminate an old textual problem: a crux arising from the 1623 Folio's description of Falstaff's death in *Henry V*. Today's media, it argues, help to explain the crux as they reveal textual features obscured by centuries of performance and print history.

LOUISE GEDDES

Unlearning Shakespeare Studies: Speculative Criticism and the Place of Fan Activism
Fan reading is a form of speculative critical praxis, built around affective relationships that connect a text with its transhistorical network of cultural affiliations. 'Unlearning Shakespeare Studies' suggests that the intersection of traditional critical reading and fan creativity in the Mercutio fandom generates radical new perspectives on *Romeo and Juliet*.

MARK HUTCHINGS

***Titus Andronicus* and Trapdoors at the Rose and Newington Butts**
This article presents a preliminary exploration of the trapdoor, which we tend to assume was ubiquitous. Examination of the evidence suggests this was not necessarily so: thus, the case of *Titus Andronicus* at the Rose and Newington Butts in 1594 may offer exceptional rather than representative evidence of its use.

ABSTRACTS OF ARTICLES IN *SHAKESPEARE SURVEY 71*

ROBERT STAGG

Shakespeare's Bewitching Line

This article considers Shakespeare's use of the seven-syllable line, at once critical to his writing (particularly of the supernatural) and criticized by his contemporaries. It examines the origins of the line (the patronage of James I, in particular) and its afterlives in Jonson and Middleton.

AMY LIDSTER

At the Sign of the Angel: The Influence of Andrew Wise on Shakespeare in Print

This article argues that Andrew Wise – one of the first publishers to concentrate on plays by Shakespeare – contributed to the selection, presentation, and reputation of Shakespeare's plays in print. It highlights the influence of Wise's business location and the role of patronage connections in this process.

TOM MCALINDON

Shakespeare and Hardy: The Tragi-comic Nexus

For commercial as well as artistic reasons, Hardy exploited his natural gift for comedy in his major tragic novels, looking to Shakespeare as model and justification. Seeing how Shakespeare mixed modes in *A Midsummmer's Night Dream* and *Romeo and Juliet*, Hardy used the technique in *The Return of the Native*, *The Mayor of Casterbridge*, and *Tess of the D'Urbervilles*.

JONATHAN CREWE

Queer Iago: A Brief History

Initially, psychoanalytic criticism diagnosed Iago as a 'paranoid homosexual'. This pathologizing approach yielded eventually to more sympathetic consideration of a 'gay' or 'queer' Iago. If, however, psychoanalysis of Iago has a future, perhaps it is the 'no future' projected by Lee Edelman, with the villain Iago recast as *sinthomosexual*.

MARK THORNTON BURNETT

Global Shakespeare and the Censor: Adaptation, Context, and *Shakespeare Must Die*, a Thai Film Adaptation of *Macbeth*

This article discusses *Shakespeare Must Die*, a 2012 Thai film adaptation of *Macbeth*, which has been banned by the Thai Film Censorship Board. It explores the film's engagement with contemporary Thai politics, its relation to popular protest and the conflicting ways in which Shakespeare circulates as a global commodity.

KATHERINE WEST SCHEIL

Hathaway Farm: Commemorating Warwickshire Will Between the Wars

This article examines a particular commemoration of Shakespeare between the two world wars, at Hathaway Farm, a tourist attraction near Anne Hathaway's Cottage. Hathaway Farm was run by Midlands solicitor Philip Baker, who sought to recreate a mythical and idealized version of Shakespeare's Warwickshire life.

INDEX

INDEX

INDEX

INDEX

INDEX

INDEX